PRAISE FOR *THE THIRD REICH*

"A narrative masterpiece that displays both Childers's profound expertise and genius for storytelling."

—Walter A. McDougall, Professor of History and Alloy-Ansin Professor of International Relations, University of Pennsylvania, and Pulitzer Prize–winning historian

"Riveting. . . . An elegantly composed study, important and even timely, given current trends in American and global politics."

—*Kirkus Reviews* (starred review)

"Historian Childers does a magnificent job of balancing many details within an overarching narrative of the Nazis' rise to power. . . . Essential reading for World War II enthusiasts and those interested in the origins of the Nazi Party and the resulting Holocaust."

—*Library Journal* (starred review)

"[Childers] is a master of English prose, writing with clarity, elegance, and wit; his account of Nazi Germany is every bit as readable as Shirer's and deserves a wide audience. . . . Offers a series of important correctives to Shirer's narrative, based on a comprehensive knowledge of the research carried out in the half-century and more since *The Rise and Fall of the Third Reich* was first published."

—Richard J. Evans, *The Nation*

"An exhaustive but powerful timeline of the rise and fall of the Third Reich. Childers dispels some common misconceptions about early Nazi history, while not sugarcoating their heinous atrocities. This book is a historical reminder of what happens when power goes unchecked."

—Philip Zozzaro, *San Francisco Review of Books*

"The new definitive volume on the subject, supplanting William Shirer's gold standard *The Rise and Fall of the Third Reich*. . . . The book's main strength lies in its chapters on the rise and early years of the party. And with newly unearthed documents—many from Germany—that the author had access to."

—Bob Ruggiero, *Houston Press*

T0002817

THE THIRD REICH

A HISTORY OF NAZI GERMANY

THOMAS CHILDERS

Simon & Schuster Paperbacks
New York London Toronto Sydney New Delhi

Simon & Schuster Paperbacks
An Imprint of Simon & Schuster, Inc.
1230 Avenue of the Americas
New York, NY 10020

First Simon & Schuster trade paperback edition October 2018

SIMON & SCHUSTER PAPERBACKS and colophon are registered trademarks of
Simon & Schuster, Inc.

For information about special discounts for bulk purchases, please contact Simon &
Schuster Special Sales at 1-866-506-1949 or business@simonandschuster.com.

The Simon & Schuster Speakers Bureau can bring authors to your live event.
For more information or to book an event, contact the Simon & Schuster Speakers Bureau
at 1-866-248-3049 or visit our website at www.simonspeakers.com.

Interior design by Silverglass Design

Manufactured in the United States of America

10   9   8   7   6   5   4   3

Library of Congress Cataloging-in-Publication Data is available.

1: Bundesarchiv, Bild 102-00344A / photo: Heinrich Hoffmann; 2: (top) Bundesarchiv,
Bild 183-1989-0630-504, (bottom left) Bundesarchiv, Bild 183-S00017 / photo: o.Ang,
(bottom right) Bundesarchiv, Bild 183-B0527-0001-020 / photo: o.Ang; 3: Bundesarchiv,
Bild 102-12403 / photo: Georg Pahl; 4-5: Bundesarchiv, Bild 183-h28422 / photo: o.Ang;
6: (left) Bundesarchiv, Bild 146-1982-159-21A / photo: o.Ang, (right) Bundesarchiv, Bild
102-01894A / photo: Georg Pahl; 7: Bundesarchiv, Bild 183-S38324 / photo: o.Ang; 8:
Photo by Heinrich Hoffmann/Archive Photos/Getty Images; 9: (top) Photo by ullstein
bild via Getty Images, (bottom) Bundesarchiv, Bild 146-1992-019-20A / photo: o.Ang;
10: Bundesarchiv, Bild 101III-Bueschel-009-03 / photo: Büschel; 11: (top) Bundesarchiv,
Bild 146-1969-054-16 / photo: Heinrich Hoffmann, (bottom) Photo by Hulton Archive/
Getty Images; 12: (top) Photo by Pictures Inc./The LIFE Picture Collection/Getty Images,
(bottom) © Pictures From History/The Image Works; 13: United States Holocaust Memo-
rial Museum, courtesy of Yad Vashem (THE VIEWS OR OPINIONS EXPRESSED IN
THIS BOOK), AND THE CONTEXT IN WHICH THE IMAGES ARE USED, DO NOT
NECESSARILY REFLECT THE VIEWS OR POLICY OF, NOR IMPLY APPROVAL OR
ENDORSEMENT BY, THE UNITED STATES HOLOCAUST MEMORIAL MUSEUM);
14: Photo by Sovfoto/UIG via Getty Images; 15: (top) Photo by Hulton Archive/Getty
Images, (bottom) Bundesarchiv, Bild 146-1973-001-30 / photo: o.Ang; 16: Bundesarchiv,
Bild 183-J28836A / photo: Franz Otto Koch

ISBN 978-1-4516-5113-3
ISBN 978-1-4516-5114-0 (pbk)
ISBN 978-1-4516-5115-7 (ebook)

For Kristen

CONTENTS

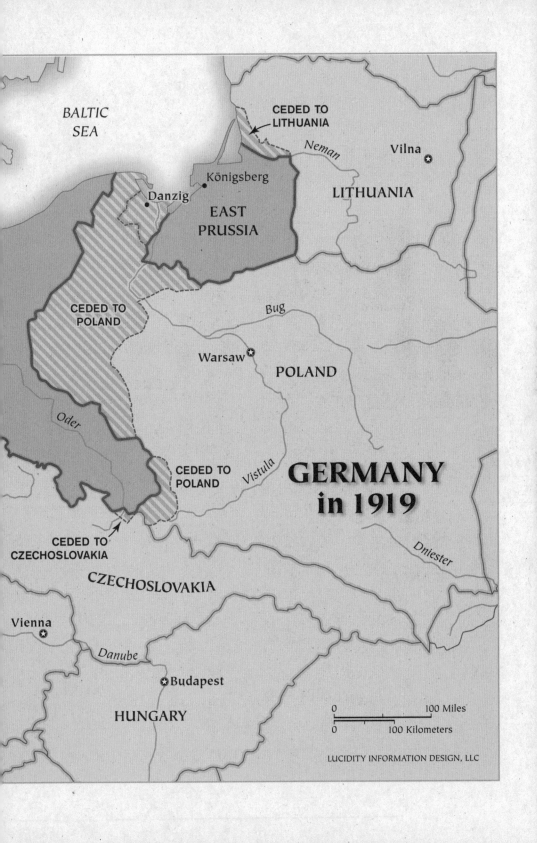

BALTIC
SEA

LITHUANIA

Neman

Vilna ✪

Königsberg

Danzig

EAST
PRUSSIA

DANZIG
AND THE
POLISH
CORRIDOR

Vistula

Bug

Warsaw ✪

POLAND

Oder

Vistula

GERMANY
in 1939

ANNEXED BY
POLAND

Dniester

BOHEMIA-
MORAVIA
March 1939

SLOVAKIA
March 1939

ANNEXED BY
HUNGARY

Vienna ✪

ANNEXED BY
HUNGARY

Danube

Budapest ✪

HUNGARY

0   100 Miles

0   100 Kilometers

LUCIDITY INFORMATION DESIGN, LLC

THE GERMAN PARTY SYSTEM

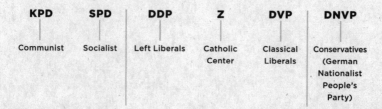

KPD	SPD	DDP	Z	DVP	DNVP
Communist	Socialist	Left Liberals	Catholic Center	Classical Liberals	Conservatives (German Nationalist People's Party)

NSDAP

National Socialist German Workers Party (Nazis)

GLOSSARY OF GERMAN TERMS

Ahnenpass ("racial passport")
Bürgfrieden (political truce)
Deutschlandflug (flight over Germany)
Einzelaktionen (individual/independent actions)
Gauleiter (district leader)
Hofoper (Court Opera House–Vienna)
Landespolizei (State Police)
Lebensraum (living space)
Mischling (mix/hybrid)
Ortsgruppen (local party chapters)
Realschule (technical school)
Salonfähig (respectable)
Schaffenden (productive)
Stimmungsbericht (morale report)
Völkisch (populist)
Volksbewegung (people's movement)
Volksempfänger (people's radio)
Volksgemeinschaft (people's community)
Volksgenossen (people's comrades)
Volkskörper (body of the people)
Wählerei (choice/vote)

THE THIRD REICH
1919–1945

THE SERPENT'S EGG

Adolf Hitler was born on April 20, 1889, in the Austrian town of Braunau am Inn on the German-Austrian border. His father, Alois Hitler, was a provincial customs official of liberal views who had risen from an unpromising background to the respectable status of middle-grade civil servant of the Habsburg Empire. Alois's patrimony was a source of controversy and rumor. He was the illegitimate son of Maria Anna Schicklgruber and an unknown father. In 1842 Maria Anna married Johann Georg Hiedler, and in 1876 Alois adopted the name of his stepfather, later changing the spelling to Hitler. As the Nazis came to prominence and Adolf Hitler emerged a national political figure, there was some speculation that Adolf's unknown grandfather was Jewish, but no credible evidence to support such rumors has ever surfaced.

The family moved several times, from Braunau to Passau to Linz, where Adolf spent most of his unexceptional youth. There was nothing notable about him in his early life, nothing to suggest potential of any sort. He read, he daydreamed—he was a great artist, a great architect, the builder of monumental buildings and grand cities, a Wagnerian hero. None of these dreams translated into serious work or training. He loved music, especially the operas of Richard Wagner, but had only a rudimentary knowledge of music. He liked to sketch, to paint in watercolors, but he had neither the talent nor the work ethic to achieve the grandiose successes he envisioned.

Hitler's father provided a comfortable existence for the family. He hoped that young Adolf would follow him into government service, and he had little patience with his son's dreaminess. He was a gruff, authoritarian *paterfamilias*, a strict disciplinarian who terrorized his indolent son. Beatings were not infrequent. Adolf took refuge with his mother, Klara, who doted on him. Alois had three children from an earlier marriage but three of his children with Klara died, two brothers and a sister, before Adolf was born, and Klara was determined to protect this son spared by providence. Sickly as a baby, he grew to be very much a mamma's boy, lazy, self-indulgent, and coddled. His father died in 1903, when Adolf was fourteen, easing some of the tension in the Hitler household.

Young Adolf was a loner, a perpetual outsider. He had few friends, in fact, only one to speak of. He showed little interest in girls, had no sweethearts or even friendly relationships with the opposite sex. He shied away from physical contact, only reluctantly shaking hands; he was "almost pathologically sensitive about anything concerning the body," according to his one genuine friend, the son of an upholsterer in Linz, August Kubizek, who aspired to be a musician. Together the boys roamed the Danubian countryside, strolled the streets of Linz, and attended the opera, Adolf expounding all the while on his many enthusiasms. Kubizek's essential qualification for Hitler's friendship was that he was a good listener. Impressionable and unassertive, he hung on Adolf's every word. In return he was granted visiting rights into Hitler's intense fantasy world, a world of grand illusions in which Adolf Hitler would be recognized as an artistic giant, an architectural genius, a shaper of worlds.

Hitler was, to put it generously, an indifferent student. His grades were so poor at the technical school (*Realschule*)—he failed math; he failed German!—that he was held back a year and forced to take qualifying exams to avoid being held back a second time. Misunderstood and unappreciated, by his lights, he had had enough, and at age sixteen he left school without a degree. He set his sights on a career in art and hoped to gain admission to the Academy of Fine Arts in Vienna. In July 1907 he convinced his mother that he should go to Vienna to prepare for the entrance exam, which was held every year in October. Initially he was captivated by the city, especially its magisterial buildings—the Opera, the Parliament, all the grand structures along the Ringstrasse. It was the great world, far from provincial Linz.

Supremely confident in his own talents, he did little in the way of preparation for the exam. He submitted a portfolio of his drawings and sat for the exam, but to his utter astonishment he failed. "I was so convinced that I would be successful that when I received my rejection, it struck me as a bolt from the blue." It is telling that while Hitler was a passable draftsman—he could draw buildings, street scenes, structures of all kinds—he was unable to render the human form. He was hopelessly unqualified for painting, one examiner told him. Perhaps he was better suited for architecture. Hitler liked the idea, but the academy's School of Architecture required a high school degree or at least some previous technical training, which thanks to his own negligence he could not provide. There was, he realized, no chance that he could study painting *or* architecture. Hitler kept this humiliating rejection a secret, never telling his gravely ill mother and waiting months before confessing it to his loyal friend Kubizek. In December 1907, his mother died after a painful and protracted battle with cancer. Adolf rushed back to Linz to care for her in her final days and was devastated when she finally succumbed. His mother's death shook Hitler to the core. The family doctor, a Jewish physician from Linz, later recalled that he had never seen anyone so overcome with grief as eighteen-year-old Adolf.

After settling his mother's affairs and arranging for his orphan's pension to be forwarded, he returned to Vienna in January 1908, still hoping to pursue his dream of becoming a great artist. He settled back into his dingy room in the Stumpergasse, located in a derelict section of the city near the West Train Station. When he learned that Kubizek was preparing for the entrance exam at the Conservatory for Music, Hitler convinced him to share his quarters. The two young men, neither yet twenty, lived together for five intense months, from February to the end of July in 1908. Kubizek provided the perfect audience for his friend's endless lectures. Adolf had opinions, passionate opinions, about everything—art, opera, architecture, politics, morality, even diet. When Kubizek meekly ventured to offer his own opinion, Hitler would burst into a rage, storming around their shabby room, shouting imprecations, pounding on the door, the walls, and Kubizek's rented piano. He would tolerate no dissent. He was determined to retake the academy's admission exam, but he could not be moved to prepare. While Kubizek studied diligently and passed his entrance exam to the conservatory, Hitler spent his time developing fantastical schemes of all kinds—he would write an opera, a play, reform workers' housing in Vienna, rebuild the city of Linz; he would establish a traveling symphony orchestra and even develop a new soft drink. His feverish imagination lurched from one grandiose project to the next without missing a beat. When a new inspiration seized him, he would talk obsessively about it for days, sometimes weeks; he would make notes, write scenes, draw sketches, only to drop the whole thing from one day to the next, never to mention it again. He could never complete a project.

As long as the money from home lasted, Adolf led a life of idleness. He dallied in cafés, read the free newspapers available there; he went to the opera; he visited the museums and art galleries. It was a bohemian existence, staying up to all hours, sleeping late, bound by no fixed schedule—a routine that he would maintain throughout the Third Reich, even into the darkest days of the Second World War. He had few physical needs. He neither smoked nor drank and rarely ate meat. There were no women in his life during the Vienna years. He was fascinated but frightened by sex, afraid of women, and he remained terrified of syphilis until the end of his life. The two young men lived frugally, eating spartan meals, buying little but the bare necessities. They subsisted in their cheap, dimly lit room, with its "crumbling walls, bug infested furniture and constant smell of kerosene," and considered themselves in solidarity with the long-suffering lower classes they found all around them—a solidarity, however, that did not include mingling or interacting with them. All the while Hitler was receiving his monthly orphan's pension and a portion of his father's estate, the remainder to be paid when he turned twenty-four. He lived frugally, but he was not, as he would later imply, on the brink of starvation or in desperate straits.

His one extravagance was the opera. Hitler and Kubizek were regulars at the magnificent *Hofoper*, standing in line for hours hoping to buy tickets for the cheap seats or standing room for several nights of the week. For Hitler it was money well spent. He appreciated Verdi and Puccini, but he strongly preferred German composers and was utterly enthralled by Wagner. He was a keen analyst of the productions, paying particular attention to all the elements of stagecraft—lighting, scenery, special effects, the placement of the actors, and their dramatic entrances and exits from the stage—all of which he later employed to great effect in Nazi propaganda. His nights at the opera were far more than a musical experience for him; they were his spiritual sustenance, his inspiration, and his escape. Listening to *Lohengrin*, his favorite, or *Parsifal* or the *Ring*, he would be mesmerized for hours, transported into Wagner's mythical world of fog-shrouded mountains and doomed Nordic heroes. These were the only occasions, Kubizek realized, that Hitler seemed calm and at peace. Yet, he was an angry man. His moods alternated between frenzied elation and the darkest depression. His friend worried that Adolf "had become unbalanced. He would fly into a temper at the slightest thing," Kubizek recalled. "He was at odds with the world. Wherever he looked, he saw injustice, hate and enmity. Nothing was free from his criticism; nothing found favor in his eyes." At the slightest provocation, he railed against "the times, against the whole world; choking with his catalogue of hates, he would pour his fury over everything, against mankind in general who did not understand him, who did not appreciate him and by whom he was persecuted."

In July 1908, while Kubizek was away in Linz for his summer break, Hitler was once again turned down by the academy. This second rejection came as an even more devastating blow than the first, for after reviewing his drawings the admissions committee dismissed them as being without merit and pronounced young Hitler unqualified even to sit for the entrance exam. This time he was not so much shocked as enraged. Who were these pompous professors to reject him? How could these pedants have failed to appreciate his work, his potential, his genius! They were nothing but "a lot of old-fashioned fossilized civil servants, bureaucrats, devoid of understanding, stupid lumps of officials. The whole Academy," he thundered, "ought to be blown up." In the fall of 1908, with no career training, no position, and no prospects, he promised himself that he would continue his "studies" on his own; he would show all those who had scorned him and conspired against him.

In spite of these setbacks, Hitler remained supremely confident, possessed of a stunning amalgam of arrogance, anger, and self-pity that would remain the core of his personality for the rest of his life. His failure at the academy did not motivate him to undertake any systematic study. He remained a hopeless dilettante, dabbling, fantisizing, and sliding ever deeper into a world of illusion, where he would yet emerge, like Wagner, as the triumphant artist hero who would stun the world with his ascent from obscurity to greatness.

Almost out of money and embarrassed by his second humiliating failure at the academy, he did not want to face Kubizek again. He gave notice, paid his portion of the rent, and, while his friend was still away in Linz, simply vanished, leaving no forwarding address. Kubizek would not see him again for thirty years. After slipping his moorings in the Stumpergasse, Hitler drifted from squalid room to squalid room, beginning a gradual descent into the dismal netherworld of Vienna. He had squandered most of his father's legacy, and his orphan's pension was hardly enough to live on. He lost contact with his family—his Aunt Johanna, his half-sister Angela, and little sister Paula had no idea where he was. For months he lived on the streets; he slept in parks and all-night cafés, under bridges, on doorsteps, finding occasional refuge in flophouses and homeless shelters. He ate in charity kitchens. He had no overcoat; his once neat clothes were tattered and stained from the disinfectant used in the homeless shelters, and his dilapidated shoes were falling apart, their soles worn paper thin. In winter he was forced to take shelter during the day in a series of "warming rooms" provided by churches and other charitable organizations. He slept, when he could, in the Shelter for Homeless Men at Meidling, which provided a warm, cavernous dormitory, a meal of bread and soup, a shower, and a simple cot for the night. Every morning he was turned out for the day, and every evening found him once again standing in line with other wretched souls, the down-and-out flotsam of Vienna, hoping to be admitted to the shelter for the night. He had hit rock bottom.

In later years Hitler, without the slightest corroboration, maintained that during this gloomy period he found occasional work as a day laborer in construction, sometimes carrying bags at the railway station and shoveling snow. For much of 1909 he subsisted on a meager diet of milk, bread, and thin soup and was so blade thin, so obviously frail that he might easily have passed for a consumptive. He certainly did not work "for years in the building trade," and it is unlikely that any construction foreman in 1908 would have hired this sallow, unkempt young man when he had so many healthy jobless candidates to choose from. Carrying luggage and shoveling snow seem just as improbable.

In January 1910 with the aid of a small-time operator and habitué of the Meidling shelter, Reinhold Hanisch, he landed a spot in a well-appointed home for the laboring poor. Administered by the government and funded by contributions from prominent Jewish families, the Home for Men in the Meldemannstrasse was no cheap flophouse. Along with the usual derelicts and desperate cases, its inhabitants also included veterans, workers, respectable, educated men temporarily down on their luck, trying to keep their nose above water until times improved. It provided a simple meal in the evening, a communal kitchen where the men could cook their own meals, a cubicle for each inhabitant that allowed the men a modicum of privacy, and maintained a library and reading room. Ensconced in the library of the home, Hitler read voraciously with all the scattershot miscellany of the autodidact, supplementing the pamphlets and penny press of the cafés with bits and pieces of philosophy, history, art, and music. He later claimed to have read five hundred books while living in the Meldemannstrasse home, but this was a typical exaggeration. His reading appears to have been concentrated primarily on newspapers, pamphlets, and condensations of serious works found on the library shelves.

During his time in the men's home between 1909 and 1913, he survived by painting postcards of Viennese landmarks. In order to purchase his art supplies, he broke his silence and, at the prompting of Hanisch, contacted his Aunt Johanna. Fighting back his shame, he asked for a loan, probably implying that it was to help him with his studies. She responded not with a loan but with a generous gift, and possibly sent occasional funds to him thereafter. Thus equipped, he worked from photographs and prints, copying them mechanically in the home's reading room. He rarely ventured forth to sell them—too much direct contact with the public. Instead, he made an arrangement with Hanisch, who hawked them in the cafés and pubs and to small-time, mostly Jewish art dealers. Hanisch also sold some slightly larger paintings to frame shops and furniture dealers, who attached them as a sales decoration to the backs of sofas—a common practice in showrooms. Hitler and his partners—later a Hungarian Jew named Jacob Neubauer and others took over for Hanisch—split the meager proceeds fifty-fifty. It was a hand-to-mouth existence, but it was stable, and it offered more than a modicum of comfort.

While at the Men's Home, Hitler engaged in almost daily disputations, sometimes about art, sometimes about music, but often about politics and the miserable state of affairs in Vienna, the city he had come to loathe. He lectured; he argued; he harangued. At the first hint of a political discussion he would spring from his chair, leaving his postcards unfinished, to thunder at his fellow patrons. He fulminated against the Slavs, the Socialists, the labor unions. His favorite targets were "the Jesuits and the Reds," but, oddly enough considering the violent anti-Semitic obsession that would later come to dominate his life, not the Jews. Sometimes the men fired back at him; sometimes they just laughed at his earnest, overheated rhetoric, a reaction that sent a chagrined Hitler back to his cubicle to be consoled by Hanisch. Hitler in this period was an ardent German nationalist, a champion of all things German and contemptuous of the moldering multinational Habsburg Empire, with its polyglot population of Germans, Poles, Czechs, Slovaks, Slovenes, Hungarians, Italians, and Jews. Nowhere was that exotic brew of ethnicities, languages, and national cultures more in evidence than in Vienna. Hitler sometimes attended the sessions of the Austrian Parliament where he watched from the gallery as representatives of the various nationalities spewed venom at one another in a cacophony of languages, and the sessions disintegrated into chaos. The delegates rang cowbells, sang competing national songs, chanted party slogans, and sometimes even fought in the aisles. These rancorous displays of ethnic and class conflict filled Hitler with disgust, revealing to him the depths of Habsburg impotence and the chaos and dysfunction at the core of parliamentary democracy.

During Hitler's years in Vienna an air of decay, of impending crisis hung in its narrow streets and its broad sunlit boulevards. The city was experiencing a fin de siècle cultural flowering—it was the center of the European avant-garde, home to composers Arnold Schoenberg and Gustav Mahler, to literary figures Arthur Schnitzler and Hugo von Hofmannsthal, and to painters such as Gustav Klimt; it was the cradle of psychotherapy, the home of Sigmund Freud. Hitler had no interest in any of these manifestations of the Modern. His Vienna was a city of slums and squalor, soup kitchens and homeless shelters. It was a cold, pitiless dog-eat-dog world where the strong prevailed and the weak fell by the wayside, a dynamic that permanently shaped his view of the world and its most elemental principles.

Vienna was also a city bristling with class and ethnic hatreds. In 1908 it was the sixth largest city in the world, and its population was growing by thirty thousand each month. Although the Germans had long enjoyed a position of power and privilege in the city (and in the empire), that predominance was increasingly threatened, especially after the introduction of universal male suffrage in 1907. Like many Germans appalled by the specter of being overwhelmed by the "inferior peoples" of the empire, Hitler was an ardent admirer of Georg Ritter von Schönerer, the leader of the Austrian Pan-German movement. Schönerer rose to political prominence in the aftermath of the Austro-Prussian War of 1866, when he appeared on the scene as a rabid German nationalist, deploring Austria's exclusion from the Bismarckian Reich and lamenting the dilution of German preeminence in the Habsburg Empire. In the last decades of the nineteenth century Schönerer's Pan-German movement gained a prominence far beyond its numbers, as its leaflets, pamphlets, and newspapers carried Schönerer's words into every German corner of the empire.

Above all else, he protested the influx of Eastern European Jews into Vienna, and in 1884 introduced a bill to block Jewish immigration into the capital. Schönerer's brand of anti-Semitism was a new phenomenon in Austria; it was not only religious and socioeconomic but racial in nature. The motto of his Pan-German movement was "Through Purity to Unity," and Schönerer famously declared that "a Jew remains a Jew, whether he is baptized or not." He favored a strict separation of the races, arguing that whoever refused to embrace anti-Semitism was a "traitor to the German Volk" and "a slave of the Jews." The Jews were "like vampires" who derived their strength by "sucking the blood of the Aryan peoples." Hence, "every German had the duty to help . . . eliminate Jewry."

He also launched an "Away from Rome" campaign against the Catholic Church and engaged in a running battle with the liberal "Jewish press." He inveighed against big business and liberal economic policies that hurt tradesmen and small farmers. In addition to its anti-Semitic and anti-Catholic stance, the Pan-German movement called on its followers to adhere to a strict dietary regimen—"Aryans" should be vegetarians and should abstain from tobacco and alcohol. As the movement gained momentum, it produced a full-blown Schönerer cult, generating songs and poems devoted to its self-styled "Führer" and introduced the phrase *Heil dem Führer* (Hail to the Leader!) into the country's political lexicon.

Hitler admired Schönerer and his Pan-German movement, but when he arrived in Vienna, it was the city's rabble-rousing populist mayor, Karl Lueger, who most impressed him. Lueger, who had been mayor since 1897, had once been an admirer of Schönerer, but Lueger was not a German nationalist but a devout Catholic and a loyal subject of the Habsburg monarchy. He did, however, share Schönerer's rabid anti-Semitism, becoming, even more than Schönerer, the very embodiment of the anti-Semitic movement in Austria. In contrast to Schönerer, Lueger's anti-Semitism was not racial but religious, though for many the distinction was moot. A master politician who was, even an opponent acknowledged, "the uncrowned king" of the city, he understood how to tap the anti-Semitic paranoia stirred up by Schönerer to mobilize support among his largely lower-middle-class following.

The influx of Eastern European Jews into the empire in the late nineteenth century was an incandescent issue, and Lueger vigorously exploited it. "Greater Vienna," he warned, "must not become greater Jerusalem." In Vienna, he complained, Jews had become as plentiful as "sand on the beach." The Jews dominated the city, controlling the press, the banks, big capital, and even the Social Democrats were nothing more than "the protection squad of the Jews." So inflammatory was his rhetoric, so demagogic his public appearances that despite Lueger's electoral victories in 1895 and 1896 the aged Emperor Franz Joseph refused to recognize him as mayor for two years.

It was not so much Lueger's ideological views that most impressed Hitler but his unrivaled ability to mobilize popular support. In an emerging age of mass politics Lueger presented himself as the "tribune of the people." Always image conscious, he paid great attention to the theatrics of politics, and his numerous public appearances were carefully staged for maximum impact. Lueger was an exemplar of a new kind of politician. A charismatic speaker, he did not appeal to the educated, cultured Vienna. He spoke in a populist idiom, often lapsing into dialect, and his ability to move crowds, to agitate, and to mobilize the only recently enfranchised lower middle class made a deep impression on Hitler.

While Schönerer relentlessly linked the Jews with big capital and liberals, Lueger was determined to associate Jews with the Social Democratic movement as well. Just as in Germany, the Social Democrats and the labor unions were making steady, sometimes spectacular gains in Austria, and the reaction to the threat they posed was swift and shrill. Typical was the headline in Lueger's *Deutsches Volksblatt*: "Who leads Social Democracy? The Jews. . . . Who aids them with the public? The entire Jewish press.

And who gives them money: Jewish high finance. Just as in Russia, the Jews are the agitators and instigators [of disorder]." When the Socialists held a rally for an expanded suffrage in 1908, the Lueger press countered with the slogan: "Down with the Terrorism of Jewry."

Hitler's fear and loathing of Marxism, embodied in the Social Democratic movement and the labor unions, certainly had its origins in Vienna. He was frightened by the militant Social Democrats but also impressed by their mastery of propaganda and mass mobilization. He later wrote that after watching a Social Democratic demonstration, for the first time he "understood the infamous spiritual terror which this movement exerts, particularly on the bourgeoisie, which is neither morally nor mentally equal to such attacks." At a given signal, the Socialists could unleash "a veritable barrage of lies and slanders against whatever adversary seems most dangerous, until the nerves of the attacked persons break down. . . . This is a tactic based on precise calculation of all human weaknesses, and its result will lead to success with almost mathematical certainty." The Social Democrats also taught Hitler another important lesson, one he would employ to great effect during his rise to power and, most terrifyingly, in the Third Reich: "an understanding of the importance of physical terror toward the individual and the masses."

Given the torrent of anti-Semitic influences churning around him during his Vienna years, it seems reasonable to locate the origins of Hitler's pathological hatred of the Jews at that time and place. And yet, firsthand testimony about Hitler's attitudes toward Jews in those years is both sparse and contradictory. Kubizek maintained that Hitler arrived in Vienna already an anti-Semite, and that these feelings only intensified in the charged atmosphere of the city. Writing a decade later, Hitler, too, claimed that he "left Vienna as an absolute Anti-Semite, as a mortal enemy of the entire Marxist world view." He was no doubt influenced by Schönerer and Lueger and the powerful current of vicious anti-Semitism that coursed through Austrian and especially Viennese political culture in the early years of the twentieth century. He certainly read the anti-Semitic newspapers and broadsheets that could easily be found in the cafés and newsstands and on the benches of the shelters.

And yet Hanisch, his close associate in the homeless shelters, claimed never to have heard him utter an anti-Semitic remark. "In those days,"

Hanisch declared, "Hitler was by no means a Jew hater." Hitler, he reports, was on friendly terms with Jews in the shelter, had good relations with Jewish art dealers, and his closest associate in the Meldemannstrasse home, Jacob Neubauer, was a Hungarian Jew. Neubauer helped obtain a winter coat for Hitler, and the two even planned a trip to Munich together. Of course, it could be that anti-Semitism was such a commonplace in his surroundings that his anti-Jewish views were simply too unexceptional to be noticed or remembered. Never open with his feelings, Hitler might also have kept his views to himself for quite pragmatic reasons—he needed the assistance of Jewish associates in the men's home and the goodwill of the Jewish art dealers who bought his paintings. Both are quite possible, but the fact remains that there is no documented evidence of Hitler making anti-Semitic remarks or displaying anti-Semitic attitudes while in Vienna.

Still, whatever can be surmised from his personal relations with individual Jews, there can be no doubt that during his years in Vienna Hitler absorbed the rampant anti-Semitism of the city—possibly the most odious in Europe—reading from the scurrilous Jew-baiting gutter press available in the downtrodden neighborhoods he haunted. He clearly internalized the anti-Semitic language of Lueger and Schönerer, their slogans, their clichés, their appeals, their hatreds. "Vienna," he later wrote, "was and remained for me the hardest, though most thorough, school of my life. I had set foot in this town while still half a boy and I left it a man grown quiet and grave. In it I obtained the foundations for a philosophy in general and a political view in particular which later I only needed to supplement in detail, but which never left me." Yet when he left Vienna in 1913, his anti-Semitic and anti-Marxist attitudes amounted to little more than a jumble of inchoate ideas, personal prejudices, resentments, and fears that had not yet crystallized into a systematic worldview or ideology. That would come only in the aftermath of the First World War, in the turbulent crucible of revolutionary Munich.

What Hitler did learn in Vienna was hate, distrust, suspicion, a Darwinian view of human relations, and a lifelong resentment against comfortable bourgeois convention and the establishment that had crushed his ambitions, humiliated him, and reduced him to the pitiless life of homeless shelters, warming rooms, and soup kitchens. This was the deeply ingrained view of the world that would not change. In those prewar years, he did not have friends and did not want or need them. This was not simple shyness or social awkwardness. For all his maudlin statements later about loneliness, a friend, even a close associate, was unwelcome. Anyone who might intrude into his private world where his views, his enthusiasms, his hatreds, his delusions held sway was a threat. In spite of the fact that he was an utter failure in Vienna, a nobody, in the interior world of his co-lossal narcissism, he was neither shy nor awkward nor diffident. There he reigned supreme. There he was the maker of worlds.

Hitler left Vienna in May 1913. His destination was Munich. He had long dreamed of living in Germany, and Munich, whose many museums and galleries he had once visited as a boy, exerted an almost magnetic attraction for him. There he would continue his "studies" and finally achieve the artistic recognition that had been so cruelly denied him in Vienna. Two more immediate events triggered his move. On April 20, 1913, his twenty-fourth birthday, he received the balance of his father's legacy, and for the first time had the resources to fulfill his dream. He could buy suitable clothes, look presentable; he could purchase a railway ticket; he could afford a modest room. More pressing was a far less pleasant incentive. In 1909 he had failed to register for the Austrian draft as required by law. Nor had he done so in subsequent years. He had no intention of serving in the army of the empire he detested. Although he later claimed to have left Austria "for primarily political reasons," implying some sort of principled political protest, he left to avoid military service. Having passed safely into Germany, he believed that the Austrian authorities had forgotten him and that he was at any rate beyond their reach. But that was not the case. Far from forgetting him, the Linz police were on his trail, and unbeknownst to him, they were closing in. Failing to register for military service was a serious offense, but leaving the country under these circumstances amounted to desertion, which carried a severe prison sentence. By 1913 he was officially classified a draft dodger.

For months Hitler lived undisturbed in Munich. He was painting postcards again, now of Munich landmarks, and selling them in the cafés and beer halls that dotted the city. He took a room in the home of a respectable family and continued to live the life bohemian, sleeping late, lounging in cafés, reading deep into the night. He had no friends. His landlady would later recall that in the year that young Herr Hitler was her boarder, he had no visitors. Still, reminiscing nostalgically about his time in Munich, he would write that these fifteen months were "the happiest and by far the most contented of my life."

Then in January 1914, a shock. Answering a knock at his door, he opened it to find an officer of the Munich criminal police waiting for him. He was taken into custody and delivered to the Austrian consulate, where he would be formally charged and returned to Linz. In a series of frantic telegrams and letters between Hitler and the Linz police, he pled his case. In a three-and-a-half-page letter he accepted responsibility but claimed it had all been a misunderstanding. He had, indeed, failed to register in 1909 when he was down and out in Vienna but had done so in 1910; then he had heard nothing further from the Linz authorities, and he had let the matter slide. He made such an abjectly humble impression that the consul took pity on him and agreed to allow him to report to nearby Salzburg rather than returning to Linz for his induction. In Salzburg, frail and visibly weak, he was declared physically unfit for military service.

Shaken but relieved, he returned to Munich, where he continued to drift along. He would later claim that during this period in Munich he made a study of Marxism, but he participated in no organized political activity; he joined no party or political association, and there is scant evidence that he actually read Marx. At any rate, as he later acknowledged, he read to confirm his views, not to learn. He was apparently content to live the life of a beer hall intellectual, a café radical, haranguing anyone who would listen to his views on the mounting threats to Germany. Still directionless, he was living day to day, treading water, with no plan, no career, and no future. In Munich, as in Vienna, he remained a nonentity, a mere shadow.

Then came the war.

August 2, 1914, the day after war was declared, found a twenty-five-year-old Hitler in the cheering throng gathered on the Odeonsplatz, waving his hat in jubilation, singing "Deutschland über Alles" and "Die Wacht am Rhein." It was, he later wrote, the happiest day of his life. "To me, those hours seemed like a release from the painful feelings of my youth. . . . Overpowered by stormy enthusiasm, I fell down on my knees and thanked Heaven from an overflowing heart for granting me the good fortune of being permitted to live at this time." The country was swept up in a typhoon of patriotic enthusiasm. Schoolboys rushed to the colors; married men enlisted; jubilant civilians reveled in the streets, as if suddenly released from years of pent-up tension. The Kaiser issued a dramatic call for national unity, a *Burgfrieden* or political truce, summoning all Germans to put aside their deep social and political differences while the enemy was at the gates. From this day forward, he declared, he would no longer recognize parties; he would recognize only Germans. Even the Social Democratic Party (SPD), a party with an ostensibly radical Marxist platform and an implacable critic of the government, overcame its pacifist scruples and joined the war effort. This was a major victory for the regime, which viewed the Social Democrats as dangerous subversives determined to undermine the capitalist system and the conservative political order with it. Between 1890 and the outbreak of war, the SPD had become the largest, most energetic party in the Reich, relentlessly pressing for fundamental political and social reforms. Like all socialist parties in Europe, it was also officially pacifist. But in the "spirit of 1914," the bitterly divisive social and political issues that had rent the country for decades seemed swept beneath the surface as the nation girded for war.

Although he was an Austrian citizen, Hitler immediately enlisted in the German army (no questions were asked) and he was assigned to the 16th Reserve Regiment of the 1st Bavarian Infantry Division, called the List Regiment after its commander Julius von List. The unit received rudimentary training in Munich and was promptly dispatched to Flanders, where it was thrown into the heavy fighting near Ypres. It was a disaster. In the regiment's first few months of combat, it suffered roughly 70 percent casualties, including the death of its commanding officer. For four brutal years, Hitler served on the Western Front as a dispatch runner, carrying messages from regimental headquarters to the front lines. Although he was never a soldier in the trenches, as he subsequently implied, his was a dangerous job, and he performed it with distinction. Twice wounded, he was awarded the Iron Cross second class in 1916, and two years later the Iron Cross first class for bravery, a rare achievement for an enlisted man, especially a dispatch runner. Later the Nazi propaganda machine would greatly embellish Hitler's war record, claiming among other fictions that he had won his Iron Cross first class by singlehandedly capturing seven

French soldiers. Still, his war was dangerous enough. In September 1916 he was hit in the thigh by a shard of English shrapnel when an artillery shell slammed into regimental messengers' dugout two kilometers behind the front, killing and severely wounding almost everyone there.

Hitler spent nearly two months recuperating in Germany, where he was allowed a brief visit to Berlin before being transferred to a replacement battalion in Munich. He had not been in Germany since the outbreak of the war, and he found the mood drastically changed. He was appalled by the widespread disaffection and defeatism he found among both the soldiers and the hard-strapped civilian population. In Berlin "there was dire misery everywhere. The big city was suffering from hunger. Discontent was great." Defeatism was rampant among the troops he encountered in the hospital and elsewhere, as "shirkers" ridiculed the army and bragged about their ruses to avoid combat. "But," he added, "Munich was much worse." He hardly recognized the city. There he found "anger, discontent, cursing" wherever he went. "The general mood was miserable: to be a slacker passed almost as a sign of higher wisdom, while loyal steadfastness was considered a symptom of inner weakness and narrow-mindedness."

The patriotic unity of 1914 had long since dissolved, worn away by the remorselessly mounting casualties and the dreary hardships on the home front. For roughly two years the political truce had held, but by 1916 domestic solidarity, already frayed by mounting labor unrest, began to unravel. Frustrated by its party's continued support of "an imperialist war," the SPD's left wing bolted to form a new party (the USPD or Independent Social Democratic Party). In an effort to avert a further radicalization of the left, the Kaiser announced his intention of granting universal suffrage and other electoral changes long demanded by the Social Democrats, but, he added, any democratizing reforms would come only after the successful conclusion of hostilities.

The Kaiser's Easter message of 1917 satisfied no one, either on the right or the left. That was underscored in July when a disillusioned Reichstag, almost forgotten since 1914, passed a resolution calling for a negotiated end to the war and rejecting the expansionist war aims demanded by the government and the right. Inspired by Matthias Erzberger of the Catholic Zentrum Party, the resolution was supported by a broad coalition of Social Democrats, Zentrum, and the left-liberal Progressives. After the patriotic summer of 1914 the Reichstag and even the Kaiser had faded from view, and since 1916 army commanders Field Marshal Paul von Hindenburg and General Erich Ludendorff ruled the country from behind the scenes in a "silent dictatorship." The army simply ignored the resolution, removed the presiding chancellor from office, installed a pliant figurehead, and tightened its grip on the state. The Reichstag Peace Resolution, as it came to be called, infuriated the right, which accused the Reichstag of being under the thumb of the "internationalist" Social Democrats and their fellow travelers in the Zentrum and among the democratic liberals.

In response, the Fatherland Party, founded by a coalition of right-wing organizations in December 1916, howled against the left, the liberals, and the Jews, all of whom, they claimed, were undermining the war effort. The Fatherland Party was particularly savage in its attacks on Jews. Jewish financial interests, they insisted, dominated the German war economy, reaping enormous profits while true Germans were fighting and dying for the fatherland. Amid a growing mood of fear and mounting paranoia, a tidal wave of anti-Semitic agitation washed over the country. Right-wing groups such as the Pan-German League, the Colonial Society, and the small but aggressively anti-Semitic Thule Society—in fact, all those groups that vigorously supported Germany's expansionist war aims—shared these anti-Jewish views and aggressively pressed them on the public.

Before the war, anti-Semitism had not played a major role in German political life. In the early 1890s a number of small regional parties had made anti-Semitism the central focus of their appeal, and in 1893 the German Conservative Party, in an effort to revive its sagging popularity, drafted an anti-Semitic plank in its Tivoli Program. By 1914 these small anti-Semitic parties had evaporated into well-deserved oblivion, and the Tivoli Program signally failed to boost the electoral fortunes of the Conservatives, whose vote continued to plummet. And yet, while it was not enough to rally any significant popular support, anti-Semitism percolated through German political culture during the prewar years. By 1914, though hardly mainstream, it had become respectable, an undeniable element of political discourse.

In 1916–17, amid signs of deepening social and economic tensions, groups on the right charged that Jews controlled the war economy and were dodging military service. Even those Jews who were in the army, they claimed, were not serving on the front lines. These spurious charges became so intense that in 1916 the Reichstag launched an investigation into the role of Jews in Germany's war industries, and the Ministry of War undertook a survey to determine the number of Jews serving in the army, and especially in frontline outfits. These investigations indicated that Jews were neither overrepresented in the war economy nor underrepresented in the armed forces—not at the front or in the casualty reports. One hundred thousand Jews served in the military during the war; 12,000 were killed in action; and 35,000 were decorated for bravery. But the results of the army's *Judenzählung* were never made public, and the vicious accusations from the right continued unabated.

Contributing to the atmosphere of mounting suspicion and discord, Germany was beginning to experience the full force of the very effective English blockade, leading to severe shortages of food and fuel for heating. The country was slowly starving—a condition that would reach catastrophic proportions in the frigid "Turnip Winter" of 1916–17 when 250,000 civilians died of starvation or maladies resulting from malnutrition. Food riots broke out in several cities, and the first signs of labor unrest burst onto the surface. In 1915 Germany had experienced 137 strikes; in 1916, 240; in 1917, the number soared to 561. Then in January 1918, 400,000 strikers appeared on the streets of Berlin, and similar, though smaller, strikes followed in Düsseldorf, Kiel, Cologne, and Hamburg. By the end of the year, revolution would engulf the country.

The dramatic surge of labor unrest, especially in the vital munitions industry, spiked Hitler's loathing of the Social Democrats and labor unions. A comrade recalled, "Hitler became furious and shouted in a terrible voice that the pacifists and shirkers were losing the war." "What was the army fighting for if the homeland itself no longer wanted victory?" Hitler fumed. "For whom the immense sacrifices and privations? The soldier is expected to fight for victory and the homeland goes on strike against it." Hitler, one fellow soldier remembered, would sit "in a corner of our mess holding his head between his hands, in deep contemplation. Suddenly he would leap up, and, running about excitedly, say that in spite of our big guns victory would be denied us, for the invisible foes of the German people were a greater danger than the biggest cannon of the enemy." Already in 1915 he had written to an acquaintance in Munich that at war's end he hoped to find the German homeland "purer and cleansed from foreign influence," so that "not only will Germany's enemies from the outside be smashed but also our domestic internationalism will be broken up." His hatred of the Reds steadily escalated during the last two years of the war, and on his rare visits back to Germany he felt himself adrift in alien territory, surrounded by cynics, shirkers, socialists, and Jews. He was always eager to return to the front.

Hitler had found a home in the army. The war gave his life discipline and direction, and the army offered the perpetual outsider a sense of belonging that he had never before experienced. And yet, even among his closest comrades, he remained something of an oddity, "a white crow," as one put it, "that didn't go along with us when we damned the war to hell." While other soldiers had families or lovers or jobs waiting for them at home, Hitler did not. He received few letters or packages, even at Christmas, and he chose not to visit his family in Austria on any of his rare leaves. The men respected his bravery and reliability but found him peculiar—too quiet, too humorless, too much the prude. He didn't drink or smoke and would not join their banter about their sexual exploits and fantasies. He refused to visit the French prostitutes with his comrades— that was a betrayal of Germany's honor, he piously intoned, and besides, he was obsessed by a morbid fear of syphilis. The other men also found him a bit too zealous in his duties, too much devoted to the army, too much the idealist, the single-minded nationalist. He never indulged in the usual bellyaching about the tedious demands and discomforts of army life, and he grew irate at any stray remark that smacked of war weariness.

As the war dragged on, Hitler's identification with his adopted country became complete. Germany *had* to win the war; defeat—failure— was terrifying, a calamity too appalling, too shameful, to contemplate. Except for a few offhand comments, politics were off-limits in the early years of the war. "I was a soldier then," Hitler later explained, "and I didn't want to talk about politics. And really it was not the time for it." That began to change as Germany's military position deteriorated in 1917–18 and demoralization spread like a contagion through the troops. During those final years of the war the men close to him were startled at Hitler's furious outbursts against the Reds and the slackers, a theme that would soon grow into a pathological obsession by war's end. The Social Democrats and labor unions remained the primary targets of Hitler's vitriol, and, ironically given later developments, his comrades could not recall Hitler expressing anything other than mild, commonplace comments about Jews. One recalled that even when Hitler spoke of his bitter Vienna period and the strong Jewish presence there, it was "without spitefulness." Citing Hitler's good relations with the Jewish officers and men of the regiment, Captain Fritz Wiedemann, his immediate superior, simply could not believe that Hitler's "hatred of Jews dated back to that time." It was a Jewish officer, Hugo Gutmann, who had recommended Hitler for the Iron Cross first class. Even after Hitler rose to political prominence and they were badgered by the press and the party for their recollections of the Führer, his wartime comrades were hard-pressed to remember anything notable about his views on Jews or anti-Semitism— or about him at all.

There was, however, one striking feature of his military experience that deserves comment. Despite his lengthy service at the front and his two Iron Crosses, Hitler was repeatedly passed over for promotion and remained a lance corporal for the duration of the war. It could be that he was not eager for promotion since that would most likely have meant leaving his comfortable home in the regiment, but there were other, more troubling concerns. One of his superiors believed that Hitler was unsuited for command on account of "his mental instability," and, as Captain Wiedemann later reported, it was felt that Corporal Hitler simply lacked "the capacity for leadership."

In early October 1918, Hitler was blinded by mustard gas in a British attack near Ypres. After initial treatment in Flanders, he was transferred to a military hospital in Pasewalk, northeast of Berlin. The initial blindness passed, as was common in mild mustard gas cases, and Hitler's condition was not considered serious. The doctors concluded that his lingering blindness was largely psychosomatic, a psychological reaction to shock. He was being treated not in the ophthalmic but in the psychiatric section of the hospital. It was there, on November 10, that he heard the stunning news that the war was over, that Germany had signed an armistice—in effect, surrendered—the Kaiser had abdicated, and revolutionaries were on the streets of Berlin. On hearing this devastating report, Hitler suffered a sudden and highly unusual second onset of blindness, which the doctors were convinced was not the result of mustard gas poisoning but of hysteria. One examining psychiatrist is reported to have diagnosed Hitler as a "psychopath suffering from hysteria."

Hitler's deep shock at this shattering turn of events was shared by most Germans. Ignorant of the true military situation and misled by relentlessly upbeat bulletins from the Supreme Military Command that confidently announced that there was light at the end of the tunnel, that victory lay just around the bend, after the next offensive or the next or the next, the public was wholly unprepared for this utterly devastating news. It was simply inconceivable. After all, no enemy troops stood on German soil; German forces were still inside France and occupied virtually all of Belgium; Russia was defeated and in the throes of revolution; mutinies threatened the French army; and England was at the breaking point. But the position of the German army, the High Command understood, was desperate. Ludendorff's much vaunted spring offensive had failed, though the full extent of the catastrophe had been withheld not only from the people but also from the civilian government, such as it was. The final straw came in September when the Western Allies, buoyed by the arrival of American troops, launched a major offensive that threatened to break through German lines at any moment. If such a breach occurred, and the High Command feared that it was inevitable, Allied troops would steamroll into Germany. The situation was hopeless. To the great surprise of the parties in the Reichstag, Ludendorff, who operated virtually as a military dictator during the last two years of the war, demanded that the German government seek an immediate armistice. He now desperately sought not only to prevent an Allied breakthrough, which would reveal the utter failure of the army's High Command, but, equally important, to shift the responsibility for the defeat—and defeat it certainly was—onto the Reichstag.

News that Germany was seeking an armistice sent shockwaves across the country. The war-weary public, which had endured four years of suffering and sacrifice, desperately wanted peace, and the exhausted troops were in a state of near rebellion. Discipline broke down; soldiers defied their commanders, and many simply disappeared, deserting their units to make their way home. No one wanted to die in the last days of a lost war. Matters came to a head on November 4 at the naval station in Kiel when rebellious sailors mutinied, refusing orders to steam out of port to engage the British fleet in what would clearly have been a suicide mission. The mutiny at Kiel ignited a wildfire of uprising that quickly swept across the country. Workers surged into the streets, and workers' and soldiers' councils (*Räte*), following the Bolshevik example, sprang up spontaneously in almost every town and city. Revolutionary workers tore the insignia from the uniforms of returning soldiers. Red flags fluttered from city halls.

On November 9, with no viable options left to him and the situation deteriorating by the hour, Kaiser Wilhelm II passed into exile, and with him the proud German Empire of Bismarck and the Hohenzollerns was gone. Proceeding in uncharted constitutional waters, the last chancellor of Imperial Germany, Max von Baden, turned to the Social Democratic leader Friedrich Ebert to form a government. Ebert quickly formed a provisional government dominated by the two Socialist parties (the SPD, divided now into two parties—the majority Social Democrats and the more radical USPD, the Independent Social Democrats) and called a national congress of Workers, Soldiers, and Peasants Councils to convene in Berlin in December. With the country descending into violence, its task was to determine the form and future of a new German state. That congress, dominated by the moderate socialists, called for national elections to a constitutional convention that would draft a constitution for a democratic republic. Before those elections, the first in which women could vote, could take place, elements of the far left rose in revolt, hoping to derail the election and move the revolution onto a more radical course.

In a desperate move that would produce a fatal rift between the forces of the left, the provisional government enlisted Reichswehr troops and irregular formations of returning veterans (Free Corps) to suppress the Communist uprising. In a week of vicious street fighting in Berlin, radical leaders Rosa Luxemburg and Karl Liebknecht were brutally murdered. Despite lingering violence, the national election went forward, resulting in a sweeping victory for the democratic center and moderate left. The parties of the Peace Resolution carried three quarters of the vote and assembled a national constitutional convention in the small Thuringian city of Weimar, safely away from the sporadic street fighting and revolutionary tumult that continued to rock Berlin. The choice of venue also carried a symbolic message: Weimar was the city of Goethe and Schiller, the home of German humanism, and its selection was intended to demonstrate not only to the German public but to the Allies that the new Germany had turned away from Prussian authoritarianism and militarism.

For Hitler, these developments were much more than a bitter shock. Germany's defeat was *his* failure; Germany's humiliation, *his* disgrace, another degrading rejection of his innermost self. The German army, he believed—*had* to believe—had not lost the war. With victory virtually within its grasp, it had been stabbed in the back by the "pacifists and internationalists" at home. That, for Hitler, was the only explanation he could allow himself to believe, and with Germany's stunning collapse, a linkage, long on the cusp of his consciousness, now crystallized before him: the nation had been betrayed by an invidious conspiracy of Marxists and Jews. And with that appalling realization, all that he had absorbed in Vienna, all that he had internalized in the cafés and homeless shelters, came boiling to the surface in a blistering eruption of rage and hate. As he lay in his hospital bed in Pasewalk, "the shame of indignation and disgrace burned my brow . . . and hatred grew in me, hatred for those responsible for this deed."

Millions of returning soldiers were being discharged, finding their way through the revolutionary chaos to reach home. But Hitler was not eager to leave the war behind. "In the world of peace," the journalist Konrad Heiden astutely observed, "Hitler had been a foreigner, in the world of war he felt at home." Now he had nowhere to go. The army was dissolving, revolutionary workers' and soldiers' councils were sprouting all across the country, the Social Democrats, the ultimate outsiders of Imperial Germany, held power in Berlin, and revolution was in the air. In late November, as he struggled to come to grips with this nightmarish turn of events, Hitler was released from the hospital and ordered to report to the regimental reserve in Munich. With his usual flair for self-dramatization he would later claim that it was then, as he prepared to depart Pasewalk, that he made the momentous decision "to go into politics." In fact, he left the hospital with no other goal than to stay in the army for as long as possible, where he was guaranteed food, shelter, and for the time being regular pay. At twenty-nine years of age, he would soon be mustered out of the army and would again be, just as he had been in Vienna and prewar Munich, a mere face in the crowd, an unknown, with no profession, no prospects, and no future.

HITLER AND THE CHAOS OF POSTWAR GERMANY

W hen Hitler arrived in Munich in late November of 1918, he found a city roiling in political turmoil. Earlier in the month a Socialist revolution led by Kurt Eisner of the USPD, who had spent a year in prison for publicly opposing the war, had brushed aside the ancient Wittelsbach monarchy and proclaimed a Bavarian Socialist Republic. The Socialist government struggled to establish some semblance of order, but with food scarce, unemployment rampant, and thousands of armed veterans roaming the streets, it proved unable to master the deteriorating situation. On February 21, 1919, Eisner was assassinated by a reactionary fanatic, setting off a chain reaction of political violence that reduced Munich to virtual chaos. A cabinet headed by Majority Social Democrat (the MSPD) Johannes Hoffmann assumed power, but on April 7, a group of frustrated radicals, more anarchist and bohemian than Communist (some referred to them derisively as "coffeehouse revolutionaries") declared the creation of a government based on the Workers, Soldiers, and Peasants Councils. In the mounting disorder that ensued, the Hoffmann cabinet fled to Bamberg in northern Bavaria and refused to recognize this new Councils Republic (*Räterepublik*).

Led by a twenty-five-year-old poet and playwright, Ernst Toller, the Councils Republic fired off a barrage of reforms, some of them radical, others spectacularly idiosyncratic—capitalism would be abolished and free money issued; all banks and industrial firms were to be nationalized; agriculture was to be collectivized; a red army would be raised, and revolutionary tribunals were created to ferret out counterrevolutionary activities.

The new regime also ordered that poems by Hölderlin and Schiller be published on the front pages of all the city's newspapers, and its Commissar for Foreign Affairs, only recently released from an insane asylum, declared war on Württemberg and Switzerland because "these dogs" had failed to loan him badly needed locomotives. He also cabled Lenin and the pope indignantly complaining that his predecessor had absconded with the key to the ministerial toilet. It hardly came as a surprise when the *Räterepublik* fell after a mere six days, ousted by militant Communists who declared the creation of a Bavarian Soviet Republic on the Bolshevik model. The Communist takeover was led by two Russian Bolsheviks, Max Levien and Eugen Leviné, who proclaimed that this government, unlike its dilettantish predecessor, would represent "the genuine rule of the proletariat." They immediately called for a general strike, disarmed the Munich police, and set about creating a Red Army, manned by veterans and radical labor unionists. To pay for this force, they plundered homes in the better sections of town, and commanded all civilians to turn over their cash in return for government-backed credit vouchers. Following directives from Moscow, they ordered the arrest of aristocrats and prominent members of the upper middle class, fifty of whom were held hostage in a local high school. Bavaria, they proudly proclaimed, would constitute the advance outpost of a Communist archipelago that would stretch from Russia, to Hungary, to Austria, and into Western Europe.

In Bamberg, the Hoffmann cabinet appealed to the provisional government in Berlin to recruit a force of some 35,000 Free Corps troops to march against the Communist government in Munich. These Free Corps units were paramilitary associations formed spontaneously all across Germany in 1919 as six million veterans flooded back into the country and were being rapidly mustered out of the army. For the most part they were composed of demobilized soldiers, junior-grade officers, and enlisted men whose formative experience had been war and who found themselves unable or unwilling to demobilize psychologically. They were joined by an admixture of eager university students and young men who had missed out on the war and were impatient for action. They tended to be ultranationalist, anti-Marxist, and often anti-Semitic.

Far from being threatened by these paramilitary organizations, the Reichswehr viewed the Free Corps as useful auxiliaries to the severely reduced army and provided funds for their operations. The provisional government in Berlin engaged Free Corps units to protect Germany's eastern frontier against the Poles and Bolsheviks, but also deployed them against domestic enemies on the far left. Although their ostensible mission was to restore law and order, their actions amounted to a bloody crusade against the radical left. In the spring of 1919, Free Corps units, acting on government orders, brutally suppressed a Communist-inspired strike movement in the Ruhr and attacked strongholds of the radical left elsewhere in Germany. Germany was teetering on the cusp of civil war. It was a reflection of the near chaotic conditions prevailing in Germany that these quasi-legal armed formations could roam the country like the freebooters of the Thirty Years War, fighting the perceived threats from the left everywhere. Although they acted independently and were never united under a single command, these Free Corps units in 1919–20 numbered between 300,000 and 400,000 men, roughly four times the size of the regular army.

In late April 1919 Free Corps forces encircled "Red Munich," and then in an orgy of pitiless brutality during the first days of May, Free Corps troops, using heavy weapons and even flamethrowers, crushed the severely overmatched "Red Army." The leaders of the Red Republic were shot or beaten to death or executed after perfunctory trials; the fortunate ones escaped across the frontier. In all, some 600 people—1,200 by some estimates—died in the fighting and its bloody aftermath, leaving behind an indelible impression of Bolshevik terror and counterrevolutionary suppression.

Stationed in Munich throughout the most violent period of the revolution, Hitler witnessed firsthand the ferocious Marxist demons of his nightmares, the "un-German" revolutionaries who had sabotaged the Reich and delivered Germany to the rapacious Allies. Here he also found confirmation of his association of Jews with the radical left. Many of the Communist leaders were indeed Jewish. Of course, most Jews were not radicals and most radicals were not Jews, but many, and not just on the radical right, came to share this bogus notion during the postwar period of chaos, revolution, and violence. Those seeking a scapegoat for Germany's downfall had found one.

Contrary to his brief and obfuscating account of those turbulent days in *Mein Kampf*, Hitler did not take part in resisting, much less defeating, the Reds. As best he could, he kept his head down, serving unobtrusively and opportunistically the successive Socialist governments in the regular Bavarian army. He was relieved to escape Munich for almost two months, staying out of harm's way in Traunstein as a guard at a POW camp and returning to Munich in early February. Once back, his only duty was to guard the main railway station and later to inform on members of his unit whom he suspected of leftist sympathies, a task he performed with his usual zeal. Munich in the spring of 1919 was essentially under military rule, and the Bavarian Reichswehr was determined to ferret out and extinguish any lingering subversive sentiments among the troops. To this end, it established a military intelligence bureau that initiated a program to indoctrinate the troops in the proper anti-Marxist, nationalist values. A set of "speakers courses" was created to train "suitable personalities from among the troops" who seemed to have the potential to be effective instructors, and in early June Hitler was assigned to this program. The courses, taught largely by faculty at the university, included such offerings as "German History Since the Reformation," "The Political History of the War," "Socialism in Theory and Practice," and "Our Economic Situation and the Peace Conditions." All the instructors had impeccable nationalist credentials, but one in particular made a strong impression on Hitler. Gottfried Feder, an engineer by training and a self-taught economist, lectured on his concept of "interest slavery," drawing a distinction between capital derived from productive labor and capital accruing from stock market speculation and interest. Jews, he argued fiercely, were masters of the latter, of international finance that exploited and enslaved honest Germans by their unproductive manipulation of capital. The topic of his first lecture, "Breaking Interest Slavery," would soon be embedded in the National Socialist program. It was, Hitler believed, "a theoretical truth which would inevitably be of immense importance for the future of the German people."

One day, during a break between classes, Karl Alexander von Müller, one of Hitler's instructors, noticed a group of students gathered around one of their number, engaging in a fierce discussion. "The men seemed spellbound by a man in their midst, who railed at them uninterruptedly in a strangely guttural yet passionate voice. I had the unsettling feeling that their excitement was his work and simultaneously the source of his own power. I saw a pale, thin face under an unsoldierly shock of hanging hair, and striking large light blue eyes that glittered fanatically." Later he remarked to Captain Mayr, head of the program, "Do you know you have a natural orator in your group?" Hitler very quickly emerged as the star of the program. His oddly gripping manner of speech, his fanatical intensity, and his populist language provoked enthusiastic, stormy responses from the soldiers who formed his captive audiences. He had discovered a hidden talent. "For all at once I was offered an opportunity of speaking before a larger audience; and the thing I had always presumed from pure feeling without knowing it was now corroborated: I could 'speak.'"

In July, Mayr chose him as one of a small number of agents to conduct a five-day indoctrination course at a Reichswehr camp near Augsburg, where returning POWs were said to be harboring Communist sentiments. His speeches were thunderous attacks on the Marxists, the "November criminals" who had stabbed the army in the back, and the universally hated Treaty of Versailles, signed in June. "Herr Hitler," one of the soldiers in his audience remarked, "is the born people's speaker, and by his fanaticism and his crowd appeal he clearly compels the attention of his listeners, and makes them think his way." He was particularly fierce when speaking of the Jews. So extreme, so inflammatory were his anti-Jewish harangues that the camp commander actually requested Hitler to tone down his anti-Semitic rhetoric. By the time he returned to Munich Hitler had acquired the reputation as something of an expert on Jewish matters, so much so that when Mayr received a letter from a Herr Adolf Gemlich asking for clarification on the "Jewish question," he turned to Hitler to write the response.

Was it the case, Gemlich wanted to know, that the Jews were a threat, as some saw them to be, or was their "corruptive influence" being overestimated? Hitler began his letter by affirming that "the danger posed by Jewry for our people" was very real and must be combated. But "anti-Semitism as a political movement," he insisted, could "not be defined by emotional impulses, but by recognition of the facts," the first and most important of which was that Jewry was "a race not a religious community." The Jew "lives amongst us as a non-German alien race," with the full rights of citizenship, while corrupting German society by its obsession with money. In the Jew's striving for money and power, he is "unscrupulous in the choice of methods and pitiless in their employment. . . . His power is the power of money, which multiplies in his hands effortlessly and endlessly through interest"—echoes of Feder. "Every higher goal men strive for—religion, democracy, socialism—is to the Jew only a means to an end, the way to satisfy his lust for gold and domination." In what would be one of his many ominous biological metaphors, the Jew, he asserted, was "a racial tuberculosis of the nations."

Emotional anti-Semitism might bring temporary satisfaction but would produce only senseless pogroms. But "anti-Semitism based on reason" would lead to a systematic legal campaign against the Jews and the elimination of their privileges. This could not be accomplished by a weak democratic government led by "irresponsible majorities" with "internationalist phrases and slogans." Needed instead was a powerful state led by "nationally minded leadership personalities." The rights and privileges of this alien, corrosive race must be curbed or eliminated, but "the ultimate objective," he concluded, "must be the irrevocable removal of the Jews in general."

Hitler's letter, dated September 16, 1919, is his first recorded written pronouncement on the "Jewish question," indeed, his first recorded political statement, and it offers a foreshadowing of the basic elements of National Socialist ideology—a powerful national state led by a ruthless, determined leadership, rejection of democratic government, a spiritual rebirth of the nation from within, and radical, racial anti-Semitism. It also reveals that by the fall of 1919 the potent brew of prejudices, hatreds, and resentments formed in Vienna and stirred during the war was hardening into a cohesive political vision. Hitler was acquiring a political education; he was poised for an entry into politics.

In addition to investigating and combating Marxist subversion among the troops, Mayr's unit was also charged with the surveillance of Munich's raucous political scene. He sent his agents to monitor the numerous political parties and organizations that were springing up all around the city. Some might be dangerous, some useful. On Friday, September 12, 1919, he dispatched Hitler to report on a meeting of an obscure political group that called itself the German Workers' Party (Deutsche Arbeiterpartei or DAP). Held in a cramped backroom in the Sterneckerbräu Beer Hall, the meeting was an unimpressive affair, attended by only a smattering of unimposing men. Founded earlier in the year by Anton Drexler, a railway mechanic, and Karl Harrer, a sportswriter associated with the semisecret right-wing Thule Society, the party had few members and even fewer sources of financial support. It had the air of a sleepy, down-at-the-heels debating club.

The speaker that evening was Gottfried Feder, who spoke on "How and by What Means Can Capitalism Be Eliminated." It was one of Feder's favorite themes and one that held Hitler's attention, but he was most interested in the discussion that followed. Although he was there to monitor the proceedings, he could not resist throwing himself into the fray when a university professor in the tiny crowd asserted that Bavaria should secede from Germany and form a union with Austria. Hitler's withering demolition of that position so impressed Drexler that he turned to a colleague on the platform and commented: "Man, this one has a mouth on him. We could use him!" When the meeting broke up, Drexler pressed a copy of his pamphlet *My Political Awakening* into Hitler's hands and invited him to come to the next meeting. Hitler left underwhelmed.

The pamphlet, however, piqued his interest. In it, Drexler inveighed against the twin evils of Marxism and Jewish finance capital and called for a national revival by bringing the working and middle classes together in a genuine *Volksgemeinschaft*, a people's community, united under a strong authoritarian national government. Hitler was surprised a few days later when he received a card informing him that he had been admitted as a member of the DAP and inviting him to the next meeting of the executive committee. He was initially disinclined to accept the unsolicited offer, but on reflection realized that the little party offered some intriguing possibilities. Its small size would allow him to enter on the ground floor, a virtual founder, and its very sleepiness along with its lack of strong personalities meant that he could immediately exert his influence. After securing the army's permission, he joined the party as member number 550—a rather misleading status since the party rolls began with number 500.

When he attended the next meeting at an even smaller and dingier locale, he discovered that the party had no program, no plans, no advertising, no typewriter, no mimeograph machine, not even a rubber stamp (a vital necessity for any German organization). It was also virtually penniless. The executive committee, chaired by Drexler and Harrer, wanted to expand the membership but had no idea how to go about it. Hitler suggested advertising an upcoming meeting in the local press, not simply plastering posters about town and sending handwritten invitations to likely supporters. The executive committee was skeptical but followed Hitler's suggestion. The meeting at the Hofbräukeller on October 16 drew a modest crowd of 111, but it was by far the largest the party had ever attracted. A week later an audience of over three hundred filled the Eberl-keller to attend a DAP rally, at which Hitler spoke again. Hitler was still on the Reichswehr payroll (he would be until the summer of 1920), which meant that he had plenty of time to devote to political activities. Mayr's intelligence unit was pleased to have an agent inside the party (Hitler no doubt inflated its importance in his report) and even provided a modest subsidy for the party. Hitler was tireless, always looking for ways to draw attention to the party, to himself. He assumed direction of the party's propaganda, such as it was, and began to transform the party from an insignificant men's club to an active, high-profile political organization. He pressed the leadership to establish a permanent office, a small windowless space in the Sterneckerbräu Beer Hall, and begin acquiring office machinery, printed membership cards, stationery, and a business manager.

As 1919 turned to 1920, Hitler was fast winning a reputation as a firebrand speaker; his appearances were a spectacle. He seemed to be everywhere. He spoke in beer halls, in auditoriums, theaters, on street corners, in parks, in front of crowds large and small. The themes never varied: the November criminals, the bankruptcy of democracy, the Jewish world conspiracy, the menace of Marxism. All delivered at a fever pitch of rage and fury that found ample resonance in the climate of fear and resentment and anger that prevailed in post-revolutionary Munich.

Those feelings of betrayal were stoked by the actions of the victorious Allies, who in the summer of 1919 delivered a body blow to the progressive forces attempting to establish Germany's first working democracy. In January 1919 when representatives of the new, democratic Germany were summoned to the Bourbon palace at Versailles, they were informed that, contrary to their expectations, they were not there to negotiate but to receive the terms of the victors. The Germans had placed their hopes for fair treatment in the American president, Woodrow Wilson, whose famous "Fourteen Points" had, among other things, called for a peace without annexations and trumpeted the principle of national self-determination of peoples. The Germans had hoped—and believed—that Wilson's terms would be the basis for the talks. But Wilson proved no match for David Lloyd George and Georges Clemenceau, whose nations,

after five years of privation and slaughter, were not inclined to be generous. They were determined to weaken Germany by squeezing it, as the
British prime minister so graphically put it, "until the pips squeak." They
proceeded to do just that by detaching territory from the Reich, imposing stiff reparations, and dismantling Germany's military establishment.
In the east, Germany was forced to cede West Prussia and Posen to the
new Polish state, creating a Polish Corridor to the Baltic that separated
East Prussia from Germany proper. To give the Poles a port on the sea,
the German city of Danzig was placed under the administration of the
League of Nations, and Memel, a narrow strip of German territory along
the Baltic, was ceded to Lithuania.

In the west, Alsace and Lorraine, annexed by Germany in 1871, were
returned to France, and the thoroughly German Saar region was placed
under League of Nations administration for fifteen years. Other smaller
bits of territory were lost to Denmark and Belgium. Germany also forfeited
all its overseas colonial territories in Africa and the South Pacific. But most
shocking, and to the Germans most unjust, the British and French refused
to allow a union of German Austria with the new German state. The Austrians made clear their desire for such a union, but the Allies were not
about to see Germany, democratic or not, emerge from the war larger than
it had been in 1914. To the Germans this merely proved that the treaty's
much heralded principle of national self-determination was nothing but a
fraud, applying only in instances when it hurt German interests and not
when it benefited the new democratic state.

Though not as controversial but equally humiliating, the armaments
clauses of the treaty essentially stripped Germany of its military establishment, destroying its ability to make war—and, the Germans complained,
to defend itself. A large strip of territory in the Rhineland was declared a
demilitarized zone, making it possible for French forces to march directly
into Germany's industrial heartland if they so chose. The army was reduced
to 100,000 troops; Germany was allowed no air force, no tanks, or heavy
artillery; the General Staff was disbanded; no conscription was allowed;
and the navy was permitted only six warships and no submarines. The
German army, pride of the nation, had virtually ceased to exist, rendering
Germany, as its delegates bitterly complained, essentially defenseless.

Finally, the Allies presented Germany with a bill for the financial losses suffered by the victorious powers, but no final sum was set at the conference. Germany was compelled to sign a blank check for reparations owed. Most galling, a war guilt clause, Article 231, forced Germany to accept sole responsibility for the outbreak of the war; it was the ultimate justification for the reparations and the other harsh clauses of the treaty.

The terms of the treaty were made public in May 1919, igniting a firestorm of indignation in Germany. The armistice had been an unexpected jolt of harsh reality; the treaty was a profoundly destabilizing aftershock. Everyone from the far left to the far right was outraged by this "dictated peace," this *Diktat*. Conveniently forgotten in their indignation were the draconian terms Germany had imposed on a defeated Russia in the Treaty of Brest-Litovsk only a year before, and there was little doubt that Germany was prepared to make equally extensive territorial demands and reparations claims against the Western Allies, had it won the Great War. Also dismissed was the fact that by agreeing to these terms Germany would avoid military occupation.

So outraged was the German delegation that it refused to sign and left for Berlin. But the provisional government faced harsh realities. The British blockade was still in effect and would remain so until Germany agreed to the treaty, and the threat of Allied invasion loomed ominously over the proceedings. The Germans were given only five days to accept the terms or face military occupation. The deadline was extended by forty-eight hours because the current cabinet resigned in protest and a new government had to be formed. Finally, on June 28, 1919, the demoralized German delegation signed the treaty in the ornate Hall of Mirrors at Versailles.

The Versailles Treaty was a catastrophe for the new Republic and a boon to its enemies. It was to prove one of the treaty's most profound weaknesses that the Allies, following Wilson's lead, refused to deal with representatives of the old regime, allowing the Kaiser and his generals to evade responsibility for the catastrophe they had brought on the country—and Europe. Instead, the Allies compelled the democratic parties of the fledgling Republic to accept the humiliating terms. The timing could not have been worse. Since January elected representatives had been laboring in the provincial town of Weimar to write a constitution for the new state. Their deliberations resulted in a constitution for a democratic welfare state, with guarantees of individual rights, the enfranchisement of women, and universal suffrage, as well as a radical system of proportional representation that ensured that almost all views would be heard in the Reichstag.

But these progressive accomplishments were buried under an avalanche of outrage from across the political spectrum when almost simultaneously the Allies presented their final peace terms in Paris. Although the parties that drafted the constitution of the Weimar Republic, as it quickly came to be called, had not been responsible for the disastrous conduct of the war or Germany's capitulation, the new Republic would be saddled with the corrosive legacy of both. At the very outset of its tenuous existence, the Weimar Republic was identified with Germany's defeat and the universally unpopular treaty that followed from it. It was a legacy the new democratic state never overcame.

For Hitler, the treaty provided welcome ammunition for his assault on the "November criminals" and the democratic government they were trying to establish. It was, Hitler charged, a "treaty of shame," a "second betrayal of the people," its terms "the shackles of Versailles." And, of course, it was the creation of the Jews. It became a staple of his speeches that by the end of 1919 were drawing increasing public attention to him. Initially, the DAP turned to more established speakers from the racialist (*Völkisch*) nationalist right to attract an audience, but it gradually became apparent that Hitler, who often spoke second on the program, was the real attraction. At the party's first mass meeting, held in the spacious festival hall of the Hofbräuhaus on February 20, 1920, the keynote speaker was a well-known figure in right-wing circles. He spoke for two hours, and his address was met with polite applause from the roughly two thousand in attendance. When he finished, Hitler took the podium and began an expansive discussion of the party's new program—the Twenty-five Points—which he and Drexler had recently formulated. As he spoke, the mood in the crowded hall underwent a dramatic change. It was as if an electrical charge had jolted the crowd, showering sparks of excitement throughout the giant hall. The audience repeatedly interrupted Hitler with thunderous applause; fights broke out between loyalists and hecklers from the left, but Hitler continued on, carrying his audience with him. He had stolen the show.

Hitler's appearances soon became pieces of political theater, where confrontation was as important as the content of his remarks. Battles with the Communists and Socialists, who often appeared at the DAP's public meetings, became a regular occurrence, adding an element of danger and excitement to a Hitler event. During one Hitler speech, which would go down in Nazi lore as the "Battle of the Hall," a wild, chair-throwing melee erupted in the crowded Festival Hall of the Hofbräuhaus, but Hitler, dodging bottles and beer steins, stood his ground at the podium, refusing to yield or flee. On another occasion a group of toughs led by Hitler invaded a talk by a prominent Bavarian separatist, dragged the speaker off the platform, beat him, and took over the proceedings. For that brazen act of public mayhem, Hitler was arrested and sentenced to three months imprisonment—a typically light sentence for right-wing offenders—and then he spent only one month in Stadelheim prison. Among his followers, the jail sentence merely added to Hitler's reputation as a stalwart hero persecuted for his courageous acts of defiance.

Hitler carefully honed his skills as a public speaker, studying his gestures and expressions before a mirror. His photographer Heinrich Hoffmann took shots of Hitler auditioning different poses. His speeches were his own—no ghostwriter, no assistant. He wrote out notes on several large sheets of paper, which he kept to his left on the podium. When he finished with one sheet, he passed it unostentatiously to the right and continued. The notes served as an outline, and the impression he gave was that of a man consumed by passion, speaking extemporaneously from the heart. The effect on his audience was spectacular. Even his critics—and there were many—acknowledged the power he exerted over his listeners. He seemed to possess an instinctive ability to read a crowd, to speak their language, and to project his own disappointments and resentments as theirs, as Germany's. The journalist Konrad Heiden, a particularly tenacious critic who closely followed Hitler's career, was struck by the incongruities of his private person and his public being: "Silent in a circle of three and sluggish in conversation, without interest in his own private life, this miserable human nothing could think only in public terms, feel only the feeling of the mass, and when the nothing spoke with the people, it was as though the voice of the people were speaking."

Hearing Hitler address a large crowd on Munich's Königsplatz, one observer was overwhelmed by the performance—a reaction that was not uncommon.

Critically I studied this slight, pale man, his dark hair parted on one side and falling again and again over his sweating brow. Threatening and beseeching, with small, pleading hands and flaming, steel-blue eyes, he had the look of a fanatic. . . . I do not know how to describe the emotions that swept over me as I heard this man. His words were like a scourge. When he spoke of the disgrace of Germany, I felt ready to spring on any enemy. His appeal to German manhood was a call to arms, the gospel he preached a sacred truth. He seemed another Luther. I forgot everything but the man; then, glancing round, I saw that his magnetism was holding these thousands as one. . . . The intense will of the man, the passion of his sincerity seemed to flow from him into me. I experienced an exaltation that could be likened only to religious conversion.

With each passing month, the crowds grew larger, and Hitler's influence within the DAP mushroomed. At his insistence, the party in 1920 changed its name to the National Socialist German Workers Party or NSDAP, conjuring up highly unorthodox—and confusing—associations with both the left and right. It was a mouthful, and its enemies were fond of calling its followers *Nazis*, a diminutive for *Nationalsozialisten*, just as the Socialists were often referred to as *Sozis*. Hitler displayed an uncanny, instinctive feel for propaganda, for marketing. He believed that the party needed a symbol, an emblem that would be instantly recognized and associated with the NSDAP. He selected the swastika, an ancient Sanskrit symbol that was also found among the native tribes of North America. It was occasionally painted on the helmets of the Free Corps and other right-wing groups, but the Nazis would make it their own. The party needed a flag, a banner to be carried in parades and to be draped on podiums at meetings. A black swastika emblazoned in the center of a stark white circle on a background of bright red was the design Hitler hit upon. The red, he reasoned, would appeal to workers, while the combination of black, white, and red, the old imperial colors, would reassure nationalists and others on the right. The party also adopted a handful of short pithy slogans—"the common good before the individual good" (*Gemeinnutz geht vor Eigennutz*) and "Germany Awaken!" (*Deutschland Erwache!*) to appear on posters, leaflets, and other official publications of the party. With an easily recognizable symbol, a new and unusual name, a flag, and catchy slogans, Hitler, in modern advertising parlance, was creating a brand.

Working with Drexler, Hitler had rewritten the party's program, producing the "Twenty-five Points," which would remain the core of the "unalterable" National Socialist platform throughout the party's existence. The new program, echoed in hundreds of stump speeches, pamphlets, and later in Hitler's *Mein Kampf*, called for the nationalization of trusts and cartels, the establishment of consumer cooperatives, "profit sharing in big business," the "breaking of interest slavery" (whatever that meant—even Hitler seemed unclear), and the ennoblement of the German worker. Its language borrowed heavily from the left, referring to members as "party comrades," invoking "German socialism," and calling for a classless "*Volksgemeinschaft*," a people's community to overcome Germany's traditional social, regional, and religious cleavages.

The program also courted the middle class, especially small-business interests, calling for "the creation and maintenance of a sound *Mittelstand*." It demanded "the immediate communalization of the big department stores and their leasing to small shopkeepers at low rents." Since the major department store chains were Jewish-owned, the attack on them, the party believed, was a major selling point in its anti-Semitic agenda. In all government contracts and purchases, the party promised "the most favorable consideration to small businessmen . . . whether on the national, state, or local levels." It also advocated the creation of corporatist "chambers based on occupation and profession" as a counterweight to the powerful labor unions and corporate giants.

Like all rightist organizations and parties, the NSDAP's program was bellicosely nationalistic and expansionist, calling for "the union of all Germans . . . in a Greater Germany" and "living space" (*Lebensraum*) in the East "for the nourishment of our people and the settlement of our excess population." It reviled the odious Treaty of Versailles, with its fraudulent promises of the national self-determination of peoples, and its demilitarization of Germany that left the Reich virtually defenseless. It promised to undo the repellent clauses of the treaty, indeed, to smash this "treaty of shame" and liberate Germany from its shackles. It pledged to make Germany great again.

Its most strident element, however, was its radical anti-Semitism. The party pledged to fight "against all those who create no values, who make high profits without any mental or physical work." These profiteers and stock market capitalists, the party made clear, "are mostly Jews. They live the good life, reaping where they have not sown. They control and rule us with their money." Germany should be governed only by Germans, and citizenship in the promised classless people's community was to be a matter of race. Only people "of German blood" could become people's comrades (*Volksgenossen*) and only people's comrades could become citizens of the Greater German Reich. As Point Four of the program emphatically declared, "No Jew, therefore, can be a *Volksgenosse*." Jews and other non-Germans were to be excluded from the rights of citizenship and expelled from all public offices at all levels of government. There was little new or original about such ideas; most were staples of virtually every far-right party and organization in Germany. What was distinctive was the insistent interweaving of left and right in the program and the party's robust determination to win support from Germany's working class. Certainly the NSDAP was, as Bavaria's interior minister put it, "the noisiest and stormiest of the nationalist groups," but, he added, the party's most salient feature in 1920 was its virulent, unrelenting anti-Semitism. Although other right-wing parties indulged in anti-Semitic rhetoric, none could compare with the Nazis' vicious diatribes against the Jews. For Hitler and the NSDAP, anti-Semitism was not ancillary to the party's message of anti-Marxism and radical nationalism; it was the connective tissue that held the program together, the sinews of the party's propaganda, the core of its ideology.

As Hitler shrilly proclaimed in speech after speech, the Jews were behind "Bolshevism," "Free Masonry," "Pacifism," "Wall Street capitalism," "the rapacious Allies." They were responsible for the loss of the war, for the inflation, for the French occupation of the Rhineland. The British press was "99 percent" Jewish; "the Jewish-democratic press of America" did the bidding of "large Jewish firms." Who had enslaved the German proletariat? "Jews again!" Who controlled the League of Nations, and dominated "the history of the world over the heads of Kings and Presidents" and managed "brutally to enslave all peoples—Once more the Jews!" These and similar charges, made daily in Hitler's speeches and in the party press, went far beyond the official program. Although Hitler and others within the party would repeatedly invoke the "immutable" Twenty-five Points, as if they were engraved in tablets of stone, the formal program slipped into the background, serving merely as a point of departure for more expansive, more plastic appeals.

The Nazis always impressed observers with their raw energy and activism, but it was more than their "noisiness" that separated them from their right-wing competitors; it was the very nature of the party itself. Hitler was determined that the NSDAP would not be a conventional political party, but a movement driven by an all-embracing ideological vision that would challenge and ultimately vanquish the "Jewish Marxism" of the left. And it would pursue its vision with ruthless, fanatical zeal. The party would tolerate no compromises, no half measures, no dialogue. "There is no making pacts with Jews," Hitler later warned in *Mein Kampf*. "There can only be the hard 'either—or.'"

Hitler's radicalism, his growing mastery over crowds, and his emphasis on action attracted a wide variety of men and transformed the character and identity of the party. While the DAP of Drexler and Harrer drew followers who were for the most part nonunion workers, craftsmen, and small shopkeepers, Hitler attracted a different element. He began by recruiting men from his old regiment, from the barracks, and other combat veterans. These were men with few ties to a middle-class past and who had contempt for the moral confines of bourgeois life. They were comfortable in uniform, with weapons, military discipline, and violence, men of action who would not be constrained either by bourgeois convention or even law. They believed that they could do anything, accomplish anything through iron will, determination, and, when necessary, by force—men, in other words, cut from the same cloth as Hitler. As Hitler's reputation grew, such men flooded into the little DAP and quickly swamped the original membership. Although he did not directly challenge the party's executive committee, Hitler built a cadre of men loyal to him that gradually undermined its authority. Dietrich Eckart, a hard-drinking poet and journalist with good connections in artistic and social circles, acted as something of a mentor to the younger Hitler. Eckart was a ferocious Jew hater and published a scurrilously anti-Semitic sheet called *Auf Gut Deutsch* (*In Plain German*). After hearing Hitler speak for the first time, Eckart believed he had discovered the "messiah" who could unite the country and lead Germany out of the leftist, pacifist darkness. He introduced the untutored Hitler not only to important figures in the *Völkisch* movement but to moneyed members of the Munich social elite as well. It was Eckart and his connections who raised the funds to buy the tiny *Münchner Beobachter*, which, as the *Völkischer Beobachter* (*People's Observer*), would become the party's official newspaper.

Also drawn to Hitler by his speeches was Alfred Rosenberg, a Baltic German who was of a philosophical disposition, given to conspiracy theories involving Jews, Freemasons, and Marxists. His prolific writings in the *Völkisch* press, with titles such as his 1919 books *The Tracks of the Jews Through the Ages* and *Immorality in the Talmud*, fairly bristled with crackpot ideas and were couched in exactly the turgid, pseudo-profound language that appealed to the autodidact Hitler. Rosenberg also introduced Hitler to the sensational *Protocols of the Elders of Zion*, a fraudulent Russian work that purported to reveal a Jewish conspiracy to dominate the world. The *Protocols* was making the rounds in Europe, and although it was obviously a work of pure invention, it stirred anti-Semitic sentiments across the continent. In 1923 Hitler would appoint Rosenberg to the editorship of the *Völkischer Beobachter*.

Another new party member, Rudolf Hess, had been trained as a combat pilot toward the end of the war, and as a student in postwar Munich had been profoundly influenced by Professor Karl Haushofer's concept of *Lebensraum*, living space, as the key to a nation's power. Haushofer argued that culturally superior but "land-starved" states must expand territorially or slip into inevitable decline. Germany's only hope for survival as a great power lay in acquiring land in the East, by which he meant Russia. Hess introduced these ideas to Hitler. Several years younger than Hitler, Hess was not terribly bright, but he became slavishly devoted to Hitler and would serve as his loyal personal secretary.

Also among this group of early Hitler converts was twenty-year-old Hermann Esser, a flamboyant character so thoroughly disreputable in his private life that Hitler openly referred to him as a scoundrel—but a useful one. Esser carried on a variety of unsavory sexual affairs and was said to live exclusively on the income of his various mistresses, but in these early days he proved to be, after Hitler, the party's most popular speaker. When Hitler became official leader of the NSDAP in 1921 he placed Esser in charge of the party's propaganda.

At thirty-nine a veritable tribal elder by the Nazis' youthful standards, Julius Streicher was a notoriously crude character. Short and stocky with a barrel chest, a shaven head, and an intimidating, blustering manner, Streicher was perhaps the most violently anti-Semitic of the Nazi leaders, a position for which there was keen competition. In early 1923 he began publishing a weekly newspaper, *Der Stürmer* (*The Striker*), a particularly vulgar tabloid that specialized in salacious depictions of grotesquely distorted Jews molesting pure Aryan women, their clothes torn, breasts exposed. Although Streicher's paper was and would remain an embarrassment to many party leaders, it had Hitler's full support. Streicher earned Hitler's enduring gratitude when in 1921 he deserted the German Socialist Party (despite its name, a right-wing party) and joined the NSDAP, bringing his many followers with him, a move that virtually doubled the size of the Nazi party.

These men, more militant and active than the executive committee, transformed the NSDAP into a more radical, revolutionary party. Some in the leadership were uncomfortable with Hitler's raw ambition and feared that he was moving the party too far, too fast—and that they were losing control. But efforts to rein in Hitler proved unsuccessful, and Harrer resigned from the executive committee. Although Drexler assumed the chairmanship, it was increasingly clear that Hitler had eclipsed the stodgy executive committee and had become the catalyst of the party.

Hitler's leadership was officially confirmed at a membership meeting in January 1922. The party's membership was growing, chapters (*Ortsgruppen*) were opening in other towns, and another set of adherents, energetic, ruthless men drawn less by ideology than by Hitler's dynamism and call to action, joined the party. Hermann Göring was a celebrated war hero, winner of *Pour le Mérite*, Germany's highest award for bravery in combat, and the last group commander of the illustrious Richthofen squadron. After the war he had bounced from one job to another—he flew as a stunt pilot in air circuses in Denmark and Sweden, where he married a Swedish baroness; he became a commercial pilot, an aircraft salesman for Fokker; he enrolled at the university in Munich. Too restless to settle down, he found peacetime sorely lacking in the adventure he had enjoyed during the war. In 1921 he walked into the party's new office in the Corneliusstrasse and offered his services. Hitler was delighted to have a genuine war hero onboard. Göring, who ultimately became Hitler's extremely powerful deputy and second in command of the Third Reich, projected an image of a dashing man of action, jolly, outgoing, a hail-fellow-well-met. He was also utterly ruthless. Although he shared Hitler's xenophobia and anti-Semitism, he was less interested in ideology than in action and power. He joined the Nazi party, he later remarked, not because of any ideological nonsense but because it was revolutionary.

Göring was not the portly, almost clownish figure he would later become, but a man of soldierly bearing and physique. It was precisely his distinguished military background and his swaggering persona that prompted Hitler to put him in charge of a new party formation whose ostensible task was to protect the party's speakers from enemies at public meetings and rallies. These men were the rough and ready of the party, ex-soldiers, Free Corps veterans, and thugs eager to smash heads, to meet the Communists and Social Democrats in battle and lay claim to the streets. Initially called the Gymnastic and Sports Division, an appellation that fooled no one, in late 1921 the organization was renamed the Sturmabteilung (Storm Section) or SA. Although they did not yet wear the yellowish brown uniforms that would become ubiquitous features of the German political landscape, in the summer of 1922 the Storm Troopers appeared in the beer halls and streets of Munich, quickly earning a reputation for violence and thuggery.

Göring was officially in charge of the SA, but Ernst Röhm was its real driving force. Like Eckart, Rosenberg, and Hess, Röhm had joined the DAP in 1919, and he was the most important of the Hitler loyalists. Wounded in the war, his face badly scarred by gunfire, Röhm was above all a soldier, and like Hitler he was unwilling to leave the war behind. "War and unrest," he wrote in a 1928 memoir, "appeal to me more than the orderly life of your respectable burgher." He had fought for four years in the trenches, was a recipient of the Iron Cross first class, and was still a captain in the army in the early postwar years.

His duties in the new Reichswehr included liaising with the various right-wing organizations that were sprouting like weeds around Munich. Röhm had contacts with a variety of right-wing paramilitary groups, from which he funneled men into the DAP. He was committed to establishing a fighting force for the party and hoped ultimately to forge a coalition of rightist paramilitary organizations that would combat the Marxists. He convinced the army to train SA men in the military arts, and he was also in charge of a stockpile of weapons from the demobilized army and Free Corps. In what proved to be a crucial ingredient of right-wing terror, he surreptitiously supplied various counterrevolutionary groups, especially the SA, with small arms.

Röhm envisioned the SA as a private army under his command and largely independent of the party leadership. Hitler, who respected Röhm as a fellow front soldier—he was one of the very few who addressed Hitler with the familiar *du*—was also keen to have such a paramilitary organization, but he took a quite different view of its role. For Hitler, the Storm Troopers were to be subordinate to the party leadership and serve as an important weapon to be wielded by the party for its agitation and propaganda activities. Blurred in these early years of the NSDAP's existence, those conflicting visions would strain the relationship between the SA and the party down to 1934.

By 1922 Hitler had become a local phenomenon, not only a major figure in Munich's right-wing demimonde but something of a minor celebrity about town. He was seen at the opera, at concerts, at films—he was a great fan of the movies, especially the Hollywood variety—and met regularly for social evenings at the Café Neumayer, overlooking the Viktualienmarkt, with his cronies and admirers—Göring, Rosenberg, Esser; and Max Amann, his former sergeant and since 1921 business manager of the party; Ulrich Graf, a wrestler and barroom bouncer who served as his bodyguard; Emil Maurice, his driver and general factotum; Heinrich Hoffmann, who became Hitler's personal photographer. At the end of an evening of Hitler monologues, an armed escort would accompany their leader back to his narrow, one-room flat in the Thierschstrasse.

Hitler's reputation as an eccentric and political maverick piqued the interest of some in the city's more refined social set. Ernst "Putzi" Hanfstaengl, heir to a lucrative international art reproduction firm, was won over to Hitler after hearing him speak to a mass meeting in the Kindlkeller in November 1922. Tall and gangly, Hanfstaengl was a well-heeled, Harvard-educated bon vivant with connections to the business and social worlds of Munich. He was also a man of culture, an accomplished amateur musician whose vigorous piano playing, especially of Wagner, entranced Hitler.

Hanfstaengl took it upon himself to introduce Hitler into polite society, where he was a hit with a number of society ladies who adopted this thrilling—and delightfully dangerous—bohemian with a thick Austrian accent and peculiarly clipped mustache. Helene Bechstein of the Bechstein piano fortune, and Elsa Bruckmann, whose family owned a major publishing firm in Munich, took a particular interest in him, treating him much like a bright son in need of social instruction. They mothered him, gave him money, advised him on matters of etiquette and attire, and held soirees for him at their salons in Munich and Berlin. On such occasions his behavior was decidedly odd: he might chat with courtly Viennese charm or sit through dinner in stony silence. If asked a question on some political or social matter, he might abruptly jump to his feet and deliver a passionate speech, bellowing as if he were addressing a crowd of thousands at the Hofbräuhaus. Then he would just as abruptly bow to his host and depart. He never failed to make an impression.

For Hitler, the pinnacle of these social connections was to come in Bayreuth where Helene Bechstein introduced him to Wagner's son Siegfried and his wife, Winifred, and to the ancient Houston Stewart Chamberlain, the expatriate Englishman who had married one of Wagner's daughters and become a fervent German nationalist and racist. The Wagners were surprised and impressed by Hitler's extensive knowledge of the Master's operas. Winifred was utterly charmed by Hitler and saw him as the "coming man" in German politics. Siegfried tolerated him, indulging his wife and treating the exotic, sallow-faced Austrian rather like a not quite housebroken mascot.

Hitler was generally indifferent to his appearance; he wore distinctly eccentric attire—not the usual conservative uniform favored by politicians—black suits and shoes, starched shirts, stiff collars, cravats. Aside from the lederhosen, knee stockings, incongruous brown leather vest, and traditional Bavarian jacket he sometimes donned for outdoor events, he could be seen around the city wearing a black slouch hat and a seedy trench coat, which made him look less like an aspiring politician than a Chicago mobster. He also carried a dog whip and pistol, which shocked and titillated his society patrons. He owned a cheap blue suit, which he wore when speaking in the beer halls and when introduced into the salons of the elite. On such occasions, as Hanfstaengl remarked, Hitler looked "like a waiter in a railway station restaurant." Frau Bechstein insisted on buying her rough-edged protégé formal evening clothes and patent leather shoes, which he was careful not to wear in public. Hitler *was* very fond of the shoes, which he did wear, but understood that he could hardly project himself as a man of the people if he were seen in a dinner jacket and white tie.

Although Hitler received occasional money from the Bechsteins, Bruckmanns, and lesser society patrons, their contributions to his career were not merely financial. More importantly, they imparted to Hitler the basic tenets of acceptable social behavior when interacting with moneyed interests that might contribute to his cause. By opening their salons to him, these wealthy benefactors gave him credibility in mainstream conservative circles where he was generally viewed as a vulgar, rabble-rousing philistine. By 1922, doors were opening. In the spring of that year he was twice invited to speak at the National Club in Berlin, and in Munich he addressed an informal meeting of the League of Bavarian Industrialists and delivered a well-attended talk to business leaders at the Merchants' Guild Hall. When addressing these business groups, Hitler emphasized the party's opposition to Marxism, underscoring his determination to pry workers away from the left and reintegrate them into the national community. Attacks on Versailles, especially the reparations clauses, were de rigueur on such occasions, and the anticapitalist, anti–big business rhetoric that occupied such a central position in the party's program and in so many of his rousing public speeches was notably absent.

These appearances opened the pocketbooks of some in the business community. Ernst von Borsig, a powerful manufacturer of locomotives and heavy machinery in Berlin, and the Ruhr industrialist Fritz Thyssen were impressed with Hitler and funneled cash to the party. There were other contributors, drawn mostly from Munich business circles, and the party even received funds from anti-Marxist groups abroad. These business contributions were important but sporadic and were supplemented by secret funds from the Bavarian Reichswehr, which saw in the NSDAP a useful weapon in the anti-Marxist cause. As Hitler's popularity grew, however, the party was increasingly financed by its own rank and file. It scrupulously collected membership dues, charged admission to Hitler events, passed the hat at rallies, and launched collection campaigns asking members to make contributions for special causes or occasions—11 million reichsmarks, for example, were collected in celebration of Hitler's birthday.

Although still a small splinter party, barely known beyond the borders of Bavaria, the NSDAP was growing rapidly. By fall 1923 the party could claim a membership of 55,000, roughly double what it had been in 1922 and up from 6,000 in 1921. Over half had joined in the first months of 1923 alone. In February 1923, with funds supplied by Hanfstaengl and Röhm, the party acquired two modern rotary presses for the *Völkischer Beobachter*, which allowed it to print a full-sized paper that would appear on newsstands every day. The party established a theater troupe, which performed its own plays at theaters around the city. The party was now filling larger and larger halls—the Bürgerbräukeller, the Hofbräuhaus, and the gigantic Zirkus Krone, drawing audiences of three to six thousand enthusiastic listeners. Some journalists began calling Hitler "the king of Munich."

And Munich in the early postwar years provided a particularly fertile breeding ground for Hitler and his party. Since the end of the war and more specifically since the revolution, the city had become a powerful magnet for anti-leftist, anti-Republican nationalist groups. Still reeling from the trauma of the Munich revolution and with the Republican government in Berlin led by Socialists, the traditional Bavarian hostility toward Prussia revived with a vengeance. A strong separatist movement took hold, as some saw in the collapse of the empire and the weakness of the Weimar Republic an opportunity to establish an independent Bavarian state. Some hoped to see a restoration of the Wittelsbach monarchy; others envisioned a Danubian confederation of Bavaria, Austria, and Hungary. The Munich authorities proved distinctly hostile to "Red Berlin," often refusing to implement directives and decrees from the central government. Efforts by Berlin to curb the vicious right-wing groups in the Reich were ostentatiously spurned by the Bavarian authorities, and as a result this largely conservative Catholic state became, ironically, a haven for counterrevolutionary nationalist-*Völkisch* extremists of all kinds. It is impossible to overstate the crucial importance of this tolerant, even supportive, posture to Hitler's early success.

The situation in 1922 seemed particularly ripe for an assault on the embattled Republic. Between 1918 and 1924 Germany suffered from a severe case of cabinet instability—nine different governments since 1920, none with a workable majority in the Reichstag; a plague of political terrorism, and attempts to overthrow the fledgling Republic from both the radical left and right. The Reichstag elections in June 1920, held in the shadow of the Versailles Treaty, resulted in a devastating defeat for the parties of the Weimar coalition: the left-liberals, now called the Democratic Party, saw their vote cut in half, and the Social Democrats and Catholic Zentrum also experienced serious losses. The Conservatives were the big winners but were not strong enough to form a government. As a result, a string of minority cabinets and patchwork coalitions presided over the country, sometimes invoking Article 48 of the constitution, which gave the chancellor, with the approval of the Reich President, the power to take measures by emergency decree.

In 1920 a conspiracy of conservative monarchists under the leadership of Wolfgang Kapp sent troops angry at their demobilization orders into Berlin and declared the establishment of a dictatorship. The army, while refusing to defend the government, also declined to throw support behind the coup. Without that support, the Kapp Putsch collapsed after a mere six days, brought down by an effective general strike called by the labor unions. The trouble did not end there. Workers in the Ruhr were not ready to end the strike without guarantees for reform and meaningful action against the Free Corps. They formed a "Red Army of the Ruhr" to protect themselves from the anticipated reaction of the army. Indeed, the army showed no qualms about moving vigorously against the left; reinforced by Free Corps units, the army smashed the workers' uprising, executing many and murdering others.

The ongoing unrest in the Reich prompted the Allies to demand that all paramilitary groups in Germany be disbanded or Germany would face invasion. The Reich government agreed, but Bavaria refused to comply. Under pressure from the Allies, Berlin at last demanded that Bavaria submit or face invasion from the north. With great reluctance the ultra-conservative government of Bavarian monarchist Gustav Ritter von Kahr at last complied. By mid-1921 the various paramilitary organizations in Bavaria were dissolved, their members drifting to the NSDAP and other counterrevolutionary parties. Predictably, right-wing outrage against the Republic intensified, stoking the smoldering Bavarian resentment at Berlin.

Adding to the instability was a rising tide of political murder that swept across the country in these years. Hugo Haase, leader of the USPD, was assassinated in 1919; Matthias Erzberger, signatory of the Armistice and long vilified as one of the "November criminals," was murdered while vacationing in the Black Forest in 1921; and a year later so was Walther Rathenau, the liberal Jewish foreign minister. All were committed by right-wing terrorists, many with ties to groups in Munich. Almost all escaped without serious consequences. Anti-republican police officials tolerated and in some cases colluded with right-wing fugitives, helping them to escape the law, and judges were notoriously lenient with those who were tried. When the Munich police chief Ernst Pöhner, who helped Erzberger's killers flee across the Czech border, was asked if he was aware that there were "political murder gangs" operating in the city, he is said to have replied, "Yes, but not enough of them."

The murder of these prominent national figures was but the tip of the iceberg. Numerous pro-Republican regional leaders as well as outspoken local supporters of the Republic fell victim to right-wing hit squads. Between 1919 and 1922, Germany recorded over three hundred political murders; in the first six months of 1922 alone, the number climbed to 376. Only twenty-two of these attacks were committed by leftists. "It was the time," Konrad Heiden remarked, "when murder could be had for small change."

The brazen murder of Rathenau in June 1922 was the final straw. The Reich government enacted the Law for the Protection of the Republic, which instituted stiff penalties for attacks against Republican institutions and officials, and called for a nationwide crackdown on extremist groups. It also created a special tribunal within the Supreme Court in Leipzig to hear cases of political terrorism and laid out regulations for strict monitoring of political parties and societies, including their meetings and printed propaganda materials. In Munich the Bavarian authorities refused to honor the law, claiming that it amounted to unconstitutional meddling in Bavarian affairs. Bavaria would deal with terrorism in its own fashion and enacted its own legislation, which, Bavarian leaders insisted, superseded the Reich law. Little changed. As 1922 turned to 1923, the Weimar Republic was still very much in peril, and the forces of the right were gathering strength.

The reparations issue continued to haunt the Weimar government. The Versailles Treaty had not set a specific amount for Germany's reparations obligations, but in 1921 the Allied Reparations Commission had finally presented the German government with a figure. The bill was 123 billion gold marks, not counting payments amounting to 26 percent of Germany's exports. In what was called the London Ultimatum, Germany had been given six days to accept or the Allies would occupy the Ruhr. The Republic had only with great reluctance bowed to the ultimatum, prompting another round of accusations of betrayal and cowardice from the political extremes. Although the government had accepted the terms, it also employed a variety of economic stratagems to avoid making the payments—disputing the value of payments in kind, especially timber and coal, the value of the mark, and the schedule of installments. In January 1923, France and Belgium, exasperated by Germany's consistent evasion, invaded and occupied the Ruhr, setting off an economic and political crisis that threatened to unravel the delicate fabric of Weimar democracy. The German government called for a policy of passive resistance and let the printing presses of the treasury roll. Inflation, which had been mounting since the end of the war, spiraled into an utterly surrealistic hyperinflation. At the outbreak of the war in 1914 a dollar was worth 5 reichsmark (RM); at war's end, 64 RM; in January 1923 following the Franco-Belgian invasion, 17,972 RM. Thereafter the value of the reichsmark was almost impossible to calculate for more than a few hours. In August 1923 a dollar was worth 109,996 RM; by November, 420,000,000,000 RM.

Banks received government permission to print their own currency, sometimes on paper (small bills printed on one side that looked rather like Monopoly money), later on bedsheets and pillowcases. Often banks simply stamped zeros on existing denominations, transforming a 5 RM note into a 5,000 or 500,000 or 5,000,000 bill. In November, a streetcar ticket in Berlin cost 150,000,000 RM; a kilo of potatoes 90,000,000,000 RM; a beer in Munich 500,000,000,000. Children constructed elaborate castles with stacks of worthless paper currency; women shopped with wheelbarrows heaped high with bills. Shopkeepers hoarded their goods, refusing to sell their merchandise since it would be impossible to replenish their inventory tomorrow with today's now worthless currency. People were paid three times a day. Upon arriving at work in the morning, they received a payment and immediately dispatched an accompanying family member (often a child) to buy lunch; if they waited until lunch break, the morning's pay would be worthless; at the midday break the process was repeated, with a runner sent to buy food for dinner. Finally at the end of the workday, workers and employees were paid again and bought food for the next morning, when the whole process would begin again. "Life," one German glumly lamented, was "madness, nightmare, desperation and chaos." It was the end of the world, "the death of money."

With the economy careening toward utter collapse, the foundations of the Republic began to crumble. In late summer two Rhenish separatist movements, cheered on by the French, declared independent Rhineland republics, one in Aachen, the other in Koblenz; in Saxony and Thuringia, where the Communists and Socialists had formed a legitimate governing alliance, rumors of a leftist coup prompted Berlin to send in troops, disband the leftist government, and impose martial law. A Communist uprising in Hamburg in October was crushed by the army, leaving the country poised on the cusp of anarchy and civil war. It was in this cauldron of economic crisis and political instability that Hitler and the NSDAP made their first appearance on the national political scene.

Throughout the early months of 1923 Hitler had continued his feverish agitation against the Republic, heaping abuse on Berlin's policy of passive resistance. It was, he roared, the Republic's craven behavior, the government's disgraceful inability to stand up to the Allies that had led Germany to this catastrophe. In January the NSDAP had held its first National Party Day. The party rented out a dozen of Munich's largest beer halls, and throughout the day and into the night Hitler spoke in all twelve. He also presided over an imposing parade by the SA on the Marsfeld, where he stood in review of the passing columns for over two hours. In all, the police estimated the attendance at the Nazis' Party Day events at 100,000. There were setbacks—on May Day an embarrassing confrontation with government forces, when a massive show of force by the Nazis was frustrated by the Bavarian Reichswehr and State Police (Landespolizei), who disarmed and dispersed the thousands of paramilitary men gathered on the Oberwiesenfeld. Hitler was humiliated, and yet despite this embarrassment, huge crowds still continued to flock to hear him speak.

In the late summer, as the economy spun out of control and the political situation deteriorated, rumors of an impending coup d'état swirled through the city. Pressure was building from the far right as well as separatist forces. On September 1–2, General Erich Ludendorff, an implacable enemy of the Republic and the hero of the far right, presided over a "German Day" celebration in Nuremberg. Over 100,000 militants from right-wing groups, veterans' associations, and paramilitary organizations swarmed into the city. At the German Day event, Röhm managed to bring the right-wing organizations Reich War Flag, the Bund Oberland, and the SA into a new militant coalition, the German Battle League (Kampfbund). Remarkably, Hitler, who had always resisted entering into an alliance with other parties, had agreed to allow the SA to join as well. Hitler was recognized by the other groups as the "political leader" of the alliance, though exactly what that meant was not at all clear; retired Lieutenant Colonel Hermann Kriebel was to be its military commander, while Ludendorff was generally viewed as the future dictator of Germany. All three stood together on the podium at the impressive German Day demonstration, exhibiting an unusual degree of right-wing solidarity, and fresh rumors of an impending coup swept throughout Munich.

Hitler had succeeded in galvanizing popular opposition to the Bavarian Republic, but Röhm and others in his inner circle were worried that the party could not keep its followers at a fever pitch indefinitely. Hitler had preached action, revolutionary action. If he did not move, and soon, they would begin drifting away. Beyond the party faithful, the broader public was growing desperate. Unemployment was rapidly rising; food prices were exploding; savings were disappearing. In late October, reports from regional officials brought alarming news: in Upper Bavaria, one district office reported that the mood of the local population "is close to the mood of the November days of 1918 and April 1919," and Bavarian officials were "expecting riots at any moment." The people were demanding a solution to their economic distress. The time was ripe; the party had to act.

In November 1923 real power in Munich was in the hands of a triumvirate consisting of State Commissar Gustav Ritter von Kahr; Colonel Hans Ritter von Seisser, director of the State Police; and General Otto von Lossow, commander of the Bavarian Reichswehr. The last weeks of

October were taut with intrigue and suspicion, as Hitler, Ludendorff, and other leaders of the Kampfbund held meetings with members of the triumvirate. Each pressed its vision of the future on the other, but little agreement could be reached. A veil of mutual mistrust hung over the meetings. Both groups wanted to hurry the demise of the democratic state they abhorred, but beyond that little common ground could be found. The triumvirate wanted the Republic overthrown and replaced by a dictatorship backed by the Reichswehr and led by an oligarchic group of conservative political leaders in Berlin. Kahr was engaged in talks to win support for such a plan in Berlin, without, however, gaining much traction. Especially disheartening was his failure to win over Reichswehr commander General Hans von Seeckt, whose support would be pivotal.

At a meeting with leaders of the Kampfbund on November 6, Kahr, backed by Lossow and Seisser, emphasized that any attempt to bring down the Republic would take time and careful planning, and he wanted no part of a Putsch, especially one led by Ludendorff and Hitler. All must act in concert; this was no time for unilateral moves. Hitler had not been at the meeting, and he was unsettled by Kahr's intransigence. He wanted revolutionary action and was not inclined to wait. Still, he realized that any Putsch would need the support of the Munich police and the Bavarian Reichswehr, and he hoped to coax Kahr to back—or at least not block—such a move. On the night of the 6th he tried to arrange a meeting with Kahr for the next day, but the commissar refused to see him. That night, after conferring with his top advisors, Hitler decided that the time for the Putsch had come. Then on November 7, Kahr made an unexpected announcement: he would hold an important speech at the Bürgerbräu Beer Hall on the following evening. All Munich's prominent political players, business leaders, military men, and social movers and shakers were to be in attendance. Hitler took Kahr's refusal to meet with him as an ominous sign, and when Kahr again refused to meet with him on the 8th, either before or after his Bürgerbräu address, the Nazis were convinced that the commissar intended to exclude Hitler from his plans altogether. Of more immediate concern, Hitler and his lieutenants feared that Kahr might use his Bürgerbräu speech to announce his intention to break with Berlin, restore the Wittelsbach monarchy, and declare an independent Bavaria. Kahr's hand would have to be forced.

That morning, Hitler conferred with his inner circle. He sensed a potential opportunity. With Munich's top civilian and military leaders all gathered in one place, he would crash the meeting, hijack the proceedings, and launch his own Putsch from the Bürgerbräukeller. He would force Kahr, Lossow, and Seisser to endorse the Putsch. He convinced himself that the army would fall in line behind them. It was a desperate roll of the dice, a long shot, but, as he would demonstrate again and again in the coming years, Hitler was a gambler.

In the afternoon of November 7, the plan was finalized. It called for SA and Kampfbund troops to take control of all the major cities in Bavaria—Nuremberg, Augsburg, Regensburg, Ingolstadt, Würzburg, and Munich. They would seize railways, bridges, communications centers, radio stations, government buildings, and police headquarters. The offices of the labor unions, Social Democrats, and Communists were to be occupied and their leaders arrested. SA units from the surrounding countryside would converge on Munich, coming by truck and train. SA and Kampfbund leaders would be given their orders by telephone or courier. They were to alert their men for action the next day, although they were not to inform them of their mission. Secrecy was essential. Lieutenant Colonel Kriebel, the military leader of the Putsch, calculated that Hitler could count on roughly four thousand armed men arrayed against an army and police force of about half that number. But Hitler did not intend to use force. He hoped that no violence would be necessary. If the triumvirate could be convinced—or coerced—to cooperate with the Putsch, the Bavarian authorities, the municipal police, and the Bavarian Reichswehr would fall into line and together they would move on Berlin. It was to be, as historian Alan Bullock put it, "a revolution by sheer bluff."

It was dark when Hitler and his entourage left party headquarters bound for the Bürgerbräukeller. The beer hall sat on a gentle rise on the east side of the Isar River, about a half mile from the Marienplatz in the center of the city. It was one of Munich's largest beer halls, flanked by gardens and surrounded by a low stone wall. Its main hall could seat some three thousand people. It tended to draw a somewhat more upscale crowd than the earthier Hofbräuhaus or Löwenbräukeller, and that would certainly be the case for Commissar Kahr's address. Aware of the possibility of trouble, a contingent of 125 municipal police was in place in and around the sprawling grounds, and a company of State Police was held in readiness at a nearby barracks.

Commissar Kahr's address began promptly at eight o'clock. The hall was filled to capacity. Seated at dozens of round wooden tables before him were bankers and businessmen, military officers, newspaper editors, members of the Bavarian cabinet, and political figures from the center-right. His theme for the evening was the evils of Marxism, punctuated by the usual paeans to German nationalism, always a hit with this crowd. Kahr was deep into his remarks when Hitler arrived in his red Mercedes, bluffed his way through the police cordon, and, accompanied by his armed entourage, stepped into the lobby. Outside a stream of trucks began arriving. Within minutes they had disgorged their load of heavily armed SA men and helmeted members of Hitler's special guard, the Shock Troop Adolf Hitler. Within minutes they had brushed aside the police cordon, surrounded the building, and blocked all the exits. Then, at just past 8:30, as Kahr droned on, the door to the hall burst open and in stormed Göring, "with all his medals clinking," followed by two dozen uniformed shock troops brandishing pistols and machine guns. Behind them, in the entrance to the main hall, SA men mounted a heavy machine gun, training it directly on the audience.

In the general uproar, Hitler, surrounded by his Shock Troop guards, pushed his way through the crowd. Shouts of protest rang out, tables and chairs were overturned, beer mugs crashed to the floor. Just in front of the podium Hitler clambered onto a chair, gave a signal to the SA man on his right, and a pistol shot was fired into the ceiling. In the sudden silence, Hitler bellowed, "The German revolution has broken out! This hall is surrounded." The response was not what he had anticipated. Many in the distinguished audience whistled and stamped their disapproval; others shouted "Mexico" or "South America." This was no banana republic!

Dripping sweat, Hitler stripped off his rumpled trench coat, and to the surprise (and amusement) of some, stood before them in a long-tailed black cutaway. He appeared, one bemused onlooker remarked, "like a cross between Charlie Chaplin and a headwaiter." But this was no laughing matter. Hitler climbed down from his chair and moved to the speaker's platform where Kahr, Seisser, and Lossow stood as if paralyzed. After guaranteeing their safety, Hitler politely asked the three gentlemen to follow him into an adjoining room. There he apologized for the nature of his actions, but told them, "It is done and cannot now be undone." He was creating a new Bavarian government in preparation for a move on Berlin. He assured them that all three would hold leading positions in that new government, and he hoped he could count on their cooperation. His manner seemed to swing between the respectful and the intimidating, pleading for their support one minute and at another threatening to shoot the "traitors" and then himself if his enterprise should fail.

The triumvirate did not immediately agree to cooperate. After fifteen minutes of alternately cajoling, menacing, and finally subjecting them to a hectoring speech about their patriotic duty, Hitler returned to the hall to address the crowd, which had grown restless in his absence. At one point Göring had to fire a shot into the ceiling to restore order, screaming that a new Germany was in the making. Everyone should settle down with their beer and be patient. When Hitler finally reappeared without Kahr and company, the crowd again grew raucous and did not subside when he tried to speak. Finally Hitler drew his pistol and fired yet another shot into the ceiling. If order wasn't restored, he shouted, he would order a machine gun placed in the gallery.

The crowd noise subsided, and Hitler began to speak. At first he seemed shaky, unsure of himself, but he quickly rebounded, gaining confidence with every fiery word. A new government was being formed, Hitler told the crowd. General Ludendorff would assume command of the army; the triumvirate would all have prominent positions in the new government. With the army restored to its former glory and with the support of the people, the provisional government would "begin the march against Berlin, that sink of iniquity, with all the might of this state and the accumulated power of every province in Germany."

In the audience was the peripatetic professor Karl Alexander von Müller, who had taught Hitler in the Reichswehr's speakers course in 1919. He was thunderstruck. Hitler's words, according to Müller, had an electrifying effect on the crowd. In a flash, the audience, sullen and skeptical at the outset, swung behind Hitler. His performance was "an oratorical masterpiece, which any actor might envy. . . . I cannot remember in my entire life such a change in the attitude of a crowd in a few minutes, almost a few seconds. . . . Hitler had turned them inside out, as one turns a glove inside out, with a few sentences. It had almost something of hocus-pocus, of magic about it. Loud approval roared forth, no further opposition was to be heard." Hitler told the crowd that Kahr, Seisser, and Lossow were in an adjoining room, trying to decide whether to support the new government. Could he report to them that "you will stand behind them?" The room was filled with boisterous cries of "Yes, yes!"

Back with the sequestered triumvirate, Hitler was frustrated to discover that they were still wavering. The situation was saved only when General Ludendorff appeared, dressed in his impressive uniform from the Great War, topped off by the pointed *Pickelhaube* helmet. Ludendorff commanded great respect as the leader of the nationalist right, and together with Pöhner the general managed to convince the recalcitrant trio to join the cause, though Kahr still insisted that he was merely acting as regent in preparation for a restoration of the Wittelsbach monarchy. Hitler had no intention of restoring the monarchy but was happy to let Kahr posture as he would. The group now reappeared on the platform, joined by Ludendorff. Unity achieved, a beaming Hitler ostentatiously shook hands all around, projecting an image of harmony and solidarity. The crowd broke into thunderous applause. It was pure political theater. While this display of goodwill reigned onstage, contingents of SA men began rounding up members of the Bavarian cabinet in the hall. They would be held as hostages.

While these dramatic events were unfolding in the Bürgerbräukeller, Ernst Röhm and Hermann Esser were addressing a large Kampfbund crowd at the Löwenbräukeller. At about nine o'clock, Röhm received a short telephone message: "Safely delivered." It was the signal he had been waiting for: Hitler had succeeded; the Putsch was successfully under way. Röhm strode to the podium and announced that the Kahr government had been deposed and Adolf Hitler had declared a national revolution. His words were met with wild cheering. He called for everyone to march on the Bürgerbräukeller to join the revolutionary troops there. But as the two thousand excited men began moving down the street, a motorcycle courier stopped them with a new order from Hitler. They were to proceed to the Reichswehr's District IV headquarters and seize it. Another contingent was to collect some three thousand rifles from a monastery basement on St. Annaplatz. All across the city Kampfbund troops were moving on their assigned objectives.

Back at the Bürgerbräu, things had begun to go wrong. Hitler received a message that Kampfbund forces were in a standoff with government troops at the barracks of the army engineers. Believing that he might resolve the situation, Hitler sped to the scene, leaving Ludendorff in charge of the Bürgerbräukeller. Shortly after Hitler left, Lossow asked Ludendorff if he might leave the building to attend to matters at his office—after all, he had important orders to issue. He gave a solemn promise not to undertake any action that would harm the Putsch. Kahr and Seisser echoed Lossow's request, and Ludendorff permitted them all to leave. When Hitler returned, he was flabbergasted at what Ludendorff had done. Didn't the general realize that they could sabotage the whole enterprise? Ludendorff was surprised and offended. Didn't Hitler, a corporal, understand that a German officer would never break his oath?

Hitler's suspicions were well founded. As soon as Kahr and company gained their freedom, they renounced their pledge to Hitler, explaining that they were not bound by a promise made under duress, and immediately began working to rally government forces against the Putsch. Lossow and Seisser worked the phones to alert military and police units around the city to resist the rebels and issued orders to troops from the outlying districts to move on Munich. Inexplicably and contrary to their hastily drawn up plans, the Putschists had not taken the key communications and transportation centers that were so crucial to the success of their endeavor.

By ten o'clock Röhm had taken control of the Reichswehr headquarters without firing a shot, some bridges were occupied, and placards declaring the creation of the revolutionary government were being posted about town. Roving SA bands were harassing Jews, beating some, dragging others off to the Bürgerbräu, where they were thrown into the cellar to be held as hostages. But in the cold midnight hours, the Putsch began to fall apart. Efforts to seize the Municipal Police Directorate, the Office of the State Commissariat, the City Military Command, army barracks, and police installations had misfired. As the night wore on, it was becoming increasingly clear to Hitler and his allies that the Putsch had failed.

The crowd in the Bürgerbräukeller had long departed, and in the great hall hundreds of restless Storm Troopers stood about or tried to get a little rest, dozing on tabletops, in chairs pulled together, and on the floor. The frenzied excitement of the Putsch's first hours was long gone, as were the beer and bread and pretzels (the management would later present the party with a bill of over 11 million marks). Still the leaders had no new orders to give them. As dawn approached and the unraveling of their plans sank in, the leadership debated its next move. In the hurried, improvised planning of the Putsch, Hitler had given little thought to the possibility of failure. There was no backup plan. Grasping at straws, Hitler dispatched a messenger to Crown Prince Ruppert in Berchtesgaden, hoping that he would intervene with Kahr and convince him to back the uprising. It was symptomatic of the Putsch's disorganization that the messenger could not find a car and had to travel by train, arriving in the afternoon. Ruppert flatly refused. He had, in fact, already encouraged Kahr to crush the rebellion. Kriebel, the military commander of the Putsch, recommended pulling out of Munich and regrouping in Rosenheim on the nearby Austrian border. There they could count on the support of the local population. Göring agreed, but Ludendorff, who had gone home to rest and returned in civilian clothes, wouldn't hear of it. "The movement cannot end in the ditch of some obscure country lane," he snorted.

In the late morning, with the situation deteriorating with each passing hour and no resolution reached, Ludendorff made a straightforward declaration that sounded like an order: "We will march!" Röhm and his men were barricaded in the Reichswehr headquarters, surrounded by government troops. The Putschists would march through the city and liberate them. The idea of a march appealed to Hitler (so much so that he later claimed that it was his own). Freeing Röhm was the ostensible objective of the march, but as Hitler envisioned it, a march through the center of the city with banners flying and a band leading the way would stir support for the Putsch among the people. The public simply didn't know about the revolution—that was the problem—and this display of power by the rebels would turn the tide. It was an exercise in the sort of performance politics that Hitler so enthusiastically practiced. The government troops would not dare fire on the aroused people; indeed, they would join their ranks, and Kahr and his allies would be forced to cooperate with the national revolution after all. Even in his desperation, Hitler must have realized that this was more of a hope than a realistic expectation.

As they made preparations to march, Hitler sent Feder, Streicher, and other party leaders into the streets to rouse the people. They were to hold speeches on public squares, explaining the goals of the national revolution, whipping up support. At 11 a.m. things at last began to move at the Bürgerbräukeller. Two thousand men, many of them exhausted from little sleep, hungover, and stiff in the bracing morning chill, began pouring out of the hall, forming up in the Rosenheimerstrasse. It was a ragtag assemblage. The Shock Troop Hitler, in Reichswehr helmets and outfitted with army-issue rifles and grenades, bore some resemblance to a military unit; the regiments of the Munich SA wore gray-green jackets, topped with Norwegian ski caps. Others were dressed in an array of civilian clothes—workers' overalls and business suits with bits and pieces of wartime uniforms peeking through. All wore red swastika armbands and almost all were armed.

Kriebel quickly organized the men into columns, with ranks of eight across in the front, followed by ranks of four for the SA and other trailing units. Swastika banners and the black-white-red battle flags of the old imperial army sprouted at intervals throughout the formation. Leading the procession in the first rank were Hitler in his tightly belted trench coat, Ludendorff in hunting jacket and overcoat; Göring in a black leather coat, his *Pour le Mérite* visible at the neck, topped by a steel helmet with a white swastika painted on the front; and assorted other party officials. The brass band, which Hitler had engaged in the morning, played one uninspiring march as the troops assembled and then departed, angry that they had not had breakfast and had not been paid.

Finally, the procession lurched into motion, swinging westward down the sloping Rosenheimerstrasse to the Ludwigsbrücke, where they encountered a police blockade. The formation pushed through the outmanned police and continued across the river toward the Isar Gate. Along the way, curious onlookers lined the streets, uncertain of just what they were witnessing. Some shouted their support; some on the crowded sidewalks waved small Nazi flags; others jeered. Finally, the procession reached the Marienplatz, where it was swallowed up in an immense throng. An enormous Nazi flag fluttered from the balcony of the Rathaus, and smaller swastika banners flew from windows all around the square. Whipped up by Strasser and other Nazi speakers, the crowd greeted the Putschists with rousing cheers and shouts of *Heil*. Some joined the marchers, as if on parade. The spirits of the marchers soared. They sang as they marched. It was an encouraging sign that Hitler's hope of an aroused public storming to support the Putsch might actually work.

The goal of the march had not been made clear to most of the men, and no one expected an armed confrontation. Some thought that having made a show of force, the formation would return to the Bürgerbräukeller in preparation for a next step. But Ludendorff was determined to liberate Röhm and his men trapped in the Reichswehr headquarters and pushed on. Reluctantly Hitler went along. Ludendorff led the procession away from the Marienplatz down a narrow street just off the Rathaus, then into the even narrower Residenzstrasse, barely wide enough for the eight-man ranks walking abreast. One hundred meters or so down the Residenz-strasse, the street widened into the broad Odeonsplatz, where nine years before Hitler had stood in the exultant multitude cheering the outbreak of war. Beyond the Odeonsplatz lay the Reichswehr headquarters.

Just as the marchers reached the Feldherrnhalle, a massive stone structure honoring Bavaria's military heroes, at the mouth of the Odeons-platz, the procession encountered a line of blue-uniformed State Police. This time the police did not buckle. As the marchers pushed forward, a shot rang out, echoing up the canyon walls of the tapered street. Then a frantic volley of gunfire. The shooting lasted no more than thirty sec-onds. When it stopped, eighteen men were lying dead in the street— fourteen Nazis and four policemen. The Putschists fell back in disarray. Hitler, his arm locked with another's, was dragged down with such vi-olence that his shoulder was separated. Göring was badly wounded, hit in the upper thigh. Rosenberg and Streicher, in the second rank, turned and fled. They saw Weber, leader of the Bund Oberland, pressed against a wall, weeping hysterically. Ludendorff, who immediately hit the cob-blestones when the shots were fired, regained his feet and, certain that no troops would dare shoot the hero of the Great War, marched ramrod stiff through the police lines, where he was politely greeted by the officer in charge and escorted to safety in the Residenz. In the chaos, Hitler and Göring were dragged to safety and escaped the scene.

The ranks now dissolved in panic. Those in the rear of the formation were still singing patriotic marching songs when they heard the shots. They had no idea what had happened—no one expected a battle—but saw those in front of them frantically retreating from the Feldherrn-halle. The long column abruptly halted and began to scatter. During the afternoon the State Police rounded up hundreds of Putschists and disarmed them, taking the Bürgerbräukeller without any resistance from the dispirited revolutionaries. Hitler managed to evade capture until the 11th, when he was found hiding at the Hanfstaengl villa south of the city. By that time the NSDAP was officially banned, its newspaper closed down; its leaders either on their way to prison or hiding in exile. Hitler's daring bid for power had lasted less than twenty-four hours and ended in an ignominious fiasco.

Hitler was removed to Landsberg Prison about forty miles west of Munich and placed in cell number 7. Defeated and humiliated, he wanted to see no one; he refused to talk to the interrogators from the state's attorney's office; he began a hunger strike. Formal charges of high treason were filed against him, Ludendorff, and several other Nazis. The trial date was set for February 27, 1924. By the time the court was called into session in the new year, Hitler and his Putsch were yesterday's news. His short-lived political career seemed to be at an end—and by all rights should have been. The Putsch was almost universally ridiculed as hopelessly amateurish, almost laughable, an Italian comic opera led by a delusional self-important dilettante. But Hitler's political obituary, as the trial would dramatically prove, was premature.

The timing and location of the proceedings proved crucial for his political resurrection. The Reichstag elected in June 1920 had been dissolved, and new elections called for May 4, 1924. The campaign was not officially under way when the trial opened at the end of February, but the national press, seeing it as a prelude to the election, descended on the courtroom, giving it front-page coverage for a full month. The venue was just as important. By law, the case should have been tried before the German high court in Leipzig, but in another reflection of the strained relations between Berlin and Munich, the Bavarian government claimed jurisdiction, and the central government relented.

The trial would be held before the Bavarian People's Court in Munich. This proved to be of enormous significance. It was Hitler's home turf, providing him a far more favorable environment than would have prevailed in Saxon Leipzig. And there was another advantage. Throughout the trial and forever after, Hitler, with his inexhaustible penchant for self-dramatization, projected an image of the lonely man of conviction, the upright common man, the front soldier, standing up boldly to the overpowering authority of a treasonous state. It was a self-conscious evocation of Luther at Worms, the simple German monk defiantly speaking his conscience before the combined might of the emperor and the papacy. It was a narrative that became engraved in Nazi legend.

In fact, even before the trial began, Hitler was confident of a sympathetic hearing. He had already come before the presiding judge, Franz Neidhardt, well known for his right-wing nationalist sympathies. In May Neidhardt had presided over Hitler's trial for assault arising from a beer hall brawl and imposed the lightest possible sentence on the defendant: three months. He also sanctioned Hitler's release from Stadelheim prison after serving only thirty days. With Neidhardt's indulgence, the trial provided Hitler with exactly the national stage he craved. Although Ludendorff was by far the most well known of the defendants, from the beginning this was Hitler's show.

Hitler appeared before the court in civilian clothes, his Iron Cross displayed on his chest. After the initial bout of despair in prison, his spirits had been lifted by visits from Drexler, Helene Hanfstaengl, Frau Bechstein, and others who brought encouraging words from his loyal followers. His self-confidence surged. And no wonder. From the opening gavel, the court proceedings were a scandal. Neidhardt allowed Hitler to interrupt the prosecutor, to cross-examine witnesses, and to give perorations of up to four hours. Hitler heaped scorn on the state's witnesses, especially Lossow, Seisser, and Kahr, branding them cowards, hypocrites, and co-conspirators desperately trying to cover their tracks. He was allowed to ramble on at length about his political vision, about the November criminals, the Treaty of Versailles, Germany's future foreign policy under his direction. He inveighed against parliamentary democracy and called for a dictatorship, immodestly laying claim to the role of Germany's savior, its future dictator. The other defendants entered pleas of not guilty. Hitler defiantly took responsibility for all that had happened. He proudly admitted his guilt for wanting to reclaim the honor of Germany, to restore the glory of the German army, to free Germany from the grip of the November criminals who had enslaved the nation. Above all, he thundered, he was "resolved to be the destroyer of Marxism."

In his closing statement he delivered one of his most impressive speeches, explaining that he and the National Socialists "wanted to create in Germany the preconditions that alone will make it possible for the iron grip of our enemies to be removed from us. We wanted to create order in the state, throw out the drones, take up the fight against international stock exchange slavery. Against our whole economy being cornered by stock exchange slavery, against the politicizing of the trade unions, and above all, for the highest honorable duty which we, as Germans, know should be once more introduced—the duty of bearing arms, military service. And now, I ask you: Is what we wanted high treason?"

He closed with a warning:

> The army we have formed is growing from day to day, from hour to hour, and faster. Especially in these days I nourish the proud hope that one day the hour will come when these wild companies will grow to battalions, the battalions to regiments, the regiments to divisions; that the old cockade will be taken from the filth, that the old flags will wave again, that there will be a reconciliation at the last great divine judgment, which we are prepared to face. Then from our bones and our graves the voice of that court will speak, which alone is entitled to sit in judgment over us. For it is not you, gentlemen, who pronounce judgment upon us. The judgment is spoken by the eternal court of history. . . . What judgment you will hand down, I know. But that court will not ask us: "Did you commit high treason or did you not?"

No, he went on, that court would judge the men of November 9 as "Germans, who wanted and desired only the good of their people and fatherland; who wanted to fight and die. You may pronounce us guilty a thousand times over, the goddess of the eternal court of history will smile and tear to tatters the brief of the state's attorney and the sentence of the court; for she acquits us."

The crowd was with him, the judge was with him; even the state prosecutor praised his motives, if not his methods. On the day the sentence was to be announced, expectant crowds swarmed around the redbrick structure that served as courthouse and jail. The six defendants posed proudly on the steps of the building for a group photo. They looked stern but confident. Inside, the state prosecutors found the courtroom sprinkled with women carrying flowers for their hero; one even asked if she might bathe in Hitler's bathtub. The international press and journalists from around Germany, on the other hand, were appalled by what one called the "Munich carnival" in the courtroom. Even ministers in the Bavarian government, some of whom had been held hostage in the Bürgerbräukeller, complained about Neidhardt's indulgent handling of Hitler. When censured by a minister of state for allowing Hitler to speak for hours, Neidhardt lamely responded: "It is impossible to keep Hitler from talking."

The worst fears of the Republic's supporters were realized when the court rendered its final verdict on April 1. All evidence to the contrary, Ludendorff was acquitted outright. "Adolf Hitler [was] practically acquitted and all the rest of the accused [were] either freed without further ado or punished with such ridiculous sentences that they are to all intents and purposes free men. . . . To put the sentences in a nutshell," *The New York Times* commented, "every one of the accused is as free as a mountain bird except Hitler, Kriebel, and Weber, and all Germany is convinced that they will likewise be free as soon as they have served the Munich court's idea of punishment which a traitor to the German Republic should suffer— six months imprisonment" minus time already served. It was, most observers agreed, a farce. "All Munich is chuckling over the verdict which is regarded as an excellent joke for All Fools Day." But while supporters of the Republic could only shake their heads in dismay, "reactionary Munich is delighted at the verdict," the *Times* reported, "though some dissatisfaction is expressed that Hitler was not freed with Ludendorff." In delivering Hitler's sentence of five years—the minimum allowed by law— Neidhardt emphasized that the Nazi leader would be eligible for parole in six months, minus the four months already served. In other words, Hitler could be back on the streets in eight weeks. There was consternation in the international press. As the reporter for *The New York Times* cryptically put it: "To plot against the Constitution of the Republic is not considered a serious crime in Munich."

Some had hoped that Hitler, still an Austrian citizen, would at a minimum be deported when released. They were sorely disappointed. "In the opinion of the court," the final judgment read, "a man who thinks and feels as German as Hitler, a man who voluntarily served four and a half years in the German army during the war, who earned high war decorations for bravery in the face of the enemy, who was wounded and whose health was impaired . . . should not be subjected to the Law for the Protection of the Republic." It was a remarkable turnaround. Ingloriously defeated in his attempt to overthrow the legitimate government of Germany by force, Hitler had turned the trial into a major triumph. The trial had given him a national stage on which to spout his views, and he had delivered a propaganda masterpiece. Still, most assumed that his newfound notoriety would quickly fade. After all, he had no national following to speak of; he was still very much a regional phenomenon; and despite his dramatic courtroom theatrics, he would now disappear into prison. His party was in disarray, declared illegal, its leaders scattered, in exile or in prison. Germany, most believed, had seen the last of Adolf Hitler.

ON THE FRINGE, 1925–28

When Hitler returned to Landsberg Prison on April 1, 1924, his old cell was waiting. He had left the prison for his trial an obscure street corner agitator whose notoriety was confined largely to Bavaria. When he returned, he was the "martyr of Munich," a hero of the radical right. The disastrous Putsch had been ridiculed everywhere as a bumbling, almost farcical calamity, but Hitler's virtuoso performance in the courtroom had transformed him into a national figure. Now he was Landsberg's "prisoner of honor," a celebrity to the other conspirators, the jailers, and the prison officials.

In the wing of Landsberg Prison reserved for political prisoners—a commodity with which Bavaria, given its turbulent postwar history, was well stocked—Hitler was again assigned cell 7 on the upper floor, reserved for the most important prisoners. His cell was small but comfortable, holding a table, two chairs, a cupboard, and bed. Light poured in from two large windows, and although Hitler complained about the bars, his view was of shrubbery, trees, and hills. Visitors brought geraniums and other flowers.

Under the circumstances, he had all he could ask for. He dressed in his own clothes, usually lederhosen and the traditional Tyrolean jacket, white shirt, and sometimes a tie. Telegrams and letters from loyal party members and doting admirers poured into the prison; some sent books, others packages of food.(Hitler was partial to Viennese pastries and fretted about his weight). Hitler's cell, Putzi Hanfstaengl later remarked, "looked like a delicatessen. You could have opened up a flower and fruit and a wine shop with all the stuff stacked in there."

Although visitors were to be restricted, the sympathetic prison authorities turned a blind eye to the rising tide of visitors who arrived for an audience with "the hero of Munich." On some days Hitler spent up to six hours receiving guests. Even his dog was allowed a visit. By summer Hitler was besieged by so many visitors that he asked the jailers to admit only those with a written appointment. The prisoners were granted two hour-long sessions of physical exercise, including boxing and gymnastics. Hitler sometimes refereed the contests but usually preferred to walk—after all, the leader of the movement could hardly enter into a physical competition with his followers.

Even as a prisoner, Hitler was very much in command, the master of his surroundings. When a new prisoner was assigned to the block, he was taken immediately to report to Hitler. At meals in the common room Hitler presided over the table, holding court. One fellow conspirator wrote to a friend that every day at 10 a.m. "there is normally an hour's discussion with the Chief or better still an address by the Chief." The jailers and other prison staff often listened from beyond the doorway, and were as impressed as the prisoners. When Hitler spoke, "the warders gathered outside on the staircase and listened without making a sound . . . the men of the police guard unit would form up in the courtyard outside and none of these listeners ever made even the smallest disturbance."

Hitler's main occupation while at Landsberg was writing. He had in mind to write a book about his wartime experiences, his political awakening, and the beginnings of the NSDAP. A second volume might be necessary to explain National Socialism's *Weltanschauung*, its ideological goals and assumptions. Together the two volumes would constitute an autobiographical political manifesto. Visitors supplied him with paper, pen, and ink, even a typewriter, on which he tapped out the pages, using the two finger method. Sometimes he dictated to fellow conspirators Emil Maurice or Rudolf Hess. One jailer remarked that "all day long and late into the night the typewriter would be tapping and one could hear Hitler in his small room dictating to his friend Hess. On Saturday evenings he would generally read the completed sections to his fellow prisoners who sat around him like schoolboys."

Hitler was not altogether unhappy with this respite from the frenetic rough and tumble of politics. Since his entry into the party, he had found little time to reflect and write. His considerable energies had been de-voted to speaking, organizing, and attempting to hold the rambunctious NSDAP together. Now, with the enforced discipline and quiet of prison, he could turn at last to developing his ideas in a more systematic form. As he would recall many years later, his book would never have been written had it not been for his time in prison. In Landsberg, with few diversions, he threw himself into his writing. He had high hopes for the book. He intended to call it *Four and a Half Years of Struggle Against Lies, Corruption, and Cowardice*, but was dissuaded by his old army comrade and publisher Max Amann, who gingerly suggested that the title might not be as compelling to potential readers as it was to Hitler. Amann suggested a shorter, pithier title: *Mein Kampf* (*My Struggle*).

Although Hitler was kept informed about developments beyond the prison walls, he refused to become involved in the incessant wrangling among his lieutenants. While awaiting trial, he had deputized Alfred Rosen-berg, the editor of the *Völkischer Beobachter*, to act as caretaker for the party in his absence. It was a curious choice. Pedantic, aloof, and bereft of any personal charisma, Rosenberg liked to think of himself as the philos-opher of the party. He had no administrative experience and no personal following. Many believed that Hitler had chosen him for precisely these reasons. Rosenberg was in no danger of usurping his power, nor would he be a threat to his position as leader when he returned.

Almost immediately Rosenberg encountered challenges on several fronts. Little had been done to prepare for the possibility that the coup might fail, and Rosenberg discovered that the party's organization was in almost hopeless disarray. Hoping to establish a caretaker organization for the banned NSDAP, he founded the Greater German People's Community (Grossdeutsche Volksgemeinschaft or GVG) on January 1, 1924, but few party leaders were ready to accept him as leader. Many Hitler loyalists re-mained aloof, and by summer Esser and Streicher had assumed control of the GVG. Other Nazi leaders attached themselves to a rival radical party, the German *Völkisch* Freedom Party (DVFP), headquartered in Berlin and headed by Ludendorff and Albrecht von Graefe, who had marched in the failed Putsch. What was left of the NSDAP was fragmenting by the day, splintering into mutually mistrustful factions.

Complicating matters further, the Nazis were confronted by the approach of the first national elections since 1920. Hitler had always vehemently opposed participation in democratic elections, but the situation in early 1924 seemed to offer rich possibilities. Between November 1923 and the spring of 1924 the Reich government, using emergency decree powers provided by Article 48 of the Weimar constitution, introduced a series of stringent deflationary measures that led to an immediate stabilization of the economy but also had serious social and political ramifications. They entailed the de facto suspension of the eight-hour workday, a massive and unprecedented dismissal of civil servants and public employees, a severe restriction of credit, which produced a flood of bankruptcies, especially by small businesses, and a startling rise in unemployment, most striking among white-collar personnel. In addition, the government's Third Emergency Tax Decree, which revalued debts and mortgages at only 15 percent of their original value, triggered a volcanic eruption of protest from creditors. The inflation crisis of 1923 quickly gave way to the stabilization crisis of 1924.

Contributing to the furor raised by the government's harsh stabilization measures was the revival of the reparations issue. The question—how much, in what form, and on what schedule Germany would pay—had not been settled at Versailles or at subsequent international conferences. It would prove to be the most intractable issue in postwar international politics. In early 1924, an international committee of economic experts, appointed by the League of Nations' Reparations Commission and chaired by the American banker Charles Dawes, drafted a new scheme of payment to be presented to the German government. In early April, with the Reichstag campaign just getting under way, the committee presented its report to the commission. Quickly dubbed the Dawes Plan, this bundle of recommendations called for a graduated schedule of payments, beginning with approximately one billion marks in 1925–26 and rising to a normal annual payment of 2.5 billion by 1928–29. To Berlin's dismay, it did not, however, establish Germany's total liability, and hence the ominous prospect of paying and paying endlessly into the future loomed over the negotiations.

Among the most galling aspects of the plan were provisions that were widely viewed as infringements on Germany's sovereignty. The plan called for the creation of an international general council with broad powers to oversee the German economy. Since a stable currency and a balanced budget were viewed as prerequisites for German recovery, the operations of the German central bank (Reichsbank) were to be closely supervised by the international general council, and an Allied reparations agent was to be stationed in Berlin to direct the transfer of reparations payments. As sweeteners, the committee indicated that acceptance of the Dawes Plan and a good-faith effort to put Germany's economic house in order would prompt a much needed influx of foreign capital that would allow the country to get back on its feet again. Although not formally part of the plan, the Allies also suggested that evacuation of the Ruhr within one year could be expected if the Germans cooperated and accepted the report.

As soon as the details of the Dawes Plan—and its positive reception by the German government—were made public, a nationwide furor erupted. The Conservatives, Nazis, and *Völkisch* parties as well as the Communists denounced the plan as a "second Versailles," another link in the chains of slavery imposed on Germany by the vindictive Allied governments. Although the press referred to it as the "inflation election," the government's harsh stabilization policies and the Dawes Plan quickly became the central issues of the ensuing campaign, galvanizing all the enemies of the Republic.

With the election scheduled for May 4, the Nazis would have to make a decision on whether to participate—and quickly. It was a highly contentious issue. Held in the shadow of the hyperinflation and the draconian stabilization that followed, the spring campaign of 1924 seemed to offer anti-Republican forces a tremendous launching pad. Anger over the destruction of the currency and the severe measures undertaken to stabilize the economy—all unpopular and all by emergency decree—was running high. At the same time, the extensive media coverage of the Hitler trial had thrown a spotlight on the National Socialists just as the campaign was getting under way, and although Hitler was no longer on the scene, many within the party believed that the moment should not be wasted.

The foremost advocate of this position was Gregor Strasser, a thirty-two-year-old druggist who in 1924 emerged as one of the most energetic and influential leaders of the NSDAP. Like Hitler, Strasser was a decorated war veteran, a militant nationalist, and an anti-Semite. After four years in the trenches, he returned home to Bavaria, finished his degree in pharmacology at Erlangen, and began a career as an apothecary. In 1919 he signed on with Franz Ritter von Epp's Free Corps to overthrow the

Bavarian Socialist Republic; two years later he joined Hitler's fledgling party. Big, gruff in appearance, Strasser had a commanding personality, boundless energy, and a talent for organization. He founded an SA unit in Landshut, acted as SA chief for all of Lower Bavaria, and worked assiduously to establish party chapters in other Bavarian towns. A former army officer, a man of action, he also enjoyed reading Homer in the original classical Greek. Strasser had participated in the Putsch but was cast in a minor role. A few days later he was arrested, charged not for his minimal participation in the coup but with attempting to recruit a soldier for the now-outlawed NSDAP. His stay in prison was brief; he was released in late April 1924 after he was elected to the Bavarian state legislature, a reflection of his burgeoning regional stature.

Strasser was convinced that the party should dive into the Reichstag campaign, even if it meant an alliance with other parties, and he vigorously championed a coalition with the German *Völkisch* Freedom Party (DVFP). This might be a short-term accommodation, Strasser acknowledged, but he hoped to exploit the DVFP's connections in northern Germany to expand Nazi influence beyond Bavaria. His plans met stiff resistance from Esser and Streicher, leaders of the Bavarian clique that dominated party headquarters in Munich. Despite their considerable personal liabilities, both were longtime party men. They were slavishly devoted to Hitler, who returned their loyalty and trust in equal measure. Both rejected even a temporary alliance with the DVFP and scorned Strasser's efforts to thrust the NSDAP into electoral politics. Didn't he understand that Hitler had always rejected collaboration with other parties and had opposed on principle any participation in Weimar's corrupt parliamentary system?

In spite of these rancorous disagreements within the Nazi camp—or perhaps because of them—Graefe and Ludendorff relentlessly pressed the case for a joint Nazi-*Völkisch* venture. They saw in Hitler's absence an opportunity to assume the leadership of the entire *Völkisch* movement and score a major electoral victory. With Strasser's support, Graefe began negotiations with Rosenberg and other Nazi leaders for an amalgamation of the two organizations. At a January meeting in Salzburg, Rosenberg refused to accept a merger but did agree to the formation of a temporary electoral alliance. The DVFP would focus primarily (but not exclusively) on the north, the Nazis on the south—and policy would be determined by consultation between the leadership of the two parties. It would be the Nazis' first election campaign.

Although the Nazis had to operate under the banner of the DVFP, the spring campaign displayed all the basic themes of National Socialist ideology. Denouncing class struggle, the Nazis were determined to break down social barriers and establish a "genuine people's community" (*Volksgemeinschaft*) that would bridge the deep divides of German society. The "ultimate cause" of Germany's collapse in 1918 lay precisely in this "hate-filled divisiveness," which had been "systematically fostered by Jewish Marxism." After having driven the kings from their thrones in 1918, the workers now confronted the "kings of finance." "International bank and stock-market capital" had assumed absolute power, with the greatest financial clout resting in the hands of the Jews, who "maintain a powerful network covering the whole world." The central issue confronting the German people, the Nazis warned, was not left or right, Nationalist or Socialist, but "for or against the Jews."

With the aftershocks of the political and economic eruptions of 1923 still reverberating, Germans went to the polls on May 4, and the extent of their disaffection was reflected in a dramatic surge of the radical, antidemocratic parties. The anti-Republican Conservatives, whose vote jumped from 14 percent in 1920 to 19.5 percent, were the big winners, but with 6.5 percent of the vote, the DVFP made a surprisingly strong showing. Despite organizational difficulties, bitter personal rivalries, and internecine bickering, the Nazis and their partners collected almost two million votes, surpassing each of the small special interest and regional parties and the mainstream Democratic Party (DDP) as well. As expected, support for the Nazis was centered in the south, particularly in Bavaria, but the ability of the Nazi-*Völkisch* coalition to win votes in the north served notice that the appeal of National Socialism was hardly a regional phenomenon.

With the anti-Republican forces of both right and left claiming almost 40 percent of the vote and the democratic parties divided on a number of issues, the creation of a stable majority cabinet proved elusive, and in October, after much wrangling, the Reichstag was dissolved again and new elections called for December. But the political and economic environment had undergone a considerable transformation since May. The ominous sense of impending doom that had clouded the spring campaign had dissipated. Passage of the Dawes legislation triggered a massive infusion of foreign, especially American, capital, which acted as a catalyst to economic revival. Unemployment dropped, real wages rose, and the desperate pall of economic calamity that had lingered throughout the spring had begun to lift before the fall campaign began. The threat of Rhenish and Bavarian separatism as well as armed insurrection by the political extremes had also greatly diminished. French and Belgian troops were evacuating the Ruhr. The Republic, against all odds, had managed to survive.

For the Nazi-*Völkisch* alliance none of these developments was welcome news. Following their surprisingly strong showing in May, the forces of the radical right were unable to bridge the steadily widening rifts in their coalition. In late August, Strasser and Rosenberg decided to join Ludendorff in founding a new party of *Völkisch* unity, the National Socialist Freedom Movement (NSFB), in time for the new election. But in Bavaria, Streicher and Esser refused to join the new national party and established their own rival organization. The NSFB was apparently neither sufficiently anti-Semitic nor xenophobic enough to suit their tastes. They denounced the Ludendorff-Strasser creation as hopelessly bourgeois and urged Bavarian National Socialists to boycott the approaching elections.

Although repelled by Esser and Streicher, many Nazi leaders shared their aversion to parliamentary elections and particularly disliked any formal association with the NSFB. They openly advocated total abstention from the new campaign, even encouraging those Nazis who did vote to cast Conservative ballots. To no one's surprise, the radical right lost over half of its constituency in the December election. With a paltry 3 percent of the vote, the Nazis and the *Völkisch* right began a drift back to the periphery of German politics, where they remained firmly anchored until the onset of the Great Depression in 1929.

Cocooned in Landsberg, Hitler chose to sit on the sidelines. Until the ill-fated Kampfbund, he had always disparaged cooperation, not to mention merger, with other right-wing parties, and he had condemned any participation in parliamentary politics. But removed from the scene and unable to stay abreast of developments, he seemed surprisingly ambivalent, evasive. Rival leaders who made the pilgrimage to Landsberg seeking

Hitler's blessing for their plans often departed believing that they had secured his support, only to discover that he had offered similar encouragement to their adversaries. It often seemed to depend on who had seen him last. When Ludendorff made two visits to Landsberg in May, hoping to coax Hitler into agreeing to a union of the NSDAP with the much stronger DVFP, Hitler temporized. Ludendorff responded by issuing a press release claiming that Hitler had, in fact, endorsed the merger. When Hitler publicly disavowed the article, it merely added to the confusion. Hitler was livid, furious at his own powerlessness and at the treachery of Ludendorff. The event vividly underscored just how little he was able to manage events from the confines of prison.

So frustrated with the situation was Hitler that in early July he announced his temporary withdrawal from active politics and requested that no more delegations from the different party factions visit him. He had had enough. He explained that he could not be responsible for developments while still in prison. He would bide his time, finish his book, and would, he hoped, be released in the not too distant future. Hitler's announcement surprised and disappointed many party leaders, some of whom lashed out at his curious disengagement, his passivity. Hitler, they felt, was simply drifting along, allowing the rudderless party to disintegrate.

Hitler fully understood this. But he had little incentive to try to sort out matters, to referee the conflicts between the different factions of his movement. Why should he be involved in matters over which he had no control? It was clear to him—and to all others—that no real unity in the movement could be attained without him, and he was more than content to await events. He was due for parole in September; then he would leave Landsberg as the savior of a revived National Socialist movement.

Hitler was denied parole in September, but against the recommendation of the state prosecutor was released from Landsberg on December 20, 1924, two weeks after the party's electoral fiasco. In all, he had spent thirteen months in prison for attempting the violent overthrow of the duly constituted government of Germany. Beyond the right-wing fringe, his release stirred little interest. A small news item in *The New York Times* on the day of his discharge—"Hitler Tamed by Prison"—was typical:

Adolf Hitler, the demigod of the reactionary extremists, was released on parole from imprisonment at Fortress Landsberg, Bavaria, today and immediately left in an auto for Munich. He looked a much sadder and wiser man today than last spring when he, with Ludendorff and other radical extremists, appeared before a Munich court charged with conspiracy to overthrow the government. His behavior during his imprisonment convinced the authorities that, like his political organization, he was no longer to be feared. It is believed he will retire to private life and return to Austria, the country of his birth.

Hitler, of course, had no intention of fading meekly into a quiet retirement in Austria. He left prison determined to achieve two objectives: to reestablish the party and to assert his undisputed leadership of it. Both would be daunting tasks. The centrifugal forces that had threatened to tear the movement asunder during his detention were still strong, and when he returned to Munich a free man, his status as leader was far from clear. Before the Putsch, he had been at best only one of several figures vying for leadership of the *Völkisch* right. The trial had catapulted him momentarily onto the national stage, and his time in prison lent him a mysterious aura, which he assiduously cultivated. But while everyone paid homage to the heroic Hitler of Landsberg, the flesh-and-blood Hitler freed from prison and back on the streets of Munich was another matter. Some leaders on the far right, especially those in the north, were not inclined to accept him as the "Führer" of the anti-Republican *Völkisch* movement. At a meeting in Berlin on January 17, 1925, intended to find common ground between representatives of the *Völkisch* right and the National Socialists, *Völkisch* leaders dismissed Hitler as little more than "a drummer," a successful agitator, but hardly the stuff from which national political leaders are made. What had he actually accomplished? By what right could he claim undisputed leadership of the *Völkisch* right? After all, Graefe was far more active, and Ludendorff enjoyed far greater national recognition than Hitler. Furious, the Nazi representatives stormed out of the meeting.

On that same day some three hundred miles to the south Hitler announced his intention to reestablish the NSDAP. Since his release from prison, he had met several times with Bavarian minister president Heinrich

Held to convince him that he had learned his lesson, that a refounded National Socialist Party would follow a path of legality in its future activities. No more violence, no more attempts to overthrow the government by force. It was, as usual with Hitler, a persuasive performance. With some misgivings, Held lifted the ban on the NSDAP on February 16, 1925.

Ten days later the first issue of the revived *Völkischer Beobachter* appeared on the newsstands. It carried several announcements and declarations from Hitler, beginning with an appeal to the squabbling factions of the movement to put their quarrels behind them and come together behind the party's banner. He was not interested in the conflicts of the past, he wrote. There would be no questions asked, no settling of scores. All that was behind them. He was interested only in the present and future, in men who were committed National Socialists, devoted to "the idea." Above all, "every split in the struggle is to be avoided," Hitler insisted. "The entire strength of the movement must be thrown against the most fearsome enemy of the German people: Jewry and Marxism as well as the parties allied with or supportive of them."

There would be some organizational reforms within the party, but "the political and propaganda struggle of the new movement," he proclaimed, would "be uniformly led according to the principles of the old movement. The program of the movement and the more detailed guidelines issued by the leadership will be the deciding factor for this." The role of leader—his role—was key. "First [comes] the Führer, then the organization and not the other way around." His claim to leadership was total. He would take sole responsibility for the party, its policies, organizations, and goals, and he would brook no interference or sniping. If, after a year, the party was dissatisfied with his leadership, he would step aside. The leader was more than a political leader; he was to be the very embodiment of the National Socialist idea. The message was clear: To oppose Hitler was to oppose National Socialism. His time in Landsberg had convinced him that he was the chosen one, the savior ordained by History to liberate the German people from their "enslavement," to preserve the endangered Aryan race, and to lead the German nation again to greatness. Now he needed to convince his fractious party of that calling.

On February 27 Hitler made his first public appearance since his trial. As the venue, he chose the Bürgerbräukeller. His speech was scheduled for eight, but by late afternoon a large crowd had begun gathering outside. More than three thousand of the party faithful finally squeezed into the hall, while thousands more jostled outside as the police finally barred the doors. Those in the expectant audience paid one mark for an admission ticket—the party needed the money, and Hitler remained its biggest attraction.

Speaking in the cavernous auditorium beneath wagon-wheel-shaped lamps that hung pendulously from the ceiling, Hitler spoke for two hours, his rasping voice rising and falling in the familiar frenzied cadences, his arms flailing, his raised right hand stabbing the air for emphasis, his body straining into the odd contortions so familiar to the party faithful. He called for a revival of the German spirit, of German power, of German self-reliance. He railed against the weakness of the bourgeoisie, the cowardice of their parties, and the pacifism of the left. Above all he fulminated against that "devilish power that had plunged Germany into this misery . . . Marxism and the carrier of that world pestilence and scourge, the Jew."

The Jewish Marxist threat was not simply a matter of ideology, of political philosophies locked in mortal combat. The peril penetrated far deeper and was more insidious than that. "The greatest threat . . . for us," he warned his spellbound listeners, was "the alien poison in our body. All other dangers are transitory. . . . Only this one alone is . . . for us eternal." The National Socialists could break the Versailles Treaty, refuse to pay the reparations; they could eliminate political parties, "but blood, once contaminated, can't be changed. It continues to degenerate, pushing us year after year down deeper and deeper." If today his audience wondered about the fractiousness of the German people, the cause was as simple as it was sinister: it was merely the corruption of their contaminated blood manifesting itself.

The evening ended, revival fashion, with leaders who only days— even hours—before had been at each other's throats, climbing onto the garland-draped platform to shake hands and embrace, to swear brotherhood to each other and fealty to the Führer. They stood on chairs and tables, cheered and laughed and wept; they roared their approval. Their Führer Adolf Hitler was back; the old fanaticism still burned.

Hitler had carried it off, energizing the troops, demanding obedience and party unity, declaring war on the movement's enemies. Yet outside the fragile bubble of far-right politics, Hitler's return to the stage was hardly newsworthy. He was no longer a figure of national significance; the party was half the size it had been in November 1923 and was riddled with seemingly intractable internal conflicts. In one sense, however, Hitler's appearance at the Bürgerbräukeller had succeeded altogether too well. Alarmed by the inflammatory radicalism of Hitler's speech, especially his violent rhetoric about the life-and-death struggle against his enemies, the Bavarian government on March 9 issued an edict prohibiting Hitler from speaking in public. He would be permitted to address closed party functions, but nothing more, nothing in the public arena. Shortly thereafter, virtually every German state issued a similar ban.

Coming at a time when he was attempting to reinvigorate the party and to restore his leadership over it, the ban was a potentially serious blow. His oratory, his ability to energize crowds, had always been his greatest political asset, and now at a critical juncture it was lost. In the spring of 1925 his claim to leadership of the radical right was tenuous, his position challenged from a number of quarters—by Graefe and the *Völkisch* crowd, even by some within the NSDAP, and, most seriously, by Erich Ludendorff. The general was viewed by many as a unity figure who could transcend all the petty differences that had bedeviled the radical right in 1924. He was certainly the most visible figure on the right-wing fringe, and he still commanded the allegiance of many, even within the NSDAP. If Hitler were to challenge him, he would need to proceed with caution. In all his official statements Hitler was careful to show great deference to the general, to praise his service to the nation, but he was determined to undermine him and then, at the right moment, push him aside. Just how he would do this was not clear. But events, as they so often did in Hitler's career, came to his rescue.

On February 28, Reich President Friedrich Ebert died suddenly of complications from an appendectomy. Ebert's death at fifty-four was a tragedy for Weimar democracy but a godsend for Hitler. There would be presidential elections, and Hitler recognized an opportunity to deal a blow to Ludendorff. Playing to the general's vanity, Hitler convinced him to enter the race as the National Socialist candidate. Some in Hitler's inner circle felt this a risky move, but Hitler was convinced that Ludendorff could not win and saw in it the possibility of eliminating him as a serious rival. The general took the bait. Throughout the March campaign, the *Völkischer Beobachter*, with its modest and overwhelmingly regional readership, issued perfunctory endorsements, and Hitler sounded all the right notes. But the party's ability to mobilize was still weak, and Hitler's support was a masterpiece of understatement. He wrote respectfully of Ludendorff, addressing him always as "his Excellency," and as "the military leader" of the *Völkisch* right, a formulation that implicitly if none too subtly suggested that he, Adolf Hitler, was its true political leader. Adding to Ludendorff's meager prospects, the other *Völkisch* organizations chose to back another candidate—Karl Jarres—put forward by the mainstream Conservatives.

Underfunded and poorly organized, Ludendorff's candidacy proved to be exactly the disaster that Hitler had anticipated. Out of the roughly two million votes cast in the first round of the election on March 29, only 285,793 Germans cast ballots for the general—a humiliating 14 percent of the total. Since no candidate won a majority of the vote, a second round was necessary. The discredited Ludendorff chose not to enter the runoff, and the Nazis shifted their support to another hero of the Great War, Field Marshal Paul von Hindenburg. Standing as a man above party and supported by a combination of right/center-right parties, Hindenburg carried the election with a mere plurality. At seventy-seven years of age, Hindenburg was a living legend, associated with the glories of the old empire. He had been called out of retirement in 1914 and dealt the Russians a major defeat at Tannenberg—the first great German victory of the war. Hindenburg quickly became Germany's most celebrated war hero, and by 1916 was by far the most revered man in the Reich. Although he was a conservative, a devout monarchist, in fact, the very embodiment of the old order, he took his oath to defend the Republic seriously, as a matter of honor. Despite his reservations about parliamentary democracy, his assumption of the Reich presidency lent the struggling Republic a degree of legitimacy it had hitherto lacked. Yet, unlike Ebert, Hindenburg was hardly devoted to the Weimar Republic he agreed to serve, and in time he would play a crucial role in the final collapse of German democracy.

The elections of 1925 shattered Ludendorff's standing as leader of the "national opposition," and in the following years his increasingly eccentric views pushed him beyond even the outer fringes of German politics. He launched occasional thunderbolts aimed most frequently at the Catholic Church, but his threat to Hitler's leadership of the radical right was at an end. The *Völkisch* party began a slow but relentless slide into irrelevance.

Its followers drifted gradually to the NSDAP, joined by many of its leaders, and after 1928 it virtually vanished from the political stage.

With Ludendorff's position gravely weakened and the DVFP's influence rapidly ebbing, Hitler faced another, potentially more serious problem, one arising from within the party's ranks. In the run-up to the Putsch, Ernst Röhm had worked assiduously to build bridges to other right-wing paramilitary organizations. He had played a central role in the events of November 9, 1923, and had spent two months in prison as a consequence. Upon being granted parole, he once again took up the organizational reins, hoping to bring about an amalgamation of the same armed groups with which he had worked in 1923. Traveling around the country, he made contact with different paramilitary organizations and began welding them into an umbrella organization, the Frontbann, which he hoped would function as a purely military formation, free from the endemic factional bickering that plagued the right in 1924. The Frontbann, as Röhm envisioned it, would be the military arm of the NSDAP but remain an autonomous organization within the party owing allegiance to him personally.

Röhm's extensive military experience, his contacts with the army and other paramilitary leaders, as well as his determination to transform the SA into a mass organization made him an invaluable asset for the party, but his vision of an autonomous SA, technically subordinate to the party but in fact largely independent, was unacceptable to Hitler. The Storm Troopers, in Hitler's view, were to be integrated into the party and subordinated to his leadership. The SA was to be an instrument of the party's political strategy—providing protection for Nazi speakers at mass rallies, handing out leaflets, posting placards, staging gigantic parades and other demonstrations. The SA was to be an integral part of the party's propaganda offensives. Above all, Adolf Hitler, not Ernst Röhm, would be its supreme leader.

During 1924 Röhm made several visits to Hitler in Landsberg, hoping to convince him of his plans, only to be rebuffed time and again. With the reestablishment of the NSDAP in 1925, matters came to a head. In Hitler's first programmatic statement in the *Völkischer Beobachter*, he spelled out the SA's role as an instrument for political agitation. In mid-April Röhm presented Hitler with a memorandum that suggested that the thirty thousand men he had organized in the Frontbann could serve as the basis for a national political organization, albeit under his control. When Hitler failed to respond, Röhm issued an ultimatum, threatening to resign from his post as leader of the SA. This he intended as an opening gambit in a difficult bargaining process, and he was shocked when Hitler simply refused to reply. In fact, Hitler never offered a response of any kind to his old comrade.

In late April, Röhm formally resigned his position as head of the SA and the Frontbann. He made several personal appeals to Hitler, appeals in which he used the familiar "*du*," and invoked the "memory of the fine and difficult days we have lived through together," begging Hitler "not to exclude me from your personal friendship." Hitler still did not reply, leaving Röhm offended and deeply hurt. To a party colleague he grumbled about Hitler's unwillingness to tolerate any opposition to his ideas and his notorious indecisiveness when faced with difficult choices. When problems arose, Röhm complained, Hitler would resolve them "suddenly, at the very last minute," after allowing the situation to fester, sometimes for weeks or months on end. The situation often became "intolerable and dangerous only because he vacillates and procrastinates." Hitler wanted "things his own way and gets mad when he strikes firm opposition." He didn't "realize how he can wear on one's nerves," and he didn't understand "that he fools only himself and those worms around him" with his fits and histrionics. For the time being the SA question was not so much resolved as simply left in limbo. Göring, formerly head of the SA, was still in exile (he would not return to Germany for five years when the Reich government issued an amnesty for political criminals) and SA units were to organize themselves at the local level, with little in the way of a national structure or clear chain of command. It was symptomatic of Hitler's leadership style that he did not address the SA question or move to appoint a new leader of the Storm Troopers for more than a year.

Meanwhile another threat was brewing in the north. In March 1925, only days after he was banned from speaking, Hitler deputized Gregor Strasser to take charge of the party in northern Germany. From his days working with the NSFB in the Nazi-*Völkisch* alliance of the previous year, Strasser had many contacts in the north, and, armed with the free railroad pass given to all Reichstag deputies (he had been elected in December 1924), he crisscrossed northern Germany, giving speeches, founding local chapters of the party, and revitalizing old ones. With Hitler sidelined, Strasser spoke at ninety-one Nazi events in 1925, the vast majority in the north. As one political commentator observed, Strasser lacked "Hitler's oratorical gift, but possessed something just as rare: the power to move an audience by his very personality." He also proved to be a master organizer. By the end of the year, the northern party could boast 272 local chapters compared to a mere 71 prior to the Putsch, and Strasser had become the most visible Nazi leader in the country.

Leaders in northern Germany were drawn to Strasser both for his strong anticapitalist, "socialist" stance and his emerging role as a counterpoise to the domination of the party by the Bavarian faction. Many were also disturbed by Hitler's apparent indifference to their concerns. Banned from speaking in public, Hitler spent much of 1925 concentrating his energies almost exclusively on Bavaria and, inexplicably to many party leaders, spent long weeks virtually secluded in the mountains outside Berchtesgaden writing the second volume of *Mein Kampf*. Leaders in the north, many of whom had never actually met Hitler, grew increasingly restless. They chafed at what they considered Munich's attempt to impose its control over the entire party and hoped to break the dominance of the Bavarian camarilla at party headquarters. They were convinced that Esser, Streicher, and Amann were leading Hitler astray, pushing him in a bourgeois, reactionary direction that might play well in rural Bavaria but would ultimately limit the party's appeal in urban Germany. They were also increasingly frustrated by Hitler's inattention to party matters—a passivity that de facto left Esser, Streicher, and the Munich clique in charge.

In the course of 1925 they gravitated naturally toward Strasser, who operated out of Berlin and was visible on the ground all across northern Germany. He organized meetings of regional district leaders (*Gauleiter*) from the north and west where disgruntled leaders could voice their frustration with Munich—and by implication, Hitler. In September, inspired by Strasser, these leaders formed the Working Group of Northern and Western German *Gauleiter* of the NSDAP (Arbeitsgemeinschaft or AG), intended to be a sounding board for like-minded *Gauleiter* and a counterweight to party headquarters. They insisted that they were not challenging Hitler's leadership, but the northern leaders were determined to create an alternative center of power to Munich.

Strasser was loyal to Hitler, recognizing him as the indispensable leader of the party, the glue that held it together. But, like Röhm, he considered himself a "colleague" of Hitler rather than a follower. Strasser's unwavering loyalty to Hitler did not, however, extend to the program or the Munich headquarters. He believed that the program—the "immutable" Twenty-five Points of 1920—needed serious revision. Like many leaders in the industrial north, Strasser believed that the party should place far greater stress on its radical "socialist" impulses. He was wary of the southern faction's heavy emphasis on fanatical nationalism and anti-Semitism and was convinced that the NSDAP should develop a labor-oriented, anticapitalist stance that would appeal to the industrial working class. His brand of "socialism," as he made clear on numerous occasions, was not a form of Marxism but a radical *national* socialism, a German socialism rooted in the *Volk*. Speaking in the Reichstag in November 1925, Strasser explained: "We National Socialists want the economic revolution involving the nationalization of the economy. . . . We want in place of an exploitative capitalist economic system a real socialism, maintained not by a soulless Jewish-materialist outlook but by the believing, sacrificial, and unselfish old German community sentiment, community purpose and community feeling. We want the social revolution in order to bring about the national revolution."

To provide a platform for these views, he and his younger brother Otto established their own publishing house, the Kampfverlag (Struggle Publishing), in Berlin, which would publish a variety of National Socialist newspapers and journals. Foremost among them was the daily *Workers' Press* (*Arbeiterzeitung*), which focused largely on Berlin, and the *National Socialist Letters*, a bimonthly journal that was intended to produce serious intellectual articles devoted to National Socialist ideology and strategy. Strasser was the Kampfverlag's publisher, but for its managing editor (and chief writer) he selected a young Rhinelander, a university graduate, would-be novelist, poet, freelance journalist, and political agitator who had joined the party only in late 1924. Dr. Joseph Goebbels (he received his PhD in Romantic Literature from Heidelberg in 1921) was short in stature and slight of build; he walked with a pronounced limp due to a crippled foot from a childhood illness. He was filled with a deep-seated rage at his failed career aspirations and his physical deformity, a burning resentment that he projected onto the German nation and its unjust treatment by Fate. Inspired by Hitler's defiant words in the

Munich courtroom, he became a fervent adherent, worshipping Hitler from afar as the ordained savior who would restore the soul of Germany and lead the nation once more to greatness.

Based in Elberfeld in the Rhineland and working as a freelance journalist, Goebbels was drawn to the NSDAP and to Strasser, acquiring a reputation as a firebrand, both for his incendiary articles in the *Völkisch* press and his equally biting oratory. He proved to be a creative and gifted public speaker, sharp-tongued, clever, a master of unabashed demagoguery. He quickly became a popular speaker at National Socialist and *Völkisch* gatherings throughout the Rhineland and across northern Germany, drawing on an extensive repertoire of radical rhetoric. Goebbels shared Strasser's vision of National Socialism that emphasized the socialist strains of the party's ideology, at times swerving toward a form of national Bolshevism. In 1925 he was appointed business manager of the *Gau* (party district) Rhineland-North, overseeing its press and its propaganda. He showed remarkable skill at both.

During the winter of 1925–26 Strasser and Goebbels set to work on a draft of a revised party program and distributed copies to a number of district leaders in the north. In it they endorsed a closer relationship with Russia and emphasized the party's socialism and its determination to crush corrupt capitalism. To demonstrate the party's leftist credentials they also advocated Nazi participation in a Communist- and Socialist-sponsored referendum to block a government plan that would compensate aristocratic and princely families for property lost in the 1919 revolution.

They chose not to inform Hitler about this draft revision, though it was widely discussed by National Socialist leaders in the Northern Working Group. The draft did not find universal approval even in the North, but it was, by its very existence, a challenge to the established powers within the party. It was not until February 1926 that Hitler, informed by an incensed Gottfried Feder, came to understand fully the threat posed by Strasser and his draft. He immediately called a conference of party leaders to set matters straight. The meeting was to be held in the Baroque city of Bamberg, in Upper Franconia (northern Bavaria), in February. Goebbels and Strasser traveled to the conference intending to press their ideas, hopeful that Hitler could be won over to their views.

But Hitler preempted them. The audience of some sixty participants consisted largely of leaders from the south, and Hitler, speaking first, delivered a powerful address of some two hours, scornfully dismissing the draft and insisting that the program of 1920 was inviolate.

Without mentioning Strasser or Goebbels by name, he restated the party's commitment to the principle of private property and firmly rejected any National Socialist participation in the leftist referendum on princely property. It would undermine the NSDAP's standing with the already nervous middle class and undermine his efforts to win financial backing from prominent business interests. Most of all, the NSDAP could not, under any circumstances, afford to be seen as working with the Communists and Socialists. He was equally adamant about the party's foreign policy. He restated his conviction that France was Germany's implacable enemy and hence England and Italy offered the most as potential allies. Cooperation with Russia was unthinkable. "Anyone who talks about a Russo-German alliance hasn't realized that such an alliance would result in the immediate political bolshevization of Germany and thus national suicide."

When he at last rose to speak, Strasser was clearly intimidated. He stumbled haltingly through his remarks, and Goebbels decided to pass on his opportunity to address the room. Both had assumed that Hitler would be sympathetic to their ideas and were shocked by his performance. "What Hitler is this? A reactionary?" Goebbels agonized in his diary that night. "Incredibly clumsy and uncertain. Russian question completely beside the point. Italy and England [Germany's] natural allies. Awful! Our mission is the destruction of Bolshevism. Bolshevism and its Jewish progenitors." Germany, Hitler had insisted, must ultimately secure Russia, with its vast lands and natural resources. Germany was to pursue a colonial policy, not in Asia or Africa, but on the European continent. On the home front, National Socialism must not shake the principle of private property. The party's program, Hitler declared, was sufficient as it was. To Goebbels's disgust, Hitler was obviously satisfied with it. "Feder nods. Ley nods. Streicher nods. Esser nods. It hurts me to the bottom of my soul," Goebbels confided to his diary, "to see you in this company."

Bamberg was a decisive moment in the evolution of the NSDAP. At Bamberg, Hitler reasserted his control over the party. The National Socialists were fond of invoking "the idea" of the movement, but at Bamberg it was not so much this nebulous ideological idea that carried the day but Hitler's powerful personality. He had become the embodiment of the "idea," and to oppose the program was to oppose him. The NSDAP was now unequivocally Hitler's party, and the leaders at Bamberg overwhelmingly swore fealty to him. He and he alone would ultimately decide the content of the program. Isolated in Bamberg, Strasser and Goebbels beat a hasty retreat. Hitler demanded that Strasser destroy all copies of his draft program, which he did. And Goebbels, mortified by Hitler's speech, returned to Ebersfeld shaken, wondering how he could have been so wrong about Hitler.

In May, delegates at the party congress formally pronounced the NSDAP's Twenty-five Points immutable, and early in the summer Hitler prohibited the existence of working groups within the party. To placate Strasser and his followers, Hitler courted leading men among the northern leaders, embracing those who were a potential threat to his leadership. He tapped Franz Pfeffer von Salomon, a member of Strasser's Northern Working Group, to assume the national leadership of the SA, a position he had left vacant since Röhm's departure in April of the previous year. Pfeffer had a long history of right-wing militancy—he was a Free Corps leader, a participant in the Kapp Putsch, and a resistance fighter against the French occupation of the Ruhr. In 1925—at age twenty-five—he became the *Gauleiter* of the important Westphalian/Ruhr district. On accepting Hitler's offer on November 1, 1926, he changed his name to von Pfeffer, feeling that Pfeffer von Salomon sounded too Jewish. He understood his mission and the place of the SA in Hitler's plans. As Hitler had unsuccessfully tried to impress upon Röhm, the SA was to be neither a secret band of conspirators nor an armed militia but an instrument of party policy, subordinate to the political leadership in Munich and, above all, to the Führer. Although tension between the regional SA and the political leadership would linger for years to come, under Pfeffer's leadership the friction receded, and by early 1927, the SA seemed firmly under Hitler's control.

Hitler also had plans for Strasser's chief lieutenant, Joseph Goebbels. Shortly after the Bamberg conference, Hitler launched a personal offensive to lure Goebbels away from his mentor. He invited Goebbels to Munich to give a speech at the Bürgerbräukeller, the Nazi holy of holies, and when he arrived at the station, he found Hitler's gleaming black Mercedes waiting for him. As he was driven through the city, Goebbels noticed gigantic blood-red placards plastered everywhere announcing his speech. It was, Goebbels thought, "a noble reception."

For several days Hitler played the genial host; he invited Goebbels to join him and a lady friend for dinner; Hitler supplied tickets for concerts and the opera and offered his chauffeured car for tours of the Bavarian countryside; they had conversations tête-à-tête about party matters, each move calculated to convince Goebbels that he was a valued figure in the party, even a trusted friend of the Führer. Dr. Goebbels did not need Strasser, Hitler implied, he could stand on his own. In private discussion with a small circle of party leaders, Hitler chastised those who had challenged him at Bamberg, then proceeded to expand on the views he had propounded so fiercely at the conference. "We ask questions," Goebbels wrote, "he answers brilliantly. I love him. A mixture of collectivism and individualism. Land to the people. Production, where one creates, individualism. Corporations, trusts, finished goods, transportation, etc. socialized." Goebbels was overwhelmed. The disenchantment he had experienced at Bamberg was swept away by Hitler's attentions, his show of friendship, his charisma. Goebbels succumbed entirely. Hitler "has thought everything through . . . always sees the big picture." Such a man, Goebbels gushed adoringly, "can be my leader. I bow to the greater man, the political genius."

Hitler rewarded him by appointing him to head the Berlin NSDAP. It was a tough assignment, but Goebbels seemed up to the challenge. He spoke the language of revolutionary politics; he espoused a nebulous, non-Marxist form of socialism, and his attacks on capitalism, mixed with a particularly toxic dose of anti-Semitism, were vicious and unrelenting. When he arrived in the capital, the Berlin party was disorganized and in disarray, with barely eight hundred members, and the city—the "asphalt desert," as Goebbels sometimes referred to it—was the epicenter of left-wing politics in Germany, a stronghold of both the Social Democrats and the Communists. Goebbels threw himself into the fray with utter fanaticism. He wrote incendiary articles in the party press, he pushed the SA into the streets; he provoked violent confrontations with the Communists' powerful paramilitary Red Front. He had a natural propensity for theatricality, for public spectacle, which he would develop to great effect in the following years. After only a few difficult months, he had injected new energy, new confidence, and aggressiveness into the Berlin party, greatly expanded its membership, and given it a much higher profile in Berlin politics.

Goebbels would prove to be an inspired choice, both in Berlin and nationally, but Hitler's most important move at this juncture was to strike a deal with Gregor Strasser. In the aftermath of Bamberg, Strasser agreed to disband the Northern Working Group, and Hitler agreed to remove the loathsome Esser from the party leadership. He then asked Strasser to take charge of the party's propaganda department. Then a devastating car crash in March 1926 left him seriously injured and bedridden through much of the spring, and Hitler was forced to name an interim director to manage the Propaganda Section until Strasser's appointment was formally announced in mid-September. But Strasser was brought back into the fold.

A tireless organizer and campaigner, Strasser seemed ideal for the position, and he took up his new task with the same boundless energy that characterized all his political actions. Between 1926 and 1928, the Propaganda Section initiated a set of organizational reforms intended to tighten the leadership's control of the party and to enhance Nazi campaign performance. He crafted a vertical organizational structure that established a clear chain of command. He redrew the NSDAP's regional boundaries to conform to the Reichstag thirty-five electoral districts, and the authority of the regional Chiefs, the *Gauleiter,* was substantially strengthened in each area. It was the *Gauleiter* and their propaganda staffs that were charged with executing the party's campaign directives.

This emphasis on propaganda, its organization and content, came as a result of Hitler's decision, made while in prison, to take a new strategic tack. He had learned his lessons from the failed Putsch. "From now on," he said to a follower during a visit to Landsberg, "we must follow a new line of action. . . . When I resume active work, it will be necessary to pursue a new policy. Instead of working to achieve power by an armed coup, we shall have to hold our noses and enter the Reichstag." The party would embrace parliamentary politics not to save German democracy but to destroy it. "Sooner or later," he said, "we shall have a majority—and after that Germany."

The key was propaganda, and here Hitler had quite specific ideas. Propaganda, he argued, "must be aimed at the emotions and only to a very limited degree at the so-called intellect." Propaganda appeals, therefore, "must be adjusted to the most limited intelligence among those it is addressed to." The art of propaganda lay "in understanding the emotional ideas of the great masses and finding, through a psychologically correct form, the way to the attention and thence to the heart of the broad masses." To do this, it was necessary to have only a few major themes. "The receptivity of the great masses is very limited," he added scornfully, "their intelligence is small, but their power of forgetting is enormous. In consequence . . . all effective propaganda must be limited to a very few points and must harp on these in slogans until the last member of the public understands what you want him to understand by your slogan." "The people in their overwhelming majority are so feminine by nature and attitude that sober reasoning determines their thoughts and actions far less than emotion." Given the limited intelligence and "primitive sentiments" of the broad masses, it was, therefore, necessary to restrict appeals "to a few points and repeat them over and over." Equally important, due to "the primitive simplicity" of their minds, the "great masses of the people . . . more easily fall a victim to a big lie than to a little one, since they themselves lie in little things, but would be ashamed of lies that were too big. Such a falsehood will never enter their heads, and they will not be able to believe in the possibility of such monstrous effrontery and infamous misrepresentation in others." The "Jews and their Marxist fighting organizations" operate on this "sound principle," and, in self-defense, so, too, should the National Socialists.

The party, for Hitler, existed for propaganda, and these were the principles on which the party's propaganda would be based. Street propaganda, recruitment drives, and mobilization for elections now became the raison d'être of all National Socialist activities. Hitler's first priority, after establishing his control over the movement, was to create a broadly based, centrally directed party organization necessary for the NSDAP's entry onto the stage of Weimar electoral politics. The *Völkisch* campaigns of 1924 had been too disjoined, lacking clarity and central direction. With the reestablishment of the party in 1925, Hitler hoped to concentrate responsibility for the conduct of nationwide propaganda in the hands of the party leadership in Munich. He was convinced that if the reconstructed NSDAP was to compete successfully in democratic elections, it needed a grassroots organization capable of attracting dues-paying members and mobilizing voters.

In the spring of 1926 the party took the first steps toward creating a tightly organized and energetic propaganda operation. Reorganization of the party's propaganda apparatus was to be taken at the grass roots. Each local party chapter (*Ortsgruppe*) was ordered to organize a propaganda cell to be staffed by party members from diverse occupational backgrounds who were "infused with a fanatical, fiery spirit for our movement." To broaden the social and cultural perspective of local propaganda operations, one third of cell operatives were to be women. As a measure to increase centralized control over local propaganda, the leadership instructed the cells to bypass their regional leaders (*Gauleiter*) and establish direct contact with the Propaganda Leadership in Munich.

The drive to create this network of propaganda cells, inspired by the Communist example, was launched in 1926, but the party had neither the financial resources nor the membership to generate the sort of national grassroots activity that Hitler and Strasser envisioned. Goebbels suggested another approach. He praised the party's expanding organizational network but warned that the party should have no illusions about its strength or effectiveness. The network of propaganda cells was "ready to break in some places," while in others it was "too finely spun, as delicate as a spider's web." On the other hand, Goebbels noted that the party was truly well organized in three or four areas, and rather than expending its energies on a nationwide effort, the NSDAP should concentrate its resources in these places. He argued that "our objective in the coming winter must be to transform one, maybe two dozen large metropolitan areas into unshakable bulwarks of the movement." These cities must be carefully chosen, and then, only after the most exhaustive and detailed preparation, subjected to an intensive propaganda barrage. Following centralized direction and guidelines from the Propaganda Section in Munich, these propaganda offensives would saturate the selected cities with leaflets, placards, parades, pamphlets, rallies, and special appearances by the party's "big guns." In this way, the party could maximize its very limited financial resources, employ its best speakers, and devastate its overwhelmed enemies in the targeted cities. Having secured such urban bastions, the NSDAP could launch an assault on the surrounding countryside.

Although Goebbels's plan found a favorable reception in the party's leadership, it was not implemented in 1926. Instead, Hitler opted to continue the party's emphasis on national grassroots expansion and to tighten the party's central control over its burgeoning but loose apparatus. He confirmed that decision at the NSDAP's first Party Day congress at Weimar, when he officially clarified the national chain of command. The local party chapters were explicitly subordinated to the regional chiefs (*Gauleiter*), who were in turn selected by Hitler. The local party chapters (*Ortsgruppen*) were required to submit monthly reports on their propaganda activities to the regional party leadership, where the *Gauleiter* and his propaganda staff would then pass them on to the Reich Propaganda Leadership in Munich. There they would be analyzed and used to formulate the party's propaganda and campaign strategy.

From 1926 to late 1927, the thrust of the party's propaganda was set by Strasser in his role as propaganda chief, but the ideological message remained blurred. Appeals to farmers, shopkeepers, and clerks did not cease, but Strasser relentlessly pressed for greater efforts to mobilize the urban proletariat, stressing the revolutionary, anticapitalist themes calculated to attract working-class support. That position was vigorously opposed by other Nazi leaders in the less industrial south. They contended that the future of National Socialism lay not in the cities, where the Communists and Social Democrats dominated working-class politics, but in the towns and villages of the countryside, where the small-town, rural population would be more attracted to radical nationalist and anti-Semitic themes.

Hitler chose not to intervene in these disputes. His interests at this point were primarily organizational, not ideological, and he was willing to tolerate considerable internal controversy so long as the rival factions recognized his ultimate authority to determine party policy. But since his own views remained typically vague, conflicts within the NSDAP persisted, and ideological murkiness continued to characterize the NSDAP as it entered the vigorous regional campaigns of the mid-1920s.

Behind these campaigns was a vision of propaganda that was shared by Strasser and Goebbels. Whatever theme the party chose to emphasize, the forms, dictated by Munich, were to be the same. Even when the party was an obscure fringe phenomenon, the Nazis envisioned nothing less than the creation of an alternative political universe, a new political myth, complete with their own festivals, rituals, songs, symbols, and language. By 1927, when the party published its first propaganda handbook for local Nazi officials, the basic forms of Nazi propaganda had already emerged. The handbook described the different officially sanctioned types of meetings, festivals, celebrations, and demonstrations; it set guidelines for their organizational format, advertising, and security; and it offered instructions on how to make the most effective use of leaflets and placards, the party press, films, and other forms of agitational activity. Included among these activities were the major festivals on the National Socialist calendar: the celebration of Hitler's birthday on April 20; the summer solstice festival on June 22; the Day of Mourning, a memorial service in honor of fallen party comrades; a reenactment of the march to the Feldherrnhalle on November 9; and Christmas. Later, the party's increasingly elaborate annual rally at Nuremberg during September, which would acquire monumental dimensions after Hitler's assumption of power in 1933, would be added to the list.

In between these fixed dates on the calendar, the party encouraged the holding of other propaganda events: "German Days" or "German Evenings"; SA marches and parades; flag dedications; memorial services for war veterans. Regardless of region or featured speaker, these ceremonies were intended to follow a set of standard procedures. The sight of the SA marching through a small town or big-city neighborhood to a wreath-laying ceremony at the local war memorial followed by a military religious service, either in church, under a tent, or in the open air, became a familiar spectacle throughout Germany after 1925.

These Nazi festivals followed a set ceremonial form. Some ritual events might consume hours or, in some instances, days. A typical German Day festival might begin with a torchlight parade from a neighboring town, where a ceremonial military retreat was followed by a public rally. The evening would then conclude with a concert by the local SA band and a speech in the hall of a hotel. The next morning was to be given over to a ceremony honoring Germany's fallen heroes, followed by church services, and a musical concert in the marketplace. After lunch, a "propaganda march" to neighboring villages would be planned, with brief rallies and a short concert in each, before returning for another concert at the marketplace and a speech in the town hall. Marches, music, and masses were the essential ingredients of this National Socialist event.

The "public mass meeting" was a particularly favored option on the Nazi propaganda menu. Following the party's guidelines, it called for a major speech and a public discussion. In the last turbulent years of the Weimar Republic, this sort of meeting, advertised in the local press, was viewed as an effective means of recruitment. Since Communists and Social Democrats regularly attended these meetings, catcalls, insults, threats, and finally bottle-throwing melees often ensued. Such fracases were not only accorded wide coverage in the local press, giving the party heightened visibility, they were also widely seen as a rough form of local entertainment.

The party sought to attract not the local elite, but respected representatives of the different occupational, professional, and social groups who might then lead the way for others to join. If the local bookseller or schoolteacher or farmer saw something in the NSDAP, then maybe the Nazis were not so out of bounds after all. These notables were invited to special recruitment evenings that included a ritual ceremony of great solemnity that combined many of the basic elements of the NSDAP's propaganda repertory. Instructions for the evening were detailed down to the minute.

Beyond these grassroots forms of propaganda, the NSDAP in 1926 held the first of what came in subsequent years to be its signature event: the national party rally. The event was held in Weimar in the summer, and attendance was modest, with only seven to eight thousand in attendance, roughly half of whom were Storm Troopers. In their brown caps, shirts, and trousers, which became their official uniform in 1926, they marched in massed formation past Hitler, who, with arm outstretched in the Nazi salute, reviewed the troops. Trumpets, drums, torchlight parades, the solemn military ritual of the retreat at day's end—all would be essential elements in the annual rallies that would later be staged with increasing grandiosity in Nuremberg.

The Weimar rally marked the first public appearance of a new National Socialist formation, the Security Staff or SS (Schutzstaffel). Unlike the mass SA, the SS was a small elite organization, founded in November of the previous year as an heir to Hitler's personal bodyguard, the Shock Troop Adolf Hitler. In these early days, the SS, with its jet black uniforms with silver trim, was a mysterious unit; its duties were ambiguous and its place in the National Socialist hierarchy unclear. It was officially subordinate to the SA, but, in fact, owed its allegiance directly to Hitler.

It gradually took on policing duties, ferreting out spies within the party, compiling lists of Jews and enemies of the NSDAP, and was always alert for opportunities to expand its influence. But during the party's formative years the SS remained a small, select organization operating in the shadow of the much larger SA. It had yet to acquire the bone-chilling reputation for cold-eyed murder, sadism, and unthinkable cruelty that it would develop in the Third Reich.

It was also at the Weimar rally that Hitler introduced the "blood flag" into the National Socialist liturgy. The flag had been carried at the head of the procession on November 9, 1923, stained, presumably, with the blood of the "martyrs" who died at the Feldherrnhalle. In a reverent, almost mystical ceremony enacted before the massed formation of the party's uniformed minions, Hitler solemnly touched the sacred blood flag to the banner of each SA and SS unit, an act of consecration that symbolically bound the Storm Troopers and SS men to him in eternal loyalty. It was a ceremony to be enacted with solemn piety at all subsequent national party rallies.

By the end of 1927, with Hitler's dominance over the NSDAP firmly established, a "Führer cult" gradually took hold within the party. Before the Putsch, he was simply "Herr Hitler" or "the boss," but after his release from prison, Hess and then others began referring to him as "the Führer," the leader. It caught on. The "German greeting" of "Heil" morphed into "Heil Hitler," and although the idea did not originate with Hitler, he did nothing to discourage it. Adding to his mystique, he grew more aloof in his personal and professional activities, a being apart, hard to reach, his movements, his whereabouts, shrouded in mystery. Even high-ranking party officials often had to wait days or weeks before being granted an audience.

Much of 1926 he spent away from Munich, retreating to the Alpine village of Berchtesgaden, where he worked feverishly on the second volume of *Mein Kampf*. There above the village on the slopes of the Obersalzberg he rented a cottage, Haus Wachenfeld, from a widowed party member. Within a short time he was able to buy the cottage on very favorable terms and expanded it gradually, until, during the Third Reich, it was transformed into the grand villa, the Berghof. The first volume of *Mein Kampf* appeared in July 1925, the second in December 1927. The book registered only modest sales but contributed mightily to his reputation within the party as a political visionary, a man of piercing political insights and profound philosophical depths. Couched in portentous biblical imagery, Hitler presented himself as the prophet called by providence to unite the German peoples of Europe and lead them from the depths of their humiliation to redemption. "Today," the book begins, "it seems to me providential that Fate should have chosen Braunau on the Inn as my birthplace. For this little town lies on the boundary between two German states which we of the younger generation at least have made it our life work to reunite by every means at our disposal." Sounding the essential racial and expansionist themes that reverberated through the roughly thousand pages of text that followed, he proclaimed that "one blood demands one Reich. . . . Only when the Reich borders include the very last German, but can no longer guarantee his daily bread, will the moral right to acquire foreign soil arise from the distress of our own people. Their sword will become our plow, and from the tears of war the daily bread of future generations will grow. And so this little city on the border seems to me the symbol of a great mission."

Aside from detailing his ideas about marketing for a mass public, *Mein Kampf* offered nothing new to the party faithful. Hitler's obsessive racial anti-Semitism and his genocidal rhetoric; his determination to expunge "Judeo-Marxism" from the face of the earth; his calls for *Lebensraum* in the East had been loudly proclaimed in innumerable speeches and articles for years. Readers of the book might find it convoluted, contradictory, turgid, and virtually unreadable (it was, and they did), but party members were wise to have a copy on hand. The book was a collection of dubious aphorisms, backward projections of Hitler's views, a semifictional portrayal of his past, stray thoughts on alcohol, diet, dress, and sex, historical observations, and a tangled effort at theory. What came through loud and clear was Hitler's insatiable hatred, his enraged self-pity. Sales of *Mein Kampf* remained disappointing until the Nazi electoral breakthrough in 1930, when the book's popularity followed the sharp upward curve of Nazi electoral fortunes. Even then, the tragic irony of *Mein Kampf* was not that people read it and were convinced by it, but that people did *not* read it.

While Hitler in private appeared distant, disconnected to those around him, an empty shell, he came alive when he strode onstage. To read Hitler's speeches is to miss entirely the passion, the power, and electricity of his performances. Parades, spectacles, rallies were important, but for Hitler "the power which has always started the greatest religions and political avalanches in history rolling has from time immemorial been the magic power of the spoken word, and that alone." The "broad masses of the people," he declared, "can be moved only by the power of speech. All great movements are popular movements, stirred either by the cruel Goddess of Distress or by the firebrand of the word hurled among the masses. . . . Only a storm of hot passion can turn the destinies of peoples, and he alone can rouse passion who bears it within himself. It alone gives its chosen one the words which like hammer blows can open the gates to the heart of a people."

Between 1925 and 1928 Hitler's grand vision of propaganda was the ideal; practice was another matter. For most of the period the party relied on the regional chiefs and a cadre of dedicated activists sprinkled thinly across the country. The Storm Troopers, whose parades, demonstrations, house-to-house canvassing, and other activities Hitler considered essential to political mobilization, were certainly the most visible and energetic elements of Nazi propaganda. The party had neither the money nor the manpower to create a national network of propaganda cells, and its organization was still too loose to guarantee the party leadership the degree of control it desired. The *Gauleiter*, although appointed by Hitler and loyal to him, displayed a tenacious independence, choosing to emphasize the themes they favored and to target the constituencies they thought most susceptible in their area. As a consequence, while the forms and techniques of Nazi political mobilization were becoming more uniform, the party could look quite different from region to region.

In January 1926, Strasser left the Propaganda Leadership to take command of the party's Organization Section, recommending his young adjutant Heinrich Himmler to run the party's national propaganda operation. Himmler, twenty-eight with a degree in agriculture from Munich's Technical University, had participated in the Putsch and thereafter served as Strasser's deputy in Lower Bavaria in 1924–25, hurrying on his motorbike along narrow country lanes to deliver messages, give speeches, and arrange meetings. When Strasser moved to Berlin in 1925, Himmler served as his surrogate in Lower Bavaria. Strasser found Himmler, with his thick rimless glasses and pale owlish face, humorless and uncomfortably formal, but he recommended him to the party leadership nonetheless. Punctilious, obsessed with detail and discipline, Himmler combined a prodigious bureaucratic talent for organization with a cold ideological fervor. Hitler was duly impressed. In January 1928 Himmler assumed the reins of the Propaganda Section and began preparations for the first national election since 1924.

The party, though still very small, was better organized and prepared for a national campaign than four years earlier, but major problems remained. Communications between Munich and the regional and local party organizations were unreliable, compelling the Propaganda Section on occasion to publish directives openly in the *Völkischer Beobachter*, to which all party chapters were required to subscribe. Mixups and miscommunication were common. The Propaganda Section found itself fielding endless queries and complaints on matters large and small.

Complaints and demands went both ways. If a local group decided to draft its own leaflets, the text had to be first submitted to and approved by the Propaganda Section. Himmler chided affiliates that failed to comply with directives from Munich. All chapters were ordered to send regular reports on their activities and those of the party's enemies to the Propaganda Section, and if Himmler discovered an *Ortsgruppe* or district underperforming, he fired off threatening dispatches. He always seemed to be watching, attentive to even the smallest detail. Whereas Strasser drew followers to him through the strength of his personality, Himmler compelled cooperation with pettifogging harassment of the local groups.

With much enthusiasm but also with a campaign apparatus that was underfunded and far from the smooth-functioning organization Hitler envisioned, the NSDAP prepared for Reichstag elections on May 20, 1928. The Nazis wanted to enter the Reichstag, Goebbels forthrightly stated, in order "to arm ourselves with democracy's weapons. If democracy is foolish enough to give us free railway passes and salaries that is its problem. It does not concern us. Any way of bringing about the revolution is fine by us." This was the very public position the party had taken since 1925, and it had paid very poor dividends. The NSDAP had staggered through the regional state elections of 1926 and 1927, faring miserably all across the board. In none of the ten provincial elections of the period could the NSDAP muster even 4 percent of the vote. Despite the fierce intensity of their efforts, the Nazis had shown themselves remarkably inept in the arts of democratic electoral politics.

The NSDAP's poor performance at the polls was not simply a consequence of its organizational shortcomings; it also reflected the effects of a hopeful though fragile economic recovery. The Dawes Plan had ushered in a period of relative economic stability and political calm, wedged between the seismic disruptions of the hyperinflation and the Great Depression. The Golden Twenties, as the period from 1924 to 1929 came to be called, saw a resurgence of the pro-Weimar parties and a serious setback for both the conservative and radical right. For the first time in Germany's tumultuous postwar history, it seemed to have achieved a measure of domestic stability. The Weimar government also jettisoned its policy of noncompliance and obfuscation and moved to reintegrate Germany into the European state system. In 1926 Germany signed the Locarno Pact with England, France, Belgium, and Italy recognizing the western borders of the Reich as set by Versailles and pledging not to go to war with its western neighbors. Significantly, no such agreement was reached on Germany's eastern frontier. In 1928, Germany was a signatory to the Kellogg-Briand Pact, an international agreement in which signatory states promised not to resort to war to resolve "disputes or conflicts of whatever nature or of whatever origin they may be, which may arise among them." Germany was at last admitted to the League of Nations and reentered the community of nations. It was no longer a pariah state.

The Reichstag election of May 1928 seemed to confirm that newfound economic and political stability. The Nazis could muster only a dismal 2.6 percent of the vote. Many, using the poor performance of the anti-Republican parties as a yardstick, have interpreted the 1928 elections as a triumph of Weimar democracy, and used the abysmal Nazi vote as a baseline from which to measure its dramatic breakthrough in 1930 and its breathtaking ascent thereafter. After all, for the first time since 1923, a Social Democrat, Hermann Müller, assumed the chancellorship, leading a broadly based pro-democratic coalition (the Great Coalition) that stretched from the SPD to the liberal but right-of-center German People's Party.

Yet the elections of 1928 reveal not that German democracy was on solid ground but rather offer subtle manifestations of a momentous transformation within the Weimar party system and within the middle-class electorate in particular. This trend was not reflected in the growth of radicalism but in the steady growth of special-interest, single-issue, and regional parties. Greatly facilitated by Weimar's radical system of proportional representation, sixty thousand votes nationwide earned a party a seat in the Reichstag, parties such as the Bavarian Peasants Party, the Hanoverian Party, the Homeowners Party, the Christian Service and Peoples Party, the Christian-National Peasants and Rural People's Party, the People's Justice Party, the Revalorization and Reconstruction Party, not to be confused with the Revalorization and *Con*struction Party, both representing people who were irate at the government's harsh stabilization of the economy after the hyperinflation. Altogether some thirty such parties crowded onto the ballot in every state.

These small splinter parties drew their support almost exclusively from middle-class voters and although they claimed to be "above politics," their programs contained an implicit ideological message. They attacked big business, big labor, and big government. They dismissed Weimar's parliamentary system as the tool of powerful special interests and assailed the liberal and conservative parties that had sold out the small businessman, the small farmer, the small homeowner, civil servants, and pensioners. Instead, they advocated various forms of corporatist government, where representation would be based on occupational or interest blocs, each given equal weight. In this way, the "disenfranchised" of the Weimar system could compete on equal terms with the powerful entrenched interests. Although most of these parties were not radical, they represented a mounting anti-system protest that went far beyond simple interest politics. Under more desperate circumstances, circumstances that would soon come with the onset of the Great Depression, their message of protest could—and would—be nestled quite snugly within the ideological framework of National Socialism.

Individually these small splinter parties were utterly insignificant, but together they attracted a sizable chunk of the middle-class electorate, revealing in the process that traditional political allegiances had been badly shaken and that a major migration of middle-class voters was under way. In 1919 and 1920 these Lilliputian parties had garnered only 3 percent of the national vote; by 1924 they won 10 percent, and even when the economy rebounded during the Golden Twenties, their vote inched upward in regional elections, while the liberals and conservatives stumbled. In May 1928, they captured 13.7 percent of the national vote, matching the

Conservatives and surpassing the two liberal parties combined. More than a year before the Great Depression crashed over Germany, roughly one third of the middle-class electorate had deserted their traditional parties and were clearly searching for political alternatives.

In 1928, the high-water mark of Weimar stability, Germans, especially middle-class Germans, were not ready to embrace the radical politics of Hitler and the NSDAP, but they were increasingly disenchanted with the political mainstream. The Nazis were not yet able to capitalize on this growing disaffection, and for them the outcome of the Reichstag election of 1928 was a disappointing surprise. After all the reorganization, all the propaganda innovations, all the ideological fervor, the party had actually lost ground since 1924. With 2.6 percent of the vote, the NSDAP was again relegated to the fringes of German politics, and Hitler, the Führer, the self-proclaimed savior of Germany, seemed condemned to remain a marginal, quixotic figure in German political life. That was the verdict of an undercover official from the Reich Ministry of the Interior whose confidential report on the NSDAP declared: "This is a party that is not going anywhere. It is a numerically insignificant . . . radical revolutionary splinter group incapable of exerting any noticeable influence on the great mass of the population and the course of political events." On the eve of the Great Depression, few would have disputed his judgment.

INTO THE MAINSTREAM

The Nazis desperately needed an issue, something that would thrust them into the mainstream of German political consciousness. The Wall Street crash and the onset of the Great Depression in the fall of 1929 did just that. As the stock market in New York collapsed, the Americans withdrew their short-term loans, and the German economy, so dependent on those loans, careened downward like the tail of a falling kite. Between June 1928 and May 1930, industrial production in Germany dropped by 31 percent; unemployment, especially among blue-collar workers, catapulted by 200 percent, and the government deficit mushroomed as claims for unemployment compensation skyrocketed. Bankruptcies soared, as small businesses failed in record numbers. It was only the beginning. By the summer of 1932, over one third of the German labor force was out of work, and over two million more had simply vanished from the unemployment rolls, having exhausted their meager benefits. Armies of shabby, jobless men drifted through the streets; bread lines and soup kitchens appeared in every community and squalid shantytowns sprouted like weeds on the fringes of the cities. A rising wave of foreclosures swept across the rural countryside, leaving hundreds of family farms up for auction. For three dismal years the economic news remained grim: there was no light at the end of the tunnel, no recovery predicted for the next quarter, or the next, or the next. The economy plunged in a free fall, and an atmosphere of mounting fear, tinged with anger, settled over the country. It was just the situation the Nazis needed.

In the aftermath of the party's poor showing in the 1928 elections, the Nazi leadership began a reevaluation of the NSDAP's considerably muddled public image. Especially dispiriting for Nazi strategists was the party's consistently poor performance in the large cities. Despite years of intense agitation, the Nazis had made only marginal inroads into the urban working class. In 1928, however, the NSDAP had done surprisingly well in a number of rural areas, notably the farm communities of Schleswig-Holstein, Lower Saxony, Thuringia, and Upper Bavaria. Almost immediately, party leaders renewed their calls for a greater cultivation of the rural and small-town electorate as well as a sharper focus on the middle class. While the Social Democrats and Communists blocked the Nazi advance into the mainstream of working-class politics, the declining popularity of the traditional liberal and conservative parties seemed to offer a promising opportunity for a revitalized NSDAP. Evaluating the outcome of the election, the *Völkischer Beobachter* of May 31, 1928, signaled the party's new direction. "The results in the countryside have shown that greater successes can be achieved with less expenditure of energy, money, and time than in the large cities. National Socialist rallies with good speakers are real events in small towns and villages and are talked about for weeks. In the large cities, on the other hand, even rallies with three or four thousand people disappear and are forgotten."

As a result of these considerations, the Nazis undertook a significant shift in the focus of their propaganda. Without reducing its efforts to win a blue-collar following, the NSDAP intensified and broadened its campaign to cultivate support within the middle class. Although the party's program remained essentially unchanged, the social revolutionary strategy advocated by Strasser and his followers assumed an increasingly subordinate role in Nazi policy. Even Strasser's thinking underwent a gradual transformation after the 1928 debacle; he was not prepared to give up on the working class but recognized the need for a shift in emphasis. Hitler himself had presaged the party's reorientation by publicly reaffirming the NSDAP's strong support for private property during the 1928 campaign, explaining that Nazi demands "to expropriate the owners without compensation of any land needed for the common purpose," Point Seventeen of the party's Twenty-five Points, applied only to "alien" or "antisocial"— that is, Jewish—businesses and farms. Building on this foundation, the party gradually intensified its vilification of the department stores and consumer cooperatives so resented by small business and launched a major campaign to enhance its appeal to the rural, landowning population.

In addition to these propaganda offensives, the party also accelerated its efforts to infiltrate existing middle-class organizations and clubs as well as to sponsor occupational associations of its own. Between 1928 and 1930, the NSDAP founded its own organizations for doctors, lawyers, and students, while creating a National Socialist farm association as well. The NSDAP had not abandoned its determination to become a party of mass integration, bridging the great social divides of German politics, but it had become increasingly clear that a solid base of support within the fractious *Mittelstand* (middle class) offered the most promising foundation on which to build.

At the same time, the party introduced changes in its approach to political agitation. Recognizing its very limited resources and its determination to attract maximum public attention, the party adopted a variation of the plan first suggested by Goebbels two years earlier. In a memorandum of December 1928, Heinrich Himmler, chief of the Propaganda Section, announced his intention of conducting concentrated propaganda offensives "from time to time in every region of Germany" that would "surpass . . . our previous agitational activities." These "propaganda actions" were to be carefully prepared and coordinated in one area after another. Seventy to two hundred rallies would be held in the selected districts (*Gaue*) within a period of seven to ten days. Motorized SA parades would be launched, well-known party figures would make appearances, and thousands of leaflets would be distributed in more than a hundred villages, towns, and cities in the area. An official list of the party's most popular speakers would be made available to the local groups along with instructions on how to place requests for their favorites with the *Gau* and national headquarters. The objective of such saturation campaigns would be to concentrate the party's energies and meager financial resources on specially selected locales, where the national party would rouse local Nazi activists, spark the growth of the party press, and stimulate recruitment for the SA and other party organizations. Most important, these propaganda actions would be mounted not only during election campaigns but were intended to provide the NSDAP with a high public profile in the fallow periods between elections.

These organizational and strategic reforms coincided with the first tremors of the oncoming world economic crisis, but the party was still groping for some issue that would provide the NSDAP with the national visibility it lacked. The revival of the highly volatile reparations issue in 1929 offered the party precisely the opportunity it needed. A new plan sought to establish exactly what Germany owed and to arrange a final schedule of payments. Drafted by an international committee of economic experts under the chairmanship of American businessman Owen Young, a final report was released on June 9, 1929, known as the Young Plan, and called for Germany to make payments over a period of fifty-nine years with annuities mounting gradually to a maximum of approximately 2.4 billion marks. Although that figure was considerably lower than the original Allied claim of 132 billion marks, the plan provoked a storm of protest in Germany. When the Great Coalition government accepted the report as the basis for negotiations, Alfred Hugenberg, the chairman of the conservative DNVP, opened talks with several right-wing organizations, including the Pan-German League, the Stahlhelm, and the NSDAP, to form a "front of national opposition" against the proposed settlement.

Hugenberg was a wealthy industrialist and press magnate and the leader of the DNVP's far right wing. He had assumed the leadership of the DNVP in the aftermath of the party's terrible showing in the 1928 election when its vote plunged from 20 percent in 1924 to 14 percent. He was determined to push the conservative right in a more radical, anti-Republican direction. With his extensive network of newspapers behind him, Hugenberg hoped to lead a "national opposition" in a referendum against the plan, and a draft bill, the so-called Freedom Law, condemning the Young Plan, was composed for submission to the Reichstag and ultimately to the general public.

Although some Nazi militants opposed even limited cooperation with the conservatives, Hitler was convinced that a temporary alliance would serve the party's interests. Utilizing its new organizational structure and drawing considerable financial support from conservative sources, the Nazis played by far the most prominent role in the campaign waged against the plan and its supporters. While Hugenberg provided the funding and the extensive press coverage, it was the brown-shirted Nazis the public saw on the streets collecting signatures, distributing anti-Young leaflets, and leading demonstrations against the plan.

The Young Plan, the Nazis wailed, was a "pact with the devil" forced on Germany by the rapacious victor states. It would produce an "insane indebtedness" that would destroy "all economic credit," eliminate "job opportunities for millions," and lead to "the ruin of Germany's economy, its agriculture, its middle class, and its small businesses." It would be, after the Dawes Plan, "a third Versailles," which would enslave Germans for decades to come. Generations of Germans yet unborn would be paying tribute to the vengeful Allies until 1988! The Nazi propaganda offensive dominated Germany's national press for months, and Hitler, rather than Hugenberg, occupied center stage throughout. But the Freedom Law was decisively defeated in the Reichstag in late November and a national referendum on the Young Plan held on December 22, 1929, received less than one third of the required votes. Yet, despite its failure to sabotage the new plan, the anti-Young campaign had served its purpose for Hitler. Association with Hugenberg's DNVP lent the Nazis a touch of respectability in conservative circles that they had previously lacked and constituted a major step in revising public perceptions of the party. Following the conclusion of the campaign, police reports on Nazi activities noted that "more and more frequently members of the *Mittelstand* and the so-called better classes are seen [at Nazi events]." The coarse, unruly Nazis were becoming socially acceptable. Even more important, the NSDAP had clearly emerged as the most prominent and aggressive voice of the anti-Republican right at a time when the beleaguered government parties were vainly attempting to cope with the onset of the Great Depression.

Timing was key. Just as the anti-Young campaign drew to a close in late 1929, the world economic crisis hit Germany with the force of a howling gale. Industrial production began a precipitous slide, and as production fell, unemployment rose. By January 1930, over three million Germans were unemployed, and with tax revenue shrinking and the government deficit soaring, the Great Coalition government found it increasingly difficult to fund the now desperately needed unemployment insurance program. While the national liberal DVP, supported by the major employers' associations, insisted on a reduction of benefits, the Social Democrats, backed by powerful labor unions, countered by demanding greater government contributions to the fund. Neither party was willing to abandon its "principles," and compromise proved impossible. Finally, after securing the Reichstag's approval of the Young Plan, the Great Coalition government dissolved in March 1930. It would be the last majority government of the Weimar era.

With the collapse of the Great Coalition, government based on a sound parliamentary basis proved unattainable. After surveying the bleak political landscape and finding no viable majority combination, Reich President Hindenburg turned to Heinrich Brüning, leader of the Catholic Zentrum's Reichstag delegation, to form a government "above parties." His name was suggested to Hindenburg by General Kurt von Schleicher, a "desk general" who had served on Hindenburg's staff during the world war. In that post he had acted as a monitor of the political scene, and, although only a captain, became a trusted advisor to the General Staff in political matters. After the war, as he rose rapidly in rank, he continued to act as a link between the army and the government. He preferred to work behind the scenes, and he made connections with a wide variety of political and government figures. Intrigue was his milieu. A political sphinx, he was a schemer—his very name in German means "creeper." Many felt that it was apt.

In 1928 he became chief of the Minister's Office, a new post created especially for him, with vague responsibility for representing the military in its relations with the government. He acted, in effect, as an unofficial cabinet member, and his influence, always shadowy, soared. He was a longtime friend of Hindenburg's son Oskar, with whom he had served during the war, and he remained a close confidant of the Reich President. He was convinced, as were many within the army, that the Republic was beyond repair and some form of authoritarian regime was needed to save Germany from chaos. In the climactic years of the Republic, when power became concentrated in a few individuals close to the Reich President, Schleicher would play a critical—and destructive—role.

Brüning recommended himself to Schleicher in part because of his financial expertise but also because of his standing on the right wing of the Catholic Zentrum. Brüning had served with distinction as an officer in the army during the war, he was the holder of the Iron Cross first class, and his political preferences inclined decidedly toward an authoritarian—though not radical—solution to Germany's problems. He had little confidence in the Reichstag and the vicissitudes of parliamentary politics, especially under current circumstances. He also hoped to dismantle Weimar's extensive welfare state, which he held responsible for much of Germany's economic distress. In the process, he would reduce the power of organized labor and of the Social Democrats. Although Brüning was able to convince members of the liberal parties, the Zentrum, and, temporarily, the conservative DNVP to hold posts in the new cabinet, their parties were not bound by the cabinet's decisions. The government clearly rested solely on the confidence of the aging Reich President, and Hindenburg was determined to steer the unwieldy parliamentary system in a more authoritarian direction.

Following the economic orthodoxy of the day, Brüning viewed a balanced budget and thus a sharp reduction of government spending as the critical first step toward a reversal of the Republic's disastrous economic fortunes. Between March and July he submitted a series of stringent fiscal reforms to the Reichstag, only to have each rejected for quite different reasons by a majority composed of Social Democrats, Communists, Conservatives, and Nazis. In late July, with a national deficit of more than one billion marks, Brüning presented a final budgetary plan, which, in effect, would have increased the government contribution to the unemployment fund but would also have ultimately reduced benefits. When the proposed legislation met with stiff resistance in the Reichstag, he moved to implement the plan by emergency decree. Shortly thereafter a motion calling for the abrogation of the decrees received majority support in the Reichstag, but Brüning refused to back down. Instead of resigning, he asked Hindenburg to dissolve the recalcitrant Reichstag and call for new elections in September.

Brüning's decision proved a disastrous blunder. Using its expanded organizational network and its strategy of political saturation, the NSDAP had scored disquieting gains in a series of regional elections in late 1929 and early 1930. The upward curve of Nazi electoral fortunes began in October in Baden with a modest 7 percent of the vote, but less than a month before Brüning's announcement of new national elections, the Nazis stunned observers by winning 15 percent of the vote in Saxony, a traditional stronghold of the left. Two years earlier the NSDAP had attracted less than 3 percent of the vote.

The big losers in these regional elections were not the parties of the Marxist left, nor were they the small splinter parties. Instead, they were the traditional parties of the liberal center and the conservative right. Voter dissatisfaction with these traditional alternatives of middle-class politics, which had begun to crystallize before the onset of the Great Depression, continued in 1929–30, accelerated by their inability to deal effectively with the nation's deteriorating economic condition. After months of internal dissension and public recriminations between the liberal parties and the relentless bickering within the fragmented conservative camp, the parties of the traditional center and right were ill-prepared for the approaching battle.

The NSDAP, on the other hand, was primed for action. In the fall of 1930 the Nazis were better organized and better financed than at any time in their brief history. The party's prominent role in the anti-Young campaign had given the Nazis a high national profile and a growing sense of self-confidence. Party membership was virtually three times as large as in 1923, and it was no longer confined largely to the south. New local chapters were springing up all over the country, and new recruits were flooding into the NSDAP.

Hitler, who was as uninterested in organizational matters as he was in mediating ideological disputes within the party, turned the job of managing the party's burgeoning organization over to Gregor Strasser. Between 1928 and 1930, Strasser initiated a set of organizational reforms intended to tighten the leadership's grip on the party and to enhance Nazi campaign performance. He crafted a vertical organizational structure, established a clear chain of command, delineated responsibilities, and created a team of inspectors, responsible to him, to ensure that Munich's directives were being properly carried out. He redrew the NSDAP's regional boundaries to conform to the Reichstag thirty-five electoral districts, and the authority of the *Gauleiter* was substantially strengthened in each area. The *Gauleiter* and his propaganda staff were now charged with executing the party's campaign directives.

Working with this structure, Munich now assumed responsibility for the direction of all Nazi propaganda activities throughout the country. Since 1928 Hitler had been acting head of the Propaganda Section, with Himmler serving as his deputy. In the spring of 1930 Hitler appointed Joseph Goebbels to lead the party's propaganda efforts. It was an inspired choice. Goebbels had distinguished himself as the energetic and combative *Gauleiter* of Berlin, where he was in perpetual conflict with the powerful leftist parties. He was creative and unflagging in his efforts to provoke and humiliate the Reds, to wean Berlin's workers away from the Marxists and win them for National Socialism. His newspaper, *Der Angriff* (*The Attack*), established in 1927, aggressively courted workers, printing savage attacks on "the bosses of capitalism" that were in tone and content virtually indistinguishable from that of the Communists. From his position on the front lines of Berlin, he spearheaded the party's efforts to win working-class support. Just as important as his ideological commitment, he was devoted to Hitler. "In Goebbels," the journalist Konrad Heiden remarked, "Hitler found a man who would listen for days to his endless speeches; the arduously cultivated enthusiasm in his eyes never abated." Goebbels, Hitler was said to have remarked, was "a man who burns like a flame."

For some time Goebbels had been locked in a bitter conflict with the Strasser brothers, Gregor and his younger sibling Otto. It was less a doctrinal battle than a turf war. In spite of the Twenty-five Points, there was no official party line to be toed in the NSDAP, only unquestioned obedience to the Führer, and many variants of National Socialism flourished, with different ideological emphases and target constituencies. Otto Strasser's brand was a compound of strident anticapitalism, rabid nationalism, anti-Semitism, and a revolutionary rejection of all things bourgeois. He was deeply concerned that Hitler and "the Munich clique" around him were not committed to the radical social revolutionary vision he espoused, that they were too timid, too willing to court the conservative right. The Strassers used their Berlin publishing house, the Kampfverlag, and daily and weekly newspapers as a platform for their views, hurting in the process the sales of Goebbels's *Der Angriff*. By early spring 1930, the rivalry had reached the boiling point.

Otto and Gregor Strasser were committed National Socialists, but they were not blind adherents of the Hitler cult that had emerged after 1925. Each maintained a degree of quasi-independence and believed that the party, the "idea" of National Socialism, was larger and more important than any individual, including Hitler. Goebbels complained to Hitler that Otto Strasser was undermining his authority in Berlin, not adhering to party directives, and ignoring orders from Munich. Hitler promised to take action against Strasser but characteristically let the matter slide. "Munich, the Chief, has lost all credit with me," Goebbels grumbled to his diary in mid-March 1930. "Hitler has—for whatever reason—broken his word to me five times. . . . Hitler withdraws into himself; he makes no decisions; he doesn't lead any more but lets things happen." Finally, in mid-April, after Otto Strasser had ignored a direct Hitler order by publishing an article critical of Hitler's decision to break with the anti-Young coalition, Hitler again promised to purge the Strasser faction. Again he hesitated. "That's the old Hitler," Goebbels complained bitterly. "The procrastinator! Forever putting things off!" It was a common complaint. Only in midsummer was the conflict resolved—not by Hitler but by Otto Strasser, who read the handwriting on the wall and announced his decision to withdraw from the NSDAP. Gregor Strasser, a far more important figure in the party, did not follow him; he renounced his brother's ideas, resigned as managing editor of the Kampfverlag, and pledged his unequivocal loyalty to Hitler. Goebbels was disappointed that Hitler had not purged the elder Strasser from the party, but the crisis was over for the present. The situation, as it so often did, had resolved itself.

Goebbels was now not only the *Gauleiter* of Berlin but head of Nazi propaganda throughout the country, and he quickly showed his talents. Under his leadership, the increasingly sophisticated National Socialist campaign machine pioneered a breathtaking array of modern political techniques—an innovative form of survey research, direct mailings, highly coordinated press and leaflet campaigns, films, slide shows, phonograph records, torchlight parades, motorcades through the countryside, and entertainment events to draw crowds and raise money. The party established a speaker's school and a nine-month correspondence course for local Nazi operatives, with lessons in National Socialist ideology and propaganda techniques. Each regional party organization was required to enroll two speakers each term. "The major burden of the party's campaign must be carried by the speakers," Goebbels emphasized in a 1930 circular, because the party did not yet possess "the means necessary to saturate the entire country with propaganda material." In addition to weekly communiqués and instructions, Goebbels's staff produced monthly notes for speakers that offered analyses of international and domestic issues and provided suggestions for more effective local mobilization—everything from musical selections for entertainment events to the color of posters and handbills to how best to position busts of Hitler during recruitment meetings.

Shortly after the dissolution of the Reichstag on July 18, Goebbels and the reorganized Propaganda Section moved into action. At a meeting with members of the national leadership, the district chiefs, and the NSDAP's tiny Reichstag delegation in late July, Hitler laid out in broad strokes the basic outline of the party's campaign. As always, he confined himself to the big picture. Goebbels's task was to translate Hitler's general objectives into action on the ground. He and his young staff would manage the actual conduct of the campaign, plotting day-to-day strategy and coordinating the party's propaganda activities. It was an arrangement that remained unchanged throughout the last Nazi campaigns of the Weimar era—indeed, would be a hallmark of Hitler's leadership style throughout the Third Reich.

In the torrent of memoranda that followed that July meeting, Goebbels stressed to the regional party chieftains the importance of conducting the party's campaign "in the most uniform possible manner." At the outset of the campaign, the Propaganda Section issued a lengthy circular to the district leaders outlining the NSDAP's strategic goals, explaining the major themes to be developed, and defining the slogans to be used. The party's "entire campaign propaganda" was to revolve around the theme "For or Against Young," launching a ruthless offensive "against the war guilt lie, against the Young Treaty, against the beneficiaries of the policy of fulfillment, against the jailer parties of enslaving capitalism."

To ensure conformity with its objectives, Goebbels expressly forbade the local chapters to "make electoral propaganda on their own." They were "to operate only according to the guidelines determined by the Propaganda Section and with campaign materials provided to them." This centralized control was necessary to achieve the party's strategic goals and to keep the entire party apparatus on message. "Everywhere in Germany the same placards will be posted, the same leaflets distributed, and the same stickers will appear." The typewritten texts of all leaflets and other campaign literature would be wired from Munich to the district leaders, who were responsible for their printing and distribution. In this way, the flow of material to the locals could be closely monitored and coordinated. The circular also dealt extensively with propaganda techniques and acquainted the party's functionaries with the services and propaganda aids that were available from either the regional or national headquarters. Locals were reminded that newspaper off-prints, leaflets, flyers, stickers, brochures, and special illustrated posters were available. It recommended that direct mailings be undertaken by the local chapters, using a personally addressed form letter to every inhabitant of a given area. Using local Address Books that listed the occupation of the head of the household, the party was able to subdivide the population by occupation and deliver letters that spoke directly to issues relating to farmers, shopkeepers, civil servants, white-collar personnel, workers, and retirees. The party also printed special election postcards and swastika-bedecked stamps for correspondence or display on windows, books, briefcases, etc. In a political culture dominated by print media, the distribution of leaflets, as usual, received special attention. Goebbels instructed the local leaders that "flyers, leaflets, etc. should be passed out early on . . . Sunday," the day when the parties were most active, "so that the worker, the civil servant, and the petit bourgeois has them in hand before the expected flood of trash sets in." Parades led by trucks with large placards and filled with storm troopers were also recommended as "a propaganda device that should not be underestimated."

The content of these Nazi appeals was based on a crude system of marketing research that was, for its time, unparalleled in sophistication. District leaders were urged to send their functionaries into "the bakeries, butcher shops, grocery stores, and taverns," to sample public opinion and find out for whom the people had voted and why. Local Nazi propaganda operatives filed weekly reports detailing which techniques worked and which didn't, what sort of pitch appealed to farmers, to shopkeepers, to workers. What were civil servants, office clerks, homeowners, and tenants angry about? What worried Catholics, Protestants, and women? How had "the system" failed each, and how could the NSDAP articulate a set of appeals that would exploit their sense of grievance? This information could then be used by the national leadership in developing the party's campaign strategy. Appeals and techniques that had originated and worked well in one locale were reported to the Propaganda Division and then incorporated into its monthly reports to all regional offices. In this way, a circular flow of valuable intelligence was generated that would serve the party well in the following campaigns.

Offering specific solutions to the country's problems was not important, and ideological appeals based on the party's famous Twenty-five Points were shuffled into the background. Gregor Strasser was surprisingly candid in his explanation of the Nazi message. "Everything which is detrimental to the existing order of things has our support . . . because we want catastrophe. . . . everything which hastens the beginning of catastrophe in the present system . . . every strike, every governmental crisis, every erosion of state power, every weakening of the System . . . is good, very good for us . . . and it will always and constantly be our endeavor to strengthen such difficulties . . . in order to expedite the death of this system." Nor did the Nazis feel themselves constrained by a need for ideological consistency. When a confused supporter asked Goebbels if the NSDAP was still committed to "breaking interest slavery," one of the party's demands in the original, "immutable" platform of 1920, the propaganda chief responded, "I wish to God we had never heard of these miserable Twenty-Five Points." For all their bluster about "the idea" of National Socialism, the Nazis campaigned not on a program or an ideology, but on a mood, and as anger and fear in Germany mounted, they touched a raw public nerve.

Throughout the campaign, the Propaganda Division issued updates, refining instructions, coordinating speaking dates, and announcing rallies or appearances by Hitler. The Nazi campaign was largely negative and bereft of anything in the way of specifics, directing instead a relentless assault on the corrupt, ineffectual Weimar "system" and "the heap of special interests" that controlled it.

More important than any particular theme was image. Hitler and Goebbels were intent on creating the impression of a vigorous, dynamic, youthful movement standing in sharp contrast to the dispirited, enervated parties of the bourgeois center and right. Energy, activism, and a fanatical determination to sweep away the old, Goebbels believed, were the keys to Nazi success. "By September 14," he declared, "there must be no city, no village, no spot-in-the-road where we National Socialists have not appeared in a great rally." On August 18 the *Völkischer Beobachter* announced that a total of 34,000 rallies were planned for the final four weeks of the election campaign, and while that figure was probably exaggerated, the high-octane activism of the NSDAP could not be matched by the fading bourgeois parties. Relentlessly spurring his propaganda operatives into ever more frenzied activity, Goebbels concluded, "We want to conduct a campaign such as the corrupt parliamentary parties (*Bonzenparteien*) have never seen before."

The plan was for the campaign to gather momentum throughout August, before reaching a crescendo in the last weeks before the election. But with election day only two weeks away and all progressing according to plan, a crisis broke suddenly over the party. Tension between the Berlin SA and the party had been simmering for some time. SA leaders felt underappreciated, underfinanced, and, most galling, under the thumb of the party's political organization. Walter Stennes, the leader of the powerful Berlin SA, wanted Storm Troopers to be put on the party's electoral ballot and additional funding for the organization; most unsettling, Stennes expressed the SA's growing impatience with Hitler's insistence on legality. The SA wanted action that would bring about social revolution and feared that Hitler and the "party bosses" in Munich, with their relentless calls for restraint, for maintaining the policy of legality, were less committed to that revolutionary vision. "Some things must be changed after the election," Goebbels complained. The SA "under Pfeffer and Stennes was too independent and positively hostile to politics." Above all he didn't trust Stennes.

On August 30, Goebbels had just delivered a speech in Breslau, his sixth in four days, and was resting in his hotel, when he received an alarming message from Berlin. There were rumors that elements of the SA were planning a rebellion. "They are going to give us an ultimatum and if their terms are not met, they will go on the attack," he wrote. "In the middle of a battle! I can't believe it." Later in the night those preliminary reports were confirmed. Things were worse than Goebbels had expected. SA men had stormed into party headquarters in the Hedemannstrasse, brushed aside the SS guards, smashed up the furniture and files. They were occupying the building; they were making demands; they were "in open rebellion against the *Gau* and against Munich. . . . Stennes is a traitor."

Both Goebbels and Hitler, who was attending the annual Wagner festival in Bayreuth, rushed to Berlin. In the early-morning hours, the two met with Stennes at the Duke of Coburg Hotel beside the Anhalt Station. Stennes complained of broken promises—Goebbels had agreed to place SA men on the party's electoral list and to consult with him about suitable candidates, but had not; he complained about the burden placed on the SA and its poor financial situation; he expressed the widespread SA frustration at the course of legality pursued by the party.

Hitler's initial reaction was to reject Stennes's demands out of hand, but during a night of consultation with Goebbels, he softened his stance. That night, while Hitler and Goebbels were conferring at the Goebbels private residence, Stennes and a group of SA leaders appeared, followed by a host of angry Storm Troopers. As Stennes presented his demands, the mob "stood outside chanting, growing more and more rebellious. . . . Stennes has organized his mutiny brilliantly." Hitler listened and finally agreed to allow the SA to keep more of the dues it collected—the remainder was sent to the Munich HQ—and explained his position to Stennes. Later at a gathering of some two thousand SA men, Hitler swore his fervent allegiance to them and assured them that the revolution they—and he—so desperately wanted would come, but it would come *not before but after* the seizure of power. The takeover of the government must come by legal means, by mobilizing the masses, by participation in elections. The SA's role in this strategy was crucial, their loyalty imperative, their fighting spirit essential.

To thunderous cheers, he announced that he was now personally assuming the leadership of both the SA and SS. Undercover police agents monitoring the meeting were struck by Hitler's nervousness as he repeatedly appealed to the SA to trust him. With "his overstrained voice rising to an almost hysterical scream," Hitler pleaded for their loyalty. "We will vow in this hour that nothing can divide us, as truly as God can help us against all devils! May almighty God bless our struggle!" The assembled SA men broke into shouts of "Heil!" Hitler had succeeded in defusing the situation. The immediate crisis passed, but the tension between the party leadership and the SA did not; it merely slipped beneath the surface, ready to erupt again at any moment.

September 14, election day, Hitler proclaimed, was "the beginning of Germany's reckoning" with the "criminals of the November Republic," the "judgment day for the Young parties." Everyone sensed a palpable change in the air when the polls opened on Sunday morning. Voters were pouring into the polling stations all over the country. Turnout, which had dipped in 1928, was exceptionally high. The Nazis were confident of making significant gains, but in spite of their tireless campaigning and vigorous predictions of victory, few within the leadership were prepared for the magnitude of the party's surge. As the returns were tabulated on the evening of September 14–15, the outcome sent shock waves across the political world and plunged the already embattled Weimar Republic into crisis. The Nazi vote had lurched from a mere 800,000 in 1928 to an astonishing 6,000,000. With 18 percent of the electorate, Hitler's obscure NSDAP had overnight become the second-largest party in Germany after the Social Democrats.

The outcome came as a surprise even to the Nazis. "Fantastic," Goebbels exulted in his diary, "an unbelievable advance." At an election night rally at the Sportpalast, the largest arena in Berlin, he witnessed an explosion of enthusiasm and excitement "like 1914. . . . The Sportpalast a madhouse." Ecstatic Storm Troopers carried him through the hall on their shoulders. He dropped in on one SA pub after another until four in the morning. Everywhere he was "greeted with the same scene—joy and fighting spirit." It was, Hitler prophesied, the dawning of a new era in German politics, an era of radical political change that would sweep away the ineffectual sham democracy of the November criminals, return power to the people, and make Germany great again. Germany, he proclaimed, had awakened.

Brüning had anticipated a spike in the Nazi vote and even hoped to use the rising threat of right-wing radicalism to convince the other parties to cooperate with his government, but neither he nor anyone else in Germany was prepared for the seismic shift in the political landscape produced by the Nazi breakthrough. Only twelve Nazis had held seats in the old Reichstag; when the new Reichstag convened in October, 107 brown-clad National Socialist deputies filed into the chamber; only the Social Democratic delegation was larger. Hitler and his party were no longer specters haunting the lunatic fringes of German public consciousness. To the surprise of all, they had swept into the mainstream of German politics.

As Goebbels and his staff analyzed the election results, it was immediately clear that the Nazi breakthrough, though impressive virtually everywhere, was especially striking in the Protestant north. Even a cursory perusal of the election returns revealed that the Nazis, as anticipated, had done exceptionally well in rural areas and small towns hard hit by the lengthy agricultural depression. In some provincial counties, the party captured an unheard of 50 to 60 percent of the vote. In the large northern states of

Prussia, Pomerania, Mecklenburg, and Hanover, the party's vote surged past 20 percent. In Schleswig-Holstein, where two years before the Nazis had claimed a mere 4 percent of the vote, their total vaulted to 27 percent.

Just as they had before, Nazi appeals found their greatest resonance among elements of the anxious middle class—small shopkeepers, farmers, artisans (plumbers, electricians, carpenters), lower-level civil servants, teachers, and some white-collar workers. It was a constellation of social forces that would constitute the party's base throughout its rise to power. For small businesses, the onrushing economic crisis had been little short of catastrophic. Caught between the large department stores owned, as the Nazis always pointed out, by Jews, and the socialist consumer cooperatives, the small shopkeepers and artisans were growing desperate. In 1930 bankruptcies were twice as high as they were two years before, with small businesses representing over half the total. Bankruptcies in the retail trade had risen by approximately 150 percent since 1928. Businesses that had somehow managed to survive the hyperinflation and harsh stabilization of the 1920s now found themselves confronting financial ruin, and Brüning's austerity program offered little hope of immediate salvation. Germany was mired in a "battle between the rich and the impoverished," the Nazis brayed, and under the present system, "this battle will proletarianize more and more members of the middle class," bringing "ever greater numbers of reinforcements to the army of the unemployed." Only the NSDAP could keep the "uprooted and expropriated" from "falling into the clutches of international capital" and the big conglomerates; only the NSDAP would provide "protection of small business" against "the pestilence of Jewish department stores."

The situation for farmers was even bleaker. Already suffering from a deep agricultural recession in 1928, the Depression threatened to hurl farmers—especially small farmers—into the abyss. Between 1928 and 1930 foreclosures and forced sales of agricultural property almost doubled. Banks conducted auctions of family farms all across rural Germany, unleashing a tsunami of outrage in farm communities. While the government introduced programs to rescue the large agrarian estates of the east, it seemed remarkably indifferent to the suffering of the small farmer. Already in 1928 a protest movement, the *Landvolk* (Rural People's Movement), had organized demonstrations against the banks, the government, the big agricultural lobbies, and even the DNVP, the traditional party of choice for farmers. The *Landvolk* called for a tax revolt among farmers; bankers were ambushed, auctioneers shot; suicides skyrocketed. The Conservatives tried to co-opt the movement but discovered that it could neither manage nor contain the spreading protest in the countryside. "Day by day the farmer sinks deeper into debt and misery," the Nazis charged in 1928. "In the end he will be driven from his hearth and home while international money and Jewish capital take possession of his land." By 1930 that dire prophesy, the Nazis claimed, had been fulfilled.

Support for the party in 1930 was not, however, confined to the frightened petit bourgeoisie that contemporary commentators—and generations of historians—believed. Although still widely perceived as raucous and crude, its leaders vulgar and uneducated, the NSDAP was picking up support among elements of the established upper middle class—civil servants, professionals, especially doctors, and residents of affluent neighborhoods in the cities and towns. No one felt insulated from the crisis; no one, even the well-off upper middle class, was immune to the spreading virus of fear and uncertainty. The NSDAP was no longer simply a lower-middle-class phenomenon, a revolt of the frightened little men of German society. It was becoming far more broad based, less class bound, more dangerous.

In spite of the NSDAP's sharper focus on the *Mittelstand*, the Nazis were determined to make a major breakthrough among working-class Germans. In January 1930 the party founded its own labor union, the NSBO, or National Socialist Shop Floor Organization. Although it was hardly a challenge to the Social Democratic labor organizations, its timing was propitious. With real wages plummeting and unemployment climbing, here at last was the opening Hitler had looked for. But the vast majority of those standing in the unemployment lines were blue-collar workers, many of them union members, a group that had been consistently resistant to Nazi blandishments in the past. Unemployment among workers in the major industrial sectors was rampant. The highest rate of unemployment was recorded among unskilled and unorganized day laborers who flooded the job-referral and unemployment agencies in 1929–30. Even for those desperately clinging to a full-time job, reduced wages and the constant fear of layoffs haunted their daily lives. Everywhere one looked, the economic landscape yielded the same desolate view.

Instead of offering concrete plans to overcome the unemployment crisis and put people back to work, the Nazis chose to lambast the Social Democrats for their betrayal of the working class, their shameless "collaboration" with Brüning and his austerity program. The Social Democrats had produced nothing for the workers in the twelve years of Weimar democracy, the Nazis charged, "but hunger, misery, and slavery." If the German working class wanted to set itself free, it would have "to break the chains" of both capitalism and Marxism, and "only a National Socialist regime could offer the working people of Germany genuine liberation." Under Hitler, the German worker would no longer be a social pariah but would be "integrated into the nation with full rights and obligations" and guaranteed "social justice, work . . . a decent living, and bread." In the National Socialist people's community (*Volksgemeinschaft*), class distinctions would be a thing of the past. Neither the Communists nor the Social Democrats, whose very existence was based on struggle between the classes, could achieve this. "Only a new movement, which rejects the distinction between bourgeois and proletarian, could free German society from its destructive tradition of class conflict." The Social Democrats and Communists, of course, ridiculed Nazi "socialism" and its professed concern for the working class as a cynical fraud, claiming that the NSDAP was nothing more than "the last bulwark of big capital." Both parties warned working-class audiences that Fascism could be defeated only by proletarian unity and then proceeded to accuse each other of sabotaging that unity. Both blasted the "counterfeit socialism" of the Nazis, but saved their most vicious invective for each other.

In appealing to working-class audiences, Nazis could also give free rein to their anticapitalist rhetoric, often lacing it with rabid anti-Semitism. Nazi appeals to working-class audiences typically linked Social Democracy with the "system" and with "the Jewish wire pullers of international capitalism." Over and over again in the industrial cities of the Ruhr, Nazi speakers inveighed against "stock market swindlers, the powers of international capital, and the Jews who stood behind them." The Nazis were "fighting Marxism, international big capital and Jewry," as one speaker explained. Jewry possessed "power over the banks and industrial enterprises, and works hand in hand with the Social Democrats to bolster the existing corrupt system." Under the Weimar system, "lice-covered Jews were allowed to cross Germany's eastern border, insinuate themselves in German social, economic, and cultural life." They had "taken control of the banks and stock market, and carried off to Switzerland the money they have swindled from the German people." That money "must be taken from them and returned to the working people." Workers could not really expect the SPD to correct the system, when the Social Democratic leadership was shot through with Jews. "As soon as the NSDAP has the rudder of government in its hands," another speaker declared, "there will be no place for Jews in the German Fatherland."

Despite the NSDAP's most energetic efforts to gain a beachhead on the embattled shores of working-class politics, the parties of the bitterly divided left held their own, gathering 37 percent of the vote. The Nazis had made some headway, gaining support among unorganized workers who stood outside working-class subculture and the influence of the labor unions, but it was obvious to all that movement within working-class politics tended to remain largely confined to crossovers between the SPD and the KPD, with the more disaffected and radical sliding from the former to the latter. The Nazis were by no means daunted by their modest successes. Their vigorous efforts to win adherents within the working class were a source of growing alarm to both the Social Democrats and Communists, but at a time when the energies of the two leftist parties might have been directed more forcefully toward defeating the upstart Nazis, they were instead wasted in a bitter internecine struggle against one another.

Another problem for Nazi strategists was the continuing trouble the NSDAP experienced in predominantly Catholic areas, where the Zentrum maintained its dominance and where the Church, with its extensive network of social and cultural organizations, exerted enormous influence. In Catholic Germany, parish priests issued condemnations of Nazi heathenism on election day, declaring that a vote for either godless Communism or pagan National Socialism was inconsistent with the Christian faith. Shortly after the election, the Nazi press officer in Hessen inquired of Church officials in Mainz if, as a local priest had declared from the pulpit, it was the Church's official position that "1) Catholics were forbidden to be members of the Hitler party, 2) that as long as a Catholic remained a member of the NSDAP, he was not permitted to participate in funerals and other Church rites, and 3) could not receive the sacraments." The Church informed him that it was so. Similar declarations followed from the Catholic provinces across the country, confirming the Church's position that National Socialism was fundamentally incompatible with the teachings of Christianity and the Catholic Church.

The party's image problem with the Catholic Church was not helped by the appearance of Nazi "philosopher" Alfred Rosenberg's *The Myth of the Twentieth Century*, an impenetrable book that was both rabidly anti-Semitic *and* anti-Christian. Rosenberg, whose ideological fanaticism was undiluted by either reason or serious learning, attacked Christian ideals and institutions, calling for a return to the mystical religious practices of the ancient Germanic peoples, complete with the celebrations of the solstices, rune stones, and Norse gods. Although Hitler never officially endorsed such ideas and kept his distance from Rosenberg's positions on religious matters, the damage had been done. The party, Goebbels concluded, would have to make a concerted effort to allay the fears of Christians, especially the Catholic Church whose "internationalism" came under particularly vitriolic attack by Rosenberg. This would prove to be a tall order.

In the aftermath of the election, the formation of a viable parliamentary coalition was virtually impossible. The devastating losses suffered by the parties of the center and right dashed Brüning's hopes of reviving a *Bürgerblock* coalition, and the chancellor was not seriously interested in tempting the Nazis—or Social Democrats—into some form of participation in the government. Hugenberg also quickly informed the chancellor that the DNVP was not interested in serving in another Weimar cabinet. Brüning was not altogether displeased with this turn of events. After only desultory efforts to find a workable parliamentary majority, he was able to convince Reich President Hindenburg to allow him to continue the convenient presidential government based on emergency decrees. Afraid that a failure of the Brüning cabinet and new elections would only result in even more massive gains for both the radical right and left, the Social Democrats, still the largest party, were reluctantly willing to tolerate Brüning's emergency rule.

Already paralyzed by the political extremes and deserted by the parties of the center, Weimar democracy now began a precipitous descent into authoritarian rule. The new Nazi Reichstag deputies were not interested in discussing policy, introducing bills, or passing legislation that might actually address the problems of the country; they were there to poison the well. In the chamber they chanted Nazi slogans, shouted down government spokesmen, whistled, and baited the smaller Communist delegation. The Communists responded, singing "The Internationale" and hurling insults across the chamber at the Nazis. Working sessions in the chamber became impossible. When in February 1931 the Reichstag considered a measure that would make it more difficult for the extremists to disrupt the proceedings, the Nazi and Communist delegates marched out of the chamber in protest. They did not return until October, leaving the Reichstag paralyzed.

Between 1920 and 1930 the Reichstag met in session for an average of one hundred days a year. Between the 1930 elections and March of 1931 it convened only fifty times; between March 1931 and the July elections of 1932, only twenty-four. After that, the Reichstag held only three working sessions. While the Reichstag virtually disappeared from public awareness in 1931, Brüning issued forty-four emergency decrees; in the following year, three successive Reich governments enacted no fewer than fifty-seven such measures. Government by emergency decree had become the norm. Almost three years before Hitler assumed the reins of power, Brüning had embarked on a course that resulted in the end of parliamentary government in Germany.

While the Nazis and Communists confronted one another on the floor of the Reichstag, the SA and paramilitary formations of the left fought deadly battles in the streets. Every day, in almost every town and city across Germany, Nazis clashed with the Communist Red Front and the Social Democratic Reichsbanner. Although the violence was most intense and relentless in the cities, no town, no village was out of the line of fire. The political terrorism that had lacerated the country in the early years of the Republic had subsided during the so-called Golden Twenties, but in 1929–30 it erupted with unprecedented savagery, threatening to plunge the country into chaos and civil war. Formations of armed Storm Troopers marched defiantly into working-class neighborhoods, intent on showing the swastika, on provocation. They succeeded. Advancing in ranks of four abreast, they poured into the courtyards of massive apartment complexes, the tread of their jackboots echoing from the cobblestones. They sang Nazi songs; they chanted call-and-response choruses.

"*Wer hat euch verratten?*" (Who has betrayed you?), the SA troop leader would call out. "*Die Sozialdemokraten*" (the Social Democrats) came the lusty response from the ranks. "*Wer macht euch frei?*" (Who will set you free?), answered by "*Die Hitlerpartei*" (the Hitler party). Phone calls and messengers would go out to the pubs that served as neighborhood command posts for the KPD, and within minutes armed men of the Red Front rushed to the scene. Brass knuckles, blackjacks, knives, pistols, and clubs materialized; blood flowed. Adding to the spectacle, flowerpots, ashtrays, clumps of coal, shards of glass rained down from apartment windows, and the casualties rose—just as they were intended to do. The overmatched police would arrive, make arrests, dispatch the wounded to hospitals, and make reports to headquarters. In almost every instance, the authorities tended to see the Communists as the source of the trouble, and the conservative press eagerly picked up the story and the official interpretation.

As the violence escalated, a culture of political martyrdom emerged on both sides of the ideological divide—men felled in heroic battle with the partisan enemy were given elaborate funerals attended by party dignitaries, guarded by paramilitary troops, and given extensive coverage in the party press. The *Völkischer Beobachter, The Red Flag*, and *Forward* carried photographs and commentary, punctuated by rhetoric that combined eulogistic commemoration with menacing intimations of revenge. For the Nazis, the model for this ritual celebration of party martyrdom was created by Goebbels in the winter of 1930, when a twenty-one-year-old SA man, Horst Wessel, was shot dead in his Berlin apartment by a Communist gunman. Goebbels launched a barrage of invective against the KPD and its "hired thugs" who were murdering National Socialists all around the country. The Communists responded by denying that Wessel's murder had been politically motivated or ordered by the party. It was instead the result of a sordid private dispute. Wessel, they maintained, was a common pimp, living with his prostitute, and had refused to pay his rent to the widow of a fallen Communist. Wessel was well known in Nazi circles in the city and beyond both for his fearless assault on Communists in Friedrichshain, a working-class section of the capital, where he lived, and for a number of political songs he had written. One in particular, "Die Fahne Hoch!" (Raise the Banner), was a Goebbels favorite and already was being sung at party gatherings around the country.

Despite the murky circumstances surrounding the murder, Goebbels saw the propaganda potential in Wessel's death. Using his Berlin newspaper, *Der Angriff,* he transformed the young SA man into a National Socialist martyr, a fallen hero in the epic struggle between the NSDAP and the predatory forces of the left. Goebbels orchestrated an elaborate show of Nazi strength for Wessel's funeral. A lengthy funeral cortege followed by columns of Storm Troopers passed solemnly through the city, pelted and heckled along the way by Communist onlookers in the enormous crowds. At one point, a riot broke out as Communists tried to break through the police cordon and overturn the carriage carrying Wessel's body. At the gates of the cemetery the funeral procession faced yet another affront, a brazen, blood-red epitaph scrawled across the walls during the night by Communists: "A Final 'Heil Hitler' to the Pimp Horst Wessel." Some thirty thousand Berliners attended the funeral, and at the graveside Goebbels, speaking above the hoots and chants of the Communists beyond the gates, delivered a lengthy homily, an inspirational tribute to Wessel—the common SA man who was now ascending into the Valhalla of Nazi heroes.

Each year, the Nazis staged garland-draped memorial services on the anniversary of Wessel's death; major figures from the party attended; the party press eulogized the fallen hero; party photographers snapped shots of the mournful proceedings. It was a hallowed event in the crowded calendar of Nazi spectacles, and "Die Fahne Hoch," popularly referred to simply as the "Horst Wessel Song," acquired the status of party anthem, played at every National Socialist occasion into the last days of the Third Reich. Other show funerals followed, as the brutal clashes between the Nazis and the left grew more frequent in 1931–32—pageants of political martyrdom that were, from Goebbels's point of view, pitch-perfect propaganda for the party.

Frustrated by the rampant violence unleashed by the Nazis and Communists, Brüning produced an emergency decree in March 1931 that required all political meetings to be registered in advance with the police and subjected all political posters and leaflets to police censorship. It also gave the Reich government wide-ranging powers to combat "political excesses." Fearful that the chancellor would invoke his new emergency powers to ban the party, Hitler issued an order to the SA to halt the street battles and to avoid violence for the foreseeable future—an order that did not sit well with the Storm Troopers. He used every opportunity to emphasize his commitment to taking power by constitutional means. There would be no Nazi Putsch. To underscore this position, Hitler volunteered in March to testify for the defense at a much publicized trial of three junior Reichswehr officers who were charged with forming an illegal Nazi cell in the army garrison in Ulm. As he had done in his 1923 trial, Hitler exploited the opportunity to make a dramatic political statement. He solemnly declared that the NSDAP was committed to a policy of legality, that it had no need to think of revolution since the party would win a majority in the next two or three elections and would then, having been put legally in power, proceed to transform the state. When the skeptical judge pressed him, asking what would happen to those who had opposed him, Hitler at first demurred, but finally responded, "When the National Socialist movement is victorious in its struggle, there will be a National Socialist court of justice; November 1918 will be expiated, and heads will roll."

In spite of Hitler's assurances of the party's commitment to the path of legality, it proved difficult to keep the lid on the rambunctious SA. In the spring of 1931 the strains boiled over into open conflict when Walter Stennes, the disgruntled SA leader in Berlin who had been a source of trouble the previous August, attempted to lead a revolt of the eastern SA against Hitler and the party leadership. Fed up with Hitler's "timidity" and outright "cowardice," Stennes wrote a letter of complaint to SA headquarters in Munich, condemning Hitler's orders to refrain from street battles and pointedly warning that no leader could expect to go unpunished in the long run if he acts "against the sentiments of the best element of the people, in this case against the sentiments of the SA." Hitler saw this as a direct challenge to his leadership and immediately called a meeting of Nazi leaders in Weimar, where he proceeded to expel Stennes from the party.

Stennes responded by declaring his withdrawal from the NSDAP and his "takeover of the movement" in Berlin and the eastern provinces. He seized the party's Berlin headquarters and the offices of *Der Angriff* and published an edition on April 2, in which he launched a direct assault on Hitler's "un-German and boundless party despotism and the irresponsible demagogy." In the following days, he remained on the attack, picking up support among frustrated SA men in Silesia, Schleswig-Holstein, and

Pomerania. Party leaders condemned Stennes's treachery and his rhetoric as "socialist" and "revolutionary," but it was clear that he was expressing a view widely shared in SA circles that the Storm Trooper was not a handmaiden of the party bosses in Munich and their local functionaries.

Stennes's actions represented, in Goebbels's view, "the most serious crisis the party has had to go through," and Hitler responded quickly to the threat. He published an emotional appeal to the SA in the *Völkischer Beobachter*, asking the Storm Troopers to choose between Stennes, "the retired police sergeant," or "the founder of the National Socialist Movement and the Supreme Leader of your SA, Adolf Hitler." There could be no separation between the National Socialist "idea" and the "person" of the Führer, Hitler insisted. Within days the rebellion began to unravel. Although many SA men shared Stennes's dissatisfaction with the party's insistence on a policy of legality, few were willing to follow his open break with Hitler. The short-lived rebellion ended in both a purge of some five hundred Storm Troopers and a renewed effort by the political leadership to bring the SA under tighter control. But the tensions that had surged to the surface in this second Stennes episode continued to simmer.

Although Hitler had assumed leadership of the SA during the first Stennes revolt in the previous August, that move was little more than a dramatic gesture, a personal call for loyalty and obedience to his leadership. He was neither interested in nor capable of managing a growing, boisterous organization like the SA, and in an attempt to establish discipline among the Storm Troopers, Hitler turned to his old comrade Ernst Röhm. Röhm had been serving as a military advisor to the Bolivian government since 1925 when Hitler recalled him in December 1930. He assumed the post of chief of staff for the SA in January 1931, and began his work immediately. At first his appointment was met with grumbling by some SA leaders—and by Gregor Strasser. Röhm's homosexuality was well known and a topic of considerable gossip, both inside the NSDAP and beyond. The objections became so insistent that in February, Hitler felt compelled to issue a defense of his appointment. "The top SA leadership has presented a number of charges against the SA chief," Hitler wrote, "foremost among them attacks on his private life." These were matters that did not pertain to Röhm's leadership role in the party but that lay "entirely in the private realm." The SA, he reminded

Röhm's detractors, was not "a moral establishment for the education of proper young ladies but a band of rough fighters."

Röhm repaid Hitler's confidence with loyalty, energy, and a talent for organization that guided the SA through a period of stunning growth. Röhm did not support Stennes, although he shared the social revolutionary orientation of the rank and file and, like Stennes, viewed the SA primarily as an autonomous fighting force independent of the political leadership. He also saw himself primarily as a military man; the SA he envisioned was a disciplined military formation, the vital nucleus of a people's army, which would work with the Reichswehr—at least for the time being. He was also apparently content to see the SA as an instrument of the political leadership, operating on the implicit assumption that as the membership grew, so, too, would its influence. He instituted far-reaching organizational reforms, established soup kitchens and barracks for unemployed SA men, and managed the integration of thousands of new recruits. Under his command, the SA grew dramatically during 1931. In January the SA counted 88,000 men; by April, 119,000; by year's end, 260,000.

The economy meanwhile continued its free fall into the abyss. Between 1929 and 1932, industrial production plunged by almost 50 percent, the most precipitous drop coming in 1931. In roughly the same period, individual savings dwindled, bankruptcies soared, and unemployment lines grew steadily. In the winter of 1929–30, three million Germans had been out of work. During the following year that figure almost doubled, climbing to six million in early 1932. As grim as these official statistics appeared, they were certainly conservative. By 1932 perhaps as many as a million jobless men and women had exhausted their eligibility for unemployment benefits and in their despair no longer bothered to register at job referral agencies. In the midst of the prevailing economic gloom, a severe banking crisis battered the financial markets. In the summer of 1931, several major banks—among them the powerful Darmstädter and Dresdner, financial institutions thought too big to fail—teetered on the verge of collapse. The government moved to bail them out, avoiding runs on the banks like those that were occurring in the United States, but the already palpable crisis of public confidence in the beleaguered

Weimar "system" only deepened. As joblessness increased, government expenditure on unemployment compensation and related benefits began an inexorable rise, while tax revenue continued to shrink.

Afraid that growing government deficits would ignite a new inflation, Brüning introduced a series of stringent austerity measures that he believed to be the preconditions for recovery. The chancellor also hoped to score a major foreign policy success by forming a customs union with Austria—an initiative blocked by France—and by convincing the Allies to reduce or even terminate Germany's reparations obligations. A balanced budget, he felt, was a necessary precondition to demonstrate Germany's commitment to fiscal responsibility. Realizing that he would take political heat for these policies, he nonetheless produced a package of harsh deflationary measures that systematically slashed wages, prices, rents, pensions, and social services while raising some existing taxes and introducing new ones to cover government expenditures. The nation had to drink this bitter medicine, he argued, and all the parties knew it, but none was willing to take responsibility for administering it to the patient.

Brüning proceeded to enact his grim austerity program by emergency decree, eliciting howls of indignation across the political spectrum. He issued emergency decrees that slashed salaries and wages in the public sector, amounting to a 20 percent reduction in pay for civil servants and public employees. He made painful cuts in pensions and other retirement benefits; he reduced public assistance for veterans and invalids, and subsidies for children and public housing. He encouraged state governments to enact similar austerity measures by dramatically reducing the level of national funding for the states. The resulting cuts were particularly harsh in the field of education, leading to significant layoffs of schoolteachers and university staff. To cut the national deficit still further, he introduced an emergency income tax for the self-employed and white-collar workers in the private sector, a blow that was felt keenly by small business. Even President Herbert Hoover's moratorium on war debts and reparations payments in the summer of 1931—which only a year before would have been viewed as a dramatic diplomatic and economic triumph for Brüning's policies—produced hardly a ripple of support for his government. It was, quite simply, too little, too late.

Exacerbating his problems, Brüning was incapable of selling his program, either to the parliament or to the public. Ramrod stiff in appearance, severe and aloof in his personal bearing, he seemed the very incarnation of the stern, forbidding German schoolmaster. Where Hitler thundered and inspired, Brüning lectured. While he had been a competent floor leader of the Zentrum in the Reichstag, operating smoothly with parliamentary colleagues, he never grew comfortable dealing with the public. He could not move audiences with his speeches or mingle with crowds or shake hands or pat children's heads, and every day the contrast between this distant, dry, formal man and the energetic populist Nazi leader grew more glaring. Whether speaking on the radio or in public appearances, he seemed remote, out of touch with the suffering of ordinary people. Freed from the Reichstag and reliant only on the Reich President, he saw little need in trying to convince a desperate nation of the necessity of his chosen course. He was right, and he knew it, and in time the ungrateful public would recognize it as well. As the year wore on, the austere Brüning became the most reviled man in German politics, the "hunger Chancellor" who was reduced to moving about the country in a train carriage with the curtains down to hide from the public. If crowds spotted him they were apt to throw rocks. Worse still, his deeply unpopular deflationary measures failed to halt or even slow the economy's inexorable plunge. They did, however, inflame political passions and provide an inviting target for anti-Republican protest.

The NSDAP led the assault. Although the party's now imposing Reichstag delegation led by Hermann Göring could, and did, exploit parliamentary proceedings as a forum for Nazi propaganda, the NSDAP's political energies continued to be focused on the streets. Between the Reichstag elections of 1930 and 1932 the Nazis did not relax or slacken the pace of their agitation. Instead, the party continued to centralize its propaganda apparatus and to pursue its policy of perpetual campaigning. This strategy had evolved gradually since the adoption of Himmler's "propaganda action" campaigns in 1928–29, and with membership rising dramatically, it was now possible to keep the agitation at a fever pitch. Between 1928 and September 1930, the party's membership almost tripled, lurching from 108,717 to 293,000. Then in the wake of the 1930 campaign, applications for membership jumped yet again. Between September and the end of the year, the Nazis registered almost 100,000 new names on the party rolls. Even without the benefit of a national campaign in 1931, the NSDAP doubled its membership again. Each of these members paid regular party dues, filling the Nazis' rapidly expanding war chest and funding in large part the party's propaganda campaigns. By the close of 1932, a year dominated by a plethora of national and regional elections, the NSDAP boasted a membership of almost 1.5 million.

The rapidly growing membership made work in the party's modest headquarters in the Schellingstrasse increasingly difficult, and in 1930 the party, flush with funds from membership dues and a sizable contribution from the industrialist Fritz Thyssen, acquired an ornate *palais* on the Brienner Strasse just off the renowned Königsplatz. It quickly became known as the Brown House and served as party headquarters until January 1945, when it was badly damaged by Allied bombs. The building was extensively renovated in grand style by Hitler's favorite architect, Paul Ludwig Troost, and was ready for occupancy by early 1931. Engraved above its entry portal was the party's signature slogan: "Germany Awaken!" Along with offices for the party leadership and staff was a "hall of flags," at the center of which the party's "Blood Flag" from the 1923 Putsch was reverently displayed. By 1931 the NSDAP was no longer a fly-by-night enterprise but an established political institution, able to organize mass rallies and stage elaborate parades of the uniformed SA in every corner of the country. These activities were intended to create a dynamic, peripatetic public image for the party, bridging the gaps between national and regional elections. While the other parties, especially those of the bourgeois center and right, tended to go into hibernation between elections, the Nazis operated in a state of perpetual mobilization. As a circular to Nazi functionaries in the Rhineland emphasized in May 1931, all the other parties would be "going into their deep summer slumber and the legislatures [would] be closing their doors—[they think] it's too hot for politics—[but] for us National Socialists there is no pause. . . . We have no time to rest. Now is the time to intensify our propaganda work."

When no elections were on the horizon, the Nazis resorted to stunts. On December 4, 1930, the film version of Erich Maria Remarque's antiwar novel *All Quiet on the Western Front* opened in Berlin. The film had been cleared for release by the Social Democratic authorities, and for days in advance of the premiere, Goebbels and the Nazi press inveighed against this "affront to German honor." On opening night at the palatial Mozartsaal on Nollendorfplatz, 150 Storm Troopers reduced the theater to sheer bedlam. They rampaged through the theater, threw stink bombs from the balcony, released hundreds of mice in the orchestra, and, shouting "*Juden raus,*" (Jews out!) roughed up anyone they thought to be Jewish. Following their spectacular sabotage of its premiere, the Nazis mounted a series of mass demonstrations against the film, punctuated by violent clashes with the police. Within days, the country's Film Board, responding to the public outcry drummed up by the Nazis, reversed itself and rescinded its approval of *All Quiet.* The film was withdrawn from distribution, and the Nazis boasted that they had won a major triumph. "We are once again in the spotlight of public interest. The Republic rages in fury about our film victory." It could not have been grander, Goebbels gloated.

The Nazi campaign against *All Quiet* was but one manifestation of a broad assault on what it considered the un-German, cosmopolitan decadence of postwar Germany. In the aftermath of the Great War and the social and political tumult of the hyperinflation, the nation, censorious social critics lamented, had plunged into a morass of hedonistic squalor. Some blamed the war, some economic woes, others women's suffrage, but all agreed that the frenetic pleasure-seeking disregard of the traditional values of family, faith, and fidelity had sent the country plummeting into a state of "moral collapse. The boulevard press—tabloids—were filled with lurid stories of crime and sex, and were, of course, tremendously popular. The appalling evidence of the country's moral decay was everywhere: sex, jazz, flappers, homosexuality, "the New Woman," and an orgy of wild uninhibited dancing, all challenges to traditional values, all foreign, especially American, imports.

The Nazis launched assaults on all these manifestations of postwar popular culture, posing as the stalwart defenders of traditional "German" values. They reviled the postwar cinema, with its sordid sexuality, and condemned the new art, exemplified by Kandinsky, Klee, Beckmann, and other Expressionist painters. All had existed before the war but became centerpieces of what came to be called Weimar culture. The new atonal music arriving from Vienna, the futuristic architecture and furnishings of the Bauhaus, the seductive cynicism of Bertolt Brecht's plays all seemed urban, foreign, far from the image of an idyllic pastoral Germany, which had, like most objects of nostalgic yearning, hardly existed.

Cultural critics and many ordinary Germans shared these views, but the Nazis placed them in an ideological context. The degenerate developments that were corroding German cultural life from high to low were the creations of the Jews and amounted to nothing less than "cultural bolshevism." The actors, directors, musicians, novelists, playwrights, publishers, and architects who now dominated the German cultural scene were either "Jews or were swimming completely in the Jewish backwash." Indeed, all German culture had become "jewified" (*verjudet*). "Everywhere we look Jews. . . . They saturate the body of our people and stamp their mentality on it," a mentality whose essence was "money and eroticism." Not rooted in any indigenous national culture, "they recognize no traditional values. Always desirous for the New, they crave the sensational." It was the task of National Socialism "to once again warn the people and save them from the abyss."

Giving coverage to these views, the Nazis could now rely on a vastly expanded party press. Before the great electoral breakthrough in September 1930, the NSDAP controlled forty-nine newspapers, only six of which were dailies. By 1932 the number had expanded to 127, with a circulation in excess of a million. The party's *Völkischer Beobachter*, published daily in both Munich and Berlin, saw its circulation rise steadily from 26,000 in 1929 to over 100,000 in 1931, and Goebbels's Berlin-based *Der Angriff* became a daily for the first time in November 1930. All brought much needed revenue to the party treasury in Munich.

Utilizing their expanding membership and their increasingly sophisticated propaganda apparatus, the Nazis marched aggressively through a series of regional elections in 1931, registering significant gains in Oldenburg, Hamburg, Hessen, and Anhalt, while the traditional bourgeois parties faltered badly. Between these elections, Hitler enlisted the party in another referendum campaign, this time in a bizarre coalition of antidemocratic forces that ranged from the DNVP to the Communists. The referendum was an attempt to unseat the democratically elected Prussian state legislature, which was controlled by the parties of the Weimar coalition—the SPD, Zentrum, and left-liberals (DDP). It was the all-important power base of the Social Democrats in Germany, and the referendum was intended to undermine this bastion of pro-democracy forces. Beginning in April, the campaign raged across Germany's largest state until August, when the Prussian public went at last to the polls. The referendum failed—it received just 36 percent of the vote—but, just as the anti-Young campaign had done, it offered the NSDAP another opportunity for national exposure.

The Prussian referendum was hardly over when the Nazis were given another important boost by a revival of the anti-Young alliance. Organized by Hugenberg, the alliance was intended to mobilize the "national opposition" under the DNVP's leadership. Hugenberg, who was determined to project himself as the leader of the anti-system right, invited the Nazis to join the Stahlhelm (Steel Helmet), the largest of the veterans organizations, the Pan-German League, and other right-wing organizations in a mass demonstration of anti-Republican unity at the resort town of Bad Harzburg in October. Hitler played a double game during the gathering—on the one hand he threw his party into the "national opposition," and a powerful show of strength by the Storm Troopers was the highlight of the event. On the other hand, he made a point of keeping his distance from Hugenberg and the Stahlhelm leaders Franz Seldte and Theodor Duesterberg. He did not join them for the official dinner and refused to be photographed with them, actions that were deeply resented by his "allies." At that highly publicized event and in the months that followed, it became clear that Hitler, not Hugenberg, was the dominant figure in the antidemocratic alliance.

That preeminent position was underscored just a few weeks after Bad Harzburg, when, in an unparalleled display of the movement's power, Hitler reviewed a parade of more than 100,000 Storm Troopers in Braunschweig. It was the largest gathering of the SA to date and required more than two hours for the brown-shirted ranks to pass before their leader's salute. The loose cooperation between the Nazis and their reactionary Harzburg allies lasted only until the presidential election of the following spring and ended in considerable bitterness. But the Harzburg Front had been a success for Hitler, providing him with extensive national exposure and marking another stage in the legitimation of National Socialism in traditional conservative circles.

In spite of Hitler's repeated efforts to reassure the government, the police, and the conservative public that the NSDAP was committed to a policy of legality, the threat of an SA Putsch just would not go away. In November 1931 state authorities in Hessen came into possession of a set of documents that laid out plans for a Nazi coup in the event of a Communist uprising. The documents were the product of discussions by a small group of Nazis at the Boxheimer Hof, a farm in rural Hessen, and came to be known as the *Boxheimer Dokumente*. They offered a hair-raising catalogue of virtually every radical idea ever attributed to the Nazis. According to the documents, armed Nazi groups, including the SA, would declare a state of emergency, round up all political opponents and deliver them to concentration camps that would be constructed to house them. "Resistance," especially by government officials, the document declared, "will be punished by death." Anyone failing to turn in weapons within twenty-four hours or who participated in strikes or efforts at sabotage would be shot. Among other measures, the documents called for the abolition of the right to private property, the obligation to pay debts, interest on savings, and of private incomes. The SA was also empowered to administer the property of the state, and, in fact, all private property.

Publication of the documents created a sensation. The liberal and leftist press erupted. *Vorwärts* described them as "the blood plans of Hessen," declaring that for the Nazis, governing meant shooting others. Hitler vehemently denied all knowledge of such plans, a denial that seems, in this case, to have been true. The Boxheim Documents, he insisted, in no way reflected Nazi policy but were the unofficial, private conjectures of a small group, nothing more. Why, after all, would the NSDAP consider such a project? Looking ahead to the presidential elections in the spring, he explained in a newspaper interview, "A party that can count on 15 million votes doesn't need to take an illegal step."

Ultimately, the court agreed with Hitler and dropped the charges, but the Boxheim affair was an embarrassment to Hitler, especially at a time when the party was not only attempting to placate suspicious government authorities but openly courting the business community. The specter of a violent Nazi revolution, combined with the fiery quasi-socialist rhetoric issuing from some elements of the party, had long been a source of deep concern to business circles. With the growing political influence of the NSDAP, business leaders, who had been skeptical of the Nazis and their vague, inconsistent, and apparently radical economic views, thought it prudent to take a fresh look at Hitler. The NSDAP's rigid anti-Marxist and anti-union stance had long found a receptive audience in business circles, but the party's strong anticapitalist rhetoric and the "socialist" demands of the party's Twenty-five Points program—breaking interest slavery, the nationalization of all corporations and trusts—were deeply unsettling. The leaders of German big business, especially in the powerful coal, iron, and steel industries, were hardly champions of the Weimar Republic, convinced as they were that Weimar's extensive welfare state and its protection of the rights of organized labor had been prime factors in Germany's economic demise. But what were they to make of the unsystematic, sometimes blatantly contradictory economic pronouncements of the National Socialists? Some industrialists had provided occasional contributions to individual Nazis—to Strasser, Göring, and men they viewed as more reasonable and more moderate, at least in economic matters, than firebrands like Goebbels and Streicher. Just where Hitler stood in all this remained a mystery.

In 1931 contacts between the Nazis and big business multiplied. Nazi leaders were invited to speak before business audiences in Berlin and in the Ruhr, and the Nazis reciprocated by asking important business leaders to attend Nazi forums dealing with economic issues. In mid-October, Walther Funk, Hitler's top economic advisor, spoke to the exclusive Gentlemen's Club (Herrenklub) in Berlin; a few weeks later Gottfried Feder, one of Hitler's economic advisors, addressed an invited audience of coal industry representatives in Essen; in November, Feder and Otto Wagener, head of the party's Economic Policy Section, appeared in Düsseldorf before an audience of eight hundred, including many business leaders, at a special Nazi conference devoted to economic policy; and in December, Gregor Strasser gave an after-dinner speech to some thirty coal executives in Essen. With this flurry of activity, the Nazis sought to dispel fears in the business community about their presumed radical socialist intentions, while cautious business leaders hoped to cultivate the more moderate elements of the party, or, at the very least, to win friends in a movement that had become a major player in German politics.

The highlight of these efforts came in two appearances by Hitler before audiences of prominent figures in German industry and finance. In December he was invited to address the conservative National Club in Hamburg, and in January Fritz Thyssen, the powerful steel magnate, arranged for him to speak at the influential Düsseldorf Industrial Club. The themes of his Hamburg address were repeated again in Düsseldorf, but his speech there, in the heart of the industrial Ruhr, generated far more interest and news coverage. More than six hundred of the club's eight hundred members crowded into the grand ballroom to hear Hitler's views on Germany's economic future. Instead of his brown party uniform and swastika armband, Hitler appeared at the posh Park Hotel wearing a respectable blue business suit, the proper, understated man of affairs.

His reception was decidedly cool. Many in the room were intrigued by Hitler, but those hoping to learn anything specific about Nazi economic policy were sorely disappointed.

Hitler delivered a rambling two-and-a-half-hour speech that was calculated to reassure business leaders that the party did not harbor radical anticapitalist tendencies, to emphasize its determination to stand as a bulwark against Marxism, and to demonstrate that the NSDAP was a party that could be trusted to provide responsible leadership of the state. He spoke at some length about the rising danger of Communism, a threat that could not be countered by anemic, ineffectual democratic government. It had to be fought mercilessly, day and night, in every corner of the land, and only the NSDAP had the courage, power, and will to carry out this crucial mission. Emergency decrees and their economic palliatives could not save Germany, only the forceful exercise of political power. Politics, not economics, would revitalize the nation. "It was not German business that conquered the world, followed by the development of German power, but the powerful state (*Machtstaat*) which created for the business world the general conditions for its subsequent prosperity." There could be no economic life "unless behind this economic life there stands the determined political will of the nation absolutely ready to strike—and to strike hard. . . . The essential thing is the formation of the political will of the nation: that is the starting point for political action." Unless Germany could overcome its internal divisions, no measures of the Reichstag, no ephemeral foreign policy triumph could halt the decline of the German nation, and only the NSDAP, standing above class, above petty interest politics and driven by an unstoppable political will, could bring that unity.

He went on to assail Versailles, reparations, and the perfidy of the victor states; he spoke vaguely about international trade, markets, the value of the mark, closing with the assertion that in order to sustain itself and ensure growth, Germany must acquire *Lebensraum* in the East. But the prerequisite for all was the indomitable political will of a united German nation, and that was the goal of the National Socialist movement. About the economy he spoke, as usual, in maddening generalities, eschewing specifics and emphasizing his belief in the primacy of individual initiative, of private enterprise, and of the disastrous effects of weak democratic government. On the whole, the presentation seemed one of calculated ambiguity.

While business leaders may have come away from these encounters somewhat reassured about Nazi radicalism and the party's commitment to lead the fight against Communism, they were decidedly unimpressed by the Nazi leadership's feeble grasp of economic matters. Aside from "cheap demagoguery," as one business leader summarized his impressions, the presentations by the party's economic experts revealed "an astounding economic dilettantism"; another was struck by the "great shallowness, flaccidity, and primitiveness" of Nazi economic thinking. Some business leaders viewed National Socialism as a passing phenomenon, a product of extreme economic distress that would fade away as economic conditions improved. A handful of business leaders, such as Thyssen and Hjalmar Schacht, the highly respected former head of the Reichsbank, were impressed with Hitler and urged financial support for the NSDAP. But the general conclusion drawn from these interactions was that it might be possible—and prudent—to influence the Nazis, to educate them about economic affairs, and to discourage the party's radical elements by cultivating contacts with the more reasonable among them. For the most part, however, business leaders, with a few notable exceptions, remained at arm's length from the party. Despite contemporary accusations, especially by the parties of the left, that big business was bankrolling the NSDAP, the business community continued to be wary of the Nazis and preferred the more predictable center-right parties, especially the DNVP and DVP.

Hitler was not unduly upset with this state of affairs. It was not necessary to convert the leaders of big business to National Socialism, he believed, only to ensure that they did not use their influence to thwart the party's drive toward power. Modest contributions from business sources were made in 1931 and into 1932, but the Nazis were not in need of their contributions. They were proud of the fact that the party did not rely on donations from special interests to fund its activities but relied almost exclusively on grassroots sources of funding—membership dues, subscriptions to the party press, admission to party events, and so forth. Despite considerable investigation, the police authorities in the Ruhr, for example, could find no evidence of significant donations from big business to the NSDAP in 1931. Nazi propaganda—the dances, the "German Evenings," the concerts, the speeches—was a moneymaking operation. The party received occasional donations from business sources, but only after the July elections of 1932, with the party treasury exhausted, did the party turn to big business for loans or direct contributions.

As 1931 drew to a close, the Nazis had every reason to feel buoyant about the future. At each municipal and state election, the party was gaining ground. The obscure fringe party of 1928 had captured the public's attention; even the establishment, however reluctant, however reserved, had come calling. The Nazis had grabbed the spotlight, and they intended to hold it. They were new and energetic, they were exciting, and they were on the move. Elections in Germany's two largest states would be held in the spring, and there was even the possibility of presidential elections. With the promise of new triumphs and with the prospect of power, the new year beckoned.

MAKING GERMANY GREAT AGAIN

As the new year dawned, Hitler looked forward to what promised to be the year of decision. Elections were scheduled for the spring in Prussia and Bavaria, the country's two largest states, and the NSDAP was well financed, well organized, and brimming with confidence. The Nazis were riding a wave of inevitability. Every election—shop floor, student government, town council, it didn't matter—the Nazis contested them all, and in locale after locale, they were scoring spectacular gains. Hitler had every reason to feel optimistic. The NSDAP stood on the threshold of power.

The Nazis opened the year in impressive fashion, winning 30 percent of the vote in the tiny state of Lippe. For the first time, the NSDAP surpassed the combined totals of the center-right parties and exceeded the Social Democratic vote as well. The elections in Bavaria and Prussia were tantamount to a national election, and contests in Anhalt, Hamburg, and Württemberg were also scheduled for the early spring. In fact, elections would be held in virtually every German state before the high days of summer. But beyond those important contests, a much more enticing prize loomed on the near horizon. Hindenburg's term as Reich President was due to expire in May 1932. In an effort to forestall a new election, Brüning, whose continued presence as Reich Chancellor depended on Hindenburg, appealed to "the Old Gentleman" to stay on. But Hindenburg was reluctant—at eighty-four, he could not face the rigors of a national campaign. Encouraged by General Schleicher, Brüning floated a plan that would allow Hindenburg's term to be extended for another seven years— in effect, for life. Working the backstairs, Schleicher believed that it would be possible to convince the Nazis to support a rightist government that would have the backing of the Reich President, the army, and big business. With the popular support the Nazis would bring, this constellation of forces could then ditch the Weimar constitution and install the sort of authoritarian system they had long preferred. But extending Hindenburg's presidency without an election would mean a revision of the constitution and that, in turn, would require passage by a two-thirds majority in the Reichstag. For this Brüning would need the support of the NSDAP.

When first approached in November, Hitler was reluctant to agree—after all, he piously objected, this amounted to a serious breach of the constitution. For weeks in December and January a dazed public was treated to the unlikely spectacle of Adolf Hitler wrapping himself reverently in the constitution, posing as the principled defender of a constitutional order he had publicly pledged to destroy. Behind the scenes, he was more amenable. He held talks with Schleicher, with Brüning, and finally with Hindenburg. He told the Reich President that he would put aside his constitutional scruples if Hindenburg would agree to dismiss Brüning, dissolve the Reichstag, and call for new elections. Hindenburg balked, and in January 1932, with the country mired in the depths of economic despair and political passions running at a fever pitch, a presidential campaign became inevitable.

Hitler did not relish the prospect of challenging the highly venerated Hindenburg. The old field marshal was the most respected figure in German political life. Although a conservative and, in his heart of hearts, a monarchist, he was viewed as a man "above politics," the last bulwark of stability amid the chaos, violence, and polarization of German politics. He was also a living link with a glorious German past. Opposing him would be an enormous gamble for Hitler. So much of the NSDAP's rising prestige and Hitler's mystique rested on an image of unbroken momentum, of a relentlessly rising tide of public support that was sweeping them inexorably into power. Challenging Hindenburg, which Strasser and other party leaders feared would end in certain defeat, risked undoing all that Nazi propaganda had labored so assiduously to create.

Throughout January and much of February Hitler wavered. Although he projected a public image of unswerving resolve and decisive action, Hitler tended to be hesitant, vacillating sometimes for weeks before making important decisions—a tendency that would characterize his leadership throughout his political career. Once he had reached his decision, however, he would cling to it with fanatical resolve, and nothing and no one could change his mind. Goebbels and Röhm strongly favored contesting the election. Hitler *had* to run. How, after all the clamoring for power, could the Führer of NSDAP sit out the election? Goebbels's diary entries for January and February bear ample testimony to his mounting frustration. Hitler's procrastination was maddening; the "eternal waiting [was] creating low morale in the party." Many in the leadership feared that Hitler had waited too long. "When will Hitler decide," Goebbels asked on January 30, "does he lack the necessary courage? We must give it to him."

While Hitler struggled with his decision, Goebbels was already hard at work planning for a presidential campaign. He and his staff were drafting speeches and slogans, creating leaflets and placards, outlining themes and a plan of attack for the campaign. But before a Hitler candidacy could become a reality, there was a small technical problem that demanded his attention: Adolf Hitler was not a German citizen. In 1925, fearing deportation to Austria after his release from Landsberg, he had renounced his Austrian citizenship and had remained officially stateless since. In 1929, he had applied to the Bavarian authorities for naturalization, only to be brusquely denied. But according to a peculiarity of German law, an appointment to a government post, either at the Reich or regional level, brought with it automatic citizenship. The situation was resolved when in March 1932 Hitler was appointed government councilor in the Office of Culture and Measurement in Braunschweig, the only state in which a National Socialist held a position in the government.

All that remained was Hitler's commitment to run. On February 5, Goebbels briefed the Führer on his plans for the campaign. Hitler seemed impressed and on the verge of declaring his candidacy. "Everything is ready," Goebbels assured him. "Just press the button and the avalanche will begin." Still, to Goebbels's dismay, Hitler procrastinated. "We must begin the battle," Goebbels wrote in exasperation two weeks later. "Slogans [for Hitler's candidacy] have been postponed for yet another day. This eternal waiting is frightful. Hitler is hesitating too long."

By early February, the preparations for the campaign were complete, the themes laid out in a memorandum drafted on February 4. "It must be made clear to the masses . . . that the National Socialist movement is determined to use the presidential elections to put an end to the entire system of 1918. The two words '*Schluss Jetzt!*' "—End It Now!—"represent the most direct and forceful formulation of that determination. As the final words of every leaflet and placard this slogan must be relentlessly hammered into the head of the reader and voter. In ten days no one in Germany should be talking about anything but this slogan." The presidential election was to be framed "as the decisive battle between National Socialism and the system. It must be pounded into the masses that this system will inevitably lead to Bolshevist chaos." Only the NSDAP could "overcome the threatening specter of Bolshevism and . . . create a true people's community of all productive [*schaffenden*] Germans." The time had come to "End It Now!"

Finally, on February 22, Hitler gave the green light. Goebbels could announce his candidacy that night at a mass meeting in Berlin's cavernous Sportpalast. The news, proclaimed with all the stormy theatricality Goebbels could muster, was greeted with wild cheering that went on for twenty minutes. It was an auspicious beginning. Despite the infuriating delays, Goebbels was confident that the party was well prepared for the coming battle. "It will be a campaign that will leave all previous ones in the shadows," he predicted. "Everything is ready. . . . The election is already won. Poor Hindenburg."

The field of candidates reflected the shifting topography of late Weimar politics. Hindenburg, the conservative, the monarchist, was spurned by the DNVP and other right-wing organizations, who put forward Theodor Duesterberg of the Stahlhelm as their candidate. Hindenburg *was*, however, supported by the Social Democrats, Zentrum, and the rapidly shrinking parties of the moderate center. The Social Democrats were hardly enthusiastic but considered Hindenburg the lesser of several evils. The Communists put forward their leader, Ernst Thälmann.

Hindenburg was a reluctant candidate, uncomfortable from the outset. He refused to go out on the campaign trail—it was beneath his sense of dignity and beyond his physical endurance—preferring instead to campaign from the halls of the Presidential Palace. It was at best a lackluster effort. He pointedly offered no endorsement of the Brüning government, which he had himself installed. He did not attend any rallies, and he made only one radio address to the nation. Symptomatic of his aloofness were two short campaign films that were as unexciting and detached as the old gentleman himself. In one, he read ploddingly through prepared remarks about his decision to enter the race, his eyes never leaving the page he held in his hands. In a second film he did not appear on camera at all. Instead, an actor stood on stage, script in hand, and declaimed in arch-thespian style Hindenburg's record of achievement. Interspersed with his peroration were newsreel clips of Hindenburg at various state ceremonies. It was Brüning who bore the brunt of Hindenburg's campaign, Brüning who was out on the hustings, the face of the campaign.

With its propaganda machine well organized and well financed, the NSDAP launched a massive media blitz the likes of which had never been seen in German politics. In February Goebbels moved the RPL, the Propaganda Leadership, from Munich to Berlin, where he would direct the campaign. Every day the new offices in the Hedemannstrasse bustled with frantic activity: the rooms were full, the atmosphere electric. The clatter of typewriters echoed from every room in the building; telephones jangled without stop. Hourly reports poured in from all over the country. The staff produced fifty thousand phonograph records, small enough to slip into a postal envelope, and several short films for distribution. The films, none longer than fifteen minutes, featured speeches by Hitler, Goebbels, and other Nazi leaders. They would not be shown in theaters but in public plazas in major cities and market towns. Otto Dietrich, head of the Nazi press corps and a rival of Goebbels for Hitler's affection, mobilized the party's daily and weekly newspapers, adding campaign extras and articles to its big-city dailies and smaller regional weeklies. In the torrent of printed matter that rained down on the country, special leaflets were addressed to every conceivable social and demographic group—shopkeepers, civil servants, farmers, workers, Catholics, Protestants, the old, the young, women. The content of these appeals was based on an analysis by the party's market research. In Department III, on the second floor, a group of young men, most in their twenties and early thirties, analyzed reports submitted from the party's regional propaganda affiliates. They sifted through them all, preparing summaries for Goebbels, their chief, who would evaluate them.

For weeks the party saturated the country with pamphlets, rallies, and theatrically orchestrated appearances by Nazi leaders. In addition to the mass of printed materials provided to regional leaders on an almost daily basis, the RPL earmarked some for public distribution on specific dates. Their appearance on the designated dates was intended to coincide with important speeches or rallies devoted to a particular social group or political issue. "The placards must appear, whether in the press, as leaflets, or as posters on exactly the date for which they are marked," the RPL stressed. "The end effect must be that on the same day all over Germany our attack on the system and its parties has been launched as a unified assault." Such coordinated propaganda offensives became hallmarks of the National Socialist campaigns in 1932, and they produced the desired effect: on a given date, from Königsberg to Aachen, from the Baltic to the Alps, Nazis would be on the streets distributing the same leaflets, posting similar placards, and holding highly publicized speeches or rallies on the designated topic of the day. This degree of nationwide coordination was unrivaled by the other parties and gave the NSDAP a tremendous advantage in the day-to-day conduct of national campaigning.

Along with these displays of national coordination and centralized control, the party targeted virtually every group, with farmers, civil servants, and workers leading the list. No group was too small, too insignificant for the NSDAP to mobilize. The message generated in a variety of ways was simple, direct, and shorn of any nuance, couched in a few snappy catchphrases, a handful of images, and easily recognized code words—sound bites, in today's vernacular—that could be easily remembered and passed on. The local party chapters studied their area's *Addressbuch*, a forerunner of telephone directories, which listed the occupation of the head of the household. Using that information as a guide, the Nazis were able to design leaflets and short pamphlets that addressed the specific woes of the shopkeeper, the civil servant, farmer, white-collar employee, and worker. These were then delivered in person, and the recipient was invited to a follow-up meeting for his particular occupational group.

These printed materials were accompanied by the usual reminders about other propaganda aids available from the national or *Gau* headquarters. The party's list of such aids and services had grown considerably since 1930, including not only films and phonograph records, but loudspeakers, motorcycles, trucks, and, for the most affluent and important regions, even airplanes. The RPL also continued to offer detailed instructions on virtually every aspect of campaigning from the sort of music to play at rallies to the colors of campaign placards and the frequency with which they should be changed to hold public attention. In each of the 1932 campaigns, the NSDAP continued to concentrate on what the RPL referred to as "systematic work at the grass-roots level (*Kleinarbeit*)." No detail was to be ignored.

The Nazis staged more than thirty thousand events, distributed eight million leaflets, and plastered the walls of every town and city with Nazi posters. Goebbels's office circulated regular propaganda updates, designating new themes and target groups for particular emphasis. But the main attractions of the campaign were the public appearances of Hitler, Goebbels, Strasser, and Göring, whose public profile had risen dramatically since he returned from exile in 1927 to lead the party's Reichstag delegation. Other big guns of the party also spoke, but Hitler and Goebbels were the headliners. Between the announcement of Hitler's candidacy of February 22 and election day on March 13, Goebbels made nineteen speeches in Berlin, and addressed mass meetings in nine other towns scattered across Germany. Hitler kept to an exhausting schedule, speaking in twelve cities in eleven days, traveling always by car. He raced from engagement to engagement in a small convoy of automobiles, accompanied by his usual team of bodyguards, secretaries, drivers, and a changeable entourage of party figures. At the edge of every town or city, the convoy would be met by local Nazi officials, who were in charge of security for the event. Hitler, sitting beside his driver, always kept a map on his knees, marking the route, careful to avoid known Communist strongholds. He also carried a revolver. Everywhere he drew monster crowds, who often waited patiently through hours of delay for his arrival. In the last frenetic days of the campaign, Hitler addressed mass meetings in Berlin, Hamburg, Stettin, Breslau, Leipzig, Bad Blankenburg, Weimar, Frankfurt, Nuremberg, Stuttgart, Dortmund, and Hanover, where crowds of sixty to one hundred thousand turned out for his well-choreographed appearances.

Throughout the campaign, the party handled the ancient *Feldmarschall* with uncharacteristic restraint. The strategy was to praise Hindenburg's great service to the fatherland, in both war and peace, to show respect (a rare exercise for the Nazis) for his patriotism and person, while at the same time suggesting that *der Alte* (the Old One) was being manipulated and misused by an unscrupulous chancellor—a strategy that tied

Hindenburg to Brüning while at the same time serving as an indirect, if not very subtle, reminder of Hindenburg's age. A vote for Hindenburg, the Nazis insisted, was a vote for Brüning and his emergency decrees. It was time for new leadership.

There were bright clear skies over Germany on election day, March 13— "Hitler weather," Goebbels prophesized. "Everyone is confident of victory. [Hitler], too." From early in the day reports from around the country indicated a massive turnout. Polling places everywhere were teeming with activity. Long lines snaked along crowded sidewalks. "Fate, do not help us," Goebbels prayed, "but be just. . . . We await your judgment. Evening should find us joyful."

As he left his office in the Hedemannstrasse in the early evening, he was struck by the mood of excitement and anticipation he saw on the streets. "Everywhere victory fever prevails." That night a small crowd of friends and party colleagues gathered in his house to listen to the returns. The early results from cruise ships leaving Hamburg and Bremen harbors reported "a fantastic win for Hitler," a good omen. But as the evening wore on and more returns began trickling in, the optimistic mood evaporated. "Things look bad. . . . Around ten one can sense the final result. We have been beaten," Goebbels conceded glumly. The outlook was "frightful." By 2 a.m. everyone was "dejected and discouraged." It was depressingly clear, he concluded, that "we had set our goals too high." He placed a call to Hitler in Munich. The Führer was "completely surprised by the results," Goebbels thought, but was determined to go on, to get back down to work. "In that," Goebbels gushed, "he is great."

Putzi Hanfstaengl, Hitler's piano player, foreign press chief, and general factotum, had a rather different recollection of Hitler's reaction to the defeat. Hitler listened to the returns in his office at the Brown House surrounded by Hanfstaengl, Hess, his secretary Martin Bormann, and the party's business manager Philipp Bouhler. In the early-morning hours, when the final verdict was in, a heavy pall settled over the little group. The telephone began to ring. Calls from various party leaders. "Goebbels was completely distraught and cried with disappointment," Hanfstaengl remembered. Göring kept his head and pointed out that due to Hindenburg's advanced years, he would never survive a runoff. Hitler hardly uttered a word. He rose stiffly from his chair and departed as if in a trance. Sometime later Hanfstaengl drove to Hitler's apartment on the Prinzregentenplatz and found the Führer sitting alone in a darkened room, staring into the shadows, brooding. He was, Hanfstaengl thought, "the very picture of a disappointed, dejected gambler who had wagered beyond his means."

Although deflated by the results, the Nazis had captured eleven and a half million votes, almost double their total from 1930, and with 30 percent of the vote, Hitler left Duesterberg (6.8 percent) and the KPD's Thälmann (10 percent) in the dust. Hindenburg had prevailed, the outcome not even close. With more than eighteen million votes, he was the clear winner. And yet when the final results were officially tabulated, there was a problem. In order to avoid a runoff, a candidate needed at least 50 percent of the vote. Now it was the Hindenburg camp's turn to be disappointed. The old field marshal had captured 49.6 percent. A second round would be necessary.

Initially Strasser and Göring were reluctant to embark on a new campaign. With the other candidates eliminated, a direct Hindenburg-Hitler contest could only end in another, possibly more damaging setback. Even the Harzburg parties, still smarting from Hitler's refusal to back Duesterberg in the first round, were urging their voters to abstain rather than endorse Hitler. But having once decided to challenge Hindenburg, Hitler was not about to back out now. He would confront Hindenburg in the runoff. On March 14, a special edition of the *Völkischer Beobachter* appeared, carrying the party's new rallying cry: "The first election campaign is over," Hitler wrote. "The second has begun today. I will lead it."

The party's propaganda machine shifted immediately into high gear. Drawing on reports from their regional propaganda operatives, the RPL was convinced that the party had failed to attract sufficient support from civil servants, pensioners, and women. Hindenburg's strong showing, Goebbels believed, could be "traced to the typical mentality of certain bourgeois circles, especially the German petit bourgeois whose vote was won with sentimentality and the fear of the unknown; the woman whose vote was swayed by appeals to the tear ducts and fear of war; and the pensioner and public official who were misled by references to inflation, cuts in benefits, and National Socialist hostility toward civil servants." To counter such charges, Goebbels and his staff deluged regional leaders with drafts of leaflets directed to precisely these groups.

As the campaign unfolded, the Nazis avoided a frontal assault on the Reich President and directed their fire to the parties that supported him. Hindenburg was the candidate of the "system parties," and what did they stand for? "The SPD—Marxism, socialization. 'Property is theft,' hate of the army, nationalism"; they were "the treasonous guarantors of Versailles [and] enemies of the church"; the Zentrum was assailed for its "misuse of religion" and "working arm in arm with atheists." The liberals merited hardly a mention. They were simply the tools of "Jewish money bag interests." The Nazis again sought to tar Hindenburg with Brüning's unpopular emergency decrees, repeatedly reminding voters that "if you vote for Hindenburg, you're voting for Brüning, and whoever votes for Brüning casts his ballot for the emergency decrees."

At the same time, the RPL chose to concentrate on candidate Hitler, implicitly contrasting his youth, energy, and populist magnetism with the ancient Prussian field marshal. Hindenburg was a great and honorable man but a man whose day had passed. It was time for a new generation to take up the torch. Day after day the public was bombarded with articles about Hitler—his humble beginnings (not the privileged background of a Prussian Junker), his service as a common front soldier, his creation of a movement of political, social, and cultural renewal that, against all odds, was taking the country by storm. Typical was a series of leaflets composed by Goebbels that would appear nationwide on four consecutive days: "Adolf Hitler as Human Being," March 29; "Adolf Hitler as Comrade," March 30; "Adolf Hitler as Political Fighter," March 31; "Adolf Hitler as Statesman," April 1. By election day, his stern visage looked down from every wall, every kiosk. Hitler preferred one poster in particular—his chalk-white face staring hypnotically out from the center of a solid black background, presumably capturing his fanatical magnetism. The caption read only: "Hitler."

Hitler touched on all these themes in a campaign declaration entitled "My Program," released on April 2. As in almost all Hitler's public utterances, "My Program" began with a recapitulation of his unlikely rise from political obscurity, depicting himself as a lonely visionary engaged in a long and bitter struggle against the establishment, the insiders, the power brokers. The story did not lack for melodrama—or false humility. Hitler's fanatical devotion to the cause of Germany's revival (in the Nazi lexicon "fanatical" was an adjective of the highest praise) was a defining leitmotif of the campaign. Delivered in a tone of aggrieved self-righteousness, he thundered against the system that had relentlessly persecuted him and his movement. The authorities had banned the movement's newspapers, suppressed its organizations, prohibited him from speaking in different states, charged the party's leaders with slander, libel, and sedition, and thrown others into prison. "When thirteen years ago," he typically began, "an unknown man and German soldier, entered political life, I listened only to the dictates of my conscience. . . . I could not convince myself, as millions of others did, to keep quiet and go along . . . with those whose actions were driving Germany to ruin. For thirteen years of hard struggle . . . I have followed my sense of duty and founded a movement to fight against those . . . responsible for Germany's collapse." The "system parties," he wrote, "have tried to silence me; they have scorned me; they could prohibit my speaking, suppress the movement, gag our propaganda, just as today they ban my newspapers, confiscate our leaflets, and deny us access to the radio. All this they can do and have for thirteen years. But one thing they have failed to do: they have not been able to show me wrong."

In the campaign's most dramatic stroke, Hitler took to the skies in a highly publicized "flight over Germany" (*Deutschlandflug*), appearing in twenty-one cities in six days. It was a sensation. He was the first German—or for that matter, European or American—politician to campaign by airplane, and the image of a daring, innovative leader literally descending from the heavens spearheaded the Nazi propaganda offensive. When his plane touched down for the last rally of the whirlwind tour, he had spoken to a half million people.

At each of his stops Hitler was greeted by boisterous, adoring crowds, and at each he thundered with fury, his rasping voice rising to a piercing crescendo, as he gave vent to all their anger, frustration, and resentment. He spewed venom at the Marxists, the November criminals, the system parties, who were responsible for Germany's disgrace and his audience's personal misery. He, and he alone, could make Germany great again by toppling the rule of Weimar's corrupt and divisive party system and forging a new Germany united in one cohesive people's community (*Volksgemeinschaft*) that would transcend class, religion, and region. That, he promised, was Germany's future under a National Socialist regime. To his many opponents, these melodramatic tirades were the sheerest demagoguery, a paranoid amalgam of vacuous shibboleths, hate, distortions, and outright lies. To those angry multitudes caught up in the frenzy, it hardly mattered.

As election day approached, the atmosphere in Germany was electric. Every day the SA clashed in vicious street battles with the Red Front and the SPD's Reichsbanner. Columns of Storm Troopers marched through the streets; buildings were festooned with placards; discarded leaflets littered the streets; party banners fluttered from windows. "Berlin," Goebbels wrote, "is no longer recognizable. Everything is in motion." On April 10, Hitler again fell short, but this time there was not a whisper of disappointment in the Nazi camp. Hitler had captured more than thirteen million votes (36.6 percent of the total), an increase of more than two million over the first round. "For us an overwhelming victory," Goebbels gushed, almost in disbelief. In "red Berlin" alone, the Nazi vote had jumped from 300,000 to more than 800,000. "Fantastic numbers. Hitler is completely happy. Now we have a springboard for the Prussian elections." While Hindenburg claimed 53 percent of the vote, Hitler had dwarfed the other leaders of the anti-Republican right and left. He was now *the* anti-system alternative. Equally important, he had demonstrated the stature to stand on the same national platform with the venerated Hindenburg.

First incubated within the NSDAP after 1925 and largely confined to the party's true believers, the presidential campaigns had thrust the Führer cult into the mainstream of national political consciousness. Hitler was now not only a political force of the first magnitude, he was a national celebrity, easily the most recognizable—and controversial—figure in German political life. Even his enemies—and they were legion—were obsessed with him. His habits, his tastes, his background, his personal life were the topics of endless speculation, gossip, and analysis.

Yet for all the attention and public scrutiny, Hitler remained an enigma, his personal life a mystery. Away from Berlin and Munich, he liked to relax in lederhosen, the traditional leather shorts worn in southern Germany. He almost always carried a whip. He loved dogs and was fond of children, with whom he was frequently photographed. He took pride in his highly publicized "Spartan" lifestyle, his simplicity in dress and diet;

he was, after all, marketed as "a man of the people." But by 1932, Hitler led anything but the simple life. For years, from 1920 to 1929, he had lived in a narrow, one-room apartment on the Thierschstrasse, its worn linoleum floor covered by cheap, threadbare carpets. But in 1929 a wealthy benefactor secured for him a luxurious nine-room apartment on the posh Prinzregentenplatz, which would remain his personal residence for the remainder of his life. His spacious Munich apartment; his Alpine retreat— Haus Wachenfeld—outside Berchtesgaden; his lengthy stays at the ornate Kaiserhof Hotel in Berlin; his ubiquitous detachment of bodyguards, drivers, secretaries, and advisors; his massive chauffeur-driven Mercedes; and his innate restlessness that kept him and his entourage almost constantly on the move—all reflected a very different reality.

He made a great point of not drawing a salary from the party or taking honoraria for his speeches, but he did accept gifts from admirers, was paid handsomely for articles published in the party press and interviews he gave to foreign newspapers, and his expenses from his numerous speaking engagements were lavishly—and excessively—reimbursed. Sales of *Mein Kampf*, which had been a disappointment—the second volume published in 1927 had sold only thirteen thousand copies by 1929—began to rise after the breakthrough of 1930 and continued to climb, reaching eighty thousand in 1932. He was a best-selling author and financially independent.

Although constantly surrounded by obsequious lieutenants and fawning admirers, he had no friends, no close confidants. It was, after all, difficult to be on familiar terms with a deity. Sefton Delmer, an English reporter who was allowed to accompany Hitler during his campaigns in 1932, observed that

Hitler was either completely silent during his meals or he was laying down the law, expounding at length with all the dogmatic assurance of the self-taught man. He had no small talk. And he did not like others to have any either. . . . Argument was taboo. Only questions were welcome. And his companions took care that the questions they asked . . . should be questions that would provide him with an opening to lecture them on some favorite topic. What he liked talking about most was war, war of the future and war of the past, particularly the war of 1914–1918.

Only Röhm and Strasser, old comrades from the early days of the movement, dared address him with the familiar "*du*." Although he liked the company of women, especially young, attractive women, he was unmarried and had no romantic connections. His one serious attachment ended in tragedy and scandal. He appears to have fallen in love with his twenty-three-year-old niece, Geli Raubal, who had come along with her mother, Angela (Hitler's half-sister), to look after "Uncle Alf's" house outside Berchtesgaden. In 1929 Hitler invited her to live with him at his new Munich apartment. Geli was attractive and outgoing; she drew the attention of men. For two years they were photographed around Munich, in the cafés, at the opera, the cinema. Salacious stories circulated, embarrassing Goebbels and his handlers, but Hitler didn't seem to care. More than twenty years her senior, he was almost pathologically possessive. In time Geli grew weary of Hitler's jealousy and domineering control, and expressed a desire to return to Vienna to pursue a singing career. He refused to let her go.

On September 19, 1931, while he was away giving a speech in Nuremberg, Geli was found shot dead in Hitler's apartment, his pistol by her side. The death was ruled a suicide, though rumors persisted that Hitler had murdered her or that Himmler or Goebbels or Strasser had had her removed to protect Hitler and the movement from further scandal. Hitler's opponents couldn't get enough of the story, the opposition press publishing one lurid rumor after another. Insinuations of domestic violence and sexual perversions of the most varied sorts made the rounds.

Hitler was genuinely shocked at Geli's death. For days he was despondent, unable to focus. Close associates had never seen him like this; some feared that he might be suicidal. Then, within days after her funeral in Vienna, he seemed to snap out of it. He plunged again into his political work, and the scandal gradually faded. The nature of his relationship with Geli remained shrouded in obscurity, but Hitler ordered her room to be left just as she left it, and he kept a shrine to his niece in his residence in Berlin, in Berchtesgaden, and even in the *Führerbunker* where he ended his life. No one outside a small coterie within the party leadership knew as yet about another young woman, in many respects very similar to Geli, whom Hitler had met in 1929. Eva Braun would remain a secret until well into the Third Reich.

The votes in the presidential elections were still being counted when Goebbels began preparing for important regional elections on April 24. On that day, voters in Prussia, Bavaria, Anhalt, Hamburg, and Württemberg would go to the polls. With four fifths of the country's population voting, the regional elections amounted to yet another national campaign. The party's propaganda apparatus was fully mobilized and ready, its coffers full. But before the campaign could get under way, Brüning convinced Minister of the Interior General Wilhelm Groener to issue a decree dissolving the SA and the SS. Once before he had tried to rein in the Storm Troopers, who were so integral a part of Nazi campaigning. At the close of 1931 Brüning enacted a decree that prohibited the wearing of uniforms by party formations. The Storm Troopers had flouted that decree by putting away their brown shirts and appearing the next day in white shirts—or in some cases no shirts at all. The prohibition was quickly dropped. But the level of political violence had escalated dramatically during the two rounds of the presidential elections, and with regional campaigns looming, Brüning felt that something had to be done.

The decree went into effect on April 13. The Nazi press was quick to point out that no such order was issued regarding the Reichsbanner or the Red Front. It was yet another example, Hitler complained, of the government's remorseless campaign of persecution against the NSDAP. At first Röhm considered resisting the decree—after all, the SA now numbered roughly 400,000 men, four times as many as the Reichswehr. Hitler, however, disagreed, and appealed to the SA and SS, again urging patience and a renewed commitment to participation in elections. "I understand your feelings," he wrote in an address directed to them. "For years you have been true to my directives about winning political power by legal means. You are horribly persecuted and harassed. Yet in spite of all the gruesome agony perpetrated against you by today's momentarily ruling parties, you have remained upright and honorable Germans." He urged them to continue the fight as party comrades, to cooperate more than ever with local party groups in the upcoming campaigns, and "to give the current rulers no cause, under any circumstances, to set aside the elections. If you do your duty, our propaganda will strike a blow at General Groener and his accomplices a thousand times harder [than he has delivered against us]."

Still, he was uneasy. As he had done during the SA unrest of the previous year, he pledged his loyalty to the Storm Troopers and demanded their fealty in return. "I will give my all for this struggle and for Germany. You will follow me, for in spite of General Groener, I belong to you as long as I live and you belong to me."

Two days later, on April 15, Hitler once again embarked on a "flight over Germany." Following an itinerary determined by Goebbels, he criss-crossed the country, landing in smaller aerodromes, speaking in smaller venues. In all, he spoke in twenty-six towns in just over a week. The great prize was, of course, Prussia, where three fifths of the country's population lived and where a coalition of Social Democrats, Zentrum, and left-liberals had held power since the early years of the Republic. It was a bastion of pro-democracy forces, with an administration and police force second in size only to the Reich government.

Navigating the sociopolitical geography of German politics, Goebbels directed the party's campaign in Prussia against the ruling Social Democrats and targeted the blue-collar worker for special attention. An RPL memorandum of April 2 instructed the local chapters to do all they could to remove working-class mistrust of the NSDAP and "to interest the worker in us, to bring him into our rallies, to win him." To help with this task, the RPL bombarded local leaders with an almost ceaseless barrage of leaflets addressed explicitly to working-class voters, detailing Nazi positions on labor-oriented issues while ruthlessly assailing the parties of the Marxist left for their failures. In Bavaria, on the other hand, the party concentrated less on the working-class vote than on the Catholic electorate, and the local chapters were instructed to emphasize the NSDAP's defense of religious values against Weimar's cultural decadence, the shameless misuse of religion by the Zentrum, and the onslaught of godless Marxism. There the campaign theme was to be a "National Socialist Bavaria as a bulwark against centralization [from Berlin] and Godlessness."

On April 24 the NSDAP rolled to impressive victories all across the board. Despite the government's efforts to reduce the party's public presence, the NSDAP captured 36 percent of the vote in Prussia, 32 percent in Bavaria, 26 percent in Württemberg, and 31 percent in "red Hamburg." The results in Prussia were particularly striking. Since 1928 only six Nazis had sat in the state legislature; National Socialists now occupied

162 seats, becoming the largest delegation in the chamber. In May, the parade of Nazi triumphs continued. In Oldenburg the Nazis took a spectacular 48 percent of the vote, while in Hessen, traditionally a Social Democratic stronghold, the NSDAP captured 44 percent. The specter of a Nazi majority was in sight.

Confronted by this tidal wave of support for the NSDAP, Brüning found himself floundering in increasingly hostile seas. He was convinced that his unpopular economic initiatives were on the verge of bearing fruit, that signs of recovery would be evident by summer or early fall, and that Hitler's popularity would fade as that recovery took hold. He also hoped to score foreign policy victories in Lausanne, where he was pressing for a final end to reparations and war debts as well as greater arms equity at a League of Nations disarmament conference. It was imperative, even in the face of growing radicalism and continued economic suffering, to stay the course. But not only had his austerity program lost all credibility with the public, powerful economic interests were increasingly disenchanted with Brüning and his policies. His failure to make headway in dismantling Weimar's welfare state had alienated leaders of the business community, especially in heavy industry, and his plan, floated in May, to seize fatally indebted agrarian estates in the east, subdivide them into small farms, and resettle the country's unemployed there enraged powerful agrarian interests close to the Reich President. The chancellor's plan, in their view, amounted to nothing less than "agrarian Bolshevism."

Perhaps more important was Brüning's continuing failure to coax Hitler into some sort of positive relationship with the government. Brüning had tried on several occasions in 1931 and early 1932 to lure the Nazis into the cabinet, always as a junior partner, always subordinate to other coalition parties. It was crucial, he believed, to have Hitler sharing the burden of government responsibility rather than assaulting it from the outside. Brüning's inability to strike a deal with the Nazis was especially disappointing to the leadership of the Reichswehr. In the aftermath of the May state elections, General Schleicher, who had played a major role in maneuvering Brüning into power, came to the conclusion that the chancellor had outlived his usefulness. Schleicher clung to the illusion that it would be possible to enlist the Nazis in a coalition of right-wing forces that would enjoy the backing of business and agrarian leaders, the DNVP, the Reich

President, and, most importantly, the Reichswehr. Supremely confident of his own Machiavellian skills, he was convinced that the Nazis could be "tamed" and used to drum up popular support for a new authoritarian regime. Like many military leaders, Schleicher tended to dismiss Hitler's radical campaign rhetoric as mere demagoguery for the masses; he shared their view that Hitler was actually a restraining influence on the revolutionary hotheads in his party.

Based on a number of behind-the-scenes meetings with Hitler and Göring, Schleicher and other military leaders had come to the conclusion that the NSDAP and the Reichswehr shared a number of common interests. In those secret discussions Hitler was sweet reason itself, at pains to emphasize that the NSDAP was eager to cooperate with the Reichswehr. After all, both were determined to reshape the German state on an authoritarian basis and to smash the armaments clauses of the Versailles Treaty. Hitler advocated a rapid buildup of the German military, music to the ears of the High Command. Nazi extremism, Reichswehr leaders convinced themselves, was a reaction to the discriminatory treatment and outright persecution the party had suffered from the Republican authorities. With more careful and accommodating handling, Hitler and the Nazis could be put to productive use.

Schleicher began courting the Nazis before the spring regional elections, letting Hitler know by back channels that he had opposed the SA ban and believed Brüning's days were numbered. In May, as Brüning contemplated another emergency decree that would further reduce pensions and other benefits, Schleicher persuaded Hindenburg that the time had come to dismiss him. He convinced the Reich President that a new right-of-center cabinet could secure the support of both the DNVP and the Nazis, providing a parliamentary base of support for a rightward shift. On May 29, Hindenburg stunned the public by unceremoniously sacking the chancellor who only weeks before had helped secure his reelection as Reich President. Even more surprising was his installation of Franz von Papen, an obscure representative of the Zentrum in the Prussian legislature, in the Reich Chancellery. Hindenburg's choice, French ambassador André François-Poncet quipped, was met with scarcely concealed "incredulity." Everyone "smiled or tittered or laughed because Papen enjoyed the peculiarity of being taken seriously by neither his friends nor his enemies." He was also "regarded as superficial, mischief-making, deceitful, ambitious, vain, crafty, given to intrigue," observations that events would soon prove to be all too true.

Papen was a lively, dapper man, a Catholic aristocrat with charm and excellent social connections. He married the daughter of a wealthy Saar industrialist and enjoyed close ties to business leaders. Before entering politics, he had made a career in the military. During the war, he had served as military attaché in Mexico and Washington but was expelled from the United States in 1916 for attempting to sabotage American military shipments to Canada. Thereafter he served briefly as a battalion commander in France and then as a staff officer in Turkey. Following the war, he embarked on a political career as a member of the Zentrum and gravitated immediately to its far right wing. Despite being almost completely unknown, his aristocratic heritage, business connections, military background, and antidemocratic sentiments all recommended him to Schleicher, who referred to his creation condescendingly as Fränzchen, little Franz. He was the ideal front man to lead the authoritarian transformation of the German state Schleicher and the High Command envisioned.

Papen's was to be a government of national concentration, which would stand above parties. The cabinet, selected by Schleicher, was composed almost exclusively of conservative aristocrats without formal party affiliation. It contained no figure of national prominence, in either government or business, and commanded virtually no support in the Reichstag. No matter. It was a government that was never intended to rely on the support of the public or the parties, only on the favor of Hindenburg and his military entourage. Its opponents disdainfully christened it "the cabinet of barons." Virtually every parliamentary party, including Papen's own Zentrum, immediately denounced this new chancellor sprung on the country by Hindenburg and Schleicher. Only Hugenberg's DNVP and the tiny business-oriented DVP threw their meager support behind the Papen government, leaving it with an even smaller parliamentary base than its late and unlamented predecessor.

Key to the new cabinet's success was the attitude of the NSDAP. Schleicher believed that he had secured the cooperation, if not outright support, of the Nazis. In secret meetings in May he had struck a bargain with Hitler, or so he thought. In return for a Nazi pledge to refrain from attacking the new government, Papen would lift the ban on the SA and SS and call for new elections, two demands made by Hitler. It was to be a policy of toleration, a political truce that Schleicher hoped would evolve into close cooperation.

Lacking any sign of public support and demonstrating precious little interest in it, Papen openly courted business and industrial leaders. His government, he claimed, was "the last great chance" to save private enterprise and halt Germany's calamitous slide into state socialism. He indicated that tax credits for industry and a retreat from the binding nature of wage contracts, steps long sought by business, were on the way, and he promised a sharp reduction in government spending on social programs. As a sign of his determination to dismantle Weimar's welfare programs, he used his first emergency decree in June to announce substantial reductions in unemployment and health benefits, while suggesting that government spending in certain areas—transportation and housing construction, in particular—might stimulate economic activity in the private sector. These harsh measures outraged labor but found considerable resonance in the wary business community.

While sending encouraging signals to business, Papen also openly courted the political right, hoping to bind Hitler and conservative leader Hugenberg in one manner or another to his government. Following through on Schleicher's deal with Hitler, he lifted the ban on the SA and SS on June 16, despite strong objections from several state governments, and he used his emergency powers to dissolve the Reichstag and call for new elections to be held on July 31. Papen apparently hoped that new elections would further weaken the moderate center and left, while providing broad popular support for his authoritarian designs. "The system is collapsing," Goebbels gleefully confided to his diary. Papen might be chancellor for now, but the people were to be called to the polls once again. "Voting, voting! Out to the people. We're all very happy."

No sooner had the ban on the SA been lifted than a firestorm of political terrorism raged through the country. Storm Troopers surged back onto the streets, and violent clashes with the Red Front and Reichsbanner became everyday occurrences. In the last half of June, the police reported seventeen political murders, and during the run-up to the election on July 31, no fewer than eighty-six killings and literally hundreds of wounded were recorded. The dead and wounded were for the most part Nazis and Communists. "Berlin was in a state of civil war," wrote Christopher Isherwood, the English writer, who was living in the city that summer. "Hate exploded suddenly without warning, out of nowhere; at street corners, in restaurants, cinemas, dance halls, swimming baths; at midnight, after breakfast, in the middle of the afternoon. Knives were whipped out, blows were dealt with spiked rings, beer-mugs, chair legs or leaded clubs; bullets slashed the advertisements on the poster columns, rebounded from the iron roofs of latrines."

During seven days in mid-July, the carnage in the streets reached a murderous crescendo. On Sunday, July 17, some seven thousand Storm Troopers marched into the Communist stronghold of Altona, a working-class suburb of Hamburg, where they encountered thousands of heavily armed men of the Red Front. Stones were thrown; shots fired; a pitched battle raged through the narrow streets. When the police finally established order, eighteen people, many of them innocent bystanders, were dead and more than a hundred wounded. Despite all the mayhem and bloodshed Germany had endured since 1929, "Bloody Sunday" came as a shock.

On the day after the Altona riot, the Papen government issued an emergency decree that prohibited all outdoor rallies and marches. The measure had little effect. The fighting continued; the casualties mounted. Then, on July 20, claiming that the inability of the Prussian authorities to preserve public order forced him to act, Papen dismissed the Social Democratic government of Prussia and declared himself Reich commissar for Germany's largest state. It was nothing more than a thinly veiled coup d'état carried out against the last lingering stronghold of Weimar democracy.

Papen hoped that this bold—and illegal—move would establish his anti-Marxist credentials and allow him to present himself to the public as a strong law-and-order leader, and it did win praise in conservative, nationalist circles. But the parties of the moderate center and left were unalterably opposed to Papen and his action. Even the DNVP and DVP, while applauding the chancellor's "Prussian coup," were not enthusiastic about mounting a pro-Papen campaign. The Nazis remained true to their pledge to "tolerate" the Papen government, but toleration, they insisted, did not imply support. Although the Nazi campaign refrained from a direct assault on Papen, Goebbels, in a secret memorandum, warned the party's regional leaders that they "should refuse most strenuously to be associated with this cabinet." The Nazis heaped ridicule on the emergency decrees of the Papen government, but the primary target of the Nazi campaign was not Papen but "the bankrupt system parties," which were trying to divert attention from their own dismal history of failure by attacking the newly installed government. The Social Democrats and Communists were responsible for the "bloodbath in the streets," the Nazis insisted, and "the red civil war" raging over Germany was "the product of a Marxist-Jewish murder campaign." The chief goal of the campaign was therefore "to destroy the bourgeois splinters, to make inroads for the first time into the ranks of the Zentrum, and to drive the Marxists from power once and for all."

During the campaigns of 1932, the Nazis raised the already shrill pitch of negative campaigning into an entirely new register. Rather than emphasizing the party's radical *Weltanschauung* or the specifics of its own vague program, the Nazis chose to hammer away at Weimar democracy's political and economic failures. The existing "system" was a swindle, the Nazis howled, and the other parties were the puppets of special interests—especially big business and big labor. The mainstream parties—the liberals, the Conservatives, the Social Democrats—had sold out the farmer, the shopkeeper, and the worker to the corporate giants and corrupt union bosses. What had this democracy delivered but an unbroken string of economic disasters, social strife, and humiliating international oppression?

Hitler again took to the skies, carrying this message to fifty cities in the final fortnight of the campaign. His public appearances were carefully choreographed events. The RPL dispatched special instructions to the party authorities where Hitler was to speak, and an advance team checked the venue, musical selections, the parade route, security, and the roster of preliminary speakers—the warm-up acts for the main performance. Propaganda, the Nazis understood, was not about information; it was about emotions, it was about spectacle, about showmanship. Goebbels and his staff were particularly sensitive to the entertainment value of campaign events, especially Hitler's public appearances. They understood the marketing concept of branding—and the merchandising associated with it. At each stop on Hitler's speaking tour, they peddled photographs of Hitler, Goebbels, Strasser, and other top party leaders; they hawked swastika-crested pens, scarves, pendants, bookmarks, and copies of *Mein Kampf.*

Theirs was a politics of presentation, and certain tactical considerations were axiomatic: always rent a room too small—better to have spectators scrambling to get in, waiting outside, straining to hear, than to rent a large hall that might be only half full. Place loudspeakers outside so those unfortunates who couldn't manage a ticket could experience some of the excitement inside. Always provide warm-up acts—either local Nazi political leaders or a speaker from the party's official list—to work the crowd. The star attraction should always arrive late, allowing the anticipation to build to a fever pitch. In their staging, these Nazi productions resemble nothing in our current public life so much as a rock concert. The stagecraft, the timing, the theatricality was everything.

Even the daily confrontations and violence seemed scripted. Nazi campaign speeches were intended to provoke, and they did. At many campaign events, local Communists would appear, as if on cue, to sing Communist songs and hurl taunts at Nazi speakers. A brawl would erupt, windows would be smashed, heads broken. The fight would be discussed in the taverns and barbershops for days. Between 1930 and 1933 these clashes became virtual rituals, a drama with a discernible narrative arc, and everyone, from the Nazi speakers and Storm Troopers to the Communist Red Front, understood their roles. It was entertainment; it was spectacle. You didn't want to miss it.

Hitler and Goebbels understood that to an electorate grown cynical and angry, the details, the facts didn't matter. The public, they were convinced, did not want a nuanced discussion of the issues. The party certainly had detailed position papers on everything from fertilizer for farmers to foreign policy, but this was not what Nazi campaigns were selling. For those who bothered to examine the party's appeals, blatant contradictions abounded—the Nazis promised farmers higher prices for their livestock and produce while pledging lower food prices to city dwellers—and opposing parties never tired of pointing them out.

Nazi promises didn't add up, their exasperated opponents complained in frustration. The Nazis were promising everything to everybody, essentially asking people to believe that two and two equal five. Such criticism did not faze the Nazis in the least. They either ignored it or turned it on its head: that sort of whining and impotent criticism was what was wrong with German politics. The other parties—the liberals, the Conservatives, the Communists and Socialist Democrats—were paralyzed by pessimism. They could only wring their hands helplessly while the country sank deeper into chaos and despair. They understood only why things wouldn't work. But there are times, Hitler understood, when desperate, angry people *want* two and two to be five, and National Socialism would make it so. There would be a "triumph of the will" over ineffectual rationalism. In the toxic political atmosphere of Depression Germany, slurs, smears, innuendo, and character assassination became the norm as the level of political discourse plummeted. The truth, the facts, hardly mattered, only the successful spin.

In his countless speeches, Hitler offered no specific policy solutions to the country's crushing economic problems—that, too, was left to party journals and position papers, which few, either inside the party or in the general public, bothered to read. The RPL warned party speakers and local organizations not to worry about the specifics. "These things don't need to be discussed in propaganda," it explained. "Currency questions, autarky, and financial issues don't belong in rallies. They are technical problems to be handled by specialists." Party functionaries were instructed to confine themselves to the general campaign slogans and talking points developed at headquarters.

Hitler was most comfortable pounding away at one theme—the criminal failures of the ineffectual Weimar system, the perfidy of the parliamentary parties, and the determination of the National Socialists to destroy both. Intermingled with this negative assault was a positive message, a vision of an "awakened" National Socialist Germany that would liberate itself from international subjugation and unleash its own energies and talents that had been suppressed by class conflict, religious division, and parochial regional loyalties. Hitler and only Hitler could make Germany great again. This was Hitler's basic stump speech, delivered literally hundreds of times. It was a speech that combined lofty calls for national unity and common purpose with a wickedly sarcastic caricature of the current system that invariably drew appreciative applause and knowing laughter from the crowd. One did not need to be a

Nazi sympathizer or a committed Nazi to find this critique of Germany's political plight on target.

These themes were on vivid display in a brief speech Hitler delivered in Eberswalde in the last days of July—a speech important enough for Goebbels to film for national distribution. Having utterly failed the worker, the artisan, the shopkeeper, the farmer for the past thirteen years, the system parties, Hitler charged, did not care to talk about their past performance; they preferred instead to focus only on the past six weeks of the campaign and its violence. "They say: For these past six weeks the National Socialists are responsible." How this could be so, he didn't quite see—the National Socialists had not appointed Herr von Papen. Hindenburg and the parties that support him had done that. "But," moving to the punch line, "even if it were so, I would gladly take responsibility for the last six weeks, but the gentlemen should be so kind as to take responsibility for the past thirteen years. . . . For thirteen long years they have proven what they are capable of accomplishing: A nation destroyed economically, the farmers ruined, the middle class in misery, the finances in the Reich, the states, the towns in shambles,' everything bankrupt and millions unemployed. They can twist it any way they want to—*but for all this they are responsible.*" The line always brought storms of applause.

Did anyone really believe that a nation could achieve anything worthwhile, he continued, when its "political life is so mangled and mutilated as ours in Germany." He had just glanced at the ballot in Hessen-Nassau—"thirty-four parties," he exclaimed, his words dripping with sarcasm.

The workers their own party, and not just one, that would be too few, it had to be three, four; the middle class, which is so intelligent, must have even more parties; business interests their parties; the farmer his own particular party—also two, three; and the gentlemen homeowners must have their specific interests of a political and philosophical nature represented in a party; and naturally the gentlemen renters can't be left behind; and the Catholics a party and the Protestants a party, and the Bavarians a party and the Thuringians their own party and the Württembergers an extra special party, and so on and on. Thirty-four parties in one tiny state and that at a time when we are facing monumental challenges that can only be solved if the entire strength of the nation is pulled together. . . . I have set myself one goal, and that is to sweep these thirty-four parties out of Germany.

He closed with the usual rousing rhetorical flourish:

We don't want to be the representatives of one occupation, one class, one estate, one religion, or one region. No, we want to educate the German to understand that there can be no life without justice, and there can be no justice without power, and that there can be no power without strength and that that strength must reside in our own people.

Surprisingly underplayed in Hitler's campaign speeches in 1932 were the vicious anti-Semitic tirades of earlier years. Hitler was an ideological fanatic, and anti-Semitism was at the very core of National Socialist ideology, but he was also a cunning, cold-eyed political strategist. Selling Nazi ideology, he and his staff concluded, had attracted a small but intensely loyal hard core of supporters—the 3 to 6 percent of the electorate the party had received during the first decade of its obscure existence. But ideological appeals could not be expected to attract more.

While Hitler rarely spoke directly to the "Jewish question" during the campaigns of 1932, the party's anti-Semitism had hardly gone into total eclipse. It was always there, always in plain sight. Hitler might soar above the ugly, hate-fueled rhetoric when addressing large crowds of potentially undecided voters—after all, everyone presumably knew his views—but out on the campaign trail, the party's regional speakers railed against the pernicious influence of the Jews, and much of the graphic material produced by the RPL—the leaflets, pamphlets, and posters that blanketed the streets during the campaigns—portrayed the most repellent anti-Semitic stereotypes. Those images, some bordering on the pornographic, were a prominent feature of Julius Streicher's scurrilous *Der Stürmer* and found their way into the party's *Illustriert Beobachter* (*Illustrated Observer*), the NSDAP's contribution to the country's popular picture press.

For most Germans the most visible manifestation of National Socialism in their daily lives was the ubiquitous presence of the brown-shirted SA—Storm Troopers handing out leaflets, canvassing, marching in never-ending parades, collecting money for various National Socialist causes—and it was among the SA that the public encountered the most violent expressions of Nazi anti-Semitism. The pitched battles with the Communists and Social Democrats drew the most extensive coverage in the press, but the Storm Troopers also regularly harassed Jews on the streets and smashed up Jewish shops. SA battle songs spewed hatred against the Jews and issued appallingly bloodthirsty threats. "Sharpen the long knives on the pavement," one such song began, "let the knives plunge into the body of the Jew, blood must flow in streams, and we shit on the freedom of this Jew Republic."

Nor were the party's anti-Semitic pitches limited to lower-middle-class audiences, as is so often assumed, but appeared frequently in Nazi appeals to workers, where anti-Semitism could be interwoven with the party's anticapitalist rants. Aimed primarily at a working-class readership, *Der Angriff* was saturated with images of the Jew as "the wirepuller of international capital," and articles with headlines such as "Vote for Communism and Jewry," or "SPD—the Jewish Party," appeared with regularity. So relentless was *Der Angriff* in its attacks on Jews that the Prussian government banned the paper for a week in January for "holding the Jewish religion up to contempt."

Nazi strategists clearly believed that anti-Semitism was not enough to galvanize voters and propel the party into power. "People became anti-Semites because they became Nazis," one historian has argued, "not the other way around," and there is much truth to that. And yet, anti-Semitism had entered the bloodstream of German politics, and the fact that none of the other parties felt moved to challenge the Nazis for their brutish Jew baiting is in itself revealing. All the mainstream parties except the Conservatives, who sought to exploit it for their own ends, issued perfunctory condemnations of Nazi anti-Semitism and then moved on to more pressing problems. The Communists and Social Democrats were quick to dismiss anti-Semitism as shallow demaguery intended to divert attention from the reactionary nature of National Socialism, while the left-liberal DDP, the party of choice for many middle-class Jews, downplayed anti-Semitism as "a fire made of straw—it flames up brightly but quickly burns out." Left-liberals simply could not believe that it was an issue to be taken seriously. On a more unsettling note, they may also have calculated that in the end there were no votes to be gained by making it one.

On July 31, the NSDAP took 38.8 percent of the vote. The parties of mainstream center and right—the system parties so reviled by Hitler—suffered staggering losses, as their constituents defected to the NSDAP in droves. Together the liberal parties managed to win only 2 percent of the vote, the Conservatives a mere 5.9 percent, and the bevy of special-interest, regional, and single-issue parties saw their vote plummet to 3 percent. On the other side of the social divide, the Social Democrats sustained serious losses as well, falling from 24.5 percent in 1930 to 20.4 percent, while the Communist vote nudged upward from 13.1 to 14.3 percent. The NSDAP, a party that only four years before had been unable to attract even 3 percent of the electorate, had become Germany's largest political party. It was the most dramatic ascent in modern political history. The man with the funny mustache (it looked strange to Germans, too), thick Austrian accent, appalling grammar, and odd mannerisms, an unelectable outsider ridiculed by the national press and Berlin intelligentsia, stood improbably on the threshold of power.

Contemporary analysts, political opponents, and many subsequent historians were convinced that the apparently unstoppable surge of National Socialist support could be explained as a "revolt of the lower middle class," a movement of the undereducated, downwardly mobile, and economically marginal who deserted the traditional parties of the moderate center and right after 1928. Driven by economic despair and desperately afraid of "proletarianization," so the argument goes, the resentful and frightened "little men" of German society flocked to the NSDAP. It is true that the base of the Nazi support was to be found among the shopkeepers, small farmers, schoolteachers, and clerks of the embattled *Mittelstand*, but by 1932 the NSDAP was far from being a party of the lower middle class.

The Nazis always vehemently rejected such characterizations, claiming that National Socialism represented "a new political synthesis of seemingly antagonistic and contradictory currents." It was, they claimed, a *Volksbewegung*, a people's movement that stood above class, region, and religion, and as such a novelty in German political culture. The other parties scoffed. Virtually all the parties maintained that they were *Volksparteien*; virtually all invoked "the people's community" well before the NSDAP appropriated it. What was striking—and baffling—to contemporaries was the fact that the Nazis *actually attempted to translate that claim into political reality*, to mobilize support in every sector of German society, in every occupational group, in every demographic, in every region, and in both Protestant and Catholic populations. It mounted serious campaigns to recruit not only the small shopkeeper and farmer but the day laborer and steelworker as well, attacking both Marxist socialism and large-scale corporate capitalism in the process.

According to well-established traditions of German political culture, parties made little effort to cross social boundaries in mobilizing support. The parties of the left appealed to workers, the liberals and conservatives to elements of the middle class. This practice extended back into the Wilhelmine period but was greatly exacerbated by the Weimar electoral system. If a party secured 60,000 in one of the country's 35 electoral districts, it earned a seat in the Reichstag for every additional sixty thousand votes it received nationwide, securing its base—the operational imperative of all campaigning. If a party picked up votes here and there beyond that base, well and good, but securing the base was the key to its success. The parties of the middle class—the liberals and conservatives and the plethora of special interest parties—were, therefore, determined above all else to establish their credentials as stalwart defenders of middle-class interests against the threat of the Marxist left. Similarly, the Social Democrats and Communists competed fiercely for the blue-collar vote but made little effort to draw support from the fractious bourgeoisie. Only the Catholic Zentrum, whose appeal was based on religious affiliation, sought to straddle the great social divide of German politics, but almost exclusively within the Catholic community.

From the beginning, the NSDAP refused to follow in these well-worn grooves of German politics. The Nazis were charting a radically new course, pursuing a catchall strategy that aimed at capturing support from all across the social and cultural landscape. The result was considerable uncertainty as to the party's proper placement on the political spectrum—was it a party of the reactionary right, as the Communists and Social Democrats maintained, or, as the conservatives charged, a party of the socialist left? Even within the NSDAP's own ranks, local party officials occasionally expressed confusion about the social locus of the movement. "Are we a worker's party or a middle-class party?" one perplexed member of the Stuttgart NSDAP inquired of the leadership in 1923. The question might just as easily have been posed ten years later.

In pursuing this catch-all strategy, the Nazis had two major assets. Unlike the other parties, the NSDAP was neither associated with any clearly defined set of economic interests nor had it been saddled with government responsibility in the discredited Weimar state. It could not be held responsible for any failed policy or unpopular measure. The Communists, too, stood on the outside, free of the taint of participation in the discredited Weimar state, but while the KPD continued to confine its recruitment efforts to the working class, the Nazis cast their net wide. The NSDAP's unique appeal across the traditional social divides of German politics and its simultaneous insistence that it stood above special interests, that it was, in fact, a genuine people's party, carried a significant measure of plausibility to an increasingly desperate public. It also positioned the Nazis to assume the mantle of the bold outsider fighting the debilitating corruption and divisiveness of the system. They alone could give voice to the protest of the angry masses against the failed establishment. While the other parties talked, the NSDAP projected itself as a party of action, of dynamism and energy. The Nazis would get things done. And Hitler, the ultimate anti-establishment candidate, could posture as the unsullied idealist at war with the Berlin insiders, foreign oppressors, stock market swindlers, and the special interests, a role he played with consummate skill.

The NSDAP that emerged triumphant from the 1932 elections was far more than a party of angry *déclassés* and petit bourgeois misfits. Between 1929 and 1933 Hitler managed to attract a following of unprecedented demographic diversity, drawing support from elements of the affluent upper crust, the blue-collar labor force, and the lower middle class in both town and countryside. To the surprise of many, the party had done unexpectedly well in affluent, upper-middle-class neighborhoods and among civil servants of the upper ranks. Even more unprecedented, the NSDAP had found considerable support within the German working class, considered by many, both then and for decades afterward, to be immune to Nazi appeals. Although the Nazis proved unable to make dramatic inroads into the industrial strongholds of the SPD and KPD, they did succeed in attracting a substantial following among workers in handicrafts, small-scale manufacturing, and agriculture. These workers were usually employed in small plants, in government enterprises, or in the countryside, and were rarely integrated into the ranks of organized labor. It has been estimated that as much as 40 percent of the National Socialist vote by 1932 was drawn from these elements of the working class. Despite sustained efforts to court the Church and its flock (as an act of piety, the SA in many towns even marched to church—in uniform), the Nazis continued to have problems in Catholic areas. As the frustrated *Gauleiter* of Cologne-Aachen reported in March 1932, "the effectiveness of our work was hindered by the systematic counter activities of the Catholic clergy, who . . . proceeded to proclaim from the confessional box, from the pulpit, and in the press that Catholics could not work or vote for the National Socialists if they wished to receive the holy sacraments." The clergy continued to characterize National Socialism as a pagan, anti-religious, anti-church movement and in doing so, the *Gauleiter* complained, "has made the most unbelievable accusations." Still, in 1932 support for the party among Catholics was increasing but it was a work in progress.

From the earliest days of the party, the NSDAP had relentlessly projected an image of youthful dynamism, proclaiming itself "the party of young Germany." Its leaders, especially by German standards, were young: Goebbels was thirty-four; Himmler, thirty-two; Göring, thirty-nine; Röhm, forty-five; Hitler, forty-one; Gregor Strasser, forty; Rosenberg, thirty-nine; and 60 percent of the party's Reichstag deputies in 1930 were under forty—compared to the SPD's 10 percent. Its membership was also young. Of the 720,000 new members who joined the NSDAP between 1930 and 1933, 43 percent were between the ages of eighteen and thirty; another 27 percent were between thirty and forty. Between 1930 and 1932 the party made impressive gains in student elections in various German universities; the party also established a youth organization for boys ages sixteen to eighteen that would evolve into the Hitler Youth (*Hitlerjugend* or HJ) in 1932 and a similar organization for girls, the League of German Girls (*Bund deutscher Mädel* or BdM).

At the same time, the Nazis made a systematic, sustained, and surprisingly successful effort to attract older Germans to the cause, especially pensioners, widows, and veterans. Since 1930 the Nazis had remorselessly lambasted Brüning's austerity program, warning older voters that it would lead to a reduction of their health benefits and pensions—a claim given credibility by the government's first emergency decree in July 1930. In every regional and national campaign in 1932 they accused the Brüning and Papen governments of attempting to balance the budget by slashing the benefits of veterans, especially disabled veterans, and retirees. The deepest cuts came in Papen's emergency decree of June 14, and the Nazis loudly demanded a restoration of the funds. "With one stroke of the pen," the chancellor, operating by emergency decree, had "taken away the rights of pensioners," reducing their benefits to little more than "beggars' pennies." They fumed against the cold insensitivity of a system that would swindle society's most vulnerable, while giving tax breaks to the rich. Millions of ordinary Germans had "saved and paid for decades in order to have a secure retirement," only to be fleeced by a heartless government and the feckless middle-class parties that "no longer have either the strength or the will to help you." Only the NSDAP could save retirees and the disabled heroes of the Great War. The Nazis would not only preserve retirement and health benefits but increase payments and services. The strategy paid off. In 1932 the "party of youth" drew considerable support from fearful older Germans trying to stay afloat.

Even women, who had been the most reluctant demographic to embrace the Nazis, were turning to the party in ever-increasing numbers. In July 1931 the party created its own national women's organization, the National Socialist Women's League (*Nationalsozialistische Frauenschaft* (NS-F). The NS-F, as its first declaration of principles stated, stood for "a German women's spirit which is rooted in God, nature, family, nation, and homeland." Although it tended to be underfunded and encountered some resistance from regional party leaders, the NSDAP lavished increasing attention on its new women's organization, especially during the campaigns of 1932. The party sought to mobilize middle-class women with appeals that pledged the NSDAP's support for the traditional religious and cultural values of *Kinder, Kirche, und Küche*. In addressing working women, the party attacked Weimar's "sham liberation" of women, which had merely exposed them to shameless exploitation by greedy capitalists and deprived them of their most cherished role, that of wife and mother. National Socialism would restore the honor of women, who, safe in their domestic sphere, would play a central role in the creation of the Third Reich. The Nazis, as one historian has cogently put it, were offering women emancipation from emancipation. "The woman judges things primarily with the heart," a Nazi women's leader asserted. "For her it is not logical and purely reasoned considerations that are decisive but the intuitive recognition of the moral and spiritual worth of a person or an idea. . . . At the same time the woman wants to be instructed and lifted up, whether by the spoken or written word."

These efforts were not without effect. Although women still tended to favor parties with a strong religious orientation and remained underrepresented in the party's membership, the NSDAP made enormous strides with women voters after 1930, especially in 1932. In those areas where votes were tabulated by sex, women for the first time outnumbered men in the Nazi constituency in Protestant areas but still lagged behind in Catholic districts. Fighting off charges of misogyny, the Nazis discovered that women, no less than men, were disillusioned with the failures of the system and were searching for alternatives.

By the summer of 1932 the NSDAP could claim, with some credibility, that it was what it always claimed to be—a genuine people's party. Although the hard core of its following was composed overwhelmingly of elements of the lower middle class, what made the party such a powerful political force was its ability in a period of severe economic and political crisis to reach far beyond this limited reservoir of support and mobilize protest voters from a surprisingly broad range of social and demographic groups. Germany had seen nothing like it.

But there was a problem lurking behind the party's spectacular election numbers. As a catchall party of protest, its surprisingly diverse following was a highly unstable political compound. Goebbels recognized that the millions who had flocked to the NSDAP were not drawn to the cause by a commitment to National Socialist ideology, to the "idea." What held the party's uniquely heterogeneous following together was the conviction that the political system in Germany was broken, its institutions hopelessly dysfunctional, and its mainstream parties ineffective, fatally contaminated by participation in the hapless government at one time or another. As Weimar's most relentlessly militant and uncompromised critic, the NSDAP skillfully mobilized that sense of protest in each of the elections of the Depression era. Why not let Hitler have a go, many people felt. Maybe the Nazis could shake things up, make things work. Anyway, how could they be worse than those who had wielded power and gotten Germany into this abysmal situation?

Manipulating this deep-seated anger and anxiety had served the party well in the short term, but maintaining a firm grip on a socially diverse mass constituency held together less by a commitment to Nazi ideology than by protest and vague, often contradictory promises of dramatic "change" would grow increasingly problematic if the party did not actually come to power—and soon. Nazi leaders understood the potential perils of the party's position. As Goebbels noted in his diary in the full afterglow of the party's greatest triumph, "Now we must come to power and annihilate Marxism. One way or the other. Something has to happen. The time for talk is over. Now action!"

THE NAZIS HIT A WALL

In the heady days of late summer, Hitler seemed to stand on the threshold of power. All parliamentary logic dictated that as leader of the largest party in the Reichstag, he would be summoned to form a government. Within the party's rank and file anticipation of the long-awaited "seizure of power" skyrocketed. The Storm Troopers were straining at the leash, poised for action. Many units had been given specific orders for actions to be taken, radio stations, courthouses, municipal buildings to be seized, once Hitler's appointment was announced. The party's political functionaries were almost giddy with expectation. At last, after years of struggle, power was virtually within their grasp.

And yet, beneath the chest-thumping headlines of the *Völkischer Beobachter* there flowed an undercurrent of palpable nervousness. The party had won almost 38 percent of the vote and had become the largest party in Germany. Its thirteen million votes more than doubled its 1930 totals, and 230 Nazi brown-shirted deputies would march into the Reichstag when it convened—more than the Communists and Social Democrats combined. But expectations had soared so unrealistically high that many in the party felt an undeniable twinge of disappointment. They had managed to convince themselves that the party might actually capture an absolute majority, something no German party had ever achieved, and impressive as the party's thirteen million votes appeared, it had barely moved the needle from the NSDAP's showing in the last round of presidential elections. The party had picked up only 300,000 more votes than in April—"a tiny trifle," Goebbels mused. And the Marxists had made gains, climbing ahead of the Nazis in Berlin. Could it be that the Nazi juggernaut had finally hit a wall, that the party had reached the outer limits of its mass appeal? Some within the hierarchy, especially Strasser, thought so; Papen and Schleicher hoped so. A vulnerable Hitler, they thought, might prove more amenable to compromise in the coming negotiations.

Hitler spent the first days of August at his mountain retreat on the Obersalzberg, awaiting events, consulting with his inner circle, plotting strategy. Messengers came and went. Rumors of intrigues circulated. A call from Berlin, from the office of the Reich President, was expected at any moment. "High expectations filled the air," Goebbels wrote, "the whole party is ready to take power. The SA are leaving their work places to prepare for this. Our political leaders are making ready for the great hour. If things go well, everything will be all right. If they do not," Goebbels worried, "it will be a terrible setback."

Hitler was determined to accept nothing less than the chancellorship of a presidential government, armed with emergency decree power, free from the troublesome inconveniences of parliamentary politics. He would also demand the installation of a National Socialist as minister president of Prussia, as minister of the interior (and hence the police) in both the Reich and in Prussia, the minister of justice (and hence the courts), agriculture, aviation, and the creation of a new Ministry of "People's Education." He pondered possible candidates to fill those posts; went over plans for the assumption of power. He would insist on an "enabling act" (*Ermächtigungsgesetz*) to govern without interference from the Reichstag. "Once we attain power," Goebbels wrote prophetically in his diary, "we will never give it up until our dead bodies are carried from office."

Strasser had grave doubts about this course of action. Nothing more could be done with propaganda and mass mobilization. The party had finally exhausted its electoral potential, he feared, and the time had come to consider entering into a coalition government. Hitler should be open to entering a cabinet, even as vice chancellor. Taking a hard line about the chancellorship was a serious mistake. Hitler's "all or nothing" strategy would drive the party into a ditch. If the NSDAP, having reached the limits of its electoral potential, remained in fruitless opposition, it would lose credibility, not only with the rank and file but with the millions who had voted Nazi expecting some immediate impact on the government. His was a minority view. Phone calls and emissaries from Berlin brought almost hourly news and rumors. The Catholic Zentrum had taken soundings about the possibility of a Nazi-Zentrum coalition, which would command a majority in the Reichstag. Strasser was interested in the possibilities of such an arrangement, but Hitler was skeptical, and suspicions in both parties proved insurmountable. Trust was everywhere thin on the ground. Hitler, it was understood, would demand the chancellorship "with full governmental powers," and Hindenburg, it was also understood, was staunchly opposed to such an appointment. Undeterred, Papen and Schleicher, now minister of defense in the cabinet, were both eager to entice Hitler into the government, hoping that he could be persuaded to serve as vice chancellor in a reconstituted Papen cabinet.

Events moved quickly. On August 6, Schleicher invited Hitler to meet with him at an army installation just north of Berlin, and the general appeared receptive to Hitler's demands for the chancellorship, but warned that there might be trouble with the Reich President. Indeed, there was. When Schleicher raised the possibility with Hindenburg a few days later, the Old One dismissed it out of hand. Still smarting from the bitter presidential campaigns of the spring, Hindenburg declared that his decision was unalterable. On August 10, Papen tried his hand with the Reich President, raising the possibility of a Hitler chancellorship, perhaps presiding over a National Socialist–Zentrum majority in the Reichstag. Hindenburg wouldn't hear of it. He would never make that loathsome "Bohemian corporal" chancellor of the Reich.

Feverish negotiations continued. The streets of the government quarter teemed with expectant crowds. The Berlin papers fairly sizzled with speculation about different combinations. A decision would be made soon. Meanwhile, the Berlin SA was making preparations for a Nazi takeover of the city. "The SA is gathering around Berlin," Goebbels noted. "It makes the gentlemen nervous," and "that," he smirked, "is the purpose of the exercise."

Acting as Hitler's emissary, Röhm met with Schleicher and Papen on August 12. Opposition to a Hitler chancellorship, Röhm reported to Hitler, appeared to be hardening, and Hindenburg would make a decision very soon. It was time for the Führer and his entourage to come to Berlin. Before the day was out, a long caravan of black automobiles departed the Obersalzberg for the capital. Some party leaders raced on ahead by train, but Hitler preferred the lengthy trip by car. Arriving in the dead of night, he chose to stay at Goebbels's country house outside the city at Caputh, a lakeside village where, among other luminaries, Albert Einstein owned a vacation home. "The Führer is facing some tough decisions," Goebbels wrote that night, as he watched Hitler pace the terrace of the villa. "Without full power he cannot master the situation. If he doesn't receive full power, he must refuse the offer." But if he did refuse, there "would be a mighty depression in the movement and in the electorate." After all, the party had "only this one iron in the fire."

Hitler understood the high-stakes game he was playing. On the one hand, entering a Papen cabinet would certainly alienate the radicals within the party, especially within the impatient SA, whose Storm Troopers were ready for action against both the Marxists *and* the reactionaries. On the other hand, by refusing to enter a coalition government, Hitler risked undermining his credibility with the party's newly expanded electorate. Many, in fact most of the party's voters on July 31, Goebbels realized, were not staunch National Socialists drawn to the party by ideological conviction but protest voters fed up with the paralyzed "Weimar system." They expected change, rapid change. Would they understand?

Despite Strasser's insistent warnings about a failure to enter a coalition government, Hitler never seriously considered that alternative. If he agreed to join the cabinet as vice chancellor, he would be a diminished figure, binding himself to precisely the reactionary "Cabinet of Barons" he had campaigned so vigorously against. The "Führer mystique" he had carefully nurtured would be shattered, and he would be exploited by Papen, Schleicher, and the reactionaries he detested. He would be isolated in the cabinet and reduced to the role of "drummer," winning mass support for a government that without him had as good as none. It was a role he was not going to play. "Hitler under Papen," Goebbels sniffed: "a grotesque absurdity."

On the morning of the 13th, Hitler, accompanied by Göring and Röhm, met first with Schleicher and then with Papen. Both conveyed the same message. They were determined to set aside the Weimar constitution and install an authoritarian government, and they wanted his help. But for now, a Hitler chancellorship was out of the question. Hindenburg was utterly opposed. Papen hinted that if Hitler entered the cabinet now, his moment would come, and soon. He even suggested that after sweeping away the remnants of the failed Republic and establishing an authoritarian regime, he would cede the chancellorship to Hitler. It could be a matter of months, perhaps even weeks. But Hitler's cooperation now was essential. He should prove his willingness to work together, to demonstrate a sense of political responsibility by serving the conservative cabinet. Hindenburg's opposition to a Hitler chancellorship might then be overcome. Hitler flatly refused, and the sometimes heated interview came to a close.

In the afternoon, a frustrated and angry Hitler was summoned for an audience with the Reich President. He was reluctant to go since he had heard from emissaries that Hindenburg had already decided to pass over him. Papen would remain chancellor. But Hindenburg wanted to discuss the matter with Hitler one last time. Maybe Hitler could be convinced to serve in the existing government or at least to cooperate with Papen. Or perhaps Hitler, with his mighty oratorical skills and personal magnetism, might persuade the old *Feldmarschall* to overcome his reservations and appoint a National Socialist government after all.

At the meeting in the Presidential Palace Hindenburg made no headway. Serving in the Papen government was out of the question, Hitler replied, and renewed his demand for the "leadership of the state to its full extent." On this, Hindenburg simply could not be moved. He could not answer "before God, his conscience, and the Fatherland," he told Hitler, "if he handed over the entire power of the government to a single party, and one which was so intolerant towards others with different views." He feared that "a presidential cabinet headed by you would inevitably develop into a party dictatorship . . . something that he could never reconcile with his oath and his conscience."

Hitler left the meeting enraged. The whole affair had been a setup, arranged by Papen to humiliate him, to put him in his place. "The notion of the Führer as Vice-Chancellor of a bourgeois cabinet is too grotesque to be taken seriously," Goebbels scoffed after Hitler's return from the meeting. The party, after its sensational electoral victory, would now be thrown back into opposition. That night Hitler and Röhm briefed disappointed SA leaders on the state of affairs, hoping to defuse a potentially explosive situation. Their task, Goebbels recorded, would be a difficult one. "Who knows if . . . [the SA] units will be able to hold together.

Nothing is harder than to tell troops already sure of victory that this victory has come to naught." They had good reason to be nervous.

While this debate occupied Hitler and the leadership during the late summer and early autumn, the monthly activity reports flowing in from the NSDAP's regional propaganda operatives left little doubt about the impact of Hitler's decision on the party's grassroots appeal. In its monthly situation report for August, the RPL soberly acknowledged that Hitler's refusal to enter the cabinet had generated considerable problems within the party's membership and electorate and predicted serious difficulties for the NSDAP in any upcoming campaign. The prevailing mood "could be expressed with the words: 'This time I voted for Hitler and again nothing has happened. Next time I won't vote.'" The message from the party's grassroots propaganda apparatus was both unmistakable and unsettling.

Another, more immediate and equally vexing problem confronted Hitler in the aftermath of the July election. If many middle-class voters were disappointed with his refusal to enter the government, impatient party militants, especially within the SA, were frustrated that the "march order" for action had not been given. They were ready to storm the battlements of the moribund Republic, and they could not understand why the leadership had backed away from a violent confrontation.

During the July campaign the brutal wave of political terror that had swept Germany since 1928 had crashed with unparalleled fury, and the violence did not stop with the conclusion of the campaign. In the first week of August, while Hitler and the leadership consulted and negotiated, frustrated SA units, bitterly disappointed by the party's failure to seize power, unleashed a ferocious terror campaign all across East Prussia and Silesia. The wave of bombings, shootings, and arson began on August 1 in Königsberg. Acting on their own initiative, groups of SA men, convinced that only revolutionary action could now thrust the NSDAP into power, went on a binge of political violence that terrorized an entire city. Within hours, the terror spread beyond the East Prussian capital, engulfing the entire province. On August 2, Silesia also erupted in violence as SA units, acting for the most part on orders from their regional and district leaders, went on a rampage against union halls, consumer cooperatives, department stores, newspaper offices, banks, and even a police station. Their targets were not only Social Democrats and Communists but citizens prominently associated with the Catholic Zentrum as well as liberals and conservatives. SA thugs assaulted Jews, Poles, and others identified as enemies of the party, raising the already high level of political violence to unparalleled heights. On August 9, the Reich government finally took action. Papen issued two emergency decrees to deal with the escalating political violence, stiffening penalties for terrorist actions and creating special courts to try cases arising from the new decrees. Convictions for political murder were now punishable by death, and, Papen made clear, the special courts would act swiftly.

Although dozens of people were killed or wounded in the first ten days of August, one particularly vicious episode caught the attention of the public throughout Germany. In the small Silesian village of Potempa, a band of drunken SA men broke into the home of an unemployed Polish worker with Communist leanings and bludgeoned him to death while his family looked on in horror. The Potempa murder was given wide national coverage, especially since the trial of the SA assailants was the first to be conducted under the new anti-terrorism act. The evidence was overwhelming, and the Nazi defendants were convicted in short order. On August 22, five received death sentences. With the nation's attention riveted on the trial, Hitler, in a move that shocked many even on the usually sympathetic conservative right, sent a public telegram to the condemned men, deploring "this most monstrous blood verdict" and expressing his solidarity with them. "From this moment onward," he wrote, "your freedom is a question of our honor; the struggle against a regime under which this was possible is our duty."

In an interview just days after the verdict, Hitler continued to claim that the violent actions of the SA were justifiable acts of self-defense and revenge for comrades murdered by the left. "The number of terrorist acts by the Marxist parties against our movement is in the tens upon tens of thousands. The number of dead is over three hundred, the number of our wounded in the past year was over six thousand, and in this year, in seven and a half months, already over 8,200. . . . We will not be talked out of a right to self-defense with such stupid phrases as 'law and order.'" A week later he gave an ominous preview of law under a National Socialist regime. "I refuse to comprehend how five National Socialists can be sent to the guillotine for the sake of a Polish insurgent who once fought against our German brothers in Silesia." For Hitler and the National Socialist movement, "whoever struggles and lives, fights and, if it has to be, dies for Germany has every right, and anyone who turns against Germany has no rights at all."

Hitler's defiant support of the Potempa killers and, in fact, the entire SA rampage in the east was a vivid reflection of his deep unease about SA loyalty in the late summer of 1932. It also highlighted a growing dilemma for the party. To a remarkable extent the authorities and the conservative press, while deploring these breaches of public order, tended to accept Nazi claims that leftist radicals were responsible for the bloodshed and mayhem. But the SA rampage in the east included vicious attacks on conservatives, on moderates, even on the police. Middle-class Germans who had previously seen the Nazis as defenders of law and order found this spasm of violence and the party's support for it difficult to accept. The Nazis had always trod a fine line between "roughness and respectability," successfully portraying their battles with the left as roughness in defense of respectability, suggesting that the NSDAP alone could restore public order and that the only obstacle to its restoration was a truculent and aggressive left. In the summer of 1932, the Nazis stumbled off that line.

The Potempa case marked the climax of the SA's campaign of violence, but SA resentment continued to simmer into the early fall. Morale in many SA units was low, and rumors of defections to the Communists and other radical formations had begun to circulate. So worried about SA reliability was Hitler that he ordered an inquiry to determine the mood of the Storm Troopers, and in September Röhm dispatched a questionnaire to SA units all over the country. The responses, which arrived at the party's Munich headquarters late in the month, were anything but reassuring.

Disaffection with the party's policy of "legality" and its emphasis on electoral campaigning had grown steadily within the SA during this "year of elections" and by late summer had become a serious problem. "The mass of SA [men] don't fully understand the repeated postponements of [decisive action]," one unit in Hessen-Darmstadt reported. "They are pressing for the attack. To them, an open fight is preferable to this incessant voting, which in the final analysis leads to nothing, or at least to very little." From Hanover, SA leaders explained that "the activist SA man doesn't understand why [we don't] move against Hindenburg and Papen with all our might." An SA leader in Baden put it most bluntly: "We, the SA don't talk, we act. The Third Reich will not come through the babble of the political speakers and leaders but through the fists of the SA. We'll clean house after November 6. The elections have no value."

The mounting resentment voiced by so many Storm Troopers had been exacerbated by the fact that plans with specific timetables and objectives had been set for SA "actions" to be taken after each election in 1932. SA units had been on alarm status, ready to take "military action" to ensure the promised Nazi seizure of power. In each instance, these operations had been canceled, and the result was a growing exasperation within the SA.

Adding to the sense of desperation expressed by many SA men was their dismal economic situation. Many SA units were in desperate financial shape and were increasingly unable to provide aid to their often destitute members. These SA men, many of whom were unemployed, laid great hopes on a Nazi seizure of power to provide an immediate solution to their economic problems. This mounting economic pressure, some SA leaders were convinced, greatly aggravated their exasperation at the repeated postponements of the long-anticipated "march orders." As an SA commander in Schleswig-Holstein warned in September, "the material and spiritual misery is so great with many SA men that they can no longer hold out." The situation was critical. "The lofty political expectations of the recent past on the one hand and the economic despair, even hunger, on the other," an SA leader from Baden urgently implored, "demand an act of deliverance."

Although the intensity of these complaints was troubling to the political leadership, their substance hardly came as a surprise. Dissatisfaction with the lack of financial support from the party, with efforts of party leaders to subordinate the SA to their needs, and with the party's emphasis on electoral campaigning had long been a source of friction. SA men and their leaders cherished their identity as "soldiers of the Third Reich," military men belonging to an elite, uniformed party organization that stood outside the hierarchy, with special military tasks. But the party's political leadership, and especially Goebbels and his propaganda staff, insisted that the Storm Troopers were "political soldiers," important instruments to be employed in the party's critical grassroots agitation. With their marches, parades, canvassing, and, not least, their violent confrontations with the left, the Brown Shirts were indispensable in the party's campaign activities.

Some SA leaders tried to support the party's efforts to change the organization's self-image, but tensions between the party and the SA lingered, and the September morale reports were punctuated with complaints about party leaders who exceeded their authority, interfered in SA matters, or did not understand the special mission of the SA. In language usually reserved for the "bosses" of the Marxist left, some SA commanders continued to complain bitterly about local party leaders, dismissing them as "arrogant little political bureaucrats" and "paper pushers." Party officials at all levels expressed mounting concern that the restless Storm Troopers were becoming sullen and unruly.

Aggravating these problems was the introduction in 1932 of uniforms for the NSDAP's political functionaries. Much of the SA's sense of elitism, of superiority over the other elements of the NSDAP, was bound up in its conception of its unique role as the uniformed branch of the party. To discover that all party officials were now entitled to wear uniforms was a harsh blow to SA self-esteem and yet another diminution of its status by the party. The September morale reports burned with the acid contempt with which the new uniforms were greeted by the SA rank and file. "The SA man does not recognize these National Socialists stuck in brown shirts and bursting with overflowing badges and braids," the Dessau SA indignantly reported. "The magnificent preening of the political functionaries has provoked the indignation of the SA," the Upper Bavaria SA acknowledged. "The SA man who proudly wears his plain brown shirt, which until now has been the robe of honor of the active fighter, cannot understand how the brown shirt can be debased in this way."

For all these troubles, the NSDAP *was* the largest party in Germany, its leader, along with Hindenburg, the most recognizable political figure in the country, and a functioning government without Nazi participation or at least toleration was impossible. The Papen government had few supporters within the Reichstag before July 31; it had fewer now. Worse still, two parties that were determined to destroy the embattled Republic now held a majority in the Reichstag. Adding insult to injury, Hermann Göring, as representative of the largest party, assumed the position of president of the Reichstag.

In this impossible situation, Papen was determined to dissolve the Reichstag before a vote of no confidence could be taken, rule by emergency decree, and postpone new elections indefinitely, although elections within sixty days of a dissolution were required by law. This plan was brought to naught by a dramatic turn of events in the Reichstag itself. As soon as Göring gaveled the first working session to order on September 12, the Communists called for a vote of no confidence in the government. Papen had not even delivered his opening remarks. In a raucous scene, never before witnessed in the Reichstag chamber, Göring simply ignored parliamentary procedure and the outraged protests of the chancellor, who stood furiously waving his opening address, and allowed the vote to proceed. Göring's action was a blatant violation of the parliamentary practice, which stipulated that the session was not officially convened until the sitting chancellor had spoken. In the tumult, few seemed to care. The result was not only a humiliating defeat for Papen—544 deputies voted against his government; only 42 deputies from the DNVP and DVP stood by him—but one more nail in the coffin of German democracy. The cabinet could not produce a parliamentary majority, and the Reichstag had been dissolved before it had even been officially convened. Already convulsed by economic calamity, social ferment, and political terrorism, parliamentary government in Germany had been reduced to farce. Who could take such a circus seriously? How could such an impotent, dysfunctional system solve Germany's glaring problems? In this chaotic atmosphere, with no realistic parliamentary solution in sight, Hindenburg finally called for new elections. The date was fixed for November 6. It would be the fourth national campaign of the year.

Although the party's treasury was greatly depleted and the organization near exhaustion, the RPL geared up once again for a national campaign. "Down with the Reaction! Power to Hitler!" was to be the party's central theme for the new campaign. In the summer election, the Nazis had targeted the parties of the left, emphasizing their defense of the middle class against the ravages of Marxism; in the fall campaign the Nazis would train their fire on Papen and his reactionary government. "Papen is already finished," Goebbels wrote to regional leaders in October. "A feeling of utter panic about Papen must be awakened in the broad masses, a feeling so strong that Papen and his cabinet will be completely discredited and can no longer be seen as a bulwark by the wavering middle class."

As usual, the NSDAP waged an aggressive, often violent campaign, blasting the Marxist left but also unleashing a ferocious assault on "Papen's reactionary gentlemen's club." With the liberal and special interest parties virtually eliminated as serious political competitors, the battle for the middle-class vote would be waged between Hugenberg's DNVP and the NSDAP, so the Nazis were at pains to maintain their anti-Marxist credentials. At the same time, the party's campaign strained to portray National Socialism as a dedicated enemy of the Reaction and a stalwart champion of the German worker. As the campaign progressed, Nazi attacks on Papen and the special interests behind him became so steeped in the language of class struggle that they might have been spoken by the Communists. At one point, Hitler, acting through his deputy Rudolf Hess, intervened, cautioning against the "class warfare tendencies" in the party's propaganda and ordering the RPL to tone down its rhetoric against those forces associated with the traditional right. After all, many of the voters who cast ballots for the NSDAP in July were presumably crossovers from the conservative right, and it would hardly do to alienate them.

Goebbels was also convinced that in July the party had allowed its radical anti-Semitism to slide too much into the background. As the party prepared for yet another national election, he issued a secret directive to the party's propaganda operatives, ordering that "In the coming campaign, the Jewish question must be pushed more than before into the foreground. Again and again we must make it clear to broad masses that Papen is praised by the Jewish press, that his economic program comes from the Jew [banker] Jakob Goldschmidt, that his cabinet is supported by Jewish money interests. There is only one salvation from this Jewish peril in Germany and that is Hitler and the NSDAP."

Goebbels did make a halfhearted attempt to tamp down the party's offensive against the right, but the blistering attacks on the reactionary nature of the Papen government did not subside. At the same time, the NSDAP was determined to burnish its "socialist" image. Under the watchword "Work and Bread," its appeals to workers stressed the party's support for full employment, the right to work, and other measures to cast off the crushing burden of joblessness. Winning working-class votes was essential, Goebbels stressed, but these efforts had to be done in a way that would not frighten away middle-class voters. It was a balancing act that not even the RPL could manage.

The party's pronounced "swing to the left," as its conservative opponents repeatedly described it, reached a dramatic crescendo during the final week of the campaign, when Goebbels, acting on his own, decided to throw Nazi support behind a wildcat strike of the Berlin transportation workers— a strike with high national visibility and one vigorously championed by the Communists. For days the public witnessed the spectacle of Nazis and Communists working side by side, as buses, trams, and subways staggered to a halt, paralyzing the capital. Coming as it did in the very first days of November, Nazi support for the strikers was a calculated gamble, drawing heightened attention to Nazi "socialism" at a critical stage of the campaign.

Goebbels certainly understood the risk, but felt it was one worth taking. "The entire press is furious with us and calls it 'Bolshevism,' but as a matter of fact we had no alternative. If we had held ourselves aloof from this strike . . . our position among the working classes, so far firm, would have been shaken." The strike offered "a great opportunity . . . to demonstrate to the public . . . that the line we have taken up in politics is dictated by a true sympathy with the people." Many in "bourgeois circles" would no doubt be "frightened off by our participation in the strike. But that's not decisive. These circles can later be very easily won back. But if we'd have once lost the workers, they'd have been lost forever."

Despite Goebbels's effort to rouse the troops, the party faced daunting challenges. After months of intense, almost constant campaigning symptoms of strain had begun to surface. The party treasury was virtually empty, and complaints about the lack of money poured into party headquarters. Four major campaigns in nine months had left the party's organization on the brink of exhaustion. An RPL memorandum to the regional leadership in October expressed concern about flagging energy in the midst of an important political campaign and urged district leaders to press on with the expected vigor. The RPL complained that "the entire movement must display more activity. . . . From now on the National Socialist press must concentrate entirely on the election. . . . Every article and essay must close with conclusion that Adolf Hitler is the only salvation and that one must therefore vote NSDAP."

Hitler once again undertook a *Deutschlandflug*—his fourth of the year—but the novelty had clearly faded. Crowds were smaller, empty seats sprinkled the once-packed auditoriums even as his schedule, as before, was frantic. Although Hitler tried to focus the public's attention on the failures of Papen, "a chancellor without a people," and his government—the controversy surrounding his August 13 decision not to join the government simply would not go away. It hounded him throughout the campaign. In cities large and small, in hamlets and country villages, he was repeatedly forced to address the issue. His basic stump speech, which by November his audience could repeat almost verbatim, offered up the same explanation. "What you want to hear from me," he began, typically, at a campaign stop in Breslau, "is the answer to a single question, the question that has been directed at me in past weeks from countless newspapers, countless politicians, elected representatives, and speakers: 'Why,' say these bourgeois politicians and their newspapers, 'Herr Hitler, did you not climb aboard the train? It was your big chance; why did you say no and reject the offer?'"

The answer was, of course, always the same. "Why would I climb aboard when I knew full well that I would soon have to get off, since I could not support the actions of the reactionaries who drove the train." Anyway, it was better to besiege the castle from the outside, than to be a prisoner inside. He was not a bourgeois politician, who joins first this coalition and then that, bargaining for ministerial posts here and there. He could not compromise his principles or weaken his unshakable commitment to the "Idea"; he could not play the parliamentary game. National Socialism was a *Weltanschauung*, a movement of ideological conviction, not ready to abandon its fundamental values, its mission, for momentary advantage. He was not afraid of assuming government responsibility, as Papen and the reactionaries had charged. He was ready and able to take the reins of power in hand. And, he invariably concluded, "If we do one day achieve power, we will hold on to it, so help us God. We will not allow them to take it away from us again." By election day, Hitler had delivered a variant of this speech no fewer than forty-five times.

The Nazi press hailed Hitler's campaign swing through the country as a victory tour with huge crowds shouting their support, straining for a view of the Führer. But behind these blustering headlines, party leaders were anxious. From the very outset of the campaign there were disquieting signs that the party's propaganda machine, after months of operating at full throttle, was at last beginning to sputter. Reports from all across the country made clear that the party's regional and local organizations were deeply in debt from the year's campaigns and that even loyal party activists were distressed at the prospect of yet another major effort. Goebbels's orders to regional propaganda leaders were punctuated by increasingly insistent demands for greater energy and enthusiasm. Implicitly acknowledging a morale problem within the ranks, the RPL's directives during the final weeks of the campaign repeatedly emphasized the need to convince voters that "public opinion has undergone a powerful shift in favor of the NSDAP," and that after an admittedly sluggish start, the party's campaign was at last gathering "the old momentum."

For all the brave talk about renewed energy in the last days of the campaign, the party leadership was privately preparing itself for a setback. Both Hitler and Goebbels thought the party would almost certainly lose some votes, but Strasser was far more pessimistic. He feared that Hitler's "all or nothing" strategy had led the party into a dead end, and that Hitler's refusal to enter the government in August was a missed opportunity that would come back to haunt the party. "It will not be too serious a matter even if we do lose a few million votes," Goebbels gamely rationalized in his diary, "for what actually counts is not the outcome of this or that particular contest, but which party has the last battalion to throw into the fray." Three days later, with the election at hand, the possibility of a disappointing outcome was still on his mind.

On election night, Goebbels listened to the returns with a mounting sense of foreboding. "The results are not as bad as the pessimists had feared," he wrote in the whistling-past-the-graveyard tone that characterized his last diary entries before November 6, "but it still leaves a disgusting taste in one's mouth to hear it over the radio. Every new announcement brings word of another defeat." The results were, in fact, every bit as bad as Strasser and the pessimists had predicted. Less than four months after the party's greatest triumph, the Nazis suffered a stunning defeat, losing more than two million votes and seeing their share of the national total tumble to 33 percent. The NSDAP would still be the largest party in the new Reichstag, if that body ever convened, but for the first time since the party had begun its astounding ascent in the fall of 1929, it had absorbed a serious setback, puncturing its aura of invincibility and casting doubt on its promises of an inevitable—and imminent—seizure of power. There was no way around it: "We have suffered a blow," Goebbels conceded forlornly.

Goebbels's first reaction was to blame the party's failure to enter the government on Hitler's August 13 decision and to claim that voters, especially middle-class voters, simply had not understood the party's support for the Berlin strike. If only there had been more time to make the party's position clear. Hitler's refusal to enter the government in August was also a major contributing factor to the party's decline. "August 13 accounts for it," he decided. "The masses . . . have as yet not quite grasped the significance of the events of that day." But that, as Goebbels realized, was hardly a sufficient explanation for the debacle. He wanted to hear from the party's grassroots organizations, and he turned immediately to his national propaganda network for answers. Local propaganda leaders throughout the country were called upon to submit reports to their regional chiefs, who would evaluate their views and send a summary report to the RPL. There the regional reports were carefully analyzed and their important findings presented in a top secret document, a morale report, which was completed later in November and circulated among only the very highest leadership of the NSDAP. So sensitive was that document that only Hitler, Strasser, Hess, party treasurer Franz Xavier Schwarz, and party business manager Philipp Bouhler received a copy. Though struggling to accentuate the positive, the report was profoundly unsettling.

Turning first to the questions of turnout and organizational fatigue, the RPL maintained rather philosophically that the public, exhausted by months of political campaigning, had not turned away from the NSDAP alone but was disillusioned with the entire system of party politics. Growing public apathy had been clearly signaled by consistently low attendance at Nazi events through the fall, especially in the rural areas where the party had previously found an enthusiastic audience. In addition to election fatigue, the continued deterioration of the economy, the report went on, meant that the willingness of the public to make financial sacrifices for political causes had contracted sharply, and the ability of the local chapters to mount their usual propaganda operations had been severely impaired. The party treasury was running on empty, and because of the desperate financial situation, the NSDAP had nothing to spare for the regional organizations. In fact, the locals were expected to make contributions to the party treasury in Munich. This had forced them to scale back their rallies and leaflet campaigns and to concentrate instead on less costly forms of propaganda—man-to-man canvassing, the display of flags, stickers, party badges, etc. In many cases they were reduced to "chalk campaigns," scrawling slogans on walls, and *Sprechchöre*—call-and-response political choruses chanted by party activists on street corners and public squares. Many impoverished local groups complained that the party's opponents, especially the SPD and DNVP, were able to spend more and run better campaigns—a disheartening reversal of roles since the spring and summer.

Above all Goebbels wanted to know which voters had deserted the party or merely stayed at home November 6—and why? The party's grassroots organizations provided an unequivocal answer to those questions. With startling candor, the RPL concluded that "the decline in our votes can in many ways be attributed to the fact that Hitler did not enter the government. Many quite simply have no understanding of our explanation." The middle-class voter, in particular, had been led by his "neutral press" to believe "Hitler had to enter the Papen cabinet after August 13, and no campaign slogan could disabuse him of that notion." The local chapters were unanimous in their conviction that middle-class voters were slipping away, and there was little to suggest that the party had been able to compensate for that loss by tapping into a reservoir of blue-collar support. Whether in the form of direct crossovers to the DNVP or DVP or in the form of no-shows, the NSDAP had suffered a massive hemorrhage of middle-class voters on November 6, and this had serious implications for Nazi strategy. The party's unorthodox catchall strategy and its negative campaigning had proven remarkably successful after 1928 as anti-system anger boiled over and the traditional parties appeared both compromised and weak. But by the fall of 1932, after a year of relentless campaigning and intense public scrutiny, the difficulties of sustaining this anti-system, catchall strategy were becoming increasingly apparent to the NSDAP's leadership.

"In previous campaigns," the RPL explained with its usual cynicism, "appeals to the nationalist heart were enough to win the middle-class masses, and the socialist tendencies of the NSDAP could step into the background." During the fall campaign that strategy had proven impossible. Since the party's unstinting attacks on Papen and the Reaction were coupled with appeals to working-class Germans—appeals that often seemed indistinguishable from those of the Communists—the NSDAP confronted a serious dilemma. "National Socialism," the RPL admitted, "found itself forced into an unequivocal stand against the 'national reaction,' rejecting compromises and placing itself—especially in the strike question—on the side of the German workers fighting for their rights." A situation had been allowed to develop "in which we could not avoid doing things that the middle class will never understand . . . and a defection of the bourgeois masses had to follow."

Papen and the conservatives sought to capitalize on the NSDAP's dilemma, and in the aftermath of November 6 the Nazi leadership was convinced that they had succeeded only too well. Surveying the damage, the RPL concluded that the party's aggressive efforts to win workers for the party had alienated important elements of the middle class. Reports from the party's grass roots indicated that rural voters—since 1928 the mainstay of the party's constantly expanding electorate—were shocked by the party's apparent cooperation with the Communists in the Berlin strike, and in many cases simply refused to come to the polls as a consequence. This emerging schism between committed National Socialists and "fickle" one- or two-time supporters formed the leitmotif in the regional reports. A memorandum drafted by the Nazi county leader of Heilsberg in East Prussia offered a glimpse of the widespread bitterness toward such defectors. With a tone suffused simultaneously with aggression and anxiety, he claimed that those fair-weather bourgeois defectors "who recognized in time that they did after all belong to the gentlemen's club or smelled a profit there for their egotistical souls, may wish to help the Reaction shield Jewish liberal capitalism from the deadly thrust our movement will deliver."

In the face of this criticism, Goebbels doggedly insisted that the party had, in fact, made significant inroads into the working class, but his claims resounded with the hollow ring of forced optimism. Confronted by the mounting difficulties of maintaining a firm grip on the party's socially diverse electorate and the unmistakable erosion of the party's middle-class base, the RPL strongly implied that the moment for hard sociopolitical choices was at hand. Although the report did not advocate discarding the NSDAP's revolutionary catchall strategy, it did endorse a propaganda more sharply focused on the working class. The outcome of the election had revealed that "the worker, once converted and embraced by National Socialist organization, is a thousand times more dependable than the middle class with its nationalist traditions." The RPL acknowledged that "the largely unionized blue-collar labor force still approaches the NSDAP with a certain mistrust," but strongly urged that efforts to win working-class voters continue. "In future propaganda, tactical concessions to the middle classes at the expense of the working class must cease."

This plea for a shift in the social emphasis of Nazi propaganda was doubly significant. It clearly indicated a conviction that the NSDAP had reached the outer limits of its appeal to middle-class Germans and that even *maintaining* the party's broad-based support within the *Mittelstand* at anything like the levels of the spring and summer was at best problematic. On the other hand, an intensified effort to win greater working-class support could only exacerbate the NSDAP's problems within its volatile middle-class base, while hurtling the party into a more direct and doubtfully successful competition with the Social Democrats and Communists. After all, the two leftist parties together had won more votes than the Nazis in November. Equally distressing, the Nazis had not been particularly successful in mobilizing support among the unemployed, the vast majority of whom were workers and who on the whole seemed far more inclined to gravitate to the radical left than to the National Socialists.

As the implications of the election began to sink in, the spirits of the party plummeted. "Everywhere," Goebbels wrote, "we find trouble, conflicts, and dissension." Especially disturbing were reports of SA refusals to cooperate with local Nazi political leaders in the conduct of the campaign. The RPL reported that "approximately 60 percent of the party districts were dissatisfied with the SA's propaganda efforts during the fall campaign." Several districts even attributed a major share of the responsibility for the loss of voters in their region to the Storm Troopers.

While some districts registered disappointment with this mood of uncooperative resentment, other regional officials complained that vulgar, violent, and generally unruly behavior by the Brown Shirts had cost the party dearly at the polls. Understandably, such complaints were loudest in the east, where SA violence had been rampant since August and where relations between local Nazi political leaders and SA units had deteriorated dangerously. Party officials in Lower Silesia claimed that "a great segment of the electorate was deeply offended by the rowdy behavior of the SA, who have become a genuine pestilence in the land following the elections of 31 July." In Central Silesia, Nazi political functionaries stated that "if we had more SA men who knew how to behave like decent people on the street," the party's propaganda operations could be conducted effectively. "It must be made clear to the SS and SA that they are parts of a political movement and as such must cooperate instead of striking out on their own often misguided ways."

This image of an unruly horde of violent freebooters ran through the regional reports, almost all of which demanded tighter control over and greater political training for the SA. The Storm Troopers had gotten out of hand and something had to be done. "The SA man should not only be a soldier in the military sense but a political soldier as well," the propaganda leader of Upper Silesia complained. He should "view himself as the representative of the National Socialist *Weltanschauung* and always conduct himself . . . in a manner consistent with this ideology." The Storm Trooper, however, "creates the impression of mercenaries who have joined the NSDAP out of love of adventure . . . rather than out of ideological conviction."

Nazi propaganda officials at all levels had ample reason for wanting to shift the responsibility for the party's November slide to the SA, but it was painfully obvious to all that the NSDAP was confronting a very serious internal crisis at the close of 1932. It is indicative of the magnitude of that conflict that at a meeting of the Nazi leadership in Munich on November 8, SA leaders reportedly responded to charges of undermining the campaign effort by lashing out at Hitler's policy of legality, claiming that it, not the SA, was losing support for the NSDAP. "The people are no longer satisfied with Hitler's decisions," they were quoted as saying. "It doesn't work to keep on merely talking about continuing the parliamentary and propaganda struggle. That will lead the party to ruin, as the last elections have shown. . . . The people urgently demand a revolutionary act." What was clear to Nazi propaganda operatives at all levels was that the party had failed to convert the legions of protest voters who had, for a variety of reasons, been attracted to the NSDAP since 1930. Some might be convinced to cast a protest vote once, twice, three times, or maybe even more, but the longer the party campaigned without being able to deliver on its promise to change the discredited system, the less likely it would be to maintain the credibility of its protest appeal. This problem was particularly dangerous to the NSDAP, since, as Goebbels understood, these millions of protest voters were not committed ideologically to National Socialism, and in November it appeared that it was to a large extent these volatile, uncommitted voters who had either defected or simply stayed home.

The propaganda leader of Hanover–South Braunschweig, in reporting on the provincial election, echoed the RPL's criticism of Hitler's strategy. Hundreds of thousands of former Nazi supporters, the RPL believed, "had registered their disapproval" by simply refusing to vote at all. Much of this election fatigue could undoubtedly be attributed to simple exhaustion after a year of nonstop campaigning. By November, funding, enthusiasm, and endurance were running low in all the Weimar parties, but for the NSDAP, as a party of protest that counted on voter anger, the growing public apathy was particularly ominous. The longer the NSDAP was forced to campaign without being able to deliver on its promises, the less convincing its image of irrepressible dynamism and power was bound to become and the less appealing its fanatical and yet fruitless anti-system stance would appear. As the year wore on, with four national elections and regional campaigns in almost every German state, Nazi propaganda strategists became increasingly aware of this problem. Goebbels had noted in his diary as early as April, when the NSDAP's political star was still on the rise, that "we have to come to power in the near future or we will win ourselves to death in these elections." The party's window of opportunity was small, and its ability to sustain its protest-oriented appeal over time was tenuous at best.

By the close of 1932 party leaders realized that the NSDAP had reached the limits of its middle-class appeal, and any serious attempt to broaden the party's base by more aggressive efforts to recruit working-class voters ran the very substantial risk of alienating the NSDAP's essential middle-class base. The impact of the party's radical quasi-socialist rhetoric and, more directly, its support for the Berlin transportation strike seemed to have demonstrated precisely that. On the other hand, if the party were now forced to fall back on a more traditional class-based strategy, the NSDAP would be admitting the end of its electoral expansion and would forfeit its cherished claim to be a genuine *Volkspartei*.

The RPL acknowledged this when it concluded that although the party had suffered serious losses in November, "the results proved that the hard core of the party remained unshaken and [had] by no means wavered." Even

though stated very confidently, this conclusion had to be extremely sobering to Nazi strategists. If the party were unable to sustain its mass protest
appeal and were once again reduced to its lower-middle-class base, it would
be forced inexorably back to the periphery of German political life.

While the NSDAP was attempting to cope with these dilemmas, the
Papen cabinet, with no parliamentary majority in sight, resigned on November 17, and in a reprise of the August negotiations, a new round of
discussions among Papen, Schleicher, Hindenburg, and Hitler took place.
Far from being chastened by the November defeat, Hitler continued to
insist on the chancellorship and full power in a presidential government,
while Papen and Schleicher renewed their efforts to coax the Nazis into a
coalition of right-wing forces. Hitler met twice with the Reich President,
and although the latter man appealed to Hitler's patriotism to "meet me
half way," Hitler could not be moved.

Hindenburg's tone in these meetings had softened—even addressing
Hitler as a fellow soldier, a comrade-in-arms of the Great War—but his
unwillingness to appoint Hitler chancellor had not. Hindenburg informed
Hitler that he could not justify "handing presidential power over to the
leader of a party that has never renounced its claim to absolute power"
and that he feared that "a presidential cabinet headed by you would necessarily develop into a party dictatorship with all the consequences this
implies." After one of his frustrating encounters with Hitler in the Presidential Palace, a scornful Hindenburg turned to his advisor Otto Meissner
and asked if it was true that the Nazi leader had been a housepainter in
Munich before the war. It wasn't, but without waiting for an answer, he
remarked, "One can't put a house painter in Bismarck's chair."

As Hindenburg groped for a solution to this impasse, Papen approached
him with a bold plan. It called for the Reich President to dissolve the
Reichstag and declare a state of emergency. Although according to Article
25 of the Weimar constitution, elections were to take place no later than
sixty days after a dissolution of the Reichstag, Papen now insisted that
Hindenburg postpone elections indefinitely—a clear breach of the constitution. Papen would then rule by emergency decree, effecting the transition
from stalemated Republic to authoritarian regime.

Although sympathetic to Papen's goals, Hindenburg had deep reservations about such a course of action. He was not comfortable with such

a blatant violation of the constitution, especially since the responsibility for such a move would rest squarely on him. Some members of Papen's cabinet shared his reluctance, fearing that the chancellor's plan would provoke a civil war, with both the Communists and Nazis rising against the government. Among those opposed to Papen's strategy was his patron and minister of defense, Kurt von Schleicher. Although he had engineered Papen's remarkable elevation to the chancellorship in June, he had grown increasingly irritated at Papen's tendency to act independently, ignoring Schleicher's advice. He, too, was convinced that a continuation of the massively unpopular Papen government would lead to serious unrest. It was time to make a change. At a meeting of the cabinet on December 2, Schleicher spoke out against Papen's plan and produced an army study showing that the military, with its hundred thousand troops, would be no match for the paramilitary forces of both radical parties. Civil war would be the inevitable result, and the outcome would be very much in doubt.

Schleicher's study, with its military imprimatur, made a strong impression on Hindenburg. Although he was quite fond of Papen, who treated him and his son Oskar with feudal obeisance and had become a close family friend, he had to act. With great reluctance, he asked for Papen's resignation, and on December 3 turned to Schleicher to form a new government. The Reichstag, which had still not convened, was not consulted. Now a career military man with even less parliamentary backing than Papen was chancellor of the German Republic.

A virtual unknown to the public, Schleicher now stepped boldly from the shadows into the spotlight. He announced his intention of forming a government that would stand above parties, which was fortunate since he commanded, if possible, even less popular support than his predecessor. His government's economic policy, he asserted, would transcend both capitalism and socialism, though just what this meant no one, perhaps not even the general, really understood. Schleicher was not burdened by Papen's reactionary reputation (he favored, for example, a jobs creation program that Papen had opposed), and he had unorthodox ideas about forging a broad coalition that would bring together elements of the labor unions, the agrarian associations, and disaffected National Socialists. Such a government, he believed, would enjoy the support of the army and industrial interests. Schleicher liked to be called "the social general," but most would have agreed with Leon Trotsky's famous description that he was "a question mark in the epaulettes of a general."

Feeling that a sobered Hitler might be more tractable in defeat, Schleicher renewed efforts to win his support, holding out the prospect of important cabinet positions in his government, but Hitler was in no mood for compromise. His strategy since the heady days of summer had been "all or nothing," and even now he was not prepared to deviate from that hard-line stance. Schleicher opened secret negotiations with Strasser, though those talks soon became public news, and offered him the post of vice chancellor. He hinted that other National Socialists might also assume important cabinet posts. He hoped that Strasser, who commanded a strong following with the NSDAP, could bring a large contingent of Nazi Reichstag deputies into the fold. Schleicher also labored under the illusion that the more reasonable Nazis under Strasser might join with the Zentrum, the DNVP, DVP, and, most improbably, the Social Democrats to form a viable basis for the new government. Failing that, he held out the hope that an offer of important positions in the cabinet would finally tempt Hitler into joining forces with the new Reich government.

Strasser *was* tempted. His disaffection with Hitler had been building since the aftermath of the July 31 election. Strasser was one of the few inside the party who dared to question Hitler's decisions, and his disapproval of "the chief's" refusal to enter a coalition government in August was an open secret within the party hierarchy. Strasser was a deeply committed National Socialist, and he had worked tirelessly to build up the party's imposing national organization. His differences with Hitler were tactical, not ideological, and he believed that he was negotiating with Schleicher in good faith as a true National Socialist.

His approach to politics was more pragmatic than Hitler's, more oriented toward administrative structures, details, planning. Hitler was famously uninterested in the party's organization except as an instrument for propaganda and campaigning. Despite the November setback and his unsuccessful negotiations with Hindenburg, Hitler was still confident that more intensive propaganda and "fanatical" campaigning would ultimately sweep the party into power. That moment, Strasser believed, had passed, and Hitler's obstinate refusal to enter a coalition government was a disastrous mistake.

He was also painfully aware that he was being marginalized in strategy decisions, shouldered aside by his rivals Goebbels, Göring, and Röhm, all of whom scrambled over one another to win the ear of the Führer—a dynamic that would only grow worse once the party was in power. It was a symptom of his fading influence in the Führer's inner circle that Hitler had unceremoniously renounced Strasser's ideas for an emergency economic program at the outset of the fall campaign, and by November Strasser had lost all patience with Hitler and the circle of sycophants who surrounded him. To one fellow Nazi, he complained that "Hindenburg, a man of honor . . . honestly and decently offers him [Hitler] a place in the government, and there stands the delusional Lohengrin-Hitler with his darkly menacing boys." The future for the party looked bleak. Göring was "a brutal egotist who cares nothing for Germany as long as he gets something [for himself]"; Goebbels was "a limping devil and basically two-faced," while Röhm was "a pig." These were the toadies who now surrounded the Führer, slavishly encouraging him as he led the party into inevitable decline. The situation, he lamented, was a disaster.

Matters came to a head on December 5. In a turbulent session at the Kaiserhof, Strasser pleaded with Hitler to accept Schleicher's offer. He pointed out that before the election the National Socialists in the Reichstag might have formed a majority with the Zentrum, but now this possibility had ended. The votes were no longer there. Given Hindenburg's resistance, the chancellorship would have to wait, but it wasn't too late to make a deal that would put Hitler and the NSDAP into a position of power. Hitler, encouraged by Goebbels, rejected any such compromise.

Two days later, Strasser made one last personal appeal to Hitler. Meeting again at the Kaiserhof, the conversation quickly degenerated into mutual recrimination and charges of betrayal. Hitler accused Strasser of treason, of attempting to destroy the party from within and rob him of the chancellorship. Strasser held his ground. "Herr Hitler, I am no more a traitor than any other willing messenger," Strasser responded. "My plan is to prevent a further deterioration of the party, not to bring it about." The meeting ended with an enraged Strasser storming out, slamming the door behind him in disgust.

While this crisis within the leadership mounted, the bad electoral news just kept coming. In a series of local elections in Saxony, Bremen, and Lübeck in late November and Thuringia in early December, the NSDAP suffered catastrophic losses. "The situation in the Reich is disastrous," Goebbels dolefully noted in early December: "In Thuringia . . . we have a loss of nearly 40 percent since July 31." The campaign had been lethargic, the old verve absent. "This defeat is very unwelcome at the present moment," Goebbels admitted. "In the future there must be no election in which we lose a single vote."

Then, on December 8, a bombshell. With the party reeling from the setback in Thuringia, Strasser shocked the party and the country by publicly announcing his resignation from all his posts in the party leadership and declaring his intention to withdraw from politics. In a letter delivered to Hitler's suite in the Kaiserhof around noon, Strasser reiterated his conviction that the Führer's unbending stand against entering the cabinet had led the party into a cul-de-sac of futile opposition. With the flood tide of National Socialist victories now clearly ebbing, Hitler's stubborn refusal to enter the government in both August and November had been a strategic blunder for which the party was now paying dearly. Thanks to Hitler's intransigence, the NSDAP was no closer to power than it had been in January, and now the bottom was falling out. The great task of the age, his letter read, was "the creation of a great broad front of constructive people and their integration into the new-styled state." In a rebuke to Hitler, he went on: "The single-minded hope that chaos will produce the party's hour of destiny is, I believe, erroneous, dangerous, and not in the interests of Germany as a whole." He closed by insisting that "as I refuse under all circumstances to become the focal point of oppositional endeavors or conflict of such kind, I am leaving Berlin today and subsequently leaving Germany for a considerable period." The next morning he departed Berlin for a vacation in Italy.

The national press exploded with jubilant speculation. "The Jewish papers can hardly hide their satisfaction at Strasser's step," Goebbels grumbled. "The Führer and the party are given up by all. 'Hitler's star has faded,' is the refrain of Jewish elation. One is almost ashamed to meet acquaintances in the street, and would like to hide one's diminished head. . . . Everywhere the rats flee from the sinking ship," he wrote in a tangle of mixed metaphors. "Among them are the grave robbers . . . who come to take part in the execution of the will. Wild rumors are afloat. Strasser's defection is the talk of the day. He has a good Jewish press and deserves it, too."

Coming on the heels of the party's disastrous electoral performance, Strasser's resignation confronted Hitler with a very real possibility that the party would disintegrate, splintering into competing factions. And for the first time, his nerve seemed to desert him. He hurriedly gathered party leaders and pleaded for their support; he convened a meeting of the Nazi Reichstag delegation to explain the situation and reassure them that he was in control. To Goebbels, he was not so confident. "If the party falls apart," he told his startled propaganda chief, "I'll finish myself off with a pistol within three minutes."

"It is high time we attained power," Goebbels noted forlornly, "although for the moment there is not the slightest chance of it." He found it difficult to be upbeat. "Deep depression reigns in the organization," Goebbels wrote in early December. "We are all very downhearted, above all because the danger now exists that the entire party will fall apart and all our work will have been done for nothing."

Compounding these problems, the party's financial situation was little short of catastrophic. Membership dues, subscriptions to party publications, and paid attendance at Nazi events had dropped precipitously, and contributions from backers in the business community, always exaggerated both then and subsequently, had virtually evaporated. Even the firm that printed the *Völkischer Beobachter* threatened several times in November and December to stop printing unless the party paid up. So deeply in debt was the party that wages to party employees were cut, and National Socialist Reichstag deputies were even ordered to forgo the customary Christmas tips to porters. SA men, who only weeks before had been planning to take the government by storm, could now be seen on Berlin street corners collecting money from passersby. They stood, Konrad Heiden observed with satisfaction, "in their thin shirts, shivering with the cold . . . rattling their tin collection cups and crying lamentably: 'Give something to the wicked Nazis!'"

Only six months after reaching the very threshold of power, the NSDAP was poised on the cusp of decline and disintegration. In evaluating the party's options, the RPL concluded that the cluster of strategic dilemmas facing the NSDAP could not be resolved in the context of a free and competitive parliamentary system. After an ascent of unparalleled swiftness, the Nazis had reached the limits of their popular support and now faced almost certain decline. The policy of legality, of mass mobilization for electoral campaigning, had failed. Only a National Socialist seizure of power could ensure the survival of the party as a mass phenomenon. Quoting from a local propaganda leader whose views it obviously endorsed, the RPL concluded its postmortem of the November election with the stunning conclusion that "On the basis of numerous contacts with our supporters, we are of the opinion that little can be salvaged by way of propaganda. . . . New paths must be taken. Nothing more is to be accomplished with words, placards, and leaflets. Now we must act!"

But above all else, the RPL asserted with uncommon frankness, "it must not come to another election. The results could not be imagined." It was a sobering admission for the party's proud propaganda operatives but one that accurately gauged the NSDAP's grim electoral prospects. There was still hope, the RPL concluded, "if Adolf Hitler succeeds in bringing about a political transformation in Germany and appears before the German people as a man of action." In December 1932 that prospect seemed remote indeed.

As "the year of elections" drew to a close, the great expectations of the spring and summer had dissolved. Hitler remained as far from the Reich Chancellery as ever, and none of the fundamental strategic dilemmas that had plagued the party in the fall had been resolved. The party's narrow window of opportunity seemed to have been wedged firmly shut. Local elections in November and December had confirmed the verdict of the Reichstag campaign. It was becoming increasingly obvious that the disappointing results of the November election had not been a fluke but marked the onset of an undeniable trend. The volatile Nazi constituency was fragmenting; the party's treasury was empty; and the Storm Troopers were fed up with the endless campaigns and impatient for action. Strasser's resignation and the fear that he might lead a revolt within the ranks merely deepened the shadows that hung over the party and cast a lengthening pall over its future.

Reflecting back over the triumphs and travails of the past year, Goebbels could muster little optimism for the future. "The year 1932 was an endless run of bad luck," he mused in late December. "Outside the peace of Christmas reigns in the streets. I am at home alone, pondering over my life. The past was sad, and the future looks dark and gloomy; all prospects and hopes have completely failed."

THE IMPOSSIBLE HAPPENS

By the close of 1932, Hitler's road to power seemed blocked. Nazi popular appeal was waning, its catchall strategy had run aground; its organization was demoralized, its militants disillusioned. The Storm Troopers were once again at the point of revolt, and the party was deeply in debt. Hitler, virtually everyone agreed, had missed his chance. Now he was wandering in the wilderness, his run at power stalled. "The mighty National Socialist assault on the democratic state," the liberal *Frankfurter Zeitung* declared in its New Year's Day edition, "has been repulsed." The threat of National Socialism seemed to have passed.

But the situation of the Weimar government had hardly improved since Schleicher had become chancellor in December. The Reichstag, the centerpiece of Weimar's democratic system, had been rendered irrelevant, stymied by almost three years of political polarization and rule by emergency decree. Of the Weimar parties, only the SPD and the Zentrum remained staunch defenders of the democratic constitution and its institutions. Although bitter enemies, together the Nazis and Communists held a majority in the Reichstag and were determined to destroy it. The liberal parties, long in decline, had receded almost to the vanishing point. The moderate center of German politics had dissolved; the margins had become the mainstream. With the political system mired in hopeless paralysis, real power devolved onto a small group of insiders from Germany's agrarian, industrial, and military elites. They, not the dispirited parties or the disillusioned public, would decide Germany's destiny.

That fate would be sealed during four intense weeks in January 1933, enacted in a drama played out almost entirely behind the scenes. Occasionally the curtain would lift for a brief moment, offering tantalizing glimpses of the high-stakes drama that was unfolding offstage, but little more. Many—politicians, pundits, diplomats, and journalists—speculated about the possible twists of plot, but few anticipated the fantastic resolution. By the end of the month, the last act of Weimar's tragedy had been played, and when the house lights went up, Germans were startled to discover that the impossible had happened.

Between 1928 and January 1933, German politics had been driven by large-scale economic and political developments—the Great Depression, mass unemployment, political polarization, institutional paralysis, and a rising tide of violence and chaos. Those wrenching macro-level forces had provided the context and catalyst for the rise of the Nazis and had delivered Hitler to the very threshold of power, but they could not push him across. January 1933 would change all that. It was a month of intrigue, of plots and subplots, more suited to the conspiratorial intricacies of a Renaissance court than the age of mass politics. Ironically it was not Hitler, the presumed protagonist of the piece, who drove the action forward—Hitler played a supporting and surprisingly secondary role—but former chancellor Franz von Papen and a handful of other powerful players whose connivances propelled events. Their motives and ambitions differed, but they shared one overriding and ultimately fatal illusion: all believed that Adolf Hitler and the NSDAP could be "tamed" and used for their political purposes.

Through much of December and into January Schleicher made overtures to the socialist labor unions, to the SPD, the Christian trade unions, the DNVP, and to the National Socialists. He hoped to fashion a broad base of support stretching from the right wing of the SPD and labor unions to the Conservatives and the Nazis. He was convinced that he would succeed where Papen had failed and would lure the more reasonable elements of the NSDAP into some sort of cooperation. Just the threat of that, he thought, might be enough to prompt Hitler into support for a right-wing government.

In an effort to win support from labor, Schleicher repealed Papen's immensely unpopular emergency decree that had allowed employers to reduce wages below levels set by collective bargaining agreements, and he voided Papen's decree that mandated a means test for unemployment compensation. Whereas Papen had attempted to stimulate the economy by giving tax breaks and other incentives to business, Schleicher favored a stimulus package to jump-start the economy and proposed a major public works bill that he hoped would make an immediate dent in Germany's still-astronomical unemployment. Although the unions looked favorably upon these moves, it was not enough to overcome their deep reservations about the "red general," as Schleicher was sometimes called. In the end, none of these moves met with success. The labor unions distrusted the former general, and the Social Democrats wanted no part of him or his government. The irascible Hugenberg kept his distance, and Hitler, even with his diminished stature, remained intractable. These pro-labor initiatives did, however, succeed in unsettling many in the business community, who interpreted them as populist pandering and yet another example of the profligate government spending that had crippled the German economy. Papen, with his unvarnished pro-business stance, remained the option of choice for the country's industrial and financial elites.

In a move more damaging than his troubles with business, Schleicher also incurred the wrath of the powerful agrarian lobby. The Reich Agricultural League (*Reichslandbund*), dominated by large eastern landowners, turned with a fury on Schleicher for his refusal to raise tariffs on agricultural imports, a step, the chancellor correctly believed, that would be vigorously opposed by labor and by consumers. Exacerbating his problems, Schleicher also exhumed Brüning's ill-fated plan to resettle the unemployed on bankrupt agrarian estates in the east, reviving near-hysterical charges of "agrarian Bolshevism." Hindenburg, who was proud of his Junker heritage and his status as an estate owner, came under heavy pressure from his friends and turned that pressure on Schleicher. Overstepping the bounds of his constitutional authority, he intervened directly in the dispute and insisted that Schleicher resolve these difficulties immediately.

While Schleicher struggled with these problems, his troubles were greatly exacerbated by a scandal that erupted in mid-January over alleged improprieties in the Eastern Aid (*Osthilfe*) program. A Reichstag oversight committee claimed that some East Elbian landowners had misused the funds to take luxury vacation trips to the south of France, to purchase expensive automobiles, and indulge in other extravagances. Some of the implicated landowners were friends of the Reich President, and in the course of the hearings it came to light that Hindenburg's ancestral estate, bought for him in 1928 by industrialist friends, had been registered in his son's name to avoid inheritance taxes. The Agricultural League was furious that the Schleicher government had let the inquiry go forward, and Hindenburg was incensed that Schleicher had allowed his name to be connected with the scandal.

For all his vaunted political skills, Schleicher found himself increasingly isolated. Without allies in industry, agriculture, or labor he was more than ever dependent on the favor of the Reich President, and to his dismay his relations with Hindenburg had deteriorated perceptibly. Whereas Papen had shown virtually feudal deference to Hindenburg and his son Oskar, Schleicher's conduct, his imperious manner and overconfident presumption of Hindenburg's support, grated on the Old Gentleman. The *Osthilfe* scandal didn't help.

Above all, Hindenburg resented Schleicher pushing him to dismiss Papen in December. Despite Papen's utter lack of popular support, Hindenburg preferred him to the Machiavellian general. During Papen's roughly six months as chancellor, Hindenburg had come to look on him as a close family friend and advisor and wanted to keep him close by. So reluctant to part with him was Hindenburg that he allowed Papen to remain in his apartment in the Ministry of the Interior after his dismissal. That allowed Papen to pass unnoticed through the extensive back gardens that linked the Ministry of Interior, the Foreign Office, and the Chancellery, where Hindenburg resided while the Presidential Palace was undergoing renovations. While Schleicher had infrequent meetings with Hindenburg, Papen had direct and frequent access. The aristocratic and unloved Papen had disappeared from public view in December, but he had not abandoned his political ambitions: he was determined to use his influence with Hindenburg to undermine Schleicher and to return to power.

In early January, Kurt von Schröder, a Rhineland banker with connections to both the Hitler and Papen camps, arranged a clandestine meeting between the two bitter rivals at his home outside Cologne. Long a Nazi sympathizer, Schröder was apparently acting on his own, not as a representative of big business as it seemed to many at the time—and later. The meeting took place on January 4 in Schröder's lavish townhouse and was intended to be held in complete secrecy. Papen arrived alone by taxi at around noon to find Hitler, Himmler, party secretary Rudolf Hess, and a Nazi economic advisor waiting for him.

When Schröder took the two principals into the next room for a private discussion, the meeting began on an unpromising note. So much bad blood had flowed between them. Hitler began by reciting from his extensive catalogue of grievances against Papen, especially his actions in the previous summer when, he was convinced, Papen had blocked his appointment as chancellor. Papen insisted that it was Schleicher who had poisoned Hindenburg's mind about that possibility. Whether Hitler accepted this highly creative inversion of events is unknown, but he was impressed by Papen's obvious antipathy toward Schleicher and his determination to bring him down. Playing on Hitler's rabid anti-Marxism, Papen expressed his conviction that a rightist coalition government could be formed that would smash the left once and for all. Was Hitler interested in joining forces in this undertaking? Although neither trusted the other, each had something to gain from a bargain. Papen had no popular base; Hitler did. Hitler, on the other hand, had no access to Hindenburg, the gatekeeper to the corridors of power; Papen did. "He has the old man's ear," Goebbels wrote hopefully of Papen. It was the basis for a marriage of convenience.

The two men could not, however, agree on the shape of a new government or who should lead it. Papen argued that owing to Hindenburg's continuing aversion to the Nazi leader, Hitler should, at least for the time being, accept Nazi control over two powerful ministries in the new government—Interior and Defense. Hitler was still unwilling to accept anything less than the chancellorship, but he seemed less dogmatic, more flexible and open to other possibilities than he previously had been. Mulling over the possible combinations, they even discussed ruling jointly as a "duumvirate," but that had little appeal to either. The meeting ended without any agreement on the thorny question of the chancellorship, but it was a beginning. They agreed to further discussions, but no firm arrangements were made. The Nazis left the meeting encouraged, having learned something of vital importance: "Papen wants to oust Schleicher," Goebbels offered in summation. "Bravo! We can use him."

Despite elaborate measures to hold the meeting in complete secrecy, there had been a leak. As soon as Papen had stepped from his taxi upon arriving, a photographer, stationed at Schröder's door, had snapped his picture. The next day the meeting was national news. Speculation dominated the front pages, usually under such headlines as the *Tägliche Rundschau*'s "Hitler and Papen Against Schleicher." The two men promptly issued a joint statement denying any conspiracy against the Schleicher government, with Papen insisting that the meeting was intended merely to explore the possibilities of a broad right-wing coalition that would support the Schleicher cabinet.

No one, except, oddly enough, Schleicher, seemed to buy this disingenuous explanation. Schleicher simply couldn't believe that his feckless protégé, his Fränzchen, had acted behind his back. To French ambassador François-Poncet he scoffed at the idea that Papen had intended any intrigue. "He is frivolous," Schleicher commented dismissively. "He imagined that he was going to pull off a master stroke and serve up Hitler to us on a platter. As if Hitler had not shown many times that he was not to be trusted! . . . I won't scold him. I'll just say to him: 'My Fränzchen, you've committed another blunder.'" He did, however, press the Reich President to order Papen to refrain from such unauthorized initiatives in the future.

For Hitler, the meeting with Papen was of tremendous significance. It put him back in the headlines when he seemed increasingly like yesterday's news; it revealed the vulnerability of Schleicher's position; and at a time when the NSDAP's fortunes were at a low ebb and the path to the Chancellery blocked, new possibilities appeared. Instead of languishing in a political no-man's-land, the door to Hindenburg—and power—seemed at last to open ever so slightly. But now more than ever, the Nazis desperately needed to demonstrate their political relevance, that their losses in November and December had been merely temporary setbacks, that the party had recovered its balance and was once again on the upswing.

An opportunity beckoned. On January 15 an election would be held in the Lilliputian state of Lippe. Demographically this small political backwater in the northwest was ideally suited for the Nazis—rural, Protestant, a region of small towns, small shopkeepers, small farmers, and a relatively small Social Democratic and Communist presence. With an electorate of only about ninety thousand in a small, compact area, it offered the financially strapped NSDAP an opportunity to concentrate its limited resources for a major propaganda effort. No new *Deutschlandflug* was necessary, no far-flung speaking engagements. But it was a risk. If the Nazis suffered another defeat, it would confirm their downward spiral, sending the party into a potentially fatal tailspin. Hitler understood the stakes, and he launched the party into the campaign with a vengeance born of desperation. "The electoral contest in Lippe is beginning," Goebbels recorded in his notes on January 3. "With much effort we have succeeded in scraping together the necessary money for it. We will concentrate all our energy on this small state in order to obtain the prestige of a success. The party must . . . show that it can still be victorious."

For the first two weeks of January, all the party's financial and human resources were marshaled and hurled into the campaign. Hitler kept up his usual frenetic pace, speaking seventeen times in ten days. All the party's top speakers made appearances, addressing modest crowds in chilly tents on cold windswept nights. The audiences, Goebbels recorded, were "only peasants and little people, but that [was] fine and most seem convinced." For two weeks a blizzard of leaflets, pamphlets, and posters blanketed the countryside; SA men, bused in from the surrounding states, went door-to-door, distributing flyers, inviting residents to party rallies. They marched in parades, and toured the countryside in caravans of trucks carrying loudspeakers that blared out Nazi slogans. No village, no hamlet was bypassed. It was the most concentrated, most intense campaign the Nazis had ever conducted.

The message of the campaign had a by now familiar ring. Hitler offered the usual recapitulations of National Socialist philosophy, its determination to overcome Germany's social, religious, and regional prejudices, to awaken the dormant powers of the people and turn a divided Germany into a genuine *Volksgemeinschaft* that would restore Germany's place in the world—the same shibboleths that had formed the content of Nazi appeals for well over a year.

But if the party's message was familiar, the targets and the tone shifted. There were fewer harangues against the system parties or even Schleicher. Both were savaged but in a surprisingly perfunctory fashion, as if they were no longer of any relevance. Nazi speeches carried a sharper, more insistent ideological tone and focused on another, more ominous menace: Bolshevism. Jewish Bolshevism. The official slogan of the campaign was "Down with Marxism," and the linkage of Bolshevism and Jews, a staple of Nazi ideology, came front and center. "The danger of Bolshevism is gigantic,"

Hitler warned in his annual New Year's Declaration to the party faithful, "a threat to all of Europe. . . . The slogan, 'Proletarians of the world unite,' has become the rallying cry of sub-humanity [*Untermenschentum*]," and behind this threat, he claimed darkly, lurked the "international Jew . . . the intellectual inspiration in almost every country of the world in a struggle of the less gifted lower races against higher humanity. . . . Jewish intellectual leadership of world revolution" had already conquered Russia, and its tentacles stretched now into all the countries of Europe.

Other parties might be content to fight for a few ministerial posts in a new cabinet, a few more seats in the Reichstag, but the National Socialist movement was embarked on a world-historical struggle, an ideological crusade for the soul of Germany. The NSDAP, as Hitler rasped in a speech in Detmold before about three thousand shivering spectators, "doesn't see forming a government as its goal. Its ultimate mission is winning *people*. Race, *Volk* and land are the eternal sources from which the life of a people is constructed." In Berlin, Goebbels, who shuttled back and forth from the capital to Lippe, underscored the sharper ideological tone of the campaign. Speaking to a crowd of 100,000 in Berlin's Lustgarten, Goebbels delivered "a sharp denunciation of the Jews. The masses," he wrote afterward, "were delirious."

But something was amiss. Maybe it was the weather. Bone-chilling cold and freezing rain, frosts and frigid winds buffeted the campaign. Many events were held in large, poorly heated tents, and Hitler, with his usual late arrivals, often appeared hours behind schedule. He seemed tired. So did the message—and the audience. His predictable recitation of the party's history and his own spectacular rise from obscurity, the betrayal of 1918, and the predatory Allies were refrains his audiences could recite from memory. His appearances always drew a full house, the numbers always grossly inflated in the Nazi press, but while Goebbels hailed them as stunning successes, the public response, as more neutral reports indicated, was often lukewarm. One local newspaper reported that while Hitler's "remarks sometimes displayed his inner agitation," his speech in Detmold was "not interrupted by applause until the last part," when he turned to the political issues of the day. A Hitler speech in Lipperode just three days before the balloting elicited a similar response. Hitler's lengthy "introduction into the world of National Socialist political thinking . . . brought him no applause. Not until the second part of his speech, when he took up current political questions, did his speech stir interest."

Adding to Hitler's sense of crisis, the party continued to be plagued by internal dissension. Throughout December and January the specter of Gregor Strasser haunted the party. Rumors ran riot—Strasser had entered into talks with Schleicher, with Hindenburg, even with Papen, raising the possibility that he would split the party and enter the government, taking other Nazi leaders with him. Some believed that he was planning to found his own party. So concerned was Hitler that since mid-December he traveled the country speaking to party leaders, from the highest to the lowest, to reaffirm their loyalty. Strasser remained a member of the party, and Hitler was reluctant to expel him, but in mid-December he dismissed Strasser loyalists from their positions in the party leadership, dismantled his network of inspectors (the *Amtswälter*), reshuffled its personnel, and assigned their tasks to men whose fealty was beyond suspicion.

At the same time he issued a memorandum to party leaders that, while not explicitly denouncing Strasser, highlighted the differences in their views and underscored Hitler's "unalterable" vision of the party's organization and its mission. "The basis of political organization," it began, "is loyalty." Loyalty and obedience could "never be replaced by formal technical measures and structures, no matter what their type." The victory of the National Socialist idea was "the goal of our struggle," and the party's organization was merely "a means to achieve this end." In an expression of Hitler's careless approach to organization that would characterize his regime after 1933, he stated that "It is a mistake to assume that the organization would be better, the more extensive and structured its apparatus. The opposite is correct. . . . A *Weltanschauung* doesn't need bureaucrats . . . but fanatical apostles."

Despite these moves to erase Strasser's influence in the party, the rumors persisted. Goebbels's diary obsessively recorded each new Strasser sighting, each new bit of Strasser gossip. There was much to report. "The Berlin papers have a new theme," he wrote on January 3. "Strasser will enter the Schleicher cabinet. . . . They are nattering that he has already had a number of talks with the General . . . and we already have proof of it. This is the most unscrupulous act of treachery that has ever been committed against the party." Some days later he feared that Strasser was "about to betray us to Schleicher. . . . But he will pay for this." On the eve of the election in Lippe he learned that Strasser had met with Hindenburg. "That's just how I imagine a traitor," Goebbels groused. "I have always seen through him. Hitler is very distressed. Everything hangs in the balance. . . . Everything now hangs on Lippe."

Strasser wasn't the only source of trouble. Overtaxed by the exertions of 1932, the party's organization seemed to be fracturing under the strain. The tensions between the NSDAP's political leadership and the SA that had plagued the party in 1932 had not subsided following the November election. Bursts of SA violence and acts of criminality (petty larceny, armed robberies, extortion) continued to embarrass the party, and SA resentment against the political leadership continued to smolder. During December an acrimonious dispute between the top SA commander in the Nazi stronghold of Franconia, Wilhelm Stegmann, and the powerful *Gauleiter* of the area, Julius Streicher, burst into the open. Stegmann accused the *Gauleiter* of failing to honor a commitment to reimburse the SA for expenses incurred in the November election, and Streicher, in turn, accused Stegmann of embezzling party funds.

Streicher appealed for support to the top leadership of the SA; Stegmann called on local SA leaders in Franconia to back him. After removing several Streicher loyalists from their posts, Stegmann's men stormed into SA offices in Nuremberg. Fighting broke out, and the police had to be called in to restore order. The opposition press gloried in all the embarrassing details. "Hitler SA smashes SA Heads," *Vorwärts* gleefully reported. Röhm initiated an investigation, and relieved Stegmann of his command pending the outcome of the probe. Stegmann did not protest; he did not complain; he simply ignored the order. It was symptomatic of the tenuous control exerted by the party over the SA that Stegmann, relying on grassroots support from the Franconian SA, defied the Munich leadership and continued on in his position. Hitler appeared to have arranged reconciliation between the warring factions, but on the eve of the voting in Lippe, the conflict in Franconia flared again.

So serious was the situation that Röhm, who was enjoying a romantic getaway on Capri, was immediately ordered back to Germany to deal with his recalcitrant Storm Troopers. On election eve Hitler summoned

Stegmann to a meeting, where, under considerable duress, Stegmann signed a public statement pledging his loyalty and obedience to the Führer. It was crucial, Hitler insisted, for the party to project an image of unity as voters went to the polls. As events would soon demonstrate, the trouble was far from over.

By the time the polls closed in Lippe on January 15, Hitler, Goebbels, and the high echelons of the party had returned to Berlin to await the results. The party simply could not endure another setback. By late evening it was clear that the NSDAP could lay claim to a victory. "The party is on the march again," Goebbels sighed with relief. "It has paid off after all." With 39.6 percent of the vote, the party had surpassed its November figure of 34 percent, and the Nazi press heralded the outcome in Lippe a great triumph, a turning point. But while Goebbels was selling Lippe as a historic victory—in the Nazi lexicon all triumphs were "decisive" and "historic"—few were buying it. True, the Nazis had picked up some five thousand votes over the previous November, mostly at the expense of the Conservatives, whose vote tumbled, but their numbers still fell some 3,500 short of the party's July figures. Other parties, with far less funding and far less effort, had achieved bigger gains—to the Nazi 17 percent surge, the tiny Democratic Party had gained 60 percent, the liberal DVP 20 percent. These were small parties, but the Social Democrats also registered a gain of 15 percent. Together the Social Democrats and Communists had outpolled the Nazis. Little wonder that so few were impressed with the NSDAP's "historic triumph." Typical was a withering editorial assessment in the liberal *Berliner Tageblatt*: "Hitler has brought home from his heroic struggle in Lippe only a fly impaled on the tip of *his sword*."

His confidence revived by the Lippe "victory," Hitler convened a meeting of all the *Gauleiter* in Weimar. He would now settle the Strasser problem once and for all; the time had come for "tough intransigence . . . no compromises." For three hours he harangued the assembled leaders. His remarks were blunt, going into all the sordid details of Strasser's alleged betrayal. The *Gauleiter*, according to Goebbels, were shaken. Then one after another they joined in the escalating denunciation. Strasser's "best friends are deserting him," Goebbels rejoiced.

Martin Mutschmann, *Gauleiter* of Saxony, "characterized him as a Jew. Judas would be better." At the end of the day, Hitler had "achieved a complete victory. The Strasser case is done. Finis. Poor Gregor," Goebbels gloated, "his best friends have slaughtered him."

The leadership would continue to fret about Strasser—obsessively, it often seemed—but the threat he posed was more phantom than fact. Strasser did meet with Schleicher and with Hindenburg in January, but he was, to the surprise of all, sincere in his determination to leave the squalid world of late Weimar politics and was not angling for a position in the Schleicher government. As he later explained to a friend, he made his decision to leave the party only after much deliberation and after "my view that we had to participate in the running of the state and appeal to the people with deeds rather than words had been utterly rejected." His goal was "the coming together of all constructive-minded people, no matter where they come from, on the basis of new ideas in government, the economy and the cultural sphere." He had no desire to split the NSDAP or make a permanent break with Hitler, but he was "convinced that the time of agitation and of parties is fast disappearing and that the immediate future calls for men who are prepared to come into government with courage and a sense of responsibility" and "who . . . attempt finally to draw conclusions from an understanding of the present time, and achieve results." It was obvious why Schleicher found Strasser such an appealing possibility.

Had Strasser stayed on and fought for his views, he might well have carried many followers with him, dealing Hitler a serious blow and perhaps leading a truncated NSDAP in a different, less radical direction. But for all his energy and organizational talent, Strasser, in the final analysis, lacked the political toughness and the ruthless will to power for a fight with Hitler. He would continue to haunt the party—there was always a phantom Strasser lurking in the wings—but by mid-January he had exited the stage, bringing his role as the organizational mastermind of the NSDAP to a close.

While the Nazis were focused on the electoral contest in Lippe, Papen was working assiduously behind the scenes to undermine Schleicher. As a first step, he hoped to convince Hugenberg to bring his Conservatives into a Papen-Hitler government. Hugenberg loathed Schleicher and was willing to listen, but he was more than a little skeptical about Hitler—he had painful memories of his previous attempts to collaborate with the Nazi leader.

Hitler, he felt, was utterly unscrupulous, a view he expressed to both Papen and Hindenburg. Still, in any new government, preferably one headed by Papen, his price for support was the Ministry of Economics and Agriculture in both Prussia and the Reich. Nothing was settled. Hugenberg continued to have reservations, but he was, Papen felt, definitely in play.

Hitler also tried his hand with Hugenberg at a meeting on January 17. The conservative leader voiced reservations about a Hitler chancellorship, though he stopped short of outright opposition. He did, however, express strong objections to a National Socialist being put in charge of the Prussian Ministry of the Interior, a move that would place the fifty-thousand-strong Prussian police force under direct Nazi control. He also strongly disapproved of Hitler's demand for new Reichstag elections—elections in which the Conservatives could hardly expect to improve their position. For Hitler, new Reichstag elections were essential. He was confident that new elections, conducted while a Hitler-Papen government held the instruments of power—and coercion—would deliver the necessary majority to pass an enabling law. Such a law would allow him to govern without the Reichstag *and* also without presidential decrees. It would, in other words, free him from any institutional restraints on his exercise of power. Hugenberg, however, would not be moved, and Hitler left the meeting frustrated.

Still scrambling for traction, Hitler arranged for another secret meeting with Papen. On January 18, accompanied by Himmler and Röhm, he met with Papen at the villa of Joachim von Ribbentrop in Dahlem, a fashionable section of Berlin. Ribbentrop, a wealthy Nazi Reichstag deputy who fancied himself possessed of considerable diplomatic skills (he would later rise to be foreign minister in the Third Reich), had served with Papen in Turkey during the World War, and he was eager to act as intermediary between Hitler and the former chancellor. When the two had met earlier in the month in Cologne, Hitler seemed prepared to drop his demand for the chancellorship and the minister presidency of Prussia and to accept a more modest National Socialist role in a Papen cabinet—maybe the ministries of the Interior and Defense. But over lunch on the 18th, buoyed by the party's showing in Lippe, Hitler renewed his demands for the chancellorship and the minister presidency of Prussia. Papen replied that he did not believe he had enough influence to overcome Hindenburg's resistance to a Hitler cabinet, and the meeting ended inconclusively.

On the following day another meeting was arranged for the 22nd. Arriving at the Ribbentrop estate at ten in the evening, Hitler, Wilhelm Frick, Hitler's advisor in legal matters, and later Göring found Papen, Oskar von Hindenburg, and Otto Meissner, the influential state secretary to the Reich President, waiting for them. Hitler was still adamant about the chancellorship but expressed his willingness to have only two other National Socialists in the cabinet. Frick was to be minister of the interior and something should be found for Göring, but the other positions in the cabinet, Hitler magnanimously offered, could be filled by conservatives acceptable to the Reich President. Papen, who would serve as vice chancellor, found these terms more reasonable than Hitler had previously put forward and felt that Hindenburg might finally agree to a Hitler government. The question of Prussia was left open. Oskar von Hindenburg left the meeting still harboring deep reservations about Hitler, but Meissner was surprised by Hitler's apparent willingness to make concessions and felt that the terms discussed might be acceptable to the Reich President. Papen agreed. Armed with these terms, he felt that he could now approach the Reich President with a reasonable chance of success.

The meetings at the Ribbentrop villa were intended to be secret, but the press quickly uncovered both, and the Berlin papers reveled in speculation. Rumors swarmed through the government quarter like bats from a cave. Hitler and Papen, of course, denied that anything was afoot, and, of course, no one believed them. Schleicher, who was at last beginning to appreciate the danger he was in, appealed to Hindenburg to grant him permission to dissolve the Reichstag before it reconvened on January 31. Without a presidential order to dissolve, Schleicher faced a certain vote of no confidence. If, on the other hand, the Reichstag could be dissolved by presidential order, he could remain in office and buy time. The effects of his reforms might be felt in the near future. The economy, analysts were now saying, had bottomed out in late summer of 1932, and although improvements in unemployment could not yet be felt on the street, expectations were that there would be a significant uptick in the economy by summer.

On January 23 Schleicher pressed Hindenburg not only for the dissolution order but also a promise to delay new elections indefinitely, a move that was a direct violation of the constitution. With no pressure from the Reichstag and governing by emergency decree, Schleicher could put Germany's political house in order and await improvement in the economic situation. The Nazis might choose to support the government or, if not, simply wither on the vine of fruitless opposition. Anyway, Schleicher was convinced that Hitler was "on the verge of desperation." Speaking off the record at a dinner for journalists, he was confident that now Hitler realized "that his party is falling apart under him without his ever seeing it attain a position of power." With a patronizing smile, he waved away the threat of the Nazis. "I'll take care of them," he said confidently. "They'll soon be eating out of my hand."

Hindenburg was not so confident. Hadn't he heard all this before? Wasn't Schleicher's plan exactly the same course of action Papen had advocated in December and that Schleicher had so effectively demolished that it led to Papen's fall? Such a blatantly unconstitutional action, Schleicher had argued then, would provoke an uprising of both the radical left and right that would lead to civil war. In such a situation, the army could not gurantee its ability to prevail. Hindenburg was no keener on the plan now than when Papen had proposed it and needed time to consider his options.

With Hitler's talks with Hugenberg and Papen stalled, a new outbreak of trouble with the SA threatened to plunge the NSDAP once again into crisis. Again it was Stegmann. Back in Franconia after his meeting with Hitler, the SA leader showed no sign of having learned his lesson. He openly renewed his feud with Streicher, leaving a frustrated and angry Hitler no alternative but to expel him from the party. Far from being intimidated, Stegmann responded by founding his own "Free Corps Franconia," taking some three thousand followers—roughly half the Franconian SA—with him. The new paramilitary organization lashed out at Hitler's policy of legality and at the party bosses in Munich. At an SA rally in Nuremberg on the 24th, Stegmann declared that the party "had missed its historic opportunity of coming to power through legal means"; now it was time for a "more brutal and revolutionary fight." Stegmann's call for rebellion struck a chord among disgruntled SA men around the country. Dissident Storm Troopers formed their own breakaway Free Corps groups in the Ruhr, the Upper Rhine, and Hessen. More mutinies were cropping up elsewhere. There appeared a very real possibility that Stegmann's revolt might sweep the entire country, rending the NSDAP asunder at a critical juncture.

Adding to Nazi anxiety was the party's continuing financial despera-tion. Early in the month Goebbels complained about the "bad financial sit-uation of the organization," noting that the party would have to find ways to economize. Creditors were demanding payment for loans extended over the past year, and membership dues continued to shrink dramatically as did revenues from poorly attended party events. Hitler's meeting with Schröder was not about money but about politics, and there is little ev-idence to suggest a sudden influx of funding from business sources. The party's financial situation was further strained by the all-out campaign in Lippe. With the sources of domestic financing drying up and the party in desperate need of cash, Göring took the extraordinary step of inquiring of an American diplomat about the possibility of securing a loan for the party in the United States.

With the NSDAP's fortunes sinking fast, Papen threw Hitler a lifeline. On the morning of the 23rd he met with the Reich President, Meissner, and Oskar von Hindenburg and laid out the case for a Hitler chancellorship. To a reluctant Hindenburg, Meissner argued that Papen's proposal offered the best way to break the political gridlock. Hitler would at last be saddled with governmental responsibility and would be safely held in check by Papen and the conservative members of the cabinet. Hindenburg listened but remained unconvinced, a skepticism shared by his son. Both still be-lieved if the Schleicher government were to fall, as now seemed inevitable, Papen would be the best alternative.

As late as January 27 Hindenburg was still reassuring associates that he had no intention of naming Hitler chancellor. Many feared—and with good reason—that the Old One would return the dangerously divisive Papen to the Chancellery, a step that virtually everyone from right to left, but especially the anxious army leadership, felt certain would trigger a bloody civil war. So unpopular was the former chancellor that although many in positions of power had deep reservations about the Nazis, a Hitler cabinet actually seemed less dangerous than a second Papen government. The moderate center and right were also dead set against a reprise of the Papen cabinet but took comfort in the belief that Hindenburg would never appoint the "little Bohemian corporal" to head a government. But with Schleicher's ouster imminent and opposition to Papen (even Papen had come to understand this), Hindenburg discovered that he had little room for maneuver. Perhaps, after all, with the proper precautions and restraints, the time for Hitler had arrived.

Meanwhile, Hitler was in a gloomy frame of mind. Exasperated by his failure to make headway in his various negotiations, he was ready to quit the city and leave for Munich. This sudden change in attitude caught his close confederates by surprise. Those who met him in those tense January days, even those who distrusted or detested him, were often struck by his sense of unwavering confidence, his unshakable conviction that his was the only path to power. Throughout the frenetic campaigning and daily intrigues, Hitler retained an almost preternatural calm. Despite the mounting political pressures, he even insisted on maintaining something of his bohemian style of life. He still rose late, usually around eleven, chatted through the hours, lingered over afternoon tea and cakes at the Kaiserhof café, went to the cinema, and attended the opera.

Through all the ups and downs of the previous years, it had always been Hitler's unshakable confidence that had boosted the spirits of his lieutenants. Now it was their turn to pick him up. On the 27th Hitler huddled with Göring and Ribbentrop and expressed his soaring frustration with the situation. He was fed up, ready to leave Berlin altogether and return to Munich. Göring insisted that "the situation is far from hopeless" and counseled another meeting with Hindenburg; Ribbentrop offered to arrange another session with Papen. Hitler rejected both out of hand. He had already said "all there is to say to the Field Marshal," and did "not know what to add." Only with considerable difficulty were Göring and Ribbentrop able to calm him and prevail upon him to stay in Berlin a bit longer. Finally, and with great reluctance, he agreed to meet that afternoon with Hugenberg. But the interview did not go well. The querulous Conservative leader again raised objections to Hitler's plans and stated numerous conditions for his support, displaying, in Hitler's view, "a greed for portfolios out of all proportion to the strength of his party." The meeting ended with such rancor that "Hitler, very indignant," announced his intention "to leave for Munich immediately." Ribbentrop had never seen him in such a state.

That night Ribbentrop met alone with Papen and restated the Nazi position that the only solution that made any political sense was a Hitler chancellorship backed by a strong national front. Hugenberg would be a problem, but perhaps he could be brought around. To his surprise, Papen readily agreed. Papen was "now absolutely in favor of Hitler becoming Chancellor." This represented, according to Ribbentrop, "the decisive change in Papen's attitude." It was, he believed, "the turning point." Papen was to meet with Hindenburg at ten in the morning. Ribbentrop promised to produce Hitler at eleven.

Papen's scheme had now reached a crucial stage, and events began to move quickly. On the 28th Hindenburg informed Schleicher that he would not authorize the dissolution of the Reichstag. Knowing that he faced a vote of no confidence when that body reconvened on the 31st, Schleicher submitted his resignation. He had misplayed his hand, assuming until too late that he had Hindenburg's support, and he had grossly underestimated his erstwhile protégé. It was not until word of the meetings at Ribbentrop's estate reached him that he fully realized that Papen had hatched a conspiracy to bring him down. By the evening of the 28th, he had tendered his resignation and vacated his office in the Chancellery.

The next morning Papen met with Hindenburg. The Old One at last seemed reconciled to the prospect of a Hitler government, with Papen as vice chancellor and supported by the Conservatives, the Stahlhelm, and other right-of-center groups. Papen then hurried to his appointment with Hitler. But when, just after eleven, he opened his door, he found only Ribbentrop. "Where is Hitler?" he demanded. Ribbentrop feared that Hitler had already departed for Munich. Papen said that he had to be brought back without delay; a breakthrough with Hindenburg had occurred, and a Hitler chancellorship was now definitely possible. Ribbentrop left immediately and discovered from Göring that Hitler had not yet left the Kaiserhof. A quick telephone call, and a meeting with Papen was arranged for the following morning.

At that meeting on January 29, Hitler's mood improved dramatically when Papen confirmed that he was solidly committed to a Hitler chancellorship and that Hindenburg now seemed prepared to accept a Hitler-Papen government. The two men were able to reach agreement on the composition of the cabinet—all posts but two, the chancellorship and Ministry of the Interior, would be filled by conservatives. Hitler agreed that the Foreign Office, Finance Ministry, and Defense were to be headed by Hindenburg favorites. The important Ministry of Justice would for the time being be left vacant. Hitler also grudgingly dropped his demand for the minister presidency of Prussia, conceding that position to Papen. As compensation, he suggested that Göring be appointed as Papen's minister of the interior in Prussia.

Later in the day Papen held talks with Hugenberg, who still vigorously objected to Nazi demands for new elections. But when Papen offered him the Ministry of Economics, a position he had long coveted, he tentatively agreed to participate in a Hitler-Papen government. When one conservative whom Papen hoped to entice into the cabinet voiced his concerns about a Hitler government, Papen sought to allay his fears: "What do you want? I have the confidence of Hindenburg. In two months we'll have pushed Hitler so far into a corner that he'll squeal." To another prospective cabinet minister who voiced reservations, worrying that Hitler was untrustworthy and would cause a world of trouble, Papen responded, "You're wrong. We've hired him."

Hoping to create a firm right-wing base of support for the new government, Papen was convinced he needed the backing of the powerful right-wing veterans organization the Stahlhelm. He invited the two Stahlhelm leaders, Theodor Duesterberg and Franz Seldte, to join him and Hugenberg at Papen's apartment. There Papen offered Seldte the Labor Ministry, but Duesterberg, who still smarted from vicious Nazi attacks on him during the presidential elections, wanted no part of a Hitler government. Appointing someone as ruthless and dishonest as Hitler was a recipe for disaster, he argued. Hugenberg intervened in an attempt to reassure him, pointing out that Hindenburg would still be in command of the army, that Papen would be vice chancellor, that he would be in charge of the entire economic sphere, and that conservatives would dominate the new cabinet. "We're boxing Hitler in," he boasted. Duesterberg was unmoved. "One night," he warned, "you will find yourself running through the ministerial garden in your underpants to avoid arrest."

At the Kaiserhof, Hitler and his entourage mulled over the situation. Could they trust Papen? Hindenburg? "Hitler is very skeptical and mistrustful," Goebbels noted. "With good reason. Those over there [at the Chancellery] are a big band of swindlers. . . . The Old One is unpredictable. . . . At least we are rid of Schleicher. The Old One basically threw him out." That was "a perfect punishment" for a schemer like Schleicher. "Tomorrow the tug of war [for power] begins."

Despite all the mutual suspicions and misgivings, by the evening of January 29 Papen had maneuvered all the pieces into place. Hitler was satisfied, Hugenberg was tentatively onboard; all the proposed cabinet officers were in agreement. Even the reluctant Duesterberg grudgingly dropped his opposition to the cabinet, and Seldte agreed to be minister of labor. The Stahlhelm was ready to support the new government. Some potential problems remained to be resolved, especially Hugenberg's adamant opposition to new elections, which Hitler considered essential. But everything seemed set. Even Hindenburg's resistance to a Hitler chancellorship had apparently been overcome, at least for the moment, and a Hitler government would be sworn in at the Chancellery at eleven o'clock in the morning.

"One doesn't dare to believe it yet," Goebbels wrote that night. "Is Papen honest? Who knows?" And Hindenburg was so unreliable, so changeable. Then, suddenly, a new and more ominous menace appeared. A messenger arrived at Goebbels's apartment bearing word that Hindenburg had decided, after all, to appoint Papen chancellor. The army was vehemently opposed. Rumors had surfaced that in order to block a return of the Papen cabinet, plans were now under way at army headquarters to arrest Oskar von Hindenburg, while the Reich President would be taken away to his estate at Neudeck and held incommunicado. Army troops would occupy the city. Some believed that Schleicher was behind it; others thought Commander-in-Chief Kurt von Hammerstein-Equord. It was to be a military coup, and the outcome would be a military dictatorship, undoing all Hitler's calculations just when it seemed that power was within his grasp.

Göring and Hitler, who were also present in Goebbels's apartment, swung into action. Göring immediately warned Meissner and Papen, and Hindenburg sent word to General Werner von Blomberg. The Reich President ordered the general, who was attending the Disarmament Conference in Geneva, back to Berlin immediately, warning him to proceed directly to the Reich Chancellery to be sworn in as minister of defense—a post that would make him commander-in-chief of the army. Hitler meanwhile telephoned the commander of the Berlin SA, and ordered him to put the SA on alert around the city. The Storm Troopers should be prepared for a showdown with Army troops. "We must not lose our nerve now," Goebbels wrote. "Who knows if this is a serious threat or just childishness?" At the Kaiserhof, Hitler's inner circle sat and waited, while he stalked silently through the suite, lost in thought. No new reports reached them. The hours ground slowly by, and as daybreak approached, nothing had happened. No troops from the Potsdam garrison, no arrests. Finally, at five in the morning, the men allowed themselves a brief sleep. The tension was still high—something could still go wrong—Hindenburg might have a change of heart, Papen might yet betray them, the army might march. The anticipation was almost unbearable. Snowflakes were filtering through the weak winter sunlight as the first crowds began to form outside the Chancellery, sensing that something momentous was going to happen. "We have only to wait a few more hours," Goebbels anxiously noted, "then the great moment will be here."

Early that morning, as rumors of an impending military Putsch seized the government quarter, Oskar von Hindenburg was dispatched to the Anhalter railway station to fetch General Blomberg. The Reich President's conviction that something was afoot was reinforced when the younger Hindenburg discovered a staff officer sent by General Hammerstein stationed on the train platform, apparently under orders to bring Blomberg directly to army headquarters in Potsdam. Instead, Blomberg was whisked straightaway to the Reich President. In a tense meeting at the Chancellery, Hindenburg briefed him on the situation, warning him to be prepared to suppress an imminent coup d'état.

An air of anticipation gripped the city. Expectant crowds filled the Wilhelmstrasse, flocking into the square that separated the Kaiserhof from the Chancellery. Around ten, Hitler and Hugenberg slipped through a back garden into Papen's residence for a last discussion before proceeding to their audience with Hindenburg. When in the course of the conversation, Hugenberg learned for the first time that the issue of new elections had not been settled, he flew into a rage. He had entered into this arrangement with the understanding that there would be no new elections. Hitler, for his part, was taken aback that Papen had not actually secured Hugenberg's agreement beforehand. Under these circumstances, Hugenberg threatened to back out of the deal, and Hitler's efforts to reassure him that there would be no changes in the cabinet no matter what the outcome of the elections fell on deaf ears. Finally, Papen, at wits' end, interjected: "If the new government is not formed by eleven o'clock, the army is going to march. Schleicher may establish a military dictatorship." It was approaching eleven before the men, still arguing, marched through the snow-dusted back gardens and into presidential secretary Meissner's office in the Reich Chancellery, where the presumptive ministers of the new cabinet had gathered.

With Hindenburg waiting impatiently in the next room, the row over new elections flared again. Once more Hitler tried to reassure Hugenberg, promising that no matter what might come he would hold his position as economics and agriculture minister—he would be economics czar, a term that greatly appealed to Hugenberg's vanity. Papen seconded those promises, but Hugenberg could not be mollified. At that point Meissner reminded them that it was already five past eleven, and they were keeping the Reich President waiting. When this warning failed to move the implacable Hugenberg, Papen asked plaintively, "Do you want to risk the national unity which has finally been achieved after so many difficult negotiations? You cannot possibly doubt the solemn word of a German man." The argument was still sputtering on when Meissner reappeared from Hindenburg's office, watch in hand, and announced: "The President requests you not to keep him waiting any longer. It is now eleven-fifteen. The Old Gentleman may retire at any moment."

Meissner's anxious words seemed to jolt Hugenberg into motion, and, with agreement hanging by a gossamer thread, the triumvirate marched at last into Hindenburg's presence. So irritated with the situation was Hindenburg that he could not bring himself to offer the cabinet the ceremonial welcoming speech. Unfazed, Hitler, too, broke with protocol and surprised the company by plunging into a short speech of his own. He solemnly promised the Reich President that he would uphold the Weimar constitution, find a majority in the Reichstag so that emergency decrees would no longer be necessary, resolve Germany's economic crisis, and restore unity to a divided and downtrodden German people. When he finished, a startled and still peeved Hindenburg offered no comment, except to utter a perfunctory "And now, gentlemen, forward with God!"

Across the square at the Kaiserhof, Hitler's entourage waited anxiously. "The inward excitement almost takes our breath away," Goebbels wrote. "In the street below the crowd stands silently between the Kaiserhof and the Chancellery. What is happening there? We are torn between doubt, hope, joy and despair. We have been deceived too often to be able wholeheartedly to believe in the great miracle." Röhm stood at the window, watching the door of the Chancellery from which the Führer would emerge. "We will be able to judge by his face if the interview has gone well," Goebbels worried. "Torturous hours of waiting! At last a car draws up in front of the entrance. The crowd cheers. They seem to feel that a great change is taking place or has already begun. The Führer is coming."

A few minutes later, Hitler entered the suite that had served as his headquarters. At first he did not speak. Overwhelmed, he looked at his disciples in silence. "He says nothing, and we all remain silent also," Goebbels wrote, overflowing with unctuous piety. "His eyes are full of tears. It has come! . . . Germany is at a turning point in its history." Adolf Hitler, the indifferent student, the failed artist, the tramp, the obscure soldier of the Great War, the vulgar beer hall agitator, was, improbably, chancellor of Germany. "It was," Goebbels wrote, "like a dream, a fairy tale."

There was nothing inevitable about that day, about Hitler's rise to power. He was not voted into office, not swept into power on a tidal wave of public support. At the height of their electoral popularity in July the Nazis had received only 38 percent of the vote, and although they could not know it at the time, it was the largest vote they would ever claim in a free election. Then in November, in the last truly unfettered elections of the Weimar era, the Nazi vote fell to 33 percent and continued to plummet in state and local elections that followed. As they had done through virtually all the elections from 1928 to 1933, more Germans had voted for the tragically divided parties of the left than for the Nazis. These figures do not mean that those who voted for other parties were voting against the NSDAP or that they rejected all that National Socialism stood for. But it does mean that when given a free choice, even in the depths of the Great Depression, two thirds of the German population preferred someone else.

It, therefore, constitutes a monstrous historical irony that Adolf Hitler was inserted into power at a moment when the party's popularity was rapidly receding, its street organization was in revolt, and its treasury empty. What Hitler and the NSDAP's sophisticated propaganda apparatus had failed to achieve at the apex of the party's popular appeal in 1932, a group of highly placed conservative figures managed by engineering a backroom deal to create a Hitler cabinet. They believed, as Papen put it, that the National Socialist demagogue could be "tamed," that they had "sandbagged

Hitler." But, as they would soon discover, they had made a fatal miscalculation, disastrously underestimating Hitler's limitless ambition, his capacity for treachery, and his ruthless political acumen. They would not be the last to make such an error. Just a day after Hitler's appointment, Hugenberg was already experiencing buyer's regret. "Yesterday," he is reported to have said, "I committed the greatest stupidity of my life. I joined forces with the greatest demagogue in world history."

Dusk was settling over the city, the street lamps just springing to life, when the first elements of the vast parade came into view. The streets of the government quarter were thronged with people, the sidewalks packed, young boys perched in the branches of trees, bands playing, impromptu choruses chanting Nazi songs. To a thunderous rumbling of drums, column after column of SA men, Hitler Youth, SS, and Stahlhelm holding torches aloft emerged from the darkness of the Tiergarten and surged onto Unter den Linden. French ambassador François-Poncet watched in awe as the massed columns, "flanked by bands that played martial airs to the muffled beat of their big drums . . . passed under the triumphal arch of the Brandenburg Gate. The torches they brandished formed a river of fire, a river with hastening, unquenchable waves . . . sweeping . . . over the very heart of the city. From these brown-shirted, jack booted men, as they marched by in perfect discipline and alignment, their well-pitched voices bawling warlike songs, there rose an enthusiasm and dynamism that were extraordinary. The onlookers, drawn up on either side of the marching columns, burst into a vast clamor." For three interminable hours the procession passed beneath the windows of the Reich Chancellery Annex where Hitler, nodding and extending his arm in his abbreviated version of the Nazi salute, beamed down upon them. Just beyond, the ancient Hindenburg stood at his window, "a towering, dignified heroic figure," Goebbels now gushed, "invested with a touch of old time marvel. Now and then, he beats time to the military marches with his cane," perhaps wondering at what he had done. For Goebbels it was "the rising of a nation. Germany has awakened."

Far from the tumultuous scene in the Wilhelmstrasse, Erich Ludendorff penned a note to Hindenburg. Ludendorff had been Hindenburg's partner in commanding Germany's military effort in the Great War, and in 1923 had been Hitler's co-conspirator in the failed Putsch attempt. He was widely considered something of a crank. But he knew a few things about Hitler and on that fateful January day, he sent an ominous warning to the aged Reich President: "I solemnly prophesy," he wrote, "that this accursed man will cast our Reich into the abyss and bring our nation to inconceivable misery. Future generations will damn you in your grave for what you have done."

SEIZING POWER

Around the country Nazis celebrated through the night. Bonfires burned in the countryside, columns of SA men tramped through village streets; swastika banners fluttered on public buildings. Germany, the National Socialist press proclaimed, had reached a "historic turning point," and January 30, 1933, was "an event like nothing that has come before in Germany's post-war evolution. With a strong National Socialist advance guard our leaders have moved into the government to clear the road to freedom for the German people." The discredited Weimar Republic had been dispatched; the new Germany had ridden to the rescue of a country long mired in confusion and despair. This, at any rate, was the National Socialist version of January 30—a glorious new chapter in the official Nazi narrative of events. Reality, as usual, was more prosaic, and more complicated. While the Nazis hyperventilated over the new cabinet, most Germans greeted the announcement of the Hitler government with something of a wait-and-see shrug. There were a few outbreaks of violence, but bloody confrontations were far fewer than had been anticipated. As *The New York Times* reported, "everything is going on much as usual in the country." So many cabinets had come and gone; so little had changed.

Most informed opinion, both in Germany and abroad, assumed that Hitler had been outfoxed by Papen. The wily ex-chancellor had lured the Nazi leader into heading a coalition government in which he would be outnumbered by Conservatives and overshadowed by his own vice chancellor. All agreed that Hitler had little room for maneuver. "The composition of the cabinet leaves Herr Hitler no scope for gratification of any dictatorial ambition," *The New York Times* confidently proclaimed. "Nationalists to Dominate in Government Led by National Socialist" was a typical headline. Hitler had "merely been taken in tow . . ." It was generally felt that "the government is Colonel von Papen's show . . ." He was expected "to be a buffer to National Socialist influence in the Cabinet. . . . There is also a very definite impression in political circles that the Vice Chancellor has received a certain vetoing authority that he can oppose to any radical action Herr Hitler may attempt to undertake."

Others claimed to be gratified that Hitler had at last been enticed into a position of responsibility and that his days of savaging the government from the safety of the sidelines were over. And, of course, behind this view was the plausible assumption that he would be no more capable of dealing with Germany's colossal economic problems than his predecessors. While conceding that the appointment of Hitler was "a severe blow to Social Democracy," France's *Le Temps* suggested that "it is possible that the new Chancellor will be quickly exhausted by this exposure and his reputation as a worker of miracles will vanish." The editors of *Le Temps* were also convinced that "it will be impossible for the new Chancellor to make good the madly demagogic program that succeeded in attracting the support of the German people."

The German papers were more ambivalent. The liberal *Frankfurter Zeitung* sounded the alarm, calling on the public to rally "to the defense of the rights of the working population, fundamentals of democracy, freedom of thought and justice and social economic rationality." The leftist press anticipated a crackdown, but tended to see Hitler as a mere figurehead. Hewing to the Comintern line from Moscow, the Communists held that Hitler was nothing more than a tool of monopoly capitalism, and that the real power in the new government was that representative of big business and big agriculture Alfred Hugenberg. More common was the view of the left-liberal *Berliner Tageblatt* that the Nazis for all their fanatical zeal posed little cause for concern. "There is the Socialist Hitler under the business supervision of the foxy capitalist Hugenberg and an ex-corporal amidst a Count and four Barons." But at least this cabinet was better than Papen's because of "the disenchantment that will now come to Hitler's followers."

For his part, Hitler was content to encourage this public perception. In cabinet meetings he was cooperative, even deferential, eager to indulge his conservative partners. Publicly, the Nazi propaganda machine was careful not to describe the events of January 30 as a National Socialist revolution but a "national uprising" of all anti-Marxist, nationalist forces, a term intended to reassure. Such illusions did not last long.

Hitler had promised Hindenburg that he would conduct negotiations with the Zentrum, whose votes in the Reichstag would give the government a parliamentary majority, and, apparently true to his word, he began talks with the Zentrum leadership on the morning of his first full working day in the Chancellery. Hindenburg had grown weary of issuing repeated emergency decrees to keep minority cabinets afloat—a burden that had weighed heavily on him since 1930, but especially in 1932. Hitler went dutifully through the motions, but he had no intention of coaxing the Catholic party into "the Government of National Concentration," as it was now being called. After only a brief meeting with Prelate Ludwig Kaas, the Zentrum leader, Hitler reported to Hindenburg and the cabinet that unfortunately no progress in the talks was possible. The Zentrum was not prepared to join the government. No one was more surprised to learn this than Kaas, who was, in fact, open to entering the coalition and believed that his conversation with Hitler was only the beginning of negotiations. Hitler was misrepresenting his position, he protested to Hindenburg, but it was too late. The Reich President had already signed a decree dissolving the Reichstag and calling for new elections to be held on March 5. It was exactly what Hitler wanted.

Hitler was hopeful that with the power of the state behind him, the elections of March 5 would yield a Nazi majority, freeing the party from Hindenburg and its conservative coalition partners. With a working majority in place, he would pass an "enabling law," granting the government the power to act independently for a period of time—four years is what he had in mind—without interference from the Reichstag and its quagmire of wrangling parties. It was an idea Hitler—and also Papen—had put forward in November, and which Hindenburg had rebuffed, but the Old Gentleman had softened, and this "Government of National Concentration," he realized, seemed to offer the last best chance for a workable, meaning right-wing, parliamentary government.

On the night of February 1, Hitler addressed the nation for the first time as Reich chancellor. For many who had never actually heard him speak but knew his reputation as a blustering firebrand and fanatic, the national radio address must have come as something of a surprise. It was a different Hitler whose voice crackled over the airwaves that winter night. Missing was the usual bombast, the bellicose tirades, the fanatical anti-Semitic rants. Instead, a surprisingly measured, statesmanlike Hitler pleaded for national unity, mouthing platitudes about national self-reliance, German greatness, and world peace. He called for the restoration of Germany's right to defend itself, a reference to the international disarmament conference under way in Geneva, but rather than excoriating the victorious Allies, as he had routinely done for more than a decade, he expressed his "most sincere wish for the welfare of Europe, and more, for the welfare of the whole world." He was committed to the "preservation and maintenance of a peace which the world needs now more than ever before." He even invoked the Almighty, piously pledging that his government would "extend its strong, protecting hand over Christianity as the basis of our entire morality and the family as the germ cell of the body of our people and state."

Turning to the most pressing issue of the day, he announced a four-year plan to rebuild the economy, which would put the jobless back to work, rescue the peasantry from poverty, and restore middle-class prosperity, but he offered no specifics. There was a glancing reference to "a compulsory labor service" and a commitment to "the performance of social duties for the sick and aged," but little else. To a nation battered by a progression of economic calamities—the hyperinflation, harsh stabilization, and the Great Depression—he sought to assure the public and the business community that there would be no radical experiments that would destabilize the currency or hurl Germany into even greater economic despair.

None of this could be achieved, however, until the scourge of Marxism was expunged from German life. If the Communists were to seize power, Hitler warned, it would be "a catastrophe of unfathomable dimensions. . . . Beginning with the family and ranging through all of the concepts of honor and loyalty, *Volk und Vaterland*, culture and economy, all the way to the eternal foundation of our morality and our faith, nothing has been spared by this negating, all destroying dogma." Fourteen years of Marxism had ruined Germany; one year of Bolshevism would destroy it. Alarming signs of Communist subversion were everywhere. "In a single gigantic offensive of willpower and violence, the Communist method of madness is attempting to poison and disrupt the Volk." The Communists represented a clear and present danger to the political, economic, and moral health of the people, and cleansing Germany of this toxic pollutant would be the first priority of the new government. "Now, German people," he concluded, "give us four years, and then pass judgment upon us! True to the order of the Field Marshal, we shall begin. May Almighty God look mercifully on our work, lead our will on the right path, bless our wisdom, and reward us with the confidence of our people. We are not fighting for ourselves, but for Germany!"

In a revealing reflection of his priorities, Hitler, on the next day, moved to win the support—or at the very least the benevolent neutrality—of the army. It was arranged for General Blomberg, the new minister of defense, to invite Hitler to address a group of generals at the home of General Hammerstein, commander of the army. Blomberg was sympathetic to the Nazis; Hammerstein was not, and as long as Hindenburg was alive, the army was a potential threat to the new government. Hitler began by reassuring the generals that the army would remain the only armed force in Germany; he had no intention of transforming the SA into a people's army—a concern that had grown steadily throughout 1932 thanks to provocative remarks by Röhm and other SA commanders. They were also relieved to hear that Hitler intended to keep the army out of politics and that it would not be expected to intervene in the event of domestic unrest, a possibility that in February 1933 seemed quite likely. Perhaps most importantly, Hitler announced that rearmament would be the government's highest priority. The army would be vastly expanded and would be well equipped not only to defend Germany's frontiers but to be prepared for an expansion to the east, which, Hitler declared, was essential for the future health of the German people. Despite the initially cool reception he received and lingering reservations privately expressed by some of those present, Hitler's remarks met with general approval. Few were enthusiastic supporters of Hitler, but for most the political alternatives in Germany seemed to be either the Nazis or the Reds, and for them that was no choice at all.

With the army apparently pacified, the Government of National Concentration wasted little time in translating Hitler's words into action. Many
Germans worried that Hitler's assumption of power would push the country into civil war, a fear vigorously stoked by the Nazi press, which filled
its pages with alleged leftist plots to overthrow the government. After all,
the Social Democrats and Communists, implacable foes of the Nazis, were
a force to be reckoned with. Together the two parties continued to draw an
electorate larger than that of the NSDAP, and both commanded powerful
street organizations. Surely the showdown would now come.

That anxiety was heightened when on January 31 the Communists called
for a general strike to protest Hitler's appointment as chancellor. It was, the
Nazis claimed, the opening salvo of the expected Communist assault. Under
the circumstances, it took little effort to convince Hindenburg—and much
of the public—that the nation was in peril, and on February 2 the Reich
President issued an emergency decree, "For the Protection of the German
People." The decree empowered the government to ban all public meetings,
newspapers, leaflets, and pamphlets that brought the new government and
its officials "into contempt." In effect, it permitted the government to suppress Communist and Social Democratic campaign events, harass and arrest
their functionaries, and to close any publication that offered even a hint of
criticism of the Government of National Concentration. With a Reichstag
election looming, the decree dealt a crippling blow to the Social Democratic
and Communist campaigns, made criticism of the government a crime, and
opened the door to "legal" harassment of opposing parties.

That decree was immediately followed by another that dissolved all
elected bodies in Prussia, the country's largest state and a stronghold of
pro-democratic forces, and transferred all power to the national government. Both measures were blatantly unconstitutional, but aside from a protest to the Reichstag Rules Committee by the Social Democrats and their
initiation of legal proceedings against the government in the Supreme Court,
these actions provoked little public outcry and no sustained resistance.

The critical question was who would enforce these measures and how.
The answer was not long in coming. Although still technically subordinate
to Papen, Göring, acting in his capacity as Reich commissar for the Prussian Ministry of the Interior, immediately assumed control over all police
forces in three fifths of Germany. Göring had played an important role

in the frantic backdoor negotiations in the months leading to Hitler's appointment as chancellor, but held no formal position in the party hierarchy nor had he built up a cohort of followers within the ranks. Yet in the first crucial weeks of the Hitler government, it was Göring, with his boundless energy and naked ambition, who drove events, and it was his ruthless will to power that set the tone of cold-blooded brutality and utter contempt for law that would define Nazi rule.

He did not wait for orders from Papen or even from Hitler. In his first days in office, he detached the section of the Berlin Police Presidium that had dealt with political matters during the Weimar years and created a separate entity that would report directly to him. It would be a secret state police or Gestapo, short for Geheime Staatspolizei, to gather information and conduct investigations of political events and personalities that might have criminal implications. To head the Gestapo he turned not to a fellow Nazi but to Rudolf Diels, a conservative, high-ranking career official in the Interior Ministry. Then, acting on his own, he immediately initiated a massive purge of the Prussian civil government at all levels, dismissing hundreds of officials—Social Democrats, liberals, Jews—anyone whose loyalty to the new Reich government was in question. Most important, he purged top police officials in fourteen major Prussian cities, replacing them with Nazis and hard-line conservatives. That was only the beginning. On February 17 he issued an order demanding that "the police must in all circumstances avoid even the appearance of a hostile attitude, still less the impression of persecution, against the patriotic associations"—the SA and Stahlhelm. "I expect from all police authorities that they maintain the best relations with these organizations which comprise the most important state-constructive forces. Patriotic activities and propaganda are to be supported by every means." Furthermore, it was to be "the business of the police to abet every form of national propaganda."

The activities of "subversive organizations," on the other hand, were "to be combated with the most drastic methods." The police were to move against "Communist terrorist acts" with "all severity." When necessary, "weapons must be ruthlessly used." To emphasize the point, Göring explained that "police officers who make use of firearms in the execution of their duties will, without regard to the consequences of such use, benefit by my protection. . . . Every official must bear in mind that failure to act will be regarded more seriously than an error due to taking action." A few days later, at a closed meeting with police officials who were sworn to secrecy, he informed them that he knew that many of his instructions "conflicted with the present rights and laws of the Reich and its member states," but he assured them that "every official who follows my instructions may be sure of my absolute protection." Police officials need not worry that they might afterward be found guilty of violating the constitution. "There will be no attorney and no judge to punish an official for following the new course."

On February 20, Göring summoned some two dozen leading industrialists to join him at his official residence to discuss economic matters with Hitler. Many of those leaders arrived at Göring's offices expecting a discussion such as they had had with previous chancellors, a give-and-take about economic issues. Gustav Krupp von Bohlen, president of the powerful Reich Association of German Industrialists, had prepared a statement, listing business concerns about Nazi economic policy as well as a series of questions for the new government. Krupp and the assembled leaders of industry were in for a rude shock. First, Göring kept these influential gentlemen waiting for a quarter hour, and Hitler, true to form, arrived later still. After perfunctory handshakes all around, he launched into a rambling monologue of an hour and a half that betrayed little understanding of or interest in economic matters. Hitler assured his listeners that the new government would undertake no economic experiments and recapitulated his well-known views about the primacy of politics over economics, his support for the fundamentals of capitalism, and the crucial importance of the upcoming election. He warned of the looming danger of Communism and his determination to smash it once and for all. "Now we stand before the final election," he declared. "Whatever the outcome, there will be no retreat. One way or another, if the election does not decide, the decision will be brought about by other means." No questions were invited, no opinions sought, but as Hitler exited the room, no one was in any doubt about the ominous meaning of his words.

Göring then took the floor and spoke more bluntly, explaining to the assembled businessmen their role in the "national uprising." He did not mince words. Underscoring the importance of the ongoing campaign, he indicated that the government needed money for this crucial showdown and darkly suggested that those who were not on the front lines of the conflict had an obligation to make financial sacrifices for the cause. This might be easier for them to bear, he added, if the gentlemen understood that the March 5 election would be "the last for the next five years, probably even for the next hundred years." (The Nazis were inordinately fond of predictions that this or that would last for one hundred years or maybe even a thousand.) When he finished his remarks, he departed the meeting as abruptly as Hitler.

At Göring's departure, Hjalmar Schacht, the highly respected former president of the Reichsbank, who had long been a Nazi sympathizer and had helped organize the meeting, rose to speak. Whereas Göring had been aggressive but vague, Schacht presented the assembled gentlemen with the tab. The government expected a contribution of three million marks for the campaign. This, his listeners realized, had been the hidden agenda of the meeting all along. There was some grousing. Some still labored under the assumption that Papen, a favorite of the business community, was an equal partner in the cabinet, and insisted that a portion of their contributions go to the Battle Front Black-White-Red, an electoral alliance formed by Papen, Hugenberg, and Seldte of the Stahlhelm. The meeting, as one historian aptly described it, amounted to nothing more than a shakedown. The industrialists did their duty. That evening and in subsequent days Schacht was able to collect pledges of the full three million marks. In March Hitler would reward him by reinstalling him as president of the Reichsbank and a year later naming him Reich minister of economics.

After Göring's meeting with the industrialists, funds began pouring into the party's war chest. "Money is there," Goebbels reported on February 22. "Now we can get going." With the necessary cash at last on hand and the Brown Shirts conducting a campaign of intimidation and terror against the party's enemies, a National Socialist landslide did not seem at all far-fetched.

Still, the party wanted to leave nothing to chance. On February 22, claiming that the Communist threat was so menacing that the police lacked the manpower to meet the challenge, Göring announced the creation of an auxiliary police force to be staffed by "volunteers." Where would the state find these volunteers? Almost overnight, some fifty thousand SA, SS, and Stahlhelm men "volunteered" and were sworn in as "*Hilfspolizei*," or auxiliary police. They immediately appeared on the streets all across Prussia wearing their brown Nazi uniforms with the swastika on the left arm, and on the right a white armband signifying auxiliary police. Technically they were under the authority of the regular police, but this was an obvious fiction. These volunteers were the same thugs who for years had clashed with the police, fought pitched battles with the Communists, committed murder and arson, and harassed ordinary citizens on the streets. Now *they* were the law. Less than a month after Hitler assumed the chancellorship, a state-sanctioned reign of terror had begun.

Among the new and most potent weapons Goebbels wielded in the campaign was the radio. In previous campaigns the government parties had denied Hitler access to the radio; now the tables would be turned. "We make no bones about it," Goebbels told a group of radio general managers and directors he had summoned to Berlin, "the radio belongs to us, to no one else! And we will place the radio at the service of our idea, no other idea shall be expressed through it." Virtually every night throughout the campaign, Goebbels flooded the airwaves with speeches by Nazi leaders, monopolizing evening programming. He arranged for Hitler to speak in every town that had its own broadcasting station, and his speeches would be carried nationwide. Loudspeakers were to be strategically placed so that Hitler's voice would blare through every street and square, reverberating in the shops and restaurants and bars. Goebbels provided a dramatic introduction to Hitler's appearances, setting the scene in a breathless tone intended to "convey . . . the magical atmosphere of our huge demonstrations."

In one radio broadcast Goebbels also issued a chilling warning to the party's opponents. "If the Jewish press"—in the Nazi lexicon any non-Nazi newspaper was "Jewish" or "Marxist" or both—"complains that the National Socialist movement is broadcasting Hitler's speeches nationwide, then I say to them, 'what you've shown us how to do, we are now doing ourselves.'" Then, in a voice literally brimming with menace, he added: "If the Jewish newspapers try to get around our emergency decrees or think that they can intimidate our movement, then I say to them: 'You should beware. One day our patience will come to an end, and then we will stuff shut your lying Jewish mouths.'"

The Nazis wove two major motifs into their campaign. One was a positive message: Hitler was rebuilding the nation, putting things right after fourteen years of democratic misrule, cowardice, and corruption. He called on patriotic Germans to join him in his fight to overcome the religious, regional, and class cleavages that had sapped German strength and eroded its resolve. He needed their help. Second and far more prominent was his determination to eradicate Marxism. Both themes were on display in Hitler's first public appearance as chancellor on February 10 at the Berlin Sportpalast. It was also his first campaign speech for the March 5 election, and on this occasion Hitler the reserved statesman, the conciliatory chancellor, retreated to the wings, while Hitler the demagogic leader of the National Socialist movement strode boldly onto center stage. Gone were the dark blue business suit, black tie, and patent leather shoes; he marched through the wildly cheering crowd in his brown party uniform, the red swastika armband in place; his polished jack boots gleaming in the bright lights. All around the great oval auditorium a stream of swastika banners proclaimed anti-Marxist slogans.

As was so often the case, Hitler began haltingly but picked up steam as he rumbled onto familiar tracks. He recounted his spectacular rise from obscurity; he recapitulated the obligatory broadsides against the men of November 1918; condemned the corrosive system that for fourteen years had produced nothing but misery and despair, leaving millions without work and thousands with bankrupt businesses and family farms lost to the banks. He lamented the degradation of the culture and the loss of pride in being German. It was time to save the nation, and just as he had built a party of twelve million from a tiny group of seven, he would rebuild Germany, restore its faith and self-respect. These efforts would be guided by one realization, one conviction: "We shall never believe in foreign help, never in help which lies outside our own nation, outside our own Volk. The future of the German Volk lies in itself alone.

"Our opponents are asking about our program," he thundered. "They say 'Show us the details of your program. . . . '" Well, he might well ask the worthy gentlemen, "'Where was *your* program over the past fourteen years?'" Surely, he said mockingly, you don't "intend to now suddenly recall that you bear the responsibility for [these] fourteen years." After the endless string of calamities they had inflicted on Germany, "the German people must be rebuilt from top to bottom, just as you destroyed it from top to bottom! That is our program!"

In order to rebuild the nation "we must eliminate the causes of our own disintegration and thus bring about the reconciliation of the German classes. . . . The parties which support this division can . . . be certain that as long as the Almighty keeps me alive, my resolve and my will to destroy them will know no bounds. Never, never," Hitler bellowed, his rasping voice ramping ever higher, "will I stray from the task of stamping out Marxism and its side effects in Germany, and never will I be willing to make any compromise on this point. There can be only one victor: either Marxism or the German Volk! And Germany will triumph."

As the campaign began, a wave of intimidation and terror broke over the country. SA gangs roamed the streets; the police were co-opted, the courts paralyzed; legal norms turned upside down; the very meaning of law in flux. Storm Troopers disrupted political gatherings, arrested Social Democratic and Communist officials, and assaulted Jews. Leftist newspapers were banned for a few days here and there, their offices raided, their campaign rallies broken up. "It is a disgrace which gets worse with every day that passes," Viktor Klemperer, a Jewish professor of philology in Dresden, confided to his diary on February 21. "And there's not a sound from anyone and everyone's keeping his head down, Jewry most of all and their democratic press. . . . What is strangest of all is how one is blind in the face of events, how no one has a clue to the real balance of power."

On February 24 the SA auxiliary police raided the Karl Liebknecht House, the Communist headquarters in Berlin. Only a few clerks and low-level functionaries were in the building and almost all of the party's documents had already been removed. This did not prevent Göring from claiming to have found "tons of seditious material," clearly revealing that a Communist coup was in the works. None of these incriminating documents were produced in the following days (or ever), even for the Nazi press, which did nothing to tamp down the party's hysteria about an imminent Communist uprising.

Then, in the night of February 27–28, with the campaign going as the Nazis planned and the election only one week away, an event occurred that dramatically altered the pace of events. Hitler was enjoying an evening of relaxation with Goebbels and his wife, Magda, at their home when shortly after 9:30 Putzi Hanfstaengl telephoned with startling news: from the window of his quarters in the Wilhelmstrasse he could see rippling sheets of flame rising from the Reichstag. Goebbels was skeptical—was this another of Putzi's bad jokes? Come see for yourself, Hanfstaengl told him brusquely and hung up. Stepping outside into the darkness, Hitler could see an ominous crimson glow beyond the black treetops of the Tiergarten. Within minutes Hitler and Goebbels arrived on the scene. Climbing out of their black limousines, they found the area cordoned off, fire brigades and police units swarming everywhere. Swollen fire hoses tessellated the pavement, sirens wailed, and through the tumult of soot and flying grit the sound of crackling flames, breaking glass, and falling timbers. The imposing glass dome of the building had shattered. The wood-paneled plenary chamber, with its ancient benches and cushioned chairs, its heavy curtains and dry-as-a-bone flooring, had gone up like a tinderbox.

Göring, dressed in an expensive camel-hair coat and wearing a brown hat turned up in front in the stylish Potsdam manner, was already on the scene, bustling about, bellowing commands. The fire was largely under control, he reported, as Hitler and his party approached. He had initially been worried about the Gobelin tapestries, but they had been saved. "It's the Communists," he declared. There was no doubt about it. A number of Communist deputies had been seen in the building only twenty minutes before the fire broke out. Surely this was the beginning of the long-anticipated Communist uprising. "God grant that this may be the Communists," Hitler remarked to Sefton Delmer, an English journalist who managed to accompany Hitler and his party as they toured the still-burning Reichstag. "If the Communists got hold of Europe and had control of it six months—what am I saying!— two months—the whole continent would be aflame like this building." To an impeccably dressed Papen, who arrived fresh from a formal dinner party in Hindenburg's honor, Hitler added, "This is a God-given signal, Herr Vice Chancellor! If this fire, as I believe, is the work of the Communists, then we must crush out this murderous pest with an iron fist!"

Moments later Rudolf Diels, the career police official whom Göring had promoted to head the new Prussian secret state police (Gestapo), reported that a suspect had been apprehended in the building—a young, soot-covered Dutchman with strong anti-Fascist sentiments and vague ties to the Dutch Communist Party. The man, twenty-four-year-old Marinus van der Lubbe, defiantly admitted to starting the fire and steadfastly claimed to have acted alone. Over the past week he had set fires in other government buildings, he boasted, though not as successfully as the Reichstag conflagration. His actions were intended as a cry of protest against the new government. His confession, Diels thought, had the ring of truth to it and expressed skepticism that this was the signal for a Communist insurrection. From his numerous interrogations of arrested KPD officials and his review of confiscated Communist documents, he had come to the conclusion that the Communists were in disarray and were simply incapable of organizing a mass action to overthrow the government. The call for a general strike, the threats of a popular uprising, were all talk, his sources told him, intended above all to embarrass the Social Democrats and reveal their timidity.

When Diels tried to explain this, Hitler, his face flaming red with heat and excitement, wasn't having it. In an outburst of rage that bordered on hysteria, he shrieked, "Now we'll show them! Anyone who stands in our way will be mown down! The German people have been soft too long. Every Communist official must be shot. All Communist deputies must be hanged this very night. All friends of the Communists must be locked up. And that goes for the Social Democrats and the Reichsbanner as well!" After listening to this unbridled rant, Diels turned to the Reichstag building inspector standing beside him and muttered, "This is a madhouse."

The little group adjourned to the Reichstag President's office in the building, where Hitler continued his tirade. Still in a fury, Hitler ordered Göring to take all necessary measures to crush the Communist uprising, and Göring, himself highly agitated, quickly obeyed. He hurriedly issued a flood of sweeping and confusing instructions to Diels, ordering him to put all police on emergency footing with instructions for the mass arrest of Communists and Social Democrats, and a "shoot to kill" order in the event of resistance. Later a directive was sent by police radio to all law enforcement officials to arrest not only all Communist delegates in the Reichstag, but in all provincial legislatures and town councils as well. All Communist functionaries were to be rounded up, all Communist newspapers were to be suppressed. Some seven thousand Communist functionaries, legislative deputies, journalists, and fellow travelers were arrested.

Hitler and Goebbels left the still-burning Reichstag, convinced that they had witnessed the first shot in the Communist insurrection. They rushed to the Prussian Ministry of the Interior, where they convened an impromptu conference of police and government officials. Hitler repeated his order for the mass arrest of Communists, and one official suggested that a new emergency decree against arson and terroristic attacks be issued to give legal cover for the arrests to follow. Hitler agreed but decided that it should be discussed at a meeting of the cabinet he would call for the next morning. From there Hitler and Goebbels rushed to the offices of the *Völkischer Beobachter* where they supervised the paper's coverage of the crime. So far there had been no discussion of more sweeping measures.

The next morning, the Reich cabinet met in emergency session. The first item on the agenda was Hitler's insistence that despite the expected Communist uprising, the March 5 elections must go forward. Papen favored declaring martial law, handing power over to the army (and Hindenburg), which Hitler was not about to do. Besides, no election could be held under martial law, and Hitler was convinced that after the Reichstag fire and the ensuing anti-Communist hysteria, the Nazis would prevail in the election, perhaps winning a majority. Wilhelm Frick then produced a short draft of a measure he had drawn up in preparation for the meeting. The gist of the document was that the regime would impose a form of martial law to be enforced not by the army but by the civilian government. The model was Papen's July 20 seizure of power in Prussia during the previous year. The draft suspended freedom of the press, freedom of expression, freedom of association, freedom of assembly, and arrogated to the government the authority to open private mail and to place wiretaps on telephones. It also gave the regime the right to make arrests without warrant or judicial review and to detain persons for an unlimited amount of time. The police would be empowered to conduct warrantless searches and confiscate property "beyond the legal limits otherwise proscribed."

The draft was accepted with little discussion or demur, and that same day Reich President Hindenburg was prevailed upon to issue an emergency decree, "For the Protection of People and State." Hitler was careful to frame the decree as a purely defensive measure, intended as "a ruthless settling of accounts" with the Communists, something the conservative cabinet majority could certainly endorse, and, he insisted, the execution of the decree "must not be dependent on legal considerations." The blanket suspension of civil rights embodied in the decree provoked no opposition. Under the circumstances, it did not seem so ominous. After all, it was to be only a temporary measure, the conservatives still held a majority in the cabinet, and, they complacently believed, still held the real power in

the new government. To further allay fears of an emerging Nazi dictatorship, Hitler solemnly declared that the suspension of civil rights was
only temporary. As he declared to Sefton Delmer, "I myself am only too
anxious for the normal state of affairs to be restored as quickly as possible.
. . . First, however, we must crush Communism out of existence."

Although it is not clear that Hitler at first perceived the full implications of
the hastily drafted edict, the Reichstag Fire Decree, as it came to be known,
put an end to all civil rights guaranteed by the Weimar constitution and provided the legal basis for Nazi suppression of all opposition by "enemies of the
state." In four short paragraphs it sounded the death knell of democracy in
Germany and served as the founding document of the Third Reich.

The Communists meanwhile vehemently denied any responsibility for
the fire, claiming instead that the Nazis had set the blaze, and international opinion tended to agree. After all, the Nazis were the obvious beneficiaries of the fire, and the swift Nazi response seemed less a spontaneous
reaction than an act of premeditation. Virtually no one believed that the
enormous conflagration had been the work of one man, least of all van
der Lubbe, whose police photographs seemed to offer pictorial evidence
that the young man was mentally defective. (He was not.) So either the
Communists had torched the building or the Nazis. Variations on exactly
how and by whom were myriad, but in this view the Nazi reaction was so
rapid and radical that it had to be a Nazi plot, planned and executed as
justification for a severe crackdown on the left.

No definitive evidence of responsibility for the fire has ever emerged,
but much hangs on the interpretation. Some historians have claimed that
the Reichstag fire was part of a Nazi plan to establish the regime's total
domination over state and society, a calculated pretext for the oppressive
measures that followed. Among other suggestive evidence, they point to
the fact that a tunnel ran from Göring's office directly to the speaker's
podium in the Reichstag, where, they hypothesize, the blaze began. They
also note suspicious comments attributed to various SA men and other
party leaders, especially Göring, in the preceding days, as they loudly
claimed that the Communists were planning a campaign of public unrest
and arson against government buildings. It remains a plausible case.

But the most compelling evidence to date strongly suggests that *neither* the Nazis nor the Communists set the fire, but that, unlikely as it

might seem, Marinus van der Lubbe acted alone. But if the Nazis had not planned it, Hitler and the Nazi leadership saw in the Reichstag fire an un-anticipated opportunity for decisive action against the Communists. It was exactly the sort of improvisation that would characterize the first months of Nazi rule—indeed, for much of the Third Reich. The Nazis certainly made every effort to link the Communists to the crime, arresting hundreds of Communist functionaries and formally charging Ernst Torgler, head of the Communist Reichstag delegation, and Georgi Dimitrov, a representative of the Communist International living in Berlin, and two other Bulgarian Communists who happened to be in the city. These actions were not simply for propaganda purposes; Hitler's fear and rage were not feigned. Göring, Hitler, and the Nazi leadership were convinced that the long anticipated Communist revolution had finally come. There could be no doubt, Goebbels recorded in his diary on February 27, that the Reichstag fire represented "a final Communist attempt to use arson and terror to create disorder and in the resultant general panic to seize power. The decisive moment has come. Göring has set everything in motion." Despite an utter lack of evidence, the Nazis had for years so demonized the Communists, had so stoked their own imagination with fantastic charges of devilish Bolshevik plots that they came to believe it themselves. They had expected a Communist uprising; now it had come. Nazi actions around the Reichstag fire were driven less by clever design than their own feverish fantasies.

Göring boasted publicly about the incriminating documents he had discovered in the Karl Liebknecht House—documents that revealed that the Communists were hatching a vast plot to overthrow the government. They intended to spread terror by setting fire to public buildings in Berlin and elsewhere; they planned to disrupt the nation's electrical grid, murder public figures, and kidnap their wives and children; they even intended to poison the water supply. Despite Diels's plea not to do so, Göring insisted that there should be a trial before the German Supreme Court in Leipzig, in which he would act as special prosecutor. It was to be a show trial of the first order. But the damning evidence Göring claimed to have found did not materialize in the Nazi press or at the trial. Publishing in exile, the left-leaning journal *Die Weltbühne* claimed that the cabinet, upon ex-amining the documents, had insisted that they were such clumsy forger-ies that they could not be presented to the court. In a humiliating blow to Göring, the court found no firm evidence of a Communist conspiracy and acquitted Torgler, Dimitrov, and the Bulgarian Communists. Van der Lubbe alone was convicted in September and beheaded in January 1934.

Regardless of who started the fire, the Nazis wasted no time in exploiting it. On March 2, Göring made the regime's intentions brutally clear: "It will be my chief objective to expunge the pestilence of Communism. . . . I don't need the Reichstag fire to move against Communism, and I'm not betraying any secret when I say that if it were left to Hitler and me, the perpetrators would already be swinging on the gallows." In a directive to police officials across Germany, he made clear that they were to interpret the Reichstag Fire Decree broadly. The police and their auxiliaries were to move against the Communists "but also those who work with Communists, or support or further, even indirectly, their criminal goals." It was open season not only on the left but on anyone suspected of opposition, no matter how insignificant, to the regime.

The enactment of the Reichstag Fire Decree removed the last gossamer restraints on the SA. All across Germany the Brown Shirts unleashed a campaign of unrestrained terror. Storm Troopers and party radicals, acting on their own initiative, seized city halls, purged police departments, schools, and cultural institutions. Jails and prisons overflowed with political prisoners taken into "protective custody"; Jews, Social Democrats, Communists, troublesome clergy, anyone who had crossed them, found themselves under assault. Grudges were settled, revenge taken. Ali Höhler, the convicted killer of Horst Wessel, was torn from his prison cell and murdered in a forest near Berlin. The police made some formal arrests and filed charges, but the SA acted as a law unto itself—as, indeed, it was. Storm Troopers dragged their victims to old warehouses, empty factories and schools, into cellars, where they were beaten and tortured. These makeshift prisons, or camps as they were called, sprouted like poisonous weeds all across the country—there were more than one hundred in Berlin alone. They followed no order from above; there was no coordinated plan of action for these spontaneous prison camps. As Rudolf Diels remarked, these hellholes "weren't established; one day they were just there."

Formal charges were rarely filed; few records kept; prisoners were tortured, beaten to death, hanged, or shot, their battered bodies dumped in vacant lots, alleyways, forest paths, or left floating in ponds and canals.

Some "committed suicide" by leaping from a high window; others were "shot while trying to escape." There was no public outcry. "No one dares to say anything more," Viktor Klemperer wrote in his diary, "everyone is afraid. . . . It is shocking how day after day naked acts of violence, breaches of the law, barbaric opinions appear quite undisguised as official decree. . . . I can no longer get rid of the feeling of disgust and shame. And no one stirs; everyone trembles, keeps out of sight."

Attention was now focused on the March 5 election. The Communist press was suppressed indefinitely and Social Democratic newspapers were prohibited for two weeks—until after the election. Neither party held campaign rallies or other public events. Many of their leaders and functionaries were arrested by the police—the entire KPD Reichstag delegation was in jail—or held in makeshift SA prisons. Some had gone underground; others escaped abroad. Gangs of Brown Shirts roamed the cities, pounding on doors, "getting out the vote"; truckloads of Storm Troopers cruised through the streets, whipping up enthusiasm—and fear. On election day voters faced widespread intimidation. In some smaller towns the Nazis themselves manned the polling places; in others the secret ballot was discarded altogether, and, with SA men looking on, voters were "encouraged" to cast their ballots publicly. Many people felt so threatened, so afraid that the Nazis were listening to their phone calls, reading their mail, and opening their ballots that they complied without complaint.

The election of March 1933 was not the last free election of the Weimar era; it was the first sham election of the Third Reich. Under the circumstances, the Nazis were expected to prevail, and it came as no surprise that the party rebounded from its dismal November performance, its vote jumping from 11,737,821 to 17,200,000. Goebbels hailed the outcome as an overwhelming victory, a crowning achievement to his years of work. "We are the masters of the Reich and in Prussia. Everything else shrinks to insignificance." Yet despite all the intimidation, coercion, and outright violence, the Nazis were still unable to attain the majority they sought. Prevented from mounting anything like a full-fledged campaign, the Social Democrats still drew a remarkable 7,100,000 votes, the Communists 4,800,000, the Catholic Zentrum and its Bavarian sister party, 5,400,000.

The Conservatives, despite being Hitler's coalition partners, insisted on running an independent campaign and captured another 3,100,000 votes. Altogether these parties received roughly 56 percent of the vote, leading journalist Konrad Heiden to observe that "a majority did not want Hitler, but it wanted nothing else. There was no united will to confront the united will of the National Socialists." The Nazis had captured 43.9 percent of the vote, and with the 8 percent garnered by their Conservative partners polled, the Government of National Concentration now held a majority of seats in the new Reichstag. Hitler felt it something of a disappointment that he would still be dependent on the Conservatives and ultimately on Hindenburg, but he acted immediately to take advantage of the situation.

The first priority of the new regime was to sweep away all organized opposition and to assume control of the civil administration at every level of government. The Nazis referred to this policy as "Gleichschaltung," a term derived from electrical usage, meaning all switches were put onto the same circuit so that all could be activated by throwing a single master switch. The term is usually translated as "coordination," but is more aptly rendered as "bringing onto line." Initially it referred to bringing all governmental departments and agencies under Nazi control, dismissing unreliable personnel, especially Jews, Social Democrats, and other political "undesirables," and installing Nazis in their positions. Göring had begun the process in Prussia in February, and within a week of the March 5 election the Nazis seized control of all the German states. Between March 5 and March 9, Hitler dispatched Reich commissars—Nazi governors—to all the German states not already headed by National Socialists. Their ostensible mission was to curb unrest and restore order, although the only civil unrest being stirred up in Germany was the work of Storm Troopers and other Nazi militants. The initial impetus came from Berlin, but the Nazi seizure of power was to a surprising extent an exercise in grassroots politics, as fanatical local Nazis, acting without explicit orders from above, took matters into their own hands. Everywhere they bullied local authorities into submission, pushing aside city councils and state governments. In fact, Hitler appointed the Reich commissars not so much to deal with threats from the left, recalcitrant clergy, or other enemies of the regime but to ride herd on party radicals whose violent excesses and calls for a "revolution from below" were a growing source of concern.

Bavaria, which had historically resisted every threat to its independence, was the last state government to succumb to Nazi pressure. Munich's possible resistance had worried the party leadership, but on March 9 the Bavarian government meekly ceded power to Hitler's appointee, General Ritter von Epp, who appeared in Munich backed by a phalanx of armed Storm Troopers. Epp was well known and respected in Bavaria. He had commanded Bavarian troops in the Great War and had led the Free Corps's bloody suppression of the Bavarian Communist Republic in 1919. Foremost among the many Nazi stalwarts who assumed powerful positions in the new Bavarian government were SA commander Ernst Röhm as minister without portfolio and SS leader Heinrich Himmler, who assumed leadership of the Munich police. Himmler quickly appointed his SS deputy Reinhard Heydrich to take charge of the Bavarian Political Police. Since 1930 Heydrich had led the party's Security Service (Sicherheitsdienst or SD), gathering intelligence on the NSDAP's enemies, real and imagined. Although it had hardly seemed so at the time, these appointments proved to be the first stepping-stone to ultimate power for Himmler, Heydrich, and the SS.

The dispatch of the Reich commissars, however, did little to restrain the SA. Storm Troopers attacked German citizens on the streets for failing to give the Hitler salute to passing SA formations or join in the singing of the Nazi Party anthem; they roughed up—sometimes severely—foreign businessmen, tourists, and even diplomats and their families. Formal complaints from foreign governments flooded into the Foreign Office, and on March 10 Hitler made an effort to bring the SA under control. Disingenuously claiming that these excesses were mostly the work of Communist spies who had infiltrated the SA, he nonetheless made an appeal to the Storm Troopers and other radicals to show restraint. "Unprincipled characters . . . are attempting to compromise the Party with individual actions (*Einzelaktionen*) which are not in any way related to the great task of the national uprising and can only damage and belittle the accomplishments of our Movement. . . . Men of the SA and SS! You must apprehend such creatures yourselves . . . and call them to account for their actions; you must turn them over to the police without delay, regardless of who they may be." He reminded them that "as of today, the National Government has the executive power in Germany in its hands" and reassured them that "the national uprising will continue to be carried out methodically," but "under control from above. . . . From this moment on all individual actions must cease. From now on, whoever attempts to disrupt our administrative and social life through *Einzelaktionen*, is acting consciously against the national regime." These admonitions were largely ignored at the grass roots, where beatings, murder, and unauthorized arrests continued. The response of SA leaders was "That's what the Führer must say for foreign consumption. We know he wants the opposite." Some of the more egregious excesses subsided, but despite Hitler's order, few practical steps were taken to rein in the SA. The radicals had read him correctly.

Insubordination by radical SA troops bent on exacting revenge against all opponents, real and imagined, was a potential problem but one Hitler was willing to tolerate in the first critical months of the regime. He needed them as enforcers, as threats to potential opponents. At this point, the most disturbing threat to the Nazi consolidation of power was the Reich President, and behind him the army. What would happen, Nazi leaders worried, if Hindenburg awoke one morning and decided that the "national revolution" had gone too far? Might he push the recently installed Hitler government aside and install a military dictatorship as a prelude to a restoration of the monarchy?

In a bow to the traditional fixtures of the old right, the Nazis decided to use the occasion of the opening session of the new Reichstag to stage an extravagant display of reverence for the venerable field marshal and the Prussian military tradition. The time and place for the ceremony were intended to project a compelling symbolic meaning. It was to be held in Potsdam, the historic residence of the Hohenzollern monarchy, in the storied Potsdam Garrison Church, which held the tombs of Frederick William I, "the Soldier King," and his son, Frederick the Great. It was hallowed ground, steeped in Prussian dynastic and military history, and the date, March 21, was the anniversary of Bismarck's convening of the first Reichstag in the newly united Germany in 1871.

The day began with religious services at the St. Nicholai Church for the Protestant dignitaries and in St. Peter and Paul for Catholics. Hitler and Goebbels chose not to attend either and instead visited the graves of fallen Nazi "martyrs" in a Berlin cemetery before motoring to Potsdam. It was a telling choice. On March 21, the streets of Potsdam were draped in the black, white, and red of the Empire, interspersed with brilliant swastika banners. Reichswehr troops in their steel helmets and field gray uniforms lined the route. Hitler, incongruously sporting a top hat and cutaway, and Hindenburg, in the uniform of an Imperial field marshal, spiked helmet, and the grand cordon of the Black Eagle, arrived together, cheered along their way by a multitude of enthusiastic well-wishers. Prominent among the guests of honor were generals of the Reichswehr, the crown prince in his army regalia, and military notables from past wars, all resplendent in their antediluvian dress uniforms—this, the setting proclaimed, was Potsdam, not Weimar.

Assembled in the crowded interior of the church were the Imperial family, foreign dignitaries, ambassadors, the ministers of the Hitler cabinet, and the newly elected Reichstag deputies. The Communists, of course, were nowhere to be seen—they were locked away in jail—and the Social Democrats refused to attend such a shameless paean to Hitler and the faded grandees of the old order. All rose when Hindenburg, accompanied by a respectful Hitler, entered. "Hitler," French ambassador François-Poncet observed, "looked like a timid newcomer being introduced by an important protector into a company to which he does not belong. Who could have believed that this wan man with such vulgar features, dressed in an ill-fitting coat and in appearance so respectful and so modest, was the more powerful of the two personages." An awed hush fell upon the guests as Hindenburg turned to the gallery where was seated the Imperial family and raised his field marshal's baton in a solemn salute to the empty chair of his exiled Kaiser Wilhelm II.

In his brief opening address, Hindenburg praised the new legally elected majority cabinet and exhorted it to be guided, in its exuberant youth, by the virtues and values of old Prussia—honor, duty, loyalty, and hard work. Hitler then took his position at the ornate rostrum, and, facing Hindenburg seated just a few feet away, gave an abbreviated recapitulation of his standard stump speech—Weimar's failures, the ignominy of Versailles, the calumny of the Allies in assigning guilt for the war to the German state and its people, all well-worn themes. Notably absent, however, was the usual stormy rhetoric, the angry bombast. On this occasion a solemn Hitler reached for the inspirational, summoning the nation to join with him in his struggle to restore Germany's prosperity, patriotism, and standing in a peaceful world.

After the shameful end to the Great War, he declared, "while the German people and the German Reich . . . became mired in internal political conflict and discord and the economy drifted into ruin, a new group of Germans gathered, Germans who with faithful trust in their own people, wished to form it into a new community. It was to this young Germany that you, Herr *Generalfeldmarschall*, entrusted the leadership of the Reich." On March 5, the people had given the new government a majority and in so doing had "restored the national honor within a few short weeks and, thanks to your understanding, Herr Reich President, consummated the marriage between the symbols of old glory and young strength." At the conclusion of these two sober declarations, Hindenburg rose and stepped stiffly down into the crypt, where, head bowed, he communed in silence with the two long dead Prussian kings.

The festivities inside over, the party adjourned to the steps of the church where they reviewed marching columns of Storm Troopers, SS men, Stahlhelm, and Reichswehr troops. Cannons fired in salute; military bands played. During the military review Hitler was content to remain in the background, yielding center stage to Hindenburg, who must have thought himself transported back to the glories of the old empire. In such a scene it was easy to imagine that Hitler was preparing the ground for a restoration of the monarchy. For weeks he had hinted to conservatives that he was at least open to such a move. Certainly the crown prince seemed to think so, watching the passing troops as if they were marching in review for him. The most compelling image of the day came when Hitler, in a studied display of deference, bowed low and offered his hand to the field marshal who towered above him like a stone pillar. It was, in today's political idiom, a staged photo op, and that image, captured in a photograph, appeared on postcards and in newspapers throughout the country. It was the message of the day, and it proved wildly popular. That night, torchlight parades were held in cities around the country, each with this same theme of fusion between the glories of the old and the revivifying energies of the new. The Day of Potsdam had been a triumph.

That same day, some three hundred miles away in a small Bavarian village, another side of the "national revolution" was on display. While national radio gave minute-by-minute coverage of the events in Potsdam, Heinrich Himmler, in his capacity as police president of Munich, announced the opening of "a concentration camp for political prisoners" at Dachau. This new institution, he explained, would hold some five thousand prisoners, primarily Communists, who were too dangerous to be released from the already clogged jails. Contrary to the widely circulating rumors, he reassured the public that the prisoners would be well treated and would be held only as long as necessary for their "reeducation." Press releases, some with accompanying photographs, emphasized that the camp, and others that were being built around the country, were necessary to preserve law and order, to keep hardened "enemies of the Reich" under lock and key, and to relieve overcrowding in the prisons.

The first of these installations, called concentration camps, was located at the edge of the village of Dachau, about fifteen miles from Munich. It was hardly a secret. The camp was given extensive publicity in the press, always emphasizing the humane treatment of prisoners, always stressing that the inmates were primarily Communist subversives who were being reeducated so that they could rejoin society as loyal, productive "people's comrades." The prisoners would learn the virtues of honest labor and discipline while enjoying the fresh air of a clean rural environment. This motif ran through news stories about all the camps (Oranienburg near Berlin, the Emsland camps in Baden) established in the early days of the regime. At first, the city fathers of Dachau were excited about the prospect of much needed business coming to the town; some even speculated that it would be something of a tourist attraction, though the locals were warned to keep their distance from the camp. Local boosters were soon calling it "the most famous town in the Fatherland." This benevolent glow vanished soon enough. Within a year, Dachau would become an internationally reviled synonym for suffering, sadism, and oppression, a name that produced revulsion and dread in all who heard it.

A day after the camp at Dachau opened, the first working session of the Reichstag got under way in the Kroll Opera House, close by the ruined Reichstag building. SA and SS troops cordoned off the building, and inside the main chamber Nazi deputies in their brown party uniforms took their places, and armed SA and SS men loitered ominously in the corridors. Behind the speaker's podium loomed a gigantic swastika banner. Hitler had already announced that he would demand the passage of an "enabling act," which would amend the constitution to allow the Reich government to rule without legislative or presidential interference for a period of four years. The passage of such a measure, however, would require a two-thirds majority in the Reichstag. The Communists were not a worry—the KPD's elected representatives were either dead, in jail, or in hiding—but the Social Democrats had already proclaimed their opposition to such a measure. Crucial to attaining the necessary two-thirds majority was the Zentrum, and its leader, Prelate Ludwig Kaas, insisted on assurances that the rights and institutions of the Church would be unaffected by the act. Hitler eagerly provided such guarantees, but Kaas demanded that his promise be put in writing. Hitler agreed but then evaded producing such a document. To the surprise of no one, perhaps even Kaas, the written document never materialized. Fearing that the Nazis would simply outlaw the party if it defied the regime, the Zentrum dropped its opposition to the proposal, leaving the Social Democrats alone to resist the "Law for Removing the Distress of People and Reich."

During his prepared remarks, Hitler's demeanor was moderate; his message, restrained. He reiterated Germany's deep desire for peace and equality in international affairs, affirmed the government's regard for "Christianity as the unshakeable foundation of the ethics and morality of the people," and stated his determination to establish friendly relations with the Vatican. He also pledged that the government would make use of "this authorization" only if it was necessary "for the implementation of vital measures." It would "always be the first and foremost task of the Government to bring about inner consensus with its aims." Neither the Reichstag nor the Reichsrat (where the individual states were represented) was endangered. The position of the Reich President would remain inviolate. The states would not be abolished; "the rights of the Churches" would "not be curtailed and their position vis-à-vis the State will not be altered." Furthermore, he assured his audience that "the number of cases in which there is an internal necessity for taking refuge in such a law is, in and of itself, limited."

The Enabling Act tightened the Nazi grip on the state, and its passage also removed the few remaining restraints on the SA, whose brutal "excesses" went far beyond all that had come before. The extent of the violence was stunning. The primary targets continued to be Communists and

Social Democrats, from the top leaders to midlevel functionaries to the rank and file, but the Storm Troopers and party militants also conducted an escalating campaign of harassment against the Jews. Although the regime occasionally admonished the radicals, these uncoordinated "independent actions" (*Einzelaktionen*) continued to be tolerated and even encouraged by the regime. Since January 30 and with mounting intensity, Jews were daily being subjected to beatings, arrests, public humiliations, ransacked shops and homes, and, occasionally, murder. But with the passage of the Enabling Act, the floodgates of persecution burst wide open. On March 9, SA squads moved into a Jewish neighborhood in Berlin, rounded up dozens of Eastern European Jews, and packed them off to a concentration camp; four days later Brown Shirts in Mannheim invaded Jewish businesses, roughed up their owners, and shut down the shops; later that same day in a small Hessian town, Storm Troopers, "in search of weapons," forced their way into the homes of local Jews, ransacked the rooms, and brutalized the terrified inhabitants; in Breslau, SA men stormed brazenly into a courtroom, attacked Jewish lawyers and judges, and drove them out of the building. Such "independent actions" were not authorized or directed from above, and they were not coordinated as part of an organized campaign, but in the spring of 1933 such outrageous breaches of the law were occurring throughout the Reich on an almost daily basis.

The unprecedented scope of the violence drew international attention. While domestic criticism of the regime had been effectively stifled, the foreign press, especially in the United States, condemned Nazi outrages against the Jews. In the early spring Jewish organizations in the United States and Western Europe began an intense media campaign to raise public awareness of Nazi atrocities against Germany's Jews, and on March 27 the American Jewish Congress issued a call for an international boycott of German goods. The Nazis reacted with predictable fury. They threatened to initiate a boycott of their own against Jewish businesses in the Reich. In a bow to party radicals, Hitler appointed Julius Streicher, the party's most notorious anti-Semite, to organize a nationwide boycott. The tentative start date was set for April 1 and was intended to go on indefinitely.

As preparation for the boycott proceeded, Hitler came under pressure from within his own government, especially from Foreign Minister Constantin von Neurath, Hjalmar Schacht, president of the Reichsbank, and even Hindenburg, who feared that a boycott would seriously damage the weak German economy and undermine the country's reputation in the international community. Caught between the pragmatists and the extremists, Hitler found himself in a familiar dilemma. He was not inclined to retreat, especially since he was under pressure from party radicals to live up to his own anti-Semitic rhetoric, but he also understood the pragmatists' plea for restraint. In private he heartily embraced the boycott, even encouraged it, but in public he posed as the sensible man of moderation, trying to restrain the justifiable outrage of the German people at the vile calumny of international Jewry.

On the morning of April 1, the boycott went forward as planned. Storm Troopers stationed themselves in front of Jewish shops, department stores, and professional offices, menacing anyone who wanted to go inside. They carried anti-Semitic placards and scrawled slogans on Jewish shop windows: "Germans, defend yourselves. Don't buy from Jews." Goebbels, an enthusiastic promoter of the boycott, launched a propaganda barrage aimed at "enlightening" the public about world Jewry's "declaration of economic warfare" against Germany.

"The boycott against the world atrocity propaganda has broken out in full force in Berlin and across the entire Reich," Goebbels enthused in his diary notes. To see for himself, he drove down Tauentzienstrasse, a fashionable street with many Jewish businesses. "All the Jewish shops are closed," he beamed. "SA guards stand before the entries. Everywhere the public has declared its solidarity [with us]. Exemplary discipline dominates." All in all, it was "an impressive play." Yet, for all the furious bluster, the boycott did not produce the enthusiastic burst of public support that Goebbels desired. Some Jewish businesses simply stayed closed on that Saturday morning, and many customers ignored the boycott, brushing past the SA pickets to shop at Jewish businesses and department stores. Germans still visited their Jewish doctors and lawyers. The *Völkischer Beobachter* of April 3 reported that in Hanover some shoppers had even tried to enter a Jewish business by force, while in Munich customers had been feverishly stocking up on merchandise from Jewish shops for days prior to the boycott. Exasperated, the *Völkischer Beobachter* condemned "the lack of sense among that part of the population which forced its hard-earned money into the hands of enemies of the people and cunning slanderers." Some store windows were smashed and some proprietors and even a few customers were roughed up, but instances of outright violence were surprisingly rare. The boycott had been orderly, and the day passed in relative calm. After twenty-four hours, the Nazis, declaring victory, suspended the boycott. It would never be revived.

The April boycott was only the beginning, an ominous prelude. To pacify the disappointed radicals and to assert the state's control of Jewish policy, the regime initiated a series of anti-Jewish measures in the weeks that followed. On April 7, a hastily drafted Law for the Protection of a Professional Civil Service was enacted. Drafted by Minister of the Interior Wilhelm Frick, the law allowed the government to dismiss tenured civil servants who were known to be "politically unreliable"—leftists, liberals, and others "whose previous political activities afford no assurance that they will at all times give their fullest support to the national state." Beyond that, the law also contained an "Aryan Paragraph," as it came to be called, ordering that all "non Aryans" be dismissed immediately from the national, state, and municipal civil service. Jews were no longer allowed to serve as schoolteachers, university professors, judges, or in any other government post. For the law's purposes, anyone with one Jewish grandparent was classified a Jew. Shortly thereafter (April 11) an ordinance, also emanating from the Ministry of the Interior, denied Jews admission to the bar, and another edict later in the month banned Jews from practicing medicine through the state-run insurance programs where most Germans received their health care. Both measures encountered opposition from an unexpected source. The Reich President was distressed by the law as originally written and pressured Hitler to grant some exceptions, which he did. The law's restrictions were not to apply to combat veterans of the Great War, civil servants who had served continuously since August 1914, and those whose father or son had been killed in the war.

Draconian as these laws and ordinances were, their initial impact was not as extensive as the regime intended. With the exceptions granted, 3,167 of the country's 4,585 Jewish lawyers were allowed to continue their work; of the 717 Jewish judges and state prosecutors, 336 remained in place. Even fewer Jewish physicians, who made up 11 percent of all doctors in Germany, were affected by the laws. Here the regime trod carefully, not willing at this early stage to insert itself between those Jewish physicians and their thousands of patients. Later in the year additional edicts placed further restrictions on Jewish life in Germany—regulating, among other measures, the number of Jewish students in schools (Law to Prevent the Overcrowding of German Schools, April 29) and forbidding Jews from acquiring agricultural property (The Hereditary Farm Law, September 1933). The ideological message in these early measures was chillingly clear, sending an ominous signal about Nazi intentions regarding Germany's increasingly beleaguered Jewish community.

Hitler was coming under mounting international criticism for the violence of the SA, and on April 6 he spoke to the foreign press, defending the course of the revolution under way in Germany. During his speech introducing the Enabling Law, he had claimed that "hardly ever has a revolution on such a large scale been carried out in so disciplined and bloodless a fashion as this renaissance of the German people." Addressing the foreign journalists, he returned to that theme. In contrast to "the intolerable terrorization" of the National Socialists by the Weimar parties, "the victorious revolution" was carried out with "unheard of discipline and incomparable self-control. . . . Not only did the retaliation bear no relation to the sufferings which had been endured [by the Nazis] but even where there was retaliation it was always given rein only through the necessity to break the opposition of the November system."

The politically unreliable and racially unacceptable were driven from state offices, but the *Gleichschaltung* was far from complete. Two other groups from outside the formal power structure remained: workers and Catholics, two elements of the population that had proven most resistant to the Nazis before 1933. The Communist threat had been squashed, but millions of workers, with their traditional alliance to the parties of the left, were hostile or at least highly suspicious of the new regime. In an attempt to woo them, the Nazis, with their usual fanfare, declared May 1 "The Day of German Labor." If the Day of Potsdam was a reassuring bow to the reactionary right, May Day would be a national celebration of the German worker. The Nazis declared it a national holiday, something even the Social Democratic governments of Weimar had been unable to accomplish, and Goebbels organized a massive day-long demonstration in Berlin that would show the new regime's determination to integrate the working class into the new national community. It would be staged on the "grandest scale" and would "for the first time draw the entire Volk together," Goebbels noted in his diary, but "from that point onward, the final showdown with the unions will begin. We will never rest easy until they are completely in our hands."

The day began with nationwide celebrations and speeches lauding the German worker. At nine in the morning Hitler and Hindenburg addressed a mammoth youth rally at the Lustgarten in central Berlin; in the early afternoon Hitler received a delegation of workers from around the country in the Chancellery, and then, as an acknowledgment of their elevated status in the new national community, introduced them to the Reich President himself. Despite all the repression and brutality, some labor leaders clung to a desperate hope that a show of cooperation with the new regime might secure their continued existence. In what struck many disillusioned Social Democrats as sheer cowardice, the labor unions joined in the parades on May Day, some even marching behind swastika banners and offering speeches pledging cooperation with the new government. Not all was voluntary. Some factory owners required their workers to participate in the festivities; Storm Troopers, going house to house, bullied others into the streets, handing out small swastika pendants to all. The climax of the festivities came in the evening when a crowd of more than a million gathered on the vast field adjacent to the Tempelhof aerodrome. Searchlights raked the sky and swept across the assembled masses, until at last, as the drama built, only one glaring white spotlight cut the darkness, directed to the platform where Hitler made his appearance.

Speaking beneath billowing swastika banners, his voice carried nationwide over the radio, Hitler briefly reiterated his determination to end unemployment in Germany and announced the introduction of compulsory labor service to put the jobless back to work. But the theme for the evening was not policy but unity. Overcoming generations of class warfare would be a struggle, but the National Socialists had "the resolution to lead the German people back together, and, if necessary," Hitler added menacingly, "to force them back together." The meaning of May Day was to break down class barriers and to "honor the work, and respect the worker." The German people are strong when they are united, Hitler declared, when "you banish from your heart the spirit of class conflict and . . . discord." He summoned the people to join with the regime in this struggle, "to go forth into the cities to proclaim . . . the importance of the German peasant and go out into the country and to our thinkers and teach them the significance of the German working class.

"The fact that the world is so against us is all the more reason why we must become a unified whole," he continued. The world must be shown that it could "never break us, never force us to submit to any yoke." One day, when the work of the National Socialist regime was completed, the German people would "be able to face the Almighty and say 'You can see that we have changed. The German people is no longer a Volk of infamy, shame, self-degradation, faintheartedness, and faithlessness. No, Lord, the German Volk is once again strong in its will, strong in its persistence, strong in bearing any sacrifice. Lord, we will not give you up! Now bless our fight for our freedom and thus our German *Volk und Vaterland*." The spectacle ended with the surprisingly enthusiastic multitude singing the German national anthem and the "Horst Wessel Song" while a dazzling display of fireworks burst over the scene. Celebrations continued on into the night.

At just after nine the next morning, SA men appeared at union halls all across the country. They arrested union functionaries, plundered union offices, confiscated records, office equipment, and even furniture; they shut down union newspapers, closed union banks, and seized their assets. They encountered no resistance. Since the working men of Germany were now integrated into the National Socialist people's community, unions, the Nazis declared, were no longer necessary. They were, in fact, impediments to the national unity proclaimed by the Führer. German workers would now be represented, along with management, in a National Socialist Labor Front headed by Nazi organization leader Robert Ley. The action had been planned well in advance of the May Day celebrations. As Goebbels recorded in his diary on April 17, Hitler had discussed the operation with him, and they agreed on its essentials. First the celebration, then the seizure of the union halls. "There may be a few days of trouble, but then they will belong to us. One can't show any scruples or have any reservations." After all, the regime was only doing the worker a service by "liberating him from the parasitic [union] leadership, which has only turned his life sour. If the unions are in our hands, then the other parties and organizations won't be able to hold out for long."

And just like that they were gone. The most highly organized, well-established, and powerful socialist organization in Europe was brushed aside with hardly a whimper of resistance. No strikes, no demonstrations, no protests. Even the Nazis were surprised. Within a few weeks' time, the labor movement had been rendered leaderless; many functionaries were behind bars, while others were keeping their head down, intimidated into silence. Tens of thousands of Social Democratic and Communist operatives were locked away in jails and in unauthorized SA prisons, and more would come. Already by the end of March, the Prussian police reported that roughly twenty thousand Communists had been arrested and thrown in jail; in Bavaria, ten thousand Communists and Social Democrats were arrested in March and April; by June the number had doubled.

Nor were party activists the only targets. In the Ruhr, almost half the entire Communist membership was taken into custody. By the end of the year the total number of political arrests in Germany ran to more than 100,000 and the number of deaths while in custody reached nearly six hundred. These numbers were almost certainly understated, for many arrests and murders simply went unrecorded, as victims seized by the SA disappeared into their makeshift prisons, never to be heard from again. With their organizations demolished, their newspapers banned, their leaders imprisoned or in exile, many of the rank and file were demoralized. They were dismayed by the party leadership, disgusted with its supine surrender to the Nazis. But what were their options? Under the circumstances, some were reluctantly resigned to an uneasy coexistence with the Nazis. Few thought the Nazi regime would last longer than a few months, and the labor movement had survived Bismarck's suppression from 1878 to 1890 and emerged even stronger. Social democracy and organized labor would survive Hitler and the Nazis as well. The inevitable coup de grâce came on June 22, when the regime formally outlawed the already ravaged SPD. A Social Democratic underground would develop, dodging the Gestapo, smuggling reports on life in the Third Reich out to the SPD's Prague headquarters in exile, but labor's organized resistance in German political life was effectively over.

Disbanding the SPD was merely the first rumble of an avalanche that would soon bury the remaining parties. On June 26, Alfred Hugenberg, once thought to be the real power in the new government, was forced out of the cabinet, ostensibly for his aggressive, undiplomatic behavior at the World Economic Conference in London, where without consultation with the Foreign Office or the cabinet he had belligerently demanded, among other things, the return of Germany's colonies. With his departure, the conservative coalition that he led chose to disband itself. Its members were given the option of joining the NSDAP, and Stahlhelm troopers were offered a spot in the SA. Papen remained in the cabinet but was isolated and without influence. On June 28 and 29, the two liberal parties, long reduced to irrelevance, caved in and voluntarily dissolved themselves. For their followers there was no offer of membership in the NSDAP. By the end of June, only the Catholic Zentrum and its partner the BVP remained.

The Zentrum, with its deep reservations about National Socialism, had long been a source of trouble for the Nazis, but by the summer of 1933 it was under mounting pressure to reach an accommodation with the "national revolution." The pressure came not only from the regime, which had vividly demonstrated the unhappy fate of opposition parties, but from the Church hierarchy as well. Since January the Nazis had been attempting to find a modus vivendi with the Catholic Church, which was the spiritual home of roughly one third of the population. For its part, the Church wanted to secure a safe position within the new order and pressed Hitler for formal guarantees that Catholic institutions, organizations, and practices would be left intact. Momentum for an understanding had accelerated since Hitler's Enabling Act speech on March 23, in which he had made a point of promising that the Church would remain unmolested. In response, the Catholic hierarchy in Germany reversed course, reluctantly dropping its previous opposition to the Nazis and calling for loyalty to the new regime, actions that went a long way toward alleviating the fears of ordinary Catholics who had for years been told at mass that they could not support National Socialism and remain in good standing with the Church.

While the Nazis were wary of organized Catholicism, they anticipated little trouble from the Protestant churches, of which there were twenty-eight. The Protestant churches had a strong nationalist tradition and a history of respect for the authority of the state, and they had not displayed the same hostility toward National Socialism as had the Catholic Church. One particularly vocal minority, the German Christians, was formed in 1932 and had gone beyond a generally supportive view of National

Socialism, becoming open advocates for Hitler and his movement. Some pastors among the German Christians proclaimed their desire to be "the storm troopers of Jesus Christ." They espoused what they called "positive Christianity" and hoped to establish a unified national Protestant church under the slogan "One Volk, One Reich, One Church"—an echo of the Nazi slogan "One Volk, One Reich, One Führer."

Hitler liked the idea of a united national church, and with the enthusiastic support of the German Christians, a Nazi-controlled Reich Church was established in the spring of 1933. Hitler appointed Ludwig Müller, a former naval chaplain and an ardent Nazi, to the new post of Reich bishop. Backed by the vigorous support of the Propaganda Ministry, the German Christians, numbering perhaps 600,000 adherents, prevailed in the church elections of July 1933 and assumed control of church offices.

Protestants were generally positive about the new regime, and by summer 1933 the regime seemed to have cemented their support. Since the new Reich Church was technically a government entity, Müller insisted that it was subject to the Civil Service Law, with its Aryan Paragraph. Pressure from German Christian pastors to dismiss all Jews employed by the Church mounted. Among the more radical pastors there was even a move to push Jesus aside and elevate Hitler to the role of national savior who would return Germany to the true, un-Judaized Christianity of the traditional evangelical church. They rejected the Old Testament as a Jewish book and demanded that it be deleted from the German Bible; they argued that the Cross was a Jewish symbol and should be replaced, presumably by the swastika, though that remained unspoken. The Reich Church, in short, was to be a Nazi church.

Meanwhile, negotiations with the Vatican began in earnest in late March following the passage of the Enabling Act, with Papen serving as the lead negotiator for the Reich. Reflecting the high priority Hitler placed on an agreement, Göring, too, was dispatched to Rome for an audience with the pope. After a series of highly publicized talks, the Reich announced on July 8 that a Concordat had been signed with the Vatican. In it, the Nazis pledged to respect the rights of the Church and its lay organizations, while the Church promised to halt its relentless assaults on "heathen" National Socialism and to withdraw from politics. The Zentrum, which was little more than a bystander to the talks, found its position undermined by the

Church hierarchy, and on July 6 voted itself out of existence. The BVP disbanded on the following day, prodded no doubt by Himmler's arrest of some two thousand of its functionaries. The Concordat and the disappearance of the Zentrum/BVP marked the end of political Catholicism in Germany and slammed the final nail into the coffin of Germany's moribund party system. Two weeks later, with a malicious sense of historical irony, a new edict formally outlawed all political parties and organizations, except for the NSDAP. It was July 14, Bastille Day.

Having successfully seized the state apparatus, smashed the labor movement, abolished the parties, neutralized the churches, seduced the army, and intimidated the business community, the Nazis had been successful beyond their wildest dreams. The Nazi revolution, as Hitler had often told the impatient Storm Troopers, had come after the assumption of power, not before it, and it had achieved its astonishing victory with a rapidity that was little short of breathtaking. Perhaps most surprising to the Nazi leadership, they had managed it without plunging the country into chaos or civil war. All across the board, Germany was falling into line. The time had come for consolidation.

CONSOLIDATION OF POWER

While Hitler believed that the time had come to consolidate Nazi achievements—achievements that had come with stunning ease—consolidation was not what SA leader Ernst Röhm wanted to hear. Writing in the June 1933 issue of the influential party journal, the *Nationalsozialistische Monatshefte*, he acknowledged that "a mighty victory has been won, but not *the* victory." The ultimate goal of creating a new Germany, infused with the National Socialist spirit of revolutionary struggle, had not yet been achieved, and as long as that goal was not attained, "the bitter, passionate struggle of the SA and SS will not cease." He lashed out against timidity in the political leadership and squeamish moderation that would drain the Nazi revolution of its fanatical zeal. Invoking Prussian General Gebhard von Blücher, the German hero of Waterloo, he cautioned that "the politicians should not spoil what the soldier has won with his blood." The SA and SS, he warned, "would not tolerate [a situation in which] the German revolution goes to sleep or is betrayed by 'non-fighters' content to go only 'half way.'" Now with four million members, the SA was not going away; it would be a major power factor in the coming National Socialist state, a third pillar of the regime, alongside the army and the police. It would have "special tasks" and, he not so subtly implied, would not be content merely "to take orders." Röhm closed his article with a direct challenge to the "bourgeois souls" in the party: "Whether it suits them or not, we will continue our fight. With them, if they finally grasp what it is all about. Without them, if they don't want it. And against them, if it must be!"

Throughout the spring Röhm and other senior SA leaders continued to call for "a second revolution" that would realize the party's long-standing social revolutionary promises. The Storm Troopers, Röhm declared, were "the incorruptible guarantors of the fulfillment of the German revolution." The relationship between the party and the SA had always been prickly, and by summer 1933 the gap between the party's political leadership and the SA was widening into a chasm. From the earliest days of the party, the SA had seen itself as a military organization, its members the soldiers that fought for the National Socialist revolution—and won it. Their contempt for what they considered the bourgeois restraint of the political leadership was never far from the surface and had exploded into open conflict at intervals over the years.

Differences over ideology and strategy aside, many Brown Shirts were bitterly disappointed by the failure of the new regime to find positions for them, either in the party or state administrations. Many were still surviving on the dole, eating in SA soup kitchens, living in SA barracks, desperately in need of a job. It was their due, their just reward for fighting the party's hard battles in "the time of struggle," while others sat safely ensconced in their offices or strutted about in their un-bloodied party uniforms. Many had come to feel that Hitler's loyal "old fighters" were being passed over for opportunists who had rushed to join the party or the SA after the Enabling Act. March violets, they were derisively called. Almost 80 percent of the party's membership had joined since the March 5 election.

Although the Nazis were firmly entrenched in power, widespread SA hooliganism remained a problem, and an increasingly embarrassing one, for the regime. Despite urgent calls for a stabilization of the situation by the Justice and Interior ministries, SA leaders tenaciously resisted any interference in their affairs. In the spring and summer violent incidents involving the SA occurred throughout the Reich, but the most explosive outburst came in late June, in the Köpenick section of Berlin. There, on June 21, a young Social Democrat fought off an assault by a gang of Brown Shirts, shooting dead two of his assailants. Hundreds of Storm Troopers soon descended on the scene, and from June 21 to June 26 rampaged through the neighborhood, beating and arresting over five hundred "enemies of the state." Most were dragged off to makeshift SA prisons where they were so sadistically tortured that ninety-one of them died. These days of appalling savagery came to be known as the "blood week of Köpenick." The authorities looked the other way.

This state of affairs could not continue. The SA's unbridled thuggery, so crucial in establishing the dictatorship during the first six months of the regime, was becoming a political liability. If this unruly behavior continued unchecked, Reichsbank president Hjalmar Schacht warned, it could prove a serious deterrent to German economic recovery, frightening away much-needed foreign investment. The Justice and Interior Ministries both complained about the ongoing arbitrary arrests, extralegal internment, and the notorious SA bestiality. The SA even claimed the right to try its own men accused of crimes, asserting its immunity from the ordinary process of criminal justice. By late spring, the state authorities—all dedicated Nazis—were demanding that the SA be brought to heel and made subject to the law.

Rumors and reports of ghastly SA brutality in their unauthorized prisons came regularly to Diels and other police officials. Gradually the police, working under the aegis of the Interior Ministry, and with Göring's blessing, began a campaign to close the SA prisons. It did not go smoothly. Even when confronted with written authorization from Göring, some SA commanders resisted, demanding instead an order from *their* leader, Ernst Röhm. In some cases SA leaders simply refused to cooperate, resulting in armed standoffs as police officials attempted to close their unauthorized concentration camps. It became, as Diels described it, "a small war."

In one instance, Diels led a group of police into one such chamber of horrors in Berlin. A seasoned police official, even he was shocked by what he saw. The dark, dismal rooms were bare, the furniture removed, the floors covered in straw, soiled with blood and urine. The prisoners were little more than skeletons, starved, dehydrated, their heads lolling around on their shoulders "like a doll's." They had been forced to stand for days in cramped cabinets without food or water, their time in these vertical coffins being interrupted only for the relentless torture sessions. A dozen or so SA brutes worked in rotating shifts, so that the beatings with iron rods, rubber truncheons, and leather whips continued around the clock. Many of the prisoners were laid out in rows on the festering straw, their bones broken, teeth shattered, their eyes swollen shut. Runnels of crusted blood trailed from their nostrils. "There were none whose bodies were not covered from head to toe with blue, yellow and green bruises." As he walked through the rooms Diels heard no groaning or sobbing, only stony, deathlike silence, as prisoners stared glassy-eyed, waiting for the end or a new round of interrogation. "Hieronymus Bosch and Pieter Brueghel," Diels reflected, "had never witnessed such horror."

Although Hitler was sympathetic to the radicals, he, too, desired to shift power away from the SA to the Nazi-controlled state apparatus. Unrestrained SA violence not only endangered Germany's economic recovery, it ran the risk of alienating those members of the public who had initially viewed National Socialism as a force for the restoration of law and order. Speaking to a group of SA leaders on July 6, 1933, Hitler finally declared "The revolution is over." Revolution, he said, "is not a permanent condition" and "must not be allowed to develop into one. . . . One must guide the liberated stream of revolution into a secure bed of evolution. The education of people is therefore the most important consideration. The current state of affairs must be improved and the people . . . must be educated in the National Socialist conception of the state." The time had come for indoctrination, not terror in the streets, and that task was the provenance of Goebbels's new Ministry of Propaganda and Public Enlightenment. A second revolution to sweep away bourgeois capitalism, as some radicals in the party were demanding, was not possible at this critical juncture. Such social revolutionary impulses had to be tempered by realism and the exigencies of rebuilding a shattered economy. "We must not dismiss a businessman if he is a good businessman," Hitler insisted, "but not yet a National Socialist; especially not if the National Socialist that we put in his place understands nothing about business."

Even a firebrand like Goebbels hewed to the new party line, explaining that "revolutions that drive toward anarchy don't deserve the name [of revolution]. . . . The regime is keeping a watchful eye on any covert Bolshevist elements who speak of a second revolution." In an article directed at SA and SS leaders, Rudolf Hess warned against "spies and provocateurs who try to encourage the men to mistreatment of opponents which only leads to more atrocity lies in the foreign press." Göring also followed the script. Working with Diels, he began a systematic effort to rein in the Prussian SA, disbanding the auxiliary police he had called into being there, and the other states were quick to follow his lead. He also began closing the SA's prisons and camps, transferring the inmates to formal concentration camps. He was eager to see Röhm's influence in Prussia sharply reduced.

The level of public violence *did* drop in the months following Hitler's July declaration, and yet the unrest continued. Even in late 1933 when Interior Minister Frick won Hitler's approval for an edict that made the SA and SS subject to the law, Röhm, Himmler, and the regional party chiefs simply ignored it. In fact, many party officials at the regional level sometimes chose to disregard direct orders, arguing that the Führer had to take certain public stands but that they understood his real intentions. As one regional chief made clear, "we old Nazis don't give a damn about the remarks of some Nazi bigwig. As far as we are concerned, all we have to do is fulfill the program as the Führer wishes."

And Hitler, after his forceful intervention in the conflict in July, again withdrew to the sidelines, leaving his party and state officials to sort out matters. So the internecine struggles for power continued, with different state agencies and party formations jealously fighting to hold and extend their authority. The regime operated in a state of "organized chaos"; its guiding imperative "institutional Darwinism." In Prussia, for example, the Interior Ministry (Göring) and the Gestapo (Diels) were successful in closing the SA prisons throughout the fall and even pressed charges against SA goons for egregious mistreatment of prisoners. But in Bavaria efforts by the Nazi state authorities to investigate charges of torture in Dachau were thwarted by the SS and SD (Himmler, Heydrich) and the SA (Röhm), who maintained that charges of abuse and torture were fairy tales and, anyway, what right did the Bavarian Interior Ministry have to be snooping around for atrocity stories? Hitler, as usual, did nothing.

Exacerbating this state of affairs was the fact that no real table of organization or clear chain of command existed, even in key areas such as the economy or the police. At the top, the Third Reich resembled a medieval court, with loyal vassals jostling for Hitler's favor but acting with surprising independence. Party and state agencies competed to interpret and implement the will of the Führer. Hitler rarely interceded and never committed himself to paper; orders were verbal, notoriously vague, and not infrequently contradictory. At every level of the state and party apparatus officials sought "to work toward the Führer," but essentially operated on their own. In the general free-for-all for power and influence, personal jealousies were endemic, conflicts of interest ubiquitous, and offices with no clear lines of responsibility multiplied. The result was a highly inefficient polyocracy with multiple centers of power animated by a crude "institutional Darwinism," where the strongest, most forceful, and most persistent prevailed.

Nowhere was this dynamic more striking than in the emergence of the SS as the nation's most powerful political police organization and its transformation into one of the essential pillars of Nazi rule. In the months after Hitler's appointment as chancellor, Himmler, chief of both the SS and the Bavarian state police, undertook a systematic campaign to expand his power by seizing control of the political police in one German state after another. He was a trusted member of Hitler's inner circle, and cowed local officials assumed that he was acting on the Führer's orders. He was not. Only in Prussia did his ambitions encounter a roadblock, because there another powerful vassal of the Führer, Hermann Göring, was in charge of the police and was not so easily brushed aside. Adding a symptomatic twist to these events, Göring, who had created the Gestapo in Prussia, proceeded to open Gestapo branches in all the German states—a move for which he possessed no legal authority and which lacked Hitler's explicit authorization. These Gestapo offices were responsible not to Himmler and the SS or to the local police authorities but to Göring alone, and, just as typically Hitler did nothing to clarify the situation. He soared above such problems, leaving contrails of confusion streaming behind him.

Throughout the fall and winter of 1933 complaints about unruly, brawling Storm Troopers continued to pour in from business leaders, local, state, and party officials, from the Foreign Office and Economics Ministry. Yet, despite widespread SA violence and political abuses by the local party leaders—the "little Führers" as they were derisively called—Hitler's popularity not only remained strong but grew. After fourteen years of paralysis and ineffectuality, here at last, many Germans felt, was a man of action, a man who would get things done. Ruthless, to be sure, but he was exactly what the nation needed: a populist "people's chancellor," not from the traditional elites but an uncompromising nationalist leading the dispirited *Volk* out of its lethargy and hopelessness. This was the image that Goebbels worked tirelessly to promote, but Hitler's popularity was not simply a product of propaganda and intimidation. The adoration seemed genuine.

Already by mid-1933 a Hitler cult was effectively woven into the political fabric of the Reich, and Führer worship was widespread and growing. Hitler's birthday on April 20 turned into a semiofficial national holiday with an authentic outpouring of adulation; garlanded portraits and gold-framed Hitler photographs appeared in shop windows; parades and celebrations in his honor were held across the country. Reverential articles in the press, programs on the radio, and regular appearances in the newsreels offered quasi-religious paeans to Germany's savior. Poems and songs were written about him, streets and squares, schools and other public buildings were named for him. A village in Thuringia changed its name to Hitler Heights (Hitlerhöhe) in honor of the Führer. Blending politics and commercial opportunity, one café owner unsuccessfully requested permission to lend his shop the patriotic appellation "Café Reich Chancellor Adolf Hitler." Another entrepreneur, a gardener, asked obsequiously—and also unsuccessfully—if he might "allow myself to bestow on one of my best roses the name 'Reich Chancellor Hitler' as a gift and memento of the present great time and if I might be permitted to bring it, with the same name, onto the world market." Party officials in *Gau* Düsseldorf-Ost fielded a request from a local man who wanted to name his newborn daughter "Hitlerine." The request went all the way to the Interior Ministry, where it was denied; as a consolation officials there suggested the mellifluous "Adolfine" instead. Such requests became so numerous that in April Hitler requested his followers to refrain from naming streets and squares after him. To no avail. The trend continued on into the war.

There was, of course, an undercurrent of grumbling about various aspects of the dictatorship, especially as it revealed itself at the local level, but Hitler seemed unaffected by it. No matter what the outrage by the party or the SA, nothing seemed to stick to him. He was, in public perception, inspiring the people to shake off their pessimism and sense of inferiority and reclaim their faith and pride in Germany. His uncompromising idealism, rough as it might be, was reviving the nation, many thought, restoring its confidence, driving it forward once again. Initiatives in two areas proved extremely popular, one domestic, the other in foreign affairs. He had promised to put people back to work, and he had. Hitler inherited a fully funded work creation program from his predecessor Kurt von Schleicher, but the general had not had time to implement his public works agenda when he was sacked in January 1933. Hitler was the fortunate beneficiary. His creation of the Labor Front, which drafted the unemployed off the streets, coupled with a feverish burst of labor-intensive public works projects had reduced unemployment from six million to roughly four million in barely six months. The creation of a vast network of superhighways, the Autobahn, caught the public imagination, and Hitler was photographed shoveling not only the first spade of dirt but filling a whole wheelbarrow. The precipitous drop in unemployment during the first months of the regime could not be sustained, and by fall unemployment figures stabilized, but Hitler had acted decisively in what the Nazis referred to as "the Battle for Work," and the public was impressed. No one, even his bitterest enemies, could doubt that he had brought a new excitement and enthusiasm to German public life, rallying the people to a common purpose as no one had done in the fourteen years of Germany's tormented democracy. Within a few short months he had come to symbolize Germany's rebirth.

Bolstering Hitler's popularity at home was a dramatic display of defiance to the great powers in the autumn of 1933. A disarmament conference sponsored by the League of Nations had been convened in February 1932, and when Hitler assumed the chancellorship, his opening performance in world politics was to make a typically theatrical offer. He began, as he was to do in every international crisis over the next six years, by wrapping himself in pieties about Germany's commitment to peace. "Our boundless love for and loyalty to our own national traditions makes us respect the national claims of others and makes us desire from the bottom of our hearts to live with them in peace and friendship." But Germany alone had been forced to disarm at Versailles, rendering the country defenseless. "The Rhineland was demilitarized, the German fortresses were dismantled, our ships surrendered, our airplanes destroyed, our system of military service abandoned and the training of reserves thus prevented. Even the most indispensable weapons of defense were denied us." It was time for the other nations of Europe to demonstrate their willingness to end this terrible injustice.

Germany would be willing at any time "to undertake further obligations in regard to international security, if all the other nations are ready on their side to do the same." In particular, Germany was "perfectly ready to disband her entire military establishment and destroy the small amounts of arms remaining to her, if the neighboring countries will do the same thing with equal thoroughness." Since Germany was restricted by the Versailles Treaty to a military of only 100,000 troops, had no heavy weapons, no air force, and no battle fleet, it was an easy—and disingenuous—offer to make. If the international community was unprepared for such a radical offer, Hitler suggested more specifically that France might reduce its military down to German levels or alternatively that Germany be allowed to increase its forces to match those of France. When, not surprisingly, France balked, Hitler insisted that all Germany was seeking was to be treated as an equal in matters of international security. Had not Germany, "in her state of defenselessness and disarmament, greater justification in demanding security than the over-armed states bound together in military alliances?" But that, he implied, was apparently not the intention of the French, who seemed determined to maintain their vast military superiority over Germany. In a statement to the public on October 14, Hitler explained that since the powers gathered in Geneva were intent on perpetuating "an unjust and degrading discrimination of the German people," the Reich government could not "under these circumstances, feel itself able to participate any longer as a second-class nation without rights of its own in negotiations which can only result in further dictates. While professing its unshakable desire for peace, Germany must announce . . . that it is forced to leave the Disarmament Conference. Thus it will also announce its withdrawal from the League of Nations." In doing so, Germany was declaring its "truly honest will for peace and its willingness to reach an understanding, while maintaining its honor."

To those abroad—the French in particular—who accused him of harboring aggressive intentions and of attempting to sabotage the armaments restrictions of the Versailles treaty, Hitler replied piously that all he wanted was "to provide work and bread to the German Volk," and this he could do only if "peace and quiet" prevailed. No one should assume that "I would be so mad as to want a war. . . . I do not know how many foreign statesmen actually took part in the War. I did. I know war. But among those who are agitating against Germany today and slandering the German Volk—this is one thing I do know—not a single one has ever heard the hiss of a traveling bullet." This aggressive self-righteousness was an attitude he would routinely strike in the crises of coming years, framing acts of aggression in the most pacific language while invoking his experience in the last war and platitudes about his commitment to world peace.

Foreign statesmen were unimpressed, but his action played very well in Germany. Here at last was a German leader who would not be pushed around by the great powers. Not only was Hitler confronting Germany's enemies at home, he was standing up for Germany's rights on the international scene. Eager to display the public's enthusiastic support for the Hitler government, the Nazis staged a plebiscite on November 12, summoning the nation to approve the regime's actions since January 30. Goebbels was back in campaign form, saturating the country in the usual Nazi style. Watching the campaign unfold in Dresden, Viktor Klemperer confided to his diary: "On every commercial vehicle, post office van, mailman's bicycle, on every house and show window, on broad banners, which are stretched across the street—quotations from Hitler are everywhere and always 'Yes' for peace! It is the most monstrous of hypocrisies. . . . Demonstrations and chanting into the night, loudspeakers on the streets, vehicles (with wireless apparatus playing music mounted on top), both cars and trams." What kind of an election could it be, he asked himself, since "no one believes that the secrecy of the ballot will be protected, no one believes either in a fair counting of votes: so why be a martyr?" It came as no surprise that on November 12, 93 percent of the ballots cast were registered as "yes." Remarkably, two million had voted "no," and another 3.5 percent of the ballots were declared "invalid." Despite the widespread foreign skepticism, even the Social Democratic underground came to the conclusion that, on the whole, the outcome of the election seemed an accurate measure of popular support for the regime. In a report smuggled out of Germany in December, the underground leftist group New Beginning conceded that there was simply no denying that the election had demonstrated just how "rapid and strong the process of Nazifying society was progressing."

But despite Hitler's undeniable popularity and the general excitement of the early months of the regime, by early 1934 signs were emerging of a creeping disenchantment with the realities of Nazi rule. The enthusiasm and hope that had swept the party through much of the previous year were melting away. In February the Social Democratic underground reported "a general increase of grumbling, of dissatisfaction in broad strata" of the population, from presumably already coordinated youth to "reactionary groups (monarchists)," and elements of the working class. In spite of the Nazis' lofty promises, unemployment remained stubbornly high, business continued to stagnate, consumer goods remained scarce, and food expensive. The grumbling, however muffled, was widespread.

Aggravating the disappointment was the arrogant posturing of local Nazi bosses, preening, puffed-up "little Führers" out to exercise their new power and position. Looking daily at these men, with their swaggering, their arbitrariness, petty jealousies, turf battles, nepotism, and corruption, Germans were making the disconcerting discovery that the Nazis, rather than ideological idealists, were politicians of a familiar stripe after all. In Stettin SS men hit upon the idea of seizing prosperous individuals, throwing them into their own private concentration camp, extorting money from them, and then setting them free. This practice went on for months and came to a halt only when they overreached, arresting a leader of the local Conservative party with indirect ties to President Hindenburg. A nervous Göring rushed to Stettin, closed the camp, and sent the guilty parties before a special party tribunal. In Kiel two Nazi officials energetically collected for the Winter Relief charity but decided that charity should begin at home and kept the funds for themselves. Both were arrested, stripped of their party posts, and sent to prison. In Flensburg locals watched as the city's Nazi treasurer was arrested for embezzlement, only to see his successor follow in his footsteps. Such cases were far from rare. Remarkably, no blame was directed at Hitler. By 1934, the phrase "if the Führer only knew what was going on down here" had become a common refrain in local political discourse.

Most disturbing to the public was the SA and its unruly Storm Troopers, who continued to roam the streets, drinking, brawling, and harassing ordinary citizens. SA commanders also continued to call for a second revolution, though what exactly they had in mind was never really clear. At the close of March, with the pressure to act building, Hitler addressed Röhm and an assembly of SA leaders in Berlin. "I will energetically oppose a second revolutionary wave," he told them bluntly, "since it would unavoidably produce chaos. Anyone who rises up against the authority of the state will be severely punished, no matter what position he holds." Hardly chastened by Hitler's words, Röhm responded by once again invoking the SA's revolutionary role. "Our revolution is no national revolution; it is a National Socialist revolution," he wrote to SA commanders. "Our SA battalions represent the only safeguard against the Reaction, for they are the absolute embodiment of the revolutionary idea. . . . From day one, the brown-shirted fighter committed himself to the revolutionary path, and he won't be diverted away from it until our final goal is reached."

Matters soon came to a head. Despite Hitler's orders, Röhm continued his campaign to institutionalize the SA as an essential pillar of the Reich—there was even talk of creating an SA state—and saw himself as something akin to a minister of defense. Initially the army had viewed the SA as a sort of military auxiliary, not unlike the Free Corps of the immediate postwar years. But with the Nazis in power and the SA growing in strength, friction between the SA and the army intensified. Röhm's ambitions mounted, and he was not bashful about expressing them. He was giving voice to views that he and other SA leaders had held from the earliest days of the NSDAP, only now more openly, more stridently. The SA would not be integrated into the army, he not so discreetly hinted; the army would be absorbed by the SA in a people's militia. In an effort to appease Röhm, Hitler in December 1933 appointed him minister without portfolio in the Reich cabinet and showered him with warm personal praise as a trusted old comrade, but Röhm was not to be placated.

By 1934 the hostility between the SA and the army reached such an alarming state that in late February Hitler summoned Röhm and General Blomberg, the minister of war, to a meeting at the Reich Chancellery. At that meeting, Hitler emphatically reiterated to Röhm that the army was to be the only military force within the country. The SA would patrol the borders and provide pre-military training, but he repeated his long-held position that the mission of the SA was political, not military. Hitler had made his choice. The SA had played a crucial role in the party's rise to power and in creating the Nazi dictatorship, but in order to fulfill his expansionist foreign policy objectives, Hitler needed a powerful, well-trained, and well-equipped professional army. It was a refrain Röhm had heard many times before and understood was not a matter for negotiation. At the conclusion of the meeting, Hitler coaxed the two men to sign an agreement in his presence to end the backbiting.

Röhm dutifully signed the document, but he was furious. In a perfunctory show of goodwill, he invited Hitler and the military party to a reception just after the meeting. Hitler did not attend, but Blomberg and other high-ranking officers put in an appearance. It was an awkward occasion, the atmosphere frosty. When finally the generals departed, Röhm could contain his ire no longer. "What that ridiculous corporal says means nothing to me," he told his followers. "I have not the slightest intention of keeping this agreement. Hitler is a traitor and at the very least must go on leave. . . . If we can't get there with him, we'll get there without him." Never one for caution, he later added: "Adolf is rotten. He's betraying all of us. He only goes around with reactionaries. His old comrades aren't good enough for him. So he brings in these East Prussian generals. They're the ones he pals around with now. . . . Adolf knows perfectly well what I want. . . . Are we a revolution or aren't we? . . . Something new has to be brought in. . . . A new discipline. A new principle of organization. The generals are old fogeys. They'll never have a new idea."

These comments and others like them inevitably made their way back to Hitler and to Blomberg. Throughout the spring of 1934 tensions mounted as Röhm continued his agitation for a leading military role for the SA, and the reckless talk of a second revolution showed few signs of abating. For months Hitler had been reluctant to discipline Röhm, his old comrade in arms and the leader of the party's largest and most militant organization. After all, the Storm Troopers were fanatically devoted to Röhm, and a challenge to his leadership carried enormous political risks. But the SA had outlived its usefulness. Secretly he gave orders to Himmler and Göring, both of whom loathed Röhm and hoped to undermine him, to begin an investigation into SA activities. In an effort to reduce Röhm's power in Prussia, Göring in April agreed to hand over control of the Prussian Gestapo to Himmler and Heydrich, who proceeded to initiate their own secret investigation of Röhm and the SA. Himmler was intent on liberating the SS from the much larger SA, to which it was still technically subordinate, and with control of the Prussian Gestapo, the SS now possessed a nationwide police and surveillance network. The army, too, had been creating its own file on the SA and scrupulously reporting its findings directly to Hitler. Over the years Röhm had managed to make a host of very powerful enemies, and by 1934, those enemies were mobilized and ready to act.

Exacerbating the tension was the fact that for some time Hindenburg's health had been in steep decline. In April the eighty-seven-year-old Reich President began withdrawing from active participation in government affairs, and in early June he retreated to his Neudeck estate in East Prussia.

From there a steady stream of reports of his deteriorating health poured forth, provoking anxiety across the political scene. It was obvious that Hindenburg did not have long to live. Hitler was eager to have the old field marshal out of the way, but was nervous about the attitude of the army once Hindenburg, its supreme commander, was gone. Who would succeed him as Reich President and commander-in-chief, and how? On this, Franz von Papen, virtually forgotten since the previous spring, had ideas of his own.

For months Papen and the national Conservatives, who had done so much to insert Hitler into power, had grown increasingly dismayed by their dwindling influence and alarmed about the radical talk of a second revolution. During the spring they began sounding out like-minded conservatives and disgruntled generals who shared their unease with the radical course the Nazi revolution had taken. Their hope was to place a conservative in a caretaker role and then, supported by the army, restore the Hohenzollerns to power.

In a speech at Marburg University on June 17, Papen openly expressed their concerns and delivered a stern warning about the perils of a second revolution. He spoke with uncharacteristic boldness, arguing that Germany could not survive in a perpetual state of unrest—a second revolution would merely bring forth a third and a fourth, plunging the country into endless chaos. Hitler had sought to restore Germany's spiritual unity, and the nation had "experienced that unity in the excitement of thousands of demonstrations, rallies, flags and celebrations." But now, he suggested, the enthusiasm had waned, and the country needed "an open and manly discussion" of issues that was currently absent in German public life.

Without explicitly mentioning Hitler, he condemned "the false cult of personality," pointedly noting that "great men are not made by propaganda but grown out of their actions." And in a stinging rebuke to the regime, he stated that it should be confident enough of its power and popular support that it could tolerate "responsible criticism." It should be possible, he said, to voice reservations about this policy or that without being branded an enemy of the state and treated like a criminal. The regime "should remember the old adage that only weaklings cannot tolerate criticism." It was time to come together to "silence the doctrinaire fanatics" threatening German political life. It was a startlingly audacious speech, all the more for being the first public criticism of Hitler and the Nazis, and when he concluded, the audience broke into stormy applause.

The Marburg speech sent shockwaves through a country in which open political criticism was as extinct as a mastodon. A stunned Goebbels tried to suppress the speech; he seized newspapers, ordered all copies of the speech confiscated, and blocked its retransmission over the Frankfurt radio cable. But it was too late. Around the country Papen was greeted with cries of "Heil Marburg" instead of "Heil Hitler." The conservatives close to him believed that their moment was coming. Given the mounting tension between Hitler and Röhm, it was time to press the case for a conservative succession. Hindenburg, they felt certain, would be open to a change of government.

Hitler was furious at Papen and his circle of "reactionaries," and in a speech before an assembly of Nazi leaders in Thuringia, he blasted the "little worms" and "pygmies" of the Reaction. "If they should at any time attempt, even in a small way, to move from their criticism to a new act of perjury, they can be sure that what they are confronting today is not the cowardly and corrupt bourgeoisie of 1918 but the fist of the entire people. It is the fist of the nation that is clenched and will smash down anyone who dares to undertake even the slightest attempt at sabotage." In an ominous preview of things to come, Himmler ordered the arrest of Edgar Jung, the author of the Marburg speech.

Still, for all his rage, Hitler was wary of Papen's influence with the Reich President. He recognized the dangerous conservative disaffection with the Nazi dictatorship, and with Hindenburg's demise on the near horizon, he was concerned about a renewed conservative push to reinstate the monarchy. When on June 21 Papen threatened to resign because of Goebbels's actions, Hitler invited him to the Reich Chancellery to clear the air. At that meeting Hitler was conciliatory, expressing his understanding of Papen's honorable intent, even condemning Goebbels's overreaction, and promising to lift the ban on the Marburg speech (which he did not do). He did convince Papen to withhold his resignation until the two men could travel together to Neudeck to discuss the situation with Hindenburg. But Hitler had no intention of including Papen in such a meeting. Instead, the next day he hurried off to Hindenburg's East Prussian estate alone, where upon arriving he encountered General Blomberg. Blomberg, Hitler's minister of defense and a man favorably inclined toward National Socialism, was just leaving for Berlin after a conference with Hindenburg. On this occasion the general was not the malleable "rubber lion," as Hitler privately called him; he made it abundantly clear to Hitler that the army had had enough. If Hitler could not tame the SA and establish domestic order, the Reich President was prepared to declare martial law and the army would assume control of the country. Hindenburg sternly reinforced that position.

Coming in the wake of Papen's Marburg speech, these conversations proved to be the tipping point. Having done nothing for months to address the SA situation, Hitler now sprang into action. It was his usual pattern—wait for a situation to resolve itself, prevaricate, delay, postpone, then, when absolutely forced to make a decision, move swiftly and radically. Now the time had come to act. In the last week of June he began moving the pieces into place for a strike against both Röhm and the reactionaries. For months Himmler and Heydrich had been preparing an extensive dossier on Röhm's "treasonous actions," providing "evidence" that Röhm was plotting a coup d'état, conspiring with Strasser and even the French ambassador to bring down the Hitler government. The variations of these allegations were multiple and the evidence slight to nonexistent, but Hitler appears to have accepted them without question. On June 25 Himmler and Heydrich summoned SS and SD commanders to Berlin for a briefing on the situation. The SS men were informed that a Putsch by Röhm and the SA was imminent, and instructions were given for the countermeasures to be taken when the alert came. No date was set, but the SS was to hurry their preparations to seize SA leaders and functionaries. Hitler also conferred with Blomberg, who assured him of the military's support for an action against the SA and agreed to put the troops on high alert. The army also supplied the SS with weapons and transportation to carry out the operation.

In the last week of June, the regime escalated its warnings against would-be "saboteurs" of the National Socialist revolution. In a radio address on June 24 Hess sounded a menacing note: "The order of the Führer, to whom we have sworn our loyalty, is alone decisive. Woe betide anyone who is unfaithful to this vow of loyalty, believing that his revolt will serve the Revolution. Pity unto those who believe themselves the chosen ones who must aid the Führer by revolutionary agitation from below." Two days later, speaking to a convention of Nazi functionaries in Hamburg, Göring sharpened the rhetoric, issuing a thinly veiled threat to both the SA and the Papen circle. The regime had worked hard and been successful "because we have behind us a Volk which trusts us," adding that "anyone who gnaws away at this trust is committing a crime against the Volk; he is committing treachery and high treason. He who designs to destroy this trust, destroys Germany; he who sins against this trust has put his own head in the noose."

With rumors swirling about an SA Putsch and a backdoor conservative effort to undermine the regime, Hitler, on June 28, discovered that Papen had arranged to meet with Hindenburg on the 30th. It was, Hitler felt certain, a last-gasp effort to win the Reich President's support for a conservative assumption of power. There could be no more hesitation. That night Hitler telephoned Röhm instructing him to call a meeting of the SA leadership for June 30 in the resort village of Bad Wiessee forty miles south of Munich, where Röhm was vacationing. Hitler would come to Wiessee to address them. On June 7 Röhm had sent all SA formations on leave for a month; it was to be a cooling-off period, an opportunity for the Storm Troopers to regroup and take a much needed rest. Although Röhm would never acknowledge it, the SA leadership had considerable trouble controlling its own Brown Shirts, who seemed immune to any plea to refrain from unruly behavior, which the public found increasingly obnoxious.

On June 29, Hitler kept a busy public schedule. In Westphalia to attend the wedding of a regional party leader, he toured the Krupp works in Essen, made a short speech to the Labor Service unit near Lünen, and toured a nearby labor camp, before moving on to Bad Godesberg, where the wedding was to take place. There he was joined by Goebbels and Göring, who had flown in from Berlin. That night Hitler excused himself early from the wedding reception and retreated to his hotel room. Distressing reports from Himmler and Heydrich flooded in about SA unrest in different parts of the country. An SA Putsch, they believed, was imminent. Hitler briefed Göring and Goebbels about the situation, both of whom were surprised to learn that the primary target of the planned strike was not Papen and the conservatives but the SA. Hitler sent Göring back to Berlin to direct the action there and ordered Sepp

Dietrich, commander of his elite body guard, the *Leibstandarte Adolf Hitler*, to fly immediately to Munich, where he was to marshal two companies of SS troops. They were to rendezvous at the Hotel Hanselbauer in Bad Wiessee at 11:30 next morning.

At some point in the black early-morning hours, Hitler decided that he would fly to Munich immediately to lead the operation himself. After alerting Adolf Wagner, the *Gauleiter* and interior minister of Bavaria, to be prepared for his arrival, he boarded his private plane at 2:30 a.m. bound for Munich. It was coming on first light when Hitler's Ju 52 touched down at the Oberwiesenfeld military field outside Munich. He demanded to be taken at once to the Interior Ministry, where he learned that during the night a mob of some three thousand SA men had stormed through the streets chanting, "The Führer is against us; the Army is against us. SA men, out into the streets!" On hearing this, Hitler erupted in a towering rage. He demanded to see the two ranking SA officers on duty at once. When the bewildered men appeared before him, Hitler was not interested in information or explanations. Before they could utter a word, he ripped the insignia from their uniforms and thundered: "You're under arrest! You will be shot." They were immediately led away to Stadelheim prison to await their fate, the first of many on that long murderous night.

It was now 4:30 a.m., and Sepp Dietrich had not yet arrived with his SS troops, but Hitler, by now virtually hysterical in his fury, could wait no longer. He would go to Bad Wiessee and make the arrests himself. Accompanied by Goebbels, press chief Otto Dietrich, and several heavily armed SS men and police detectives, he set off for the resort in a convoy of three large black touring cars. At 6:45 when they reached the Hotel Hanselbauer, all was quiet—the small group of SA men were still sleeping off a night of heavy drinking; the hotel staff just beginning to stir, sorting linens for the new day, bustling about in the kitchen preparing breakfast coffee. The dining room was empty, the places set for the anticipated meeting of the SA chiefs at noon. Brandishing a pistol, Hitler bounded upstairs to Röhm's room. When the door opened, an astonished Röhm managed to blurt out a drowsy *"Heil, mein Führer,"* before Hitler, using the familiar *"du"* form, bellowed: "Ernst, you are under arrest!"

Across the hall, Edward Heines, leader of the Silesian SA, was found in bed with a young man, and after a brief scuffle was seized and led

downstairs. The other Storm Troopers were taken by surprise and offered no resistance as they were led from their rooms to the hotel laundry,
where they were locked in. Röhm, now fully dressed in civilian clothes,
demanded an explanation, but none was given. He was taken to the hotel
dining room rather than being forced to join the others in the cramped
laundry. He took a chair and waited calmly. Hitler even allowed him to be
served coffee. All had happened so quickly and so quietly that the other
hotel guests slumbered on with no idea that anything unusual was taking
place. The SA men taken at the Hotel Hanselbauer were loaded into a bus
commandeered to carry them to Munich. Their destination was Stadelheim. While Hitler was trying to decide what to do with Röhm, a troop
of about forty SA men from Röhm's Munich guard arrived. Hitler came
forward to address them. He informed them that he had assumed active
command of the SA and that they were to return to Munich in his convoy,
which would be leaving shortly for the Brown House. Hitler also sent
word to SS leaders to intercept any SA men on their way to the leadership
conference, whether at the Munich train station or on the roads leading
to Bad Wiessee.

Meanwhile, Goebbels telephoned a one-word coded message to Göring
in Berlin: "*Kolibri*"—hummingbird. It was the signal to launch the operation in the capital, and Göring wasted no time. He sent out hit squads with
a list of "conspirators" to be rounded up. They were on their way when
Papen appeared at Göring's office. He was alarmed to find it surrounded
by armed SS guards. Once inside he learned that Hitler had delegated to
Göring the legal authority to deal with the situation in Berlin. Papen protested that by law he should have been placed in charge and insisted that
President Hindenburg declare a state of emergency and mobilize the army.
Göring flatly refused. The SS and police had matters well in hand, he said
blandly, and "advised" Papen to return home and stay there. It was not safe
in the capital today. The murders began immediately. General Schleicher
and his wife were gunned down in their home; General Ferdinand von
Bredow, a friend and aide of Schleicher's, was shot at his front door; Edgar
Jung, already held by the SS, was executed in the dreaded Gestapo prison
at 8 Prinz-Albrech-Strasse. Three of Papen's conservative inner circle were
also arrested and shot. Gregor Strasser was taken to the Prinz-Albrech-
Strasse prison, where he was shot in his cell. Erich Klausner, the president

of the Catholic Action, the largest Catholic organization still in operation, was executed; various SA men and conservative government officials were shot. The killing went on throughout the day and night. Papen was spared, held under house arrest, his telephone line cut, his house surrounded. It was decided that it would be too embarrassing for the regime to have the vice chancellor executed without a trial. And, besides, how would Hindenburg react? Some of the targeted victims were taken into "protective custody," but most were murdered in cold blood—no arrests, no formal charges, no trials. The death toll continued to rise throughout the evening and into the following day.

In Munich the executions began as soon as Hitler returned from Bad Wiessee in mid-morning. He ordered Heines and the other SA leaders from Bad Wiessee shot for treason, but here he encountered unexpected trouble. Upon learning that SA leaders were being held in Stadelheim and were condemned to death, Hans Frank, the Nazi justice minister of Bavaria, protested. By what right were they to be executed? The prisoners, he argued, were to be turned over to the Bavarian state police immediately, and no executions should take place under any circumstances. There must be formal legal proceedings, he insisted. When these complaints were relayed to Hitler by telephone, he took the receiver and speaking directly to Frank stated that he himself had given the order. "These gentlemen are criminals against the Reich. I am the Reich Chancellor. It is a matter of the Reich, which is never under your jurisdiction." A similarly telling scene played out in the Brown House when the Nazi governor of Bavaria, Franz Ritter von Epp, demanded a court-martial for Röhm. He was shocked when Hitler exploded, screaming that Röhm was a proven traitor and deserved to be shot. Epp was speechless. As he left the room, he could only mutter "crazy."

At noon, Hitler addressed high-ranking SA leaders in the Senate Room of the Brown House. It was a tense meeting, and Hitler had worked himself into such a titanic fury that one observer claimed that he was literally foaming at the mouth. Röhm had betrayed him, he raged. He had committed the "worst treachery in world history." He had accepted twelve million marks from the French to have Hitler arrested and liquidated (an untrue assertion) and Germany put at the mercy of its enemies. Röhm and his co-conspirators would be shot. While asserting his "unshakable alliance with the SA," Hitler at the same time bluntly threatened that he would show no mercy in "exterminating and destroying undisciplined and disobedient characters and asocial or diseased elements." Tens of thousands of upright SA men had made the most difficult sacrifices for the movement, and he expected the leaders of every SA division to prove themselves worthy of these sacrifices. He also reminded the nervous SA leaders that he had defended Röhm for years against the most vicious attacks on his private life but that the most recent developments had forced him "to place all personal feeling second to the welfare of the Movement and to that of the State." Above all, he would "eradicate and nip in the bud any attempts to propagate a new upheaval by ludicrous circles of pretentious characters." When he finished, his listeners lustily shouted their approval.

Despite his homicidal rage, Hitler hesitated in passing sentence on Röhm. Himmler and Göring pressed him to execute the SA commander, who they maintained was the leader of the planned insurrection. At first Hitler thought to pardon him, but in the end reluctantly decided that Röhm could not be spared. He did, however, offer his old comrade the opportunity to die with a soldier's honor. On July 1, as Röhm waited in his sweltering cell in Stadelheim, two SS men, led by Theodor Eicke, the commandant of Dachau, entered. "You have forfeited your life," Eicke stated. "The Führer gives you one more chance to draw the right conclusions." With that, he placed a pistol loaded with a single round on a small table, and the three SS men left the cell. When some fifteen minutes passed and no shot was heard, Eicke and his men returned to the cell. They found Röhm standing, bare-chested, and defiant. "Chief of Staff, prepare yourself," Eicke barked. As the powerful SA chief started to speak, his executioners opened fire. According to postwar reports his last words were "My Führer, my Führer."

Within forty-eight hours more than one hundred people had been killed. Some estimates run as high as double that number. Some died as a result of mistaken identity, and many victims who had no connection with Röhm or Papen were killed to settle old scores. Gustav Ritter von Kahr, former premier of Bavaria, who had thwarted Hitler in the Beer Hall Putsch, was seized by the SS, taken out into a nearby swamp, and hacked to death with axes. His badly mutilated body was discovered days later in a muddy ditch near Dachau. For all the vicious brutality of "The Night of

Long Knives," as the purge came to be called, the violence took place out
of public view. For the citizens of Berlin and Munich, life on June 30 and
the following day went on as if nothing had happened. Press coverage was
minimal, reports vague. When the Nazi press broke the news of Röhm's
alleged plot, its stories trumpeted Hitler's heroic action in crushing the
SA traitors and their co-conspirators in Berlin and elsewhere. A purge of
the Brown Shirt leadership was for many Germans a welcome relief. With
its swaggering, drunken excesses, violent disrespect for the law, bullying
intimidation, and incessant agitation for a second revolution, the SA had
few friends by the summer of 1934.

The murders of June 30–July 2 represented only the first act. On July 3,
Hitler appeared before the cabinet and offered an extensive report on the
events of the previous days. Still enraged, he fulminated against Röhm's
treachery and defended his drastic action by comparing himself to a captain at sea confronted with a mutiny. Under the circumstances, immediate
action to crush the mutiny was imperative; a formal trial impossible. He
had saved the government and provided would-be troublemakers with a
stark example of the kind of swift justice they would receive. This was an
emergency act of state, and there would be no subsequent trials. An official
communiqué summarizing the cabinet meeting announced that the ministers had granted unanimous approval for a law governing measures for the
self-defense of the state. The law, the title of which was virtually as long as
the text, consisted of a single article—actually a single sentence. The Law
for the Emergency Defense of the State stated simply: "The measures taken
to crush the treasonous attacks against the internal and external security
of the State on June 30 and July 1 and 2, 1934, are deemed justified and
as self-defense of the state." The brutal murder of defenseless men by the
German head of state had been made retroactively legal.

Ten days passed before Hitler made a public appearance. Addressing
a nervous Reichstag, twelve of whose members had been murdered, he
took full responsibility for all that had occurred, even for measures he had
not specifically ordered. He made reference to overwhelming evidence—
meetings, plans, contacts, and conversations that pointed to conspiracy,
without, however, providing any details or proof. That would have been
difficult, because there was no hard evidence of a Putsch, no proof that
Röhm or Strasser or Schleicher and the dozens of other victims had been

conspiring to overthrow the Nazi state. None was ever forthcoming. Hitler praised the SS for its loyalty and resolute action and went on to reassert his devotion to the SA, which, he said, "has upheld its inner loyalty to me in these days which have been so difficult for both it and myself." The SA would rebound from this betrayal by its leaders and "will once again dominate German streets and clearly demonstrate to everyone that the life of National Socialist Germany has become all the stronger for having to overcome a difficult crisis."

While striking a pose of moral rectitude, he boldly confessed responsibility for the bloodbath that had just occurred. Earlier reports had set the number of deaths at seven; now Hitler admitted to seventy-seven. "I gave the order to shoot those . . . mainly responsible for this treason, and I also gave the order to burn out the tumors of our domestic poisoning . . . down to the raw flesh." Responding to critics, especially from abroad, he stated defiantly that "if anyone reproaches me and asks why we did not call upon the regular courts for sentencing, my only answer is this: in that hour, I was responsible for the fate of the German nation, and was thus the supreme judge of the German people!" And he promised more of the same. "Every person should know for all time that if he raises his hand to strike out at the state, certain death will be his lot. . . . Any nation which does not find the strength to exterminate such pests makes itself guilty." In the summer of 1934 Hitler had become the prosecutor, judge, jury, and executioner, roles he would never relinquish. German jurists contorted themselves into knots attempting to justify Hitler's actions, but there was one fact that could not be obscured: Hitler's will had become law. The highly respected legal theorist Carl Schmitt pronounced Hitler's actions the very essence of justice, since "the true Führer is always also the judge. The status of judge flows from the status of the Führer. . . . The Führer's deed was, in truth, the genuine exercise of justice. It is not subordinate to justice, but rather it is itself supreme justice."

While international opinion condemned the state-sanctioned murders, labeling Hitler a common thug, a gangster among gangsters, in Germany popular sentiment was clearly with him. The general public celebrated him as a savior, liberating them from the plague of SA viciousness. There was, Viktor Klemperer noted with dismay, "no sympathy at all for the vanquished, only delight." There were some faint murmurings of dissent. Police reported that among Catholics, news of the death of Catholic leader Klausner had met with an "extremely unfavorable response," but most were so absorbed with their immediate economic difficulties that no unrest was expected.

Hindenburg received news of the purge with relief, though he could not bring himself to believe that the Schleichers had been killed while "resisting arrest" and ordered an investigation. After a hurried Hitler visit to Neudeck, Hindenburg sent him a telegram on July 2, commending him for "your own determined action and your brave personal intervention. You have rescued the German Volk from a serious threat. For this may I extend to you my deeply felt gratitude and my sincere appreciation." A similar telegram went to Göring. The army leadership was also delighted with the elimination of Röhm and chose to overlook the murders of Generals Schleicher and Bredow, issuing a statement to the troops pledging the army's unstinting support for the Führer. The killings were still under way when Blomberg on July 1 praised Hitler for his "soldierly determination and exemplary courage" in smashing the treasonous plot of "the traitors and mutineers." Hitler, for a change, had been true to his word; he had eliminated the threat of the SA and solidified the army's power position in the Third Reich.

Along with the army, business leaders were also pleased that Hitler had struck down the social revolutionaries in the party, but the big winner of the Night of Long Knives was the SS. On July 20 Hitler ended its formal subordination to the much larger SA and elevated the SS to a position of independence, responsible only to him. Overnight Himmler's black-uniformed SS stepped from the shadow of the Storm Troopers to become the dominant force in the dictatorship. The team of Himmler and Heydrich was now in charge of virtually all police power in the state, and that power would only grow. In the following years the SS emerged as the regime's all-powerful instrument of terror and repression; it would also develop into the party's ideological elite, becoming a key player in the articulation and realization of Nazi ideology.

As for the SA, its power was broken. The organization that had played such a crucial role in the Nazi drive to power before 1933 and in the establishment of the Hitler dictatorship would no longer constitute a major power factor in the Third Reich. Twenty percent of its leadership was purged in the aftermath of the "Röhm Putsch," many lower-level commanders were dismissed, and by year's end the SA had lost 40 percent of its troops. It still played a highly visible role in Nazi ceremonial events—the endless parades, the anniversary celebrations of the 1923 Putsch, the Führer's birthday, the Nuremberg party rallies—wherever an imposing mass presence was required for a display of Nazi power. It also continued to play a very active role in the regime's relentless persecution of the Jews, harassing, threatening, bullying, and beating Jews in independent local actions that required no authorization from above. But after June 1934 its influence as an instrument of Nazi policy steadily dwindled.

While the country was still absorbing the news of Hitler's ruthless purge of the SA, Hindenburg's condition continued to deteriorate, and on August 2 he died quietly at his estate in East Prussia. On the day before, with the old field marshal lying on his deathbed, Hitler introduced a new law stipulating that on the death of Hindenburg, the offices of Reich President and chancellor would be merged, a move that was in clear violation of the Enabling Act, a technicality of interest at this point to virtually no one. Hitler's assumption of the position of Reich President also made him commander-in-chief of the armed forces. Without consulting him, General Blomberg and General Walter von Reichenau, like Blomberg a Nazi sympathizer, drafted an oath of unconditional loyalty not to the office of the president or to the constitution or to the German nation but to the person of Adolf Hitler. On August 2, in ceremonies held on all military installations, members of the armed forces swore their fealty to the Führer: "I swear by God this sacred oath to render unconditional obedience to the Führer of the German Reich and *Volk*, Adolf Hitler, the Supreme Commander of the Armed Forces, and to be willing at all times to risk my life as a brave soldier for this oath."

Hindenburg was laid to rest in a state funeral at the imposing Tannenberg Memorial in East Prussia, site of the field marshal's greatest victory of the World War. And with his burial, the basic structure of the Third Reich fell firmly into place, its domestic position secure.

Within a stunningly short period of time a dysfunctional democratic state had been dismantled, sources of organized opposition crushed or neutralized, and a dictatorial regime with totalitarian aspirations erected. But the Nazis were not content to monopolize the instruments of state power. Theirs was a far more ambitious goal.

THE PEOPLE'S COMMUNITY

While the systematic *Gleichschaltung* of the nation's political institutions was unfolding, another process, simultaneous and sinister, was under way in the everyday life of the Third Reich. The regime's goal, stated openly and acted upon with unflagging zeal, was nothing less than a complete transformation of German politics, culture, and society, coordinating not only governmental institutions but the media, the churches, schools, social clubs, youth organizations, athletic leagues, and cultural institutions of all sorts. The regime sought to mobilize all elements of society, creating National Socialist organizations for women, girls, boys, teachers, students, lawyers, physicians, craftsmen, workers, each with its own uniform, flag, party badges, and slogans ("Barbers, too, Face Great Tasks!"). No one in the "people's community" was overlooked, and no one could stand outside. Everyone was called on not simply to obey but to believe, to participate.

Hitler had offered a preview of his vision for the Third Reich in his Reichstag speech on March 23, 1933. In pressing for the passage of the Enabling Act, he explained that along with the "political purification of our public life, the Reich Government intends to undertake a thorough moral purging of the body of the people [*Volkskörper*]. The entire system of education, the theater, the cinema, literature, the press, and radio—they will be used as a means to this end and valued accordingly. They must all work to preserve the eternal values residing in the essential character of our people." Art, in all its forms, was of crucial importance in this endeavor. Art "will always remain the expression and mirror of the yearning and the reality of an era. The cosmopolitan contemplative attitude is rapidly disappearing. Heroism is arising passionately as the future shaper and leader of political destinies. The task of art is to give expression to this determining spirit of the age. Blood and Race will once more become the source of artistic intuition."

Many found it striking that in making a speech that would establish the legal foundation of the Third Reich Hitler chose to address the role of art, but over the next six years of peace Hitler repeatedly emphasized art's crucial mission in constructing a new National Socialist society. In fact, no other government in the interwar years was more obsessed with art and culture than the Nazi regime. In an "Address on Art and Politics" delivered at the 1935 Nuremberg party rally, Hitler remarked proudly that "at some future date people will be astonished to find that at the very time when National Socialism and its leaders were fighting to finish a heroic struggle for existence—a life and death struggle—the first impulses were given towards a revival and resurrection of German art." For the Nazis, art was power; it defined the National Socialist vision of the future, and the Nazis were determined to extract the maximum value from it.

The vibrant, edgy cultural flourishing of the Weimar era, the Nazis were convinced, was a force to be reckoned with. For Hitler and the Nazis, everything that emerged in German cultural life after the revolution of 1918—experimental art, jazz and atonal music, literary and architectural modernism, avant-garde theater, and Expressionist film, most of which had their origins in the prewar Empire—was corrupt, degenerate, and foreign. The Nazis reviled it as "cultural Bolshevism," a creation of leftists and Jews that had saturated the country with a spirit fundamentally alien to the German people. The eruption of artistic innovation that had made Berlin an exciting international center of postwar culture was responsible not only for degenerate art but for the collapse of all notions of traditional morality and taste. Everywhere they turned the Nazis found ample evidence of the nation's slide into decadence and decay—rampant sexual promiscuity and perversion—on the stage, in film, in countless nightclubs and cabarets, in prostitution, homosexuality, and the open flouting of traditional mores.

The purification commenced immediately. In the spring of 1933, the Law for the Restoration of the Professional Civil Service led to the immediate dismissal of all "non-Aryans" from state-subsidized theaters, orchestras, museums, schools, and research institutions. Jews, at whom the law was aimed, were immediately purged, but even those artists and teachers not directly affected by the Civil Service Law felt the prevailing chill. Many cultural institutions did not wait for the regime to institute changes; they rushed to "coordinate" themselves, voluntarily expelling anyone the Nazis might consider politically undesirable. Newspaper chiefs and magazine editors, reporters, illustrators, musicians, actors, critics, even librarians were sacked. Ufa, the largest studio in the German motion picture industry, dismissed Jews and other politically undesirable actors, directors, film editors, cameramen, screenwriters, stage managers, and others. Innovative stage directors Erwin Piscator and Max Reinhardt, filmmakers Fritz Lang and Billy Wilder, all emigrated. Wilder was Jewish, and Lang, whose films both Hitler and Goebbels admired, had a Jewish mother. He had to go.

The paintings of modernist artists Otto Dix, Paul Klee, Max Beckmann, George Grosz, Gerhard Marcks, Oscar Kokoschka, Käthe Kollwitz, and dozens of others gradually disappeared from galleries. The works of Erich Maria Remarque, author of *All Quiet on the Western Front*, Alfred Döblin, Lion Feuchtwanger, Stefan Zweig, Franz Werfel, Sigmund Freud, Albert Einstein, and many others tainted with "alien Jewish views" vanished from bookshops and library shelves, and publishers quickly dropped them from their lists. By the close of 1934, some four thousand works had been banned in that year alone. The modernist music of composers Alban Berg, Paul Hindemith, and Arnold Schönberg disappeared from the repertoires of the country's orchestras; and famed Jewish conductors Bruno Walter, Otto Klemperer, and Erich Kleiber were dismissed from their positions and fled the country. The music of Jewish classical composers Mendelssohn, Mahler, Meyerbeer, and Offenbach was no longer performed, and works with Jewish associations such as Handel's Old Testament oratorios underwent title changes. The Nazis even insisted that Mozart's *Don Giovanni, Le Nozze di Figaro, and Cosi fan tutte* be translated into German because Mozart's Italian librettist was of Jewish origin.

An exodus of actors, authors, musicians, and painters, most of them Jewish, began and gathered momentum. The Prussian Academy of Letters purged novelist Heinrich Mann (a well-known anti-Nazi), and his brother Nobel laureate Thomas Mann, Germany's most distinguished literary figure, resigned and emigrated, as did playwrights Georg Kaiser, Carl Zuckmayer, and Bertolt Brecht. After the absorption of Austria in 1938, they were joined, among others, by Jewish novelists Hermann Broch, Joseph Roth, and Stefan Zweig.

Most artists and writers, however, chose to stay; they adapted and continued their careers. Popular novelists Hans Fallada and Erich Kästner continued to write, but produced innocuous, politically safe work. Ernst Barlach went on sculpting but was prohibited from exhibiting his work. Some who stayed were forbidden to write or paint at all. Others flourished. The aged Nobel laureate Gerhart Hauptmann, musicians Wilhelm Furtwängler and Richard Strauss, popular actors Emil Jannings, Werner Kraus, and actress/filmmaker Leni Riefenstahl, to name only a few, easily adjusted to the new regime. Even leading lights of the modern dance movement such as Rudolf von Laban accommodated themselves to the new rulers. "Dance," as Fritz Böhme, Germany's most influential dance critic, put it, "is a racial question. There is no international, trans-racial form of dance."

Inspired by the Nazis, some gallery directors began mounting special exhibitions of "degenerate art" under such titles as "Chamber of Art Horrors" and "Images of Cultural Bolshevism" or "The Spirit of November: Art in the Service of Decay." By the mid-1930s, exhibitions of this type had been mounted in sixteen different cities. In 1936 Goebbels received Hitler's backing to confiscate examples of forbidden art from German museums and galleries, which he intended to display in a show of "German Degenerate Art Since 1910." He dispatched a small team headed by the artist Adolf Ziegler, a Nazi favorite, to scour the museums for representative artworks from the Weimar period. By fall 1937 more than five thousand paintings, drawings, prints, and sculptures had been seized. The confiscations would continue into 1939, by which time the team had seized seventeen thousand pieces of forbidden art.

Goebbels could always count on Hitler's absolute abhorrence of Expressionism, Cubism, Dadaism, in fact, anything that smacked of modernism. "The artist Hitler," as he was frequently described in the Nazi press, preferred nineteenth-century realism, especially pastoral landscapes, bucolic scenes of peasant life, nursing mothers, sturdy bare-breasted peasant women, and square-jawed men. These paintings were aesthetically banal, trending into kitsch, but that was not the standard by which the Nazis judged them. They were powerful ideological expressions of the National Socialist "Blood and Soil" ethos, subtly blurring the line between the overtly political and the artistic. While in painting Hitler favored the quotidian, in sculpture, as in architecture, his taste ran to the monumental, preferring Arno Breker and Josef Thorak, who carved colossal supermen that guarded the many mammoth structures created by Hitler's favorite architects, Paul Ludwig Troost and Albert Speer. Needless to say, the Bauhaus, the center of modernist architecture and design, closed in 1933 under pressure from the regime.

The climax of the campaign against "cultural bolshevism" came in the form of a major exhibition *Degenerate Art* (*Entartete Kunst*) that opened in Munich in July 1937. Six hundred fifty paintings and sculptures, all forbidden since 1933, were hauled from the storage vaults of German museums and collected for the show—Klee, Kandinsky, Mondrian, Chagall, Cézanne, van Gogh, and the usual German suspects were all there. The exhibit was mounted in a gallery on the Hofgarten arcade, a short distance from the monumental House of German Art, where a much larger exhibition of state-approved "Great German Art" opened the day before. The motivation behind the *Degenerate Art* show, as a guide to the exhibition made clear, was "to display the common roots of cultural anarchy and political anarchy and reveal the perversion of art as cultural bolshevism." The public was invited to see for themselves "what museums from all over Germany had purchased with taxpayers' hard-earned money and displayed as art."

The Nazi press was aflame with lurid descriptions of the perversions the public could view—dismembered front soldiers, pimps, whores, dope fiends, alcoholics, starving children, grotesquely fat, cigar-chomping capitalists. The exhibition was divided into nine stations, among them "Shameless Mockery of Every Religious Sensibility," "The Political Background of Degenerate Art," "Bordellos, Whores, Pimps," and "Idiots, Cretins, and the Deformed" (an underlying theme of the exhibition was a putative link between mental derangement and the distortions of the art on display). The title of one section was simply "Jews," featuring Jewish artists (there were only five in the exhibit) and their un-German work. The paintings were crowded together, hung at odd angles in poor lighting, and staggered like a twisted lattice from floor to ceiling—as if, ironically, Expressionist artists had planned the display themselves. On the walls were scribbled captions in bold black letters that ridiculed the featured artists and their works. It was, in Nazi parlance, a freak show.

Predictably the exhibition drew savage reviews in the Nazi-dominated press but also long lines, attracting more than two million visitors in Munich before it went on the road in November. *The New York Times* reported that the show had drawn three times as many visitors as the officially approved German art exhibit just down the street. "Many were foreign tourists, especially American and English, but also many German art students, for whom the show was perhaps their last opportunity to see modern art." Attendance was not hurt by the fact that admission to the museum was free, and "the common *Volk*," people who had probably never ventured into an art gallery and were not in tune with the latest artistic trends, were much in evidence.

In the fall, the *Degenerate Art* exhibit began a tour of twelve German cities that extended into 1939, always accompanied by withering commentary by local Nazi reviewers and ordinary visitors. "The artists ought to be tied up next to their pictures so that every German can spit in their face," one visitor to the Munich exhibit angrily grumbled, "but not only the artists, also the museum directors who, at a time of mass unemployment, poured vast sums into the ever-open jaws of the perpetrators of these atrocities." After inspecting the confiscated works, Goebbels was filled with contempt. It was "the sort of garbage that after a three hour inspection makes one want to vomit." He was proud that he had "cleansed the museums." He had performed a service for the Reich.

And yet, as in Munich, the show attracted unprecedented crowds in Münster, Düsseldorf, Frankfurt, Cologne, Kiel, Bonn, and Essen, as thousands flocked to the galleries to see the forbidden paintings. More people visited the *Degenerate Art* exhibition than any other in history. Everywhere the reviews were blistering—the works on display were the rotten fruit of the November Republic, pacifist, sexually degenerate, Jewish, and Bolshevik, but as one newspaper reported, "the rush to see the exhibition [in Berlin] is extraordinary. One has to find a special way over backstairs and through a courtyard to avoid the crush of the exiting masses colliding with the new arrivals." Whether the visitors were drawn by prurient curiosity or a desire to get a final glimpse of modern art that was bound for extinction is impossible to know. But when the traveling exhibition finally closed in early 1939, *Time* magazine estimated that at least three million Germans had viewed it. Goebbels considered it a great success. When the show's national tour finally closed, many of the nearly priceless works slipped into the private collections of prominent Nazis; more than nine hundred were sold abroad, the proceeds going to the Reich government; and more than four thousand were burned in the courtyard of a Berlin fire station.

Given the resounding success of the *Degenerate Art* exhibition, a show of degenerate music inevitably followed. Initiated in Düsseldorf, the program showcased and reviled atonal symphonic music. The Nazis were also appalled by American imports such as blues, jazz, and swing, which were especially popular with younger Germans, and condemned them as "Negro music." As one SA publication commented, "We, the younger German generation, are . . . aware of the fact that the legacy of a great past in the field of music places a special obligation on us. We, the people of Beethoven, Bach, Mozart, Haydn, and Handel, cannot and will not any longer allow one of the noblest blooms of cultural life to fall increasingly victim to degeneration and to ultimate degradation to satisfy the demands of big-city night clubs and international bordellos."

Speaking to representatives of German theater in May 1933, Goebbels had laid out the Nazi vision of the role of culture in the Third Reich. The National Socialist revolution, he proclaimed, was introducing a new spirit into German life, and it was the task of the artist community to infuse society with this new spirit. "Individualism will be conquered and in place of the individual and its deification, the Volk will emerge. The Volk stands in the center of all things. The revolution is conquering the Volk and public life, imprinting its stamp on culture, economy, politics and private life. It would be naïve to believe that art could remain exempt from this." Art could no longer "claim to be apolitical or nonpartisan. It could not claim to have loftier goals than politics." In an earlier time when politics was "nothing more than the battle of parliamentary parties screaming at one another," artists "might claim the right to ignore politics, but not at this historic moment." The goal of the regime, and with it Germany's artists, must be nothing less than to "conquer the soul of the nation."

While culture set the tone and symbolic content for the regime, the educational system was a critical target in the transformation of German sensibilities. The control and coordination (*Gleichschaltung*) of the university proceeded quickly and with precious little opposition. In a toxic brew of ideological zeal, petty jealousy, and personal ambition, colleagues betrayed one another, denouncing current behavior as well as actions from the pre-Nazi past. There were few genuine Nazis among the professoriate before 1933, but the Nazis could count on widespread sympathy for their vigorous nationalism, their rejection of Versailles, and their contempt for the parties that had signed the hated document. As a result, the Nazis found many fellow travelers among the academics. Opposition to the regime among the professoriate was almost unheard of, and when dissent was voiced, it invariably focused on specific policies that directly affected professional standing or practices and did not question the nature of the regime or Nazism's core values.

However much the regime might count on sympathy from conservative academics, it also sought compliance in other more draconian ways. No one could assume an academic position without first attending a six-week course conducted by the National Socialist Lecturers Association, a course that included not only political indoctrination but military drill and physical training. All schools in Germany were public institutions and hence all faculty and staff were subject to the Aryan Paragraph of the Civil Service Law of April 7, 1933, which expelled social or racial undesirables from teaching posts in primary and secondary schools as well as in universities. Despite the personal pain and despair that accompanied the expulsions, the action provoked virtually no resistance. Jews, who made up just over one percent of the population, made up 12 percent of all professors and a quarter of Germany's Nobel laureates, most in physics and mathematics. Luminaries such as Albert Einstein, Max Born, Fritz Haber, James Franck, and Hans Krebs, all of whom were or would become Nobel Prize winners, were unceremoniously pushed out of their positions or resigned under pressure. In all, some 15 percent of all university professors were dismissed; by 1934 some 1,600 out of 5,000 university faculty had been forced out, roughly one third of whom were Jews or were married to Jews. The number of dismissals in physics and chemistry was particularly high, including eleven Nobel laureates. When Bernhard Rust, the Nazi minister of education, asked the director of the prestigious Göttingen Institute for Quantum Physics if his institute had suffered as a result of the dismissal of the Jews, he responded: "Suffered? No, it hasn't suffered, Herr Minister, it just doesn't exist anymore."

While the professoriate had been lukewarm toward the Nazis before Hitler's assumption of power, university students had been among the most ardent supporters of the NSDAP. The economic woes of the 1920s had created a large academic proletariat, and the Depression worsened that situation. Each year 25,000 students graduated from the universities, most with little hope for employment, in part a result of the draconian cuts in the civil service from the Brüning and Papen austerity programs. Those hoping for a position in teaching discovered that one in three academics was unemployed, and even recent graduates in medicine and law encountered problems finding positions. A sense of gloom settled over the student body of the universities, and the Nazis were the clear beneficiaries. Already in 1931, 60 percent of all university students supported the National Socialist Students Association in nationwide student elections. Nazi-inspired anti-Semitic demonstrations took place at the universities all across the Reich as students demanded a quota for Jews in the student body. Students also found the Nazis' rabid nationalism appealing, as well as the party's unrelenting assault on "the Weimar system."

On April 12, 1933, the Nazi German Students Association's Office for Press and Propaganda announced a nationwide "Action Against the Un-German Spirit," which was to climax in a literary purge, a "cleansing" by fire. The students presented their action as a response to a worldwide Jewish "smear campaign" against Germany and "an affirmation of traditional German values." They published a blacklist of "un-German" authors, including Freud, Kästner, Remarque, Heine, Heinrich Mann, Ernest Hemingway, John Steinbeck, Emil Ludwig, and dozens of others. Local chapters were to pepper the press with news releases, sponsor well-known Nazi figures to speak at public gatherings, and negotiate for radio airtime.

The NS Student Association also drafted "Twelve Theses Against the Un-German Spirit," a manifesto that deliberately evoked Martin Luther's rebellious 95 Theses of 1517 and his burning of the Papal Bull that excommunicated him and his followers. Three hundred years later in 1817, German students, embittered by Prussia's refusal to lead a movement for national unification, reenacted Luther's act of defiance by torching, among other things, Prussian military manuals and other symbols of Prussian authoritarianism. For the students, the tradition of book burning was associated not with reactionary impulses but with defiance against authority and with strong nationalist sentiments. Placards publicized the Twelve Theses, which attacked "Jewish intellectualism," asserted the need to "purify" German language and literature, and demanded that universities be centers of German nationalism. "Germany's most dangerous adversary is the Jew," the document read. "If a Jew writes in German, he is lying. The German who writes in German but thinks in an un-German way is a traitor. We want to eliminate the lie; we want to brand the treason. . . . We demand from the German student the will and ability to overcome Jewish intellectualism and all the liberal manifestations of decay associated with it. Students and professors should be selected on the basis of their thinking in the German spirit." This month-long campaign culminated in a coordinated wave of book burnings in Munich, Dresden, Breslau, Frankfurt, Kiel, and other cities, but the dramatic torch-lit demonstration on Berlin's Opera Plaza attracted by far the most attention, both in Germany and abroad. For weeks, students had been removing "un-German" books from libraries and universities and storing them in their headquarters in the Oranienburgstrasse. After hearing a rousing speech by the new Nazi professor of political pedagogy Alfred Bäumler, hundreds of students, many wearing SA uniforms, others in their purple and green fraternity caps, gathered at the Oranienburgstrasse and piled hundreds of books into vans and private automobiles.

At just past eleven, the students began marching toward the government quarter, picking up more students along the way. Carrying torches and singing nationalist songs, they swept through the rain-slick streets toward the Opernplatz, where the cars and vans, filled with "un-German" books, parked at the edge of the wide plaza. While an SA band blared out marches and rousing Nazi songs, the students formed a human chain, passing the books hand to hand from the cars and vans to a pyre of wooden beams in the center of plaza. There a tepid fire struggled against an intermittent drizzle, and the students heaved armloads of discredited books into the flames. Speaking one after another, nine students solemnly read out their lines for the event: "Against class warfare and materialism! For the people's community and idealist way of life! I consign to the flames the writings of Marx and Kautsky. Against decadence and moral decay! For discipline and virtue in the family and the state! I consign to the flames the writings of Heinrich Mann, Ernst Glaeser and

Erich Kästner." On and on as the works of Toller, Tucholsky, Ossietzky, Preuss, Rathenau, and dozens of others disappeared into the bonfire.

At the height of the event and with cameras rolling, Goebbels addressed the crowd, urging the students on. "The age of an exaggerated Jewish intellectualism is now at an end," he declaimed into a radio microphone. "The breakthrough of the German revolution has cleared the way for the true German spirit." The students had their role to play. "When you students claim the right to throw into the flames the rotten fruit . . . then you must also see it as your duty to replace this garbage with genuine German values." The effect was not quite the dramatic conflagration that the student organizers wanted; it had rained throughout the afternoon and early evening and for a considerable period of time the great heap of books simply smoldered in the damp air, but the book burnings of May sent shockwaves around the world. In Germany, a country renowned for its learning, its education, its books, it had come to this.

By the mid-1930s there was an air of stagnation and depression in the academy, affecting both faculty and students. In 1932 university enrollment stood at roughly 118,000, approximately 20 percent of whom were women. By 1938, enrollment dropped to 51,000, only 6,300 of whom were women. Although enrollment at technical high schools rose in 1939, the regime had deprived itself of a cohort of gifted scientists and engineers. This fact would have crucial implications for the war effort. It was typical of a self-destructive streak in Nazi ideology that infected the party and the regime it controlled. Standards plummeted, and by 1939 complaints were increasingly voiced about the poor quality of university students, who in turn complained that their work suffered because of lack of time to study. After 1935 many were siphoned off to the army, whose officers complained about the low quality of their educational preparedness.

Especially debilitating to faculty and students alike was the plague of political denunciations that swept through Germany's schools. As early as February 1933 a delegation of university professors felt compelled to make a formal complaint to Vice Chancellor Papen, warning that "denunciations, lack of discipline, and slavish conformity" to political currents represented "a danger not only for the schools but the nation as a whole." Papen listened but could do little, and the situation did not improve. Denunciations became so numerous that in 1936 Education Minister

Bernhard Rust was moved to warn students to relax their vigilance and not subject their professors to political reliability tests. For the most part, the record of the students and their professors was one of accommodation and support. There was occasional carping, to be sure, but the complaints tended to be minor and were not directed against the nature of the National Socialist regime.

Nazi infiltration of society was not limited to Germany's cultural and educational elites. The Nazis sought to mobilize Germans of all ages and in all walks of life, organizing retreats, excursions, and training sessions in various occupational fields, but the young were the primary targets for indoctrination. The Hitler Youth (HJ) had been founded in the early 1920s and was treated as a sub-formation of the SA. Throughout the party's rise to power, the HJ remained a small but active organization with little funding and few followers. In 1932, at the height of Nazi popularity, it counted only 35,000 members, and had little influence in the party leadership. That changed in 1933 when membership began to climb, soaring to more than five million by the close of 1934.

"My program for educating youth is hard," Hitler declared in 1933. "Weakness must be hammered away. I want a youth before which the world will tremble . . . a brutal, domineering, fearless, cruel youth. . . . The free, splendid beast of prey must once again flash from its eyes. . . . That is how I will eradicate thousands of years of human domestication. . . . That is how I will create the New Order." Boys marched from the Young Volk (JV), ages ten to fourteen, to the Hitler Youth or HJ, ages fourteen to eighteen, where they received training with weapons, orienteering, and camping, all with a strong military flavor. Militarism, nationalism, racism, and Führer worship, along with the martial virtues of duty, obedience, honor, courage, physical strength, and ruthlessness, were the virtues they wished to inculcate in the young. "I swear to devote all my energies and my strength to the savior of our country, Adolf Hitler" read the pledge of ten-year-old boys entering the Jungvolk. "I am willing and ready to give up my life for him, so help me God. . . . We are born to die for Germany."

Speaking to the Reichstag in November 1938, Hitler proudly described the trajectory of Nazi indoctrination:

This youth does not learn anything else other than to think German, to act German and when those boys at the age of ten come into our organization and there for the first time begin to breathe fresh air, four years later they move from the JV to the HJ, and there we keep them for another four years and then we do not return them into the hands of our old originators of classes and estates but take them immediately into the party, into the Labor Front, into the SA or the SS . . . and so forth. And if they have been there for two years or a year and a half and they still have not become thorough National Socialists, then we put them in the labor service and for six or seven months they work at square bashing, all with one symbol, the German spade. And any class-consciousness and pride in one's social position still remaining after six or seven months will be taken over for further treatment by the army for two years, and when they come back after two, three, or four years then we take them immediately back into the SA, SS, and so on to prevent relapse and they will never be free for the rest of their lives.

Membership in the Hitler Youth was not compulsory until 1936, but it was wise to join. Wearing their brown shirts, black shorts, and white knee socks, they organized camping trips, hiked in the mountains, sang folk songs around the campfire, embracing many of the traditions of the German youth movement from the early twentieth century. This mobilization of school-age boys produced a series of unintended consequences. School discipline deteriorated as uniformed HJ bullied other students and disobeyed their teachers. Teachers—and parents—found maintaining order increasingly difficult, and academic performance declined as HJ and Labor Front activities cut into study time.

The HJ was also inculcating a new set of values, and young Germans increasingly looked to the HJ leaders instead of the teacher or the church or parents as role models. "We are the happy Hitler Youth," one typical HJ song of 1935 declared. "We need no Christian virtues for our Führer Adolf Hitler is always our guide. . . . We do not follow Christ but Horst Wessel. . . . I can do without the church, the Swastika is redemption on earth." Another went: "Pope and rabbi shall yield, we want to be pagans again. . . . Out with the Jews, and with the pope from the German home." Given this powerful propaganda message, it is hardly surprising that young Germans were encouraged to inform on any teacher or parent or clergy who displayed "unsocial" attitudes. By 1935 the party had managed to insert itself into the family, driving a wedge between parent and child, teacher and student, priest and young parishioner. "The totalitarian demands of the Hitler Youth, the sense of authority and self-confidence, rebellious spirit, and fanaticism of these youths, have added so much to this problem that it approaches an unbearable intensity," a report from the Social Democratic underground stated. (The Socialist underground organization smuggled reports on life inside Nazi Germany to the SPD's exiled leadership in Prague and later Paris.) The Nazis tried to reassure parents, but "all these reassurances have not changed the fact that parental influence over youth continues to diminish, and that relationships within families grow more and more tense and hostile. . . . Children denounce their parents—whereupon they lose jobs, positions, and are threatened with the loss of parental rights and personal freedom." It was probably too much to say that "those with children began to envy the childless," but there was no small amount of truth in it.

Girls, too, were mobilized, entering the Jungmädel (Young Girls, ages ten to fourteen), then the League of German Girls (Bund deutscher Mädel or BdM, ages fourteen to eighteen), where they received training in physical fitness, first aid, and domestic skills. At eighteen, they, too, began six months' service in the Labor Front, where most were sent to work on farms. The goal was to prepare young women for their ultimate role in the *Volksgemeinschaft* (people's community): to become wives, homemakers, and healthy mothers. Despite the party's official prudishness, its insistence on modest dress and decorous behavior for young women, its equally relentless emphasis on the body and procreation tended to sexualize the message. Given the regime's unrelenting grooming of young women for racial breeding and the organization's many unchaperoned activities, BdM soon acquired a reputation for looseness. In 1935 a Labor Front camp for girls in Breslau was rumored to have closed because so many of the young women became pregnant. That reputation, whether deserved or not, seemed sealed when in 1936 approximately 100,000 members of the HJ and BdM attended the annual party rally at Nuremberg, and nine hundred girls between the ages of fifteen and eighteen returned home pregnant. Such stories gave rise to numerous jokes—the Bund deutscher Mädel being referred to as Bald deutscher Mütter (Soon German Mothers) or Bund deutscher Matrozen (League of German Mattresses), or "Baldur, drück mich" ("Baldur, squeeze me").

The Nazis also made a serious effort to mobilize adult women. It was only in the last years of the Weimar Republic that the Nazis had made a sustained effort to win over women, who had previously been reluctant to associate with the party. The Nazi program was essentially a promise to return women to the family and home, relieving them of the double burden of household duties and employment, allowing them to realize every woman's most cherished wish: to marry and have a family. Well known for their swaggering machismo, violence, misogyny, and paganism, the Nazis rejected women's participation in politics and opposed women in the workplace, holding generally retrograde positions on all gender issues. Women's "liberation" of the Weimar era, the Nazis maintained, had been a swindle, in which women were free to work long hours for lower pay than men, and were denied the opportunity to fulfill their biological and societal destiny: to become wives and mothers. "'Women's Liberation' is merely a phrase invented by the Jewish intellect," Hitler declared in 1934. In the Third Reich, women did not need emancipation. National Socialism had "liberated women from liberation," restoring respect for motherhood and honoring women and the German family. The regime offered equality of the sexes, Hitler maintained, each with its own sphere. "Man's world is the state." His "world is his struggle, his willingness to devote himself to the community. . . . One might perhaps say that a woman's world is a smaller one. For her world is her husband, her family, her children, and her home. . . . Providence assigned to woman the care of this, her own world, and it is only on this foundation that the man's world can be formed and can grow."

To give symbolic weight to their celebration of German motherhood, the Nazis made Mother's Day, which had first been observed in Germany in 1923, an official national holiday. They did, however, change the date to Hitler's mother's birthday. Families were given favorable loans and tax breaks for children—women with more than six children paid no income tax at all. At the same time women continued to suffer discrimination in the labor market—they were forbidden from serving as judges, public prosecutors, or lawyers, and no women were promoted to positions of high rank in the civil service. Women teachers were also confronted by a glass ceiling, being excluded or removed from higher administrative posts in education.

Mothers were not, however, simply to stay at home knitting by the fire but were to be mobilized for active public service to the *Volk*. They were encouraged to pursue careers in fields that were "compatible with their nature"—domestic, clerical, and agricultural work. Women were also prodded to take up social work, and the Nazis established a series of women's organizations for that purpose—the National Socialist Women's Association (NS-F), headed since 1934 by Gertrud Scholtz-Klink, the German Women's Welfare (NS Frauenwerk), The National Socialist People's Welfare, and the Labor Front. This was to be the extent of their political involvement, and no woman, even Scholtz-Klink, the most prominent figure in the Nazi women's movement, was allowed to participate in decisions affecting policy toward women and the family.

Women should be content within their domestic sphere, Hitler declared to the NS Women's Congress in 1935, and

> the so-called granting of equal rights to women, which Marxism demands, in reality does not grant equal rights but constitutes a deprivation of rights, since it draws the woman into an area in which she will necessarily be inferior. It places the woman in situations that cannot strengthen her position—vis-à-vis both man and society—but only can weaken it. . . . The woman has her own battlefield. With every child she brings into the world, she fights her battle for the nation. The man stands up for the Volk, exactly as the woman stands up for the family.

And "the family," as one SA official explained, "is the most important cell of the state . . . and National Socialism has restored the family to its rightful place." But the regime did "not want any petit bourgeois ideal in the family, with its plush sofa psychology and walking mannequins, with its contempt for and degradation of the woman." For the Nazis, "the wife is a comrade, a fellow combatant." To underscore the regime's commitment to women and mothers, it provided state subsidies for mothers, offered them leisure activities, sports, courses in "feminine" subjects, degrees in home economics, and public ceremonies honoring mothers, all, of course, infused with the values of National Socialism. Scholtz-Klink and her organizations also emphasized proper hygiene and physical fitness, which were deemed essential for the health of the *Volk*. "Germany does not need women who can dance beautifully at five o'clock teas," an SS official remarked at a party meeting in 1937, "but women who have given proof of their health through accomplishments in the field of sport." The Reich Sports Medal would do. After all, "the javelin and springboard," he informed the crowd, "are more useful than lipstick in promoting health."

Beginning in 1935 and accelerating in the following years, two developments began to reshape the regime's approach to women. In 1935–36 the Nazis embarked on a major rearmament program, introducing conscription into a 500,000-man army, creating a modern air force and a new battle fleet, all blatant violations of the Versailles Treaty, and announcing an ambitious plan to make Germany economically self-sufficient within four years. With stepped-up production schedules in key war industries, more women were needed in the workplace, freeing men for service in the newly expanded armed forces. The regime began to expect women to find employment—and not only in occupations traditionally associated with women's work. Women were now required to juggle two sets of responsibilities—in the home and in the workplace, exactly the double burden the Nazis had so vehemently condemned in the first years of the Third Reich. Despite the regime's hortatory pledge to return women to the home and family, by the outbreak of war in 1939, two million more married women were working outside the home than in 1933.

Women were also expected to maintain an attractive appearance and behave in a modest, traditional way. Cosmetics, provocative dress, bobbed hair, and other fashions of the Weimar era were out, especially in the workplace. As Nazi factory officials in Lower Franconia declared, it was "a privilege to hold a job and women should be proud to have the opportunity." But it was also a woman's "duty to conduct [herself] in a true National Socialist manner." The Nazi Factory Organization (NSBO) would not tolerate "painted and powdered women," and "women who smoke in public—in hotels, in cafés, on the street, and so forth" were not welcome in Nazi factory gatherings.

After 1935 what had been at first a celebration of the mother's special role in Nazi society shifted subtly toward a more strictly biological function. Mothers were to be honored for fulfilling their biological duty by producing progeny for the people's community. Homage to the traditional family, so prominent in Nazi social policy before 1935, gradually receded almost imperceptibly into the background, and women were encouraged to have children, whether married or not. Unmarried pregnancy no longer constituted grounds for dismissal from the civil service, including for teachers, and Nazi propaganda began lauding the heroic "racially pure" unmarried mother's commitment to the Führer. Birth control was outlawed, abortion banned. Whereas motherhood and the family had been honored in the first years of the Third Reich, the Nazis increasingly dealt with mothers as baby-producing instruments of racial policy, a policy vividly displayed when, beginning in 1938, mothers with four children received a Mother's Cross of Honor third class; women with six offspring were awarded the Mother's Cross second class; and a mother with eight or more children was given the gold first class medal, a practice that continued until the collapse of the Third Reich.

The Nazis had proclaimed their determination to save the German family, the nucleus of the people's community, but gradually infiltrated it so thoroughly that loyalty to the myriad National Socialist organizations sundered the family, atomizing its members, inserting the party between parents and children, between husband and wife. So thoroughly Nazified was society that it gave rise to many of the "whispered jokes" that circulated during the Third Reich. "My father is in the SA," a girl explains to her friend in one such joke, "my oldest brother in the SS, my little brother in the Hitler Youth, my mother is part of the NS women's organization, and I'm in the League of German Girls." "Do you ever get to see each other?" asks the girl's friend. "Oh, yes, we meet every year at the party rally in Nürnberg!"

In addition to the welter of party organizations for every segment of the population, the Nazis were determined to bring their message directly into every German home. To do this, they turned to technology. For Goebbels, radio was a revolutionary means of mass communication that had the potential to bring the regime into the home of every German *Volksgenosse* (people's comrade). The radio was to so saturate the public "with the spiritual content of our time that no one can break away from it." He was determined to ensure that all German households should have a radio, and a new cheap set, the *Volksempfänger* (people's radio), began production in 1933. When Hitler came to power in 1933, only 4.3 million households possessed a radio out of a population of 66 million, far fewer than in the United States or Britain. A radio set in 1933 Germany was a rarity, a luxury item that cost approximately 100 marks, a price most German families could not afford.

In May 1933 Goebbels pressed a group of radio manufacturers to undertake mass production of a standard radio that would be significantly cheaper than any currently on the market. At the radio exhibition in Berlin in August, Goebbels introduced the set, the People's Receiver 301 (the numerical suffix referring to the date of Hitler's assumption of power on January 30), and it was an immediate hit. The supply of sets available at the exhibition sold out in one day, and manufacturers received 650,000 orders for the new set over the next twelve months. The Propaganda Ministry and private companies introduced a variety of payment schemes to help make a purchase possible. By the close of 1935, the number of sets sold had soared to one and a half million. By 1937, radios in large cities had reached 70 percent of all households, though sales still lagged in the countryside. In 1939 a smaller, cheaper set was introduced, so that at the outset of the war an even greater penetration of the population was achieved. In 1933 only one in four households had a radio; by 1939 it was one in two.

During his first year in power Hitler delivered some fifty radio addresses. His speeches were often transmitted during working hours, and factories, offices, and commercial businesses were required to suspend work so that the workers could hear the Führer's voice as it blared from a loudspeaker to the shop floor. All restaurants and cafés had to be equipped with radios for communal listening, and six thousand loudspeaker pillars were erected on street corners so that Hitler's voice would resound through the streets. Pedestrians were expected to stop in place and listen. This communal listening, the Nazis believed, contributed to a sense of shared experience, of community essential in the realization of the people's community.

The radio was an important entryway into the family and workplace, but it was not enough. The regime simultaneously sought to organize leisure, leaving the individual no activity beyond the reach of the party and state. The Nazis began by virtually doubling the number of paid holidays, from three to eight days under Weimar to between six and fifteen days. By far the most popular of the Nazi programs to dominate leisure activities and, in the process, integrate working-class Germans into the people's community, was the Strength Through Joy (*Kraft durch Freude* or KdF) program. Created in November 1933 as part of the German Labor Front (DAF) and funded by deductions from pay, this ambitious program was an attempt to court blue-collar Germans, linking work and leisure—and controlling both. It established sections for each area of leisure activity: vacations, instruction and education, travel and hiking, sports, and "the Beauty of Labor," which was devoted to creating hospitable conditions at work sites. Beauty of Labor, which was directed by Albert Speer, came in for a good deal of mockery because of its name (as did Strength Through Joy), but by 1939 the Beauty of Labor section had seen to the creation of over thirteen thousand green spaces, fifteen thousand canteens and recreation rooms, more than forty thousand workrooms, washrooms, and changing rooms in factories and plants, some two thousand "comradeship houses," and sports facilities, including swimming pools.

KdF also organized a wide variety of leisure activities—adult education classes, music lessons and recitals, traveling art exhibits, gymnastics, as well as instruction in tennis, sailing, and physical fitness. It operated more than three hundred adult education centers and thirty music schools. It bought blocks of tickets for the theater, for opera, for concerts, giving ordinary Germans who had never experienced a live stage performance the opportunity to attend. Most popular, and certainly the most highly publicized of the KdF's activities, were the subsidized vacation trips. On offer were holidays on the North Sea, in the Black Forest, Berlin, the Bavarian Alps, and the Harz Mountains. The majority of the tours consisted of excursions of up to three days, but the real showpiece of the KdF's vacation trips were excursions of two or even three weeks on one of the twelve cruise ships owned or leased by the program. These trips carried passengers in glittering white cruise ships to the fjords of Norway, to the Spanish coast, and to Italy. For many it was their first experience beyond the borders of the Reich. Between 1934 and 1939 approximately 43 million Germans—two thirds of the population—availed themselves of KdF trips.

The regime presented the KdF and its popular programs as evidence of the National Socialist people's community in operation, providing leisure opportunities for every German, regardless of class or income. "The worker sees that we are serious about raising his social position," Robert Ley proudly declared. "It is not the so-called educated classes whom we send out as representatives of the new Germany, but himself, the German worker whom we show to the world." Newspapers printed photographs of passengers waving happily from the decks; postcards and brochures featuring pictures of cruise destinations and testimonials of satisfied travelers could be found at every newsstand.

Hitler, himself a car enthusiast, also believed that every German should have an automobile to travel the new Autobahns being built throughout the country, and the plans for a "people's car," a Volkswagen, were begun. The original draft design sprang from Hitler, and the manufacturer Porsche was to produce the automobile. The program was launched with great fanfare in 1938, its loudly trumpeted goal to produce a cheap people's car for the common man. "For a large number of Germans," Social Democratic agents reported, "the announcement of the KdF car came as a pleasant surprise. There developed a real KdF-Car psychosis," becoming a big talking point among all classes of population. This obsession with the car, "which was cleverly stimulated by the Propaganda Ministry," was proving an effective diversionary tactic keeping "the masses from becoming preoccupied with a depressing [economic] situation." Citizens could place orders through the Labor Front, have payments deducted from wages and await delivery. They would have a long wait—no Volkswagen was produced for private use until after the Second World War, and the first delivery for those who had paid into the system during the Third Reich was made in 1960.

The regime also called on all Germans to participate in a series of public rituals that were designed to intensify their participation in the people's community and make an open display of their commitment to National Socialism. The German greeting—"Heil Hitler"—and Nazi salute became ubiquitous in everyday life. Postal clerks were required to give the Hitler greeting to patrons at the office; students at school to their teachers and one another, shopkeepers to their customers, and pedestrians on the street were expected to offer up a "Heil Hitler" instead of the traditional "*guten Tag*" (good day). The perpetual "Heils" inspired many jokes: An incredulous Göring arrives at Goebbels's office and tells him that on his way there he had heard one "good day" after another. If no one was going to use "Heil Hitler," maybe the regime should simply consider returning to "good day." Out of the question, Goebbels snaps, "as long as our beloved Führer lives, there will be no more 'good days' in Germany."

Flags, banners, and standards were everywhere, as were uniforms, armbands, and insignia. Swastikas adorned stamps, walls, billboards, stationery, and jewelry. It was everywhere one looked; no object, no matter how inconsequential, was too small to bear one. Victor Klemperer recorded his dismay when he discovered "toothpaste with the swastika" in his local pharmacy and shock a few days later when he spied "a children's ball with the swastika" in a toy shop. Seeing day in and day out these ubiquitous expressions of apparent support for the Nazis added to the more overt forms of pressure to conform, to accept the Nazi claim to have created a new people's community supported by all.

The Nazis filled the calendar with an endless series of charity drives, parades, rallies of different groups—the wounded veterans, teachers, women, youth. There was always a cause to mobilize the emotions of the public—the Winter Relief for the unemployed, homeless, and hungry, for disabled war veterans, for German minorities abroad. The Hitler Youth or SA man with cup in hand became a ubiquitous feature of daily life in the Third Reich. They collected not only on the streets, buses, and trolleys but went door-to-door in apartment blocks and in the countryside. Records were kept of who gave and who did not, with more than a little hint of retribution. One couldn't afford not to give. In some communities the names of those who were stingy or contributed nothing were posted in the newspaper; in some small villages the party erected "Boards of Shame," listing those who "despite financial ability refuse to make donations." In one village a banner was strung across the main street with the message "Take Note. In this village reside thirty-three traitors to their country. Anyone interested in their names need only inquire at the local party office."

While these activities put pressure on the individual to conform, the regime staged a succession of meticulously orchestrated mass spectacles that were intended to demonstrate the power and popularity of the regime.

The calendar year began with festivities marking the anniversary of Hitler's appointment as chancellor on January 30, followed by a celebration of the party's founding on February 24. In March the National Hero's Day dedicated to the fallen heroes of Germany's wars was expanded to include the "martyrs of the National Socialist movement," a fusion of the nationalist past with the Nazi present. On the last Sunday in March the new members of the Hitler Youth and the League of German Girls were sworn in, kicking off a day of speeches and parades as young Germans officially took up their duties in the *Volksgemeinschaft*. April 20, the Führer's birthday, was celebrated across the country in euphoric, quasi-religious displays of devotion to Germany's savior, and on May Day the Nazis observed a national holiday to celebrate not only the working class—the "Day of National Labor"—but all productive Germans. No longer a day devoted to a particular segment of the population, it was transformed into the "National Festival of the German People," transcending the now irrelevant boundaries of class.

Fall brought the three most hallowed events on the Nazi calendar: the party rally in Nuremberg, the Harvest Festival at the Bückeburg outside Hameln, and the reenactment of the 1923 Beer Hall Putsch in Munich. Of these, the Nuremberg rally in early September was by far the most awe-inspiring and the most theatrical in its staging. The Nazis had held their first national rally in Munich in 1923, a smallish affair that lasted barely three days; the second, in 1926, made hardly a blip on the radar screen of Weimar politics. It was poorly attended and lasted but two days. In the following year, the party gathered for the first time in Nuremberg but no national rally was held again until 1933 when Hitler declared that the annual Reich Party Rally would be held there in perpetuity.

The city recommended itself for a variety of reasons. Nuremberg, where Julius Streicher was in command, had been a hotbed of Nazi support throughout "the years of the struggle," and it was, in addition, the historic site where for centuries the diet of the Holy Roman Empire had convened. With its timbered houses, winding canals, medieval turrets, towering church spires, and cobblestone byways, the city offered the very essence of the Nazi vision of a romantic, mythical German past. And now, all through the narrow city streets, brown-shirted troops marched; Nazi flags fluttered from the mullioned windows; giant banners, three stories high, streamed down the facades of ancient buildings. Beginning in 1933, these weeklong rallies took on colossal proportions, attracting hundreds of thousands of participants—SA and SS troops; HJ and BdM; uniformed workers of the Labor Front; the Nazi Motor Corps; and the NS League of German Women—all in their distinctive uniforms and carrying different flags and standards. Alternating with the march of Storm Troopers and black-shirted SS came a parade of peasants from the different regions of the Reich, all dressed in colorful, traditional costume, fusing the traditional with the revolutionary.

The rally engulfed the entire city, but the main events were staged on the sprawling rally grounds situated on the outskirts of town. In early 1934 Hitler commissioned Albert Speer with the task of creating a vast party complex for the rallies, which would ultimately include several large arenas and parade grounds, a congress hall, a stadium, a war memorial, and, most impressive, a monumental stone structure on the Zeppelin Field. The Zeppelin Field arena was built to hold 90,000 participants on the field proper, 60,000 on the grand tribunal, and another 64,000 on the earthen embankments that formed the semicircular periphery of the arena. The tribunal and review stand made of white stone rose eighty feet high and consisted of a massive central block containing the speaker's rostrum and on either side a long colonnade that stretched 1,300 feet. Speer modeled the tribunal on the Pergamon Altar, an ancient Greek structure that was housed in a Berlin museum, but with a monumental coldness that lacked any semblance of elegance or humanity. Its message was power. Like a guiding star hovering above the tribunal, a giant swastika looked down on the assembled masses. The Luitpold Arena, built as a park and war memorial during the Weimar Republic, was expanded to hold 200,000. Its speaker's tribunal and grandstand were flanked by two gargantuan golden eagles with wings spread, fierce birds of prey perched upon giant swastikas. The sheer magnitude of these sites, especially when filled with hundreds of thousands of Storm Troopers, Hitler Youth, and SS, was awe-inspiring, just as intended.

Dozens of special trains and chartered buses delivered the multitudes to the grounds of the rally, where they were settled in vast tent encampments—acres of tents aligned in perfect military order that held field kitchens, hygienic facilities, and recreation areas. Speer created a variety of spectacular effects, the most striking of which was "the dome of light," produced by

130 giant spotlights spaced at ten-meter intervals around the periphery of the Zeppelin Field, where the main nighttime events were held. Each spotlight beamed a shaft of brilliant white light 25,000 feet into the night sky, encasing the Zeppelin Field in what British ambassador Sir Nevile Henderson called a "cathedral of ice." A mixture of awe-inspiring pageantry, mysticism, and color dominated the scene as hundreds of brilliant red swastika banners, their gold trim glittering in the dazzling light, rose over a sea of Storm Troopers and Hitler Youth.

The annual Nuremberg rally lasted five days to a week, with speeches, parades, mass gymnastics exhibitions, and, beginning in 1935, military demonstrations. Every party dignitary attended and spoke; every Nazi organization had its special role to play, its own event—the day of German youth, the day of the Labor Front, and so on. Beginning in 1933 each rally was filmed to be shown around the country—and the world—and each was given a theme reflecting momentous events of the past year. Nineteen thirty-three brought the "Victory of Faith"; the 1934 rally, captured in an extraordinary film by Leni Riefenstahl, proclaimed the "Triumph of the Will" and was held in the nervous aftermath of the Röhm purge. It emphasized the unbroken unity of the party and the loyalty of the SA to Hitler. In 1935 the "Party Rally of Freedom" marked the return of the Saar region to Germany and the emancipation of the Reich from the armaments clauses of Versailles. The last of the rallies—the "Rally of Greater Germany"—was held in 1938 after the German absorption of Austria in the spring and in the midst of the international crisis over the Sudetenland region of Czechoslovakia.

The daily events unfolded with military precision and virtually operatic theatricality, each providing the assembled multitude a visual spectacle—hundreds of thousands of SA men and Hitler Youth with their standards, more thousands of white-clad young women performing synchronized gymnastics, uniformed workers of the Labor Front performing the manual of arms with glistening spades, and Wehrmacht (the new name of the Reichswehr after 1933) troops parading before the grand tribunal on the Zeppelin Field. Peering majestically down from a raised speaker's platform of white stone, Hitler presided over it all, a solitary, heroic, all-mighty figure. He was omnipresent in every assembly, on every parade ground, his position—his pedestal—raised architecturally, the visual focal point of the proceedings. After all the awesome pageantry of the marches, assemblies, the torchlight parades, the climax of each rally was Hitler's address on the final day, delivered to a packed house in the old Congress Hall.

In the fall the Nazis mounted a harvest festival outside the village of Bückeburg in Hanover. Unlike the Nuremberg rallies, Bückeburg was not strictly a party event but a *Volksfest*, a people's festival to give thanks for the harvest. Exuberant peasants in traditional costume lined a broad stone pathway that split the massive crowd; ordinary Germans stood and sat in the fields; many brought picnics and sat on blankets.

The atmosphere at Bückeburg was different, more informal, more populist than other Nazi events. Crowds covered the hillside and the surrounding fields—a "living mountain," as Goebbels described it. Eight temporary railway stations were constructed to handle the fleet of special trains that carried hundreds of thousands to the area. In 1934, five hundred thousand spectators filled the festival grounds; three years later the crowd was estimated at more than a million. The people were not there to be propagandized—assembled en masse in their hundreds of thousands, *they were* the propaganda.

Finally, every November 8–9, veterans of the Beer Hall Putsch gathered at the Bürgerbräukeller in Munich to reenact the ill-fated but "heroic" march of 1923. Led by Julius Streicher, the procession followed the route of the Putschists across the Ludwig Bridge, to the Marienplatz, and finally to the Feldherrnhalle. Throngs lined the flag-draped streets; giant red pylons marked their path, one spaced every ten meters or so. Each was topped by an enormous cauldron from which an eternal flame flickered. On the side of each was inscribed in gold letters the name of a party martyr. At the Feldherrnhalle, where the fatal shots had been fired, the procession halted, and Hitler, standing on the top step of the monument's arcade, addressed the uniformed legions gathered below on the Odeonsplatz. Behind him, lined against the back wall of the monument, stood the iron sarcophagi of the sixteen Nazi martyrs killed on that day in 1923. In later years the sarcophagi were moved to two open "Temples of Honor" constructed on the Königsplatz, built adjacent to the Führer Building, which held Hitler's Munich office. There an even larger ceremony was staged on the broad square. The nation was invited to listen to the live broadcast of these proceedings and watch them in newsreels shown at theaters across the country. November 9 was a solemn party ritual, an integral component of the Nazi myth, and was reenacted every year down to the outbreak of the war.

These public spectacles were intended to demonstrate the irresistible psychological pull of National Socialism and to overwhelm any onlookers who still harbored reservations about the regime. They also contributed to the ever-deepening cult of the Führer and the Nazi *Volksgemeinschaft*. Historians have often been quick to dismiss this National Socialist "people's community" as mere public relations, a cover for the Nazi coordination of all social, economic, and political relations in the new dictatorship. That it served that purpose is indisputable, but the power of its appeal should not be underestimated. To a country humiliated by defeat, torn by class antagonisms, and divided by religious affiliation and regional loyalties, the Nazi motifs of racial strength and internal harmony in the face of a hostile world were enormously appealing. The relentless drumbeat of social solidarity, unity in a people's community where coal miners, peasants, shopkeepers, clerks, engineers, corporate executives, Protestants, and Catholics would stand on equal footing as Germans found considerable popular resonance. The Nazis were promoting social equality, and Hitler rarely let an opportunity pass to invoke his humble origins, his lack of formal education, his struggle up from want, and praise for the solidarity and national idealism he found in the trenches, where Germans of all backgrounds were thrown together to fight for the common cause of German survival. Re-creating and perpetuating that solidarity of the trenches constituted the basic social imperative of the *Volksgemeinschaft*.

Traditionally, German politicians and statesmen were distant, formal figures—one only had to glance at the austere Brüning or aristocratic Papen or Hindenburg's towering aloofness to get the picture; they did not plunge into crowds to shake hands with their countrymen. They could not play politics in a populist key. Hitler was different. A peripatetic Hitler was photographed with laboring men on factory floors, cutting ribbons for the launch of ships, shoveling the first—and second and third—spade of earth for Autobahn construction, walking amongst the peasants at the Bückeburg harvest festival. These were elaborate photo ops, carefully staged for the cameras, and played an important role in shaping both the "Führer cult" and the *Volksgemeinschaft*. Goebbels's propaganda machine trumpeted

Hitler as a tribune of the people, the embodiment of the egalitarian spirit of the new Germany. Although he was at the same time portrayed as a sophisticated man of the world, at home in top hat and tails at the opera, greeting foreign heads of state, assessing trends in the art world, he was still at heart the common soldier of the Great War, a folksy south German who loved the Alps and relaxed in lederhosen, a man with common tastes. He was pictured in the Reich Chancellery with top party officials eating from a large steaming pot of stew—*Eintopfessen*, a simple one-pot peasant's meal. The image caught on, and every German family was encouraged to have a one-pot meal on the first Sunday of every month. The money saved was to be contributed to the Winter Relief. Even restaurants participated. All people's comrades were doing their part for the *Volksgemeinschaft*, where the distinctions of class and region had disappeared.

The power of this populist imagery was reinforced by a number of developments that the regime could point to as triumphs of Nazi policy. From the earliest days of Nazi rule, the regime threw itself into highly publicized public works projects that signaled a single-minded determination to put the country back to work. Using uniformed men of the Labor Front, a National Socialist organization that conscripted the unemployed off the streets, the regime constructed bridges and roads, drained swamps and constructed dams—the highlight of which was the construction of the great Autobahn network, a project that was actually conceived under the last Weimar governments. Unemployment in 1932 stood at six million; in 1934 at 2.6 million; by 1937, spurred by the massive rearmament program begun in 1935, the figure had plunged to 500,000.

The regime also pointed to the new sense of social harmony, the absence of political strife, and the restoration of law and order as signs of the new national solidarity. With the Nazis entrenched in power, there were no more clashes in the streets, no bloody class conflict. For all the brutality of the SA and the looming menace of the SS, after the first months of the Nazi rule, peace and public order seemed to have been established. Gestapo arrests usually occurred at night, out of sight. People simply disappeared. Whispered rumors abounded, but it was not prudent to ask questions. Yet if Germans didn't see the brutality, it is because they didn't want to or were afraid to. After the first great wave of arrests, murders, and beatings in 1933, when more than 100,000 Social Democrats and Communists, recalcitrant clergy, obstreperous conservatives, and other suspected opponents were rounded up, *public* violence was rare. After years of political and social turmoil, stability and apparent social solidarity had been achieved—or, perhaps more accurately, imposed. Still, there could be no denying that the economic recovery that had eluded the star-crossed Weimar Republic had, thanks largely to rearmament, been achieved by the mid-1930s, and the dramatic successes of Hitler's foreign policy had expunged the humiliation of Versailles and rekindled a sense of national pride and purpose.

But behind the elaborately constructed facade of social solidarity and enthusiastic support for the regime there lurked a more complicated—and uglier—reality. With each passing year, the sinister reach of the Gestapo extended deeper and deeper into the private lives of the population. The Gestapo seemed to be everywhere, always listening, always watching. One might be arrested for "subjective crime," what one thought, in addition to "objective crime," public actions, or for being "anti-community-minded." A prisoner might be released after an hour or so, but the effect was chilling. Since arrests often occurred in the dark early-morning hours when, the Gestapo understood, people were at their most psychologically vulnerable, rumor and fear mounted. It didn't take many of these nighttime arrests to convince the public that the Gestapo had eyes and ears in every house, every apartment, in every bar and public place.

One didn't dare ask too many questions or express disappointment, not to mention disapproval, too openly. Neighbors and family members were prodded to inform on one another; each building, each city block had its *Blockwart* (monitor) who made sure that residents of his assigned area put out the flag on the Führer's birthday, contributed to the Nazi charities, and listened to the Führer's speeches on the radio. Children were encouraged to report on their parents—had they heard anything subversive at home, anything disrespectful of the regime, its policies or its leaders? A torrent of anonymous denunciations flooded Gestapo offices, as people quickly learned how to instrumentalize the system, settling old grudges by denouncing a rival in love or at work or a troublesome neighbor. The Gestapo, in fact, was quite small—much smaller than the East German Stasi of postwar years—and relied heavily on such denunciations.

For those who were not intimidated or were simply incautious, there were the camps. During the early years of the Third Reich, there was no concentration camp system. Camps sprang up across the country, some run by the SA, some by local Nazi governments, some by the regional police, some by the Gestapo. Each camp operated according to its own procedures, its own administration. These camps were not intended to be permanent installations. No long-range plans were made; no thought given as to whether they would continue to operate once the wave of mass arrests of Socialists, Communists, and other outright opponents had passed in 1933. Their purpose was to incarcerate political prisoners; they were not intended to hold Jews unless they were engaged in resistance or anti-Nazi activities.

Göring, as head of the Gestapo in 1933, began closing many of the smaller, unregulated camps, and Himmler continued the process in 1934. While expanding his control of the Gestapo to all of Germany, Himmler sought to bring all the camps under SS direction. Backed by Hitler, he established a Concentration Camp Inspectorate in the summer of 1934 and named Theodor Eicke, the brutal commandant of Dachau, to lead the organization. Eicke was an old Nazi, fanatically loyal to Himmler, and he was renowned for the iron discipline and ruthless cruelty with which he ran Dachau. Eicke's task was to bring order to the camps, which effectively meant to bring them firmly under SS control. Only installations organized by the Inspectorate were henceforth to be granted the official designation *Konzentrationslager* (KZ), concentration camp.

Armed with Himmler's authority and Hitler's support, Eicke worked assiduously to accomplish that mission. He closed some camps, expanded others, and created new ones. Using his harsh regime at Dachau as his model, he imposed uniform regulations on the operation of the camps, and he trained special units to run them. He introduced a standard uniform for the prisoners, who were no longer to wear their own clothes but were issued the coarse blue and white striped pajamas that would become symbols of Nazi slavery and oppression throughout Europe. The camps acquired paved roads, electrified wire fences, guard towers, row upon row of barracks. These were permanent facilities intended to operate in a formal concentration camp system.

But the future existence of camps was still uncertain. With camps closing and the number of prisoners falling, the SS system was a rather small-scale operation. Only five camps were still operating in the summer of 1935, and the number of their prisoners had dropped to 4,000. They were dwarfed by the official prison system, which held more than 100,000 inmates, 23,000 of them political prisoners. At this time Hitler even considered closing the camps. Were they really still necessary? Himmler talked him out of it. In 1936 Hitler appointed Himmler Reichsführer-SS and head of all German police forces, merging both state and party positions and vastly extending Himmler's power. In November 1937 Himmler told SS officers that he wanted a total of at least 20,000 prisoners for the camps. Using these powers, Himmler initiated a series of sweeps, ordering police and SS to round up beggars, pimps, prostitutes, drunks, the "work shy," and "social misfits," individuals who did not conform to the National Socialist conception of a meaningful contributor to the *Volksgemeinschaft*. The concentration camp population began to rise, and new camps were established at Sachsenhausen near Berlin in 1936, Buchenwald near Weimar in 1937, Flossenbürg on the Czech border, and Mauthausen in just annexed Austria, in 1938. Ravensbrück, a camp for women, was established in 1939. These were permanent installations, the foundation of the Nazi system of terror.

The existence of the camps cast a dark shadow over the Reich, a sinister reflection of a regime that harped incessantly on its overwhelming popularity with the German people. The American novelist Thomas Wolfe, who had traveled widely in Germany during the Weimar years, was shocked on a return trip in the mid-1930s by the dramatic changes that Hitler had wrought. He could hardly recognize the country he thought he knew. "Here was an entire nation," he wrote, ". . . infested with the contagion of an ever-present fear. It was a kind of creeping paralysis which twisted and blighted all human relations." Yet, thinking back on day-to-day life in the Third Reich, most Germans did not recall being consciously afraid. Instead they lived with a subliminal fear; developing a sixth sense for survival; learning what to say, when, and to whom was essential in daily life. A quick, almost reflexive glance over the shoulder to see who might be watching or listening nearby was dubbed the *"deutscher Blick,"* the German glance. Martha Dodd, the daughter of the American ambassador, recalled that "whenever we wanted to talk, we had to look around corners and behind doors, watch for the telephone and speak in whispers." Many were convinced that their telephone receivers were rigged to act as transmitters so that private conservations at home could be listened to by the authorities. One defense was to place a tea cozy over the telephone to muffle conversations. Berlin merchants couldn't keep them on the shelves.

Behind the elaborately constructed facade of social solidarity and support for the regime, pockets of dissent or nonconformity persisted. By the late 1930s, the Gestapo was registering increasing incidents of young people, especially but not exclusively working-class teens and young adults, who were involved in informal underground "bands, cliques, and gangs." Groups such as the Edelweiss Pirates and the Kittelsbach Pirates in the Rhineland, the Navajos from Cologne, the Pack in Leipzig, the Swing Kids in Hamburg, and others sprang up in reaction to the authoritarian character of the Hitler Youth and the stultifying conformity imposed by the Third Reich. At gatherings in pubs, amusement parks, pool halls, and private homes, they wore eccentric, nonconformist clothing and long hair; they were sexually promiscuous, and danced to American jazz, all strictly forbidden as decadent by the Nazis. They also occasionally clashed with members of the Hitler Youth, who were their sworn enemies. "Beat the HJ wherever you come across them!" was the slogan of one group.

Some were involved in petty crimes—theft, assault, breaking and entering, particularly during the war. Most of their activities were apolitical in any larger sense. Their dissent was not so much against Nazi ideology as such—its racism, anti-Semitism, and aggressive xenophobia—as an expression of rebellious nonconformity and opposition to the oppressiveness of the Nazi regime. Their opposition hardened during the war years. "Hitler's Power may lay us low," went one song, "and keep us locked in chains, But we will smash the chains one day, We'll be free again. We've got the fists and we can fight, We've got knives, and we'll get them out. We want freedom, don't we, boys? We're the fighting Navajos."

These groups, which were located primarily in urban areas, were not a direct threat to the regime; yet, in a context where the state's claim to the individual was total, their very existence, outside Nazi control, was viewed by the regime as a serious provocation. And, for these discontented youths, many of whom were fourteen to seventeen years of age, their involvement was an act of courage. HJ patrols tracked them and reported them to the authorities; the Gestapo made arrests. Ignored by the Nazi press but captured in the secret Gestapo reports, a current of juvenile delinquency flowed beneath the smooth surface of the Third Reich, escalating dramatically during the war. As the alarmed Reich Youth Leadership declared in 1942, "the forming of cliques . . . of young people outside the HJ before the war, but especially during the war, has increased to such a degree that one can now speak of a serious danger of a political, moral, and criminal disintegration of the youth."

More troublesome for the Nazis were the regime's relations with the Christian churches. Both Protestant and Catholic churches had proven remarkably pliable in the first stages of the dictatorship. The Concordat with the papacy and the takeover of the Protestant leadership by the radical German Christians in 1933 seemed to indicate smooth sailing for the regime. But the honeymoon was short lived. The Nazis had pledged that the Catholic Church and its lay organizations would remain untouched by the regime so long as the Church did not engage in politics. But almost immediately Himmler's SS began surveillance and harassment of Catholic lay organizations, which intensified as the year progressed. Mounting pressure was applied to Catholic youth organizations, when HJ leader Baldur von Schirach accused them of encouraging divisions within the *Volk*. By 1934 Catholic publications were compelled to drop "Catholic" from their mastheads, replacing it with "German." The following year, the regime began banning Catholic magazines and newspapers until by 1939 all were "brought into line."

Himmler also moved against the Church itself. Gestapo agents monitored sermons and infiltrated Catholic organizations. Priests were arrested, charged with engaging in political activity for reading from the Old Testament, for reminding their parishioners that Jesus was a Jew, and other acts of blasphemy against Nazi ideology. The party outlawed Nativity plays and other Catholic theatricals, claiming that they were ideological and hence political statements that were against the law. Some monasteries and convents were closed; some churches were shuttered, Catholic teachers furloughed, priests harassed. In 1935 the Nazi minister of education in Oldenburg decreed that all religious statuary, including crucifixes, were to be removed from all schools, parishes, and other public buildings. Not only did the local clergy protest, but the largely rural population reacted with outrage. They staged protests, circulated petitions, and created such a disruptive atmosphere that the Nazi regional governor felt compelled to retract the order. A similar incident, with the same results, occurred in Bavaria in 1937 when a local Nazi official ordered the crucifixes removed from public schools. Such civil disobedience was unheard of in the Third Reich, and it reminded the regime of the need for caution when dealing with the Church.

Alfred Rosenberg, the self-proclaimed interpreter of Nazi philosophy and author of the pagan, anti-Christian *The Myth of the Twentieth Century* (1930), could always be counted on to inflame relations between the party and the Church. An implacable enemy of Christianity, Rosenberg was at his most venomous when dealing with the Catholic Church. It had snuffed out the "Nordic Christianity" of the Early Middle Ages and allowed Jewish influence to permeate Christianity, leading to its degeneration over the centuries. He advocated a "positive Christianity" liberated from the Judaized Christianity of the Church. Despite widespread denunciations from the Catholic clergy, Rosenberg doggedly pressed his idea of merging Nazi racial ideology with a "renewed Christianity," calling for a revival of the Nordic "blood soul."

In 1935 Cardinal Clemens von Galen responded to Rosenberg in a pamphlet entitled "Studies on *The Myth of the Twentieth Century*," eviscerating Rosenberg's ideas. In a pastoral letter of the Catholic Bishops Conference at Fulda, he continued his assault, writing that "Religion cannot be based on blood, race or other dogmas of human creation, but only on divine revelation." Following his lead, parish priests then read out a stern condemnation of Rosenberg's work and the actions of the German Faith Movement. The Gestapo threatened Galen and banned the pastoral letter, but it was widely circulated nonetheless.

In this poisoned atmosphere, Goebbels launched a major propaganda offensive against Catholic institutions, charging them with financial corruption and rampant sexual abuse of children by predatory priests. Coverage of alleged sex scandals within the Church became a staple of the Nazi press. Anti-Catholic incidents multiplied; Hitler Youth disrupted church services, priests were taunted in the streets, Catholic youth groups assaulted. Himmler was relentless, applying ever-increasing pressure on Church organizations, restricting public meetings, censoring then banning Catholic publications, and arresting recalcitrant priests. Anticlericalism moved into elementary and middle schools, with Hitler Youth singing songs that ridiculed the Church and its teachings. "Their time has passed," went one such song, "but the priests remain to rob the people of their soul, and whether it is Rome or Luther they are peddling, it's all Jewish thinking. The time for the cross is now over." Finally, the Catholic hierarchy in Germany had had enough. In January 1937 a delegation of senior German bishops and cardinals, including Cardinals Michael von Faulhaber of Munich and Clemens Galen of Münster, traveled to Rome. Their mission was to deliver a scathing indictment of the Third Reich and its war against the Church. After meeting with the pope, Faulhaber was asked to draft a papal encyclical enumerating the many Nazi breaches of the Concordat and condemning its escalating persecution of the Church. Pius XI approved the draft, and the document, written in German and entitled "With Burning Concern," was smuggled into Germany. Some 300,000 copies were printed clandestinely in shops around the country and then surreptitiously passed to parish priests, who read it from pulpits all across Germany on Palm Sunday, March 21, 1937.

The papal encyclical's open condemnation of the Third Reich hit like a bombshell. "With Burning Concern" blasted the regime for its "aggressive paganism," its "secret and open measures of intimidation, the threat of economic and civic consequences, its campaign against the Church." It denounced the regime's closing of confessional schools, in flagrant disregard of the Concordat of 1933. "Catholics have a right to their children's Catholic education," as promised in the Concordat. On a more fundamental level, the document took aim at Nazi ideology. "None but superficial minds could stumble into concepts of a national God, of a national religion; or attempt to lock within the frontiers of a single people, within the narrow limits of a single race." Catholics could be certain that "the enemies of the Church who think that their time has come, will see that their joy was premature, and they may close the grave they had dug. The day will come when the *Te Deum* of liberation will succeed to the premature hymns of the enemies of Christ."

Publicly Hitler sought to reassure the Holy See and German Catholics by repeating that the regime's goal was the extirpation of Marxism, and in that life-and-death struggle the unity of the German people was essential. In private, he was outraged. The encyclical came as a complete surprise to the regime. As disturbing to Hitler as the content of the document was the uncomfortable realization that the Church had been able to produce and distribute the encyclical without being detected by the regime's security forces. It was an embarrassment for the SS and Gestapo, and it was a warning signal of what the Catholic Church was still capable of doing.

Hardly intimidated by papal intervention, the Nazis struck back with their usual fury, sharply escalating their offensive against the Church and its organizations. The Nazi press did not report the story at all, but on the day after Palm Sunday the Gestapo descended on the companies that printed the encyclical and seized all remaining copies. They also closed and sealed the firms responsible. The Church, Goebbels yammered, was a sinkhole of fiscal and sexual corruption not to be trusted with Germany's youth or money. Ordinary Catholics were being swindled by a corrupt Church and its organizations. Throughout the rest of 1937, a flood of alleged incidents of pederasty and financial misconduct rippled through the Nazi press. Priests, monks, and friars were arrested—over a thousand, it was said—and awaiting trial. "Houses of God Degraded into Brothels and Dens of Vice" was a typical headline, and the trials that occurred throughout the year were given maximum coverage. Nazi tabloids wallowed in every lurid detail provided by the Propaganda Ministry. Germany, Goebbels asserted in a national radio address in May, was confronting a systematic effort to undermine the morality of the German people. The Church, he warned, should remember, "it is not the law of the Vatican that rules here but the law of the German people."

Throughout 1938 and into 1939 the regime, having already eliminated religious instruction in public schools, moved decisively against church schools, converting them into "community schools." It was for many Catholics the last battleground. Although the party had not managed to close all church schools by the outbreak of the war, they were making steady headway. Their sustained campaign against the Church had its effect, sobering the Catholic public and weakening any inclination toward opposition to the regime. Goebbels's hope of driving a wedge between the Church and its flock seemed to be working. Despite the regime's heathenism and its actions against the Church, Hitler remained popular with German Catholics, and opposition, both from ordinary Catholics and their leadership, remained focused narrowly on specific religious matters. There was little criticism of the Nazi racial policy or its totalitarian ambitions or its oppressive intervention in everyday life. In the last years of peace the

"Church struggle," as it came to be called, continued but at a lower pitch. By the outbreak of war in 1939, Catholic cultural organizations had been smashed, its Youth League disbanded, its publications banned, and yet, for all that, the Church remained a potential source of trouble to the regime, and Gestapo surveillance remained vigilant.

The Protestant church also represented a potential problem for the Nazis, albeit of a different nature. Hitler's attempt to build a united national church led by the German Christians ran into trouble almost immediately. Ludwig Müller, Hitler's choice for bishop of the new Reich Church, failed to create the unified Protestant church the Führer wanted, and Hitler's appointment of Hanns Kerrl as head of the newly founded Reich Ministry of Church Affairs in 1935 was no more successful. The eager subservience of the new, coordinated Reich Church to the Nazi state, its willingness to allow the regime to intervene and direct its affairs, and the ham-fisted efforts of Müller and Kerrl to impose the pagan, anti-Semitic doctrine of the German Christians provoked an immediate reaction in 1933 and grew progressively stronger in 1934.

Adding to Müller's difficulties was the Church Law, enacted on September 6, 1933, which required all pastors to take an oath of loyalty to Hitler and the National Socialist state. Among the clauses of that law was the introduction of the Aryan Paragraph of the Civil Service Law into the Church. Alarmed at the law and the direction of the new church, many pastors refused to take the oath. They also explicitly rejected the incorporation of the Aryan Paragraph into Church affairs. Among the most vocal opponents of the law was Dietrich Bonhoeffer, a bright twenty-seven-year-old pastor and university lecturer. On September 27 he issued a declaration denouncing the Aryan Paragraph and Nazi racial policy more broadly, which found resonance with other dissident pastors. Especially disturbing to them was the Reich Church's racial orientation, which, in their view, made race the key element of a new Nazified theology. These pastors, with Martin Niemöller's leadership, began to organize in regional groups around the country to express their disaffection.

Niemöller was pastor of the Lutheran church in the posh Dahlem section of Berlin. He was no liberal. He had served as a submarine captain during the war, and like many Protestant pastors was a nationalist conservative. He fought in the Free Corps in the immediate postwar years and was an opponent of the Weimar Republic, which he considered too weak to represent Germany's interests abroad and too fractured and disorganized to meet the Communist threat at home. For a time he was attracted to Hitler for his staunch anti-Communism and his promise of a revivified Germany, but in the course of 1933 he became disillusioned by the regime's naked attempt to coordinate and control all the churches, Protestant as well as Catholic.

In September 1933 he joined with other recalcitrant pastors to create the Pastors' Emergency League. In the following months they met in various cities, and in May 1934 at a meeting in Barmen, attended by some three thousand pastors, they issued a declaration of principles that formally rejected the Aryan Paragraph and the attempt of the German Christians to merge Nazism with Protestant Christianity. It was an unequivocal declaration of independence from the Reich Church and delivered a strong rebuke to the German Christians and to Reich Bishop Müller for their attempts to Nazify the Church. The text of the Barmen Declaration was written by Karl Barth, a Swiss theologian who was residing in Germany. It was, in effect, the founding document of a new, anti-regime Protestant Church, the Bekennende Kirche, or Confessing Church.

The Confessing Church viewed itself as the legitimate Protestant church in Germany and was especially vocal in its rejection of "Nazi theology." As a consequence, its pastors were under perpetual Gestapo surveillance and were frequently arrested. By 1937, some seven hundred pastors of the Confessing Church had been imprisoned, including particularly prominent figures—Bishop Theophil Wurm of Württemberg in 1935 and in 1937 Niemöller himself. Niemöller had continued to give sermons highly critical of the regime and had become the national voice of the disaffected, attracting a diverse following from former Social Democrats, Communists, and Catholics. In 1937, he was tried and convicted of actions embarrassing to the state, but was released the following year since he had already served his sentence of seven months while awaiting trial. Immediately upon his release he was rearrested—a not uncommon practice in the Third Reich. He disappeared into the concentration camp at Sachsenhausen. He would spend seven years in the camps, much of it in solitary confinement, before he was liberated by the Americans in the spring of 1945.

Although they occasionally ruffled the smooth surface of the Third Reich and hundreds of clergy disappeared into the concentration camps in the prewar years, the churches posed no imminent danger to the dominance of the regime. Their criticism was mostly confined to Nazi intervention in church matters, and they remained largely silent about other criminal policies of the regime. Some smaller sects, especially the Jehovah's Witnesses, courageously refused to swear any allegiance to Hitler's new order and distributed pamphlets condemning the idolatry of Hitler and the Nazi attempts to undermine Christian beliefs. They also refused to serve in the military. They were rounded up and dispatched to the camps, most without a trial, where they constituted a major element of those arrested for religious opposition. They were an irritant but little more. And yet for the Nazis, whose goal was to leave no group outside their control, the churches were more than a nuisance: with their relative independence and their organizational networks spread across the country, their very existence represented a threat to the regime's totalitarian aspirations.

Hitler was reluctant to attack the churches directly and left the rabid anti-Christian rhetoric to Goebbels, Rosenberg, and Himmler. But in private conversations he left no doubt about his intentions. "In the long run," he explained to luncheon guests in 1941, "National Socialism and religion will no longer be able to exist together. . . . The heaviest blow that ever struck humanity was the coming of Christianity. Bolshevism is Christianity's illegitimate child. Both are inventions of the Jews." Later he confided to Speer and Himmler that he had been patient, but "we shan't be able to go on evading the religious problem. . . . The evil that is gnawing our vitals is our priests, of both creeds. . . . The time will come when I'll settle my account with them, and I'll go straight to the point. . . . They've only got to keep at it, they'll hear from me, all right. I shan't let myself be hampered by juridical scruples. . . . In less than ten years from now, things will have quite another look, I can promise them."

Terror and political indoctrination were central pillars of the Third Reich, but what the regime counted on was not just fear and not ideological commitment but apathy—each atomized individual looking for his or her own interests. Opportunists, especially among the more educated, rushed to join the party in such numbers that by the end of 1933 over half the membership of the NSDAP had joined since Hitler's appointment as chancellor. And, of course, if one had misgivings, if one disagreed, one found little or no reinforcement in public. One didn't dare confide in friends or colleagues or talk openly to strangers. Organized discussion outside National Socialist supervision became virtually impossible. Would someone inform? Werner Finck, the popular comedian at the Catacombs cabaret in Berlin, performed a routine in which a patient sitting in a dentist's chair refuses to open his mouth. When the puzzled dentist asks why, Finck responds, "I don't know you." The skit routinely brought down the house—until, inevitably, the Nazis closed the Catacombs.

And besides, official reality in the Third Reich was so relentlessly positive, so upbeat. The newspapers carried no dissenting opinions, no outraged letters to the editor; the newsreels portrayed a happy people, proud of having overcome the lost war, the Great Depression, and international oppression. Why be a troublemaker? So many seemed happy in the new *Volksgemeinschaft*. They went dancing, went to the movies, went on excursions, attended the opera. On the surface everything seemed familiar, normal. But, of course, it wasn't. Trying to describe life in the Third Reich and the insidious process by which society was diverted, seduced, tricked, threatened, and implicated, a German schoolteacher, hardly a Nazi himself, explained to a Jewish friend from America after the war:

To live in this process is absolutely not to be able to notice it—unless one has a much greater degree of political awareness, acuity, than most of us had ever had occasion to develop. Each step was so small, so inconsequential, so well explained or, on occasion, "regretted," that unless one were detached from the whole process from the beginning, unless one understood what the whole thing was in principle, what all these "little measures" that no "patriotic German" could resent must someday lead to, one no more saw it developing from day to day than a farmer in his field sees the corn growing. One day it is over his head.

And one day, too late, your principles, if you were sensible of them, all rush in upon you. The burden of self-deception has grown too heavy, and some minor incident, in my case my little boy, hardly more than a baby, saying "Jew swine," collapses it all at once, and

you see that everything, everything, has changed and changed completely under your nose. . . . You see what you are, what you have
done, or, more accurately, what you haven't done (for that was all
that was required of most of us: that we do nothing). . . . You remember everything now, and your heart breaks. Too late. You are
compromised beyond repair.

By mid-1934 it was obvious to all that this was no ordinary authoritarian dictatorship but a regime with totalitarian aspirations, a regime that
sought to dominate not only the individual's public behavior, but his private life, his thoughts. Hitler and the National Socialists had embarked on
a course of action that would seek to efface the distinction between public
and private life. "The revolution that we have made is a total revolution,"
Goebbels stated in November 1933. "It encompasses every aspect of public
life from the bottom up. . . . It has completely altered relations between individuals and utterly transformed the relationship between the individual
and the state." The Nazi goal was to "replace individuality with collective
racial consciousness and the individual with the community." In the Third
Reich, Goebbels bluntly proclaimed, there would "no longer [be] any free
realms in which the individual belongs to himself . . . the time for personal
happiness is over." Or as Robert Ley, minister of Labor, succinctly expressed it, "the individual in Germany who leads a private life is asleep."

The Beerhall Putsch defendants, gathered on the steps of
Munich courthouse, April 1, 1924.

LEFT: Heinrich Brüning,
(*below left*) Franz von
Papen, and (*below right*)
Kurt von Schleicher,
Weimar's last pre-Hitler
chancellors.

Alfred Hugenberg (*left*), who with Hitler was leader of the Harzburg Front, 1931. Hugenberg was the titular head of the alliance, but Hitler was the dominant force behind the right-wing alliance.

The first meeting of the Hitler cabinet on January 30, 1933. Only three Nazis were included, Göring (*front left*), Hitler, and Wilhelm Frick, Minister of Education (second row, standing between Göring and Hitler).

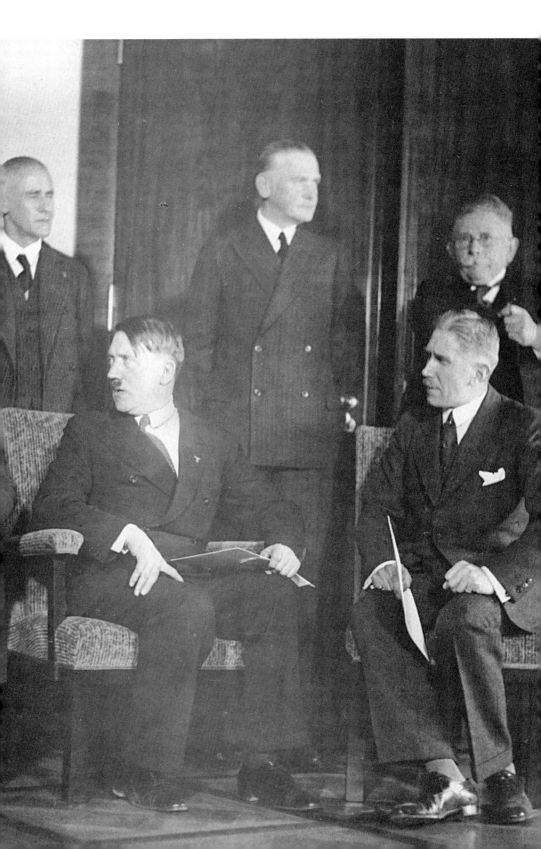

Hitler and S.A. leader Ernst Röhm in 1933, when they were still allies. Hitler had him shot in the summer of 1934.

Rabble-rousing Joseph Goebbels speaking at a propaganda rally 1932. Aside from Hitler, Goebbels was the party's most popular speaker.

Famous image of
Hitler bowing to
Reichspräsident Paul
von Hindenburg on
the Day of Potsdam,
February 1933.

ABOVE: Hitler reviewing the
S.A. at Nuremberg, 1933 or
1934. OPPOSITE TOP: The
Reichstag Fire, the morning
after, February 1933.
OPPOSITE BOTTOM: Hitler,
the "common man," working
at the groundbreaking of the
Autobahn, 1933.

Chief of the S.S.
Heinrich Himmler
in Russia in the
summer of 1941.

LEFT: Reinhard Heydrich, Head of the Reich Security Main Office, Himmler's second in command and architect of the "Final Solution." BELOW: Reichsmarshal Herman Göring; often seen as jovial and a bon vivant, this photograph captures the malevolence of his character.

OPPOSITE TOP: Hitler appears to dance with joy at the surrender of France, June 1940, Compiègne, France. OPPOSITE BOTTOM: Massacre of Jews at Babi Yar, in Ukraine, 1942. There the Germans murdered 33,000 Jews during a single weekend. ABOVE: The entrance ramp at Auschwitz, where the women and children were separated from able-bodied men and sent directly to the gas chambers. The men would be worked to death.

ABOVE: Defeated German prisoners marching into captivity, Stalingrad, February 1943. OPPOSITE TOP: Young Wehrmacht soldier weeps during the devastating defeat at Kursk, 1943. It was the last German offensive on the Eastern Front. OPPOSITE BOTTOM: Women, children, and old men were expected to defend Berlin and other cities against the onrushing Soviets.

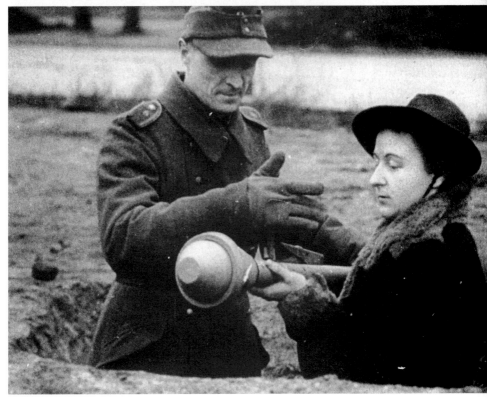

Proud recipient of the
Iron Cross, March 1945,
for his actions against
Russian tanks in Berlin.
He was twelve years old.

A RACIAL REVOLUTION

The Nazis had unleashed a revolution in Germany, but not an economic one. Hitler was not interested in economics and certainly did not intend to turn the rabid social revolutionary rhetoric of the party into reality. For all the insistent talk about *Volksgemeinschaft*, his view of the economy was strictly instrumentalist: he needed a strong industrial base and a powerful army to realize his dreams of expansion, of *Lebensraum* in the East. The fate of the small shopkeeper, farmer, or artisan, stalwart elements of the party's national support before 1933, held little interest for him. As if to drive that point home, the party leadership announced on July 7, 1933, that "active measures" to nationalize the department stores—one of the party's most strident promises before 1933—"were not indicated for the present." No action against the department stores was undertaken, then or later, and the big chains continued to operate as before, although under different—"Aryan"—management.

Property relations in the Third Reich remained largely untouched, except for the expropriation of Jewish property. Instead, the Nazis undertook a fundamental reordering of status, the most obvious expression of which was their effort to elevate the social standing of peasants and workers, two groups traditionally considered to inhabit the lower reaches of German society. National Socialism, Hitler and Goebbels were at pains to emphasize, was not defined by wealth or property, by possessions, bank accounts, stock portfolios, and income, mere material things. Nazi socialism was much deeper, more profound than Marxism, they claimed. It did not change the external order of things, but sought to fundamentally transform the relationship of man to the state. They were going to create a new man, a new people, strong and vigorous and untainted by the weaknesses of the past. The Nazis did not need to socialize the banks and factories; they were socializing the people.

Creating a united Germany liberated from the traditional divisions of class, religion, and region was merely one dimension of Hitler's agenda to establish a fundamentally new German nation. The National Socialist *Volksgemeinschaft* was to be a society bound together by blood, a nation built on a utopian vision of racial purity, cleansed of hereditary weakness and freed from the taint of foreign, especially Jewish, blood. The Third Reich would build national, by which the Nazis meant racial, solidarity by expunging the biological contaminants infecting the German people. They would cultivate a healthy, vigorous, racial community that would unchain the vast energies of a proud, revivified people.

History, Hitler believed, was driven by remorseless struggle, nation against nation, culture against culture, and ultimately race against race. In his thinking, a hierarchy of races existed, and Aryans, which he never defined in any serious anthropological way, were the most valuable race. They alone possessed the capacity "for creating and building culture." In fact, "all the results of art, science, and technology that we see before us today are almost exclusively the creative product of the Aryan." But if the Aryans bred with people of inferior racial stock, their blood would be hopelessly polluted, and the Aryan race would gradually descend into extinction. History offered overwhelming evidence "that in every mingling of Aryan blood with that of lower peoples, the result was the end of the cultured people." Indeed, "all great cultures of the past perished only because the originally creative [people] died out from blood poisoning."

The situation had now reached the tipping point. A sense of urgency prevailed. Germany stood on the brink of irreversible racial degeneration. Drastic measures had to be taken immediately to halt this defilement of Aryan blood and to improve the health of the race. This was the historic mission of the National Socialist movement. Struggle, Hitler declared, "is always a means for improving a species' health and power of resistance and, therefore, a cause of its higher development." And in this struggle between the superior and inferior, there could be no half measures, no compromises; there could be no pity. "The stronger must dominate and not blend with the weaker."

The greatest threat to Aryan purity, as it had always been, was posed by the Jew, who was responsible for all Germany's misfortunes. Hitler devoted a chapter of *Mein Kampf* to a fantastic history of the Jews, drawing on every racist stereotype, myth, and crackpot theory that had circulated in the Vienna of his youth. Invoking the fraudulent *Protocols of the Elders of Zion*, he claimed that the Jews were engaged in a global conspiracy to undermine existing states and cultures, and to seize world power. The Jews were the very incarnation of evil, parasites that feasted on the blood of their racially superior hosts. Germany's otherwise inexplicable collapse in the Great War was due to its "failure to recognize the racial problem and especially the Jewish menace." The old Reich's downfall was not the result of setbacks on the battlefield but "was brought about by that power which prepared these defeats by systematically over many decades robbing our people of the political and moral instincts and forces which alone make nations capable and hence worthy of existence."

Germany, all Europe, stood on the cusp of a great precipice; the Jewish revolution that would lead to world domination was imminent. The Jews were behind Bolshevism, liberalism, plutocratic capitalism, and pacifism, but "in gaining political power the Jew casts off the few cloaks that he still wears. . . . The democratic people's Jew becomes the blood Jew and tyrant over peoples," enslaving them, depriving them of their freedom and their strength. But "a racially pure people that is conscious of its blood can never be enslaved by the Jew," and raising that racial consciousness was the first task of National Socialism.

That last point was particularly crucial since Germany, Hitler believed, was the last best racial hope of humankind, and it was threatened by a world teeming with dangers. Racial regeneration of the German people was a precondition for a powerful state that would guarantee Germany's racial survival and would allow it to assert itself in a world driven by merciless racial struggle. Although the Nazi campaigns of the pre-1933 era had focused largely on the economic and political failures of the Weimar system, mass unemployment, and the threat of Bolshevism, the party's ultimate aim, as became quickly apparent upon Hitler's assumption of power, was to launch a racial revolution.

The outlines of such a vision had been there all along, in the pages of *Mein Kampf,* in innumerable party publications, and campaign speeches without number, but it still came as something of a surprise, even a shock to some, that among the myriad, fantastic, and contradictory promises made by the Nazis before 1933, eliminating Jews from German life would emerge as the defining element in Hitler's agenda. But this shouldn't have been a surprise. Fanatical racial anti-Semitism lay at the very core of National Socialist ideology and remained Hitler's most enduring and passionate obsession. If the German people were not ready for his radical vision before 1933—and both he and Goebbels were convinced they were not—he could wait. But once in power, the Nazis did not hesitate to begin translating that racial fixation into policy. National Socialist racial thinking followed two inextricably interwoven threads in which ferocious hatred of Jews commingled with a pseudoscientific biological interpretation of the dynamics of world history. Anti-Semitism was the most visible and vicious component of Nazi racial policy, but it represented only one dimension of a broader racist agenda. Brutal, gutter anti-Semitism, found in the pages of *Der Stürmer* and in the ranks of the SA, merged with an obsession with eugenics, referred to in the Nazi lexicon as "racial hygiene." The pseudoscientific approach to issues of race was articulated in a variety of Nazi publications such as the *People and Race, New People,* the SS's *The Black Corps,* and numerous medical journals. This spurious "scientific" racism was enthusiastically adopted by the SS, which viewed itself as the ideological vanguard of National Socialism, standing above the sort of vulgar Jew baiting found among the party's militants and the SA.

. With Hitler installed in the chancellor's office, the Nazis wasted little time in initiating a series of measures aimed at "cleansing the body of the people." This was to be accomplished by purging "racially inferior" elements from German life—from Jews and Gypsies to the mentally defective, the physically handicapped, and finally to the "socially deviant." The National Socialist regime viewed itself as a "therapeutic state" that would guarantee public health through racially driven policies of pronatalism, compulsory sterilization, and finally, in 1939, a top secret program of euthanasia.

The Nazis initiated their racial offensive in the spring of 1933 with a barrage of decrees aimed at eliminating Jews from participation in the life of the nation. Against a backdrop of daily harassment, humiliation, and violence against Jews, the Nazis introduced the Civil Service Law in April, with its Aryan Paragraph that declared that anyone with one Jewish grandparent was not an Aryan and hence was to be retired from the civil service. (In May *all* non-Aryan public employees were dismissed.) Regional and local governments soon followed suit. A follow-up decree in March limited non-Aryan access to the practice of medicine, and another, the Law to Prevent the Overcrowding in German Schools and Universities, restricted the matriculation of new Jewish students in any German school or university to 1.5 percent of the total applicants. At no educational institution could Jews constitute more than 5 percent of the total student body. The boycott of Jewish businesses on April 1 was an attempt to incite the public to displays of anti-Jewish sentiment, though the public response was disappointing.

In June a decree prohibited Jews from working as dentists or dental technicians in public insurance programs, then another extended that ban to Germans in the medical field who were married to non-Aryans. In September the Hereditary Farm Law prohibited Jews from owning land or engaging in agriculture. The Aryan Paragraph was also extended to the armed forces, banning Jews from conscription and prohibiting Jews already in the military from serving as officers. Later measures were introduced that sought to drive Jews from the press, especially forbidding Jews from working as newspaper editors, just as Goebbels's newly created Reich Culture Chamber took steps to expunge Jews from all areas of German cultural life. These laws promulgated at the national level represented only the tip of the iceberg; states, municipalities, and private institutions imposed additional restrictions on the Jewish community so that numerous regional variations existed. These laws served another purpose: through them, Achim Gercke, a specialist on racial matters in the Interior Ministry, argued "the entire national community becomes enlightened about the Jewish question; it learns that the national community is a community of blood; for the first time it understands race thinking and, instead of an overly theoretical approach to the Jewish question, it is confronted with a concrete solution."

Already in 1933 Germans were expected to carry a "racial passport" (*Ahnenpass*) to prove their pure "Aryan" heritage. This quasi-official document was not issued by the state, but given the mounting offensive against the Jews, many felt it behooved them to establish proof of their undiluted Aryan identity. Germans feverishly researched their ancestry, scouring municipal archives, church records, and census reports to establish a family tree at least through their grandparents' generation. SS personnel and their wives were required to prove their Aryan bloodlines back to 1800, and many nervous Germans thought it prudent to do the same, desperately hoping not to unearth a long-forgotten Jewish relative lurking in their past. Genealogists were in great demand. But just what constituted an "Aryan" remained unclear. Did the Civil Service Law's definition of non-Aryan apply to all areas of German life? Was that the criterion to be used in every instance? "I looked up Aryans in the encyclopedia," one puzzled woman reported to the authorities. "They live in Asia. We don't have relatives there, we're from Prenzlau."

At the same time, the regime introduced another set of laws and regulations that would dramatically affect not only the tiny Jewish community but the entire *Volk*. In June 1933, Wilhelm Frick established a Committee of Experts for Population and Racial Policy within his Interior Ministry. Its immediate task was to prepare the public for a planned law permitting compulsory sterilization of persons suffering from "hereditarily determined" disabilities. In the last days of Weimar, the Prussian government, influenced by similar laws in a number of states in the United States, had considered legislation that would have allowed sterilization of the "hereditarily ill," but this draft law, like the American versions, applied to a limited number of medical conditions and required the consent of the person in question or a legal guardian. On July 14, 1933, Frick announced the Law for the Prevention of Progeny with Hereditary Diseases, which differed in crucial ways from the draft Weimar legislation. The law dictated sterilization for individuals suffering from a significantly expanded list of allegedly inherited medical defects: schizophrenia, manic depression, hereditary blindness or deafness, hereditary epilepsy, and serious physical deformities. It was also compulsory. As the law made brutally clear, "if the court finally decides upon sterilization, the operation must be performed even if it is against the wishes of the person to be sterilized. . . . In so far as other measures prove insufficient, the use of force is permissible."

Shortly after the introduction of the sterilization law, Interior Minister Frick sought to explain the rationale behind the new policy in a national radio broadcast. His message was blunt. In earlier times, the laws of nature had ensured that the weak would perish before reaching reproductive age, but with the advances in modern medicine, the weak had been artificially kept alive, a development that had damaged the long-term health of the people. It was now a moral obligation for the state to fulfill "nature's wishes," and it was the duty of the individual to comply with the new order of things.

To implement this invasive system, the regime enacted the Unification of Health Affairs Law, which brought the entire public health system under Nazi control. Local health officials, appointed by the regime, were empowered to monitor the genetic health of citizens and to issue certificates of genetic health. They were also authorized to order the sterilization of individuals who were genetically tainted. Hospitals, asylums, welfare organizations, and physicians were required by law to submit the names of patients who would fall into one of these categories. In 1934, 181 Hereditary Health Courts, each staffed by two physicians and one lawyer, were attached to the civil courts to examine the cases reported. Their proceedings were secret, and although the law established an appeal process, barely 3 percent of such appeals were successful.

In addition to these criteria, an intelligence test, based on dubious scientific criteria, was administered to those thought to be "feeble-minded." It asked questions such as: Where are you? Where do you live? Who was Bismarck? Luther? When is it Christmas? How many days in the week? Reflecting on this test years later, Hitler wryly commented that having seen the questions, "at least three-quarters of [them] . . . would have defeated my own good mother. One I recall was: 'Why does a ship made of steel float in the water?' If this system had been introduced before my birth, I am pretty sure I should never have been born at all." Feeble-mindedness provided the most common grounds for sterilization, especially when in 1934 the diagnosis was expanded to a new, more ambiguous category: "moral feeble-mindedness." This new designation covered an elastic list of deviants: chronic alcoholics, habitual criminals, vagrants, and "the anti-community-minded," among others. Women who had many sexual partners, for example, were declared morally feeble-minded and would be sterilized. Men exhibiting similar "promiscuous" behavior were not. Women were sterilized by undergoing an operation to tie their fallopian tubes, while men underwent vasectomy or, in some cases, castration. Abortions were forbidden by law, but in dealing with the genetically unfit, the regime quietly allowed it. An amendment to the sterilization law in June 1935 allowed abortions for "hereditarily ill" women within the first six months of pregnancy.

The law made no mention of sterilization on racial grounds, and Jews were not specifically targeted. Even Germans armed with a racial passport found themselves subjected to Nazi racial oversight. In 1935 the Interior Ministry drafted a law that would require all prospective newlyweds to obtain an official certificate of genetic health from local public health authorities. Couples who could not or would not produce a certificate of health were declared ineligible for government marriage loans, tax deductions, and other benefits. And failure to present a certificate of health might also prompt an official investigation into their backgrounds, and who knew what that would turn up. Might an ordinary childhood illness be interpreted as a hereditary flaw? Would it be enough to prohibit the marriage, or worse, lead to compulsory sterilization? If the marriage was allowed, couples were incessantly reminded of their racial duty. Beginning in 1936, newlyweds were presented a copy of *Mein Kampf* as well as pamphlets with advice on how to maintain good racial stock. Most of the prescriptive literature was couched in strictly "scientific" terms, but others, such as "The Ten Commandments for Selecting a Mate," invoked both National Socialist ideology and religion. "1. Remember you are German. 2. If you are genetically healthy, you shall not remain unmarried. 3. Keep your body pure. 4. Keep your soul and mind pure. 5. As a German, select only a mate with Nordic blood. 6. When you select a mate, ask about ancestry. 7. Health is the precondition for external beauty. 8. Marry only for love. 9. Don't select a playmate. Choose a partner for life. 10. Hope for as many children as possible."

Scientific quackery also fused with Nazi prudery in advice literature. "In free love," one Nazi racial hygienist wrote, "the mutual impulse to union is contained exclusively in erotic feelings, the confluence of the germ plasma endowments of both parents is left exclusively to chance, whereas monogamy, through the elaboration of perceptible biological hereditary stocks, enables human reason to bring together high-grade hereditary stocks for human breeding and to exterminate hereditary stocks of inferior grade. In this context free love means the admission of inferior biological ancestry to human breeding and the necessary squandering of high-grade germ endowments, whereas monogamy at least offers the opportunity for biological selection and preservation of high-grade germ plasma."

In seizing control of the public health system, the Nazis had little trouble recruiting support from Germany's internationally respected medical community. Doctors, part of the German social elite, had gravitated toward National Socialism early, becoming the most overrepresented profession in the Nazi party before Hitler's assumption of power, far surpassing lawyers, teachers, and university professors. Many, especially young doctors, were happy to see Jewish competitors purged; many were deeply conservative and harbored anti-Semitic views and many were taken with Nazi ideas on race, eugenics, and preventive medicine. But the German medical profession, like the Nazi regime it served, was hardly a monolith. Many physicians were attracted by the Nazis' aggressive approach to public health, their emphasis on prenatal care, on a healthy work environment, on physical fitness, on diet, and the regime's efforts to curb alcohol and tobacco consumption. German scientists, concerned about asbestos in the workplace, were impressed by the regime's Beauty of Labor program, which sought to create a healthy workplace. The Third Reich also launched what historian of science Robert E. Proctor has called a "war against cancer." German medical scientists were leaders in identifying the link between tobacco and cancer; others researched the connection between diet and cancer, endorsing the consumption of fresh, organically grown vegetables and whole wheat bread.

These concerns found support from the nonsmoking, teetotaling, vegetarian Führer. Hitler endorsed a diet of raw vegetables and grains, and his private conversations were sprinkled with declamations, some of them crackpot, some prescient, about a healthy lifestyle. "In countries like Bulgaria," he claimed, "where people live on polenta, yoghurt, and other such foods . . . men live to a greater age than in our part of the world." Germans should eat more fish, less meat, as in Italy and the Mediterranean countries. "Japanese wrestlers, who are amongst the strongest men in the world, feed almost exclusively on vegetables. The same is true of a Turkish porter, who can move a piano by himself." Abhorring smoking, he even toyed with the idea of ending soldiers' cigarette ration during the war but wisely decided against it. None of these initiatives was very successful, but the regime was actively promoting a healthy new lifestyle for the *Volksgemeinschaft*.

For all of these reasons, German doctors quickly fell into line with the new order. They wrote ideologically tinged articles on eugenics in professional journals; they taught courses in racial hygiene, and they participated without demur in the regime's new racially directed health system. Medical professional organizations were quickly coordinated, coming under the control of the National Socialist Physicians League, whose membership catapulted from 2,800 in 1932 to 11,000 by October 1933 as eager doctors clambered to get onboard. By 1934 the backlog of doctors waiting to join the league was so great that newcomers were advised to hold their application until those already awaiting admission were processed. In that same year, medical schools began requiring courses in racial hygiene, and serious medical journals published a steady stream of articles on eugenics. Racial hygiene also became a required subject at universities. In 1933 only one university had a faculty position in racial hygiene or eugenics; by 1935 more than a dozen of Germany's most prestigious universities had appointed professors offering courses in the subject.

Already in 1933 Prussian educational authorities required that instruction in racial studies be added to the curriculum, and soon all German states followed Berlin's example. Secondary schools were required to teach heredity, racial science, and family as well as population policies. The essentials of these subjects were to be integrated into instruction in biology. Students were being groomed to think in biological categories, to distinguish between "valuable life" and its lesser, "degenerate" forms. Classrooms, indeed all of public discourse, resounded with fatuous theories about Aryan, Germanic, and Nordic peoples, the last of whom were highly praised by the Nazis.

Nazi racial hygienists offered secondary school teachers advice on how to organize their instruction on racial matters. One sample assignment for students was to compose an essay on "How We Can Learn to Recognize a Person's Race." Students were required, among other things, to

summarize the spiritual characteristics of the individual races. . . . What are the expressions, gestures, and movements which allow us to make conclusion as to the attitude of the racial soul? Determine also the physical features which go hand in hand with specific racial soul characteristics of the individual figures. Try to discover the intrinsic nature of the racial soul through the characters in stories and poetical works. Collect propaganda posters and caricatures for your race book and arrange them according to a racial scheme. . . . Observe people whose special racial features have drawn your attention also with respect to their bearing when moving or when speaking. Observe their expressions and gestures. Observe the Jew: his way of walking, his bearing, gestures, and movements when talking. What strikes you about the way a Jew talks and sings? What are the occupations engaged in by the Jews of your acquaintance?

The ultimate goal of this intense indoctrination was to condition Germans to think racially, to view the world through a biological lens, and to infuse German society with a new racial ethos. Germans were constantly reminded that they were no longer merely Germans; they were Aryans, and their first duty was to the *Volk*, defined in racial terms. Doctors, too, needed to adjust their priorities. They were no longer tending to the individual but to the *Volk*. There was no higher moral obligation. In this new biological society there could be no outmoded sympathy for the weak or for the racially inferior. Feelings of "false humanity," "exaggerated pity," and brotherly love were no longer operable values. As Walter Gross, a major figure in the articulation and implementation of Nazi racial policy, explained in a radio broadcast to the nation in July 1933, "the [Nazi] revolution that has just begun not only creates new political norms, but also new human beings and a new understanding of history. . . . New values and judgments change our views of not only the future but of the past." Borrowing terminology from Nietzsche, he explained that "this transvaluation of values marks our times and justifies it as a genuine spiritual revolution." He called on Germans to join him in "a crusade" to create "a new moral order."

To further justify the sterilization measures, the regime launched a public relations campaign emphasizing that "we do not stand alone," pointing out that the United States, Norway, Denmark, Sweden, and Finland had similar laws, neglecting, of course, to mention that in each case sterilization was voluntary. The campaign also stressed the staggering financial burden the German taxpayer was compelled to bear in caring for the severely handicapped. With stunning callousness, the Nazis produced photographs of desperately disabled children juxtaposed with rosy-cheeked healthy children, accompanied by charts that purported to document the exorbitant costs of maintaining the unfit. These illustrated charts appeared in newspapers, journals, and as posters, ostensibly documenting the drain posed by the disabled on the economy and reminding taxpayers that they were footing the bill for this false "humanitarianism"—and that in a stressful time of economic recovery. As one poster frankly stated, "The genetically ill damage the community. The healthy preserve the Volk."

To coordinate and unify all schooling and propaganda in the areas of population and racial matters, the Nazis created the Office of Racial Policy (*Rassenpolitisches Amt*) in May 1934. The *Rassenpolitisches Amt* was a party office, not a formal government department or ministry, but its influence reached into every corner of German life. Headed by the fanatical physician Walter Gross, it would become one of the most important organizations in the Third Reich. In addition to maintaining an ongoing campaign to "enlighten" the public on racial matters, it operated a training school for doctors and medical students and provided instruction for members of the SS. More than any other agency it carried Nazi racial ideology into the public arena. The range of its activities was breathtaking. In one three-month period in 1938, it sponsored 1,106 public meetings attended by 173,870 people and held 5,172 school functions in which a total of 330,972 pupils participated. It organized thousands of week-long retreats and seminars for party members; it produced 350 films whose explicit message was to belittle the "soft-headed humanism" of those who harbored moral reservations about sterilization, a message also carried in its glossy illustrated journal, *New People*. By 1939 it was staffed by 3,600 workers.

Like all organizations in Nazi Germany, it found competitors at every turn: the SS maintained its own racial section, as did the Propaganda Ministry, the party's Office for Public Health, the Interior Ministry, the Labor Front, the Physicians League, and the Education Ministry, which authorized the National Socialist Teachers League to organize retraining camps to equip teachers with educational material on heredity and race for the classroom. It is estimated that 215,000 of the Reich's 300,000 teachers attended these retreats at fifty-six regional camps and national centers that combined athletics, military exercises, and instruction in the National Socialist ideology. Even the army established an office to deal with racial affairs. By 1934 German society was thoroughly immersed in organizations and events devoted to Nazi racial indoctrination. There was no escape from it, no way to shut it out.

In 1934, the first year in which the sterilization law went into full effect, 56,000 sterilizations were performed. In subsequent years the pace did not slacken. Between 1934 and 1939 the number of sterilizations performed averaged 50,000 per year, almost equally divided between women and men. There was no public dissent or opposition. By 1941 between 350,000 and 400,000 involuntary sterilizations had been performed in the Reich. Hitler was a strong advocate of the program but early expressed the view that euthanasia would be more effective in ridding the *Volk* of its weakest elements. Such an undertaking, he observed, would be best undertaken under the cover of war, and if war came, he would authorize a nationwide program of euthanasia.

In 1939 he commissioned Dr. Karl Brandt to appoint an advisory committee to prepare for the selection and extermination of physically deformed and mentally defective children. In the chilling terminology of the National Socialist state, these candidates for liquidation represented *"lebensunwertes Leben"*—"life unworthy of life"—and should be eliminated to improve the racial health of the *Volk*. Hitler's Chancellery would be directly responsible for the operation, which was to take place in the utmost secrecy. According to the plan, physicians were required to report to local health authorities all cases of newborns with congenital defects or deformities of any kind. Doctors were also to register any child under their care up to the age of three suffering from these conditions. Lengthy questionnaires were then sent to the Berlin headquarters, located in a villa at Tiergartenstrasse 4, from which the entire operation derived its code name, T4. There they were evaluated by a committee of three physicians who would mark those chosen for "selection" with a plus sign, those allowed to live with a minus sign. The committee never examined the children in person or made follow-up inquiries with local doctors. The decisions were made solely on the basis of the questionnaires. The children selected were transported to one of twenty-eight specially equipped medical institutions. Parents were told that the transport to these facilities was necessary to improve treatment for their child. No visitations were permitted.

Methods of killing varied—lethal injections and gassing were the most common. Six of the hospitals were equipped with specially constructed gas chambers, where the first experiments with poison gas took place. At some installations the children slowly starved; in others they were left unattended in unheated rooms to die of exposure, allowing the doctors to maintain that death came of natural causes. Within a year the age parameters of the program expanded, so that children up to seven, then eight, twelve, and finally seventeen years of age could be killed.

In July 1939, the program came to include the adult population. People who might have been sterilized under the old program would now be disposed of once and for all. In 1940, specially equipped gas vans were developed that could move from installation to installation. Victims were herded into the enclosed vans and carbon monoxide introduced. Dr. Leonardo Conti, working with Brandt, had drafted a plan for the extermination of all Germany's mental patients as well as those with severe physical handicaps. It was administered by Philipp Bouhler, head of the Führer Chancellery, operating under the cover of an ad hoc front organization, the Committee for the Scientific Treatment of Severe, Genetically Determined Illness.

Parents and loved ones received a standardized form letter regretfully informing them that their son or daughter, brother or sister had died suddenly of pneumonia, brain edema, appendicitis, or other fabricated causes. Due to concerns about an epidemic, the letters read, the bodies were cremated immediately. They would receive their loved one's ashes in due course. After a time, suspicions began to be raised when relatives came to notice that other families received the identical letter with the identical cause of death and the identical date. Rumors spread, and one local police official even made arrests at one of the hospitals, only to be informed that the policy came directly from the Führer. As a result of rising public suspicions, Martin Bormann ordered T4 personnel to draft a number of different form letters, and the furor died down until July 1941, when Cardinal Clemens von Galen of Münster, in a series of blistering sermons, made public charges of forced euthanasia. The state's policy of euthanasia was "pure murder," he argued, and his sermons sparked a public sensation. The program was temporarily suspended, but by that point plans were already being made for a far more drastic solution. In fact, after a brief pause, the program resumed its operations and continued to 1945. By the time T4 was briefly suspended on July 14, 1941, 70,000 German adults and 20,000 "racially valueless children" had been exterminated. It is estimated that by the end of the war, the euthanasia program had claimed 200,000 victims in Germany and beyond.

The Third Reich's commitment to "racial hygiene" was cold-blooded and callous, rendered no less vicious by its claim to "objectivity" and its veneer of pseudoscience. Nazi anti-Semitism blended that same biological fixation with a venomous hatred that only grew more intense as the regime matured. Both obsessions were inextricably intertwined and mutually reinforcing, an ideological fusion that found explicit expression in the so-called Nuremberg Laws of 1935. Throughout 1934 the regime refined its eugenics and anti-Semitic legislation, chipping away at the exemptions for Jewish war veterans that Hindenburg had insisted upon. To their chagrin, the Nazis had discovered that those exemptions turned out to be the rule rather than the exception. Given their relentless propaganda claims that Jews had shirked their duty during the Great War, the Nazis were nonplussed to discover that 100,000 Jews had served in the military, 78,000 at the front; 12,000 Jews had died in combat, and 30,000 had received decorations for bravery. The result was that 60 percent of Jewish doctors, lawyers, teachers, and other civil servants were exempt from the Aryan Paragraph of the Civil Service Law. Not to be deterred by inconvenient facts, the regime began a rollback of those exemptions that continued piecemeal until, by the close of 1938, there were none.

After the initial burst of racial legislation in 1933–34, a relative lull in the campaign against the Jews followed—at least on the national level. No major new discriminatory laws were enacted, but the violent anti-Semitic rhetoric of the regime remained as savage as ever. "We know him, the Jew," Himmler thundered at a public ceremony for German farmers in 1935, "this people composed of the waste products of all the people and nations of this planet on which it has imprinted the features of its Jewish blood, the people whose goal is the domination of the world, whose breath is destruction, whose will is extermination, whose religion is atheism, whose idea is Bolshevism."

The regime's reluctance to take radical action against the Jews during 1934 into the early months of 1935 was the result of a number of different factors, some domestic, others in the realm of foreign relations. The crisis with the SA and its violent resolution in the summer of 1934 absorbed much of the regime's energy at home, while Hitler's decision to withdraw from the League of Nations in October 1933 and subsequent complicity in a failed coup d'état by Austrian Nazis in July 1934 put a weak Germany in an increasingly isolated international position. With a plebiscite scheduled for the Saar region to determine whether the strategically important area in the west would vote to return to Germany after fifteen years of League of Nations administration, Hitler meant to emphasize the stability of the Third Reich and downplay Nazi radicalism that might frighten away many who were not committed Nazis.

Rather than issuing new discriminatory laws, the regime tolerated, indeed, tacitly encouraged the Storm Troopers and party militants to step up grassroots harassment of Jews, and in the spring of 1935, following Hitler's landslide victory in the Saar plebiscite (90.8 percent of the vote), a new wave of anti-Semitic violence swept across the country. Local radicals organized demonstrations before Jewish shops, shattered their windows, assaulted their owners, and threatened shoppers who dared enter them. They accosted Jews on the streets, fired shots into Jewish homes, painted anti-Semitic slogans—"Death to the Jews," "Jew Perish"—on walls, vandalized synagogues, overturned gravestones in Jewish cemeteries; they intimidated Jewish children on their way to school and branded anyone who associated with them as "a slave of the Jews" (*Judenknecht*). To the police they reported the names of Jews and their Aryan partners suspected of having a romantic or intimate relationship—which was, at this time, a violation of no existing law. To all of this, the regime turned a benevolent eye. Party leaders viewed these independent actions against Jews as a much needed safety valve for radical elements of the party who were frustrated by what they considered the slow pace of the state's anti-Semitic actions. A stepped-up campaign against the Jews would then provide the Storm Troopers with a new mission and revive their flagging spirits, much shaken in the wake of the Röhm purge.

These very public acts of persecution reached a crescendo in the early months of 1935. Poisonous anti-Jewish rhetoric spewed from the party press, and a "pogrom atmosphere" settled over the country. Police in Cologne reported stones thrown through the windows of Jewish homes, Jews beaten in taverns, a synagogue trashed, its sacred objects desecrated and thrown into the street. In Rhina, a village in eastern Hesse, a gang of some twenty men, dressed in black and wearing masks, burst into a synagogue just as services were ending. Wielding rubber truncheons, they savagely attacked the male members of the congregation.

Pressure was building among party activists for some sort of government action against interracial marriages and sexual relations between Jews and non-Jews—"racial defilement" (*Rassenschande*), as the Nazis branded it. In Mannheim, during August, the regional Nazi paper published a steady stream of articles under such blaring headlines as "A Heidelberg Jew as Race Defiler," "Jewish Doctor and His Jew Love Partner in Custody," "Jewish Sadists and Race Defilers," "Race Defilers Will Be Rooted Out." In Kiel, movie owners announced that Jews would no longer be admitted to theaters.

By late summer, Nazi hooliganism directed at Jews was proving unpopular with the broader German public, unsettled by the flagrant violations of the dictatorship's much touted commitment to law and order. The chief of the state police in Aachen stated in early September that "in my district the handling of the Jewish question has provoked the greatest resentment, since the mentality of the Catholic population chiefly views Jews as human beings and only secondarily thinks to judge the matter from a racial political viewpoint." That attitude was apparent in their tepid response to the boycott, the sterilization laws, and other National Socialist initiatives in racial policy. The good citizens, he remarked sarcastically, were actually tolerant of Jews in general and emphatically rejected actions taken against individual Jews. "In the future it is therefore advisable to avoid independent action in dealing with the Jews." As the Social Democratic underground in the Palatinate put it, "it is no exaggeration to say that four-fifths of the population rejects this persecution of the Jews," but that displeasure was confined to the privacy of their homes or close family friends.

Still, the radical, often violent actions of the party militants were also proving increasingly awkward for the government. Economics Minister Schacht was concerned that these outbursts of lawlessness and instability were having a negative impact on Germany's international business relationships. The Nazis were also confronted with another restraint: with tourists and the world press descending on Germany for the Olympic Games in Berlin and Garmisch-Partenkirchen in 1936, the regime was anxious to avoid embarrassing scenes. In August, after a particularly ugly SA rampage through the Kurfürstendamm, Berlin's main shopping street, Hitler called a halt to this behavior. "JEWS NOT WANTED" signs, ubiquitous in shop windows only shortly before, were tucked discreetly away; the Nazi press toned down its anti-Semitic tirades; public displays of Jew baiting slipped into the background. The Third Reich wanted to make a good impression, to show the world this new, confident, well-ordered, and happy Germany.

But given the pressure from local militants and calls for legislation regulating the status of Jews in Germany, Hitler felt that some sort of legal action was necessary for the Reich government to regain the initiative and direct militant radicalism into manageable channels. Since 1933 the Interior Ministry had been considering measures that would strip Jews of their citizenship—it had, after all, been one of the party's original Twenty-five Points—and Hitler was quite keen on the idea. Several desultory efforts were made to draft legislation to that effect, but for a variety of reasons little progress had been made. Likewise, Roland Freisler, an influential state secretary in the Ministry of Justice and later the fanatical judge of the dreaded People's Court, had long agitated for a law that would ban marriage between Jews and Aryans and also make sexual relations between them a criminal offense—another of Hitler's long-cherished ideas.

Although the Reich government had not moved on these issues, party officials at the local level did, arresting Jews suspected of having sex with Aryans, an offense referred to as "racial treason." In some areas mobs seized suspected transgressors and turned them over to the authorities, although just what law they were breaking was not at all clear. In some communities registrars refused to issue marriage licenses to mixed couples and reported them to local Nazi authorities. To bring some order and uniformity to the situation, the Gestapo intervened, directing registrars to report all such proposed marriages, so that its agents could "enlighten" the Aryan partner of his or her impending blunder.

Such was the situation as the party prepared for the 1935 rally at Nuremberg, set to begin on September 9 and run through the 15th. The climax of the great extravaganza was always the Führer's address on the final day of the festivities, and Hitler planned to announce a new law, the Reich Flag Law, which would formally make the party's swastika banner Germany's national flag. Adding a special ideological twist to the law, Jews would be forbidden to raise the flag or show the national colors. In the Third Reich German Jews could never be accused of being unpatriotic—they were forbidden to be patriotic. It was thought that perhaps Hitler would also offer some remarks on foreign policy. To lend the occasion some additional gravitas, the virtually forgotten Reichstag was summoned to Nuremberg for a special session on the 15th. Its role in the performance was to act as chorus, chanting its superfluous approval at the appropriate moments before rubber-stamping the legislation.

But two days before he was to deliver his address, Hitler changed his mind. The Flag Law was not substantial or stirring enough. He needed something else, something with greater ideological clout. In a speech earlier in the rally, Gerhard Wagner, leader of the Nazi Physicians League, had proposed a law that would forbid mixed marriages between Jews and Aryans, and late in the night of the 12th Hitler decided that dramatic new race legislation would do. State and party officials were sent scrambling to come up with a draft. Bernhard Lösener, who manned the Interior Ministry's desk for Jewish affairs, was flown in from Berlin, and a small team of officials worked frantically through the night to craft a preliminary draft. Several versions of the proposed law, one of which was written on the back of a menu, were presented to Hitler, and at 2:30 in the morning of the 15th, only hours before his closing speech, he chose the most "moderate." At eight that evening, standing before the assembled Reichstag Hitler announced what came to be known as the Nuremberg Laws. Göring was given the honor of reading out the text.

The Reich Flag Law, by now virtually an afterthought, was overshadowed by two others, the Reich Citizenship Law and the Law for the Protection of German Blood and German Honor. The Reich Citizenship Law deprived Jews of their German citizenship; they were now to be considered "subjects" of the Reich, aliens in their own country. Although aside from political rights, of which there were precious few in Nazi Germany, the law did not remove any specific rights, it left the tiny Jewish community utterly vulnerable to the whims of the regime—and to their neighbors. Of far greater consequence was the Law for the Protection of German Blood and German Honor, often simply called the Blood Protection Law, which forbade marriage and "sexual intercourse outside of marriage between Jews and Aryans." It also prohibited the employment in Jewish households of German women under the age of forty-five—an expression of the prevailing Nazi stereotype of Jewish men as sexually voracious creatures who could not be trusted with Aryan women of child-bearing age.

Hitler's last-minute decision to enact these measures was characteristic of his leadership as it was of so much in the governance of the Third Reich.

He had not come to Nuremberg intending to announce a new initiative in Nazi race policy, nor were the laws a carefully calculated escalation of the regime's persecution of the Jews, a planned step in an inevitable march to genocide. Instead, their sudden announcement in September 1935, after a frenzied thirty-six hours of formulation in Berlin and Nuremberg, is a prime example of the improvisational nature of Nazi decision making—spontaneous and portentous action taken within an ideological context. And yet, if the timing of the laws was not calculated, their substance was hardly improvisational or spontaneous. Hitler—and many other party leaders—had long favored some sort of discriminatory legislation outlawing mixed marriage and sexual relations between Jews and Aryans, and stripping Jews of their citizenship had been a recurrent demand since the earliest days of the NSDAP. Fragmentary work on such ideas had been conducted within state and party bureaucracies since the summer of 1933.

It was also symptomatic of Hitler's modus operandi that after firing off a sweeping ideological barrage against the Jews, party and state officials were left to translate his pronouncements into practical policy, and here—again typically—little agreement could be found. In their haste to draft the laws, Nazi officials left many questions unanswered. The most important—and most vexing—was exactly who was to be classified a Jew and how. Neither Hitler nor the Nazi bureaucracy had addressed this question. Was it anyone with one Jewish grandparent, as the Civil Service law of 1933 had dictated? Two Jewish grandparents? Three? State officials, especially Economics Minister Schacht and Foreign Minister Constantin von Neurath, insisted on three grandparents; party radicals, led by Rudolf Hess, on only one. The army, concerned about manpower needs, also hoped for a more restrictive definition.

Once his broadside had been fired, Hitler, as usual, could not be bothered with the details. When, several weeks after his dramatic announcement at Nuremberg, Hitler was asked to decide the issue once and for all at a meeting of the warring factions, he typically refused to take a stand—or even address the issue. Instead, he launched into a lengthy diatribe against the nefarious role of Jews in German history and then stalked from the room, leaving party and state officials to thrash matters out. It was vintage Hitler. A month later when he discovered that an agreement over who was considered Jewish had still not been reached and that he was again expected to decide the issue at a similar gathering, he abruptly canceled the meeting, and State Secretary Hans Lammers announced to frustrated officials that the Führer had far more important things to do than officiate at a debate between clashing Nazi factions. The message was get it done, and don't bother the Führer about the details.

In the end, the state position prevailed—three Jewish grandparents was determined to be decisive. The status of racially mixed individuals—half Jews (two Jewish grandparents) or quarter Jews (one Jewish grandparent)—remained a source of conflict and confusion within the regime for years. In November a supplement to the Law for the Protection of German Blood classified anyone with two Jewish grandparents "a Mixture of the first degree" (*Mischling erster Grad*), except where the grandparents were religiously practicing, in which case the individual was declared "a full Jew." The introduction of religious practice as a consideration came as something of a surprise since it was utterly inconsistent with the party's official position that religious and environmental factors were irrelevant; blood was all. Anyone with one Jewish grandparent—a quarter Jew—was declared a *Mischling* second degree. An inquiry by the Jewish umbrella organization the Central Association of German Jews determined that 502,200 full Jews were living in Germany in May 1935, and using the categories that would be formally established as a result of the Nuremberg Laws, the study calculated the number of half Jews at 70,000 to 75,000, and quarter Jews at 25,000 to 130,000.

The classifications would have serious implications. Quarter Jews were to be treated as virtual Aryans: they were permitted to serve in the military and to marry Aryans; half Jews were not. Although *Mischlinge* of the first degree were forbidden to marry an Aryan, they could appeal to Hitler himself for a special dispensation. Few such appeals were ever successful. The Mendelian complexities created by the laws led to a plethora of unanticipated problems, as Nazi jurists gathered again and again to debate whether this or that anti-Semitic law could or should be applied in the case of *Mischlinge*. How would a child of a quarter Jew and half Jew be classified? What about the child of two quarter Jews? And what did "religiously practicing" actually mean? The permutations were myriad and were the subject of interminable debate within the party and the state bureaucracy. In all there were five supplements to the Blood Protection Law between

1935 and 1939, each attempting to clarify the status of *Mischlinge*. The question of how to treat them was still being vigorously discussed at the infamous Wannsee Conference in January 1942.

Nor was this all. Many in the party felt that forbidding "intercourse outside of marriage," as defined in the Blood Protection Law, was far too narrow to protect Germany's racial stock. That law had explicitly mentioned sexual intercourse, but this, Nazi legal specialists came to argue, was merely the starting point. As battles flared in the lower courts, the statute was extended to cover a broad range of sexual practices, and the resulting cases led regularly to extraordinarily graphic proceedings. In December 1935, the matter reached the German Supreme Court, which issued a ruling declaring that "the term sexual intercourse" included "all forms of natural and unnatural sexual intercourse—that is, coition as well as those sexual activities with the person of the opposite sex which are designed, in the manner in which they are performed, to serve in place of coition to satisfy the sex drive of at least one of the partners." Under National Socialism, German jurisprudence had come to this.

The first trials arising from the Nuremberg Laws began in December 1935, and the number rose steadily in the following years. Between those first trials and the close of 1940 German courts sentenced 1,911 persons for the crime of miscegenation. All were men; most were Jews, a reflection of Hitler's belief that in sexual matters women were essentially passive. The sentences ranged from incarceration of two or so weeks to two years. These numbers probably understate the number of cases, since in June 1937 Reinhard Heydrich, head of the Security Service (SD) and the second most powerful man in the SS, issued a decree that a suspect could be sent directly to a concentration camp without first being sentenced in court.

Under the circumstances, any sort of normal social interaction between Jews and non-Jews became impossible. "Aryan" Germans became cautious, ducking their former Jewish friends; Jews withdrew into themselves. There were some brave souls, "who carry on a friendly, neighborly relationship in Germany," but they were isolated and scorned as "servants of the Jews." In Breslau, the local Nazi newspaper published the names and addresses of "Aryan women and girls, who carry on intimate relations with Jews." Storm Troopers posted placards throughout the city, on which the names of such women and Jews were printed, and local Nazis snapped photographs of Aryan customers entering Jewish businesses.

Most of these cases were the result of anonymous denunciations. And everything was suspect. A handshake, a touch on the shoulder, a perfunctory wave of the hand, even a glance might cause someone to be turned in to the Gestapo or local police. So swamped were the authorities by these anonymous denunciations, many of which were dismissed out of hand, that the Gestapo had to issue warnings against frivolous denunciations. Still, the result was that Jews increasingly withdrew from ordinary social interaction with their German neighbors, and even longtime friendships between "Aryans" and Jews gradually disintegrated. Jews were not forced into physical segregation—there were no ghettos—but their social and psychological isolation was virtually complete. Ostracized by their neighbors, terrorized by Nazi militants, unprotected by the police, Jews kept their heads down.

The Jewish community in Germany did not collapse or wither up and die. Officials from all over the country reported increased activity by Jewish organizations—Jewish veterans, Jewish sports clubs, Jewish youth groups, Jewish welfare societies were particularly active; even Jewish newspapers, such as the widely distributed *Jüdische Rundschau*, continued to be published into 1938. Lecture series were launched; cultural evenings were held; as were concerts by Jewish musicians. Talks were held on Palestine and the possibilities of settlement there, a subject that before 1933 had drawn little interest in the German Jewish community. Some Jews held out the hope that the Nuremberg Laws, as odious as they were, would bring an end to the SA terror and set a legal framework for continued Jewish life in Nazi Germany. Now, perhaps, there would be stability and the possibility of living unmolested in their homeland.

In 1933, approximately 38,000 Jews left Germany; in 1934, 22,000 followed. In 1935 the number actually dropped to 21,000, and there was even a small trickle of Jews returning from immigration—Jews who found living a reduced existence in exile more traumatic than living in their own country, where they had roots, community, and their own German culture. The introduction of conscription and the creation of a German army in the spring of 1935 even prompted some Jews to express their interest in joining the military as good German patriots. So many had served honorably in the Great War. Their inquiries were scornfully rebuffed, amid

Nazi suspicions that such offers to enlist were nothing more than a crafty Jewish tactic to infiltrate the military and would provide an opportunity to slip back into the German mainstream.

Still, in the mid-1930s it seemed possible, albeit under drastically reduced circumstances, to live in Germany, and Jews struggled to interpret the ambiguous signals they received from the state and the public. In the years before the war, Jews confronted different local and regional practices, some of which deviated slightly from national directives. They were left to interpret mixed signals not only from the state but also from sympathetic "Aryans," a confusing situation that at least gave Jews a glimmer of hope. Despite the remarkable tenacity of Jewish organizations and a modicum of Jewish public life, Jews lived on a knife's edge. Ostracized, determined to do nothing that could draw attention to themselves, to make no open criticism of the regime, some burned their papers, letters, newspaper clippings, anything that might be construed as anti-Nazi or subversive. Many were convinced that their telephones were tapped, their correspondence opened—a fear they shared, although in a more heightened fashion, with much of the German public. Fear was their constant companion. It was dangerous even to be in the presence of anyone, "Aryans" included, who complained about any aspect, no matter how trivial, of the regime. One Jewish woman, upon hearing an Aryan neighbor in a shop grumble about the price of butter— didn't she think so?—"did not answer and hurried away without buying anything. I was frightened. Fear, fear, fear—morning, noon and night. Fear followed us into our dreams, racking on our nerves. How imprudent, how inconsiderate of the woman to speak like that in public."

In the aftermath of the Nuremberg Laws, the regime introduced no new initiatives in racial policy in 1936–37, which has led many to speak of a lull in Nazi persecution of the Jews. To some it appeared that the regime's racial harassment of the Jews had lost momentum. That was only superficially true. While no major legislation in Jewish policy was undertaken in 1936 and 1937, five supplements to the Blood Protection Law were introduced between 1935 and the close of 1938, each further constricting the lives of Germany's Jews. Jews were banned from the practice of dentistry, from the practice of law, from the distribution of stamps, from operating as druggists, from owning restaurants or pubs; Jews were forbidden to serve as auditors, dieticians, land surveyors; and the fifth supplement issued in September 1938 liquidated Jewish law firms and put an end to any form of medical practice by Jewish doctors. The status of *Mischlinge* was a major target, and with each new supplement their position deteriorated.

In these years, Nazi racial initiatives took a backseat to Hitler's dramatic foreign policy moves, which held the nation's attention and added greatly to his popularity. In 1935 he announced that Germany would build an army and an air force; he signed a naval agreement with Great Britain, which allowed Germany to begin building a high-seas fleet, including submarines. In March 1936 he sent troops into the Rhineland, German territory that according to the Versailles Treaty was to remain a demilitarized zone. And that summer the Olympic Games in Berlin brought Germany a tremendous boost in international prestige. At home they were viewed as a glowing accomplishment of the Third Reich. The year 1938 was a year of international crises and spectacular triumphs for Hitler. In March, the *Anschluss*, the absorption of Austria, brought an additional ten million ethnic Germans into the Reich along with around 200,000 Jews, an action that would have profound implications for Nazi racial policy. (Nazi foreign policy is treated in the following chapter.)

Another development occurred in the mid-1930s that would have enormous impact on the evolution of Nazi racial policy. In June 1936 Hitler named Heinrich Himmler Reichsführer-SS and placed him in command of all German police, yet another profound incursion of the party into the competencies of the state. Gradually the SS began to play an increasingly prominent role in the formulation and enforcement of the regime's Jewish policy. The dreaded Gestapo, officially a branch of the state police, was absorbed by the SS, which now engaged in its own surveillance and intelligence-gathering operations. Officially Jewish policy was directed by the Interior Ministry, but in typical Nazi fashion, other state ministries—Justice, Health, the Office of Racial Policy—and various party agencies laid claim to jurisdiction in various areas of the policy. In 1936 the SS began to assert itself, relentlessly claiming leadership in all matters relating to the Jewish community. The SS of the mid- to late 1930s functioned virtually as a government ministry, with departments for Administration, Internal Intelligence, and Foreign Intelligence. These departments in turn had numerous subsections for Ideological Opponents (the Left),

Freemasons, Political Churches, and "the Opponent Jewry." The Jewish subsection was by far the most active, and Heydrich's Security Service, the SD, assumed the leading role. The Jewish section was composed of several desks, one each for Assimilationist Jewry, Orthodox Jewry, and Zionists. The Zionist desk was presided over by an obscure ex–traveling vacuum cleaner salesman, Adolf Eichmann, who claimed, falsely, as it turned out, to have a passable knowledge of Hebrew.

Among the duties of the Jewish section was the compilation of a card index that would locate and identify every Jew living in Germany—name, address, occupation, racial classification, memberships in clubs and organizations. Where possible, the SD also unearthed the names of friends and associates for cross-reference. An effort was also made to catalogue all Jewish organizations still operating in Germany and their possible connections to similar organizations abroad. A second Jewish card index was created to determine the most important Jews in foreign countries and the contacts they might have with German Jews. The zealous ideologues of the SD, many of whom were in their twenties or early thirties—Himmler was but thirty-two, Heydrich thirty—were convinced that an international network of Jewish conspirators existed and was plotting world domination. They repeatedly uncovered evidence, all of it imaginary, of Jewish plots to assassinate Hitler, Streicher, and other Nazi leaders, large and small.

The SS/SD claimed to prefer a policy of "rational anti-Semitism," not the emotional, violent anti-Semitism found among the Storm Troopers and party militants. It was a point Hitler had made in *Mein Kampf* and in numerous party gatherings before 1933. The SS/SD's solution to the Jewish problem at this time was "the complete emigration of the Jews." An SD memorandum underscored that position in the usual cold-blooded language of the SS: "The life opportunities of the Jews have to be restricted, not only in economic terms." The "old generation may die off . . . but . . . the young generation should find it impossible to live, so that the incentive for emigrating is constantly in force. Violent mob anti-Semitism must be avoided. One does not fight rats with guns but with poison gas."

Throughout this relatively quiet period, the violent anti-Semitic rhetoric of the regime remained as scurrilous as ever, and after a comparative lull, persecution of the Jews was once again ratcheted up. In November 1937 the largest anti-Jewish exhibition, *The Eternal Jew*, opened with great fanfare in Munich at the Deutsches Museum, with Goebbels and Streicher giving speeches to launch the exhibit. Goebbels's bloodcurdling rhetoric set the tone: The Jew "is the enemy of the world, the destroyer of cultures, the parasite among the nations, the son of chaos, the incarnation of evil, the ferment of decomposition, the visible demon of the decay of humanity. . . . This Jewish pestilence must be eradicated. Totally. None of it should remain." By the close of 1937 a palpable radicalization of tone and content was evident in Nazi propaganda and actions toward the Jews, with increasingly shrill threats and occasional violence against the small and shrinking Jewish community on the rise.

The extremist rhetoric rose to an almost hysterical pitch, contributing palpably to an air of crisis that hung over the country through much of 1938. A mounting fear of war prevailed. The Austrian crisis in February and March and the attenuated and far more dangerous confrontation with Czechoslovakia in the late summer produced a virtual state of emergency. Germany, the Social Democratic secret reports emphasized, was suffering from a "war psychosis," which together with a sharp escalation in radical anti-Semitic action by local and regional party formations, left the population perpetually on edge.

At the same time, the regime was becoming more self-confident, more radical, more confrontational both at home and abroad. From 1936 onward, moderating influences on Hitler began falling away. In the following year he removed prominent conservatives in both the administration and the military who had acted as a restraint on Nazi radicalism. With the brakes, such as they were, removed, and all the high offices of the state and military now firmly in the hands of committed Nazis, Hitler could pursue a far more aggressive policy, one that would lead to expansion in Eastern Europe, confrontation with the West, and a concomitant surge of violent anti-Semitic activity at home. Those developments converged in dramatic fashion in the winter of 1938, when Germany annexed Austria, a move that set the international community on edge and was accompanied by a profound radicalization of Nazi Jewish policy. The announcement of the *Anschluss* in March triggered a storm of ferocious anti-Semitic activity by Austrian Nazis and other Jew haters that far exceeded anything that had yet occurred in Germany. Given "freedom of action" by Hitler, party radicals immediately went on the offensive, smashing Jewish houses and shops, torching synagogues, parading Jews through the streets. Public humiliations of Jewish men—and women—became an everyday occurrence. Jews, on hands and knees, scrubbing the sidewalks in front of their shops while obviously satisfied spectators surrounded and taunted them, became a shameful part of life in Austrian cities. Nazi leaders at every level simply seized Jewish property, enriching themselves in a noxious display of avarice and corruption.

Pressure on the Jewish community in Germany escalated steadily as 1938 progressed. A new wave of discriminatory decrees began with a law requiring all Jews to turn in their passports—new ones would be issued only to those who were about to emigrate. In July the regime decreed that all Jews must apply to the police for an identity card, which was to be carried at all times and produced on demand. In August, the regime decreed that beginning in January 1939 Jews whose names did not appear on a list authorized by the state—names that any German would presumably recognize as Jewish—were required to add Israel or Sara to their names.

Eichmann, head of the SD's Zionist section, was dispatched to Vienna to manage the emigration of Jews, at this time still the SS's preferred solution to the "Jewish problem." That problem was becoming acute. By the close of 1937 some 60,000 German Jews had emigrated, roughly 20,000 per year; now the *Anschluss* brought an additional 195,000 Jews into the Reich. Eichmann's solution was forced emigration, developing a system whereby wealthy Jewish emigrants were extorted to subsidize poorer Jews who were desperate to get out of Austria. Eichmann created a Bureau of Emigration to organize the forced emigration. It worked, with staggering corruption at its sinister core, as Nazi officials coerced money from frantic Jews. By late November, Eichmann was able to boast that his policy had resulted in 350 Jews leaving Austria per day. The numbers were no doubt inflated, but impressive nonetheless to Heydrich and the SD. Later in the year, Himmler established a similar bureau in Berlin based on Eichmann's Austrian model.

In the summer of 1938 Jewish emigration from the Third Reich was a matter of growing international concern, and an international conference to deal with the problem was held in the French spa Evian-les-Bains.

Called on the initiative of President Franklin Roosevelt, the conference drew thirty-two participating nations and ended in utter failure. Although virtually all the participants expressed humanitarian concerns and agreed that the problem was pressing, all showed remarkable reluctance to accept Germany's Jews. The Nazis were beside themselves with glee. The Western powers that so sanctimoniously condemned Nazi anti-Semitism had revealed themselves as hypocrites of the first order. Headlines in the *Völkischer Beobachter* screamed: "Nobody Wants Them."

Against this backdrop of growing intimidation and violence, the Nazis moved decisively to expropriate the assets of Germany's Jews. Beginning in January a series of edicts emanating from Göring's Office of the Four Year Plan, a powerful ad hoc agency created in 1936 to organize and oversee the economy, aimed at assessing the extent of Jewish wealth in the country. All Jewish assets of over 5,000 RM were to be reported to Göring's office; another regulation forbade Jews from changing family names to escape detection. It seemed ominously clear that the regime was conducting an inventory of Jewish assets in preparation for their seizure by the state. But what was a Jewish business? For small family shops determination of ownership posed few problems, but in larger enterprises, with multiple stockholders and Aryan managers or CEOs, the situation was more complex. Some Jewish owners had also struck upon the tactic of shifting the titular management of the business to a trusted "Aryan" employee or associate, some of whom proved not so trustworthy after all. Soon a decree against the camouflaging of Jewish businesses was put in place.

Many Jewish firms had already closed—"Aryanized," was the operative term—their owners liquidating properties in bankruptcy; others, deemed too large, were being prepared for Aryanization. Corruption was epidemic. At every opportunity local Nazi leaders swooped in and bought up properties from Jewish owners, paying a mere fraction of their value. Aryanization of Jewish businesses was a moneymaker, not only for the state and the party but for individual Nazi leaders whose goal was more venal than ideological. The situation became so untenable that Göring was forced to remind party leaders that Aryanization was not intended as "a charitable scheme for incompetent party members."

But it was a completely unforeseen event that would once again radicalize Nazi Jewish policy. On the afternoon of November 7, 1938, a seventeen-year-old Polish Jew, Herschel Grynszpan, entered the German embassy in Paris and asked to meet with the ambassador on a passport matter. Only days before he had received a postcard from his sister bringing him distressing news that the family, which had lived in Germany since 1918, had been "relocated" and were living in deplorable conditions in a refugee camp on the German-Polish border. They were among some seventeen thousand Jews with Polish citizenship who were arrested and prepared for deportation to Poland. But the Polish government refused to take them in, and so, dumped in a dismal refugee camp, they waited, stateless, unwanted, without a country.

Grynszpan had been living in Paris with an uncle since 1936, but his Polish passport and German exit visa had expired in August, and the French authorities had ordered him to leave within four days. Powerless and despondent, he went into hiding. He decided to take a bold, desperate step. To his uncle, he wrote: "Jews have the right to protest. In a way that the whole world hears, and with your forgiveness this I intend to do. With god's help, I couldn't do otherwise. My heart bleeds when I think of our tragedy and that of the 12,000 [sic]."

The German ambassador was not available, and so Grynszpan was ushered into the office of Ernst vom Rath, a minor Foreign Service official. There he pulled out a revolver and shot Rath at point-blank range. He made no effort to escape and was arrested by French police on the spot. To them he sobbed, "Being a Jew is not a crime. I am not a dog. I have a right to live and the Jewish people have the right to live on this earth. Where I have been I have been chased like an animal." Berlin demanded that Grynszpan be turned over to German authorities, but the French, noting that he was not a German citizen, refused. He would be held in France until his legal status could be clarified. Rath, mortally wounded, did not succumb immediately and while he lingered on the verge of death, Goebbels sensed a propaganda gold mine. He portrayed the attempted assassination in Paris as an act of war against the Reich by international Jewry, and the German press sizzled with white-hot fury.

November 9 was the fifteenth anniversary of the Beer Hall Putsch, and the party had gathered in Munich for the annual celebration. A social gathering for party leaders in the ornate Old Town Hall was to take place in the evening before the annual midnight swearing-in ceremony of new SS recruits. In the late afternoon, Goebbels received a telephone call from Dr. Brandt in Paris informing him that Rath had died. Goebbels passed on that information to Hitler, and the two held a lengthy discussion about some sort of nationwide action against the Jews—an assault against synagogues, businesses, homes, and individual Jews. Although Goebbels's propaganda network would initiate the action, his agents were to do so in civilian clothes. The uprising was to appear to be a spontaneous action of an enraged nation.

During the meeting that evening, one messenger after another arrived to confer with Goebbels, and Goebbels left his seat to confer with Hitler. They spoke in hushed tones. Shortly thereafter Hitler left the Rathaus for his private apartment in the Prinzregentenstrasse, and at 9 p.m. Goebbels announced to the assembled leaders that Rath had died. Spontaneous riots were occurring throughout the Reich. Neither the SS nor the SA had been informed, and there was considerable confusion and consternation among the leadership about what was to be done. Meanwhile reports were arriving informing the leaders that synagogues were burning in several cities, and crowds of infuriated civilians were taking matters into their own hands, torching Jewish businesses and homes. Jewish men were being arrested by the hundreds. Goebbels also made it clear that the Führer ordered that the police and fire departments were not to interfere except to prevent flames from spreading to adjoining "Aryan" homes and businesses. Party leaders rushed to the telephones, calling their regional chieftains, issuing orders to launch their own operations. Both Göring and Himmler, neither of whom was present in the Old Town Hall, were furious at Goebbels's failure to inform them of his plans. Himmler complained that "I suppose that it is Goebbels's megalomania and his stupidity which are responsible for starting this operation now, in a particularly difficult diplomatic situation."

In city after city crowds gathered in the streets to watch, sometimes in silence, sometimes cheering, as mobs of Storm Troopers, Hitler Youth, and other party radicals attacked every identifiable Jewish institution or dwelling. The scenes of destruction were shocking; rampaging Nazis invaded Jewish homes, smashed the furniture, crockery, ripped bedding, tossed expensive paintings out into the streets. Shards of shattered glass covered streets and sidewalks; the acrid smell of creosote hung in the air. The Swiss consul in Cologne reported seeing gramophones, sewing machines, and typewriters tumbling into the streets. A colleague of his "even saw a piano being thrown out of a second floor window." Jewish men were dragged out of their beds and paraded through the streets by the mob before being formally placed in "protective custody" and dispatched to concentration camps. The police stood by, watching but not intervening.

Like so many Jews who would never forget that harrowing night, Simon Ackermann from a small town near Baden-Baden vividly recalled the terrifying details of this Night of Broken Glass (*Kristallnacht*). In the late afternoon "ten Gestapo men burst into our apartment and turned everything upside down looking for weapons." A short time later a uniformed policeman and an SS man broke down the door. "The policeman threw my wife to the ground, while the SS man flailed away at me like a madman. The policeman wanted to throw my three year old daughter out the window but I held her tight." Then he snarled that "he did not yet have an order to shoot, otherwise he would already have shot all the Jews."

Ackermann was taken to police headquarters, where a crowd of Jewish men had already been assembled. At shortly after nine o'clock they "were led by the police and SS through the streets. At the front of the procession were youths who chanted '*Jew Perish*.' The whole town was on the streets. Many screamed like drunkards, yelling out 'Beat the Jews to death.' They threw stones and spit at us. . . . At the Leopoldplatz the SS men bellowed [to the crowd] 'Here you have the Jews. Do what you want to do to them.' In a flash hundreds of people gathered round and began beating us." The SS then marched the battered men to the synagogue. As they trudged along, they were forced to sing the "Horst Wessel Song," and once inside the synagogue "the SS led us one after another to the altar where we were forced to read aloud from the *Stürmer*." Then the frightened Jews were herded to a local Jewish-owned hotel. The Nazis had disconnected the interior lighting, and the men sat in darkness waiting for the next blow to fall. At 2 a.m. the cantor "was taken from the hotel; he returned after a time covered in blood and cried: " 'Our synagogue is burning.' "

Meanwhile Ackermann's wife appealed to the Gestapo chief for permission to leave the house. He refused, telling her that the people were demanding that she and her child be burned alive. Late in the afternoon she slipped away with her daughter and ran to the woods, where they hid until dark. Then they found their way to a friend's house and took shelter for the night. She had no idea what had happened to her husband. Along with the other Jewish men of the town, he was being beaten on the railway platform, where they waited for a train that would carry them to Dachau.

Sally Schlesinger was a young girl in Koblenz on *Kristallnacht.*

It was a cold, dismal morning when I was awakened by a frightful noise in the house. . . . As I came down the stairs I saw several SA men beating my Stepfather and Uncle over the head as they drove them out of the house. . . . They had smashed in the glass house door and the glass door to my parents' bedroom. My poor little mother stood in the bedroom which was so covered in glass that it was impossible to sit down and dangerous to walk. It was in the dining room where the SA had had their greatest fun. Every glass, every plate was pulled from the breakfront and shattered on the floor. Even the ceiling lamp was ripped down and smashed. Later my parents were held liable for the damages to their apartment and had to pay.

All over Germany, from cities to small villages, it was the same—a nightmarish orgy of violence, arson, looting, and beatings that left 7,500 Jewish stores demolished, 267 synagogues burned, 20,000 Jewish males arrested, and 91 Jews murdered, a figure that does not include the large number of suicides that followed. The Nazis tried to maintain that this nationwide pogrom was a spontaneous explosion of popular rage at the "cowardly Jewish attack on Germany," but, as was plain to virtually everyone, this was no independent action by local radicals. The night of wanton violence was clearly ordered and coordinated from the top of the National Socialist regime. Now even the law was no protection.

Goebbels had planned and organized the pogrom, with Hitler's apparent approval, but without consultation with Himmler or Göring. Some have speculated that Goebbels's action was prompted by a desire to regain favor with Hitler. He had for some time been carrying on an affair with a movie actress and had asked Hitler for permission to divorce his wife. But divorce, Hitler responded, was out of the question. The Führer, after all, had himself been a member of the Goebbels wedding, and the Goebbels family, with its virtual assembly line of children, to whom Hitler was godfather, had assumed the unofficial role of first family of the Third Reich. Goebbels remained a dynamo of energy, publishing, writing articles for various Nazi journals and newspapers, giving radio addresses, and directing the party's propaganda machine. But with Himmler's appointment as top police official in the Reich and Göring's new post as head of the Four Year Plan, both in 1936, the two men were fast becoming the most powerful players in the National Socialist state. Goebbels's star was fading, and he needed to do something to reestablish himself in Hitler's good graces. Be that as it may, *Kristallnacht* did not mark the onset of a new offensive against the Jews but the crest of a wave of anti-Semitic riots that had gathered momentum throughout the summer and early fall.

For the Jews of Germany, *Kristallnacht* was a sheer disaster, bringing the end of any lingering illusions about the Third Reich. Most Jews had insurance policies that should have covered much of the property damage, but the regime voided those policies and imposed a one-billion-mark indemnity on the Jews, forcing them to pay for the destruction visited on them during that terrible night. The beatings, the murders, the arson, the arrests, the concentration camps, and the failure of the police or fire departments to help made it appallingly clear that until then, German Jews still clung to the belief that the law protected them. For the most part, their incarceration in the camps was of short duration—a few weeks, a month—but it provided them with a menacing preview of a dark future.

Although many Germans complained about what they considered as irresponsible destruction of valuable property on that night, some local reports emphasized moral reservations. In what was a common refrain, the mayor of Borgentreich in Westphalia reported that "in many ways, the population didn't understand the action, or put better, didn't want to understand it. The Jews are the objects of sympathy. Especially because they lost house and home and [because] male Jews were taken to a concentration camp . . . I estimate that here at least sixty percent of the population thought like this."

Although *Kristallnacht* provoked shock in much of the German public, there were few public displays of sympathy for the Jews; open expressions of disapproval were dangerous and usually took the form of criticism of the "senseless destruction of property" and "pogrom anti-Semitism." The response of the people was definitely divided, with widespread rejection of the pogrom coexisting with a general approval of the regime's "legal" actions against the Jews. The Nazi leadership took notice and drew several important conclusions from the public's ambivalent reaction. The people, SD reports noted, were shocked by the government-sanctioned violence. Until *Kristallnacht* Germans could maintain the illusion that this kind of vicious terrorism was the doing of the unruly SA and other local radicals. Now they, like the Jewish victims of that night, were confronted by the ugly realization that this was no spontaneous "excess" by party militants. This was a savage assault on the Jews conceived, fomented, and conducted by the regime itself. To Heydrich, the lessons of that night were quite clear: there could be no more open violence against the Jews, no more vigilante action. In the future, the SS insisted, anti-Jewish measures should follow a "more rational course." Emigration—forced emigration—was the key, and since the SS had seized the initiative in Jewish emigration policy, Himmler would henceforth stake his claim to leadership in the regime's overall Jewish policy.

While the ruins of Germany's synagogues still smoldered, the regime moved quickly to complete the exclusion of the Jews from the German economy. On November 12, Göring, with Hitler's approval, convened a meeting on the "Jewish question" with leading figures in the regime as well as various police officials. Still fuming at Goebbels's reckless action and the destruction of valuable property, Göring made it clear that "something decisive must be done. . . . I have had enough of these demonstrations. It is not the Jew they harm but myself as final authority for coordinating the German economy." The solution to the "Jewish question," Göring asserted, was to be found in the complete elimination of Jews from the German economy, and since the problem was "mainly an economic one, it is from the economic angle that it will have to be tackled."

At that meeting and in subsequent days Göring issued a series of stringent economic decrees meant to drive Jews completely out of the German economy. Life was to be made so miserable, so unsustainable for the Jews that they would have no choice but to leave the country. According to the decrees of November 12, Jews were compelled to sell their retail businesses and any export mail order firms; they could not work as independent craftsmen; they could not sell any goods and services; they could not act as managers of businesses or be members of consumer cooperatives; they could not participate in the welfare system. In addition, all Jewish children were expelled from public schools, and Jews were forbidden access to certain public sites (parks, movie theaters, among others), or limited to a few hours each day; Jews were also deprived of their driver's licenses and were forbidden to own radios. At the conclusion of the November 12 meeting, Göring commented: "I would not wish to be a Jew in Germany tonight."

That meeting also marked Göring's assertion of leadership in all matters related to Jewish policy. Although he would face relentless pressure from the SS/SD, Göring confirmed his claim by issuing a December directive to all government departments that stated: "to ensure uniform treatment of the Jewish question, upon which rests the handling of economic matters, I am asking that all decrees and other important orders touching upon Jewish matters be cleared through my office and that absolutely no independent initiatives on the Jewish question be undertaken."

By the close of 1938, the economic destruction of the Jewish community was virtually complete. Aryanization was intensified, and Jews were entirely thrown back upon their own shrinking community to survive. The events of 1938 did produce a dramatic surge of Jewish emigration—more than eighty thousand fled the country. But leaving was not easy. While the SS was pursuing a policy of Jewish emigration—increasingly forced—other state ministries were, in typical Nazi fashion, making it more and more difficult for Jews to leave. Jews were forced to pay an exorbitant emigration tax and a special "Jew tax" that, along with Aryanization, Nazi extortion at the grass roots, and other exploitative economic measures, left most Jews lacking the funds necessary to acquire visas. And it was also increasingly difficult to find countries willing to take impoverished refugees from Germany, especially since most countries were still dealing with the effects of the Great Depression.

In its annual report for 1938, the SD concluded that "as far as laws and edicts are concerned, the Jewish question in Germany has been resolved." From January 1 through November 8, legislation and administrative directives were designed to exclude Jews from German society. With the action of November 9–10, the report proudly proclaimed, the removal of Jews from "all areas of public and private life has for all practical purposes been realized." Four years earlier an SD memorandum had asserted that for Jews their existence must be rendered so unbearable, so impossible that they would find Germany "a country without a future." In the aftermath of *Kristallnacht*, that dark vision had become stark reality.

COURTING DISASTER

Race and war were inextricably intertwined in Nazi thinking. While ruthlessly imposing their radical racial vision on the country, the Nazis simultaneously launched a systematic campaign to militarize German society. If Germany was to reach its rightful potential as a great—indeed, hegemonic—power and provide a self-sustaining base for the healthy cultivation of its racial stock, the Reich would have to expand beyond its cramped frontiers. Even a return to the borders of 1914 was unacceptable. The German people required *Lebensraum*, living space, that would provide the territory and resources necessary to make Germany economically self-sufficient—"autarkic" was the term favored by the regime. The acquisition of new territory and a self-sustaining economy would render Germany invulnerable to an enemy blockade and would provide the raw materials necessary for exerting German power over the European continent—and perhaps beyond. Although Hitler maintained a public pretense that this living space could be acquired by peaceful means, it was palpably obvious to both the Foreign Office and the military and increasingly to the public that it could not be attained without military conquest.

Hitler's determination to acquire *Lebensraum* was hardly a hidden agenda. Expansion meant continental expansion—and continental expansion meant the East. In this, Hitler's geopolitical aims did not differ significantly from those of Imperial Germany during the Great War, but the ideological vision underlying them did. Hitler hoped to establish a vast central European imperium, the geographic and racial nucleus of which would be a "Greater Germany," uniting all ethnic Germans and cleansed

of Jews, Gypsies, Slavs, and other racially inferior elements. Some territories would be annexed outright, their native populations expelled; others
would be transformed into satellite states. Hardy German settlers would
be dispatched to people the eastern borderlands—warrior farmers, tilling
the land and guarding the frontier against Slavs and other racial enemies.
Diplomacy would set the stage for German expansion, but ultimately
Hitler trained his sights on a war of conquest.

All of this, of course, required a full demolition of the Versailles Treaty,
but during 1933 and 1934 Hitler's attention was absorbed by the seizure
and consolidation of power. Germany was militarily weak and vulnerable
to foreign, especially French, intervention, a situation that dictated restraint
in international affairs. Hitler was careful. As he set about undermining
the Versailles settlement, his standard operating procedure was to proclaim
his fervent desire for peace and international cooperation, while privately
plotting a more aggressive strategy. Until the very brink of war in 1939, this
modus operandi never varied. Every assault on the Treaty of Versailles was
invariably couched in the language of international understanding.

Despite repeated assurances from Hitler, suspicions of German intentions were heightened in October 1933 when, in his first initiative in foreign policy, Hitler abruptly withdrew Germany from the World Disarmament Conference and the League of Nations. The disarmament conference
sponsored by the League of Nations had been convened in February 1932,
and when Hitler assumed the chancellorship, his opening performance on
the stage of world politics was to make a typically theatrical offer. "Our
boundless love for and loyalty to our own national traditions makes us respect the national claims of others and makes us desire from the bottom of
our hearts to live with them in peace and friendship." But Germany alone
had been forced to disarm at Versailles, rendering the country defenseless.
Germany would be willing at any time "to undertake further obligations
in regard to international security, if all the other nations are ready on
their side to do the same."

Since Germany was restricted by the Versailles Treaty to a military of
only 100,000 troops, had no heavy weapons, no air force, and no battle
fleet, it was an easy—and disingenuous—offer to make. If the international
community was unprepared for such a radical offer, Hitler suggested more
specifically that France might reduce its military down to German levels or

alternatively that Germany be allowed to increase its forces to match those of France. When, not surprisingly, France balked, Hitler insisted that all Germany was seeking was to be treated as an equal in matters of international security. Had not Germany, "in her state of defenselessness and disarmament, greater justification in demanding security than the over-armed states bound together in military alliances?" But that, he implied, was apparently not the intention of the French, who seemed determined to maintain their vast military superiority over Germany.

While expressing his deepest regrets, Hitler announced that Germany was forced to leave the Disarmament Conference. At the same time, he also declared Germany's withdrawal from the League of Nations. In a statement to the public on October 14, he explained that since the powers gathered in Geneva were intent on perpetuating "an unjust and degrading discrimination of the German people," the Reich government could not "under these circumstances, feel itself able to participate any longer as a second-class nation without rights of its own in negotiations which can only result in further dictates."

The move aroused uneasiness in the international community, especially in France, where Hitler's grand proposal to disarm completely if France and other states did the same was scorned as a sham—an offer that he knew would not, could not, be accepted. It was, Paris maintained, nothing more than a transparent ruse to allow Germany to cast off the armaments restrictions of Versailles. Besides, France's armed forces were the largest in Europe, and Paris was not about to forfeit its strategic advantage.

To those abroad who accused him of harboring aggressive intentions, Hitler dipped into his limitless stock of sanctimony to reply that all he wanted was "to provide work and bread to the German Volk," and this he could do only if "peace and quiet" prevailed. No one should assume that "I would be so mad as to want a war." Foreign statesmen were unimpressed, but Hitler's action played very well inside Germany. Here at last was a German leader who would not be pushed around by France and Britain. Not only was Hitler ruthlessly combating Germany's domestic enemies, he was standing up for Germany's rights in the international arena. He was bent on expunging Germany's disgrace of 1918. This theme remained a major leitmotif of Hitler's policy in these years, reprised in speeches without number.

Eager to display the public's enthusiastic support for the Hitler government, the Nazis staged an "election" on November 12, summoning the nation to approve the regime's actions since January 30. Back in fighting form, Goebbels embarked on a vigorous public campaign in the usual Nazi style. It was a plebiscite not only on Hitler's audacious foreign policy but his murderous suppression of domestic opposition. The results were not surprising. Ninety-eight percent of those voting cast a "yes" ballot in support of the regime, and although the usual intimidation no doubt played a significant role, there can be little doubt that Hitler's moves found favor with a majority of Germans.

While Germans hailed Hitler's audacity, French suspicions proved well founded. In December 1933, the German High Command, with Hitler's encouragement, drafted a program for a vast expansion of the armed forces. It called for a peacetime army of twenty-one divisions, or about 300,000 troops, by 1938 and a field army of sixty-three divisions—proposals that were a blatant violation of the armaments clauses of the Versailles Treaty. These strength levels were intended to provide Germany with a force capable of fighting a defensive war on multiple fronts. It was to be a "Peace Army," strong enough to guarantee German security. Then in the spring of 1934 Hitler demanded that these goals be attained by October, a target date the army felt was unrealistic. Yet by the end of February 1935, the German army had already reached a troop strength of 280,000. In early March, the High Command proposed a peacetime army of thirty to thirty-six divisions, numbers that Hitler gladly endorsed.

Hitler meanwhile continued to portray himself as a man of peace. In January 1934 he entered into a ten-year nonaggression pact with Poland, a move that to some seemed to signal Germany's willingness to recognize its existing eastern borders—or at least to pledge that any modification would come via peaceful negotiation. It was a step that his Weimar predecessors had signally refused to take and both his generals and Foreign Office opposed. The pact was not popular in Germany, but it strengthened Hitler's claim to be a reasonable statesman determined to revise the Versailles Treaty but willing to live in peace with his neighbors. Above all, however, it was a shrewdly calculated move to undermine the system of Eastern European alliances—the Little Entente—that France had concluded with Poland, Czechoslovakia, and Yugoslavia over the course of the 1920s.

Hitler's international credibility suffered a serious setback in July 1934 when Austrian Nazis, with unofficial support from Berlin, attempted a coup against Engelbert Dollfuss and his dictatorial government in Austria. Austrian Nazis assassinated Dollfuss, briefly seized the national radio, and battled pro-government forces all across the country. The Putsch was quickly crushed. The army remained loyal to the government; Nazis were arrested; Dollfuss's assassins were hanged; and the party slipped deeper underground. The Germans continued to insist that they had played no part in the Putsch, but their fervent protestations of innocence only served to convince international opinion of their complicity. Most important, the Putsch dealt a blow to Hitler's efforts to establish closer ties with Italian dictator Benito Mussolini, who distrusted Hitler and viewed himself as the protector of Austrian sovereignty.

For all of his reassurances, Hitler was determined to rearm, and his efforts were already under way when Germany exited the Disarmament Conference in October 1933. In his first days in office, he had pledged to military leaders that rearmament would be his highest priority, even if that meant radically reordering Germany's economic priorities, committing the country's still-fragile economy to an immense program of rearmament. Hitler interpreted the tepid response of the Western powers to his brusque withdrawal from the Disarmament Conference as evidence that Britain and France were weak, that they would do little to thwart his determination to rearm and acquire *Lebensraum* in the East. That assumption was put to the test in the spring of 1935, when on March 9 Hitler suddenly announced his intention to build an air force and hinted darkly that the process was already well under way. A week later he informed the international community that he would create a mass army of half a million troops. Germany would also introduce compulsory military service, a move explicitly forbidden by the Versailles settlement. These measures were a direct challenge to the Western powers, but they were, as usual, presented as purely defensive moves; surely, Hitler argued, Germany had the right of self-defense.

The international response was swift and daunting. In April, French foreign minister Pierre Laval and British prime minister Ramsay MacDonald joined Mussolini in the Italian city of Stresa to discuss Germany's threat to peace and stability in Europe. Their immediate aim was to reaffirm the independence of Austria, and the closing Stresa communiqué censured

Germany and declared the signatories' determination to forcefully oppose any unilateral alteration of the Versailles Treaty and the 1926 Locarno Pact according to which Germany recognized its postwar western borders.

The Stresa Front was a sobering reminder to Hitler of his virtually complete diplomatic isolation and prompted a new fusillade of reassuring rhetoric meant to defuse a potentially dangerous situation. "The government of today's German Reich will continue to do what [is] in its power to promote the cause of peace," he told an American journalist. Striking a note of great solemnity, he declared that the German government pledges "never to step beyond the bounds of preserving German honor and the freedom of the Reich and in particular shall never make of the German national arms an instrument of warlike aggression, but an instrument confined exclusively to defense and thereby to the preservation of peace."

While Hitler's dramatic announcement was unsettling to Germany's neighbors, the reaction at home was enthusiastic. "All Munich was on its feet," the Social Democratic underground reported, when Hitler arrived in the city on March 17. The jubilation that greeted Hitler's appearance in Munich that day surpassed even the wild frenzy that accompanied the call for general mobilization in August 1914. "I experienced the days of 1914," one agent reported, "and can only say that the declaration of war didn't have the impact that Hitler's reception [made] on March 17. . . . You can force a people to sing but you can't force them to sing with such enthusiasm."

That mood of patriotic exhilaration, however, soon gave way to a more sober assessment of the situation. Many, especially older Germans whose memories of the slaughter and privations of 1914–18 were still vivid, were convinced that the British and French would never permit such defiance and that war was now an inevitability. Fears were already widespread that Hitler's determination to rearm would plunge Europe into an arms race that would create the same volatile situation as on the eve of the Great War. An arms buildup was already under way in England and France, and Russia had "strengthened its army by 30 percent." In spite of such worries, the underground concluded that "the mass of the people doubtless views the reintroduction of universal military service as a desirable good, since the victors, aside from England, were determined to hold that right for themselves while denying it to Germany." Younger Germans in particular remained convinced that despite the dangers, the Führer had restored Germany's honor and had scored a great diplomatic victory. Hitler's popularity soared. As the SPD underground organization Sopade glumly reported, "he is loved by many."

Within six weeks, the Stresa Front, so imposing on paper, was already beginning to fray. The first sign of trouble came in May and from an unexpected source. Hitler had appointed Joachim von Ribbentrop as a special ambassador to London, bypassing Neurath's Foreign Office, a move symptomatic of Hitler's predilection for ad hoc or parallel appointments. Ribbentrop would report not to the Foreign Office but directly to Hitler. The ambitious Ribbentrop was convinced that some sort of arrangement with Britain could be reached on armaments questions—especially naval strength. The Foreign Office thought this highly unlikely, and was privately hoping that Ribbentrop would fall flat on his face. An international conference on naval matters was scheduled for London in June, but before it convened, Hitler made a proposal to Britain on naval armaments, and London responded immediately. Formal Anglo-German talks began in Berlin on June 4, with Ribbentrop presiding.

Hitler offered a bilateral pact under which Britain would agree to expanded German naval construction, and the Reich in turn would limit its tonnage to 35 percent of Britain's. It also allowed for German submarine construction to amount to 45 percent of the navies of the British Commonwealth. The negotiations were left in Ribbentrop's hands. The Foreign Office was not involved. Ribbentrop, whose arrogance was matched only by his blundering tactlessness, surprised the British by bluntly informing them that this was Germany's final offer and was not open to negotiation. After hesitating for a day, the British agreed to sign. To London it was clear that Hitler was intent on building not only an air force and army but also a high-seas battle fleet. Determined to hold German rearmament within limits and to avoid a debilitating arms race, Britain shocked its French ally on June 18 by concluding a separate naval treaty with the Third Reich—and on Hitler's terms.

The rationale guiding Britain's policy was to meet what it considered legitimate German demands, demands that were consistent with international law and based on the Reich's just desire for arms equality. Many in the British policy elite had come to the conclusion that the Versailles Treaty, especially the armaments clauses and certain territorial arrangements, were, indeed, unfair and had inflicted considerable damage on postwar efforts at international cooperation in Europe. Britain would, therefore, endeavor to meet Germany's legitimate demands, hoping to entangle the Germans in a thicket of treaties and international commitments that would limit German rearmament and severely restrict Hitler's freedom of action. London was convinced that military intervention to prevent German rearmament was out of the question, that it was best to agree to Germany's reasonable terms. To the British, the Anglo-German Naval Agreement of June 1935 was strategically sensible and politically pragmatic. To the French it was betrayal.

The Anglo-German Naval Agreement was a coup for Ribbentrop, whose influence with Hitler and in foreign affairs was on the rise. To Hitler, Ribbentrop's aggressive approach to international relations more fully reflected National Socialism's revolutionary dynamism than the over-cautious orientation of the professionals. Since 1934 Ribbentrop had operated an independent organization whose activities paralleled those of the Foreign Office. The Büro Ribbentrop remained largely independent of the Foreign Office, competed with it, and exploited every opportunity to usurp its role in the formulation and execution of foreign policy. The result was that the foreign policy of Nazi Germany was increasingly characterized by a system of parallel competing institutions and individuals—an organizational modus operandi symptomatic of the Third Reich.

The Anglo-German Naval Agreement represented the high-water mark of Hitler's efforts to woo the British into a closer relationship, perhaps even an alliance. He had long believed that Britain and Germany were natural allies. Their interests were compatible and, to Hitler, immanently compelling. Germany would support Britain's imperial interests around the globe, while Britain would recognize Germany's preeminence on the European continent. The Royal Navy would ensure that Germany was not vulnerable to blockade, and Britain would recognize the Third Reich as a force for stability on the continent and a bulwark against Bolshevism. It was obvious to Hitler and Ribbentrop that the interests of the two countries were also compatible for a more profound reason—they were "of common racial stock."

Britain wasn't the only weak link in the Stresa Front. In June 1935 Italy invaded Abyssinia, a first step in Mussolini's grandiose ambition to reestablish the Roman Empire in the Mediterranean. Italian troops quickly crushed the outnumbered and poorly equipped forces of Haile Selassie and occupied the country, an act of naked aggression that brought swift censure and sanctions from the League of Nations. Britain and France were especially vocal in their condemnation of Mussolini's action and voted for sanctions. Hitler, on the other hand, saw in the situation an opportunity to draw closer to the Duce, who remained suspicious of Nazi ambitions in southeastern Europe. While proclaiming a neutral stance, Hitler applauded Mussolini's defiance of the League and the Western powers, and refused to join in the League's measures. Instead, he offered Mussolini economic support in the face of sanctions. Most important, he saw in the Abyssinian War an opportunity to exploit the widening rift between Mussolini and his Stresa partners and to demonstrate his support for Fascist Italy.

His courting of Mussolini bore fruit in the following year, when Germany intervened, along with Italy, to support Francisco Franco in his military rebellion against the Spanish Republic. Hitler dispatched some seven thousand military advisors to Spain and provided Franco's forces with armaments and air support. The conflict in Spain also offered an opportunity to field-test new German aircraft and other heavy weapons. With two devastating attacks against the Spanish cities of Durango and Guernica, the latter inspiring Pablo Picasso's savage painting of the same name, the German Luftwaffe tested the efficacy of aerial bombardment. While Britain and France stood by, unwilling to invest significant support in the Republican cause, the Soviets rose to the occasion, sending aid to the faltering Republican forces. But their intervention was too little to save the Republic. Meanwhile Mussolini, though still mistrustful of Hitler's motives, was grateful for Germany's display of solidarity. The Stresa Front was dead.

With the Stresa Front in shambles, France cast about for more reliable allies and began negotiations for a mutual aid pact with the Soviet Union. The deal was signed on February 27, 1936, and Hitler immediately denounced the treaty, declaring that France had now introduced the Bolshevik state into the heart of Europe, upsetting the established power arrangements in Western Europe. And besides, Soviet Russia wasn't like other states; it was "the exponent of a revolutionary political and philosophical system" and "its creed" was "world revolution." The Franco-Soviet Pact was directly aimed at Germany, he insisted, and by concluding a military alliance with the Soviet Union, France had fatally undermined the Locarno Treaty. Given its pact with Czechoslovakia and now the Soviet Union, France, Hitler contended, was tightening a noose around the neck of the defenseless Reich.

In the face of such "provocations," Hitler decided to take bold action. He alerted General Werner von Fritsch, commander-in-chief of the army, that he intended to send German troops into the demilitarized Rhineland. Based on their feeble response to his announcement of rearmament in 1935, Hitler was convinced that neither Britain nor France would take military action to enforce the treaty. Fritsch did not share this sanguine view, and both he and Minister of War Werner von Blomberg strongly opposed such a risky undertaking. German rearmament, they reminded the Führer, was still in its early stages, and military commanders were acutely aware of France's vast military superiority. If the French sent so much as a single division into the Rhineland, Blomberg believed, they would easily rout the German troops there and force the Wehrmacht into a humiliating retreat. If Hitler could not be convinced to scrap his reckless plan, then they suggested perhaps a largely symbolic action could be undertaken—an incursion into the Demilitarized Zone, a one-day occupation of certain key points on the west bank of the Rhine, and then a withdrawal.

Hitler was not to be moved. In a memorandum to his generals, he insisted that Germany had no choice but to assert "its fundamental right . . . to secure its frontiers and ensure its possibilities of defense." Then, speaking before a hastily called Reichstag on March 7, 1936, he made a dramatic announcement: at that very moment, he informed the deputies, German troops were marching across the Rhine bridges, streaming into the Rhineland, occupying Cologne, Saarbrücken, Aachen, and other key points. "The German Government has today restored the full sovereignty of Germany in the demilitarized zone of the Rhineland." Wild cheering resounded through the crowded chamber.

Before the powers could respond, Hitler issued the by now predictable appeal to peaceable reason. He proposed the creation of a demilitarized zone on both sides of the Rhine; the conclusion of a twenty-five-year non-aggression pact between Germany, France, and Belgium, with Italy and Britain serving as guarantors of the agreement. He also floated a plan to minimize the danger of air attack, a nonaggression pact with Germany's eastern neighbors; and, since the Reich's equality of rights and full sovereignty over its territory had been restored, Germany was prepared to rejoin the League of Nations. Finally, he declared that henceforth Germany had "no territorial claims to put forward in Europe."

The French lodged a stern protest, as did the League of Nations, but, significantly, Britain did not join them. It was, after all, German territory, and it broke no international law. France vastly overestimated the number of German forces in the operation, fooled by the numerous police units that marched along with the military. The response, in other words, was largely as Hitler anticipated. He had ignored his generals and gambled, and the gamble had paid off. He had correctly read the international situation, had predicted the British and French response, and taken bold action over the objections of the generals.

The remilitarization of the Rhineland had momentous consequences. It fatally weakened the credibility of France's Eastern European alliance system. As long as the Rhineland was a demilitarized zone, French troops could march swiftly into Germany and occupy the Reich's industrial heartland. That threat alone would serve to restrain German ambitions in the East. Now that deterrent was gone. The occupation of the Rhineland also dealt another body blow to the League of Nations, one of several it suffered between 1935 and 1939, and the most significant. League sanctions had failed to deter Mussolini in Abyssinia or Spain, and in 1937 Japan simply ignored the League's censure when it invaded China and withdrew from the organization.

Perhaps as important, the seizure of the Rhineland also further eroded the confidence of Germany's military commanders in their own professional judgment. It would not be the last time. Could it be that this crude, uneducated former corporal understood the international array of forces better than they? In prevailing over his generals, the remilitarization of the Rhineland boosted Hitler's already colossal confidence in the superiority of his instinct-driven decisions. Intuition had prevailed over the caution of the professional diplomats and military men. Always aloof, in 1936 Hitler became more unapproachable, more convinced of the infallibility of his views. Brimming with self-confidence, he became virtually immune to differing opinions, whether from the party, the Wehrmacht, or the Foreign Office. From his boyhood days with his friend August Kubizek, Hitler could never abide objections to his ideas, never allowing reference to inconvenient realities to intrude into his hermetically sealed world of illusion. As he told a crowd in Munich, "I go the way that Providence dictates with the assurance of a sleepwalker."

To these dramatic foreign policy victories came the spectacular success of the 1936 Olympic Games in Berlin and Garmisch. Lavish preparations had been under way in the capital for over a year. Visitors found an enormous 100,000-seat stadium, the largest in the world, monumental statuary, flag-lined boulevards flanked by cheering crowds. Visitors were to have a good time. Bands played American music; dance halls overflowed; beer gardens flourished; and seven thousand prostitutes, who had only recently been swept off the streets, were allowed to return. The regime had ordered the removal of anti-Jewish signs from shop windows, and delivered strict orders to party officials to desist from harassing Jews in public. Many foreign visitors left impressed by the display of Nazi organization and the elaborate orchestration of the games. The Germans they saw seemed so happy, so prosperous, so proud. Where were signs of the brutal street violence, midnight arrests, anti-Semitism, and concentration camps? Many departed wondering if the horror stories they had read about Nazi oppression and brutality, especially directed at the Jews, could really be true.

Adding to the sense of German pride was the outcome of the games. Despite African American Jesse Owens's awesome achievements in track and field—he took four gold medals—Germany won the Olympic medal count, accumulating more gold, silver, and bronze than the favored United States, an achievement the Nazi propaganda machine never tired of touting. Contrary to popular belief, which tends to focus on Hitler's putative embarrassment by Jesse Owens's spectacular victories, the games represented a tremendous public relations triumph for the Third Reich. The world had come to Berlin, and Germany, under National Socialist leadership, had regained its rightful status as a great international power.

Following the Olympics, the "Jews Not Wanted" signs resurfaced, and the Nazis resumed their campaign against "the world Jewish conspiracy." At the same time, the regime escalated its anti-Soviet agitation, and the two themes merged into one. At the Nuremberg party rally in September, Goebbels unleashed a fiery diatribe against Bolshevist terror in Spain and Russia. Who was responsible for this peril? It was the Jew, "the inspirer, the author, and the beneficiary of this terrible catastrophe: look, this is the enemy of the world, the destroyer of cultures, the parasite among the nations, the son of chaos, the incarnation of evil, the ferment of decomposition, the visible demon of the decay of humanity." On the final day of the rally, Hitler underscored the pernicious link between this world Jewish conspiracy and ruinous Bolshevism. The National Socialist state was locked in battle with that dual threat; it was not an ordinary battle but "a struggle for the very essence of human culture and civilization. . . . What others profess not to see because they simply do not want to see it, is something we must unfortunately state as a bitter truth: the world is presently in the midst of an increasing upheaval, whose spiritual and factual preparation and whose leadership undoubtedly proceed from the rulers of Jewish Bolshevism."

Building on that theme and working without the knowledge of the Foreign Office, Ribbentrop engineered a treaty with Japan aimed at the looming Bolshevist menace. Although the agreement, signed on November 26, did not explicitly mention the Soviet Union, focusing instead on the Moscow-directed Communist International (Comintern), the real target was the Soviet Union. Both Japan and Germany recognized "that the aim of the Communist International . . . is to disintegrate and subdue existing states by all the means at its command." They further agreed that "the toleration of interference by the Communist International in the internal affairs of the nations not only endangers their internal peace and social well-being, but is also a menace to the peace of the world desirous of co-operating in the defense against Communist subversive activities." The parties pledged to assume a position of benevolent neutrality should one become involved in a war with another power, but beyond that, the Anti-Comintern Pact offered little that was concrete. Its value was in propaganda, a sign of Germany's growing global influence.

By year's end Hitler could point to an impressive string of accomplishments—the stunning foreign policy successes, the Olympic Games, and a striking economic recovery, albeit an uneven, shallow one. By 1936 Germany was enjoying full employment, and predictions circulated that Germany would face a labor shortage in the near future. But beneath the surface of these triumphs lurked a serious and escalating problem, one that threatened to undermine the regime's successes. Since 1934 rearmament was proceeding at an ever-accelerating pace, and military demands on the economy were growing by the month. By winter 1936 rationing had been put in place on many consumer items. The rising price of food, especially meat, led to considerable grumbling. William Shirer, an American journalist stationed in Berlin, reported in his diary that he had seen "long lines of sullen people before the food shops, that there is a shortage of meat and butter and fruit and fats, that whipped cream is *verboten*, that men's suits and women's dresses are increasingly being made out of wood pulp, gasoline out of coal, rubber out of coal and lime; that there is no coverage for the Reichsmark or for anything else, not even for vital imports." Already in the summer of 1935, state police officials in the Münster district were reporting that "the dissatisfaction mentioned over the past months has not abated but escalated. The cause is the tough economic situation that shows no sign of a quick turnaround, and can be traced back to higher prices and shortages of food." The manifestations of that rising discontent could really "only be seen in the palpable passivity of a great portion of the population toward the movement and its events." The reasons for this disenchantment could be found "in the great poverty of a large portion of the population which stands in stark contrast to the grand style of certain offices of the party and state."

It was growing increasingly clear to policymakers that the Third Reich faced an intractable dilemma: to build the military machine Hitler desired, Germany needed to import vast quantities of raw materials. To pay for these imports the Reich needed hard currency. Exports, primarily of consumer goods, had previously provided the bulk of that hard currency, but with an ever-increasing share of the economy being devoured by the military, production of consumer goods began a steep decline in 1935 and steadily gathered momentum. The man Hitler called on to manage his ambitious rearmament program was Reichsbank president Hjalmar Schacht. Appointed minister of economics in June 1934, Schacht was an internationally recognized financial wizard, and the task before him was to find the funds necessary for Hitler's ambitious rearmament plans. Schacht fully supported Hitler's desire to rearm and devised a system of off-budget financing to increase military spending that would avoid detection from

Germany's neighbors. Using a variety of financial and foreign trade strategies to fund (and disguise) Germany's rearmament in 1933 and 1934, Schacht had managed to lay the economic foundation for the military's expansion. His "New Plan" called for rearmament that would unfold in two phases, each phase taking roughly four years. The initial phase called for the creation of a defensive army, capable of protecting the Reich from all possible enemies. The second phase would be devoted to developing offensive capabilities, tanks, and other armored vehicles.

But the Wehrmacht, with Hitler's wholehearted approval, was impatient. Its demands for raw materials escalated steadily in 1934 and 1935, and astronomically thereafter. In November 1935 Minister of War Blomberg informed all the service chiefs that they were no longer to concern themselves with costs and to order anything they needed. The response was swift. In the following month the army added forty-eight tank battalions to its projected thirty-six divisions, adding an offensive capability that Schacht's plan had not foreseen until 1938. The air force also scheduled a vast expansion of its strength from forty-eight squadrons in 1935 to over two hundred by October 1938, and the navy was quick to follow suit. By 1936 military spending dominated the German economy and continued to climb; by 1938 the military accounted for 80 percent of the goods and services purchased by the Reich.

For Schacht this was altogether too much too soon. In a series of increasingly frank memoranda and meetings with Hitler, Schacht tried to impress upon the Führer that the German economy simply could not cope with such demands. The Wehrmacht desperately needed ever-greater supplies of raw materials, especially iron, rubber, and oil, and needed them as soon as possible. Other states, jolted into action by Germany's feverish rearmament, had begun to increase their military spending. There was no time to waste. The problem, as Schacht tried to explain, was that Germany lacked the necessary hard currency to procure the needed goods. Autarky had possibilities but was not the answer. Germany needed to rejoin the world economy and export. If the regime persisted in its massive rearmament and at this accelerated pace, the economy would simply implode.

To prevent an economic catastrophe, Germany must either slow the pace of rearmament or temporarily halt it. Schacht was not reticent in presenting this gloomy prognostication to Hitler, which he pressed with ever greater bluntness. Unaccustomed to hearing such direct criticism and uninterested in either of Schacht's unpalatable options, Hitler turned a deaf ear to such worries. He did not want to hear about the laws of economics as Schacht saw them and was not at all concerned about *how* the raw materials were acquired, just that they were. His overarching goal was preparation for war, and he was not about to let troublesome economic realities stand in his way. He would brook no criticism, even from his experts. The economy was there to serve the regime, to provide the state with what it required to realize its goal, and that goal was war. By 1936 he had grown weary of the economics minister's pessimism and bleak forebodings. "He must go," Goebbels noted in his diary. "He is a cancerous shadow on our politics."

In July, Hitler removed Schacht from his post as economics minister and forced him to take a leave of absence as director of the Reichsbank. Schacht would remain a member of the cabinet and continued to express his objections to the course of German economic planning, but Hitler wasn't listening. He needed someone to lead the economy who would not be deterred by economic "inconveniences" but would make his preparations for war with ruthlessness and energy. That man was Hermann Göring. At the Nuremberg party rally in September 1936, Hitler announced a new Four Year Plan that would make Germany militarily and economically prepared for war within four years. He also revealed the creation of a new ad hoc organization that would assume command of the economy. Göring would lead this Office of the Four Year Plan, and his mission was abundantly clear: he was not to worry about the balance of payments, currency issues, foreign trade, or civilian needs; his job was to ensure the Reich's preparedness for war within four years, whatever the costs. Hitler was aware of the privations being forced on the German people, but could only state that the people should be prepared to sacrifice for the good of the nation.

In December, Göring spelled out the dire situation to a gathering of industrialists. Germany was engaged in a life-or-death struggle, and "no end of rearmament is in sight. The struggle which we are approaching demands a colossal measure of productive ability." It mattered not if every investment could be amortized. "The whole deciding point to this case is victory or destruction. If we win, then business will be sufficiently compensated. . . . We are now playing for the highest stakes . . . All selfish interests must be put aside. Our whole nation is at stake. We live in a time when the final battles are in sight. We are already on the threshold of mobilization and are at war, only the guns are not yet firing."

Under Göring's management of the economy, a dramatic surge in military spending, astronomical in scope, began. To raise and equip an army of roughly three and a half million troops in only four years, large parts of German industry would have to be retooled; other manufacturing plants brought on line; workers retrained. The economy would be stretched to the limit—and beyond. By 1940 the army was to be a fully equipped fighting force of 102 divisions and more than 3.6 million men. At least five thousand tanks were to be produced in the same time frame. The Luftwaffe also issued an order that its forces should be at full strength by 1937, a full year ahead of schedule, adding more complications for economic planning. Wehrmacht thinking was no longer focused on defensive considerations but on a force trained and equipped for offensive operations.

This massive military buildup imposed serious strains on the economy. Aside from the currency and balance of payments problems, for which there was no obvious financial solution, there was the looming question of what was to happen when this massive flood of spending subsided, when the factories had filled all their orders and the production targets had been met. Would the armaments factories then function at half time, lay off millions of workers, or close their doors? If this rapacious military machine was not to be used in the near future, would armaments production at the same pace be necessary? Although the Nazis did not trouble themselves very much about such long-range questions, they had, in fact, created an economy that was based on war and expansion. As economic historian Adam Tooze has aptly put it, "War now had to be contemplated not as an option, but as the logical consequence of the preparations being made."

The year 1937 was bereft of any major foreign policy crisis, and yet amid all the frenzied military and economic activity, an air of nervousness prevailed. The Socialist underground reported that "more than ever all strata of the population are filled with the worry that war is imminent." That fear was heightened in September when the regime conducted air raid drills in Berlin, blacking out the city for three consecutive nights. Other cities were encouraged to do the same. The Socialist underground reported that "the Four-Year-Plan, the rationing of food supplies, the deployment orders for the event of a general mobilization, the heightened activity of air defense, the involvement of Germany in Spain, and the boundless agitation against the Soviet Union—all this provides constant nourishment for the war psychosis." Women in the National Socialist Women's Organization were "being trained to take over men's jobs," and "in recent months the Hitler Youth has introduced special training afternoons, during which the youths practiced throwing hand grenades and firing machine guns."

Hitler needed some sort of foreign policy success, some new surprise or dramatic exhibition of Nazi dynamism to reignite the people's enthusiasm. He decided to host a lavish state visit by Mussolini to demonstrate the newfound solidarity between Germany and Italy. Preparations on the usual Nazi scale were undertaken. For three days in late October, the Duce was saluted, celebrated, and cheered by excited crowds that greeted him wherever he appeared. Mussolini was impressed. The visit culminated on a rainy night in Berlin, when the Führer and Duce gave speeches effusively touting Fascist solidarity to a rain-soaked crowd of 62,000 on the Maifeld. It was, a rapturous Goebbels believed, the largest crowd Mussolini had ever addressed. The stadium was bathed "in a magical light . . . Unfortunately much rain. But what does that matter on this night! I am completely happy."

Nothing concrete was achieved during the visit and potential problems still remained between the two regimes, especially over the status of Austria, but both powers considered the visit a spectacular success. Mussolini returned to Rome impressed with German power, organization, and Hitler himself. For his part, Hitler could feel that Germany was no longer isolated in Europe. Shortly after the visit, on November 6, Ribbentrop announced that Italy had joined the Anti-Comintern Pact, making for a Rome-Berlin-Tokyo axis of power, an apparent sign of Germany's global reach.

It was under these circumstances that on November 5, 1937, Hitler convened a meeting of his top military commanders in the Reich Chancellery. The purpose of the meeting was ostensibly to settle mounting disagreements between the different branches of the armed forces over the allocation of increasingly scarce raw materials. Present in this small circle were Göring, in his dual capacity as head of the Four Year Plan and as commander of the Luftwaffe; Blomberg, minister of war; Fritsch, Commander; and chief-of-staff of the army, and Admiral Erich Raeder, supreme commander of the navy. Foreign Minister Constantin von Neurath was also in attendance, as was Hitler's military attaché, Friedrich Hossbach. Raeder, whose complaints about steel allocations had prompted the meeting, was particularly galled by what he considered the preferential treatment given to Göring's Luftwaffe—a grievance shared by Blomberg and other service chiefs. Raeder hoped that Hitler would resolve the dispute. Instead, and typically for Hitler, the Führer did not address the issue at hand until late in his presentation and then only fleetingly. To the surprise of his listeners, he launched into a lengthy monologue on foreign and economic policy, providing a sweeping overview of his strategic thinking. His demeanor was grim. This would be no blustery propaganda speech.

"The aim of German policy," Hitler began, was "to make secure and preserve the racial community and to enlarge it." Preservation of "the German racial core" was, above all, a question of space. Lack of *Lebensraum* represented "the greatest danger to the German race," and securing Germany's future was "wholly conditional on solving the issue of space." Over the next three hours, he assessed Germany's economic options, particularly with regard to raw materials. Tin, steel, rubber, and oil were of course essential, but the food supply drew his greatest attention. Although some gains had been made, especially in the area of synthetics, the policy of pure autarky could not solve Germany's food problems. Nor could a return to world trade, an oblique swipe at Schacht's position. Expansion was the only realistic solution, as it had been for the great empires from the Romans to Frederick the Great to Bismarck. "Germany's problem could only be solved by force and this was never without attendant risk. The only real question was 'when and how.'"

Germany's first objective was to secure its southern and eastern flanks, and that meant seizing Czechoslovakia and Austria. Austria should be absorbed, if possible without military conflict, but the Czechs deserved no such consideration. "*Die Tschechi,*" as Hitler and the Nazis referred to Czechoslovakia, was an illegitimate state, created by the victors at Versailles. It was rich in raw materials and would simply disappear into the German Reich. Hitler then reviewed the strengths and weaknesses of the major powers and their likely responses to an act of German aggression. Britain and its empire were weaker than widely assumed and did not represent a serious threat; France would not act without Britain. Poland would not intervene alone, and if the German offensive was "lightning fast," Russia would stay on the sidelines. Bolshevik Russia posed a long-term threat but, confronted by a fait accompli, would not take action. Italy, despite some difficulties regarding Austria, would be a reliable ally.

With the other powers increasing their own military spending in response to Germany's massive rearmament, the Reich could not afford a lengthy delay. Germany must act soon or lose its momentary advantage. It was his unalterable resolve that at the very latest the German economy and armed forces must be ready to act by 1943–45 or earlier if circumstances were favorable. At the conclusion of his presentation, the issue of resource allocation among the services was briefly addressed and resolved to Raeder's satisfaction. But after the Führer's remarkable talk, that question slipped distinctly into the background.

The small circle of listeners was shocked by what they heard. Although the generals were certainly familiar with the basic thrust of Hitler's ideas, never before had he laid them out so directly and so exhaustively. If they were taken aback by Hitler's presentation, they were just as surprised when he solicited their comments. He listened attentively, sometimes jotting down notes, as Generals Fritsch and Blomberg raised serious objections. They were not opposed to the idea of *Lebensraum*, but they were stunned that Hitler was considering a course of action that would certainly lead to war not only with Czechoslovakia but with Britain and France—a war for which the Wehrmacht was ill prepared. Hitler did not interrupt or try to dissuade them—Göring was left to respond to their criticisms—but he must have been disappointed. He was not accustomed to dissent and certainly not the sharpness of their objections.

No formal minutes were taken, and the only record of the proceedings are the notes written several days later by Colonel Hossbach. In the Hossbach Memorandum, many historians have seen a clear blueprint for action, an actual plan for German aggression. Others have claimed that Hitler's speech was merely a *tour d'horizon*, a typical diversionary tactic to avoid having to address the armaments issue. But Hitler carried notes with him for the meeting, although he did not refer to them, and he displayed his famous memory for details. Hitler's performance that day may have been an effort to avoid taking a side in the interservice dispute, but it seems more likely that his talk was a genuine effort to convince the generals of his vision. He clearly expected them to be carried along with him. Instead, the meeting ended with disagreement and harsh language.

Blomberg left the meeting so disturbed that he requested a meeting with Hitler the next day. After consulting with Fritsch, he attempted once again to persuade Hitler to drop what the military men saw as reckless thinking that would drive Germany into a major war. The meeting was stormy, and Hitler would not be persuaded. Neurath, equally alarmed at Hitler's overly optimistic assessment of the international situation and his conviction that Britain and France would not intervene, also sought a meeting with the Führer, but Hitler brushed him off, refusing to see him until mid-January. Slow to come to decisions, Hitler rarely changed his mind once he had made them. As Ribbentrop later remarked, "it would have been easier to shift Mont Blanc than to get the Führer to reverse a decision."

Within three months, Blomberg, Fritsch, and Neurath were forced out, and although it is often treated as a well-designed purge, the circumstances were quite different and unanticipated in each case. Blomberg was the first to fall. In January, the general married a young woman thirty-five years his junior. Blomberg sought Hitler's approval, worrying that his fellow officers would shun her. She was a common shopgirl, a girl of the people. And, indeed, the army through the person of General Fritsch did protest that such a match was intolerable. Hitler was indignant at the snobbishness of the officer class—didn't they know that there were no classes in the Third Reich? He even volunteered to serve as witness to the wedding and dragged Göring along as well. The wedding was a small, private affair and took place in the tender atmosphere of the War Ministry.

While the happy couple was vacationing, the Gestapo discovered disturbing evidence that the new Frau Blomberg was a woman with a past. They produced police files that revealed that the young bride had at one time been arrested for prostitution and that she had posed for pornographic photographs, taken, to make matters even more intolerable, by a Jewish photographer with whom she was living. Hitler, Goebbels noted, was "shattered" by these discoveries: "If a German Field Marshal marries a whore," the Führer said in disbelief, "then anything in the world is possible." The only honorable way out for Blomberg, Goebbels asserted, was the pistol. But Blomberg was a longtime Hitler supporter, and the Führer was reluctant to part with him. Unwilling to face the disgraced Blomberg under these awkward circumstances, he dispatched Göring to make the general an offer. If Blomberg would agree to annul the marriage, he would be permitted to remain at his post; if not, he would be compelled to leave. To the consternation of one and all, Blomberg refused to part with his bride and submitted his resignation.

The reverberations of the Blomberg affair were still resounding when a second scandal rocked the military. In vetting General Fritsch for the post of chief of staff of the army some three years earlier, the Gestapo had unearthed allegations that Fritsch had had a homosexual encounter with a young man from the Hitler Youth. Fritsch was a highly respected officer with an unblemished record. He categorically denied the allegations, and no charges were filed. The matter seemed settled. But with the Blomberg scandal in full bloom, Heydrich produced the earlier case file, and a new investigation was launched. The evidence gathered by the Gestapo was at best unreliable. Yet, pressed by Goebbels and Himmler, Hitler was convinced that the army, indeed, the regime, could not afford another high-profile scandal. He would not let the matter drop. Vehemently denying the charges, Fritsch resigned under pressure on February 3 but demanded a military court-martial, which Hitler reluctantly granted. On March 18 Fritsch was acquitted—it proved to be a case of mistaken identity, which Himmler and Heydrich had known for some time—but the damage was done. Fritsch was allowed to retain his rank but was removed from the command hierarchy and allowed to rejoin his old artillery unit.

The purge was not over. In the following days Hitler relieved fourteen generals and reassigned forty-six senior officers, many of whom were known to be less than committed to National Socialism. He tapped General Walther von Brauchitsch to replace Fritsch, and he rebuffed the efforts of both Göring and Himmler to succeed Blomberg as minister of war. As a consolation prize, he promoted Göring to the rank of Reich marshal. To complete the reshuffling of his military command, Hitler abolished the post of war minister and anointed himself Supreme Commander of the Armed Forces (*Oberkommando der Wehrmacht* or OKW), giving him formal control over Germany's entire military establishment. Wilhelm Keitel, a desk general known for his pliability, became chief of staff of the OKW, and General Alfred Jodl assumed the post of chief of operations. Resentment in the army ran high.

Neurath did not escape the wave of dismissals. On February 6, 1938, Hitler dismissed his foreign minister. It hardly came as a surprise. A conservative holdover from the Schleicher government, he had been a reassuring presence for the old conservative elites, who viewed him as a restraining influence on Hitler. But by 1938, his cautious approach to diplomacy was increasingly out of step with the aggressive policies now being pursued by the regime. His influence had diminished steadily since 1935, gnawed away by the peripatetic Ribbentrop and his organization. Cleaning house of the old guard, Hitler also dismissed conservative ambassadors to Rome and Tokyo, along with Franz von Papen, who had served as German ambassador in Vienna since 1934. It was to Ribbentrop that Hitler turned to replace Neurath.

The haughty Ribbentrop was almost universally disliked by other Nazi leaders, but he had steadily gained in influence with Hitler since the Anglo-German Naval Agreement, moving from the periphery of power in 1933 to its center five years later. Supremely confident of his own views and impervious to criticism, he was convinced that he understood the Führer's wishes and eagerly took them up as his own. As French ambassador François-Poncet observed, Ribbentrop seemed determined to be "more Hitlerian than Hitler," reinforcing Hitler's most bellicose tendencies. Ribbentrop had a talent for ascertaining Hitler's policy desires and then telling him exactly what he wanted to hear. In this symbiotic relationship, Hitler, not surprisingly, thought his new foreign minister brilliant.

The circumstances that led to the dismissals of Blomberg and Fritsch were unanticipated, hardly part of a carefully planned purge, but the upshot of their sacking, combined with the removal of Schacht and Neurath, was to leave Hitler in unfettered control of Germany's military, economic, and foreign establishments. His power was absolute. With little to restrain him, the Third Reich entered a new, radical phase in both foreign and domestic policy. It began unexpectedly in February 1938 when Kurt von Schuschnigg, the chancellor of Austria, cast about for a strategy to deal with an increasingly threatening Germany. In July 1936 Schuschnigg had agreed to a treaty with Germany that called for the Reich to recognize full Austrian sovereignty, to abstain from interference in Austria's domestic affairs, and for Austria to follow a policy "that was at all times in conformity with the fact that Austria considers itself a German state." But by 1938 he was becoming anxious about mounting Nazi agitation in Austria and about Hitler's menacing foreign policy posture. Within the Reich government, Göring was aggressively calling for the absorption of Austria. Acting in his capacity as head of the Four Year Plan, he pressed for a customs union with Austria and a coordination of the Austrian economy with that of Germany. Incorporation of Austria into the Reich would be even better, bringing Austria's rich iron deposits and skilled workforce into the Four Year Plan.

Austria found itself increasingly isolated, and Nazi agitation was increasing. In 1934, in the aftermath of the failed Nazi Putsch, Italy had pledged to act as a guarantor of Austrian sovereignty, but with the improved relations between Italy and Germany, Mussolini had begun to drift away from that commitment. In talks with Austrian representatives he insisted that Italy's position had not changed, that Italy still strongly favored an independent Austria, but he also intimated that this was essentially an internal German issue, a matter to be dealt with by the two German states. Perhaps, he suggested, the most fruitful course of action was a bit of face-to-face diplomacy, allowing the leaders of the two German states to talk through their difficulties. For some time, Schuschnigg had himself been interested in such a meeting, and others, in both the Austrian and German governments, endorsed this idea. Franz von Papen, whom Hitler had just sacked as ambassador to Austria, was sent scurrying back to Vienna to broach the topic with Schuschnigg.

Schuschnigg liked the idea, and Papen eagerly arranged for him to travel to Hitler's Alpine retreat on the Obersalzberg, just across the Austrian border. The meeting was set for February 12. On the night before, the Austrian chancellor arrived at Salzburg. Accompanying him were only his foreign minister and another official. The meeting was to be a secret, low-key encounter to clear the air. The next morning Papen met the small Austrian party at the border and escorted them to Hitler's vastly expanded Berghof, where over the next crisis-laden months so much diplomatic activity was centered. The roads leading from Berchtesgaden to the Berghof were so ice-covered and foggy that the party had to travel in a military tracked vehicle, adding to the pervasive atmosphere of isolation.

The meeting did not go as Schuschnigg had expected. Present in the Berghof he found Ribbentrop and three generals, led by Keitel, who had just flown in from Berlin. After a cold, formal greeting, Schuschnigg was ushered into Hitler's study for a private discussion. There all diplomatic niceties beat a hasty retreat. Hardly giving his guest a chance to speak, Hitler launched into a tirade that lasted two hours. Austria, Hitler began, had never helped Germany; "the whole history of Austria is just one uninterrupted act of treason, and," he added ferociously, "I am absolutely determined to put an end to all this." Schuschnigg made an effort to defend his homeland, but Hitler was not having it. "I have a historic mission and this mission I will fulfill because Providence has destined me to do so, I thoroughly believe in this mission; it is my life." German troops were massing on the Austrian border, merely waiting for his order to begin the invasion. The presence of the three generals, who looked terribly intimidating but said not a word the entire day, was intended to reinforce that ominous threat. At one point during a pause in the meeting, Keitel confessed to one of the Austrian party that he had no idea why he or the other military men were there. It was all theater. "You don't seriously believe you can hold me up for half an hour, do you?" Hitler sneered. "Who knows, perhaps I'll appear some time overnight in Vienna, like a spring storm. Then you'll see something."

After a break for lunch, while Hitler consulted with aides, Schuschnigg was led into a room where Ribbentrop and Papen were waiting for him. There they presented him with a draft of the agreement Germany demanded. Vienna must agree to coordinate its foreign and economic policy with the Reich and to an exchange of army officers. The Austrian government must issue an amnesty for Nazis languishing in its prisons, and all restrictions on the activities of the Austrian Nazis must be lifted. Hitler also demanded the appointment of Arthur Seyss-Inquart, a prominent Nazi sympathizer, as minister of the interior in charge of all Austrian security forces, a move ominously reminiscent of the first step in the Nazis' seizure of power in Germany. When Schuschnigg raised objections to several points, Ribbentrop warned that the agreement must be accepted unconditionally. These measures were not talking points for negotiation, Ribbentrop stressed, but demands, and they must be met immediately. It was an ultimatum.

When later in the afternoon the agreement had been typed up and Schuschnigg and Hitler again sat down together, the Führer reiterated that position. "Here is the draft of the document," he said. "There is nothing to be discussed about it. I will not change one single iota. You will either sign it as it stands or else our meeting has been useless. In that case I shall decide during the night what will be done next." Despite Hitler's bullying rants, Schuschnigg did not give in. He explained that he was willing to sign the draft agreement, but, citing the Austrian constitution, he did not have the authority to act on these matters without the consent of the Austrian president, Wilhelm Miklas. He would sign the document, as Hitler insisted, but the Führer must understand that it meant nothing without the president's signature. He would consult with President Miklas upon his return to Vienna and then communicate with Berlin. Hitler relented. With his generals looming in the background, he informed Schuschnigg that he had decided to change his mind "for the first time in my life. But I warn you," he said, "this is your very last chance. I have given you three more days before the Agreement goes into effect."

Darkness had fallen before a badly shaken Schuschnigg and his party managed to escape back down the mountain into Berchtesgaden and across the border. He mustn't worry, Papen assured him as they rode along, the next meeting would be different. "Now you have seen what the Führer can be like at times." But, he assured Schuschnigg, "the next time it will be different. You know the Führer can be absolutely charming." Having seen Hitler revealed as the gangster that he was, Schuschnigg knew that "there would be no next time. . . . There would be no more discussions about Austria." Of that he was sure. "And I also knew that there was little room for any hope."

In the following days, Schuschnigg turned to Mussolini, Austria's protector, who had no comfort to offer. Neither did France or Britain. With no international support and no viable options short of war, Schuschnigg complied with the terms of the agreement and, despite Miklas's profound reservations, appointed Seyss-Inquart interior minister. But Berlin was impatient. Hitler was scheduled to deliver a major speech on February 20, and was anxious to have the Austrian matter settled. He intended to announce the agreement with Austria, thanking Schuschnigg for his "great understanding and warmhearted readiness" to serve the interests of both countries.

Hitler's speech on that day lasted more than two hours and offered a preview of the themes that would govern Nazi policy in the coming months. Germany was only too aware of "the painful consequences of the confusion introduced to the European map and the economic and political constellation of the peoples by the insane act of Versailles." He lamented that "two of the states at our borders alone encompass a mass of over ten million Germans. . . . Against their own free will, they were prevented from uniting with the Reich by virtue of the peace treaties." That was distressing enough, but this imposed separation could not be allowed to lead to "a situation in which the races are deprived of rights . . . the general rights of *völkisch* self-determination . . . which were solemnly guaranteed to us by Wilson's Fourteen Points." This was a situation that could not be sustained in the long run. "It is unbearable for a world power to know that there are racial comrades at its side being constantly subjected to the most severe suffering because of their sympathy or affiliation with their race, its fate, and its world view."

Though Austria was ostensibly the issue of the day, Hitler was establishing a broader context for his policy, and while not mentioning either country explicitly, the linkage between Austria and Czechoslovakia was obvious. "It cannot be denied that, as long as Germany was powerless and defenseless, it had no choice but to tolerate this unremitting persecution of German beings at its borders." But now that the situation had changed, he saw it as "Germany's duty to protect those German racial comrades who are not, of their own power, in a position to secure for themselves . . . the right of general human, political, and philosophical freedom!"

Hitler's remarks on February 20 seemed to suggest that the Austrian issue was essentially resolved, but in Vienna Schuschnigg had a surprise of his own. While speaking at a mass meeting in Innsbruck on March 9, the Austrian chancellor dropped a bombshell, announcing that a national plebiscite would be held on March 13, only four days away. The people were to vote yes or no on "a free and independent, German and Christian Austria," wording that was bound to alarm the Germans. For a change, it was Hitler who was caught off guard. Beside himself with rage, he informed the army that the die was now cast. A military operation, which he had hoped to avoid, now seemed unavoidable.

From this point, events moved swiftly. Germany immediately protested, demanding postponement of the plebiscite for another two weeks.

A full-blown crisis was upon them, and a pall of uneasiness descended upon the German public. A broad "war psychosis" was everywhere, both the Gestapo and the Social Democratic underground reported. "There was not a trace of enthusiasm as there was in August 1914. On the contrary," the Sopade (Social Democratic Underground) observed, "a great worry, uneasiness, and deep anxiety prevailed. . . . One could hear comments like 'what in the end does Austria matter to us. One should just leave us in peace. Should we become involved in a war over this? What do we get out of it?'"

While the public worried, the Wehrmacht was frantically drafting an operational plan for an invasion of Austria. It was a slapdash, improvised affair. The generals were concerned about the reaction of the Czechs, who in turn were nervous about a possible German attack on their territory. Perhaps they would seize this opportunity to launch a preventive assault on the Reich. Even a mobilization of their troops would threaten the entire operation. Despite these concerns, Hitler, on March 11, issued an order for German troops to move against Austria. The order emphasized that the entire operation must "be conducted without the use of force, in the manner of a peaceful entry, welcomed by the population." However, "if resistance be encountered . . . it is to be broken with utmost ruthlessness by force of arms."

On Friday, March 11, Schuschnigg was awakened at 5:30 a.m. by a phone call from his chief of police. "The German border at Salzburg was closed completely about an hour ago," he said. "All German customs officials have been withdrawn. Railroad traffic has been stopped." A few hours later, Seyss-Inquart informed Schuschnigg that he had been in telephone contact with Göring, who gave orders to inform the Austrian chancellor that "the plebiscite has to be postponed within the hour." Instead, another plebiscite was to be announced. This was to be held in two weeks, in the same fashion but according to wording supplied by the Reich government. Seyss-Inquart was given an hour to respond. If no response was received, Göring would assume that he had been prevented from calling and would take appropriate action.

Meanwhile in some parts of the country Nazi activists had taken to the streets, and trucks, with loudspeakers blaring, had been announcing that Schuschnigg's plebiscite had been canceled. Göring upped the ante. Schuschnigg must resign immediately and Seyss-Inquart be appointed chancellor within two hours. If those conditions were not fulfilled, German troops would cross the frontier into Austria. Almost immediately Göring sent Seyss-Inquart yet another wire, ordering him to dispatch a telegram to Berlin asking for German help to deal with widespread Bolshevik rioting. There was, of course, no rioting by leftists; the only troublemakers in the streets were Nazis. When Seyss-Inquart hesitated, Göring was back on the phone. Don't bother sending Berlin such a message, he said. The troops were already moving. Seyss-Inquart need only *claim* that he had sent such a telegram. Lie compounded by lie, underwritten by threats and blatant gangsterism, was now the modus operandi of Nazi diplomacy.

Hitler did seek to reassure the British and French, who had lodged stern protests, but he expected little serious trouble from either. He had correctly anticipated the reactions of both London and Paris. Neither was willing to go to war over Austria, a country that in 1919 had chosen to be joined with Germany only to have its desire vetoed by the victorious powers. Austria could expect no help from the outside. Meanwhile Nazi agitation in the streets gathered steam. In accordance with Hitler's demands, Nazi prisoners were freed from Austrian jails and returned to their former posts—many within the police, further undermining the authority of the Austrian state. Schuschnigg tried to resign, but Miklas would not accept his resignation. That night the chancellor took to the radio to address the Austrian people.

Schuschnigg explained to his national audience how the situation had developed and called on the international community to bear witness to the fact that Austria had fulfilled the terms of agreement it had signed with Hitler. The Austrian government "protested the threatened violation of our country's sovereignty, which was as uncalled for as it was unjustifiable." Austria, he made clear, was now yielding to force. He was determined at all costs to avoid bloodshed in a fratricidal war. As a consequence an order had been issued to the army not to oppose the invading German forces. He closed his speech with a word of farewell. He had spoken for ten minutes.

President Miklas yielded to the Nazis, but refused to appoint Seyss-Inquart as chancellor, an act of defiance that the Nazis simply brushed aside. On March 12 German motorized units rolled into Austria unopposed. Far from a display of military might, their progress was glacial. One panzer division had no maps and was forced to rely on a Baedeker's guide. Low on fuel, some stopped at gas stations along the way. Many of the tanks and other vehicles broke down. Their armored carcasses littered the roads, blocking traffic in some places. While traffic to the south was snarled, Hess, Himmler, and Heydrich flew into the Vienna aerodrome before dawn. The vanguard of the Gestapo and SD was rushing to the city.

The next day, March 13, Hitler crossed the frontier, standing despite the icy cold in an open car. He had planned to stop briefly at Braunau, his birthplace, before motoring on to Linz, where he spent his boyhood. But in Braunau a large, frenetic crowd of well-wishers had gathered in the town square, and Hitler, deeply moved, responded with a heartfelt speech. In Braunau and all along the road, crowds pressed forward to get a glimpse of the Führer. They cheered; they wept with joy; they brandished Nazi flags and tossed flowers. So thick were the exuberant throngs that Hitler's motorcade could only struggle forward, not reaching Linz until well after nightfall.

There Hitler was greeted by Seyss-Inquart and other leading Nazis as well as another near-hysterical crowd of some 100,000 that had gathered in the town square. He spoke from the balcony of the city hall, his address repeatedly interrupted by chants of *"Sieg Heil"* and *"Ein Volk, ein Reich, ein Führer"* (One people, one Reich, one leader). Overwhelmed by his reception, tears ran down Hitler's cheeks. "If Providence once called me forth from this town to be the leader of the Reich," he shouted, his voice brimming with genuine emotion, "it must in so doing have charged me with a mission, and that mission could only be to restore my dear homeland to the German Reich. I have believed in this mission, I have lived and fought for it, and I believe I have now fulfilled it."

Hitler had planned to carry on to Vienna the next day, but Himmler phoned during the night to suggest that he delay his entry until the SS had completed security arrangements. Hitler spent the following day visiting the old family home and laid flowers on the graves of his parents at Leonding. He quickly toured his old school, where former classmates had gathered to greet him. Everywhere he went, he was showered with adulation. At this point, he still had not decided what was to be the fate of Austria, but his reception in Linz and all along the roadway crystallized his thoughts. Seyss-Inquart and other Nazi leaders who met him in Linz believed that the country would become a National Socialist state, a satellite, but would retain its sovereign status. This had been Hitler's rather vague idea as well. Certainly no formal plans had been made. But Linz changed all that. By the time he reached Vienna late the next day, he had made his decision. Austria would be absorbed by the German Reich.

Hitler's caravan did not reach the Austrian capital until well after dark and stopped at the elegant Hotel Imperial, a favorite of Viennese high society. As a struggling young homeless nobody, he would never have dared enter; now he was shown to the royal suite. Crowds were already gathering outside the hotel, chanting deep into the night for Hitler to appear. Again and again he stepped out onto the balcony and acknowledged them. It had been an overwhelming forty-eight hours. He had come a long way from the soup kitchens and warming rooms and the Home for Men in the Meldemannstrasse.

Next day the scene was even more madly tumultuous than in Linz. The Ringstrasse, whose grand imperial buildings he had so admired as a would-be art student, was lined with delirious supporters, and the gigantic Heldenplatz before the Hofburg, seat of the Austrian government, was a sea of 200,000 flag-waving, jubilant, ecstatic people. When Hitler alighted from his Mercedes and at last reached the balcony of the Hofburg to address the frenzied multitude, he sprang his surprise. "I now proclaim for this land its new mission," he said, his voice ringing through the loudspeakers. "The oldest eastern province of the German people shall be from now on the youngest bulwark of the German nation. I can in this hour report before history the conclusion of the greatest aim in my life: the entry of my homeland into the German Reich." Austria, he shouted, had come home; it would become an integral part of the Reich. The once grand Habsburg state, ruler of a global empire, had been annexed.

Almost overnight sixty thousand people were arrested. Schuschnigg was among them. He was destined to spend the next seven years in German concentration camps, his liberation by American troops coming in April 1945. Himmler ordered the construction of a concentration camp at Mauthausen, twelve miles from Linz, which began receiving prisoners later in the year. Like the other camps operating in the old Reich, it was intended to hold political prisoners, though some Jews were imprisoned there as well. Thousands would be worked to death in its infamous stone quarry, extracting gigantic granite slabs for Speer's colossal building projects in Berlin and Nuremberg.

At the same time Hitler's entry into the city triggered an avalanche of terror against the Jews even more extreme, more hateful than anything yet seen in Germany. Jews were forced to clean toilets in the SS barracks and, on their hands and knees, scrub pro-Schuschnigg slogans from the sidewalks, while taunting crowds gathered around to spit on them and jeer. The violence of the rampaging Nazi radicals reached new depths of cruelty and hate; a tidal wave of beatings, vandalism, and looting swept over the country. Nazi mobs dragged Jews from their homes and businesses and dispatched the men to concentration camps. Some Jews hastily fled, leaving behind virtually all their possessions. Some who had boarded trains bound for Prague and elsewhere were torn from the train at the border and returned to Vienna before landing in concentration camps in Bavaria. So savage and so public were the excesses of the Austrian Nazis that in late April Heydrich had to threaten those responsible with arrest by the Gestapo or expulsion from the SA in order to curb the violence. Like other similar orders, its effect was minimal.

Just as 1938 brought a new phase of Nazi anti-Jewish policy, the more brazen moves in Hitler's foreign policy marked a dramatic turning point. Until the *Anschluss*, Hitler's policy aimed at a revision of the loathsome Versailles Treaty. The withdrawal from the League of Nations in 1934, rearmament in 1935, and remilitarization of the Rhineland in 1936 were all moves that could be seen as revising an unfair treaty and could be supported by the traditional right. But the *Anschluss* and later in the year the Czech crisis moved beyond revision into a new realm of National Socialist ideological politics.

A plebiscite was conducted with the usual Nazi intimidation on April 10, and its results were foreordained: just over 99 percent of the Austrian voters registered their support for their homeland's incorporation in the Greater German Reich, as Hitler now called it. What the result might have been had Schuschnigg's plebiscite been allowed to proceed is impossible to say. In late 1937 the Nazis were entangled in a bitter conflict with the Christian churches, and the pope's encyclical "With Burning Concern" should have been a warning to Catholic Austria. Yet, on Hitler's triumphal arrival in Vienna, Cardinal Theodor Innitzer, Archbishop of Vienna, ordered the bells of all Catholic churches to ring, and swastika banners fluttered from steeple after steeple. There can be no denying that a substantial part of the Austrian public, perhaps a majority, embraced, with varying degrees of enthusiasm, *Anschluss* with Germany, both for nationalist reasons and in the hope that it might bring an improvement to an Austrian economy still mired in the Depression.

In Germany, the *Anschluss* propelled Hitler's popularity to new heights. After the pervasive "war psychosis" that had infected the public throughout the crisis, its triumphal conclusion prompted a tremendous burst of adulation for the Führer. No small amount of that sentiment was due to the fact that a great triumph had been achieved and war had been averted. "A powerful surge of enthusiasm and joy, a jubilation that knew almost no bounds" engulfed the country "when it became clear that the whole Austrian affair would go successfully, and that it would not come to war." It was "difficult," the Sopade concluded, "to judge how much of this general public euphoria sprang from the certainty that there would be no war because of Austria."

Throughout the Austrian crisis, Hitler and his military commanders had worried about Czech intervention. Its territory protruded into central Germany, and with its highly developed armaments industry, sizable, well-equipped army, and formidable border fortifications, Czechoslovakia presented a serious obstacle to Germany's eastward expansion. And, unlike Austria, Czechoslovakia was hardly isolated diplomatically; it had treaties with Germany's two most implacable enemies, France and the Soviet Union. For months before the unanticipated Austrian crisis, Goebbels's propaganda machine had churned out story after story of alleged Czech persecution of the German minority in the mountainous Sudeten border area. Equally intolerable, Hitler charged, Czechoslovakia and its Soviet ally were inserting Bolshevism into the very heart of Europe. Hitler loathed the Czech state: everything about it was, according to the German idiom, "a thorn in the Führer's eye." It was an illegitimate creation of the Versailles settlement; it was a parliamentary democracy; and its very existence was an impediment to Hitler's expansionist aims.

The opportunity for intervention in Austria had fallen more or less into Hitler's lap, but settling with Czechoslovakia, not Austria, had been Hitler's top priority. It was then hardly a surprise that no sooner was the *Anschluss* a reality than Hitler turned his full attention once more to the Czech problem. The Sudetenland, a ragged mountainous region that rimmed western Czechoslovakia bordering the Reich, had a largely German population. With the rise of Hitler, the Sudeten German Party led by Konrad Henlein had begun to agitate against the Prague government. Hitler's call for all ethnic Germans to come "home to the Reich" found considerable resonance among the three million Germans in the Sudetenland, especially after the *Anschluss* had brought ten million German Austrians into the Reich.

For years Berlin had covertly subsidized Henlein's party, encouraging it to ratchet up the ongoing agitation against "Czech oppression." Henlein was brought to Berlin and ordered to manufacture incidents that would whip up outrage among the German minority and provoke the Czech government to react with undue force. If a Sudeten German was shot, so much the better. Outrage piled upon outrage was Goebbels's relentless propaganda drumbeat, each providing added justification for German intervention to protect the oppressed Sudeten Germans.

During the week of May 20–22, events seemed to push Europe to the brink of war. On Thursday, May 19, intelligence reports reaching Prague, Paris, and London claimed that German troop movements were under way near the Czech border. The intelligence was persuasive. Czech president Eduard Benes placed his military on high alert and ordered mobilization of the reserves, calling some 180,000 men to the colors. Exacerbating the mounting tension that weekend, Czech police shot and killed two Sudeten Germans. The threat of war seemed very real. On May 21, Lord Halifax, the British foreign secretary, who had only recently been quite amenable to German claims on Austria, informed Ribbentrop that the French were bound by treaty to intervene if Czechoslovakia were invaded, and Germany should not assume that Britain would simply stand aside.

Confronted by this apparently united front, Hitler retreated. He had been caught off guard, all the more so since there were no German maneuvers on the Czech frontier and no plans for an immediate invasion. After all the warlike bombast of the previous weeks, he was not prepared for this. While an almost audible sigh of relief rose from the capitals of Europe, Hitler's fury was incandescent. Benes had humiliated him, and this he could not tolerate. A week later, on May 28, he summoned Keitel to prepare a revised Case Green. Originally drawn up in late 1937, Case Green was a contingency plan for an invasion of Czechoslovakia. Hitler now ordered Keitel to begin planning for a military strike against Czechoslovakia in the near future. It was not a plan to liberate the Sudeten Germans; it was a plan to destroy the Czech state. "It is my unshakable will to wipe Czechoslovakia off the map," he told a special conference of his military commanders on May 28. They must understand that the destruction of Czechoslovakia was but a step in a much larger strategy to secure *Lebensraum* for the German people. But Germany could not proceed in the East if the hostile Czech state lurked to its rear. The time to strike was now. Britain and France did not want war; the Soviets were unprepared; Italy would be supportive or at the very least neutral. October 1 was set as the target date for invasion. In the meantime Germany would wage an intense propaganda campaign against the Czechs—its purpose "to intimidate the Czechs by means of threats and wear down their power of resistance."

These plans alarmed General Ludwig Beck, chief of staff of the army. He had no qualms about moving against the Czechs at some point in the future, but he believed the German army was not yet ready for a war that would almost certainly involve Britain and France. He was not convinced by Hitler's glib assurances that there would be no intervention by the Western powers. Just two days after Hitler's conference with military leaders, Beck composed a memorandum that laid out his objections to Hitler's plan. Some were technical and strategic, but his most scathing criticism was directed at Hitler's political assumptions. An attack on Czechoslovakia was sheer madness and would almost certainly plunge Germany into catastrophe. He passed the memo along to General Brauchitsch, who agreed with its substance but chose to omit Beck's damning preamble before presenting it to Hitler. Hitler, of course, scorned Beck's memorandum, dismissing it as unworthy of discussion. He would brook no resistance; he was determined to smash Czechoslovakia.

After the weekend crisis in May, Europe enjoyed a brief respite, but it was but a fleeting moment in a summer that bristled with high-voltage tension. Stung by his retreat in May, Hitler missed no opportunity to lash out at Czechoslovakia. His hatred of the Czechs and especially Benes knew no bounds, and his speeches grew more intemperate, his warlike rhetoric more incendiary. Hardly anyone in the West could believe that

Hitler was seriously contemplating a war with the Czechs that would inevitably escalate into a major European conflict. But Hitler was unpredictable, his moods mercurial. Some, even in the diplomatic community, thought that he might be mad. Among the Nazi elite, Ribbentrop alone lent enthusiastic support to Hitler's dangerous plans, concurring with his Führer's evaluation of Britain and France. As the summer days passed and tensions mounted, Göring, who only months before had led the charge against Austria, grew more and more concerned about the international implications of an attack on Czechoslovakia.

Hitler was also encountering reservations from the military. Over the summer months Beck wrote a series of memoranda dilating on the dangers inherent in Hitler's plans and circulated his objections to other leading military figures. He finally convinced Brauchitsch to call a meeting of senior army commanders in early August to discuss the issues. Many of the generals found much to agree with in Beck's position; they, too, were deeply concerned about British and French intervention that would turn a limited war with Czechoslovakia into a European, perhaps world, war. None, however, was prepared to mount a direct challenge to the Führer. Brauchitsch approached Hitler on the matter, but after a severe tongue-lashing by the Führer, his courage deserted him. Beck's hope of confronting Hitler with an ultimatum from a united front of his military commanders found little to no support. Admiral Wilhelm Canaris, head of military intelligence (Abwehr), shared many of Beck's concerns and indicated a willingness to take action, as did a number of other generals—Erwin von Witzleben, Kurt von Hammerstein-Equord, and Franz Halder—who were considering a plan to arrest Hitler as soon as the go-order for Case Green was given. But they were at this point an isolated minority.

Hitler's drive toward war also stimulated a growing concern among the civilian population. Although the public was not aware of Hitler's plans, signs of impending war were everywhere. On June 22 Göring issued a decree giving the regime the authority to conscript workers from one industry or area and transfer them to another. Workers were drafted to work on the construction of fortifications in the west or build strategically important roads on Bavaria's eastern and northern borders with Czechoslovakia. Buses were requisitioned; labor camps erected. Air raid drills increased; civil defense formations were organized. In some areas gas masks were issued. Although a full-blown rationing system was not in place until August 1939, certain food items virtually disappeared, and artificial substitutes were introduced. Military training for the Hitler Youth was intensified, and women were being prepared to take jobs in essential economic sectors formerly held by men. These measures, accompanied by an intensified propaganda campaign against Czechoslovakia, convinced the German public that the Reich stood on the brink of war.

Yet, despite Goebbels's relentless demonization of the Czechs, the German public remained largely unmoved by the plight of their Sudeten cousins. What they did feel was considerable anxiety about the possibility of war. A Sopade report out of Silesia stated that "leading Nazi circles are convinced that the people do not want war. They have, therefore, made every effort to generate the necessary psychological preconditions for war." But it was not working. "Even people who have hardly been critical of the regime before are . . . astounded by how in the last weeks attitudes about the system have turned around. One hardly recognizes the people and the openness with which they speak out against Hitler and the whole system. They accuse Hitler and his circle of wanting war because they no longer know any way out of this extremely critical situation." Some, party activists and the young, remained enthusiastic, but most Germans were deeply ambivalent about Hitler's course of action.

No less anxious were Prague, Paris, and London. Western diplomats had already come to believe that Hitler was determined to strike Czechoslovakia and that they would be drawn into the conflict. In interviews with French and German diplomats, Hitler railed against the Czechs, against Benes personally, shrilly repeating that his patience was at an end. The German press was ablaze with hysterical headlines: "WOMEN AND CHILDREN MOWED DOWN BY CZECH ARMOURED CARS" or "BLOODY REGIME—NEW CZECH MURDERS OF GERMANS" or "EXTORTION, PLUNDERING, SHOOTING—CZECH TERROR IN SUDETEN GERMAN LAND GROWS WORSE FROM DAY TO DAY." All were the pernicious creations of the Reich Propaganda Ministry, and the offensive was unrelenting.

With a mounting sense of dread, British and French leaders assumed that Hitler would use his address at the Nuremberg party rally on September 12 to declare war on Czechoslovakia. But Hitler's speech that night was surprisingly mild. He touched on the mounting Czech crisis only briefly and in the most general, though menacing, terms, but did declare ominously that there would be "grave consequences" if the "democracies persist in their conviction to . . . accord their protection to the oppression of German men and women." He was "under no circumstances willing to stand quietly by and observe from afar the continued oppression of German *Volksgenossen* (people's comrade) in Czechoslovakia. All the Sudeten Germans were demanding was the right of national determination, a right of all peoples guaranteed by the Versailles settlement.

Shortly after Hitler's speech, demonstrations broke out in the Czech town of Eger, near the German border, where ten thousand protesters jammed the town square screaming for self-determination. When the crowd grew disorderly, Czech police opened fire, killing one and wounding a number of others. Violent demonstrations quickly spread to other cities in the Sudetenland, twenty-one people were killed, and the Czech government declared martial law in the border areas. Again rumors spread that Germany was preparing an invasion. At this point, French premier Edouard Daladier conferred with British prime minister Neville Chamberlain, declaring above all it must not come to war. He recommended that they meet with Hitler immediately. When Chamberlain wired Hitler suggesting a face-to-face meeting, Hitler jumped at the chance. He invited the British prime minister, but not Daladier, to join him the very next afternoon at the Berghof. It would be summit diplomacy, a two-person conference.

On September 15, the sixty-nine-year-old Chamberlain flew to Munich. It was his first airplane trip. From Munich, he was taken by train to Berchtesgaden, and then driven up the same mountain road that Schuschnigg had followed in February. His reception was quite different from that which greeted the Austrian prime minister. After stilted pleasantries over tea, the two men and Paul Schmidt, Hitler's interpreter, adjourned to a small wood-paneled room. Chamberlain began by saying that he was prepared to discuss the possibility of righting any German grievances so long as force was not used. This set Hitler off. In a storm of words, he angrily exclaimed that it was the Czechs who had threatened to use force in May, not Germany. "I shall not put up with this any longer. I shall settle the question in one way or another. I shall take matters into my own hands."

To Chamberlain, this sounded like an ultimatum, in which case he saw no point in continuing the meeting. He would return to London at once. This seemed to sober Hitler, who, regaining his composure, said that if Chamberlain were willing to recognize the principle of self-determination of peoples in the case of the Sudeten Germans, the talks might continue. Chamberlain responded that he could not make such guarantees without first consulting the cabinet and suggested that they suspend the discussion until he could confer with both his own government and that of France. Hitler agreed and promised not to take military action "unless a particularly atrocious incident occurred," and Chamberlain left with the impression "that here was a man who could be relied upon when he had given his word."

It was clear to Chamberlain that some transfer of territory to the Reich was essential, and Daladier agreed that some "friendly pressure" should be applied to the Czechs. European peace hung in the balance; Prague must understand that some portions of Sudeten territory must be ceded to Germany. They agreed that an international guarantee of the remaining Czech state must be made, and that not only should Britain and France participate in such a guarantee but Germany as well. When these terms were presented to Prague on September 20, Benes was shocked and refused to agree. But Chamberlain was determined to resume talks with Hitler within forty-eight hours and pressed Benes to accept. It was the best way for Czechoslovakia to retain its independence and avoid a devastating war. For his part, Benes was convinced that the Sudetenland was merely a first step in Hitler's plan to dismember the Czech state. Presented with what amounted to an ultimatum from London and Paris, he bowed to pressure and indicated his willingness to accept the terms. He issued a communiqué to the Czech people, explaining that he had "relied upon the help that our friends might have given us, but when it became evident that the European crisis was taking on too serious a character," they had abandoned the Czech state. "Our friends therefore advised us to buy freedom and peace by our sacrifice. . . . The President of the Republic and our government had no other choice, for we found ourselves alone."

The next morning, Chamberlain once again boarded a plane bound for Germany, this time to Bad Godesberg on the Rhine. There he proudly presented the results of his consultations to Hitler. He began a discussion of the complicated plans for a phased Czech turnover of territory to Germany, explaining the guarantee that Britain and France would extend to Prague and his hope that Germany would join them. Hitler listened politely, then stunned the prime minister by saying softly, "I am exceedingly sorry, Mr. Chamberlain, but I can no longer discuss these matters. This solution after the developments of the last few days is no longer practicable." He could not consider a deal with the Czechs before the claims of Poland and Hungary on Czech territory were settled. After rebutting Chamberlain's proposal point by point, he closed by stating the Sudetenland must be occupied by German troops immediately. Final frontiers could be settled at a later date. When a shocked and angry Chamberlain replied that all the conditions Hitler had insisted upon in Berchtesgaden had been met, Hitler replied, with no trace of irony, that the Czechs could not be trusted and that "if Prague fell under Bolshevik influence, or if hostages continued to be shot, he would intervene at once."

The situation seemed hopeless. Hitler was implacable, and in the following days his threats grew more reckless, his language more inflammatory. In conversations with British and French diplomats, Hitler seemed to have lost all sense of perspective. Sir Horace Wilson, among Chamberlain's closest advisors, accompanied by British ambassador Sir Nevile Henderson and senior diplomat Sir Ivone Kirkpatrick, met with Hitler on September 26, bringing a letter from the prime minister informing Hitler that the Czechs had rejected the Godesberg proposal. They had been amenable to the transfer of the Sudeten districts Hitler desired but could not accept Hitler's demands for an immediate occupation by German troops. Hitler sat restlessly through the translation of the letter, until suddenly he launched himself from his chair and shouted, "There's no point at all in going on with negotiations," and made for the door, where he must have realized that this was his office and three British diplomats were left sitting there. "It was an incredibly painful scene," Hitler's translator Paul Schmidt recalled. When Hitler gained control of himself and Schmidt reached the letter's conclusion, once more Hitler could not restrain himself. Hitler "let himself go more violently" than Schmidt "ever saw him do during a diplomatic interview." Wilson's calm attempts to persuade Hitler to be reasonable only served to heighten the

Führer's rage. Ribbentrop chimed in, fanning the flames of Hitler's fury by denouncing Benes as a "terrorist" and the Czechs as "war mongers."

That night, in addressing an enormous crowd of baying Nazis at the Sportpalast, Hitler unloosed a hate-filled tirade against Benes and the Czechs that shocked even longtime Hitler watchers in the foreign press. "The Czech state was born in a lie," he thundered, his voice quaking with scorn. "The name of the father of the lie was Benes. He convinced the framers at Versailles that there was a Czechoslovakian nation. . . . He built up a regime of terror! Back then already, a number of Germans attempted to protest against this arbitrary rape of their people. They were summarily executed. Ever since, a war has been waged to exterminate the Germans there. . . . The entire development since 1918 is proof of one thing only: Herr Benes is determined to exterminate *Deutschtum* slowly but surely." His brutal rule over the Sudeten Germans amounted to "a military occupation," but the time had come "to tell him what's what." The Reich, calumnied as a warmonger in the international press, had shown superhuman restraint in the face of Czech provocations, but Benes had gone too far. The Czech president should remember, Hitler shouted, that while he "may have seven million Czechs . . . here there is a Volk of seventy-five million." Now the Reich's "patience was at an end with regard to the Sudeten German problem! I have put forward an offer to Herr Benes, an offer that is nothing other than realization of his promises. The decision is his now! Be it war or peace! He can either accept my offer and give the Germans their freedom, or we Germans will go get it for ourselves."

Leo Amery, a Conservative politician and minister in several British governments, was in the audience that night, and described Hitler's performance as "more like the snarling of a wild animal than the utterance of a human being, and the venom and vulgarity of his personal vilifications of 'Benes the liar' almost made me feel sick. There was something terrifying and obscenely sinister in this outpouring of sheer hatred." William Shirer, who as CBS's top reporter in Germany was broadcasting from the balcony that night, observed in his diary that in all the years he had been covering Hitler, "for the first time . . . he seemed tonight to have completely lost control of himself." When Hitler finished, Goebbels leapt to the podium and roared: "One thing is sure: 1918 will never be repeated." At this, Hitler sprang to his feet and, according to Shirer, "with a fanatical look in his eyes I shall never forget brought his right hand, after a broad sweep, pounding down on the table and yelled with all the power in his mighty lungs, 'Ja!'" Then he slumped back down in his chair thoroughly spent.

The following day, Wilson sought another audience with Hitler. So stormy was their earlier meeting and so belligerent was Hitler's demeanor, that British diplomat Ivone Kirkpatrick felt an aura "of such ruthless wickedness that it was oppressive and almost nightmarish to sit in the same room." The atmospherics did not improve in this second meeting. Wilson tried to convey Britain's commitment to ensuring that the Czechs honored their agreement to transfer the territory in question, but when Wilson asked if Hitler had a message for London, the Führer replied that it was all quite simple. The Czechs had but two choices. They could either accept the Godesberg Memorandum or reject it. If they chose the latter course, Hitler bellowed, "I will smash the Czechs," a threat repeated throughout the tense meeting. When Wilson stated forcefully that if Germany attacked Czechoslovakia and Paris honored its treaty obligations, Britain would feel compelled to support the French, Hitler erupted. "If France and England strike," he shouted, "let them do so. It is a matter of complete indifference to me. I am prepared for every eventuality. . . . It is Tuesday today, and by next Monday we will all be at war." To impress the world with the nation's enthusiastic support for war, Hitler planned a military parade through the government quarter later in the day. He had ordered the High Command to publish an announcement that in the afternoon the 2nd Motorized Division would drive through the city on its way toward the Czech frontier. After the wild cheering by the carefully selected audience at the Sportpalast the night before, Hitler anticipated a passionate crowd of thousands to be gathered in the Wilhelmplatz just across from the Reich Chancellery.

The peripatetic Shirer was on the scene that afternoon as the vehicles of the 2nd Motorized Division turned down the Wilhelmstrasse toward the Reich Chancellery. Like Hitler, he expected to see a tremendous demonstration, reminiscent of those he had read about during the summer of 1914 when cheering throngs had tossed flowers at the columns of marching troops. "The hour," Shirer wrote in his diary, "was undoubtedly chosen . . . to catch hundreds of thousands of Berliners pouring out of their offices at the end of the day's work, but they ducked into the subways, refused to look on, and the handful that did stood at the curb in utter silence." No frenzied cries of *Sieg Heil*, no patriotic songs. A sparse crowd of only two hundred or so had congregated in the Wilhelmplatz. "It has been the most striking demonstration against war I've ever seen," Shirer observed. "The German people are dead set against war." Hitler, who watched the sullen, silent crowd on the Wilhelmplatz from the windows of the Chancellery, was disgusted. "With such people," he said in dismay, "I cannot wage war."

Events now were rushing toward a climax. While publicly insisting on their support to the Czechs, both the British and French were desperately seeking ways out of their obligations, pressuring Benes to accept the Godesberg Memorandum. They spoke of plebiscites, phased occupation, international commissions to oversee territorial transfers, and Anglo-French guarantees of the remainder of Czechoslovakia. But Benes responded by ordering a mobilization of Czech forces. The French unhappily followed suit, and Chamberlain, with great reluctance, ordered the mobilization of the British fleet. Chamberlain, whose entire policy was based on preserving peace, gave vent to his feelings in a surprisingly candid radio address on the evening of September 27. "How horrible, fantastic, incredible, it is that we should be digging trenches and trying on gas masks here because of a quarrel in a faraway country between people of whom we know nothing." He had done his best to save Europe from war, but, he admitted, "however much we may sympathize with a small nation confronted by a big powerful neighbor, we cannot in all circumstances undertake to involve the whole British Empire in a war on her account."

With peace perched precariously on a razor's edge, Chamberlain decided to make one final appeal to Hitler. In a letter delivered on September 26 but unread until the following day, he stated his firm conviction that the differences between the two sides had narrowed to a point where "really it was inconceivable that they could not be settled by negotiations." The British, after all, were offering a settlement according to which German troops would enter selected areas in the Sudetenland, their occupation monitored by an international commission, which would set the final borders, and finally a plebiscite would be held in the areas affected. The occupation would proceed in two phases between October 1 and October 10. It was, in essence, the Godesberg agreement, but with logistical amendments. Despite his ferocious bluster and the ongoing military plans to invade, reservations had begun to creep into Hitler's thinking. Ernst von Weizsäcker, state secretary in the Foreign Office, had long cautioned restraint, gingerly urging Hitler to draw back from the precipice. Negotiation would render the desired results without armed conflict, he insisted.

Göring also expressed his growing apprehension about British military intervention. As Hitler's September 28 deadline for Benes to accept or reject his terms loomed ever nearer, Göring grew less confident that the British were bluffing, and, he argued, it made little sense to risk a world war over details when Hitler had already gained essentially what he wanted. Goebbels, too, urged restraint. Only Ribbentrop remained unflinchingly supportive of Hitler's war plans, and Ribbentrop's judgment, Goebbels noted, was clouded by his "blind hatred against England."

Influenced by Göring and Weizsäcker, Hitler responded to Chamberlain's letter with one of his own. He denied that he had any desire to "cripple Czechoslovakia in her national existence or in her political and economic independence." He had no intention of occupying the whole country. He wanted no Czechs. The Sudetenland, as he had repeated several times in meetings with French and British diplomats, was his last territorial demand to make in Europe. The Czechs had until two o'clock on the 28th, forty-eight hours, to decide.

The ensuing hours were filled with frantic telephone messages, telegrams, and letters. On the morning of September 28, French ambassador François-Poncet delivered a message to Hitler in the Reich Chancellery, presenting a new French proposal that went further than that of the British. According to François-Poncet, France was willing to see Germany occupy the entire Sudetenland so long as force was not used and other guarantees were in place. The occupation would proceed in phases, between October 1 and October 10. If Hitler accepted the proposal, France would demand acceptance by the Czechs. At roughly the same time, Chamberlain sent a message to Berlin indicating that he would be willing to make another trip to Germany to discuss the arrangements for the transfer of territory. He also suggested that Mussolini and French premier Edouard Daladier join the discussion. Mussolini, whom he had already contacted, agreed to act as mediator.

Mussolini, whose support Hitler desperately wanted, signaled Berlin that he would stand beside the Führer come what may, but he noted that the differences between the parties were now so small that in his opinion "the proposal ought to be accepted." Hitler agreed, and sent invitations to Rome and Paris—but not to Prague or Moscow. The Duce, who was not keen on the prospect of war with Britain and France, for which Italy was unprepared, readily accepted; Daladier did as well. It was agreed that the meeting of the four major powers would take place on the following day, September 29, in Munich.

The arrangements for the conference had to be thrown together at the last moment. It was decided that the four leaders would meet in the newly completed Führer Building on the Königsplatz. Hitler's official residence in Munich was a neoclassical building of white stone with marble floors, immense hallways, interior columns, and a sweeping staircase that led to the first floor (second floor in American usage) where Hitler's office was located. The discussions were to take place in a spacious conference room just adjacent. A dinner was to be held in the evening for the participants in the banquet room.

Early in the morning Hitler decided to meet the Duce's train in Kufstein in the Tyrolean Alps near the Italian border, so that the two dictators could confer before the conference convened. Daladier arrived in Munich before noon, and shortly thereafter Chamberlain's plane touched down at the Oberwiesenfeld aerodrome after a seven-hour flight. He was met, as was Daladier, by Ribbentrop, an SS honor guard, and the obligatory band. Without stopping at the hotel, where the British delegation was to stay, he was driven through the city directly to the Führer Building in an open car. Along the way from the airport to the Königsplatz, excited, friendly crowds clogged the sidewalks, waving and cheering both men, but especially Chamberlain. He had come to save the peace.

When the four leaders gathered in the conference room, the improvised character of the conference became painfully clear. There was no agenda, no chairman, no arrangements for minutes to be taken, and not even pencil and paper for the participants. The four principals sat in plush easy chairs in a semicircle around the large marble fireplace, a low coffee table between them. As the day wore on, the room filled up, as assistants, interpreters, foreign ministers and their staffs, and other members of the different delegations came and went. It was, one of the British delegation recalled, "a hugger-bugger affair." Mussolini, the only participant who spoke all the languages represented, acted as de facto chair and presented a memorandum that was to serve as the conference's working document. He had composed it during the night, he said, but it was, in fact, based on a draft by Göring and Weizsäcker. The two men had drafted the memorandum and dispatched it to Italy without the knowledge of Ribbentrop, who remained opposed to a peaceful settlement of the crisis. The document basically reiterated the terms of the Godesberg agreement. Chamberlain and Daladier both made weak efforts to include the Czechs in the meeting, but Hitler was adamant.

The meeting dragged on into the early hours of the morning, when the four heads of state affixed their signatures to the document at 1:30 a.m. According to the terms agreed upon, German troops would occupy "predominantly German territory" beginning on October 1. The territory would be divided into four military zones, and Italy, Britain, and France would guarantee that the evacuation of Czechs would be completed by October 10 and that no military installations would be destroyed. A newly created international committee of these powers plus Germany would determine the conditions for the plebiscites to be held in certain areas and would propose a final frontier. The Munich Agreement was, in effect, the Godesberg Memorandum, with certain adjustments. The Czechoslovakian Republic had been dismantled without having a say in the matter.

Chamberlain had promised the two-man Czech delegation that was waiting in its hotel that he would negotiate with Czech interests in mind. Now he received them in his suite at the Regina Palast and broke the news of their country's dismemberment. Daladier was also present, and the two sought to explain, though not too vigorously, what had happened and why. It was, they insisted, a far better arrangement than the Godesberg Memorandum, but no words could disguise or soften their cruel betrayal. Jan Mastny, the Czech ambassador, wept. The Czechs were informed that their agreement was not really required. If Prague refused, Czechoslovakia would be left to deal with the Germans alone. "Then they were finished with us," wrote Hubert Masaryk, the other Czech representative, "and we were allowed to go."

The next morning Chamberlain paid a visit to Hitler's apartment on the Prinzregentenplatz. It was not a scheduled meeting; during a break in the proceedings on the previous day, the prime minister surprised the Führer by requesting a personal meeting, and Hitler, pleased but puzzled, agreed. When Chamberlain arrived at the apartment, he produced from his briefcase a one-page document, a declaration that pledged that the two countries would never go to war with one another again. "We regard the Agreement signed last night, and the Anglo-German Naval Agreement, as symbolic of the desire of our two peoples never to go to war with each other again," it read. Hitler hesitated momentarily, then signed to wan smiles and handshakes all round. For Chamberlain this was the crowning achievement of a successful mission to Munich, and it was this paper that he waved in triumph upon his return to London, uttering words that would soon prove painfully ironic: "I believe this means peace in our time."

Chamberlain's trip back to the Munich aerodrome was even more triumphant than on his arrival. Tumultuous crowds cheered as the hero of the hour passed by. To interpreter Paul Schmidt, riding with Chamberlain in the open car, "these obviously spontaneous and unorganized ovations for Chamberlain implied a certain criticism of Hitler." Hitler, "the man of war," received "a certain tribute of routine applause," but "it lagged far behind the spontaneous manifestations of sympathy . . . accorded to Chamberlain . . . and Daladier" outside their hotels.

For all the drama surrounding the meeting in the Führer Building, the Munich Agreement did not end the Czech crisis; it was merely the beginning of the multinational republic's dismemberment. Germany emerged from the Munich Conference with eleven thousand square miles of strategically important territory, acquiring in the process the extensive Czech system of fortifications, much of its armaments industry, and 3.5 million new German speakers. And once German troops marched into the Sudetenland, Hitler simply ignored the few restrictions and conditions the Western powers had attempted to impose on him: no plebiscites were held and the boundaries that were finally set reflected Hitler's strategic concerns more than ethnic considerations (some 250,000 Germans were left in Czechoslovakia and 800,000 Czechs were marooned in areas annexed to the Reich). The Czech state was left virtually defenseless, and within days Poland, with Hitler's encouragement, seized territory on the Czech-Polish border, the Hungarians grabbed a strip of territory in southern Slovakia, and the Slovaks, with Hitler's blessing, declared autonomy within the rump Czech state.

To Hitler, Chamberlain's Anglo-German declaration was meaningless. He had no intention of abiding by the previous night's four-power agreement, and he signed this bilateral protocol with England without a care. Although he came to view the conference as a failure, entangling him in agreements that left him far short of his goal, Hitler's prestige soared. Once again he had plunged Germany into an international crisis, and once again he had emerged triumphant without a shot being fired. But war was the ultimate terminus of Nazi policy, and after the statesmen had returned home and a sense of profound relief settled over Europe, Hitler found himself deflated, disappointed, cheated of his war. Throughout the Sudeten crisis he had possessed an enormous advantage in dealing with the Western democracies: while Britain and France scrambled to maintain the peace at virtually all costs, Hitler was not only willing to go to war, he *wanted* to go to war. Confident that Britain and France would not intervene, he was determined to have his war, though a limited one, only to find that Chamberlain had robbed him of it.

Munich had profound repercussions. It convinced Hitler that the Western powers, even when sorely provoked, would not risk war, especially over his ambitions in Eastern Europe. Britain and France were, as he had concluded after his march into the Rhineland in 1936, "no longer heroic peoples." His designs for acquiring *Lebensraum* in the East, which had animated his foreign policy from the outset, were reinforced by Western weakness. Stalin drew much the same conclusion. The West was weak and, worse, was determined to channel German aggression eastward. Although the Soviets had continued to voice their support for the beleaguered Czechs throughout the crisis, they, too, felt certain that France would not act and hence Russia would be relieved of its treaty obligations to Prague. The West, in short, was not to be trusted.

Munich also confirmed Hitler's faith in his own "intuition" and emboldened him for further action. His military, his Foreign Office, and even his ally, Mussolini, had been wrong, and he had, again, been proven right. The embryonic military conspiracy collapsed, and the army's trust in its own judgment suffered another blow, one that would keep it quiescent until the latter stages of the coming war. The peaceful conclusion of the Sudeten crisis also sent his domestic popularity skyrocketing and undermined what had been a mounting undercurrent of dissatisfaction with his reckless policies.

By the close of 1938, Hitler had gutted the Versailles Treaty, over-turned the postwar European order, and raised German power and prestige to dizzying heights, all without bloodshed. The radical turn in German foreign policy accompanied a radicalization of Nazi racial policy, culminating in the nationwide violence of *Kristallnacht* just over a month after the Munich conference. The regime, in both foreign and racial policy, had turned a corner. Nor was Hitler through. While synagogues were still smoldering all over the Reich on November 10, Hitler held a remarkably candid meeting with German journalists. "For decades, circumstances caused me to speak almost exclusively of peace," he began.

> Only by constantly emphasizing the German Volk's desire for peace and peaceful intentions was I able to gain the German prerequisite for accomplishing the next step. It is self-evident that this peace propaganda throughout the decades may well have had quite questionable effects. It might well leave the mistaken impression in the minds of many that the present regime stands for the resolution and the willingness to preserve peace under all conditions. . . . For years, I spoke only of peace because of this forced situation. Now it has become necessary to slowly prepare the German Volk psychologically for the fact that there are things that cannot be achieved by peaceful means. Some goals can only be achieved through the use of force. That meant that certain of these events needed to be portrayed in a manner in which they would automatically trigger certain reactions in the brains of the mass of the German Volk: if you cannot stop these things in a peaceful manner, then you will just have to stop them by force—in any event, things cannot go on like this.

EARLY SUCCESS

On January 30, 1939, Adolf Hitler addressed the German Reichstag on the sixth anniversary of his ascension to power, and with a year of stupendous foreign policy victories behind him, he had much to boast about. He began with a recital of the triumphs of the past year, but he could not let an opportunity pass without enumerating the perils facing the new Germany. The menace of Bolshevism, Jewry, and plutocracy had been met at home, but "the Jewish world enemy" was still lurking beyond Germany's borders, always scheming. This international Jewish conspiracy, the "wire pullers" of both Bolshevism and Wall Street plutocracy, was driving the peoples of Europe toward a cataclysmic war. These themes were inextricably entwined in Hitler's fantasies, and on this day he explicitly fused the two obsessions more directly, more menacingly than ever before.

France and England were not Germany's enemies, he declared. Germany had "no feelings of hatred towards England, America, or France." Germany wished to live "in peace and quiet," and all "the assertions about the Reich's intended attacks on other nations" were lies spread by Jewish agitators and their unwitting front men. The threat to European, indeed, world peace was not the work of a nation or a state but the machinations of a single enemy, "international Jewry." Some countries, especially the benighted democracies, refused to recognize the menace, but National Socialist Germany, with its systematic campaign of enlightenment and propaganda, was raising the alarm. Thanks to that tireless effort, the nations of Europe would "no longer be willing to die on the battlefield so that this unstable international race may profiteer from a war or satisfy its Old

Testament vengeance. The Jewish watchword 'Workers of the world unite' will be conquered by a higher realization, namely 'Workers of all classes and of all nations, recognize your common enemy!'" But if the nations of the world would not learn this lesson, Hitler offered a chilling prophecy for the future: "In the course of my life," he said,

> I have very often been a prophet and have usually been ridiculed for it. During the time of struggle for power it was in the first instance the Jewish race which only received my prophecies with laughter when I said that I would one day take over the leadership of the state, and with it that of the whole nation and that I would then among many other things settle the Jewish question. Their laughter was uproarious, but I think that now that once ringing laughter is choking in their throats. Today I will once more be a prophet: If the international Jewish financiers in and outside Europe should succeed in plunging the nations once more into a world war, then the result will not be the bolshevization of the earth, and thus the victory of Jewry, but the annihilation of the Jewish race in Europe.

The Nazis' use of such apocalyptic language was not new. For years the Nazis had spoken, with mounting ferocity, of the world Jewish conspiracy, the global enemy, and Judeo-Bolshevism. But in the crisis-laden months of 1938 and 1939, terms such as "annihilation," "eradication," and "extermination" grew exponentially and infused the already threatening environment with mounting anxiety. Nazi Jewish policy was at this time still emigration, but Nazi rhetoric grew increasingly violent. Speaking to the Czech foreign minister in January 1939, Hitler fumed that Germany had been too lenient with the Jews. "Our own kindness was nothing but weakness and we regret it. This vermin must be destroyed. The Jews are our sworn enemies and at the end of this year there will not be a Jew left in Germany." They were not going to get away with what they had done in November 1918. "The day of reckoning has come."

In 1939 war was in the air. The Munich Agreement had provided a much needed respite from the serial crises of 1938, but that pause proved to be of short duration. From the outset of the Sudeten crisis Hitler's objective, stated explicitly to his generals, was a war against Czechoslovakia that would wipe the multinational state off the map, and although he emerged from the fall crisis a great hero and savior in Germany, he was frustrated. Chamberlain, for whom he had nothing but contempt, had denied him the smashing military victory he so ardently desired. He was livid at the idea that this "old man," this senile, umbrella-toting Englishman had managed to ensnare him in international agreements that had denied him his conqueror's entry into Prague. This state of affairs could not be allowed to stand. After encouraging Poland and Hungary to seize border territory from the crumbling Czech state, he proceeded in early 1939 to foment unrest among the Slovaks and Ruthenians in Czechoslovakia's eastern provinces. Both had attained far-reaching autonomy within the rump Czech state, but now Hitler pressed separatist elements in both provinces to agitate for full independence from Prague.

Following the script that had played so well in both Austria and the Sudetenland, anti-Czech agitation reached crisis proportions among the restive Slovaks and Ruthenians. On March 6 and 9 Czech president Emil Hacha, who had succeeded Benes, disbanded first the Slovak and then the Ruthenian governments and declared martial law. Although the move was unexpected, Hitler quickly seized the initiative. German arms were slipped into Slovakia from across the former Austrian border and distributed to the well-organized German minority. On March 13, Hitler summoned Slovak leader Jozef Tiso to Berlin. There Hitler demanded that either the Slovaks declare their immediate independence, which would be guaranteed by Berlin, or be left to their own devices. Ribbentrop also noted pointedly that Hungarian troops were preparing to seize Ruthenia, and parts of Slovakia were being restrained only by Germany. Tiso rushed back to Bratislava where, before the Slovak parliament, he read out a declaration of independence that had been composed by Ribbentrop. On March 14 Slovakia became an independent nation, recognized by Germany, and another Czech crisis broke over Europe.

While these events were unfolding in the eastern provinces of the Czech state, the German press was ablaze with stories of alleged Czech atrocities against the German minority in Bohemia and Moravia. Such tales by now had a familiar ring, reprising the allegations being reported in Nazi newspapers from the previous August. Prague denied these charges, but it hardly mattered. Fearing that a German invasion was looming, Hacha and his foreign minister, Frantisek Chvalkovsky, decided, despite the unhappy experiences of Schuschnigg and Benes, to make a personal appeal to Hitler. On March 14 they traveled by train to Berlin, but the elderly Hacha, who was suffering from a serious heart condition, was kept waiting for hours before being admitted to Hitler's study. Exhausted from an already trying day, he made an abject appeal to Hitler, in which he voiced his own doubts as to whether an independent Czechoslovakian state was viable, and asked whether a German invasion might be averted if the Czech army disarmed itself. Perhaps then the Führer might recognize the rights of Czechs to live an independent national life.

It was a pitiful performance. When Hacha had finished his remarks, Hitler launched into a tirade, ranting against the reign of Benes and Masaryk and announcing that he had no confidence in the present Czech government. In just a few short hours, the German army would descend on Czechoslovakia, and the Luftwaffe would begin bombing Czech targets. Hacha had two choices: if the invasion encountered armed resistance, Czech forces would be ruthlessly crushed. The alternative was that German troops be allowed to enter in a peaceable manner. If that was the case, then Hitler would be open to the possibility of some sort of autonomy for the Czechs, who would retain something of their national freedom. This part of his offer was altogether vague, but if the Czechs resisted, the Wehrmacht would mercilessly demolish the Czech army, and Göring's Luftwaffe would destroy Prague. It was 2 a.m. German troops would begin their invasion in just four hours.

Overwrought and weary, Hacha fainted. A general panic ensued. The Nazis couldn't afford to have the president of Czechoslovakia die in the Reich Chancellery in the middle of the night. Hitler's personal physician was hastily summoned and administered an injection, and Hacha revived. He had barely come to when he was confronted by a written statement prepared by Ribbentrop, inviting the Reich to establish order in the beleaguered Czech state. At first Hacha refused to sign and was literally pursued around the table by Ribbentrop and Göring, who, cajoling and threatening, kept thrusting the agreement at him. After a second injection, a resigned and despondent Hacha signed the document, inviting German forces to enter Bohemia and Moravia and placing "the fate of the Czech people in the hands of the Führer." It was the death certificate of

Czechoslovakia. Beside himself with joy, Hitler bounded into his secretaries' room and gushed: "Kiss me, children. This is the greatest day of my life! I shall go down in history as the greatest German."

At 6 a.m. on March 15, German troops crossed the frontier. Obeying Hacha's order, the formidable Czech army offered no resistance. Later that day Hitler began an automobile journey to Prague in a blinding snowstorm. His ten-car motorcade passed through columns of German soldiers trudging in the snow and ice, until at last they reached the city and Hitler installed himself in the Hradschin Castle, ancient residence of the kings of Bohemia. Next day he signed a decree announcing the creation of the Protectorate of Bohemia and Moravia and also placed the newly independent state of Slovakia under German protection. Himmler's SS was already at work. For the Jews of Czechoslovakia, the nightmare was just beginning. Ruthenia, having served its purpose, Hitler left to the Hungarians, who eagerly gobbled it up. Three days later, Germany seized Memel, a thin slice of formerly German territory on the northeastern border of East Prussia, which had been ceded to Lithuania in the Versailles settlement. The move was unopposed.

The German occupation of Bohemia and Moravia came as a surprise to the German public and the international community and hence lacked the drama that had characterized Hitler's absorption of the Sudetenland. But it was ominously clear that a decisive turning point in the foreign policy of the Third Reich had been reached. For the first time Hitler had seized a state that could in no way be justified by invoking the principle of national self-determination. Nor was it a matter of gaining equality for Germany in the international arena or protecting an oppressed German minority. The Nazi press, of course, continued to churn out Czech atrocity stories, but few outside Germany were paying attention. It was an act of naked aggression against a sovereign state and stripped away in one stroke Hitler's mask of committed peacemaker and gallant defender of ethnic Germans stranded abroad by Versailles. No amount of high-minded rhetoric could hide what lay beneath.

Domestically the response was relief and admiration for the Führer, who had once again managed a great foreign policy coup without shedding German blood. He had created the Greater German Reich about which he had so often preached, and he had done so by audacity and daring. Despite the intense anti-Czech propaganda campaign that Goebbels had unleashed in February, the news caught the German public by surprise. Most felt that it provided yet another boost to Hitler's stature, but the level of excitement did not match the public response to the dramatic resolution of the Sudeten crisis. And there was an undercurrent of uneasiness. Some found the move at odds with Hitler's professed desire to purge Germany of all foreign elements; still others were convinced that this was not the last strike the Nazis would make. "The next would follow soon, one just doesn't know where. When would this madness end?" Another Sopade report claimed that "a great anxiety prevails among the people. Almost everyone believes that war is inevitable."

International opinion had already been shocked by the Nazi brutality of *Kristallnacht*, and Chamberlain's policy of appeasement, long under assault from Conservative leader Winston Churchill and others in the Parliament, crashed virtually overnight. In a speech in Birmingham brimming with rueful indignation, Chamberlain excoriated Hitler's brazen breach of faith. What was the world to make of Hitler's promises now? he exclaimed.

No one believed that Hitler would long be satisfied with these triumphs. The occupation of Czechoslovakia had significantly strengthened Germany's military. Large stocks of Czech military equipment fell into German hands as did the gigantic Skoda arms complex, the second largest in Europe, and Germany's eastern frontier was greatly strengthened. Seizure of Prague's foreign currency and gold reserves also reduced pressure on the German economy and eased the import for crucial raw materials. All across Europe observers now anticipated another move, and that move, it was widely assumed, would come against Poland. Germany's relations with Poland had been strained since the Versailles settlement. Not only did the new Polish state receive the German provinces of West Prussia and Posen, but in order to give it access to the sea, it had been granted a corridor along the Vistula to the Baltic that separated Germany proper from East Prussia. Danzig, for centuries a German city, was detached from the Reich and declared a free city to be administered by the League of Nations. It was to be in effect Poland's port on the Baltic. Despite these deeply resented territorial arrangements, Hitler had maintained surprisingly good relations with the conservative, anti-Marxist, anti-Russian, and notoriously anti-Semitic government of Poland during the first years of the Third Reich. In 1934 he had signed a nonaggression treaty with Warsaw, good for ten years, and at Munich had supported Polish claims to Czech territory.

Almost immediately after the fall of Prague, Ribbentrop approached the Polish ambassador, Jozef Lipski, with a proposal. The Reich desired the return of Danzig to Germany and wished to build an extraterritorial road or railway connecting East Prussia to the Reich. In return, Germany would allow Poland's use of Danzig as a free port, assure Polish economic interests in the city, and guarantee Poland's current borders. Hitler would also extend the German-Polish nonaggression treaty of 1934, even floating the idea of a mutual defense agreement aimed at the Soviet Union. Ribbentrop also suggested that the two countries might cooperate on the emigration of Jews from Poland.

The Poles flatly refused the German gambit. They had no desire to become a satellite of the Third Reich, and the Nazi liquidation of Czechoslovakia was not reassuring. Instead, on the last day of March, they reached an agreement with Britain, in which London pledged to defend Polish sovereignty and its frontiers. France quickly joined in the guarantee, and a week later that agreement was formalized in a treaty. A similar guarantee was issued by Britain and France to Greece and Romania. Announcing the pact, Chamberlain's message was unambiguous: "In the event of any action which clearly threatens Polish independence and which the Polish Government accordingly consider it vital to resist with their national forces, H.M. Government would feel themselves bound at once to lend the Polish Government all support in their power."

Hitler was furious but undaunted. He still could not bring himself to believe that if push came to shove, the British would actually intervene. Three days after Chamberlain's announcement, Hitler directed his military to begin preparations for an invasion of Poland any time after September 1. Orders for an attack on Poland, code-named Case White, were formally issued on April 11, explaining that the mission of the Wehrmacht was the swift destruction of Polish military strength while the task of the political leadership was to isolate Poland diplomatically. A few days later, in a conversation with Romania's foreign minister at the Reich Chancellery, Hitler vented his disdain for the British and his frustration at his inability to reach some sort of understanding with them. He had tried again and again to reach an agreement with London, he complained, only to be rebuffed. Well, if the British were determined to have a war, they could have it. "And it will be a war of unimaginable destructiveness," he warned. "How can the English picture a modern war when they can't even put two fully equipped divisions in the field!"

Despite these developments, Hitler still hoped to arrange a deal with Poland, recruiting Warsaw into an anti-Soviet alliance. But should Warsaw remain obdurate, plans for an invasion of Poland moved ahead. On April 15, with anxiety mounting over Hitler's next move, President Roosevelt intervened. He had recalled America's ambassador to Germany in the aftermath of *Kristallnacht*, and American newspapers had led the way in condemning the Nazi pogrom. Nearly a thousand editorials had been published in the American press in the weeks after *Kristallnacht*, Goebbels grumbled. "It is an open secret," he continued, that the American president had "gathered around him a great number of Jewish advisers. One can just imagine what they are blaring into his ear." Washington had joined London and Paris in fomenting the current "war psychosis" and was widely viewed as already allied with Great Britain.

It was perhaps then only mildly surprising when on April 15 Roosevelt addressed himself directly to the deteriorating situation in Europe. He sent what amounted to an open letter to Hitler, appealing for "assurances against further aggression." Hitler had repeatedly asserted that neither he nor the German people wanted war, but it was clear in Roosevelt's eyes—and, he implied, the world's—that Germany was the source of the pervasive international tension. If it was true that neither Hitler nor the German people wanted war, as the Nazi leader maintained, then, the president stated, "there need be no war." He went on to ask Hitler in the most straightforward terms whether he was prepared to give assurances that Germany harbored no aggressive intentions against an extensive list of countries in Europe and beyond. It was, according to Goebbels, "a shameless, hypocritical" document, composed by the "charlatan from Washington."

Hitler responded in a much anticipated speech on April 28. It was to be an address of such importance that Britain and France returned their ambassadors, withdrawn in protest of the occupation of Bohemia and Moravia, to Berlin to hear it. Speaking before a packed Reichstag in the Kroll Opera House, he began with a vigorous defense of his foreign policy, justifying German action in a crumbling Czechoslovakia as an act to preserve peace and stability in Central Europe. He valued friendship with Britain, but the British had obviously come to view war with Germany as inevitable and had acted in a manner inconsistent with the Anglo-German Naval Agreement of 1935. "Now that journalists and officials in England publicly advocate opposition to Germany in any case, and this is confirmed by the well known policy of encirclement, then the foundations on which the Anglo-German Naval Agreement rested have been destroyed." He resolved, therefore, to withdraw from the Naval Agreement. At this the Reichstag erupted in thunderous applause. As for the Poles, their new alliance with England and their refusal to enter discussions with Germany were inconsistent with the German-Polish Friendship Treaty of 1934, and he renounced that as well.

Finally, toward the close of his remarks, Hitler addressed himself directly to Roosevelt's letter. It was a masterpiece of sarcasm, a combination of faux humility and mockery that left his audience roaring with appreciative laughter. Mr. Roosevelt had lectured him on the evils of war, he said, but who should know better than the German people who for twenty years had been victimized by an unjust treaty? The president seemed to believe that all problems could be solved at the conference table, but the United States had failed to ratify the Versailles Treaty that its own president, Woodrow Wilson, had inspired and helped draft. Roosevelt had expressed hopes for disarmament, as if that might be a solution to international tension, but, Hitler reminded the president, the German people had trusted another American president only to find that they alone were forced to disarm. Germany, he declared, had had enough of unilateral disarmament.

The denouement of his response came when he turned to Roosevelt's demand for a promise that Germany would attack none of the states the president proceeded to list. Hitler rattled off the countries one by one that the president believed in danger—Latvia, Estonia, Lithuania, Poland, Belgium, Holland, France, Liechtenstein, Russia, Arabia, Iran, Turkey, Palestine, on and on, with the laughter building ever louder as the list grew longer. Hitler could barely contain himself, so delighted was he with his performance and his witty humiliation of Roosevelt. He claimed to have sounded out these countries to inquire whether they felt threatened by Germany or if they had requested the president to voice their anxieties. He had not done so, but no matter. The answer was in all cases no—except, he added with relish, that some countries—Syria, Arabia, Iran, and Palestine—were unable to respond due to their occupation by troops of the democratic nations. Nonetheless, he assured the American president that he fully understood that the "vastness of your nation and the immense wealth of your country allow you to feel responsible for the history of the whole world and the history of all nations. I, sir, am placed in a much smaller and modest sphere." He could not feel himself responsible for the fate of the world, as this world took no interest in the pitiful fate of the German people. "I have regarded myself as called upon by Providence to serve my own people alone. I have lived day and night for the single task of awakening the powers of my people, in view of our desertion by the rest of the world. . . . Conditions prevailing in your country are on such a large scale that you can find time and leisure to give your attention to universal problems." It was a bravura performance—many thought it the best speech he had ever delivered—and what it lacked in veracity or accuracy, it made up for in political theater. Goebbels, of course, exulted. Hitler had given Roosevelt "a public flogging. . . . The Führer is a genius of political tactics and strategy. No one is his equal. Compared to him, what a dwarf is a man like Roosevelt."

Hitler's speech settled no one's nerves, either in Germany or abroad. It wasn't intended to. Less than a month later, Ribbentrop pressed the Italians into signing the "Pact of Steel." It was in many ways redundant, since a treaty between the two Axis dictators also existed, but this was a more sweeping and frankly aggressive document. The two regimes, bound together by the "inner affinity of their ideologies and the comprehensive solidarity of their interests," pledged to give full political and diplomatic support to each other if their interests were threatened, and in the event of hostilities, would "act side by side and with united forces to secure their *Lebensraum* and to maintain peace." The Pact of Steel, touted by the German press as "the mightiest alliance in world history," did not cause an international stir, and it did not impress either the German public or military. Its purpose was to intimidate the West.

Shortly after this speech, Hitler summoned his top military commanders to a briefing on the Polish situation. After the Great War, Hitler began, a closed circle of victorious powers had established a balance of power without German participation. Germany's revival under National

Socialism had disturbed that balance, so that every effort by Germany to claim its legitimate rights was viewed as "breaking in." Germany's economic life demanded living space, and that could not be attained "without 'breaking in' to other countries or attacking other people's possessions." Acquiring *Lebensraum* was essential to the nation's survival, and would have to be faced either now or in ten, twenty years' time. The moment for expansion was now. "With regard to the present situation in Poland, it is not Danzig that is at stake. For us it is a matter of expanding our living space in the East and making food supplies secure. . . . Therefore there is no question of sparing Poland and we are left with the decision: *To attack Poland at the first suitable opportunity*." Germany could "not expect a repetition of Czechoslovakia," he declared bluntly. "There will be war," and the key to victory was the isolation of Poland, a political task that was his responsibility. "It must not come to a simultaneous showdown with the West. An attack on Poland will only be successful if the West keeps out of the ring." England "is our enemy and the showdown with England is a matter of life and death." There was no question of "getting out cheaply. . . . We must then burn our boats, and it will no longer be a question of right or wrong but of to be or not to be for 80,000,000 people."

Throughout the following summer months the international situation simmered. Hitler retreated to Berchtesgaden and was rarely in Berlin. The Germans made desultory overtures to the Poles—Hitler still believed that they might have a role to play in an anti-Soviet alliance—but the return of Danzig and a rail or road connection across the Corridor were the unalterable German demands for any deal. Warsaw spurned these soundings as well as overtures from Russia. The key to the diplomatic situation, however, was not to be found in London or Paris or even Warsaw but in Moscow. British and French guarantees to Poland would be effective only if placed in a context of a collective security structure that included the Soviet Union, and both the English and French worked during the summer to coax the Russians into some sort of agreement. But Chamberlain was highly mistrustful of the Soviets, a sentiment reciprocated by Stalin, and the talks dragged on with little sense of urgency. Ultimately they foundered on Stalin's conviction that the West was simply trying to force war between the Soviet Union and Nazi Germany and that the English and French could not be trusted to honor their obligations. This, for Stalin, was the lesson of Munich.

Germany, too, was seeking to improve relations with Moscow. Ribbentrop was a keen advocate of closer ties, and while a rapprochement made no ideological sense, it would serve the short-run interests of both regimes. A Nazi-Soviet pact would upset Nazi party members for whom anti-Bolshevism was a central pillar of National Socialist ideology, but conservatives, especially within the military, were more open to the possibility of an accord. After all, cooperation with Russia had been a traditional element of Prussian/German foreign policy through much of the nineteenth century, and during the Weimar era the two pariah states had signed a secret agreement that established close military cooperation. In 1922 they formalized that cooperation in the Treaty of Rapallo, whereby Germany helped train Russian troops and instructed them on modern weaponry. In return the Soviets allowed the Germans to develop and test weapons far from the prying eyes of Versailles inspectors. With the installation of Hitler in the Reich Chancellery in 1933 that cooperation had come to a halt, but by the close of the decade, the exigencies of international politics created space for some sort of agreement—not simply on trade but also on security matters.

In May Stalin signaled a shift in Soviet policy. He dismissed his foreign minister, Maxim Litvinov, a pro-Western advocate of good relations with Britain and France, the League of Nations, and collective security. Litvinov was also a Jew, and his dismissal was received in Berlin as an unmistakable message. Trade talks between the two governments sputtered intermittently along during the summer until at last, in August, the Soviets hinted that they might be open to something more. Discussions turned to security matters, and the Russians indicated that they would be interested in some sort of nonaggression pact. Ribbentrop quickly picked up the idea. Knowing that the invasion of Poland was imminent, he was eager to reach an understanding with the Soviets. Adding to his anxiety, the British and French were still negotiating with the Russians. But convinced that a Nazi-Soviet pact was a political impossibility, the British and French were in no rush.

As the days passed and the pressure mounted, Ribbentrop pressed hard for an agreement. In Berlin and Berchtesgaden nerves were frayed. Hitler, who had been initially skeptical about a deal with the Soviets, was now more eager than his foreign minister. An accord with Russia would remove the threat of a two-front war, against which he had preached since the earliest days of his political life. It would also, he believed, act as a deterrent to Western intervention. But the Soviets confirmed their reputation as difficult negotiators, and their interest for a pact with Hitler seemed to run hot and cold. Then, in mid-August, came a sudden breakthrough. Moscow presented a draft of a nonaggression pact, which thrilled Ribbentrop, but then insisted that the trade deal that had been under discussion over several months be completed first. On August 20 Hitler wrote a personal message to Stalin urging him to come to terms—and quickly. The Germans hastily agreed to sign the trade agreement, and Stalin responded directly to Hitler, inviting Ribbentrop to Moscow to sign the nonaggression pact on August 23. Hitler received the message while having dinner with Albert Speer and others at the Berghof. After scanning the note, "he stared into space for a moment," Speer recalled, "flushed deeply, then banged on the table so hard that the glasses rattled, and exclaimed in a voice breaking with excitement: 'I've got them! I've got them.' "

While the Ribbentrop delegation was preparing for its secret mission to Moscow, Hitler convened a meeting of his senior military commanders at the Berghof to brief them on the political situation. There would be a war with Poland, he stated bluntly, and it was better to act now than delay. Several factors weighed in his decision. "First of all, two personal factors: my own personality and that of Mussolini. Essentially all depends on me, on my existence, because of my political talents. Probably no one will ever again have the confidence of the German people as I have. My life is, therefore, a factor of great value. But I can be eliminated at any time by a criminal or an idiot." Hitler had become increasingly preoccupied with his own mortality and was determined to achieve his goals while he was still in good health. "No one knows how long I shall live," he said, "therefore conflict is better now."

A second factor had to be taken into the equation. The Western powers were governed by men "who are below average. No personalities. No master, no men of action." This time he was not interested in negotiations.

There would be no more Munichs. "I am only afraid," he declared, "that at the last minute some *Schweinhund* will produce a plan of mediation!" It was, of course, an enormous gamble, he understood this, but a lightning victory over Poland would leave the Western powers no viable course of military action. Speed, therefore, was everything. And once the fighting had commenced, moral considerations would play no role. "When starting and waging a war it is not right that matters," he declared, "but victory. Close your hearts to pity. Act brutally. Eighty million people must obtain what is their right. . . . The wholesale destruction of Poland is the military objective. Speed is the main thing. Pursuit until complete annihilation."

The next evening at six, in the presence of Stalin himself, Ribbentrop joined Russian foreign minister Vyacheslav Molotov in signing a German-Russian nonaggression pact that no one thought possible. The two bitter ideological enemies promised to observe benevolent neutrality in the event that one or the other should become involved in a European war. In secret clauses the pact called for a partition of Poland—an indication that this agreement was intended to address an immediate situation. The signatories also divided Eastern Europe into spheres of influence: Lithuania and Vilnius would fall to the Germans, while Finland, Estonia, and Latvia would be in the Soviet sphere. No agreement could be reached about Romania, with its rich oil fields, and the issue was tabled.

For Hitler, the Molotov-Ribbentrop Pact put an end to the threat of a two-front war. The Nazi-Soviet agreement, he was certain, would serve as a deterrent to Western interference. After all, with Russia at Germany's side, how could Britain and France hope to come to Poland's aid? Russia would also be a source of much needed raw materials—timber, grain, iron, oil, among others—and render Germany impervious to an English blockade. At some point in the future, the score would be settled with Bolshevik Russia, but for the moment, cooperation between the two dictatorships was essential.

For Stalin, the pact was a hedge against betrayal by the West, which, he was convinced, was only interested in directing Nazi aggression eastward; it shifted the Soviet frontier westward, providing a buffer between Germany and the Soviet Union. The pact also gave him time to rebuild the Red Army, which had been decimated by the military purges of 1938.

Those purges were staggering in scope: of the eighty members of the Military Soviet in 1934, only five survived. All eleven deputy commissars were eliminated; every commander of a military district, including their replacements, had been liquidated by the summer of 1938; thirteen of the fifteen army commanders, fifty-seven of the eighty-five corps commanders were purged; and 220 out of the 446 brigade commanders had been executed. But the losses didn't stop there. The greatest number of victims were junior-grade officers from the rank of colonel downward; company commanders by the score were liquidated. Distasteful as it was to many in the Soviet hierarchy, the deal with the hated Nazis would buy time for Stalin to rebuild the army he had so thoroughly eviscerated.

For Chamberlain, the news from Moscow resounded like the crack of doom. Speaking to a tense House of Commons he warned that the Germans were suffering from a "dangerous illusion" if they believed that this surprise agreement would convince the British and French to abandon their obligations to Poland. He followed these words with a stern letter to Hitler, hand-delivered by Ambassador Sir Nevile Henderson. Britain would leave no stone unturned to prevent war, but "if the need should arise, His Majesty's Government is resolved, and prepared, to employ without delay all the forces at its command, and it is impossible to foresee the end of hostilities once engaged." Chamberlain also announced that the British guarantee to Poland had been formally translated into a military alliance.

Hitler's response to the prime minister's letter was to inform Henderson defiantly that with Russia at its back, if it came to it, Germany would not shrink from a war with the West. He reminded Henderson that "this time Germany will not have to fight on two fronts." He then made a typically grandiose proposal. Germany was prepared to guarantee the continued existence of the British Empire and to offer military help "in any part of the world where such help might be needed." He was also willing to offer guarantees of frontiers in the West and a limitation on armaments. But the question of Danzig and the Corridor must be resolved without delay.

Chamberlain's stern message was reinforced by Robert Coulondre, the new French ambassador, who called at the Reich Chancellery later in the day. After listening to Hitler fume about the Poles and their alleged atrocities, Coulondre replied that "in a situation as critical as this, Herr *Reichskanzler*, misunderstandings are the most dangerous things of all.

Therefore, to make the matter quite clear, I give you my word of honor as a French officer that the French army will fight by the side of Poland if that country should be attacked." At the same time, he explained, "the French Government is prepared to do everything for the maintenance of peace right up to the last, and to work for moderation in Warsaw."

As if these declarations were not sobering enough, Bernardo Attolico, the Italian ambassador, followed Coulondre into Hitler's study and delivered an eagerly awaited letter from Mussolini. The Molotov-Ribbentrop Pact had come as a disturbing surprise to the Duce, and Hitler had written an awkward communication to Rome attempting to explain how it would actually strengthen the Axis. His message also made it clear that Italy should anticipate important developments in the near future. Mussolini's response was apologetic, embarrassed, but blunt: "In one of the most painful moments of my life, I have to inform you that Italy is not ready for war." He complained about low stocks of fuel, ammunition, iron, and other shortages that made a sustained military effort impossible.

The Duce's missive was a blow. When Hitler inquired what Mussolini would need in the way of supplies, he found that Italy's needs were so exorbitant they simply could not be met. That, of course, was Mussolini's intent. If Italy felt compelled to remain neutral, Hitler asked Mussolini to give every appearance of preparing for war. The *appearance* of Fascist solidarity was important to Hitler, as was the deterrent value of possible Italian action against France and England. Let off the hook, Mussolini readily agreed. But the Pact of Steel was badly strained, and Italian bitterness at being left in the dark and then perhaps towed into a war they did not seek was palpable.

Faced with these setbacks Hitler ordered a twenty-four-hour postponement of the invasion, scheduled to begin at dawn the next day. On August 30, Henderson delivered Chamberlain's reply to Hitler's last proposal. The British wanted good relations with Germany "but could not . . . acquiesce in a settlement which would put in jeopardy the independence of a State to whom they have given a guarantee." The note proposed resumption of direct negotiations between Germany and Poland to address their points of difference and concluded with the unambiguous declaration: "A just settlement of these questions . . . may open the way to world peace. Failure to reach it would ruin the hopes of better understanding between

Germany and Great Britain, would bring the two countries into conflict, and might well plunge the whole world into war. Such an outcome would be a calamity without parallel in history."

As the diplomatic situation deteriorated, party officials and the Socialist underground throughout Germany reported growing anxiety. Initially, the popular mood was calm, confident that "the Führer will make everything all right." But as the crisis deepened, the public's mood sobered. A Sopade informant detected "a certain nervousness" among the public, especially women, who were worried about the call-ups and generally were of the opinion that "those in Berlin don't understand the situation and the feelings of the people." There was a widespread attitude "that a war because of *Danzig* [was] madness; it is irresponsible to sacrifice possibly millions of people for the sake of one city."

The last dwindling days of August brought a series of feverish meetings, midnight telegrams, urgent appeals. The atmosphere was electric. The Reich Chancellery, teeming with generals and their adjutants, diplomats, state ministers, and party leaders, seemed more like the frenetic halls of the nearby Anhalter station than a center of government. Nerves, already frayed, were not calmed when a blackout went into effect in Berlin, casting the giant metropolis into stygian darkness. Hitler's response to the British note did little to reduce tensions. The German government was open to negotiation and would accept British mediation, Ribbentrop informed Henderson. To that end, the German Foreign Office had drafted a sixteen-point proposal that the Germans believed to be generous. Danzig would be returned to Germany; a plebiscite, administered by an international commission, would be held in the Corridor; the Poles would be guaranteed an international road and railway through territory that was to become German as well as unfettered economic rights in Danzig. Britain was to produce a Polish emissary with full powers to negotiate, and that emissary, the Germans insisted, was to arrive in Berlin on Wednesday, August 30, leaving the Poles a scant twenty-four hours to prepare. It was, as Henderson protested, an ultimatum, but the Germans refused to budge, accusing the British government of indifference to the continuing persecution of Germans in Poland. The Poles must accept this condition.

Under the circumstances, the British did not even attempt to convince the Poles to meet the German deadline. They opposed both the unreasonable time frame and the site of the talks. After the experiences of Hacha and Tiso, neither the British nor the Poles were willing to contemplate another visitation to the Reich Chancellery. Instead, Poland announced the mobilization of its forces. Though they held out little hope of success, the British now urged Warsaw at least to begin negotiations. But when Polish ambassador Jozef Lipski presented himself at the Foreign Office on August 30, Ribbentrop had only one thing to say: "Have you the authority to negotiate with us on the German proposals?" When Lipski admitted that he had not, Ribbentrop brusquely terminated the meeting. There was no point of continuing. The Germans, it was plain, were not interested in negotiations, and the Poles had seen enough of Hitler to know that he could not be trusted. They were prepared to fight.

Hitler's grand sixteen-point proposal was read out over German radio on the night of August 31. It was intended for domestic consumption, demonstrating to the German people that the Führer was striving mightily for peace and was magnanimous in his dealings with the Poles. Only Polish intransigence and blind British support for Warsaw had sabotaged Germany's last-gasp offer of a peaceful settlement. Later Hitler admitted that the proposal was nothing but a propaganda ploy, "an alibi, especially with the German people, to show them that I had done everything to maintain peace. That explains my generous offer about the settlement of Danzig and the Corridor."

Throughout these last days of August, Ribbentrop remained intent on scuttling any hint of serious negotiations. Although he realized that British intervention was a distinct possibility, he was willing to take the risk. At every opportunity he emphasized to Hitler that London was bluffing, reinforcing the Führer's gambling instincts. While Ribbentrop pressed the case for war, no policy consensus existed at the highest levels of the military or among the regime's political elite. Göring sought to use both official and backdoor channels to engage the British and avert the descent into war. In one remarkable initiative, he enlisted the services of a well-connected Swedish businessman, Birger Dahlerus, to shuttle between London and Berlin, seeking the basis for some sort of understanding. Although Dahlerus was able to engage Lord Halifax's interest, he could not dispel the deep British skepticism about Hitler's intentions. At a midnight meeting in the Reich

Chancellery on August 26, Dahlerus, just back from London, attempted to convey Britain's desire for negotiations but also its profound wariness about entering into discussions with Hitler.

Hardly listening to Dahlerus, Hitler launched into a tirade against the British, becoming more and more excited as he spoke. He listened to Dahlerus's report, but it only seemed to provoke him to greater fury. He stalked up and down the room, then, suddenly stopping, he began another rant. Hitler's voice was blurred, and his behavior that of a completely abnormal person. He spoke in staccato phrases: "If there should be war, then I shall build U-boats, build U-boats, U-boats, U-boats." His voice became more indistinct and finally one could not follow him at all. Then he pulled himself together, raised his voice as though addressing a large audience, and shrieked: "I shall build aeroplanes, build aeroplanes, aeroplanes, aeroplanes, and I shall annihilate my enemies." Finally, his rage subsided, and after a few moments he walked up to Dahlerus and said: "Herr Dahlerus, you who know England so well, can you give me any reason for my perpetual failure to come to an agreement with her?" When Dahlerus, choosing his words with care, suggested that it was the English people's lack of confidence in Hitler personally and in the Nazi regime, "Hitler flung out his right arm, striking his breast with his left hand, and exclaimed: 'Idiots, have I ever told a lie in my life?'"

Despite the feverish diplomatic activity in late August, a sense of resignation hung over the governments of Europe. War seemed inevitable. Attolico, the tireless Italian ambassador, made one last desperate attempt on August 31, urging Hitler to reconsider Mussolini's offer to mediate, but Hitler again refused. It was too late. Just after noon that day, he had issued Directive No. 1 for the conduct of the war. One and a half million troops that had been waiting anxiously for days began to move into their forward positions near the Polish frontier, ready to launch the war Hitler was determined to have. The attack on Poland was to commence at 4:45 a.m. During the night Heydrich's SD was to stage "incidents" along the German-Polish border, code-named Operation Himmler. The most elaborate of these ruses was a "Polish" raid on the German radio facility at Gleiwitz in Silesia. For the Gleiwitz attack, Heydrich produced several condemned prisoners from the concentration camps—"canned goods," as he referred to them—dressed them in Polish uniforms, provided by German counterintelligence, and transported them to the deserted Gleiwitz station. They were given a fatal injection, shot, and their bodies left strewn about the station. Before slipping away, the SD operatives screamed Polish nationalist slogans into a microphone while sounds of a struggle could be heard in the background. The German press was invited to cover the "Polish" raid, and news of this "dire violation of Germany territory," one of over twenty in the past week, was broadcast over the radio later that night. The Gleiwitz incident convinced hardly anyone beyond the frontiers of the Reich, but it served its purpose, allowing the regime to portray— however transparently false—the massive assault that followed as an act of self-defense against a rapacious Poland.

At 4:17 a.m. on September 1, 1939, the German cruiser *Schleswig-Holstein*, moored in Danzig harbor on a "courtesy visit," opened fire on the Polish military installation on the Westerplatte, a small peninsula that guarded the entrance to the harbor. The shelling was intense and Polish resistance fierce. At virtually the same time sixty divisions of German troops smashed into Poland from the north, south, and west, while fleets of Luftwaffe aircraft roared into Polish airspace to bomb airfields, munitions dumps, communications centers, and other military targets. Throughout the night German radio broadcast terse reports from the front, each indicating the rapid advance of German forces.

At 10 a.m. the following morning Hitler left the Reich Chancellery for the Kroll Opera House, where he would address a special session of the Reichstag. Berlin's usually teeming streets were virtually deserted; only a few civilians stopped to watch in silence as the Führer's car swept past. Scattered shouts of "Heil Hitler" pierced the gloomy quiet, but most Berliners, standing behind an unnecessary cordon of SA and SS troopers, simply stared, wordless, as the Führer passed by. That glum reaction was a reflection of the country's dark mood. "Everybody against the war," Shirer noted on August 31. "People talking openly. How can a country go into a major war with a population so dead set against it."

Addressing the Reichstag, an edgy Hitler declared that "this night for the first time Polish regular soldiers fired on our own territory. We have been returning fire since 5:45," he declared, confusing the time of the attack. "Henceforth, bomb will be met with bomb." He appeared that morning for the first time in a gray military tunic, which, he proclaimed, "has always been the most holy and dear to me. I shall not take it off again until after victory is ours or—I shall not live to see the day." He had labored for months, he said, to resolve the Polish situation peacefully, as he had done with Austria, the Sudetenland, and Bohemia-Moravia, but the intransigence of the Polish leadership had frustrated that effort and led to the present crisis.

He was at pains to reassure Britain and France that Germany was not "pursuing any interests in the West," and "I repeat this here, that we desire nothing of them. We shall never demand anything of them. I have assured them the border separating France and Germany is a final one. Time and time again I have offered friendship, and if necessary close cooperation, to England. But love cannot remain a one sided affair. It must be met by the other side." He was resolved to meet whatever challenges that might confront him, to suffer any hardship, to make any sacrifice. He would also "demand sacrifice from the German Volk, even the ultimate sacrifice should there be need." He had a right to do this, he proclaimed, "because today I am as willing as I was before to make any personal sacrifice. I am asking of no German man more than I myself was ready to do through four years." Then, recapitulating a theme that had been a leitmotif of National Socialism's appeal since its earliest days in the beer halls of Munich and that would resound shrilly throughout the war, he declared: "There will never be another November 1918 in German history."

As the Wehrmacht ground relentlessly toward Warsaw, using a combination of armor and airpower to devastate the overmatched Poles, Attolico made yet another effort to convince the Führer that Mussolini was prepared to convene a conference, an offer he had already made only forty-eight hours before. The Duce remained confident that he could bring the British onboard. But Hitler was not interested. Just as he expected, the Western powers were hesitating to take action, and if they did make a military move, it would be merely a face-saving, symbolic gesture before retiring. Meanwhile, the British cautiously indicated that they would be prepared to discuss Danzig, the Corridor, and other issues, but insisted that no talks could begin until German troops halted their aggressive action and withdrew from Polish territory. Still convinced that Britain would not fight, Hitler dismissed Mussolini's offer out of hand.

Then on September 2, the British informed Berlin that Ambassador Henderson would appear at the Foreign Office the following morning at nine to deliver an urgent communication from His Majesty's Government. The German government, it read, had failed to respond to Britain's message of September 1, calling for a cessation of military operations and a withdrawal of German forces from Poland. Instead, Germany had intensified its onslaught, and as a consequence, London had been compelled to draw a grim conclusion. "If His Majesty's Government has not received satisfactory assurances of the cessation of all aggressive action against Poland, and the withdrawal of German troops from that country, by 11 o'clock British Summer Time, from that time a state of war will exist between Great Britain and Germany."

Interpreter Schmidt hurried to the Reich Chancellery to report the contents of the message to Hitler. He found the Führer at his desk and Ribbentrop standing to his right at the window. "As I came in, both looked up expectantly. I stopped at some distance from Hitler's desk and then slowly translated the British ultimatum. There was complete silence when I finished. Hitler sat as though petrified, staring before him. . . . After some time, which to me appeared an eternity, he turned to Ribbentrop, who, completely paralyzed, had remained standing by the window. 'What now?' asked Hitler," glaring at his foreign minister. Ribbentrop had no answer except to mutter, "I assume that the French will hand in a similar ultimatum within the hour." He was correct.

Despite repeated warnings that Britain would honor its obligation to Poland if Germany attacked, the ultimatum came as a shock. Hitler, spurred on by Ribbentrop, had for the first time badly miscalculated. His vaunted intuition had failed him. He was certain that the pact with Russia would deter the Western Powers from intervening and that they would fold, as they had done before over rearmament, the Rhineland, the *Anschluss*, and Czechoslovakia. Chamberlain and Daladier were "little worms" and had neither the courage nor the fortitude to thwart German ambitions. "I know," Hitler told his generals. "I saw them at Munich." The war against Poland, which Hitler was determined to have, was to have been a localized war, fought in the East, while Britain and France stood aside. That set of strategic assumptions was now in peril, and Hitler was compelled to confront the prospect of war in both the East and West.

His spirits soon revived as reports from the front brought news of rapid advances and German victories. Polish forces fought tenaciously but were hopelessly overmatched. The Poles possessed few tanks or motorized vehicles—the Germans could count on a fifteen-to-one advantage—and the small Polish air force, equipped with obsolete aircraft, was vastly outnumbered by Göring's modern Luftwaffe. It was destroyed in a matter of days, leaving German dive-bombers free to terrorize Polish towns and cities—and anything that moved on the rails and roadways. Despite Hitler's assurances to the contrary, the Luftwaffe made little distinction between military and civilian targets. It was a rout.

On September 6, Cracow fell with virtually no resistance. The Corridor was taken by September 8 and the remnants of the Polish army had been pushed back into Warsaw, where they were encircled. For days German bombers pulverized the near-defenseless city, reducing it to a desolate landscape of shattered buildings and rubble-filled streets. The unnerving howl of the Stuka dive-bombers and the shrill whistling of bombs falling from the sky offered a chilling preview of an utterly new kind of war. On September 17, the date the French had promised to launch their counteroffensive (they did not), the Red Army swept into eastern Poland, taking up positions agreed to in the pact with the Reich. A demarcation line between Russian and German troops was established, and a formal treaty setting the new borders of what had been Poland was signed on September 28. Poland had been partitioned three times in the last half of the eighteenth century by Prussia, Russia, and Habsburg Austria. The Nazi-Soviet partition marked the fourth. The Russians proved as ruthless as their German allies, killing fifty thousand Poles and sending more than a million, including elements of the Polish intelligentsia—to prisons in the Soviet Union, where they were executed and deposited in mass graves.

The destruction of the Polish military was quick and decisive; organized fighting ceased by the close of September. No surrender was signed but all combat ended on October 6. In a month of combat, the Polish army had suffered 65,000 men killed and 130,000 wounded, while the Wehrmacht had lost 16,000 dead and 20,000 wounded. That was only the beginning. Before the invasion, Hitler had instructed his troops that this was to be a different sort of war, a war shorn of all previous notions of combat. The old rules of engagement would not be applied. "Genghis Khan had millions of women and men killed by his own will and with a light heart. History sees him only as a great state-builder. . . . I have sent my Death's Head [SS] units to the east with the order to kill without mercy men, women and children of the Polish race or language. Only in such a way shall we win the *Lebensraum* we need."

Moving into Poland along with regular troops were special SS commando units, Einsatzgruppen, charged with orders to carry out Hitler's racial wishes. First deployed in Austria and Czechoslovakia, they had served a limited policing function; in Poland they took on a far more extensive and sinister role. Seven Einsatzgruppen were created, numbering about 2,700 men in all. Each was attached to one of the seven armies operating in Poland. Their official mission was to secure the army's rear, which meant policing conquered territory and battling insurgents, but wholesale murder was their primary activity. They were "ideological soldiers" of the Third Reich, laying the foundations of the new racial order in Europe. Although technically subordinate to the army, these ideologically schooled death squads acted largely on their own, receiving direction from Reinhard Heydrich in his capacity as head of the newly created Reich Security Main Office (Reichssicherheitshhauptamt, RSHA). Himmler placed the RSHA in charge of all German police forces in Germany and in the occupied territories and selected Heydrich, his longtime deputy, to lead it. It was the cold-blooded Heydrich who presided over the tidal wave of terror that crashed over Poland in 1939 and who, two years later, would be the prime architect of the "Final Solution" to the "Jewish problem" in Europe.

Initially, the Nazis planned to "cleanse" those areas of Poland to be annexed to the Reich. The regime created two new states, Danzig–West Prussia and the Wartheland, both incorporated into the Greater German Reich, while the borders of Silesia and East Prussia were also pushed eastward. Poles, Gypsies, and Jews were to be removed, deported to a third region, the newly created General Government of Poland. The General Government, established in an area consisting of the Polish province of Lublin as well as parts of Cracow, the seat of its new government, and Warsaw, was not to be integrated into the Reich but was to be ruled as a colony, with a

German governor. All three of these territories were governed by hard-line Nazis, and each was determined to display his ideological zeal.

Hitler appointed Himmler Reich Commissar for the Strengthening of German Folkdom, a new title that gave him responsibility for Nazi racial policy in the occupied territories. Himmler delegated that authority to Heydrich and the RSHA, where specialists were already at work on finding a solution to the "Jewish question." In a memorandum drafted on September 19, 1939, entitled "The Jewish Question in the Occupied Territories," Heydrich laid out the foundations of Nazi policy. In those territories annexed to the Reich all non-Germans were to be expelled, a racial cleansing in preparation for future settlement by Germans. This meant evacuating thousands of Slavs and all Jews, consistent with prewar Nazi racial policy. But the very nature of "immigration" had undergone a radical change. It was one thing to insist on forced immigration, but where would the dispossessed go? Little thought had been devoted to this dimension of the evacuation program, and, symptomatically, little uniformity existed in SS policy on the ground.

Along with the Einsatzgruppen, Hitler established an Ethnic German Self-Defense Militia, which was, if anything, more independent and even more brutal than the Einsatzgruppen. As the leader of one such militia proclaimed to his troops: "You are now the master race here . . . don't be soft, be merciless, and clear out everything that is not German and could hinder us in the work of construction." Acting on their own, these militias carried out mass shootings of Polish civilians throughout the country. In one month alone, the militia massacred 2,000 Poles—men, women, and children—in Klammer; 10,000 Poles and Jews were herded by militia units to Mniszek, where they were lined up on the edge of gravel pits and shot. Aided by German soldiers, the militia marched another 8,000 into the woods near Karlshof and mowed them down. Of the 65,000 Poles and Jews murdered in the last quarter of 1939, roughly half were murdered by the militias.

Not to be outdone, the Einsatzgruppen took up their charge with stunning savagery. In Bydgoszcz they slaughtered 900 Poles and Jews; in Katowice another 750 including women and children; in the Bydgozca area, 5,000; in Zloczew, a small town in western Poland, they murdered nearly 200 people. These were not exceptional cases. Sometimes the

Einsatzgruppen and army troops claimed to be responding to "provocation" from Polish saboteurs and guerrillas and would then inflict merciless retribution. This pattern of alleged provocation and savage reprisal would characterize German operations in the East, although as the fury of war intensified, no provocation was necessary to prompt German brutality. In all, Heydrich's henchmen slaughtered some 50,000 Poles, not including the 61,000 professors, schoolteachers, police, administrators, army officers, clergy, and other groups considered to compose the country's intelligentsia.

Poland was to be left in a state of devastation, not to be rebuilt for the duration of the war. The ravaged country was to be kept in a primitive condition, its population reduced to the status of second-class citizens or, in the case of Jews, slaves. In the following months the Germans unleashed a torrent of restrictions and prohibitions on the native Polish population. Poles were forbidden to use public beaches, swimming pools, or visit municipal gardens. Polish universities closed; Polish social and cultural organizations were dissolved; Polish military uniforms and decorations could not be worn in public; all adults were required to salute Germans wearing military uniforms and to remove their hats in the presence of Nazi officials; Poles were required to sit in the back of buses, train carriages, and other public conveyances. Their food rations were cut—"a lower race needs less food," Robert Ley, head of the German Labor Front, declared— and thousands of Polish homes, especially in the countryside, were seized, their owners evicted at a moment's notice (thirty minutes or less) to make room for German settlers imported from the Baltic.

All of these restrictions and more applied to the Jews. Poland's large Jewish community offered an easy target. Poland was home to Europe's largest Jewish community, and from the beginning of the Polish campaign, Jews were singled out for especially ruthless treatment. Jews were forced to flee across the demarcation line into Soviet-held territory, while a pitiless bloodbath engulfed those left behind. In many areas the Einsatzgruppen killed Jews wherever they found them. In Bedzin, one unit burned down the local synagogue and killed about five hundred Jews in two days of terror. In Dynow, near the San River, an Einsatzgruppe consisting of SS personnel and members of the Order Police, burned alive a dozen Jews in the local synagogue, then shot another 60 in a nearby forest. Similar killing operations were conducted in neighboring villages. By September 20 the unit had murdered 560 Jews in the vicinity.

While the Nazis decided that some categories of Poles would be spared—those in key economic sectors or occupations—and others "Germanized," Jews were shown no mercy. They were simply eliminated. All Jews in the territories to be incorporated into the Reich were expelled and driven into the General Government. They left their homes, businesses, even their clothes behind, to be appropriated by Germans imported into the area. Many were killed by the militias and the Einsatzgruppen, shot, beaten to death, burned alive in schools or synagogues. For those who escaped that fate, no plans had been made in the General Government—or Berlin—for their settlement or survival. Ghettos sprang up in the major Polish cities, where in the following months, Jews died on the streets, shrunken by starvation or frozen, their bodies crumpled on sidewalks, as cold and rigid as gravestones. The first—and largest—ghetto was established in October–November in Warsaw; the Lodz ghetto in February 1940. Other ghettos and labor camps would open in other areas in roughly the same period. Most were located in or near cities with good transport facilities and were viewed as temporary holding areas or transit camps. Officially, the final solution was still forced immigration and would await further developments in the war.

While Heydrich's forces pursued their ruthless objectives, army commanders were deeply mistrustful of the SS and its leaders, and only reluctantly agreed that the Einsatzgruppen be tasked with combating "all elements in foreign territory and behind the fighting troops that are hostile to the Reich and the German people." Just exactly what this meant was unclear, but after observing the Einsatzgruppen in action and realizing just how little actual control the military exercised over these death squads, a number of army officers protested. Brauchitsch, commander-in-chief of the army, told the officers that it was the Führer's policy and that he had selected the Einsatzgruppen to carry out certain "ethnic-political" tasks in the occupied territories that were beyond the providence of local army commanders. Confusion reigned.

Halder, the army's chief of staff, noted in his war diary on September 10 that "an SS artillery unit . . . has herded Jews into a church and murdered them." He tersely added: "A court martial has given them a one year

prison sentence." Other army commanders were appalled at the bestial behavior of the SS, and sought to court-martial men under their command for
war crimes. One commander in Poland reported bluntly that the violence
of the police units demonstrated "a totally inconceivable lack of human
and moral feeling . . . a demeaning situation, which tarnished the honor of
the entire German nation." He recommended disbanding and dispersing
"all the police units, including all their senior leaders, and all the directors
of administrative offices in the General Government, and replacing them
with sound and honorable men." Nor was this disdain confined to the
military leadership. General Johannes Blaskowitz, supreme commander in
the East, was moved to report that "the attitude of the troops toward the
SS and the police fluctuates between revulsion and hatred. Every soldier
feels nauseated and repelled by the crimes being perpetrated in Poland by
men representing the state authorities. The men fail to understand how
such things . . . can go unpunished."

To put an end to the arrests and courts-martial, Hitler intervened to
make sure that those in the field understood that neither the Einsaztgrup-
pen nor soldiers were to worry about the legality of their actions: everything was allowed. Himmler gave the order that when insurgents were
encountered they were "to be shot on the spot." And insurgents there were.
The Poles organized guerrilla and saboteur groups to kill not only Wehrmacht troops but German civilians living in Poland. Outlandish stories in
the Nazi press about Polish atrocities against the German minority were
wildly exaggerated but not without some basis in fact. After the German
seizure of Czechoslovakia, the Polish government had become concerned
about German underground groups and self-defense militias and had shut
down a number of German cultural and religious institutions. When the
invasion came in 1939 they marched ten to fifteen thousand ethnic Germans away from the front, approximately two thousand of whom were
killed by Polish civilians while trudging eastward.

Efforts to rein in the Einsatzgruppen were ineffectual, and for the
most part the army simply looked the other way—or joined in. Murder
and torture were not confined to the ideologically trained SS. To clarify matters, Hitler on October 4 issued an amnesty for those whom the
army wished to punish—as far as Hitler and hence the law was concerned there were no war crimes in Poland. Torture, looting, and public

humiliation of Jews were rampant and were not only tolerated but were seen, unofficially of course, almost as an entertainment for the troops. Orthodox Jews, with their distinctive beards and side locks, were the victims of choice. They were whipped, forced to smear feces on each other, to jump, crawl, clean excrement with prayer shawls, dance around a bonfire of burning Torah scrolls; some had the Star of David carved on their foreheads. The "beard game" was by far the most popular: beards and side locks were cut or torn, roots and all, from their heads, much to the delight of the laughing soldiers gathered around. Carefree men out on a spree. They took photographs and sent them home.

Despite these radical steps and the genocidal language in which they were swathed, Hitler's plans were at this point still in flux. The solution to the Jewish problem in 1939 was still officially immigration, but with the Reich now in control of more than two million Jews, this was no longer a realistic option. It was at this time that the idea of a "Jewish reservation" somewhere in occupied Poland was discussed. The scheme seems to have been tentatively approved by Göring and Himmler but was dropped when no agreement could be reached on the location of such an installation. Hans Frank, the governor of the General Government, complained that his territory, which was the most likely site, was already being turned into a dumping ground for undesirables and could not handle a major influx of Jews. In addition to the millions of Polish Jews, the regime was now contemplating transporting Jews from Bohemia-Moravia and Austria to the General Government. The newly appointed *Gauleiter* of Danzig–West Prussia and the Wartheland were already conducting brutal deportations of Jews in a feverish competition to be the first to declare themselves as "*judenrein*" (free of Jews).

But where could they go? The Nazi authorities tried at first to push them into Russian-occupied eastern Poland or force them into the General Government. But this was obviously not an acceptable long-term solution. With the Reich now in control of Austria, Bohemia, and Moravia, and much of Poland, Heydrich and his SD specialists were facing a mounting crisis of their own making. Hitler charged Himmler with direction of overall racial policy in the East, but in practice much of that authority was delegated to Heydrich. The goal of the forced expulsions in 1939–40 was the creation of "a new ethnographic order" in Europe through forced population movements to create more racially homogeneous territories. Central to Heydrich's mission, as Hitler explained it to him, was to arrange "the liquidation of various circles of the Polish leadership," which would run "into the thousands." The "driving force" behind the Polish resistance, Hitler believed, was the intelligentsia and it must, therefore, be eliminated—a view enthusiastically shared by Stalin. On the eve of the invasion, the army leadership acquiesced to SS plans to arrest up to thirty thousand Poles, overwhelmingly civilians, and Heydrich ordered his men to prepare to liquidate them. But that was only a beginning. As the Nazis assumed control of Poland, they discovered that fulfilling Hitler's vision of "a new ethnographic order" in occupied Europe was an extraordinarily complex undertaking.

Groping for options, the SS considered another possible solution: the transport of Europe's Jews to somewhere in Africa, where the French colony of Madagascar seemed like an ideal destination. During the 1930s Poland and France had discussed the possibility of deporting Poland's unwanted Jews to the French colony off Africa's eastern coast. With its primitive conditions—few settlements, hospitals, and basic infrastructure, its hostile equatorial climate, its fevers and diseases—life in Madagascar would be unbearable for European Jews. It was a death sentence. Such plans had come to nothing, but in 1940 the Nazis revived the idea. In May, Himmler wrote a memorandum for Hitler on the "Treatment of Foreign Nationals in the East," in which he stated: "I hope to see the concept of Jews completely obliterated, with the possibility of a large migration of all Jews to Africa or else in a colony." In pursuance of this option, SS specialists drafted numerous memoranda on issues of international law and transport, but the logistical problems were ultimately deemed insurmountable. Mass deportations, ghettoization, even murder were now on the agenda. The Nazis were still seeking a "final solution" to the "Jewish problem," but it was becoming increasingly clear that for the Germans, the East had become a morally distinct area of operations. Traditional codes of conduct, of law, of morality were left behind on the border.

In the fall of 1939 and the months that followed, international attention to these ominous developments and Nazi attempts to establish a new racial order in Poland tended to recede, overshadowed by military events in the West. The speed of the German onslaught was stunning, and *Blitzkrieg*, lightning war, entered into the world's military lexicon. Mechanized warfare—the use of tanks in combination with aircraft, especially the Stuka dive-bombers and their uncanny, howling shriek— heralded a new epoch of warfare. Yet, for all the cutting-edge technology of the Wehrmacht, the German advance into Poland in 1939 was carried forward by some 300,000 horses, and most German soldiers marched in on foot, much as Napoleon's army had done more than a century before. Heavy reliance on horses would characterize all major German operations in the Second World War.

For Hitler, the campaign against Poland was a splendid success, just as he had predicted, and the British and French, beyond a declaration of war, had not intervened. Yet the war in Poland did not come without costs. The Poles fought courageously; their casualties in the German conflict reached over 70,000 deaths and another 50,000 resisting the Russians. But the assault on Poland had also taken a surprisingly stiff toll on the victorious Wehrmacht, which suffered 41,000 casualties, killed and wounded.

In October Stalin surprised both Hitler and the Western powers by sending the Red Army into neighboring Finland. Stalin wished to secure his northern flank, and the city of Leningrad was particularly vulnerable, lying only miles from the Finnish border. Soviet troops entered the snow-bound landscape of dense woods and swamps in October, and although they vastly outnumbered the Finns, their progress was glacially slow. The Finns, donning white uniforms and skis, proved masters of winter warfare, inflicting serious casualties on the Russians. For his heroic defense against overwhelming odds, the Finnish general Carl Gustav Mannerheim became something of a hero in Western Europe, hailed in Britain and France. Some in Parliament, especially Churchill, loudly advocated sending troops and supplies to Mannerheim across northern Scandinavia, but Chamberlain wisely demurred.

Hitler, who had not been informed of Stalin's plans in advance, found himself in an uncomfortable position. He yearned to aid the Finns, but due to the Nazi-Soviet pact, he could not. The lackluster performance of the Red Army in the snows of Finland confirmed his low opinion of the Soviet military power. What could one expect of a military establishment so thoroughly honeycombed by Communist commissars? It was a view widely shared by military staffs all over Europe.

HITLER TURNS WEST

While these developments were unfolding in the East, world attention was focused on the war in the West, or rather the peculiar absence of it. Germany was officially at war with England and France, but no military operations were under way along the Western Front—only a brief incursion into the Saar by the French and the occasional exchange of gunfire along the border. All was, indeed, quiet on the Western Front. It was a strange situation, dubbed by the English the "Phoney War" or "Bore War," by the French the "*Drôle de Guerre,*" or Strange War, and by the Germans the "*Sitzkrieg,*" the Sitting War. Brimming with confidence, Hitler offered a new "peace initiative," and a brief flurry of diplomatic activity followed, but no progress was made toward a settlement. The Western Allies, much to Hitler's dismay, stubbornly continued to insist that a German withdrawal from Poland was the sine qua non for talks, and, of course, Hitler was not about to relinquish what he had gained. Poland was to be the launching pad for an eventual assault on the Soviet Union and, equally important, was fast becoming a laboratory for Nazi racial policy.

Although the military leadership was cautious, an emboldened Hitler was impatient. The shooting had barely stopped in Poland when he ordered the High Command to begin preparing for an immediate offensive in Western Europe. Planning was to be completed by November 5, less than a month away, and X-Day was to be November 12. His commanders were shocked. They had anticipated a protracted period of defensive warfare in the West that would allow them time to regroup and repair their equipment, to replenish their stocks of weapons, and to integrate fresh troops into the line units. In addition to the human casualties, the Wehrmacht had lost some 300 armored vehicles, 370 heavy guns, and 5,000 other military vehicles in Poland. All Hitler's top commanders were convinced that a war against the combined forces of Britain and France would end in disaster. Generals Gerd von Rundstedt, commander of an army group in Poland, Franz Halder, chief of staff of the army, Heinz Guderian, the respected advocate of armored combat and a corps commander in Poland, and Commander-in-Chief of the Army Walther von Brauchitsch were all convinced that a war against the combined forces of Britain and France would be folly. The Allies could put more troops in the field than the Germans, and unlike the Poles, the British and French were well armed, well trained, and competently led. France possessed the largest army west of the Soviet Union and was considered the best in Europe. General Wilhelm Ritter von Leeb, commander of German forces in the West during the Polish campaign, was enormously relieved that the French had not launched an attack on his forces—they could have walked into the Ruhr, he claimed—and believed an offensive now against the British and French would be a catastrophe.

These views were reinforced by General Eduard Wagner, the army's chief supply officer, and General Georg Thomas, head of the High Command's economic section, who reported that the Polish campaign had seriously depleted the army's reserves of fuel and ammunition and that Germany's industrial base could not produce enough chemicals and steel for adequate supplies of gunpowder and artillery shells until 1941. Wagner also noted that half the tanks used in the Polish campaign were not yet repaired and would not be operational until 1940, maybe 1941. As Halder recorded in his war diary on November 3, "*none* [his emphasis] of the top commanders believes that the attack ordered by High Command promises success. A decisive success for the ground forces cannot be expected."

When the generals presented their objections to the Führer on November 4, they found that "discussion with him about these things [was] absolutely impossible." He accused the commanders of cowardice and held their foot-dragging responsible for the slow tempo of rearmament. When, at a subsequent meeting, Brauchitsch suggested that morale troubles among the troops in the West had surfaced and that "there are signs of a lack of discipline like we saw in 1917–1918," Hitler flew into a blistering rage. He would go there himself, he bellowed, and confront the trouble-makers. "He would have them shot." Brauchitsch's story was a complete fabrication—there was no morale problem among the troops. He had concocted this yarn in hopes that it would give Hitler pause and add to the arguments against an immediate attack in the West.

The generals, singly or in groups, met with Hitler over the following days and weeks, and left each of these encounters deeply troubled. As in 1938, a small number of army leaders began to contemplate "making a fundamental change," by which they meant removing Hitler from power. Even Brauchitsch and Halder were involved, though the center of the nascent conspiracy was Admiral Canaris's counterintelligence agency (the Abwehr), where Colonels Hans Oster and Helmuth Groscurth, long disillusioned by Nazi radicalism, were most active. They were also in contact with conservative civilian leaders, especially former Leipzig mayor Carl Goerdeler, Hjalmar Schacht, and retired general Ludwig Beck about forming a new post-Hitler government. Those discussions meandered through the winter months, as one postponement after another delayed the offensive again and again. There were eleven postponements between November and April, most due to weather, and while the generals were relieved that Germany had been spared certain calamity in the West, the repeated delays also took the edge off the embryonic conspiracy. As in 1938 nothing came of their plans.

Despite the disturbing outcome of their meetings with Hitler, the army's staff did produce an operational plan for an offensive in the West. The first version of Case Yellow called for a major thrust through Belgium and Holland, followed by a direct assault on French and British forces in northern France, then a drive south to Paris. The operation bore a striking resemblance to the Schlieffen Plan of 1914, and although the plan would be modified over the winter months, its central feature remained a massive assault through the Low Countries. By December, however, an important shift in German thinking was under way. The basic premise of Case Yellow was that once German troops launched their offensive, British and French forces would rush to prearranged defensive positions in Holland and Belgium to meet the German onslaught. There the decisive battle would take place. The French left substantial numbers of troops marshaled behind the Maginot Line, the elaborate string of fortifications constructed along the

Franco-German border, while fewer, mostly reserve units, were deployed to guard the Luxembourg border and the Ardennes Forest. The Maginot Line was considered impregnable, and the dense forest and narrow, winding roads of the Ardennes made an attack there virtually impossible.

Few in the army leadership were satisfied with this strategy, and alternatives were being proposed as early as October. General Erich von Manstein, Rundstedt's brilliant chief of staff, had begun pressing for a major revision of the plan that would fundamentally change the strategic thrust of the offensive. Manstein insisted that as currently construed, the plan was so unimaginative, so predictable and cautious that even if all went well, the plan could not deliver a decisive victory. The Allies would have little difficulty anticipating its moves, so that while the German offensive would gain ground, it would encounter very stiff resistance in Belgium and northern France, culminating in a stalemate similar to the static warfare of the Great War.

Manstein argued that the bulk of the Wehrmacht's armor and motorized forces should be concentrated to the south, in Rundstedt's Army Group A, and that their mission would not be defensive but offensive. The main spearhead of the offensive would be shifted from a frontal assault in the north to a surprise attack through the Ardennes Forest, where the Allies would least expect it. Leading General von Rundstedt's forces would be six armored and two motorized infantry divisions.

Manstein was inspired by the revolutionary precepts of tank warfare developed by Heinz Guderian's 1937 book entitled *Achtung Panzer!* Guderian argued that concentrated armored forces could operate independently of infantry, move swiftly to disperse enemy forces, disrupt their communications, and generally create an environment of unrelenting havoc. Essential to Guderian's vision was close coordination between mass armored attacks and air strikes. As the armored spearheads shot forward, dive-bombers and fighters would pulverize the enemy from the sky. Mechanized units would follow, trailed by infantry moving on foot. The emphasis was on speed and surprise, shock and awe. In Manstein's plan, Fedor von Bock, who had commanded troops in Austria and Poland, would attack in Holland and Belgium, drawing Allied troops northward. British and French forces, Manstein believed, would race north into Belgium to meet Bock's advance, assuming that it was the main force. Then, once the Western Allies had committed themselves in Belgium, Rundstedt's panzer divisions would come roaring out of the lightly defended Ardennes. Instead of turning south toward Paris, they would drive north by northwest toward the Channel coast, trapping the divisions of the British Expeditionary Force and the First French Army between the Channel, Bock's forces, and Rundstedt's tanks. The Allies in the north would be cut off from resupply and reinforcements and defeated.

Hitler was taken with Manstein's ideas, and in February he formally committed to the "Manstein plan," making it his own. Studies by the army's Enemy Assessment Division showed that French operational culture was characterized by cautious, detailed planning, and a great concern for security. It did not act swiftly and would be especially cautious when confronted by surprise. The British were good soldiers and well led, but, in the Wehrmacht's view, tended to be even more ponderous than their French ally. Manstein's was a plan fraught with enormous risks. Hitler and many in the High Command worried that the long, extended line of Rundstedt's spearheads would be vulnerable to a French counterattack that would cut in behind the advancing armor, springing a trap that would leave the panzers encircled. The Ruhr would then beckon to the Allies. It would be a disaster from which the Wehrmacht would not recover, and Germany would lose the war. But after hesitating in his usual manner, Hitler was committed to the plan. Always a gambler, he was drawn to high-stakes risks. He was also more convinced than ever that his fate was guided by the Almighty, who had great plans for him.

While the nervous generals talked about removing the Führer but did not act, an unknown cabinetmaker with Communist sentiments did. For weeks leading up to the annual celebration of the Beer Hall Putsch on November 8–9, Georg Elser had managed to build a bomb and plant it in a wooden, load-bearing pillar just behind the speaker's podium in the Bürgerbräukeller's great hall. On this annual occasion Hitler always addressed a packed house of party leaders, and his oration ran, as did most of his speeches, two to three hours. The speech was scheduled to begin at 8 p.m., and Elser set the bomb's fuse to ignite at 9:30. But on this occasion, Hitler, to the surprise of all, spoke for a mere hour and then abruptly departed for Berlin. He was already onboard a Berlin-bound train when the bomb detonated, devastating much of the spacious hall, killing seven and injuring dozens of the three thousand in attendance.

Elser was caught that very night attempting to cross the Swiss border and, after days of brutal interrogation at Gestapo headquarters in Berlin, was taken to Sachsenhausen concentration camp, where he lived as a "special prisoner" until April 1945, when he was transferred to Dachau and executed. The Nazi press attributed the bomb plot to the British secret service working with Elser, though the Gestapo quickly ascertained that the would-be assassin had acted alone. Hitler never believed that Elser was the lone assassin, but interpreted his "miraculous escape" as a "confirmation that Providence wishes me to attain my goals."

Two weeks after the explosion at the Bürgerbräukeller, Hitler convened his principal military commanders to explain his reasoning behind the offensive in the West. He gave an assessment of the military status of each of Germany's enemies and allies as well as the Reich's many military advantages. But the ultimate key to victory, he proclaimed with unabashed frankness, was himself. "As the last factor, I must in all modesty describe my own person: Irreplaceable. Neither a military man nor a civilian could replace me. Attempts at assassination may be repeated. I am convinced of my powers of intellect and of decision. . . . Time is working for our adversaries. Now there is a relationship of forces which can never be more propitious for us. No compromises. Hardness toward ourselves. I shall strike and not capitulate. The fate of the Reich depends only on me." The time to act had come. His generals should not concern themselves with matters of international law or conventional military practice. "Wars are always ended by the annihilation of the opponent. Anyone who believes otherwise is irresponsible. . . . Breach of neutrality of Belgium and Holland is of no importance. No one will question that when we have won."

Preparations for Case Yellow got under way in earnest in February, when German intelligence became convinced that the British were preparing to mine the approaches to Norwegian ports, which, in fact, they were. This, Admiral Raeder, head of the navy, insisted, Germany could not allow. Iron ore was a crucial resource for the Nazi war machine, and Sweden was the Reich's chief supplier. During winter months when the Baltic froze over, Swedish ore was delivered to Narvik in the far north of Norway and then proceeded by German supply ship along the Norwegian coast to Germany. If the English succeeded in mining Norway's inshore navigation route and forcing German supply ships out into the open sea, where they would be vulnerable to interdiction by the Royal Navy, the result might be fatal. Raeder also stressed that the Norwegian ports would offer important facilities for German submarines patrolling the North Atlantic. If, on other hand, the Allies secured a foothold in Norway, their airbases and naval facilities would control Germany's northern flank and threaten the Fatherland itself. Hitler was also aware of British interest in traversing northern Scandinavia to supply Finnish forces fighting the Russians. That would entail a British invasion of Norway, which the Germans could not permit. As a consequence, German planning for an invasion of Denmark and Norway commenced immediately.

On April 9, 1940, as the British mining operation commenced, Germany launched air, sea, and land operations against both Denmark and Norway. Denmark fell with virtually no opposition, but the Norwegians put up a spirited, tenacious defense. German paratroopers secured Oslo's airport on the first day of the invasion, and in the following days German forces seized all major Norwegian ports—Narvik, Trondheim, Namsos, Andalsnes, and Oslo. The Allies, not for the last time, were caught by surprise at the speed of German operations and scrambled to send troops. In late May Allied forces arrived at Narvik, besieging the heavily outnumbered Germans in the port. Although the Royal Navy inflicted heavy losses on the German Kriegsmarine (Battle Fleet), it also suffered significant losses, and on June 7, with war in Western Europe then raging, the Allies withdrew their troops, leaving the Germans in control of Denmark and Norway. It was not a good omen for the Allies, and in its aftermath the Chamberlain government fell. Daladier's fell soon thereafter.

On May 10, the ax fell on Western Europe. On a day when the newly chosen French premier, Paul Reynaud, resigned and France's supreme military commander, Maurice Gamelin, did as well, the Wehrmacht smashed into Holland and Belgium. The *Drôle de Guerre* was over. As Bock's troops drove into Holland, British and French troops, as anticipated, rushed northward to meet them. Their suspicions should have been aroused when they encountered little resistance from the Luftwaffe, allowing them to move rapidly toward their predetermined defensive positions. Using airborne troops—paratroopers and gliders—Bock scored dramatic victories over the Dutch and Belgians, as the Western Allies hurried their forces north to meet the advancing Germans.

But as Allied forces moved into place in Belgium, the Germans sprang the trap: the panzers of Rundstedt's Army Group A came roaring out of the Ardennes, catching the undermanned French by surprise. Sedan, site of Emperor Napoleon III's catastrophic defeat in 1870, fell on May 12, and by May 15 the panzers were across the Meuse bridges. Led by Generals Guderian and Erwin Rommel, the panzers did not turn north to engage the Allied forces there but drove rapidly westward toward the Channel coast. By May 20, German troops reached the coast near the mouth of the Somme and wheeled north toward the French Channel ports of Calais, Boulogne, and Dunkirk.

The British Expeditionary Force and the French First Army were trapped, cut off from the rest of their forces in France, and began a fighting withdrawal to the coast, where they hoped to be evacuated. The Germans pushed them into the port city of Dunkirk and onto its beaches. The panzers were only one and half miles from the port, primed for the final assault that would annihilate the British Expeditionary Force. It had all the makings of a sheer catastrophe. But as the panzers closed in for the coup de grâce, Hitler suddenly ordered them to halt. Convinced by Rundstedt, he argued that tanks were ill suited for the marshy terrain, and besides, he needed to have them ready for the last great push toward Paris. Halder, Guderian, and Manstein were furious. The complete annihilation of the British Army was within their grasp, and the Führer had snatched that opportunity away from them at the last moment.

Hitler assigned the reduction of Dunkirk to the Luftwaffe and Bock's infantry units pushing from the north. What followed was what the British hailed as the "miracle of Dunkirk." Between May 26 and June 4, a ragtag armada of naval vessels, fishing trawlers, tugs, and private yachts miraculously plucked roughly 338,000 British and 100,000 French troops from the coast despite incessant attacks from the air. The troops were saved, but behind them they left the wreckage of the British Expeditionary Force. All their heavy equipment—hundreds of vehicles, tanks, and artillery pieces—lay scattered in the sands of Dunkirk, and the Germans took 40,000 prisoners. Hitler later implied that he had spared the British troops as an act of goodwill, thinking that such forbearance would render the British more open to negotiations. The British certainly did not see it that way, and any interpretation of Hitler's actions based on a supposition of his "goodwill" rests more on fantasy than empirical evidence.

After the fall of Dunkirk, German forces wheeled southward, quickly broke through the defensive line established by the new French commanding general, Maxime Wegand, and moved on the capital. Paris was declared an open city; French units withdrew, and on June 14 German troops marched triumphantly down the Champs-Elysees. Church bells rang all over the Reich, boats blared their horns on the Rhine, spontaneous celebrations erupted in the cities. Meanwhile, Reynaud's reconstituted government fled first to Tours and then to Bordeaux and considered continuing the fight to the French colonies in North Africa. But with German troops racing southward, slowed more by thousands of panicked civilians crowding the roads than by the French army, Reynaud was pushed aside, and the aged Philippe Pétain, hero of the Great War, assumed leadership of the government on June 17.

Reynaud had brought the marshal out of retirement in the hope that the "savior of Verdun" would stiffen the army's will to resist, but it did not happen. Instead, Pétain, backed by the highest-ranking French generals, was convinced that the military situation was hopeless and removing the French government to North Africa was dishonorable. As for their British allies, they were doomed, willing to fight to the last drop of French blood but not beyond. Alliance with Britain was "a marriage with a corpse." Under the circumstances, he drew what he deemed the obvious, rational conclusion: he asked for an immediate armistice and integration into Hitler's New Order. The Germans readily accepted.

In a particularly cruel twist to France's humiliation, Hitler had the old railroad carriage in which the Germans had signed the Armistice in 1918 taken from a museum in Paris and delivered to a clearing in the Forest of Compiègne, to the exact spot where it had stood in November 1918. Hitler was overjoyed. In six weeks, the lowly corporal of the Great War had achieved a stunning victory that had eluded the mighty Hindenburg, Ludendorff, and the Kaiser's army for four blood-soaked years. William Shirer managed to be on the scene and watched as Hitler waited to enter the carriage. He had seen Hitler's face "many times at the great moments of his life. But Today! It is afire with scorn, anger, hate, revenge, triumph." Hitler swiftly snapped his hands on his hips, arched his shoulders, planted his feet wide apart. It was "a magnificent gesture of defiance, of burning contempt for this place now and all that it has stood for in the twenty-two years hence."

The terms of the armistice were surprisingly generous. Germany was to control Paris, the industrial north, and the coastal areas of Atlantic France—approximately two thirds of the country. Unlike Poland, France would not disappear from the map. A superficially autonomous region in central France was to be left to the new conservative government of Marshal Pétain, who would rule from the small resort town of Vichy. Hitler was eager to be rid of this conflict that he had tried to avoid or at least defer. His ambitions lay not in Western Europe, but in the East, and he did not wish to deploy large numbers of troops to occupy France. A cooperative France—Pétain suggested the term "collaborationist"—was the result. And the new regime in Vichy seemed eager to fit into Hitler's New Order in Europe.

Before leaving France, Hitler wanted to fulfill a dream that had been with him since his early years in Vienna. He wanted to see Paris. As a young man, he had studied the city's architecture in books, even knowing in great detail the interior of the Paris Opera House. On June 28, he summoned Speer and two other architects to accompany him and his entourage on a tour of Paris. Early on a gray June morning Hitler traveled through the deserted streets in an open touring car to see the sights of the city—the Pantheon, the Eiffel Tower, Sacré-Coeur, the Invalides, where he visited the tomb of Napoleon, and, of course, the Opera. By nine o'clock the sightseeing was over. He would never see Paris again.

Germany's stunningly swift conquest of France sent shockwaves throughout the world, but nowhere more than in London and isolationist Washington, where in September the first American peacetime draft was introduced in response. It had been universally assumed in military and political circles that the French would blunt the German offensive, and a long gruesome war of attrition would be the result. Now, suddenly, France was defeated; England driven back to its own shores; and Germany was the master of the European continent. France's ignominious collapse, the Nazi press explained, was due to the fact that "the French had placed leadership in the hands of the Jews," who proved to be "France's gravediggers."

Nazi propaganda notwithstanding, the key to Germany's victory in France lay elsewhere. It was not technological or numerical superiority, as is so often claimed, nor was it the oft-cited poor quality of the French troops. French soldiers, the ordinary *Poilu*, fought bravely and in highly compromised situations. All these factors played contributing roles, but by far the most significant factor in accounting for France's unexpected collapse was its military leadership. The French High Command consisted of men of the last war, men who could grasp neither the speed of German operations nor the Wehrmacht's operational strategy. Germany's lightning assault and sheer audacity were utterly unanticipated, and the Allies, well equipped and well trained, operated with a conception of speed and maneuver that was still mired in the mud of the Great War.

General Maurice Gamelin, the seventy-two-year-old commander of the joint British and French forces, was confident of victory, excessively so, and was slow to react to the German onslaught. The British Expeditionary Force was hardly more robust. While the French High Command worried excessively about signals security, which delayed its responses to the German offensive, German spearheads raced forward, sent signals in the clear, and did not wait for clearances. Speed and surprise, they gambled, would trump security. Unlike their French and English counterparts, German tanks were equipped with radios, allowing the panzers to communicate directly with one another and with Luftwaffe units providing crucial air support. The result was a degree of speed and maneuverability that kept the Allies perpetually off guard and one step behind.

The dazzling triumph over France brought Hitler to the pinnacle of his popularity in Germany and left his enemies gasping for breath. A jubilant victory parade through the center of Berlin honored the Wehrmacht and its stupendous achievements, and Hitler, in a special session of the Reichstag, awarded nine field marshal's batons to his generals and named Göring Marshal of the Reich. The victory over France, he boasted in addressing the Reichstag, was "the most daring undertaking in the history of German warfare," resulting in "the greatest and most glorious victory of all time." A sense of euphoria swept the country. France had fallen, and England had been driven from the continent. Casualties were high—27,000 dead—but the British and French had suffered greater losses. Yet, despite the parades, the speeches, the scenes of German triumph in the newsreels, there remained the troublesome realization that the war was not, in fact, over. The British had been soundly beaten but didn't seem to grasp the hopelessness of their position.

Churchill, Hitler believed, was the problem. Churchill's appointment as prime minister in May 1940 had come as a blow. For years an outspoken opponent of appeasement and National Socialism, a hotheaded "warmonger" to some in British official circles, Churchill relished his role as wartime leader. Despite the string of crushing defeats in Norway, the Low Countries, and France, Churchill was determined to stay in the fight. Anyone else at the helm in London would see reason, Hitler believed, would recognize that Britain's ability to reverse the situation on the continent was nil, and that the best solution was to strike a deal. Britian should recognize the new realities of international politics and accommodate itself to them. Hitler was prepared to recognize the integrity of the British Empire; Germany had no demands to make on Britain—perhaps some restoration of German colonies in Africa, but beyond that nothing. London had merely to accept German hegemony on the continent and take the Führer's word that Germany had no further ambitions. Yet, as the peoples of Europe had learned over the previous two years, the Führer's promises counted for little. "Hitler always meant what he said," British historian John Wheeler-Bennett once observed, "except when he gave his word." The English, whose behavior Hitler could never fathom, were not prepared to accept these conditions.

It was during these critical weeks in the summer of 1940, weeks when Britain stood alone, that Churchill delivered his most inspiring speeches, calling on the British people to persevere. They were speeches of desperation and defiance, swaddled in Churchill's soaring Augustan rhetoric defiantly summoning the nation to fight to the bitter end, to never surrender to Nazi tyranny. It would be "their finest hour." That speech was in Goebbels's view brimming with "an insolence that can hardly be exaggerated." It was "the speech of a raving lunatic. He wants to keep on fighting alone."

Nonetheless, on July 19 Hitler convened the Reichstag to give a much anticipated speech that was to contain a "magnanimous" offer to the British. There were really no issues dividing the two nations, Hitler declared. He renewed his offer to provide a military guarantee of the British Empire. But if the war continues, he warned, "Mr. Churchill should . . . trust me when as a prophet I now proclaim: A great world empire will be destroyed. A world empire which I never had the ambition to destroy or as much as harm." He was working to prevent a needless calamity and felt compelled by his conscience to make another "appeal to reason in England. . . . I am not asking for something as the vanquished, but rather, as the victor." He was "speaking in the name of reason. I see no compelling reason which could force the continuation of this war." Only "Jews and Freemasons, armaments industrialists and war profiteers, international traders and stockjobbers" wanted this war.

Here Nazi propaganda found its leitmotif for war with Britain. The threat of Judeo-Bolshevism faded temporarily, while Germany's defense against Jewish plutocracy was moved stage center. Germany was not at war with the British people, but with the plutocrats backed by the Jews who had come to dominate British politics and society. "Our Jewish-democratic world enemy succeeded in inciting the English people to a state of war against Germany," Hitler declared in the very first days of the conflict. "English and Jewish philistines," the Nazi press insisted, "had a common political and economic interest in working against the process of liberation that Germany was leading against English-Jewish capitalist domination." German journalists were to direct their attacks not against the British people but "against those eternal warmongers who act on behalf of Jewry, international capitalism, and the democracies and plutocracies." Sadly, the British upper strata had become heavily "Jewified," but at least now the German people knew who their true enemy was: "power-hungry, hate filled world Jewry." England, Goebbels proclaimed, "was in the hands of the Jews."

Goebbels's propaganda barrage against England proved enormously successful, especially with the young. "German public opinion is boiling hot," Goebbels noted with satisfaction in his diary. The German people were "aflame" with hatred of Britain, and war against England "will be a relief," Goebbels concluded. "That is what the German people want." Gestapo reports on public opinion bore this out, registering a rising impatience for a decisive blow against the warmonger Churchill and the British people. "Overwhelming is the hope that the Führer attack England immediately," one report in June claimed, and that "the British will really get it in the neck." Another noted that "people could hardly wait for the attack to start, and everybody wanted to be present at Britain's impending defeat." The jaunty popular war song "We're Going Against England," released in July, captured that sense of confidence and resentment. It played on the radio in a continuous loop, and for a change German popular opinion seemed to charge out in front of Hitler and the Nazi leadership. Hitler was frustrated and angry when the very next evening the BBC broadcast a flat refusal of his peace offering, and a day later Foreign Minister Lord Halifax officially rejected it. "The Führer," Halder recorded in his diary, "is very strongly preoccupied by the question why England is still unwilling to 'choose the way to peace.'" Hitler had given his last offer to Britain. The war would continue. Unable to coax London into a settlement, Hitler ordered preparations to begin for an invasion of Britain. He had hoped to avoid such a step; to bluff the British into an agreement. An invasion was to be a last resort. But Churchill's incomprehensible truculence left him few options. On July 16 Hitler signed Directive No. 16, "About the Preparation of a Landing Operation Against England," authorizing the Wehrmacht to begin planning for an invasion of Britain.

When on July 16 the High Command of the Armed Forces (OKW—the Supreme Command of all German armed forces) for the first time confronted the stark realities of an amphibious landing in southern England, the challenges were sobering. Unlike operations against Poland and France, both of which were the result of months of staff planning, Operation Sea Lion was from the beginning an improvisation. Not even the most rudimentary plan for an invasion of Britain had been drafted when France fell in June 1940. Yet, the target date Hitler set was August 15. An undertaking, the outcome of which could decide the war and whose success would require extraordinary coordination between the army, navy, and air force, was to be operational in one month.

The original plan for Sea Lion called for 500,000 troops to land along a two-hundred-mile coastal front in the south-southeast of England. Halder believed that an invasion in a more concentrated area would be suicidal. Admiral Raeder was mortified when he saw the plan. He lacked the necessary ships to transport troops across the Channel and began requisitioning river barges, fishing trawlers, and tugs. Having suffered heavy losses in the waters off Norway, he also lacked the warships to block the Royal Navy. These considerations convinced Hitler to postpone the launch of Sea Lion until September 15, by which time Raeder hoped to scrape together enough landing craft to ferry the army across.

The key to success for the entire endeavor was the Luftwaffe's ability to establish air superiority over the Channel and the landing zones, but the army and the navy could summon little confidence in their ability to accomplish that mission. Göring's air force would have to drive the Royal Navy from the scene, destroy the RAF, break the initial resistance of British land forces, and annihilate reserves behind the lines. With his usual bluster, Göring assured Hitler that the Luftwaffe would subdue the Royal Air Force in five weeks.

On the morning of July 10, 1,500 German bombers appeared over coastal England, attacking several port cities—Plymouth, Dover, Portsmouth, and others. For almost three weeks German bombers attacked coastal defenses and sank over forty thousand tons of British shipping but never really dented the Royal Navy's strength in the Channel. Bombing in the daytime and without the benefit of fighter escorts, the Luftwaffe lost one hundred bombers by August 1. Raids on August 13 signaled a shift in targets. German planes began an assault on British air defenses to neutralize British airpower "in the shortest possible time." The raids focused on military airfields in coastal areas, flying units, supply, and the aircraft industry. Remarkably, only one attack was made on the radar installations that dotted Britain's eastern and southeastern coastline. The Luftwaffe knew their purpose but underestimated their importance.

During these raids the Germans inflicted terrible casualties on the RAF, shooting down more than one hundred British planes, but suffered heavy losses as well. If British pilots were able to bail out, most landed on British soil and could be back in the air again quickly, while German air crews shot down over England were lost for the war. On August 24, with losses rising alarmingly, the Luftwaffe shifted its priorities once again, returning to missions against RAF airfields. During the last week of August, the RAF lost so many planes and pilots that replacements could not keep pace. Fighter Command lost almost three hundred aircraft between August 24 and September 6, far more than German fighter losses. RAF Fighter Command, and hence British air defenses, was teetering on the brink of disaster, and alarm swept the government.

During the night of August 24, German planes attempting to bomb an RAF base on the outskirts of London strayed off course and dropped bombs on the center of the city. Before hostilities had begun, all combatants had issued solemn promises to refrain from attacking civilian targets, but the Luftwaffe had already bombed Warsaw and the center of Rotterdam. Warsaw could be claimed as a military target, since the Polish army was still resisting in the city, and the May bombing of Rotterdam, Berlin maintained, was due to pilot error. The RAF had also launched several desultory raids on a number of western German cities. On May 11, Mönchengladbach in the Rhineland had become the first German city to experience an air raid, but the RAF soon hit Hamburg, Kiel, Koblenz, Düsseldorf, and other targets in the following days. These raids produced little serious damage and few casualties; one could hardly speak of a systematic bombing campaign, but the shock produced on the German public was tremendous. Germans had been led to believe that the Fatherland was invulnerable to attack from the air and could hardly believe that the vanquished British had the temerity to launch raids on the Reich.

In retaliation for the London bombing, Churchill ordered a raid on Berlin for the very next night. Göring had famously joked that if a single British bomber managed to reach Berlin, he should be called Meyer, and the population of the city had great confidence in the field marshal's boast. A British bomber would have to fly deep into German airspace, dodge concentrations of flak en route, somehow elude flocks of Luftwaffe fighters, and then penetrate the outer and inner rings of antiaircraft batteries around Berlin. An impossible task. Yet on the night of August 25, a small RAF bomber force did just that. While air raid sirens wailed and powerful searchlights raked the sky, the squadron dropped bombs on the densely populated Kreuzberg section of the city. The Görlitz train station was badly damaged, bomb craters pockmarked the neighborhood's main street, and streetcar tracks lay twisted into a tangle of bizarre shapes. Twelve civilians were killed in the raid, and over nine hundred residents were left homeless. In the following week, the RAF returned for three consecutive nights. Rousted from their beds in the middle of the night by screaming sirens, civilians groped in the fathomless darkness to find their way to cellars or official air raid shelters. There they huddled for three or four hours, waiting nervously for the all-clear to be sounded. The war had come home to the Reich.

Speaking to a full house at the Sportpalast on September 4, Hitler raged against the British terror bombing. If the Royal Air Force "drop two thousand, or three thousand, or four thousand kilograms of bombs," he shrieked, "then we will now drop 150,000; 180,000; 230,000; 306,000; 400,000; yes, one million kilograms in a single night. And should they declare they will greatly increase their attacks on our cities, then we will raze their cities to the ground. . . . The hour will come that one of us will break, and it will not be National Socialist Germany." It was a dramatic reversal of his August 1 War Directive No. 17, explicitly forbidding the Luftwaffe to launch terror raids on the civilian population unless he had given his specific permission to do so. In one of his notorious monologues over dinner at the Reich Chancellery, Hitler, who only weeks before had cautioned the Luftwaffe to avoid hitting civilians, now exclaimed: "Göring wants to use innumerable incendiary bombs of an altogether new type to create sources of fire in all parts of London. Fires everywhere. Thousands of them. Then they'll unite in one gigantic area conflagration. Göring has the right idea. Explosive bombs don't work, but it can be done with incendiary bombs—total destruction of London. What use will their fire department be once that really starts." Within six months, terror bombing of civilian targets became the norm for both Britain and Germany.

In early September, the Luftwaffe shifted its targeting priorities away from the RAF airfields to an all-out assault on London. It was a drastic change in objectives, and its timing was critical. It was not just vengeance for attacks on Berlin, Hitler claimed, but would lure more British fighters into the skies, a move that Göring believed would hasten the RAF's inevitable downfall. But, with the battered RAF on the verge of collapse, that shift in strategy would prove of decisive importance. London was heavily defended by two thousand antiaircraft guns, and for ten days in mid-September, long bright blue days, the skies over southeastern England were filled with formations of black German bombers droning toward London. Vectoring fighters from around the country to intercept, the RAF relentlessly attacked. Losses were astronomically high for both sides, but by mid-September the outcome was clear. The Germans had failed to attain their strategic objectives. The RAF had suffered grievous losses but had not been broken; British morale had not cracked, and the Luftwaffe had been unable to secure the necessary air superiority for a cross-Channel invasion. On September 17, Hitler, with some relief, ordered the indefinite postponement of Operation Sea Lion.

The Battle of Britain was over, but the German air assault continued. The raids shifted to nighttime, metastasizing into the unrestrained aerial onslaught so many had feared. Fires engulfed London, turning large areas of the city into a blazing inferno. The Blitz, as the British called the German campaign of terror bombing, raged from September 1940 into the spring of 1941. During roughly thirty-seven weeks of unrelenting horror, the Luftwaffe bombed Liverpool, Hull, Bristol, Birmingham, Manchester, Sheffield, and other cities. In a particularly devastating raid on the night of November 14–15, 449 Luftwaffe bombers dropped 1,400 high-explosive bombs and 100,000 incendiaries on the industrial city of Coventry, creating a raging firestorm that consumed 50,000 buildings and killed 568 people. In London, 28,556 people, mostly civilians, lost their lives during the course of the bombing, marking an ominous new station on the road to total war. This was terror bombing, shorn of even the flimsiest justification about military targets, and with its coming, the character of the war was radically changed. What had begun as a confrontation between the armed forces of nations had now become a savage people's war, a war in which the distinction between civilian and military targets was erased.

THE CRUSADE AGAINST
JUDEO-BOLSHEVISM

In the high summer of 1940, while bombs still rained down on England and Sea Lion had not yet been officially abandoned, Hitler ordered preliminary military planning for an invasion of the Soviet Union. After Hitler quietly suspended Sea Lion in September, he was actually relieved to be free of the operation, about which he had never been enthusiastic. It was a distraction, drawing him away from his basic ideological and geopolitical objectives. Those lay, as they always had, in the East, in Russia. A war of annihilation against Judeo-Bolshevism in the Soviet Union was the bedrock of Nazi ideology and a goal Hitler had obsessively embraced throughout his political career. It was the cause that defined and animated National Socialism; the confrontation between National Socialism and Communism was for him the main event, an epic clash of ideologies that would determine the fate of Germany, Europe, and the world. It would also vastly expand the scope and savagery of the war Hitler had unleashed, and with it, geopolitics and genocide would merge into one terrifying maelstrom, transforming the very nature of the war and bringing the merciless slaughter of millions.

An attack on the Soviet Union, he assured his generals, would not draw Germany into a dreaded two-front war. England was barely clinging to life, desperately hoping for deliverance from either the United States or the USSR. A lightning conquest of the Soviet Union would eliminate Churchill's last hope for salvation in Europe, and the Americans, despite Roosevelt's strong anti-Nazi views, were a long way from intervening. A war in the East would provide the Reich with the *Lebensraum* of Hitler's fantasies and create new opportunities to solve, once and for all, the "Jewish problem" in Europe. By late summer 1940, while German bombers blotted the skies over England and the German public was absorbed in speculation about the anticipated cross-Channel invasion, Hitler decided that he could defer his vision no longer.

On July 31 in a conference with senior military leaders, Hitler ordered planning to commence for an all-out assault on the Soviet Union. The opening portion of the conference dealt with Operation Sea Lion, but Hitler quickly moved on to the central theme he wished to emphasize. "In the event that the invasion of England does not take place," he said, "our action must be directed to eliminate all factors that let England hope for a change in the situation." After all, he said, "to all intents and purposes the war is won." France was eliminated, and Italy was pinning down British forces in the Mediterranean. "Britain's hope lies in Russia and the United States," he declared. For the time being, the Americans were absorbed with the Japanese threat in the Pacific and would not be prepared to intervene in a major war in Europe until 1942 at the earliest. "With Russia smashed, Britain's last hope would be shattered," and Germany would "then be master of Europe and the Balkans." Russia's destruction "must therefore be made a part of this struggle. The sooner Russia is crushed the better."

The war against the Soviet Union, he stressed, would achieve its purpose only if the Russian state could "be shattered to its roots with one blow." Speed was critical. He estimated that "if we start in May 1941, we would have five months to finish the job. . . . The destruction of Russian manpower" was the objective, and the campaign would be divided into three major axes of advance. The first thrust would be directed toward Kiev in Ukraine and would secure the southern flank on the Dnieper River. The second would be aimed at the Baltic region and Leningrad, and then a third drive from the center on Moscow. The northern and southern spearheads would link up. Ultimately Germany would seize the Baku oil fields, Ukraine, White Russia, and the Baltic States. It was a breathtaking, "world historical" vision, as Hitler was fond of saying, and was now formally embedded in Directive No. 21, the invasion of the Soviet Union.

An undertaking of such epic magnitude demanded a fitting code name. Operation Fritz, the army's working designation for the operation, was simply too banal and would not do. On January 18, 1941, Hitler renamed it Operation Barbarossa, for the medieval German emperor Friedrich I, known for his fiery red beard (Barbarossa) and his policy of *Drang nach Osten* (Drive to the East). According to legend, Friedrich, who drowned on the Third Crusade in the twelfth century, was not dead but was slumbering in the Kyffhäuser Mountains in Thuringia, waiting to emerge in Germany's hour of need and restore it to its ancient glories. It was just the sort of mythic aura that so enchanted the Führer's imagination.

It is striking that the German generals, who almost to a man had grave reservations about operations against the Western powers in 1940, were equally unanimous in their low estimation of the Red Army. Still feeling the effects of the purges, it had sputtered ingloriously in Finland in 1939, confirming the low regard in which it was widely held. "The Russian is inferior," Hitler assured his generals. The Red Army lacked leadership and had failed to learn the tactical lessons of the war against Poland and the West. Despite its efforts to reorganize, the Russian army would be no better in the spring. German intelligence estimated that the Red Army possessed two hundred effective divisions and was still organized around infantry formations. The move to create armored divisions on the German model had only just begun. The Russians were also inferior to the Wehrmacht in equipment. "They have a few modern artillery batteries," Hitler confidently asserted, "but everything else is rebuilt old material. Our tank III . . . has a clear superiority. The majority of the Russian tanks are poorly armored." Most important in Hitler's estimation, the Red Army was hopelessly disorganized, its morale sapped by the purges and its ranks riddled with Communism. "You have only to kick in the door," Hitler told Rundstedt, "and the whole rotten structure will come crashing down."

During a series of conferences between December 1940 and February 1941, the army presented its evolving plan for the military campaign. All agreed that the first priority was the speedy destruction of the Red Army in the western Soviet Union. If it could be annihilated—not merely defeated—in the first weeks of the campaign, all options were open. No groups capable of recuperation must be allowed to escape. Beyond that lay uncertainty. The generals favored marshaling their forces for a push toward Moscow. It was, they argued, the obvious objective: Moscow was not only the political capital, it was also a major communications and transportation hub and an industrial center. An assault on the city would also draw the best of the remaining Red Army forces into the open where they could be destroyed. While not openly disagreeing, the Führer had other ideas.

As early as December 5, Hitler signaled his priorities: the Baltic area "must be cut off"; combined air and ground operations would "destroy the sources of enemy war potential" (armaments industries, mines, oil fields) and "crush Russian manpower." That, to Hitler, meant the Baltic, especially Leningrad, and Ukraine with its abundant raw materials. By striking with powerful spearheads north and south of the Pripet Marshes, the offensive would split the Russian front, allowing German forces to "encircle the enemy in separate pockets. . . . These two outer wings must be fast and strong!" For economic reasons, Leningrad and Kiev were to be the main focus of the offensive. Moscow, Hitler informed his High Command, was "of no great importance."

It was understood that the first objective was the utter annihilation of the Red Army in western Russia. Following that, the Germans could choose their next objective. Differences between Hitler and the High Command were not so much resolved as pushed to the side. Army leaders assumed that events in the field would ultimately dictate objectives for the second phase of the offensive and that Moscow would inevitably become the top priority. By early spring, the focus of the discussions shifted from strategic objectives to the conduct of the war. In a secret meeting on March 17 Hitler revealed to army leaders the full ideological dimensions of the conflict. The Soviet intelligentsia, they were told, had to be "exterminated" and the machinery of the Stalinist regime "smashed." To achieve this end, "force must be used in its most brutal form." Although Hitler did not extend this kill order to broader elements of the Soviet population at this time, a secret army order of March 26 clearly revealed how the military had understood the thrust of his remarks.

Several days later, on March 30, Hitler addressed some two hundred commanders of what was now being referred to as the Eastern Army (Ostheer). Speaking in the Reich Chancellery he reiterated the basics of his strategic thinking—the army's mission was to crush the Red Army and destroy the Soviet state, which he clearly assumed could be accomplished in a matter of weeks. But the real thrust of Hitler's remarks that day dealt more directly with the underlying ideological nature of the coming battle. This campaign would be a conflict not bound by the international rules of war established in the Hague and Geneva Conventions. While Germany was a signatory to those agreements, the Soviets had allowed their commitment to lapse. Therefore, the army could expect the most savage, barbaric conduct from the Russians, and the troops must be prepared to respond in kind.

"This," Hitler emphasized, "is a war of extermination. If we do not grasp this, we shall still beat the enemy, but thirty years later we shall again have to fight the Communist foe. We do not wage war to preserve the enemy." He called explicitly for the "extermination of the Bolshevist commissars and the Communist intelligentsia. . . . The individual troop commanders must understand the issues at stake. They must be leaders in this fight. The troops must fight back with the methods with which they are attacked." The commissars and other party functionaries, he concluded, were "criminals and must be dealt with as such."

On May 13, Hitler issued the so-called Barbarossa Decree, which, in effect, gave the troops a virtual carte blanche in dealing with the Russian enemy, both civilian and military. Commanders were free to carry out summary executions and to take reprisals against whole villages or groups when individual culprits could not be identified. The decree granted unequivocal immunity to the military and SS units engaged in such activities, guaranteeing that they "would not be subject to the constraint of prosecution even if the action is also a military crime or misdemeanor." Hitler also pledged that there would be none of the disruptive conflicts between the army and the SS that had plagued the Polish campaign; in the Soviet Union, both were now to operate from the same script.

The generals voiced no qualms about the prospect of an invasion of the Soviet Union. Although the Red Army's equipment was bountiful—it possessed more tanks and as many aircraft as the rest of the world combined, and its manpower reserves were virtually inexhaustible—the Wehrmacht command agreed with the Führer that the Soviet Union was highly vulnerable. In making that judgment, they chose to ignore the Red Army's smashing success in a series of major clashes with the Japanese on the Manchurian-Mongolian border in 1939, which would have told a very different story. As usual, the Führer was convincing. According to General Guderian's later assessment, "Hitler succeeded in infecting his immediate military entourage with his own baseless optimism." The army's High

Command (OKH) as well as the Supreme Command of the Armed Forces (OKW) were so serenely confident of victory before winter set in that winter clothing had been prepared for only every fifth man in the army.

The geographic dimensions of the operation were staggering and yet did not unduly worry Germany's military planners. Given the vastness of the terrain, they understood that the Wehrmacht could not afford to become bogged down in positional warfare. Yet, according to the plan, German troops were ultimately to establish a line from Archangel on the Arctic Ocean to Astrakhan on the shores of the Caspian Sea, a front of some 1,600 miles. It would be the most ambitious military operation in human history. "The world," Hitler said, "will hold its breath."

Three army groups would carry the offensive: Army Group North would advance through the Baltic countries in the direction of Leningrad, while Army Group Center would drive north of the vast Pripet Marshes toward Minsk and beyond that to Smolensk. Army Group South, operating below the Marshes, would spearhead the push toward Kiev and into Ukraine. In all, 3.2 million German ground troops would be committed to the offensive, augmented by approximately 500,000 Romanian, Hungarian, Slovakian, Croatian, and Italian troops. In all, 145 divisions would be mobilized, 102 infantry, 19 armored, and 14 motorized. The offensive would employ 3,600 tanks, 27,000 aircraft, and 17,000 artillery pieces. With its tanks and aircraft, it would be the most technologically advanced military machine in history. It is nonetheless telling that Barbarossa also required the requisitioning of 750,000 horses. Horse-drawn wagons would carry much of the army's heavy equipment, and most of the Wehrmacht's invading troops would enter Russia in the same way as Napoleon's *Grande Armée* in 1812—on foot or on horse-drawn wagons.

As planning progressed a number of generals, including the commanders of the three Army Groups, expressed misgivings of one sort or another. Hitler dismissed their concerns, assuring them that the loss of Leningrad, Moscow, and Ukraine would deprive the Red Army of its economic lifeblood and compel the Kremlin to surrender. But again, speed was of the essence. A quick, decisive victory in the East was imperative not only for strategic military considerations but for economic reasons as well. The German economy was not geared for a protracted war of attrition, and Hitler wished to avoid the privations on the home front that he believed had undermined the old Reich in the Great War. The German war economy, Hitler tried to assure his military commanders, could meet the demands of the Eastern Campaign, but in February, General Georg Thomas, head of the Wehrmacht's Office of the War Economy, submitted a cautionary report that cast a gloomy light over the whole of Barbarossa. It was the first of several bleak assessments of the military's economic preparedness Thomas submitted to the High Command over the following months.

The army's fuel supply, he warned, would last only for two months; the Luftwaffe might survive on its supply through the summer but no longer; essential rubber production *might* hold until spring 1942. He also warned that the food supply for the troops was a serious concern, especially if the war dragged on into the fall. Thomas presented his findings to Wilhelm Keitel, chief of Armed Forces High Command (OKW), with the assumption that they would be forwarded to Hitler, but Keitel dismissed them out of hand. The Führer would not allow himself to be influenced by such economic considerations, he told Thomas. It is unlikely that Keitel even bothered to pass along Thomas's reports to Hitler. Göring, head of the Four Year Plan and hence Germany's war economy, was equally unfazed by Thomas's dire warnings. There was little reason to be overly concerned about these putative shortages, he assured a skeptical Thomas. The army would simply seize what it needed as it moved along.

Göring had ideas of his own about the economic exploitation of the conquered land that were as sinister if not as ferocious as Heydrich's SS operations. From the outset of the war German planners had been concerned about the food supply, not only for the advancing troops but also the civilians of the Reich. Göring adopted a strategy, monstrous in its cold-blooded callousness, of "planned famines" to deal with the situation. It called for Russian cities in the west to be systematically starved. The agricultural goods that would have gone to the urban population would now feed the soldiers of the Wehrmacht and the population of the Reich. If this "hunger plan" were effectively implemented, Göring calmly estimated that as many as thirty million Russians, many of them Jews, would starve. Hitler shared this barbaric view, commenting in July that it was his "firm decision to level Moscow and Leningrad [Russia's two largest cities] and make them uninhabitable, so as to relieve us of the necessity of having to feed the populations through the winter." The cities would be razed by the air force, producing a "national catastrophe which will deprive not only Bolshevism, but also Muscovite nationalism, of their centers."

The invasion was set to be launched on May 15, after the spring rains had subsided, giving the invading forces ample time to smash the Red Army before the onset of the Russian winter. But the spring of 1941 was especially wet; rivers across Eastern Europe were swollen and roads had turned into quagmires of glutinous mud. The invasion would have to be postponed until the panzers had firm terrain. Also contributing to the delay was Mussolini's ill-conceived invasion of Greece in April, which quickly turned into a fiasco. Like Hitler on numerous occasions, Mussolini chose not to inform his ally of his plans, and a furious Hitler was caught by surprise. Mussolini's strike prompted Britain to rush troops into the Peloponnese in response, and the Wehrmacht could not afford to have its southeastern flank exposed as it plunged into Russia, so in April German forces came to Mussolini's rescue. On April 6, Wehrmacht troops invaded both Yugoslavia and Greece and within a short time stabilized the situation in the Balkans. An armistice was signed with Yugoslavia on April 14, while the fighting in Greece dragged on until May 27. The Wehrmacht fought British troops on the Greek mainland and on Crete, where it sustained serious casualties (two thousand killed) before British forces could be evicted. It was the second time that the Reich had been forced to come to the imprudent Duce's aid, having sent German troops to North Africa to bail him out of his desert war with the British.

In the spring of 1941, facing an imminent campaign of colossal proportions in the Soviet Union, German forces were now spread thinly over the Balkans, North Africa, and Western Europe, a very different situation from that which Hitler confronted in the summer of 1940. It was estimated that at least a quarter of the Reich's troops would be stationed in these far-flung theaters of war, which meant that the size of the German army that invaded the Soviet Union was not appreciably larger than the one that had attacked Western Europe in the summer of 1940. Given these complications, the launch date for Barbarossa was pushed back to June 22—the exact date of Napoleon's fateful invasion of Russia 129 years earlier.

As preparations for Barbarossa entered their final stage, Hitler was jolted by another unhappy surprise. Rudolf Hess, his slavishly devoted deputy and since 1939 second in succession to the Führer after Göring, decided to make a dramatic move. Despite his high official rank, Hess's influence had declined precipitously in the last years of peace, and, despite his unquestioning dedication to Hitler, he had become virtually irrelevant in the Nazi hierarchy. Worst of all for the faithful Hess, he had slipped to the periphery of the Führer's inner circle. But in the spring of 1941 he concocted a clandestine plan that he hoped would restore him to Hitler's good graces. He was not briefed on the details of Barbarossa, but he did know how much Hitler desired an agreement with Britain. In secret, he hatched a bizarre scheme for his personal intervention with the British that would secure the peace—and on German terms. It would be direct diplomacy. He consulted no one.

On the evening of May 10, he took off in a twin-engine Me 110 from a military aerodrome near Augsburg. He had served as a pilot in the final stages of the Great War and had secretly familiarized himself with the aircraft. His destination was Scotland. He had a message for the Duke of Hamilton, who was a wing commander in the RAF, and whom Hess had met briefly at the 1936 Olympics. He hoped to play the role of intermediary between the British government and the Reich, and Hamilton would open the necessary doors. Hess parachuted out of his plane near the duke's castle not far from Glasgow and was taken captive by a startled Scottish farmhand who took him to his cottage and gave him a cup of tea. Hess explained that he had a message of vital importance for the duke. Men from the local Home Guard soon arrived and transported Hess to their headquarters. Calls were placed, but a skeptical duke was in no rush. He did not arrive until the following day.

When he had verified that the man was, indeed, Hitler's deputy Führer, Hamilton located the prime minister at Ditchley Park in Oxfordshire, his occasional weekend retreat from the air raids of London. Churchill was hosting a dinner party at which a Marx Brothers film, Go West, was to be the evening's entertainment when the Duke of Hamilton arrived. Hess had been positively identified. It was a coup of potentially great significance. Churchill, who initially took it for a joke, was not impressed. "Hess or no Hess," he declared, "I am going to see the Marx Brothers."

For several days British interrogators had at him and quickly determined that Hess had little real information to offer. They also concluded that their prisoner was mentally unstable, possibly delusional, and that his proposal, coated now in a film of racial mysticism, merely repeated Hitler's position, which they had already rejected. To his amazement, a bewildered Hess found himself bundled off to the Tower of London and would remain confined to a British prison for the duration of the war. In fact, he never emerged from Allied captivity, and died, at the age of ninety-three, the solitary inmate in Germany's Spandau Prison, in 1987. The news of Hess's misadventure struck Berlin and Berchtesgaden like a bolt from the blue. Hitler was stupefied. Could this be true? His faithful Hess, of all people! When presented with a letter Hess had left behind for him explaining his mission to Scotland, the Führer let loose an "inarticulate, almost animal outcry" that could be heard throughout the Berghof. He immediately sent for Göring, Ribbentrop, and other officials from his inner circle. Was a Putsch under way? Was the army behind this? What exactly did Hess know about Barbarossa? He dispatched Ribbentrop to Rome to reassure Mussolini that Germany was not trying to arrange a separate peace, and Goebbels was to formulate a propaganda strategy to explain Hess's "betrayal." When the British did not immediately acknowledge that Hess had been taken prisoner, for two days an anguished Hitler hoped that Hess's plane had crashed in the sea. He inquired of the Luftwaffe staff about Hess's chances of reaching Scotland. "Virtually none" was the reassuring response. But on May 13, only a month before the planned launch of Barbarossa, London reported that Hess was in British custody. "Hitler," Goebbels recorded in his diary, "is completely shaken."

The regime went into damage control. Goebbels decided that Hess must be portrayed as an idealist and committed Hitler loyalist who, due to enormous physical and mental stress, had suffered a breakdown. He certainly did not speak for the Führer. Despite Goebbels's best efforts, the Gestapo reported that domestically the Hess incident was a "complete train wreck (a *Deroute*). . . . Massive uneasiness dominates public opinion," Goebbels noted ruefully in his diary. "The people wonder, with justification, how a fool could be the second man after the Führer." The regime struggled to manage the story, and within a short time the Hess affair was overtaken by more momentous events, and the matter receded from public consciousness. Still, the Hess episode put nerves on edge as the launch date of Barbarossa drew near. With Hess removed from Hitler's inner circle, Martin Bormann, always alert for opportunities to increase his influence with the Führer, was appointed Hitler's secretary and head of the Party

Chancellery, posts that he would gradually transform into a position of considerable power. In doing so, he would prove to be a far more malignant force within the leadership than Hess, and as the war progressed, his influence, always exercised behind the scenes, grew.

With troops and equipment moving into their forward positions, the Wehrmacht High Command issued an order to the Eastern Army on June 6 that would pass into history as the infamous Commissar Order. The essence of that directive had been first broached in Hitler's March 30 meeting with military leaders and now took official written form. So sensitive were its contents that only thirty copies were issued to the Wehrmacht's top commanders, who were not to distribute it to their troops but to read it aloud to them. It was not in the strictest sense a military directive but a mission statement, offering guidelines for the conduct of the troops in Russia and an ideological justification for the war of annihilation that Hitler intended. "In the struggle against Bolshevism, we must *not* assume that the enemy's conduct will be based on principles of humanity or of international law," it read. In particular, "hateful, cruel, and inhuman treatment of our prisoners is to be expected from *political commissars of all kinds* as the real carriers of resistance." As a consequence, "in this struggle consideration and respect for international law with regard to these elements are wrong. . . . The originators of barbaric Asiatic methods of warfare are the political commissars. Thus, measures must be taken against them *immediately* and with full severity. Accordingly, *whether captured in battle* or *offering resistance*, they are in principle to be disposed of by arms."

Germany was embarking on a desperate life-and-death struggle that demanded "ruthless and energetic measures." The troops had to understand the enormity of their mission: "Bolshevism is the mortal enemy of the National Socialist German people," the order began. "Germany's struggle is directed against this destructive ideology and its carriers. This struggle demands ruthless and energetic measures against Bolshevik agitators, guerillas, saboteurs, Jews, and the complete elimination of every active or passive resistance." Bolshevik agitators, guerrillas, and saboteurs would, of course, be difficult to ferret out, but the Jews presented an invitingly easy target. And since in Nazi ideological thinking, Jews and Bolsheviks were one and the same enemies of the Reich, these directives amounted to a death sentence for the Jews of the Soviet Union.

Some field commanders also issued orders of their own, echoing the High Command's directive. Hitler was particularly pleased with General Walter von Reichenau's order to his troops, which called for the German soldier to be "the bearer of an inexorable national idea and the avenger of all bestialities inflicted on the German people and its racial kin. Therefore the soldier must have *full* understanding for the necessity of a severe but just atonement on Jewish subhumanity. An additional aim in this is to nip in the bud any revolts in the rear of the army, which, as experience shows, have always been instigated by Jews." The army was also to understand that in this operation the SS had orders from "the highest authority" to undertake "special tasks" in the rear of the advancing fronts and would not be subject to military command. Between March and June, Heydrich formed four task forces (Einsatzgruppen) to carry out these tasks—Einsatzgruppen A (the Baltic), B (Belorussia), C (Ukraine), and D (Romania). They ranged in size from five hundred to a thousand men and were drawn from the ranks of the SD, Gestapo, Criminal Police, and Waffen-SS; their leaders were experienced and committed Nazis. They were given special ideological training, and the leadership cadres took courses in Russian geography and other practical instruction that would help them in the execution of their mission. These forces would be augmented by units of the Order Police, an organization of all uniformed police in Germany after 1936 controlled by Himmler and the SS. Local militias as well as two brigades of SS troops under Himmler's control also took part.

With the invasion only five days away, Heydrich convened his leaders for a final briefing, spelling out their mission in the most straightforward terms. They would move in either alongside or just behind the army. Their task was officially described as policing the occupied territories, but their mission was murder. They were to eliminate all functionaries of the Red Army and the Soviet administration. They were also to encourage pogroms among the local population, though Heydrich emphasized that German forces should remain very much in the background of such actions. After the war, some Einsatzgruppen commanders testified that on this occasion Heydrich ordered the murder of *all* Jews—men, women, and children—but evidence drawn from the regular Einsatzgruppen reports and other postwar testimony by Einsatzgruppen leaders suggests that Heydrich's initial order applied only to Jewish men in service to the Soviet regime. The indiscriminate slaughter of the entire Jewish population originated not from a single Heydrich order but developed incrementally from the Einsatzgruppen on the ground.

Operating in the Baltic area, Einsatzgruppe A was the first to initiate a policy of wholesale murder, slaughtering men, women, and children from virtually the outset of the campaign. Hearing no objections from Berlin—Himmler and Heydrich explicitly approved of the mass killings once they were under way—the other groups enthusiastically followed its genocidal example. Himmler's SS brigades were, if anything, more vicious than Heydrich's Einsatzgruppen; from the very outset of their deployment they systematically massacred Jews, killing men, women, and children. Such wanton murder would saturate German operations in the East and would only grow in intensity as the war progressed.

Shortly after 3 a.m. in the darkness of June 22, German artillery opened fire along a thousand-mile front and launched what was to become the most ferocious and deadly war in the dark annals of human conflict. More people would fight and die on the Eastern Front than on all other areas of combat around the globe combined. Twenty-seven million Soviet citizens and more than four million German soldiers would perish, and the Holocaust, the systematic extermination of the Jews of Europe, would be unleashed under the deadly cover of this conflict. It was a struggle of such barbarism and cruelty, such savage, remorseless killing that even decades after its conclusion the sheer magnitude of its horror defies comprehension.

On that June morning, the Germans achieved complete tactical surprise. Despite warnings from Britain, the United States, and Soviet agents in Japan and Germany, Stalin chose to believe that Britain and the U.S. were merely trying to sow discord between Moscow and Berlin and draw the Soviet Union into the war against Germany. Determined not to incite a German assault, Stalin scrupulously fulfilled all the economic clauses of the Molotov-Ribbentrop Pact and was at pains to avoid any sort of political friction with Berlin. Trainloads of raw materials and finished goods were still rolling across the frontier into German-occupied Poland as the Wehrmacht launched its offensive. Russian forces were completely unprepared for the onslaught. Stalin had chosen to position his forces far forward on the border in a thin line of defense and had not informed those forces of a possible German attack.

In the opening phase of the assault the panzers roared forward, carving up unprepared Russian units, while overhead the Luftwaffe bore down mercilessly on Russian positions. Within forty-eight hours, the Russians lost more than two thousand aircraft, mostly in their hangars and on their hardstands, and when the Red bomber force did get aloft, five hundred were shot down on June 23 alone. The world's largest air force was decimated in a mere two days. By the first days of July, all three German army groups were hurtling forward, gobbling up vast territories at a breakneck pace, inflicting staggering casualties on panicked Russian forces, and taking hundreds of thousands of prisoners. All along the front, German armored divisions broke through Russian lines, pushed on, then swung into huge enveloping movements. While the Luftwaffe provided close air support, the infantry would then close on the surrounded enemy, engaging them and clearing the area. Meanwhile, the panzers would be off again, thrusting deeper into enemy territory. It was Blitzkrieg at its most dazzling.

In June and July all three army groups made spectacular gains. At Hitler's eastern headquarters, the Wolf's Lair, concealed in a dark, mosquito-infested forest of East Prussia, a sense of euphoria prevailed. Day after day, at his military briefings Hitler watched the flag-shaped markers on the situation map press deeper and deeper into the Soviet Union. There was dramatic progress on all fronts. Army Group North drove 155 miles through Lithuania and into Latvia in five days; by July 10, German armor stood eighty miles from Leningrad and was closing fast. Army Group Center carried out gigantic encirclements of large Russian forces at Minsk and another near Smolensk some 200 miles farther east. Bock's forces had covered 440 miles in twenty-three days and were only 200 miles from Moscow. On July 3, Halder wrote in his diary: "On the whole one can say that the task of smashing the mass of the Russian army . . . has been fulfilled. . . . It is probably not too much to say when I assert that the campaign against Russia has been won within two weeks." This did not, however, mean that the battle was over. There was still much fighting to be done, Halder warned. "The sheer geographic vastness of the country and the stubbornness of the resistance, which is carried on with all means, will claim our effort for many more weeks to come."

Advancing just behind the army, the Einsatzgruppen and attached units of the Order Police conducted a bloodbath of unimaginable savagery all across the western Soviet Union. They did not operate as complete units but broke into special commando elements, often of company or even platoon size, which acted independently. They butchered tens of thousands of Jews and other "undesirables" and submitted regular reports on their murderous achievements to Berlin, where they were evaluated in the Reich Security Main Office (RSHA) and made available to a number of other Nazi officials. Altogether Einsatzgruppe A slaughtered 229,052 Jews in the late summer and fall; Einsatzgruppe B reported that it had killed 45,467 Jews; and Einsatzgruppe C claimed 95,000 victims by December 1.

The procedures varied only slightly from one killing action to another. Describing the liquidation of the ghetto in Borisov in October 1941, its SS organizer explained the procedures in terms that were both strikingly mundane and unimaginably macabre. For two days and nights before the action the policemen who were to carry out the action were "placed under the influence of alcohol and ideologically prepared to inflict atrocities on innocent people." The commander even held a banquet in a local restaurant for them during which "the policemen had the opportunity of imbibing alcoholic drinks to excess." At the banquet the leader of the action gave a speech in an attempt "to stimulate the Nazi policy of exterminating the Jews . . . and urged the policemen not to express any feelings of compassion and humanity towards either the adult Jews or the children."

Two hundred policemen, mostly Latvians, carried out the action. Under the supervision of the German Secret Field Police they ordered Russian prisoners of war to dig three large pits about two kilometers from the town. These pits or trenches were about four hundred meters long, three meters wide, and up to two meters deep. During the night before the killing (October 8–9) the ghetto was sealed off, and at daybreak the police units swarmed over their unsuspecting victims. They stormed into Jewish homes, driving men, women, and children into the town square, where trucks waited to carry them to "the place of execution." Those who could not be crammed into the trucks were marched to the trenches in groups of seventy or eighty and were beaten pitilessly all along the way. "There was no mercy shown to old people, children, pregnant women or the sick.

Anyone who offered resistance was shot on the spot . . . or beaten half to death . . . on my order," the commander proudly reported.

The doomed Jews were positioned about fifty meters from the trenches and guarded until it was their turn to be shot. Twenty Jews at a time were stripped naked, then led into the trenches, where they were forced to lie facedown. They were shot in the back of the head, execution style; in a matter of minutes another group of victims followed them into the pit, where they lay facedown on top of the first group and were shot. Wave after monstrous wave. Throughout the day the pits were "filled with groans and cries and the continual shrieks of horror of the women and children," while the murderers ate snacks and drank schnapps in the intervals between the shootings. Many were drunk. In Berlin the action was deemed a great success: seven thousand Jews were shot in a single day.

Describing the scene of another massacre in Ukraine, a German engineer from a private firm recalled watching the arrival and execution of several hundred Jews. As the victims tumbled out of the trucks, an SS man wielding a horse whip ordered them to undress and to place their clothing on separate piles for shoes, clothing, and underwear. One pile of shoes contained approximately eight hundred to a thousand pairs, and great heaps of trousers, shirts, blouses, dresses, sweaters, and stockings rose nearby. "Without weeping or crying out these people undressed and stood together in family groups, embracing each other and saying good-bye while waiting for a sign from another SS man who stood on the edge of the ditch and also carried a whip. During the quarter of an hour in which I stood near the ditch, I did not hear a single complaint or plea for mercy." One batch of victims after another was ordered into the ditch where "the bodies were lying so tightly packed together that only their heads showed, from almost all of which blood ran down over their shoulders. Some were still moving. Others raised their hands and turned their heads to show that they were still alive. The ditch was already three quarters full. I estimate that it already held about a thousand bodies. . . . The people, completely naked, climbed down steps which had been cut into the clay wall of the ditch, stumbled over the heads of those lying there and stopped at the spot indicated by the SS man. They lay down on top of the dead or wounded; some stroked those still living and spoke quietly to them." Then he heard a series of rifle shots and "looked into the ditch and saw the bodies contorting or, the heads of the already inert, sinking on the corpses." Stunned, he turned his eyes toward the man doing the shooting. "He was an SS man; he sat, legs swinging, on the edge of the ditch. He had an automatic rifle resting on his knees and was smoking a cigarette." While he relaxed for a moment, another batch of the doomed were already descending into the pit.

The rising tide of mass murder washed across the entire front, not receding even when the German advance ebbed in late summer. In the first nine months of the Eastern Campaign the Einsatzgruppen carried out two major sweeps; the first followed the rapid advance of the army in June and July, but many Jews were left behind. During the second sweep, commencing in October, the Einsatzgruppen were reinforced by personnel from the Order Police and conducted massacres on an even grander scale. These operations reached their grisly apogee in September at a large ravine just outside Kiev called Babi Yar. There the SS shot 33,771 Jews during a three-day period. By the turn of the year the Nazi annihilation plan had already resulted in the murder of 700,000 Jews.

The army did not interfere. Instead, the troops assisted in identifying and rounding up Jews, whom they turned over to the SS. The army's policy of retribution for guerrilla actions—burning villages, arbitrarily executing whole groups of "suspects"—also contributed to the pervasive aura of unrestrained violence and murder that engulfed the war in Russia. Not surprisingly, the savagery of this mass murder took a toll on the perpetrators directly involved in them. The men who participated in these operations were not SS bureaucrats sitting comfortably behind a desk in Berlin where the deaths could be dealt with as abstractions, as numbers on the page, but men with blood on their hands, men who confronted their victims face-to-face, who watched gasoline-drenched children, not yet dead, tossed onto a flaming pyre of bodies and heard their screams long after they had moved on to another massacre.

The psychological toll on the murderers was immense and a source of concern for SS higher officials. Examining troops in the area around Bialystok, where only days before 2,600 Jews had been shot and another 6,000 were scheduled for execution in the coming days, a visiting German doctor was besieged by police officials "who were suffering from nervous breakdowns and could not participate in another killing operation." Even the SS and police leader for central Russia had to be hospitalized with serious stomach and intestinal ailments, produced by nervous strain. The medical report indicated that the man was suffering from recurring nightmares in which he relived the killing operations with which he had been involved.

Himmler received reports of "disputes, refusals to obey orders, drunken orgies, but also serious psychological illnesses," and was looking for a way to reduce the psychological strain on the men involved in the shootings. One possible solution to the problems involved in these mass shooting operations was to find another mode of killing, one more efficient, more secret, and less emotionally traumatic for the perpetrators. In August 1941 the euthanasia program in the Reich was closed down, and many of its personnel transferred to the East. They had experimented with mobile gas vans in the T4 program and by fall 1941 had developed a new, more powerful model. Using carbon monoxide gas, the vans could asphyxiate forty victims at a time by connecting a metal pipe to the exhaust gas hose and inserting it into a sealed van. The powerful engines then pumped the gas into the vehicle. The specially equipped vans were first introduced into Poltava in southern Ukraine in November, and within weeks these mobile gas vans circulated across German-occupied Eastern Europe.

At this point, the German public had only vague notions of what was transpiring on the Eastern Front. So tight was the security in the run-up to Barbarossa that the invasion had come as a shock, but in the heady rush of spectacular victories in June and July, the public was swept up in the euphoria of the High Command. In late June the Gestapo reported that "the military victory over Russia has in a short time become taken as a given by every racial comrade [*Volksgenosse*]. . . . The optimism in some circles is so strong that they no longer wager about the outcome of the war but the date of German triumph. The timing most often heard is in the neighborhood of six weeks." The public was not informed about the casualties.

So confident was Hitler that Germany would prevail soon that in mid-July he convened a conference at his headquarters to establish the principles and organizational structure of the Nazis' new order in the conquered Russian lands. Before the invasion, the army had made no plans for the occupation, having been instructed that administration of the newly acquired Eastern territories was to be handed over to party officials. Only now did the regime address the question directly. Present at the five-hour meeting on July 16 were Göring, Alfred Rosenberg, Bormann, Keitel, and

Hans Lammers, secretary in the Reich Chancellery. Hitler explained that the German occupiers were not to reveal their larger intentions publicly; instead the regime would continue the threadbare narrative that Germany had been forced to intervene to restore order. The Russian public was not to recognize that a final settlement was under way. "All necessary measures—shootings, deportations, etc.—we will and can do anyway." He did not want to make premature and unnecessary enemies among the indigenous population. "We will simply act, therefore, as if we wish to carry out a mandate. But it must be clear to us that we will never again leave these territories." Germany must emphasize that "we are the liberators," but in reality "it's a matter of dividing up the giant cake so that we can first rule it, secondly administer it, and thirdly exploit it."

Hitler was not daunted by the vast territory and the millions of subjects the Reich would acquire. It would not be too difficult to control the peoples of this vast territory, Hitler maintained. "Let's learn from the English, who with 250,000 men in all, including 50,000 soldiers govern four hundred million Indians. Russia must always be dominated by Germans. . . . We'll take the southern part of the Ukraine, especially the Crimea, and make it an exclusively German colony. There'll be no harm in pushing out the population that's there now." The native population would not be educated. "It is in our interest that the people should know just enough to recognize the signs on the roads. At present they can't read and they ought to stay that way." The German colonists would be hardy "soldier-peasants" made up of "professional soldiers," preferably NCOs. Room would also be found for Nordic settlers from Scandinavia and the Netherlands—all Aryans—and Germany would build highways that would carry German settlers and tourists into what would ultimately be a German "garden of Eden."

On July 17 Hitler selected Rosenberg to head an apparently all-powerful Reich Ministry for the Occupied Eastern Territories. But the office was an empty shell, a fact underscored by Hitler's choice of the man to lead it. Rosenberg was seen by many in the party's elite as a fuzzy-headed ideologue and propagandist with no power base in the party or state. In theory this new position placed him in charge of all matters in the Occupied Eastern Territories. But, as was the case in so many positions of ostensible power in the Third Reich, Rosenberg's authority was a mirage, hopelessly diluted by other Nazi chieftains and their organizations.

Rosenberg hoped to co-opt the nationalities into the struggle against Moscow. Treated rather leniently but under tight German control, they could become valuable allies in the war against the Bolsheviks. Himmler, whose SS and Einsatzgruppen operated throughout Rosenberg's realm, was disdainful of such ideas and pursued a policy of stunning brutality. To Himmler and Heydrich, the Slavs were racial enemies, inferiors fit only for extermination or ruthless exploitation. For his part, Göring was determined to exploit the economic resources of the East to the maximum, starving millions of Slavs in the process. Rather than establishing anything that remotely resembled administrative clarity or a coherent policy, it was the usual battle of all against all, as each sought to work independently toward the Führer. Hitler, who did not take Rosenberg's ideas seriously, was, as usual, quite content with this arrangement. He had no intention of creating a series of quasi-independent Slavic satellites.

He was taken instead with Himmler's fantastic plans for the Germanization of the East. General Plan East, Himmler boasted, would be "the greatest piece of colonization which the world has ever seen." According to this plan, presented to Hitler in July 1942, some 45 million indigenous inhabitants in the targeted areas were to be expelled to points farther east. Thirty million of these were considered by SS demographic experts as racially undesirable. In all, 80 percent of the Polish population, 64 percent of the Belorussians, and 75 percent of the Ukrainians would be driven out; those allowed to remain would be "Germanized." The RSHA calculated that as many as ten million Germans would be resettled across the East within thirty years. This vast agricultural region, sprinkled with modern cities connected by a vast transportation network, would meet the food needs of a vastly expanded German empire into the future.

In the meantime the German-occupied East was to be ruled with an iron fist, the Slavic peoples enslaved, their cultures suppressed, their intelligentsia annihilated. A policy of fear and repression was deemed more effective than cultivation and co-optation. Ironically, Rosenberg's approach held far greater potential than the brutal policies adopted by his powerful rivals, but then, their policies were more in line with Hitler's, and that, in the end, was what mattered.

Muddying the waters still more, Hitler appointed special Reich commissars for the different regions under German control. All were hard-liners, and each pursued his own policies, disregarding Rosenberg and his administration. Only the will of the Führer mattered, and each commissar interpreted that as he wished. All were petty tyrants, mostly incompetent, sometimes corrupt, always savage. Their policies were not coordinated, and if they were subordinate to any higher authority, it was not to Rosenberg and his administration but to Himmler's SS.

As the campaign in Russia gathered steam, Hitler's public speeches and his addresses to party and state officials grew more extreme, more apocalyptic. He made repeated references to his prophecy of 1939 that if the Jews once again pushed the peoples of Europe into a world war, "it would not end in the defeat of those nations but the annihilation of the Jewish race in Europe." He ranted against the "Jewish global conspiracy," and that obsessive hatred resonated throughout the Nazi regime. In speeches on October 19 and 25, and December 12 and 18, Hitler explicitly mentioned the extermination of the Jews and spoke openly about it with foreign statesmen. Goebbels and Otto Dietrich, Hitler's press chief, were instructed to emphasize "the Jewish world enemy" in Nazi propaganda—which they did with a single-minded vehemence. Germany was not fighting England and Russia, but the Jewish plutocrats and Bolsheviks who controlled both.

In this atmosphere of paranoia and loathing, Hitler did not need to give a direct order for mass murder. Genocide was in the air. After July 1941, Himmler and Heydrich certainly proceeded as if the Führer had delivered a direct order to them—a verbal order, as was his practice—and everyone throughout the Nazi system understood his meaning and endeavored to, as Ian Kershaw has put it, "work toward the Führer." There may have been no single Führer order but instead an accretion of murderous initiatives from Hitler, the Einsatzgruppen, the political commissars, the SS, the Wehrmacht, all pushing in one deadly direction, a direction derived from Nazi ideology and Hitler's own ferocious obsessions.

Hitler probably had no clear idea of how his radical Judeo-phobia could be translated into action on the ground. That the Jews must leave all of Europe—still official Nazi policy in the summer and early fall of 1941—was clear, but how would this actually be accomplished? Solving that problem fell to the leadership of the SS. In October 1939 Hitler had appointed Himmler Reich commissar for The Strengthening of German

Folkdom in the occupied areas and in September 1941 expanded his Reich Führer SS's authority to the whole of occupied Russia. As previously mentioned Himmler delegated much of that authority to Heydrich in the Reich Security Main Office, where SS specialists were already at work finding a solution to the "Jewish question."

On July 31, Heydrich met with Göring, who was still ostensibly in charge of Jewish policy. That authority was based on Göring's assertion of leadership in Jewish policy dating from the aftermath of *Kristallnacht* and, typically, had never been officially superseded. Heydrich drafted a letter and obtained Göring's signature to it that formally transferred to him the authority to "make all necessary preparations" for a "total solution of the Jewish question in the German sphere of influence in Europe." He was to produce a comprehensive plan for a "final solution to the Jewish question" and to coordinate the participation of all organizations of party and state whose jurisdiction would be affected.

At that time, a final solution as envisioned by most within the Nazi leadership remained deportation: all Jews would be removed from the German sphere of influence and transported to the frozen wastes of Siberia, where, it was assumed, they would surely perish. But Hitler and the SS leadership assumed that this would come only after the defeat of the Soviet Union, and in the summer and fall of 1941 that had not yet happened. Meanwhile, Nazi officials in the East were complaining to Himmler that they were unable to cope with more transports of Jews for "resettlement." The ghettos were overflowing, and the special camps constructed by the SS to serve as temporary reception areas were already inundated. With the Nazis now in control of the largest Jewish populations in Europe and a Soviet collapse not yet in sight, some solution to these mounting problems would have to be found. There are no indications that genocide, that is, the systematic mass murder of all European Jews, was considered a possible solution at this time. That hundreds of thousands of Jews, perhaps millions, would die—were dying!—was not seen as a prelude to a more comprehensive killing program. But that was about to change.

In the late summer, Hitler was coming under mounting pressure from regional leaders in the Reich to fulfill his promise to remove all Jews from Germany and the Protectorate of Bohemia and Moravia. Nazi chieftains within the Reich were also calling for an order compelling Jews to wear some sort of distinguishing form of identification—a yellow star of David—as they did in the East, so that they could be easily recognized by the public. Goebbels was particularly vehement in his pleas to Hitler on both scores. As *Gauleiter* of Berlin, he hoped to see the Reich capital become the first German city to be declared "free of Jews." He also led the chorus of those Nazi officials demanding that German Jews be compelled to wear some sort of badge. The Jews, he argued, were responsible for deteriorating morale at home by spreading defeatist rumors and acting as "mood spoilers." A yellow star with the word "*Jude*" in black at its center would allow every German to recognize these rumormongers and defeatists. In September Hitler at last agreed to both the star and to a limited deportation program from the Reich and the protectorate. German Jews would be rounded up, and deportations to the East would begin immediately. As he told Heydrich in early October, he wanted "all Jews removed from German space by the end of the year."

In the Reich capital these first deportations were carried out in an orderly fashion. Officials of Berlin's Jewish community were required to help compile lists of those to be deported, and notifications, on the letterhead stationery of the Berlin Jewish Organization, were sent to those scheduled for "emigration." These Jewish officials cooperated in the belief that those chosen were not being sent to their death but were being resettled in the East. In unthreatening language, the letters advised the terrified recipients of the date scheduled for their departure and outlined the procedures to be followed. Baggage, carefully labeled with names, address, and transport number, could be deposited at the collection point, often a synagogue, two days before their emigration. On the day of their departure their apartment would be sealed by the Gestapo, and the Jewish men, women, and children would proceed directly to the collection point. A leaflet was enclosed detailing items the deportees were permitted to bring along—medicines, warm clothing, underwear, umbrellas, and bedding, along with shaving utensils—everything to suggest that "resettlement" was just that. All personal documents—birth, marriage, and death certificates—were to be presented to the authorities as were all cash, jewelry, savings books, bonds, and financial papers. They were also to compile an inventory of all those possessions and household items—furniture, fittings, kitchenware, and other belongings that were to be left behind. The proceeds, minus payment of outstanding bills to utility companies, would ultimately be turned over to the state. In this process, the Gestapo remained as much as possible in the background, and representatives—auxiliaries, they were called—of the Jewish community carried out this initial stage of the evacuation. The superficial civility of the process was intended to allay fears and ensure calm among the anxious and fearful, all of whom were doomed to a short, hopeless future.

While this evacuation plan appealed to Nazi officials in the Reich, leaders in the East protested that they were already swamped with Jews and other "undesirables." There was simply no room for new arrivals. They were not to worry, Himmler and Heydrich reassured them, the overcrowding in the ghettos and reception areas would be resolved. Those Jews already held in the collection areas would be shot to make room for the German Jews. The Lodz ghetto was to be the main reception center, but it could accept no more than twenty thousand Jews. Other ghettos, especially in the East, were added as reception centers to handle the anticipated influx. The first transports from Vienna bound for Lodz left the city on October 15; a day later transports from Prague and Luxembourg headed east, and on the 18th the first transport of Berlin Jews followed. To make room for the German Jews, approximately ten thousand inhabitants of the Kovno ghetto were murdered on October 28. In the first week of November, twenty transports carrying 19,593 Jews to Riga, Kovno, and Minsk—major collection areas—set off. Many of the arrivals never entered the ghettos; upon detraining they were marched into nearby woods and shot.

Still searching for an effective solution, Himmler in mid-October met with Odilo Globocnik, SS and police leader in the Lublin district, who made a radical proposal. A fanatical Austrian Nazi who had served as the top Nazi police official in Poland since 1939, Globocnik suggested that a stationary gas chamber be constructed at Belzec, an SS camp in the Lublin district of the General Government. He had consulted with personnel from the recently suspended euthanasia program, who suggested that rather than carbon monoxide a much stronger gas, Zyklon B, a deadly, fast-acting pesticide, could be used in permanently installed gas chambers. The killing would be much more efficient, and SS personnel would be liberated from the psychological stress involved in the mass shootings. Himmler was taken with the idea, and a first test was conducted at Auschwitz, not yet a major killing center, where six hundred Soviet POWs were gassed. It was deemed a success, and construction of the Belzec camp began in November 1941. It would become operational in March of the following year. Belzec would be the first installation in a new concentration camp system, distinct from the seven camps operating inside Germany. Its function was not the collection and incarceration of political prisoners but physical extermination.

While these SS killing operations gained momentum, the German army's advance slowed in late July, and the first signs of trouble began to surface. Despite their breathtaking gains, the Germans were slowly confronting some disquieting realities. Their rapidly advancing forces had outdistanced their supplies and were encountering serious logistical difficulties. Tanks broke down and replacement parts were inadequate; ammunition and fuel were in short supply. Russian and German railways operated on different gauges, and German supply trains were forced to halt and reload their cargo into Russian trains before proceeding farther east. It was a time-consuming process, and progress was slowed even more by partisan attacks, which were becoming a constant threat. Roads were also not what German intelligence had expected. Routes that appeared on maps as highways proved to be narrow, stone-paved trails, while secondary roads were often little more than sandy cattle paths that turned to mud in wet weather.

German planners believed that they had appreciated the physical immensity of the land, but when the Wehrmacht actually plunged into the seemingly infinite vastness of western Russia, it produced a profoundly unsettling psychological impact on the troops. As one German infantryman recalled, upon entering Ukraine "we came into a land of unending horizons. Endless wide steppes and grain and sunflower fields bordered our way toward the east." Marching for days in the sweltering summer heat—once they covered sixty kilometers in less than a day—they passed through a trackless landscape of deserted huts, burned-out tanks, overturned trucks, and "endless columns of Russian prisoners in ragged brown uniforms trudging in the opposite direction." It was a world of "dust, mud, burning heat, thunderstorms, and an endless open space with only occasional clusters of sparse trees stretching to the horizon."

Russian troops and their equipment were also not what the German High Command anticipated. The Germans launched Barbarossa under the assumption that Russian equipment, though plentiful, was largely obsolete or of inferior quality. In many respects this proved true, but unhappy surprises nonetheless awaited the troops. While the German infantry walked, one *Landser* (infantry soldier, or GI in American usage) recalled, "we were astonished at how well motorized the Soviet army was, as our own artillery was represented primarily by horse drawn equipment reminiscent of World War I." More ominous, Halder noted without comment the arrival of a new Russian heavy tank on the battlefield. It was the first appearance of the T-34, which would prove to be the most advanced and effective tank in the Second World War.

The biggest surprise, however, were the Russian troops themselves. They had been utterly routed; the Blitzkrieg was working as if by textbook, and yet the Russian soldiers didn't seem to understand that they were beaten. They fought tenaciously, even when there was little or no hope of survival, inflicting in the process heavy losses on the Germans. Although the Soviets were suffering horrendous casualties, so, too, was the Wehrmacht. By the close of July, German losses already exceeded casualties suffered in the entire Western campaign—and German forces had not yet achieved their primary operational objectives.

As the front moved deeper into the limitless Russian landscape, thousands of scattered enemy troops were left behind. Many stragglers and small units dissolved into the forests and swamps, suddenly reappearing to launch hit-and-run attacks far behind German lines. They struck supply trains and support units, and disrupted communications, creating for the Germans an eerie sense of vulnerability, surrounded in a strange, hostile environment where dangers lurked everywhere around them.

On the last day of August a German map depot of the Sixth Army was settling into evening bivouac at a village just off the highway leading from Korosten to Kiev. They were far behind the front lines, secure and comfortable, fraternizing with the villagers. At dusk, the Russians began to withdraw to their homes, leaving the streets virtually deserted. Then came the sound of "thundering horses and a dust cloud rising to the south." Suddenly, one German soldier recalled, "they were upon us . . . like an American film of the wild west . . . sturdy little horses riding at a gallop through our camp. Some of the Russians were using sub-machine guns, others were swinging sabers. I saw two men killed by the sword less than ten meters from me . . . think of that, eighty years after Sadowa! [the pivotal battle of the Austro-Prussian War of 1866]. They had towed up a number of those heavy two-wheeled machine guns; after a few minutes whistles began to blow and the horsemen faded away; the machine gunners started blasting us at very close ranges . . . soon tents and lorries were ablaze and through it the screams of wounded men caught in the flames."

As unnerving as these partisan attacks were, Hitler reacted to them with characteristic ferocity. When Stalin issued an appeal to the soldiers of the Red Army on July 3 to engage in partisan warfare, Hitler welcomed it as an opportunity to escalate the violence. "This partisan warfare gives us an advantage by enabling us to destroy everything in our path. . . . In this vast area, peace must be imposed as quickly as possible, and to achieve this it is necessary to execute even anyone who doesn't give us a straight look."

Despite increasing and better organized partisan attacks, the impressive string of German victories continued through the late summer of 1941. In the last weeks of July Smolensk fell to Army Group Center. During the month-long battle the Soviets suffered staggering casualties, including the loss of 300,000 prisoners and some 3,000 tanks and guns. That victory appeared to open the path to Moscow, which Hitler seemed at last to consider. By this point, all discussion of the elimination of the Soviet Union as a preliminary step to the ultimate battle with Britain had ceased. The war against Russia was all-consuming. A coup de grâce against Moscow seemed in order. But in early August, Hitler diverted Rundstedt's forces to the south toward Kiev. While the generals lamented this diversion, the results were spectacular. Army Group South took 100,000 prisoners in the Uman pocket near Kiev, and inflicted 700,544 casualties on the overmatched Red Army. In the fighting in and around Kiev, five Soviet field armies were annihilated. It was, Hitler declared, "the greatest battle in world history," and cemented his self-proclaimed status as "the greatest field commander of all times."

Hitler was in high spirits. He talked excitedly about putting the economy back on a peacetime footing and transferring several divisions of the Eastern Army to Western Europe. He felt vindicated in his battle with the generals. But the generals, while satisfied with their success in these operations, continued to harbor serious reservations. Hitler floated blissfully above all difficulties, but the Wehrmacht's spectacular victories in

June and July masked a set of increasingly serious problems. The Soviets were suffering almost incomprehensible casualties, but in the process were inflicting heavy losses on their German enemy. On July 20, Halder had to acknowledge that "the costly battles involving some groups of our armored forces, in which the infantry divisions arriving from the west can take a hand only slowly, together with loss of time due to bad roads, which restrict movement and the weariness of the troops marching and fighting without a break, have put a damper on all higher headquarters."

By August, German losses had reached alarming levels, and the severely battered Red Army still showed no signs of collapse. Halder had to admit that "the whole situation makes it increasingly plain that we have underestimated the Russian colossus," who consistently prepared for war, he added with no trace of irony, "with that utterly ruthless determination so characteristic of totalitarian states." At the outset of the war, "we reckoned with about 200 enemy divisions. Now we have already counted 360. Their divisions indeed are not armed and equipped according to our standards, and their tactical leadership is often poor. But there they are, and if we smash a dozen of them, the Russians simply put up another dozen."

The Germans were beginning to feel the alarming effects of a glaring manpower shortage. Planning had been for a short war, and little thought given to the question of replacements or resupply. Although the number of divisions deployed on the Eastern Front increased by 43 to 179—impressive as Hitler studied the situation map—many were divisions in name only. The number of troops in the Eastern region had actually declined by 750,000 men since the outset of the campaign. Some companies consisted of no more than seventeen men; corporals were pressed into command positions, and replacements could not adequately fill the gaps. The huge German losses sustained in the first year of the Russian campaign would reach close to 1,300,000 men (excluding the sick), or 40 percent of the Eastern Army's overall manpower of 3,200,000. "Certainly," Halder grimly acknowledged in late November, "the army, as it existed in June 1941, will not be available to us again."

Still, Hitler remained confident. "If the weather remains half way favorable," he boasted to Goebbels, "the Soviet army will be essentially demolished in fourteen days." But as the Russian campaign unfolded, Hitler's constantly shifting priorities, his interference in day-to-day operations, and his frightful indecisiveness contributed to growing resentment among his commanding generals. Halder complained that Hitler's "perpetual interference in matters the circumstances of which he does not understand, is becoming a scourge which will eventually be intolerable."

Direction of the campaign was shifting from the Army High Command to the OKW, with Hitler as its leader and the compliant Alfred Jodl as chief operations officer. Many army commanders, especially in the OKH, were insistent that the time had come to position their available forces for what they had long considered a decisive war-winning push on Moscow. To them it had grown increasingly obvious that the Wehrmacht could no longer sustain three separate offensives but must marshal its resources for a concentrated drive on the Russian capital. The key to success, the generals believed, lay in Army Group Center, whose operations, they assumed, would now be directed toward Moscow.

But Hitler was still determined to deprive the Red Army of essential resources in the Baltic and in the Ukraine, and in mid-August Brauchitsch and Guderian approached Hitler directly to make the case for a concentrated drive on Moscow. Hitler remained intransigent. On August 21 Jodl, who increasingly acted as a mere liaison between Hitler and the Army High Command, relayed a message from the Führer to his nervous generals, in which Hitler stated unequivocally that army proposals for "future strategy in the East were not in accord with his views." His message then repeated that the most important objective of the campaign was not Moscow and emphasized that "it was more important, before the onset of winter, to reach the Crimea and the Donetz basin in the south and cut off Russian oil supplies from the Caucasus area." Meanwhile, Army Group Center was to halt, assuming a defensive posture, while two of its armor groups were sent to reinforce Army Group South and Army Group North. Moscow remained a distant third in Hitler's thinking.

Halder no doubt voiced the reaction of the Army High Command when he slammed—albeit in private—"the absurdity of Hitler's orders." They would, he warned, result in "a dispersal of [German] forces and bring the decisive operation to a standstill." The situation "created by the Führer's interference is unendurable. . . . No other but the Führer himself is to blame for the zigzag course caused by his successive orders." After a frustrating period of waffling on the proper strategic course, Jodl explained that the Führer "has an instinctive aversion to treading the same path as Napoleon. Moscow gives him a sinister feeling." Trying to reassure the increasingly frustrated army commanders, Jodl argued lamely that "we must not try to compel him to do something which goes against his inner convictions. His intuition has generally been right. You can't deny that."

After dawdling through much of August, unable to decide on the next phase, Hitler at last, in early September, agreed to a direct assault on Moscow. He had by no means abandoned his view that the key to victory lay in the economic strangulation of the Soviet regime, but the campaigns in both north and south had not yielded the decisive victory he anticipated, and with winter bearing down on them, the seizure of Moscow, as his generals had maintained all along, might provide the rapid conclusion he desired. It was a race against time. The new operation got under way on September 3, and the Wehrmacht surged forward with a string of dramatic victories reminiscent of June. In mid-October forward elements of the 10th Panzer Division were seventy miles from the western fringes of Moscow, and on October 19 a state of siege was declared in the city. In the first week of December German reconnaissance patrols claimed that they could see the spires of the Kremlin in the distance.

But it was a different Wehrmacht now. Its equipment was in disrepair, fuel and food stocks low, casualties were high and replacements insufficient. The once-powerful Luftwaffe was severely degraded, a result of poor logistics and severe weather that greatly impeded air operations. Of the more than three thousand planes available at the launch of Barbarosa, only one thousand remained by the end of July, and only five hundred were operational by the late fall. The overtaxed troops were also suffering from low morale. Weeks of almost continuous combat had ground them down. Already in mid-August a grim report from Army Group South warned that recent Russian successes were less the result of a "change in the enemy situation as a revised assessment of the capabilities of our own troops. The plain truth is that they are exhausted and have suffered heavy losses." That sense of growing pessimism was also beginning to be noticeable on the home front. "The hope for a quick collapse of Bolshevism has given way to a conviction that the Soviet Union cannot be defeated by the offensive war in its current form but by a war of attrition whose distant end is not yet in view."

In October the offensive was slowed by weather, first by heavy rains and mud, then dense snow in November, and then howling blizzards in December. And always the bitter, implacable cold. German forces were ill prepared for a winter war. In November, with temperatures plunging to five, ten, fifteen degrees below zero Fahrenheit, equipment froze; engine blocks cracked; fires had to be lighted beneath the tanks to start their engines; coffee froze in mugs; even basic bodily functions became a torment. The Russians had executed a scorched-earth policy on the approaches to Moscow, leaving the advancing Germans in their lightweight summer uniforms little shelter, forcing them to huddle in shallow trenches to escape the frigid winds. German troops stuffed their uniforms with paper for insulation; they stole odd bits of clothing from the local population; many wrapped their boots in newspaper and rags. In late November the temperature dropped to –49 degrees Fahrenheit, and by Christmas 100,000 men had become casualties of frostbite—more than were lost to combat wounds.

In October, before the Russian winter set in, Wehrmacht commanders had pressed Hitler to issue a public appeal to the German people to donate winter clothing—caps, gloves, overcoats, sweaters—for the troops. But Hitler refused, fearing that such a move would signal that the war would go on through the winter, something his generals already knew. When, in January 1942, the regime finally issued a call for donations of winter clothing, a surprised German public responded with patriotic zeal, but troubling questions were raised: Why had the regime waited so long? people wondered. Surely, the call would have been more effective if it had been issued in September or even October. Why hadn't the army anticipated this? The Gestapo reported a slump in German morale on the home front, caused by the unexpectedly long and deadly campaign in the East and by relentless British bombing of western German cities.

Outfitted with winter gear and undeterred by the severe weather, the Red Army launched furious local counterattacks, inflicting heavy casualties on the weary German troops. Still, the German offensive, called Operation Typhoon, struggled forward. But it was severely hampered by losses in the officer corps. During the first two years of the war 1,253 officers were killed in action; between the launch of Barbarossa in June 1941 and March 1942 the number skyrocketed to 15,000, the highest rate coming among junior combat officers.

Hitler refused to credit such ominous reports and increasingly dismissed advice from his top military commanders. On one occasion, when confronted with alarming figures on Russian tank production, Hitler flew into a titanic rage and ordered the officer who had compiled these "defeatist" numbers to be silenced. Halder, who was present at that meeting, remarked that when Hitler "went off the deep end—he was no longer a rational being . . . he foamed at the mouth and threatened me with his fists. Any rational discussion was out of the question." If an action failed, whatever the cause, it was because the commanders in charge failed to follow his orders. Angered at Brauchitsch's foot-dragging failure to execute his orders, Hitler relieved the general of his command in November and assumed leadership of the army himself. Frustrated by the slow advance of Army Group South, he also dismissed General Rundstedt, the conqueror of Rostov, at the beginning of December for his apparent inability to hold the city. Both men were highly respected officers, and their dismissal was greeted with concern within the military establishment and the German public. Hitler's assumption of command of the army, which completed the Nazi hold on the military, was greeted enthusiastically on the home front but with unmistakable undertones of worry that the situation on the Eastern Front was far more serious than officially communicated.

Hitler would hear no bad news. As Field Marshal Eric von Manstein, hero of the campaign in the West and now commander of the Eighth Army in the south, observed, "Hitler was . . . disinclined to accept any reports out of hand or minimized the assertions about the enemy's deficiencies and took refuge in endless recitations of German production figures." When that failed to make the desired impression, he fell back on what for him was the key to victory: will, his will, Hitler believed, "had only to be translated into faith down to the youngest private soldier for the correctness of his decisions to be confirmed and the success of his orders ensured." Such a belief in his "mission," Manstein concluded, made him "impervious to reason" and led him "to think that his own will can operate even beyond the limits of hard reality." There was simply no place in Hitler's world for even a whiff of failure, and any attempt to pierce the bubble of his delusional imagination was doomed to failure.

While the Wehrmacht struggled forward, Heydrich completed his plan for a "final solution" to the Jewish problem. On November 29, 1941, he sent invitations to a small group of party, state, and police officials to a secret conference on December 9 to discuss matters related to Jewish policy. It was at this conference in Berlin that he would lay out his plan and assert the SS's absolute authority over it. But the meeting could not be held on December 9. It was postponed, overtaken by events that profoundly changed the dynamics of the war. On December 5, the Soviets, buoyed by reinforcements from Siberia and the Far East, launched a massive counter-offensive before Moscow that caught the decimated Germans flat-footed. With the Soviet capital in their sights, the surprised Germans fell back in a frantic retreat as the Red Army pushed the overextended Wehrmacht back over one hundred miles. With little in the way of reserves available, the situation was desperate. Hitler issued a stand-firm order, and after giving ground, the Germans were able to establish strong defensive positions; by early January the lines stabilized and held. Moscow—and the Soviet Union—were saved.

But it was events all the way across the world and apparently unrelated to developments in Europe that transformed what had been two separate conflicts—the Sino-Japanese War and Hitler's war in Europe—into a breathtakingly colossal global war. The Japanese attack on Pearl Harbor on December 7 brought the United States at last into the war, and four days later, Hitler, to the surprise of many and the dismay of his army commanders, chose to honor Germany's obligations to its Axis ally and declared war on the United States. Far from being worried, Hitler exulted, "We can't lose the war at all; we now have an ally which has never been conquered in 3,000 years." Nazi naval commanders were delighted—the U.S., they argued, had been engaged in an undeclared war against the Reich for almost two years, and American aid to Britain had been Churchill's best hope for winning the war. Now at last German submarines could be turned loose to ravage British and American shipping.

Hitler expected that America's attention would be focused on the war in the Pacific, and it seemed doubtful that the Americans could fight two wars on fronts thousands of miles apart. Besides it would take at least another year before America could fully mobilize its economy. The decision to declare war also had profound implications for Jewish policy. Roosevelt, Hitler was convinced, was controlled by a clique of Wall Street Jews, and Hitler had hoped to use the Jews as hostages to keep America out of the war. But that consideration was no longer relevant; there was no longer any reason for restraint, and so the full fury of the Nazi state could be turned on the Jews of Europe.

The German defeat before Moscow brought the Blitzkrieg phase of the war to an end. A speedy victory over the Soviet Union, which Hitler had promised, had proven elusive, and Germany was now confronted by a war with the two largest economic powers in the world. Many, even within the military, were coming to the uncomfortable conclusion that in the end Barbarossa had tried to do too much. While the Wehrmacht was still capable of winning battles, sometimes with spectacular results, it was not capable of winning a war that was now global in scale. The life-and-death struggle Hitler had proclaimed in the run-up to Barbarossa was now upon the German people, and for them, as well as the Jews of Europe, Armageddon beckoned.

HOLOCAUST AND TOTAL WAR

I n the bitter winter of 1941–42 two exhausted armies faced one another across a frozen landscape of snow and ice. The Soviet winter offensive gained ground in December and January but staggered to a halt in February; for the duration of the long dark winter, the Eastern Front saw no significant action. Both armies were recuperating, replenishing their supplies, waiting for spring and the return of good campaigning weather. In North Africa General Erwin Rommel, with his underequipped and undermanned Afrika Korps, drove across the desert into Egypt, almost reaching Alexandria before being driven back, while in the North Atlantic, German U-boats were sinking Allied shipping at an alarming rate. For German submariners it was "the second happy time," the first having come in the first months of war in 1939–40, when the U-boats sank almost a million and a half tons of Allied shipping. But for Hitler, North Africa remained a side show and although he followed the Battle of the Atlantic with satisfaction, the real war remained in the East, where the fate of the Third Reich hung in the balance. And while an uneasy lull hovered over military operations there, Hitler's war against the Jews escalated dramatically, entering a new, even more monstrous phase.

On January 20, 1942, light snow falling from a bleak overcast sky, fifteen men—officials of the Nazi party and state—began arriving at an imposing lakefront villa in the elegant Berlin suburb of Wannsee. They were there at the invitation of Reinhard Heydrich, head of the Reich Security Main Office, to discuss developments in Nazi Jewish policy. In October, Hitler had appointed Heydrich as the Reich protector of Bohemia and Moravia.

The Protectorate occupied a particularly important role in Nazi plans for the East; unlike the other conquered territories, the protectorate, with its highly developed munitions industry and supply of skilled workers, was to be incorporated in the Greater German Reich at war's end. Heydrich's appointment signaled a radicalization of Nazi policy. Heydrich was determined to crush any hint of resistance and strictly enforce Nazi racial policies. The Protectorate would be cleansed of racial undesirables before its entry into the Greater German Reich, and Hitler believed Heydrich was the man to do it.

Among those present at noon, chatting, lunching at the buffet, were Heinrich Müller, head of the Gestapo; Josef Bühler, state secretary to Hans Frank in the General Government; Wilhelm Stuckart, coauthor of the Nuremberg Laws and state secretary in the Interior Ministry; Roland Freisler, of the Justice Ministry; Erwin Neumann, of the Four Year Plan; Martin Luther, of the Foreign Office; SS *Sturmbahnführer* Rudolf Lange, commander of the Security Police and SD in Latvia; and several other SS officials and party functionaries. Neither Hitler nor Himmler was present. This was Heydrich's show, and he presided over the meeting, dominating the proceedings. His deputy, Adolf Eichmann, from the Jewish section of the Reich Security Main Office, made the arrangements and kept the minutes.

From the beginning it was clear that the meeting had two purposes. As the first order of business, Heydrich would unveil for the first time his plan for the "final solution" to the "Jewish question," and, second, he would assert his ultimate authority over it. The plan was to be executed by the SS, and the various party and state agencies represented there were to pledge their readiness to cooperate in full with its demands. Some of those present were surprised at the thrust of Heydrich's remarks, but others were not. Josef Bühler arrived at Wannsee knowing full well what to expect. He had been briefed in December and had reported to Hans Frank, whose General Government had become, in Frank's words, an overcrowded dumping ground for unwanted Jews. Something had to be done. On December 16, Frank explained to a group of senior officials in the General Government. "As for the Jews," he said,

> I will be quite open with you—they will have to be finished off one way or the other. . . . I know that many of the measures now being taken against the Jews in the Reich are criticized. It is clear from the

reports on popular opinion that there are accusations of cruelty and harshness. . . . As an old National Socialist, I must state that if the Jewish clan were to survive the war in Europe, while we had sacrificed our best blood in the defense of Europe, then this war would only represent a partial success. With respect to the Jews, therefore, I will only operate on the assumption that they will disappear. They must go. . . . But what will happen to the Jews? Do you imagine that they will actually be settled in the *Ostland* in villages? . . . I must ask you to arm yourselves against any feelings of compassion. We must exterminate the Jews wherever we find them.

That would occur through methods beyond the framework of the legal process. "One cannot apply views held up to now to such gigantic and unique events." There were currently 3.5 million Jews in the General Government, and Frank was anxious to be rid of them. It was clear, he said, "that we cannot shoot these 3.5 million Jews; we cannot poison them, but we must be able to intervene in a way which somehow achieves a successful extermination." The General Government "must be just as free of Jews as the Reich is."

Heydrich opened the meeting by emphasizing to the participants in no uncertain terms that Reich Marshal Göring, with the Führer's approval, had commissioned him to direct the conduct of the regime's Jewish policy. Establishing the RSHA's authority over all potential challengers was the second message of the meeting. The different agencies that would be called upon to participate were expected to recognize their subordination to the SS and to pledge their cooperation. Order would now be brought to the hitherto haphazard Jewish policy of the regime; local initiative would give way to a centrally directed plan with an apparatus to execute it.

Although there was some grousing around the table and mild assertions of bureaucratic preeminence in some aspect of Jewish policy, those voices were quickly silenced by Heydrich's smooth but intimidating demeanor. He then proceeded to outline the "final solution" he had developed. There would be no more talk about emigration; instead the Jews of Europe would be "evacuated to the East"—a solution taken "with the prior permission of the Führer"—not only the Jews currently under German control but in all Europe, from Britain to Switzerland to Sweden to Spain, eleven million in total. Europe would be combed through from west to east, and the Jews would initially be moved in stages to transit ghettos before being transported farther east. The Foreign Ministry, working with the Security Police and the SD, would deal with the appropriate local authorities. Although bureaucratic euphemisms dominated the formal minutes, "evacuation," his listeners clearly understood, meant "extermination." The Nuremberg Laws would be the basis for the selection process, but the definition of who was a Jew would be significantly broadened. Due to the severe labor shortage in the Reich, able-bodied Jews would be assigned to hard labor, building roads in the East, which, Heydrich estimated, would greatly reduce their number. He did not elaborate on the fate of the others, the vast majority, but that was hardly necessary. Jews over sixty-five or Jews with military decorations would be evacuated to the newly constructed "old people's ghetto" at Theresienstadt in Bohemia, which would be shown to the outside world as a model concentration camp. A number of those present, apparently uneasy with Heydrich's cold-blooded plan for mass murder, spoke up instead for mass sterilization of the Jews, but their suggestions were cast aside.

The gigantic scale of Heydrich's evacuation plan clearly assumed a German military victory, which in the winter of 1941–42 was anything but certain. The full realization of the "final solution" would have to wait until war's end. Bühler, however, insisted that conditions in the General Government made immediate action imperative, and argued that steps could be taken there now since transportation would be no problem. Three million Jews were already there, concentrated in teeming, overcrowded ghettos, and could be easily transported. Heydrich did not disagree. With that the conference was concluded. No notes were permitted; only Eichmann's minutes. Afterward the participants stood or sat in small groups, servants passed cognac; cigars appeared, and a relieved atmosphere of conviviality prevailed. The fate of Europe's Jews had been settled in only ninety minutes.

The mass murder of the Jews in the General Government got under way almost immediately. The SS had already taken action on this front in late 1941, with mass shootings, deportations to extermination camps, and forced labor. The Belzec extermination camp had been under construction since November 1941, and the gates swung open for the first time on March 17, 1942, when a transport of between forty and sixty railcars arrived bearing Jews from the Lublin area. The camp was the first of the extermination camps to go into operation and in many ways served as a model for the others. Belzec was situated about five hundred meters from a train station, which was outfitted to look like an ordinary small-town station, with timetables and travel notices posted around the site. The camp was divided into two parts: on one side was a reception area with two barracks—one for undressing and where the women had their hair shorn and the other for storing clothes and luggage. It was called "the cloak room." Camp II contained the gas chambers and mass graves and two barracks for Jewish work details, one as living quarters and one containing a kitchen. The gas chambers were surrounded by birch trees and had camouflage nets on the roof. A narrow path some seventy-five meters in length, known as "the tube," connected the two. The Jews were herded along this path from the undressing barracks in Camp I to the gas chambers in Camp II. A powerful diesel tank engine was installed outside the chambers and its exhaust fumes were fed into the chambers. A sign on the entrance read: "To the inhalation and bath rooms." In front of the building cheerful red geraniums had been planted. As a cruel joke, a Star of David had been installed on the roof.

A witness to the killing procedure described what happened when a shipment of Jews arrived at the camp. Forty-five cattle cars carrying 6,700 people, 1,450 of whom had died in transit, arrived at the station. Ukrainian guards armed with leather whips slid open the doors, and the human cargo spilled out onto the ramp. A large loudspeaker barked instructions. The prisoners were to undress completely, including artificial limbs and spectacles. Shoes were to be tied together before they were tossed into the twenty-five-meter-high pile of shoes. Then the women and girls had their hair shorn; the fallen clumps were stuffed into potato sacks to be used as insulation on submarines. From there, the procession of men, women, and children, cripples and the aged, were marched down "the tube." The SS man in charge tried to calm their nerves. He explained soothingly that "well, naturally, the men will have to work, build houses and roads, but the women won't need to work. Only if they want to, they can do housework or help in the kitchen." But the smell, the sinister darkness of the low building, and the Ukrainian guards caused the Jews to hold back. They hesitated but entered the death chambers, driven by the others behind them or by the leather whips of the SS, the majority without saying a word. "One Jewess of about forty, eyes blazing, curses the murderers. She receives five or six lashes with the riding whip from Captain Wirth [commander of the operation] personally and then disappears into the chamber. Many people pray."

The chambers were packed tight, one person per square foot, seven to eight hundred pressed so close together they could not move, fall, or lean over. The large steel door slammed shut, and the diesel engine ground into gear. Outside the thick walls one could hear sobbing, prayers. Through a peephole the SS could watch the death throes. In twenty-five minutes the chamber was at last silent. The doors were thrown open and a special prison work detail (a *Sonderkommando* composed of Jewish prisoners) entered to empty the tomb. "The dead stand like basalt pillars . . . and even in death one can tell which are the families. They are holding hands in death and it is difficult to tear them apart in order to empty the chambers for the next batch." From the gas chamber the corpses are carried on wooden stretchers only a few meters to the ditches, which are 100 x 20 x 12 meters in size. "After a few days, the corpses swell up and then collapse so that one can throw another layer on top of this one. Then ten centimeters of sand are strewn on the top so that only the occasional head or arms stick out."

Mass exterminations using carbon monoxide gas began in the other camps in the late spring. The camp at Sobibor opened in March, Chelmno in April, and Treblinka, which would emerge as the most deadly, in July. By the end of the year, 1,274,256 had been murdered in *Aktion Reinhard* camps, 713,555 in Treblinka, another 434,598 in Belzec, 101,370 in Sobibor, and 24,733 in Majdanek, an associated camp near Warsaw. Of the original 2.3 million Jews in the General Government at the outset of the program, only 298,000 remained. Another hundred thousand Jews were murdered in Galicia in the summer and fall of 1941, and it is estimated that 1.5 million Polish Jews died in actions to clear ghettos in 1942, making *Aktion Reinhard* the largest murder campaign of the Holocaust.

Hitler never committed himself to paper on Heydrich's plan, nor was it to be discussed in his presence. But it is evident from private conversations Hitler had with Himmler in the days immediately following the Wannsee Conference and on into February that he was fully briefed. At lunch on January 23, just three days after the Wannsee meeting, the Führer, in conversation with Himmler, defended the measures taken. "One must act radically. . . . The Jew must clear out of Europe. . . . For my part, I restrict myself to telling them they must go away. . . . But if they refuse to go voluntarily, I see no other solution but extermination. . . . Where the Jews are concerned, I'm devoid of all sense of pity. They'll always be the ferment that moves peoples one against the other. They sow discord everywhere, as much between individuals as between peoples." The extermination could not be restricted to Germany, he continued. "It's entirely natural that we should concern ourselves with the question on the European level. It's clearly not enough to expel them from Germany. We cannot allow them to retain bases of withdrawal at our doors. We want to be out of danger of all kinds of infiltration." A month later, again with Himmler as his guest, Hitler dilated on the danger posed by the Jews. "The discovery of the Jewish virus is one of the greatest revolutions that have taken place in the world," he averred. "The battle in which we are engaged today is of the same sort as the battle waged, during the last century, by Pasteur and Koch. How many diseases have their origin in the Jewish virus! . . . We shall regain our health only by eliminating the Jews."

This was a matter of the utmost secrecy; it was not to be discussed in public, but broad if vague knowledge seeped throughout the regime—and the public. The Jews were being "resettled" in the East, but what did that mean? What happened to them there? Goebbels certainly knew the answer. To his diary on March 27, he confided that "beginning in Lublin, the Jews in the General Government are now being evacuated eastward. The procedure is a pretty barbaric one and not to be described here more definitively. Not much will remain of the Jews. On the whole it can be said that about 60 percent of them will have to be liquidated whereas only about 40 percent can be used for forced labor." He was impressed that Globocnik was carrying out this mission "with considerable circumspection and according to a method that does not attract too much attention." To Goebbels it was clear that "a judgment is being carried out on the Jews which is barbaric, but fully deserved. The prophecy which the Führer gave them along the way for bringing about a new world war is beginning to become true in the most terrible fashion. . . . Here, too, the Führer is the unswerving champion and spokesman of a radical solution."

While little specific was known about what awaited the Jews at the end of the train journey, the deportations, of course, were quite public, and, as the Gestapo noted, the response of the public was mixed. In Minden, "the evacuation of the Jews provoked great alarm." Some "expressed concern that, given the cold weather many Jews would die in transit." A widely circulated rumor claimed that the Jews were being transported to Russia—in passenger carriages to Warsaw and from there in cattle cars. Healthy Jews would then be subjected to hard labor in former Russian factories, while the older and infirm would be shot. Such rumors, the local Gestapo complained, triggered expressions of sympathy for the Jews. "It is beyond understanding," one people's comrade was heard to say, "how human beings could be treated so brutally, whether Jew or Aryan. . . . Germans in America would have to pay dearly because the Jews in Germany are badly treated." A Gestapo report from Bremen explained that "while the politically educated of the population generally greeted the 'evacuation of the Jews,' religious and commercial circles show no understanding [for the policy] and continue to believe that they need to speak up for the Jews." The Gestapo in Magdeburg sounded a similar refrain, reporting that "persons of German blood continue to maintain friendly relations with Jews and by that sort of behavior prove that even today they have no understanding for the most elementary principles of National Socialism."

Domestic opinion could be shaped by the regime, but international opinion was another matter. In December, the Allied powers issued a declaration accusing the Germans of conducting the systematic mass murder of the Jews in Eastern Europe, and for a brief time made such allegations the centerpiece of their public attacks on the Third Reich. Instead of attempting to mount a counter-campaign denying the charges, Goebbels surprised his subordinates by concluding that it was best if the regime simply chose to ignore the accusations. In a remarkably revealing statement to a ministerial conference on December 12, he explained quite openly that "Since the enemy reports about alleged German atrocities against the Jews and Poles are threatening to grow even more massive, we find ourselves in a situation where we don't have counter arguments to offer." Two days later he returned to the theme. "We cannot answer these things. When the Jews say we have shot two and a half million Jews in Poland . . . we can't answer that it is only two and one third million." Nineteen forty-two would prove to be the deadliest year of the Holocaust. One third of the Jews who would perish in the "Final Solution" would die in that year.

The architect of the Final Solution did not live to see it implemented. Reinhard Heydrich, who had been appointed protector of Bohemia and Moravia to crush the resistance there, was assassinated by the Czech underground while being driven in an open car through Prague. The Czech assassins had been selected by the Czech government in exile in London and trained by the British Special Operations Executive (SOE) in clandestine operations. They were dropped into a field on the outskirts of Prague with the express mission of eliminating Heydrich. On May 27, they struck, attacking him with a grenade and small arms fire. Heydrich was severely wounded and lingered for eight days before dying. Hitler gave him grandiose state funerals in both Prague and Berlin. The Czech agents were trapped in a church, fought bravely for several hours, and then committed suicide. Hitler wanted to shoot ten thousand Czechs in reprisal, but Heydrich's successor as protector, Karl Hermann Frank, managed to persuade him to make an example of one Czech village instead. On June 10, the entire population of Lidice was charged with having harbored the assassins. All the men were shot; the women were sent to Ravensbrück concentration camp. Eighty-one of the children were deemed racially unworthy and were murdered, the other seventeen were given new German identities and placed with German families. The village was burned to the ground. The Jews, Goebbels claimed, were behind the attack.

Despite a frenzy of anti-Semitic propaganda spewing from Goebbels's office, other concerns laid a greater claim on the attention of the German public in 1942. During the first two years of the war, British bombers had launched raids against German cities, primarily in the west and along the coast. These operations had been small in scale and largely ineffective, and though they were an embarrassment to the Nazi authorities, their impact on the war effort or civilian morale was minimal. The spring of 1942 would change that. On the night of March 27–28 British planes raided the city of Lübeck on the Baltic coast. Flying at two thousand feet, the attackers unleashed four hundred tons of bombs on the historic city center that night, two thirds of which were incendiaries. Three hundred inhabitants of the city were killed, by far the highest casualty count of any raid to that point, and rumors quickly spread that ten times that number were dead and three thousand left homeless. The raid sent shockwaves through the country. Before these reverberations could be absorbed, the RAF followed with a series of firebomb attacks on Rostock, another port city on the Baltic. For several days, air raid sirens, soon to be a dreaded feature of everyday life for the urban population of the Reich, howled over the city. One hundred thousand dwellings were destroyed, and one hundred thousand residents were evacuated from the city.

These raids signaled an ominous shift in the British approach to bombing. An Air Directive of February 14 indicated that the targets of future operations were to be Germany's large industrial cities. The RAF had decided to embark on a strategy of area bombing. By concentrating on cities of over 100,000 in population, large targets that were easy to find and hit, it could render over one third of the German population homeless and demoralized. Henceforth, Bomber Command would measure its success by acres of built-up area destroyed and a calculation of acres of concentrated urban devastation and industrial man-hours lost.

The man who executed this policy was the new head of Bomber Command, Arthur Harris. Harris was convinced that the way to defeat Nazi Germany was to destroy its cities, devastating the Reich's war-making capabilities and, in the process, breaking the morale of its citizens. This meant smashing the civic infrastructure of Germany's cities—housing, electricity, water, sanitation—to such an extent that their inhabitants simply could not function. It also meant large-scale killing. During the spring and summer of 1942, Harris provided a terrifying hint of what was to come. Mustering every available aircraft and all combat crews—including raw trainees and their instructors—Bomber Command launched three monster raids on German cities. On May 30–31, one thousand British planes attacked Cologne in what RAF Bomber Command called Operation Millennium. The bombers dropped 1,400 tons of explosives on the city, leaving 500 dead, 5,000 wounded, and 60,000 homeless. In early June 900 aircraft raided Essen, and 1,000 appeared in the night skies over Bremen. Harris could not sustain these numbers and the subsequent raids would be lighter, but he had made his point. In the following summer months, RAF bombers ranged far and wide over Germany, attacking not only the factory cities of the Ruhr but Frankfurt, Kassel, and deep in Bavaria, Nuremberg and Munich. The nature of the air war was undergoing a radical change.

The Americans joined the air assault on Germany in 1942, flying daylight missions to complement the British nighttime raids. In January 1943, at a conference in Casablanca, attended by Roosevelt and Churchill and their military staffs, American air commander Ira Eaker coined the term "Round the Clock Bombing." The formulation implied a coordinated plan of attack—the Americans would hit key targets during the day, the RAF would go over at night. Churchill was particularly taken with the phrase, and the Casablanca Directive from the Anglo-American Combined Chiefs of Staff ordered the two air commanders to embark on the systematic demolition of a range of German target systems as essential preliminaries to an invasion of Europe: submarine yards and bases, the German aircraft industry, ball bearings, oil, synthetic rubber, and military transportation. Yet, despite the apparent unity, genuine coordination remained something of a mirage; rather than "a Combined Bomber Offensive" there were two distinct, parallel efforts. Harris routinely ignored pressure to send his planes against the priority targets and instead continued to bomb large urban centers. These attacks occasionally overlapped with the American raids but were rarely coordinated.

Still, the Anglo-American raids presaged a dramatic intensification of the air campaign in 1942 and made a deeply unsettling impression on the German public. Events in Russia were troubling, but, the Gestapo reported, "of far greater concern to the public in all parts of the Reich is the increasing British bombing of German cities. That worry is exacerbated by the regime's failure to give information about the extent of casualties and physical damage. One fears that the coming months will see an increase in the number of British raids whose objective is to destroy one industrial city after another." Worries about the stalled war in the East, the Anglo-American bombing campaign, and a tightening of rationing as the food supply dwindled, led to the first real signs of war weariness and pessimism. "The hope for a quick collapse of Bolshevism has perhaps given way to a conviction that the Soviet Union cannot be defeated by the offensive war in its current form but by a war of attrition whose distant end is not yet in view." This was not the war the Nazis and their early, easy victories promised, not the war the German people had come to expect.

Despite the pounding the Wehrmacht had taken in the East, Hitler was preparing to undertake a new campaign in the spring of 1942. He decided to abandon the ambitious objectives of Barbarossa and concentrate his forces on one primary objective: seizing the Caucasus oil fields to deny Soviet resupply and claim this valuable asset for the Reich. The plan, code-named Operation Blue, called for a three-phase campaign in the south. First, German troops would encircle Soviet troops west of the Don River, then dash southward along the Volga to Stalingrad. There General Friedrich Paulus's Sixth Army and Hermann Hoth's Fourth Panzer Army would establish a blocking position near the city to protect the southern force. Finally, phase three—a drive deep into the Caucasus. It was not as audacious as Barbarossa, but its scale was still extraordinary—over five hundred miles from Kiev to the heart of the Caucasus, and the German army in the Soviet Union had 350,000 fewer troops than the year before. Total tank strength was slightly less than in 1941, but the offensive would concentrate them in the south. The Wehrmacht would therefore be forced to rely on Romanian, Hungarian, and Italian units, and these were neither as well equipped nor as committed as their German allies.

The Russian position was also shaky as the spring approached. The winter offensive—during the worst winter in Russia in 140 years—had left the Red Army spent. The Russians had suffered almost incomprehensible losses—both of men and matériel—and Stalin was convinced that when the Germans attacked in late spring, as he knew they would, they would renew their drive on Moscow. As a result, the Red Army's best units remained on the approaches to the capital. The Germans planned to preface their offensive in June by eliminating a Soviet salient in their line south of Kharkov. But before they could do so, they were preempted by the Russians. Kharkov was the hub of the German communications network in the south and was a prime objective. Stalin and the Russian commander there, General Semyon Timoshenko, decided to launch an offensive from the salient in May. The attack began on May 12 with great initial success, but the Russians had played into German hands. Five days later, the Germans cut off the Soviet spearhead, capturing 240,000 prisoners and destroying more than 600 tanks. To the south, Manstein, who had conquered the Crimea in the fall of 1941, began a siege of Sebastopol in early June, and although the Russians held out for a month, Sebastopol fell on July 3, yielding 100,000 more prisoners and 200 tanks. The German offensive began with a replay of 1941, and Hitler was ecstatic.

The main offensive began on June 28 and made rapid progress against weakened Soviet forces. The Russian position was made worse by the failed Kharkov offensive and by Stalin's continued conviction that the major German thrust would still be directed at Moscow. Hoth's Fourth Panzer Army drove one hundred miles in eight days, reaching the Don near Voronezh. The Russians fought tenaciously there, allowing a withdrawal toward Stalingrad. For the Russians, it had all the makings of a catastrophe. "The Russian is finished," Hitler enthused, and even the sober Halder agreed. At this point, Hitler altered the original plan of the offensive with fateful consequences. He decided that it was now possible to move to Phase Three of the operation—the advance into the Caucasus—without first securing his flank at Stalingrad. According to the plan, the Fourth Panzer Army was to lead the Sixth Army, composed of infantry units, into Stalingrad. The panzers would take the city; the infantry would hold it. But now Hitler decided to divert Hoth's tanks away from Stalingrad and left the task of securing that sprawling industrial city to Paulus's Sixth. The diversion proved costly. Hoth's panzer army would probably have reached Stalingrad before Soviet defenses were established, and its presence proved unnecessary to forces moving south across the Don.

By August, the First Panzer Army had streaked southeastward against weak Russian defenses. Within days it had pressed two hundred miles southeast of Rostov and reached the Maikop oil fields in the foothills of the Caucasus. A sense of victory surged through the German army, from headquarters to the lowly foot soldier. On July 29, a soldier in the Sixth Army recorded in his diary: "The company commander says the Russian Troops are completely broken and cannot hold out any longer. To reach the Volga and take Stalingrad is not so difficult for us. The Führer knows where the Russians' weak point is. Victory is not far away." A week later he added, "Our company is tearing ahead. Today I wrote to Elsa, 'We shall soon see each other. All of us feel that the end, victory, is near.'"

At this point Hitler made another critical decision. He split his forces, one element moving east toward the Grozny oil fields, while the other pushed south toward the Black Sea. In September, the offensive slowed, and in October, Russian resistance stiffened. German troops did reach Mount Elbrus, Europe's highest mountain, and a team of climbers placed the German flag near the summit. But here the problems began to multiply. German forces were stretched to their absolute limit; resupply was difficult and fuel was short. Army Group South had begun the offensive covering a 500-mile front. Now it was stretched dangerously thin over almost 1,300 miles. Hitler grew impatient, then furious, at the slow progress in Stalingrad and the Caucasus, and in September he sacked General Wilhelm List, commander of Army Group South, as well as Army Chief of Staff Halder, against whose cautious judgment he had constantly battled. He replaced both with younger, more pliable officers.

Meanwhile progress was being made toward Stalingrad. On August 22, the Germans broke through Russian defenses and a panzer corps fought its way into the northern suburbs, reaching the Volga the next day. The Russians seemed trapped in the city, and the Luftwaffe was called in to seal their fate. On August 23 the Luftwaffe carried out its largest raid since the opening day of Barbarossa. Air units from all over the Eastern Front were brought to bear on the city. Over half the bombs dropped were incendiaries, and the results were horrifyingly spectacular. Nearly every wooden structure, including acres of workers' housing, burned. The fires were so intense, so vast, that German soldiers could read a paper forty miles away by the light of their flames. It was a terror raid to kill civilians, overload public services, and create panic. "The whole city is on fire," a German soldier wrote home, "on the Führer's orders our Luftwaffe has sent it up in flames. That's what the Russians need, to stop them resisting."

But the city did not surrender. Instead, the Regional Party Committee proclaimed a state of siege. The Russians were grimly determined to hold the city and the Germans resolutely determined to take it. As the fighting intensified, the Battle of Stalingrad assumed epic symbolic meaning for both sides. The fighting turned into a ferocious struggle of attrition, fought block by block, house by house, floor by floor, room by room. The city itself was reduced to rubble, and movement was measured in meters. There had been nothing like it since the colossal carnage of the World War I battlefields.

In the midst of the fighting, as the German home front soberly marked the third anniversary of the war, the Gestapo reported an unmistakable mood of resignation, symptomatic, it believed, of a disconcerting war weariness. That report closed with a comment that concealed, barely, a condemnation of Hitler's war. "The mounting difficulties of supply, three years of shortages in all spheres of everyday life, the intensity and extent of the steadily increasing enemy air attacks, worries about the life of family members at the front and not least the blood sacrifices of . . . the civilian victims of the enemy air attacks are factors that exert an ever greater influence on the mood of wide circles and increasingly the desire for an end to the war soon."

By early November, the Germans held nine tenths of Stalingrad. On November 9, Hitler was in Munich, speaking to an enthusiastic crowd of party leaders on the anniversary of the Beer Hall Putsch. His topic was the epic struggle in Stalingrad. "I wanted to get to the Volga, to a certain point, near a certain town. As it happens, its name is that of Stalin himself. But please don't think I marched there for that reason—it could be called something quite different." It was an important place. There followed his usual impressive recitation of statistics—how many tons of wheat, of manganese, of oil pass through there. For that reason he wanted to take it, and, "you know," he confided smugly, "we are being modest, for we have got it! There are only a few very small places left not captured."

Ten days later, the Russians unleashed an offensive against the Romanian troops northwest and southeast of the city. In yet another intelligence failure, the German High Command was caught off guard. The Romanians quickly buckled, and on November 3 the two Russian spearheads linked up forty-five miles west of Stalingrad, encircling the entire Sixth Army. General Paulus asked Hitler's permission to break out of the devastated city, but Hitler refused. Göring promised that the Luftwaffe could supply the German forces in Stalingrad by air drop, but that proved impossible. Instead, Hitler ordered General Manstein to break the encirclement and rescue the trapped Sixth Army. To stiffen Paulus's resolve, Hitler promoted him to the rank of field marshal, a not so subtle reminder that no German field marshal had ever surrendered. Paulus should draw inspiration by this action. The field marshal's baton was parachuted into the city. The troops couldn't receive adequate food or ammunition, but a field marshal's baton would have to serve to strengthen their will to resist. They were to fight to the last man, to the last bullet. The whole issue was rendered moot by a second Russian offensive on December 16, pressing from the Don toward Rostov, with the intention of cutting off all German forces to the south. A rescue of the troops in Stalingrad was now out of the question. Hopelessly surrounded, out of food and ammunition, the Sixth Army held out in the blustery bitter cold until February 2, 1943, when Paulus at last surrendered.

It was a catastrophe of colossal proportions. The Germans and their Axis allies suffered 500,000 dead as well as the 91,000 taken prisoner, including twenty-two German generals. The Sixth Army and the Fourth Panzer Army had been destroyed, along with four Axis armies; the Luftwaffe suffered grievous losses in bombers, fighters, and Stuka dive-bombers as well as almost 500 transport planes that had attempted to deliver supplies to surrounded troops in the cauldron of Stalingrad. That Stalingrad was a turning point in the Nazi war against the Soviet Union was obvious to all. In Germany, the news of the calamity was not broadcast immediately. When it came a few days later, the announcement was accompanied by the first strains of Beethoven's Fifth Symphony. It was a funeral dirge for Hitler's ambitions in the East.

In an effort to rally German morale after the shattering defeat at Stalingrad, Goebbels took a new tack in the regime's propaganda. For some time the propaganda minister had worried that the public had fallen into a comfortable optimism about the war in the East, that the steady stream of good news from Otto Dietrich's press office had lulled the people into an unwarranted overconfidence. Victory would ultimately come, he believed, but the price was going to be high, and the public should be prepared for it. He had begun to introduce a more realistic depiction of the situation even before the disaster at Stalingrad; now he had the nation's attention. On February 18, in what would be his most famous speech, he addressed a packed Sportpalast and a national radio audience. Speaking beneath a gigantic banner that read "Total War, Shortest War," Goebbels addressed a screaming crowd of carefully selected party members, dignitaries, and wounded veterans. Germany, indeed, Western civilization, he told them, now faced an *immediate* danger, and that danger was not just the Red Army but International Jewry. Once again Jewry had revealed itself "as the incarnation of evil, as the plastic demon of decay and the bearer of an international culture-destroying chaos." It was a threat to every nation. "Jewry is a contagious infection," and Germany would not bow before this threat, "but rather intends to take the most radical measures, if necessary, in good time." In a remarkable passage, he described the onrushing Russian forces in a way that was a near-perfect description of *German* operations in the East. "Behind the oncoming Soviet divisions we see the Jewish liquidation commandos, and behind them, terror, the specter of mass starvation and complete anarchy."

Warming to his theme, he shrieked, "Total war is the demand of the hour. We must put an end to the bourgeois attitude that we have seen in this war: 'Wash my back, but don't get me wet'! The time has come," he bellowed, "to remove the kid gloves and use our fists." The frenzied crowd broke into howls of approval. He announced new measures that would express that austere situation. Luxury restaurants and spas would be closed; alcohol restricted; theaters closed, food rations cut. Women, whom Hitler had been reluctant to mobilize for industrial work, would be conscripted. "This is no time to entertain wistful dreams of peace. The German people can only rely on thoughts of war. This will not lead to a prolongation of this war, but rather an acceleration. The most radical war is also the shortest."

He closed the rousing two-hour speech by posing ten rhetorical questions to his audience, made up, he falsely claimed, of a cross section of the German people. To each question the hysterical crowd roared the appropriate response: "Are you ready to follow the Führer . . . and stand and fight with the Army and with wild determination through all turns of fate until the victory is in our hands? *'JA!'* Do you want if necessary a war more total and radical than anything you ever could have imagined? *'JA!'* The English claim that the German people are war weary—*'NEIN!'*" Amid a crescendo of frenzied screaming, the speech ended with the question of the evening: "Do you want total war?" which his audience, on its feet, answered with a resounding *"JA."* Then, with his voice rising to a thunderous cry, he bellowed the words of a Prussian poet from the days of the Napoleonic Wars: "Now people rise up, and storm burst forth!" Later Goebbels, with his unparalleled cynicism, remarked to his entourage that it had been "an hour of idiocy. . . . If I had asked these people to jump from the fourth floor of the Columbus House they would have done it."

Goebbels's derisive condescension notwithstanding, he considered the speech a great success, as did Hitler, but the psychological shock of Stalingrad was not so easily overcome. Bombast and willpower could not conceal the magnitude of the defeat or slow the mounting desperation over Germany's situation. The last months of 1942 and early months of 1943 saw the momentum of the war change dramatically. Catastrophe followed catastrophe, as Germany's ability to set the pace and direction of events slipped ineluctably away. At home criticism mounted against not only the party but, for the first time, against the Führer himself. The criticism was muted and indirect, but it was clear from Gestapo reports that Hitler's ability to insulate himself from the blunders and failures of the regime was ebbing away.

The defeat at Stalingrad was not the end of the calamities. Anglo-American troops landed in French Morocco and Algiers in November (Operation Torch), and by late fall Rommel's Afrika Korps was trapped between British general Bernard Montgomery's Eighth Army pushing westward from Egypt and Anglo-American troops surging eastward toward Tunisia. In March Rommel traveled to Hitler's headquarters in East Prussia to plead for reinforcements and supplies, or, if they were not forthcoming, for an evacuation of the Afrika Korps while there was still time. But Hitler, who had always viewed the desert war as a sideshow, brusquely refused. No surrender, no evacuation. Like the beleaguered troops at Stalingrad, the Afrika Korps should fight to the last man and die a hero's death. During that same visit Rommel was relieved of his command and ordered to take sick leave in the Austrian Alps, but Hitler made sure that the popular "Desert Fox" was celebrated as a military hero. On May 13, 1943, the last Axis forces in North Africa surrendered. The Wehrmacht had been driven from Africa, and 170,000 German soldiers were marched into captivity. In Germany the debacle was referred to as "Tunisgrad." "Military Events in Africa," the Gestapo reported, "have produced deep shock in the German public." Within the span of three months, the Third Reich had suffered two disastrous defeats, and the people's faith in the regime was badly shaken. Even within the High Command many were convinced that the war could no longer be won militarily.

More disturbing, the public had always drawn a distinction between the party and the Führer, attributing every misstep, every outrage, to the party and its functionaries. But in the wake of Stalingrad the aura of infallibility that had clung to Hitler for so long had begun to dissolve. Gestapo reports from all over the Reich indicated that for the first time criticism of Hitler, though often muted and indirect, was widespread. Some criticism was leveled against the generals who had presumably misled him or Göring's Luftwaffe that had failed him, but Stalingrad marked a turning point in what historian Ian Kershaw has called "the Hitler Myth." That myth was not punctured suddenly or in response to a specific event but slowly and steadily deflated as the promised victory seemed to be slipping away. The gap between the wildly inflated image drawn by Nazi propaganda and the dark reality Germany was experiencing was unmistakably widening, and the Führer who towered above the crassness, corruption, pettiness, and the raging fanaticism of the party was at last laid open to criticism. Without new victories to trumpet, Hitler withdrew gradually from view, rarely appearing in public or even addressing the nation via the radio. Little by little the bond between the Führer and his people began to loosen.

Most debilitating for German morale in 1943 was the relentless Allied bombing, which grew in intensity and scale as the year progressed. In March the Royal Air Force devastated the industrial city of Essen, leaving it smoldering in ruins, but that was only a grisly prelude to the RAF's horrifying attacks on Hamburg in July. Aptly named Operation Gomorrah, the raid on the night of July 27–28 was only one in a ten-day joint Allied assault on the city, but its effects were horrific. Over seven hundred aircraft dropped 2,236 tons of incendiaries in an hour's time, turning Germany's fourth largest city into a raging inferno. Cyclones of fire swept through the city; temperature at ground level reached an unbelievable 2,700 degrees Fahrenheit; asphalt bubbled and burned; people were swept into the flames or suffocated in their cellars or on the street as the uncontrollable fire created a vacuum that sucked the oxygen from the air itself. A pillar of scalding wind carrying bodies and debris rose more than ten thousand feet above the stricken city. Forty thousand people lost their lives in the raid, a nightmarish figure that boggled the imagination. In the following days the streets were littered with shrunken, carbonized corpses, and the air was yellow with sulfur. Scenes of unspeakable horror were everywhere. Rats and flies swarmed through the streets. One woman, climbing into a truck for evacuation, tripped and her suitcase fell open. Out toppled an assortment of toys and the shrunken, blackened corpse of her child.

The military effectiveness of the air raids was uncertain, but their psychological impact was unmistakable. As news of the Hamburg attack spread across the Reich, it triggered a surge of fear that bordered on panic. It was spoken of simply as "*die Katastrophe.*" Albert Speer, since February Hitler's new armaments chief, wrote, "Hamburg put the fear of God into me." To Hitler he warned that "a series of attacks of this sort, extended to six more major cities, would bring Germany's armaments production to a total halt." Unfazed, the Führer, who never visited even one of the bomb-ravaged cities, merely remarked, "You'll straighten all that out again." Hamburg was the most appallingly destructive air raid of the war in Europe, a frightful portent of things to come, and Speer could never "straighten all that out again."

Despite the cascade of disasters on the battle fronts and in German cities, the Nazi war against the Jews did not slacken but moved into a new, more sinister phase. The early actions of Operation Reinhard had systematically decimated the Jewish population of Poland, but now began a new wave of deportations from Western Europe. The Gestapo, often aided by local police forces, undertook sweeps of Holland, Belgium, and France, rounding up Jews to be transported east. Their destination was not the camps of Operation Reinhard but the rapidly expanding camp at Auschwitz.

Auschwitz was the centerpiece of this new phase of Nazi policy. Located thirty-seven miles west of Cracow in Upper Silesia, Auschwitz had been in operation since 1940, housing primarily Polish political prisoners and Soviet POWs. Until summer 1942, it had played a relatively small part in the "Final Solution." It was not part of Operation Reinhard but, like Majdanek, was controlled by the SS Economic and Administrative Central

Office in Berlin. Himmler appointed SS-*Obersturmbahnführer* Rudolf Höss, an official at Sachsenhausen, to take charge of the new camp, and in June 1941 he ordered Höss to Berlin for an important meeting. There Himmler explained that Auschwitz, which at the time held roughly ten thousand mostly Polish prisoners, was to be transformed into a major concentration camp. As Höss testified after the war, Himmler told him at that time that "the Führer has ordered the final solution of the Jewish question and we—the SS have to carry out that order." Adolf Eichmann of the RSHA would provide further details. Höss was to "maintain the strictest silence concerning this order," even vis-à-vis his superiors. "The Jews are the eternal enemies of the German people and must be exterminated. Every Jew we can lay our hands on must be exterminated during the war without exception. If we now fail to destroy the biological basis of Jewry then one day the Jews will destroy the German people."

Shortly after this meeting, Eichmann visited the camp. It was ideally suited for the sort of heavy activity that Himmler had in mind—good transportation connections, isolated area, and room to expand. Given the anticipated crush of new arrivals, a new camp was constructed at Birkenau about three kilometers from the main camp. At Birkenau, or Auschwitz II, where in 1943 most of the killing took place, two rustic cottages stood on the grounds, separated by a birch woods. At first glance they appeared innocent, well-tended peasant dwellings with thatched roofs, surrounded by fruit trees, but closer examination revealed that the cottages had no windows and an unusual number of heavy doors with rubber seals. The two cottages, one called "the little red house" because of its brick exterior, the other "the little white house" because of its plaster facade, were, in fact, bunkers with gas chambers and undressing rooms. In the camp they were referred to as Bunkers 1 and 2. With a capacity for 800 victims, Bunker 1 was dismantled in the fall of 1942, and Bunker 2, which contained four gas chambers, three undressing rooms, and a crematorium that could "accommodate" 1,200 people at a time, would continue operations until the camp was shut down in the fall of 1944. It is estimated that 1,140 corpses could be burned in this crematorium every twenty-four hours. Eventually Auschwitz-Birkenau would operate four more crematoria with attached gas chambers, where hundreds of thousands of Jewish men, women, and children would perish.

Höss was told to expect transports from all over Europe. Between July 1942 and February 1943, 46,455 Jews arrived at the expanding camp at Auschwitz; by the end of the year 42,500 French Jews were transported there. On August 24, a transport left Drancy, a French concentration camp, bound for Auschwitz. It carried 1,000 Jews, of whom 553 were children under the age of seventeen, 465 were under twelve, 131 under six. Upon arrival at Auschwitz, 92 men, age twenty to forty-five, were selected for work; the rest were dispatched immediately to the gas chambers. In Belgium approximately 25,000 Jews were deported by war's end, the largest number coming in 1943. In Norway the tiny Jewish community was hunted down and sent to their deaths; by February 1943 it had ceased to exist. In Germany, the last despairing remnants of the once proud Jewish community—some 18,000—were rounded up and deported to Auschwitz. Even the ailing patients of Berlin's Jewish hospital were sent to Theresienstadt. To make room for them, 10,000 elderly prisoners already there were shipped to Treblinka, where they were gassed. In the summer of 1943 Treblinka operated three gas chambers; within three months, the SS had added an additional ten gas chambers to deal with the mushrooming number of "evacuees." And, of course, the Nazis continued to empty the Polish ghettos, sending additional thousands to their death. The systematic mass murder of the Jews would not wait until the end of the war, as Heydrich had intimated at Wannsee. By the end of 1943, the "Final Solution" was a smoothly functioning European-wide industrial operation.

The trains with their crammed boxcars would arrive at the camp night and day, sometimes pulling in one after the other. They carried thousands of victims. The exhausted, famished Jews would tumble out onto a platform, where "selections" were made.

The unloading ramp was the site of unbearable heartbreak and chaos. "To start with," an SS man testified after the war, "the men and women are separated. Mothers wave good-bye to their sons for the last time. The two columns stand in ranks of five several meters apart from one another on the ramp. Anyone who is overcome with grief and tries to rush over to embrace his or her loved one once more and give them words of comfort is hurled back by a blow from one of the SS men." A survivor recalled that wrenching scene when as a child he arrived with his mother from the Lodz ghetto. "It was at night that we arrived at Auschwitz. We came in

the minute the gates open up, we heard screams, barking of dogs, blows.
. . . And then we got off the train. And everything went so fast: left, right,
right, left. Men separated from women. Children torn from the arms of
mothers. The elderly chased like cattle. The sick, the disabled were handled like packs of garbage. They were thrown [to the] side together with
broken suitcases, with boxes. My mother ran over to me and grabbed me
by the shoulders, and she told me, 'Leibele, I'm not going to see you no
more. Take care of your brother.'"

After the selection, those doomed to die were directed along a path to
one of the bunkers. In soothing tones SS officers told the victims that they
were to take a shower and undergo delousing. A French doctor assigned to
the Jewish "special commando" responsible for removing the bodies from
the gas chambers described the procedure. The victims "were addressed in
a very polite and friendly way: 'You have been on a journey. You are dirty.
You will take a bath. Get undressed quickly.' Towels and soap were handed
out, and then suddenly the brutes woke up and showed their true faces: this
horde of people, these men and women were driven outside with hard blows
and forced both summer and winter to go the few hundred meters to the
'Shower Room.' Above the entry door was the word 'Shower.' One could
even see shower heads which were cemented in the ceiling but never had
water flowing through them. These poor innocents were crammed together,
pressed against each other. Then panic broke out, for at last they realized
the fate in store for them. But blows with rifle butts and revolver shots soon
restored order and finally they all entered the death chamber. The doors
were shut and, ten minutes later, the temperature was high enough to facil-
itate the condensation of the hydrogen cyanide. . . . This was the 'Zyklon
B' gravel pellets saturated with twenty percent hydrogen cyanide which was
used by the German barbarians." Then the pellets were thrown in through
a small vent. One could hear fearful screams, but a few moments later there
was complete silence. Twenty to twenty-five minutes later, the door and windows were opened to ventilate the rooms and the corpses were thrown at
once into pits to be burnt. But beforehand, the dentists had searched every
mouth to pull out the gold teeth. The women were also searched to see if
they had hidden jewelry in the intimate parts of their bodies, and their hair
was cut off and methodically placed in sacks for industrial purposes." The
men who carried out these macabre tasks were Jewish prisoners selected by

the Nazis to serve as *Sonderkommandos*, or special aides. After serving in this grim capacity for a time, they were executed, and a new batch of prisoners took their place. No one would survive. There would be no witnesses. The corpses were burned in the nearby incinerators, and the ashes were buried, thrown in the river, or used for fertilizer. In some cases the dead were thrown into an open pit. The stench was unbearable.

Despite the fact that rumors about the death camps were in wide circulation, Himmler continued to insist on complete secrecy. It was imperative for three reasons. First, in order to stifle any disruption or resistance, the victims should be ignorant of their fate awaiting them at the end of the train journey. Second, Hitler was always very impressed by the success of British propaganda during World War I. Those efforts had created the image of barbaric "Germans bayoneting babies in Belgium," and he wanted to give the Allies no ammunition for new propaganda campaigns. And finally, neither he nor Himmler was convinced that the German people were ready for a confrontation with this gruesome reality. All of this was reflected in a speech delivered by Himmler to a gathering of SS men in Poznan in June 1943. "I want to talk to you quite frankly about a very grave matter," he began.

> We can talk about it quite frankly among ourselves and yet we will never speak of it publicly. . . . I am referring to the Jewish evacuation program, the extermination of the Jewish people. 'The Jewish people will be exterminated,' says every party comrade. 'It's clear, it's in our program. Elimination of the Jews, extermination and we'll do it.' . . . Not one of those who talk like that has watched it happening, not one of them has been through it. Most of you will know what it means when a hundred corpses are lying side by side, or five hundred or a thousand are lying there. To have stuck it out and—apart from a few exceptions due to human weakness—to have remained decent, that is what has made us tough. This is a glorious page in our history and one that has never been written and can never be written.

Eventually more crematoria and gas chambers were constructed to deal with hundreds of thousands of victims, and the killing continued with increasing speed and efficiency into November 1944. At the peak of its operations in the summer of 1944, Auschwitz could murder 9,000 people per day, and by the close of the year, when the giant killing factory was closed down due to the approach of the Red Army, 1.1 million people, the vast majority Jews, had been murdered at Auschwitz-Birkenau. Together with the massacres of the Einsatzgruppen, the ongoing mass murders at Treblinka, and other death camps with their dozens of brutal satellite labor camps, the Nazi crusade against Judeo-Bolshevism claimed the lives of roughly six million Jews—and millions of other undesirables—Gypsies, Jehovah's Witnesses, homosexuals, Communists, as well as millions of Polish and Russian civilians, *Untermenschen* (subhumans) all.

While the Nazi campaign against the Jews was reaching its bloody climax, the war in 1943–44 turned decisively against the Third Reich. In the East, the Russians for the first time assumed—and sustained—the offensive, initiating a series of ever-larger and -deadlier operations that drove the Wehrmacht out of the Soviet Union. It would not conclude until 1945 when Red Army troops were standing in the ruins of Berlin. In the high summer of 1943 the Red Army smashed the last German offensive at Kursk, about 320 miles south of Moscow. The Germans threw twelve panzer divisions and five panzer grenadier divisions, each employing heavy Tiger tanks and the new Panthers (*Panzers*). In a battle that raged into August, the Soviets mauled the Wehrmacht's best armored forces in the largest tank battle in history. The greatly outnumbered Germans suffered crushing losses in both infantry and armor in the fighting. After receiving word of the Allied invasion of Sicily on July 10, 1943, Hitler, over General Manstein's objections, abruptly broke off the operation, and Germany's last offensive on the Eastern Front was over. It was, Guderian ruminated, "a decisive defeat. Needless to say, the Russians exploited their victory to the full. There were to be no more periods of quiet on the Eastern Front. From now on the enemy was in undisputed possession of the initiative." With the Wehrmacht reeling, the Russians retook Orel and Kharkov, and in November they drove the Germans from Kiev. In January 1944 the long agony of Leningrad came to an end when an 872-day siege was at last lifted. By the end of the month, the Red Army had reached the prewar Soviet border of Poland.

In the course of 1943 the Germans suffered one setback after another. The Allies invaded mainland Italy in September. Mussolini was deposed by King Victor Emmanuel and his own Fascist Council, and although Hitler would install him as head of a puppet Fascist state in northern Italy, the Duce was a spent political and military force. German troops overran the country, rushing south to meet the Allied invaders, but they found themselves fighting a costly defensive war as British and American troops struggled slowly but steadily up the peninsula toward Rome. At sea, the Battle of the Atlantic was basically over, as the Allies' use of convoys and aircraft threatened to sink Germany's entire submarine force. Everywhere, Germany was in retreat. And yet, while German forces fell back on every front, the Nazi war against the Jews gathered momentum, reaching its crescendo in the lengthening shadow of the Reich's mounting defeats. Here there would be no retreat.

APOCALYPSE

As the spring of 1944 approached, German attention was focused on the anticipated Allied invasion of Northern Europe, and it was a time of mounting anxiety in the Reich. In March, the Gestapo reported that "the new developments in the East, the air war, and waiting for the invasion are making it hard to see a realistic way out of this bungled situation and to believe in a good outcome of the war." The public followed with growing dismay the Russian advance on the Reich's borderlands, and worries about the anticipated Allied invasion also weighed heavily on the home front. The outcome of that battle, Hitler believed, would be the critical turning point of the war, and in November 1943 he issued Führer Order No. 51. It read:

For the last two and a half years the bitter and costly struggle against Bolshevism has made the utmost demands upon the bulk of our military resources and energies. . . . The situation has since changed. The threat from the East remains, but an even greater danger looms in the West: the Anglo-American landing! In the East, the vastness of the space will, as a last resort, permit a loss of territory even on a major scale, without suffering a mortal blow to Germany's chance for survival. Not so in the West! If the enemy here succeeds in penetrating our defense on a wide front, consequences of staggering proportions will follow within a short time. For that reason I can no longer justify the further weakening of the West in favor of other theaters of war. I have therefore decided to strengthen the defenses in the West.

His calculation was largely political, for if the invasion failed, the Western Allies would not try again for at least a year, and the Russians might seek a separate peace, especially since even if they reached the border of 1941, they would still be a thousand miles from Berlin. He named Field Marshal von Rundstedt, whom he had dismissed in 1942, to command all German forces in the West but placed Rommel, the most popular military figure in Germany, in command of all ground units in the key coastal areas of northern France and the Low Countries. It was an unorthodox arrangement, though perfectly consistent with Hitler's leadership, and would guarantee that the essential unity of command would be in question from the very beginning. Both Rommel and Rundstedt agreed that the Pas-de-Calais in the north of France was the most likely site for the Allied landing—only twenty miles across the Strait of Dover, the narrowest part of the Channel. Initially Hitler agreed but then suddenly decided that the invasion would come in Normandy, a most unlikely spot due to its distance from Paris. It was exactly the sort of surprise that always delighted Hitler, something that he would do. The generals agreed to beef up defenses along the Normandy coast, but continued to believe that a landing in the Pas-de-Calais area offered the shortest route into France, and then a quick drive through the Low Countries into Germany and the Ruhr. That had to be prevented at all costs.

While Rundstedt and Rommel were confident that the invasion would come in Pas-de-Calais, their agreement ended there. Rommel was convinced that the Allies had to be stopped immediately on the beaches; if they were to get ashore and establish a beachhead, the battle would be lost. The first twenty-four hours of the invasion would, therefore, be what he called "the longest day," the day on which the fate of Germany would hinge. Rundstedt, on the other hand, certainly wanted a vigorous defense on the beaches, but believed that attempting to defend a coastline of several hundred miles, building up defenses on all possible landing areas, was simply impossible. Rundstedt was keenly aware of Frederick the Great's dictum that he who defends everything defends nothing. Instead, he favored mounting a mobile defense with a powerful strike force to counterattack after the main thrust of the invasion had been identified. Complicating matters further, Hitler insisted on his sole control of the so-called OKW reserves, consisting of four key panzer divisions that would be essential for a successful defense. Whether Rommel's "halt them at the beaches" or Rundstedt's mobile defense strategy was adopted, these four armor divisions would be essential to thwart the main Allied assault, and only Hitler could release them.

When at last the invasion came on the blustery dawn of June 6, it was in Normandy, and it caught the Germans by surprise. Due to a prevailing bad weather front estimated to last a week, German commanders in the West assumed that the attack would not come at that time and thought it safe to attend war games in Rouen. Rommel took the opportunity to travel home to Germany for his wife's birthday. But the Allies, who could track weather fronts across the Atlantic while the Germans could not, had detected a break in the storm and gambled that it would hold for thirty-six crucial hours on June 5–6. Although Rundstedt was at first convinced that the reported landings in Normandy were a diversion, he tried to contact Hitler in Berchtesgaden to request that the Führer release the reserve panzer divisions. But Hitler was asleep—he had taken sleeping pills—and Jodl refused to wake him. Precious hours were lost until he was awakened and briefed on the situation. Much has been made of this failure, but it is unlikely that under the circumstances Hitler would have released the panzers on June 6. In fact, for a month after the invasion began both he and Rundstedt remained convinced that a second landing would be attempted and continued to assume that it would come to the north, somewhere between the Scheldt and the Seine.

In July, a full month after the landings, the Allied breakout from Normandy finally occurred, and German forces began falling back in a disorderly retreat. American troops raced to the south-southeast; Paris fell in August, Belgium in September. To the Allies' great surprise, German forces managed to regroup, and in September repulsed a major offensive in Holland (Operation Market Garden) that would have allowed Allied forces to cross the Lower Rhine. The failure of that operation meant that the war would not be over by Christmas, as many in the West had come to believe, and it gave the Germans a chance to recover and prepare for the next Allied lunge forward. The Germans had averted disaster, but as summer turned to fall, the Wehrmacht was staggering, on the cusp of defeat.

As the vise closed on the Third Reich, grumbling on the home front mounted. Complaints were widespread, and criticism of local party officials was rampant, but given the repressive nature of the regime, such dissent, if it can be called that, did not rise to the level of systemic opposition, to say nothing of organized resistance. In the last year of the war, the Gestapo did, however, report that top leaders were increasingly coming under attack, especially Goebbels and Göring. Juvenile delinquency, which was surprisingly high in the prewar Third Reich, increased as the bombing and attendant blackouts offered ample opportunities for looting, robbery, and assault, but troubling as these developments were for the regime, they were not in the end political in nature. During the war, Gestapo, police, and judicial agencies stepped up their efforts to root out possible sources of dissent, making organized resistance virtually impossible. Any hint of dissent provoked a furious response; arrests and executions multiplied; paranoia flourished.

Despite the dangers involved, some individuals and groups did manage to engage in acts of resistance to the regime. Among the most active oppositional groups were the Communists. Although they had been hounded relentlessly since the Nazi *Machtergreifung* and their organizations were honeycombed with Gestapo spies, Communist cells remained, especially in the large cities. A network of more than twenty cells run by Robert Uhrig and Josef Römer was active in Berlin. The group printed a monthly "Information Service" pamphlet, which was distributed to Communist cells around the city as well as across Germany, calling for sabotage against industrial and military targets. Uhrig, Römer, and 150 other Communists were swept up in a Gestapo dragnet in 1942, and after two years' imprisonment in a series of prisons and concentration camps, both men were guillotined in 1944. That same sweep led to the arrest of Anton Saefkow, who had taken up where Uhrig and Römer left off, distributing leaflets and aiding fugitives. Sixty members of his group were also arrested at that time, and all were executed in 1944.

The largest of the Communist groups active in Berlin was the "Red Orchestra," led by Harro Schulze-Boysen, Arvid Harnack, and his American wife, Mildred Fish Harnack. Its primary activity was espionage, sending coded radio messages to Moscow. Because resistance radio operators were referred to as "pianists," the Gestapo gave the group its musical name. The group was tracked down by the Gestapo in 1942, and Schulze-Boysen, the Harnacks, and the majority of its members were arrested. Most were tried before a military court and executed as spies. Isolated Communist cells continued their shadowy existence into the last months of the Third Reich, printing leaflets, painting anti-Nazi slogans on city walls, and trying to stay one step ahead of the Gestapo.

The Gestapo also expressed a growing concern about a significant uptick in church attendance, which it interpreted as a symptom of growing disaffection with National Socialism. The churches, both Protestant and Catholic, had been a source of trouble for the regime since the early days, and their protest against the euthanasia program had forced the regime to suspend that operation, if only briefly. During the war, sermons in both Catholic and Protestant churches, always monitored by the Gestapo, often expressed veiled criticisms of the regime, and as the war dragged on and Germany's military fortunes sagged, many saw the church as a haven, an institution with some claim to independence. It was not the major figures of the churches that concerned the Nazis during the war, but local priests and ministers, whose sermons drew larger and larger audiences. As Germany's military situation deteriorated, Nazi authorities throughout Catholic Germany had grown increasingly concerned about "competition with the clergy." People were crowding into the churches "far more than in past years," one report to Munich party headquarters noted, especially the rural population, and the regime was groping for "an effective counterweight to the increasing influence of the church." One response was repression: more than four hundred priests were arrested and sent to Dachau.

On the whole the universities, with their starkly reduced enrollments, were quiet. But in 1942 a small group of students in Munich took bold—and suicidal—action against the regime. Calling themselves the White Rose, siblings Hans and Sophie Scholl, together with their friends Alexander Schmorell, Christoph Probst, Willi Graf, and philosophy professor Hans Huber, wrote a series of anti-Nazi leaflets, printing, and distributing them around the city. They painted slogans on walls—"FREEDOM," "HITLER MASS MURDERER," and "DOWN WITH HITLER." They mailed copies of the leaflets to students in Hamburg, Berlin, and Vienna, urging them to make copies and distribute them in their communities. Hans Scholl and Alexander Schmorell were medical students and, as required of all medical students, had spent three months serving in Russia, where they were appalled by the slaughter of young German soldiers as well as the murderous SS actions against the Jews—an experience that gave them a deepened sense of urgency and purpose.

The leaflets—there were six in all—took the form of short essays, sprinkled with literary and philosophical references, and were aggressively antiwar and anti-Nazi. They created a stir among students when they surfaced in late 1942 and early 1943; they were, after all, the first open expressions of opposition against Hitler and his regime anyone had seen. "Don't wait for someone else to take action," the first leaflet urged. It was "the responsibility of every individual as a member of Christian and western culture" to guard against "the scourge of humanity, against Fascism, and every similar system of the absolutist state. Practice passive resistance—resistance wherever you are, prevent the continued functioning of this atheistic war machine before it is too late, before the last cities are reduced to rubble, like Cologne, and before the last of the Volk's youth is bled to death for the hubris of a subhuman. Don't forget, that every people deserves the regime it gets." Although the group did not focus on Nazi crimes against the Jews, its second leaflet informed the public that "since the conquering of Poland 300,000 Jews in that country have been murdered in the most bestial way. Here we see the most frightful crimes against the dignity of man, crimes like no other in the whole of human history." Its third leaflet called for "sabotage in armaments factories, sabotage of all meetings, demonstrations, celebrations, organizations of the National Socialist Party. Prevent the smooth functioning of the war machine that works for a war that only serves for the preservation and maintenance of the National Socialist Party and its dictatorship."

On February 18, 1943, the day of Goebbels's Total War speech, the Gestapo arrested the Scholls. It had been only a matter of time. They had taken a suitcase full of leaflets to the university, left stacks of them outside the lecture halls, and finally tossed them from the top floor into the atrium below. They were observed by a maintenance man who reported them to the Gestapo. Four days later they were tried before the infamous Judge Roland Freisler of the People's Court, who screamed furious imprecations at them, rarely giving them an opportunity to utter a word. They were not afforded an attorney. At one point in the proceedings, Sophie Scholl managed to say to Freisler, "You know as well as we do that the war is lost. Why are you so cowardly that you won't admit it?" It came as no surprise when they were found guilty of treason and, together with Christoph Probst, were beheaded in Stadelheim Prison that very day. Trials of others associated with the White Rose dragged on into October; the six most closely involved with the group shared the Scholls' fate. The activities of the White Rose were courageous and idealistic; they were martyrs, living manifestations of a growing discontent in German society, and their activities added to the nervousness of the regime in the aftermath of Stalingrad. But their story did not end there. Helmut James von Moltke, leader of the Kreisau Circle, another resistance group, managed to smuggle a copy of the sixth leaflet to Scandinavia, where it made its way to London. In July, at the height of the bombing, RAF aircraft dropped tens of thousands of copies over Germany under the title "Manifesto of the Munich Students."

Since the late 1930s, a group of nationalist conservatives who wished to see the downfall of the Third Reich had gathered around Carl Goerdeler, the well-connected former mayor of Leipzig and until 1936 Reich commissar for prices. His circle included former Prussian finance minister Johannes Popitz, Ulrich von Hassell, ambassador to Rome, and other establishment conservatives. They hoped to bring about the overthrow of the Nazi regime and the establishment of a conservative government with the return of the Hohenzollern dynasty. They were mistrustful of mass democracy, which they held responsible for the rise of the populist Nazis, and in a proposed constitution advocated elections that balanced the popular vote with representatives from local councils and others nominated by the churches, trade unions, universities, and business groups. They also insisted that a post-Nazi state should include Austria, the Sudetenland, and West Prussia, all territories annexed by the Nazis, a position unlikely to find favor in Allied capitals. Goerdeler even wrote letters to Hitler and Himmler attempting to convince them that they were on the wrong course, and until late in the day believed that if only he could have a serious conversation with Hitler, he could convince the Führer to step aside.

It was clear to all involved in the resistance that their activities could not bring about the fall of the regime and that Hitler could be overthrown only by force—and that force would have to be provided by the army. Since 1936 Goerdeler had been a leading figure in efforts to recruit senior military men to join with him and his conservative allies to overthrow the Nazis. Even before the war, a number of high-ranking officers had come to the conclusion that Hitler's reckless foreign policy was leading Germany into certain catastrophe and that he must be removed. Foremost among them was General Ludwig Beck, chief of staff of the army until August 1938. Beck had supported Hitler's revitalization of the military, though he was concerned by the Führer's SS and its threat to the army.

In 1938, he was in close contact with other military leaders who were convinced that Hitler's brinkmanship over the Sudetenland would plunge Germany into a European-wide war. Beck was not opposed to smashing Czechoslovakia or Hitler's expansive plans for *Lebensraum*, but he believed that Hitler's determination to go to war in 1938 was premature. When it became clear that Hitler was not to be moved, Beck undertook a clandestine campaign for a mass resignation of army commanders, forcing Hitler to abandon his plans for an invasion. His efforts proved futile, and he resigned in August. After his resignation he kept in touch with many senior military figures, men who shared his conviction that the Nazis were pushing Germany into certain disaster. Among them was Admiral Wilhelm Canaris, head of Military Counter Intelligence (the Abwehr), who allowed his command to become a magnet for dissenters in the military. Beck also came into contact with a more activist group of army officers— Colonel Hans Oster, Friedrich Olbricht, Erwin von Witzleben, and Hans Bernd Gisevius—who were not only determined to prevent war in 1938 but were convinced that Hitler and his regime must go.

Hitler's dramatic diplomatic successes between 1936 and 1938 and his spectacular triumphs of the early war years deflated hopes for a successful military conspiracy, but the mounting disasters in 1942–43 gave new life to the regime's military opponents. Top-ranking officers were difficult to recruit, although many, including Halder and Brauchitsch, listened sympathetically but in the end took no part in the conspiracy. The fact that the conspirators could approach other officers without fear of being reported was a remarkable reflection of the code of solidarity within the military. Colonel Henning von Tresckow of Army Group Center was tireless in attempting to bring down Hitler, and in early 1944 he was behind a number of assassination attempts, but each failed to come off for one reason or another.

Things came to a head in the summer of 1944 when a young colonel, Claus Schenk von Stauffenberg, appeared on the scene. Badly wounded in Tunis—he lost an eye, an arm, and several fingers on his remaining hand—Stauffenberg was assigned to a post in Berlin where he came into contact with Beck and other like-minded military men. He also met the leaders of the conservative group around Goerdeler, whom he considered hopeless reactionaries. He was far more attracted to another set of younger resistance figures who had gathered around his cousin Peter Yorck von Wartenburg and Helmut James von Moltke. Both men were appalled by the sheer brutality of the regime, its anti-Semitism, and by the barbarism of the SS in the Soviet Union. Theirs was a moral rejection of the regime and its leader. During the course of 1943 these aristocratic scions of two renowned Prussian military families formed a heterogeneous group of civil servants, socialists, Protestant and Catholic clerics, and young aristocrats. They held meetings at Kreisau, Moltke's estate in Upper Silesia, and Yorck's small house in Berlin Lichterfelde. There they developed plans for a post-Hitler government but with a more progressive mixture of socialist and Christian ideas. They had no illusions about holding on to Hitler's annexed territories and endorsed the idea of war crimes trials. Like Stauffenberg, they considered the Goerdeler group backward-looking and far too conservative, and in 1944 Socialist members of the group sought to make contact with the Communist underground. Although some in the group, especially Moltke, were opposed to assassination on moral grounds, others, Yorck in particular, became participants in the plot to kill the Führer.

Several attempts had been made to get close to Hitler but each time the attempt was aborted. Either security was too tight or Hitler failed to keep to the anticipated schedule or Himmler was not present. The conspirators agreed that it was crucial to eliminate the Reichsführer-SS along with Hitler if the plot was to have any chance of success. In January and February 1944 the Gestapo seemed to be closing in on the conspirators. Moltke was arrested in January and Admiral Canaris a month later; Julius Leber, a Socialist leader close to the Kreisau Circle, was seized after attempting to make contact with the Communist underground. Stauffenberg's arrival—and the precipitous decline in Germany's military position—galvanized the military conspiracy anew. Although neither he nor Goerdeler liked one another, they managed to work together to bring about a Putsch that planned to remove Hitler and then establish a new post-Hitler Germany. They sounded out men they hoped would join a new German government, and Goerdeler, who was not the most cautious of men, made lists. General Beck would be the head of a provisional government, and Goerdeler would be Reich chancellor. Others would be mortified to discover that he committed these things to paper. The list included Hans Oster, Erwin von Witzleben, Henning von Tresckow, all military men as well as representatives from the Socialists (Leber), several Zentrum members, and a number of men from the conservative DNVP. Rommel, though not directly involved in the conspiracy, was aware of it, and indicated that although he would not participate in the plot to assassinate Hitler, he would support it at the appropriate time.

General Olbricht in the Reserve Army headquarters had developed a scheme to subvert an existing plan approved by Hitler to deal with the possibility of an uprising by the millions of foreign workers in Germany. Olbricht believed it possible to use the plan, code-named Valkyrie, to stage a coup once Hitler was dead. The order would be given to mobilize the Reserve Army and to use it not against rebelling foreign workers but against the SS and the Nazi elite. But first, the Führer had to be eliminated. Several abortive attempts had already been made. Then, on July 1, Stauffenberg was appointed chief of staff to General Friedrich Fromm, commander of the Reserve Army, headquartered in the Bendlerstrasse in Berlin. That not only put him at the command center of the Reserve Army but also meant that he was able to attend Hitler's military conferences as Fromm's deputy. Four times in the first weeks of July Stauffenberg attended these briefings in both the Obersalzburg and Hitler's East Prussian headquarters, the Wolf's Lair, carrying a bomb in his briefcase, but in each case he was unable to detonate the explosives. On July 20, Stauffenberg was scheduled to attend a Führer conference at the Wolf's Lair. By this time, the conspirators had decided that the assassination had to take place whether Himmler was present or not. Besides, with the Gestapo apparently closing in, the time to take action had come. Again he carried a bomb.

The conference began just after noon. Stauffenberg carried two bombs in his briefcase, but he had time to activate the timer on only one, and his aide, Werner von Haeften, took the other away. Upon entering the conference room, he placed his briefcase under the heavy oak conference table on which the situation map was spread. About twenty officers were in attendance, standing or sitting around the table. About ten minutes into the briefing, while Hitler was bent over the table studying the map, Stauffenberg said that he had to make an important call and left the room. This was not unusual at such briefings, and no suspicion was aroused. He quickly left the building and made his way toward the airfield. He and Haeften had to bluff their way through two security checkpoints at the inner and outer rings of the complex. As they reached the second checkpoint, a tremendous blast resounded, and a pall of black smoke swirled into the air, but the guard let them pass. They raced to the waiting aircraft and took off for Berlin. The explosion shattered the flimsy wooden conference building, killing four officers and critically wounding several others. But Hitler miraculously survived. At the time of the blast, he was leaning over the table, and someone had apparently shifted Stauffenberg's briefcase to the outside of the thick wedge of the table support, channeling the force of the blast away from Hitler. His right arm was wrenched, an eardrum perforated; he had cuts and bruises on his arms and legs, but he was alive.

By the time Stauffenberg reached Berlin shortly before 3:00 p.m. and phoned the conspirators in the Bendlerblock to report that Hitler was dead, he discovered that a phone call from the Wolf's Lair had already informed them that Hitler had survived. Stauffenberg did not believe it, but it was clear already that a major element of the plot had miscarried— communications between the Wolf's Lair and the outside world were to have been cut. Despite this critical setback, General Olbricht set Valkyrie in motion. Military forces acting under that plan moved against the SS in Vienna, Prague, and Paris, where the commanding officers of the SS were arrested. But soon Hitler's staff at the Wolf's Lair were phoning army commands around Europe, assuring them that the Führer was alive and that a small clique of disgruntled officers in Berlin had undertaken a Putsch. Army troops and Waffen-SS personnel descended on the Bendlerblock and after a brief exchange of gunfire, the leaders of the conspiracy were seized. Beck was allowed to commit suicide, though he botched the job and had to be finished off by an SS man. Stauffenberg, Haeften, Olbricht, and Mertz von Quirnheim were led into the courtyard and shot by a firing squad, Stauffenberg shouting out "Long live sacred Germany" just as the shots were fired.

Throughout the night and into the following day members of the conspiracy were hunted down by the Gestapo and arrested. Many, like Tresckow, committed suicide before the Gestapo came for them. Beginning on August 7, the regime staged show trials in the People's Court, with Roland Freisler serving as presiding judge. Before being led into the courtroom the accused had been tortured for days, and to humiliate them, they were dressed in ill-fitting civilian clothes, no ties or belts allowed, so that some had to tug at their trousers to keep them from falling down. In the proceedings Freisler, perched beneath an enormous swastika banner, heaped abuse on them, bullying them, shrieking so shrilly that the film crew assigned by Goebbels to record the trials reported that his screaming interfered with the recording. One of the defendants did manage to slip in a retort when Freisler roared that he would soon roast in hell. Bowing, the defendant shot back, "I'll look forward to your own imminent arrival, your honor!" Even the Nazi minister of justice complained about Freisler's outrageous conduct.

The condemned were taken directly from the courtroom to Plötzensee Prison, where they were hanged by piano wire from meat hooks. It was a slow agonizing death, in some cases taking twenty minutes before the victim finally strangled. While they were writhing in unbearable pain, guards pulled down their trousers, adding a last dose of humiliation to their horrific misery. Hitler, seething with rage and a bloodthirsty desire for vengeance, had the executions filmed. "Now I finally have the swine who have been sabotaging my work for years," Hitler raged. "Now I have proof: the whole General Staff is contaminated." The failures of the generals to produce the victories he had foreseen could now be explained. "Now I know why all my great plans in Russia had to fail in recent years. It was treason! But for these traitors we would have won long ago."

In the aftermath of the failed Putsch, more than two hundred people directly implicated in the conspiracy were arrested and executed. Yorck, Witzleben, Goerdeler, Moltke, Leber, Oster, and others were murdered over a matter of months. Goerdeler was put to death in February 1945, while Canaris and Dietrich Bonhoeffer of the Confessing Church were hanged in April. In a major police operation that followed the show trials, more than five thousand persons, many who had no connection whatsoever with the plot, were arrested. The most prominent among them was Rommel. As mentioned, Rommel knew about the plot but refused to take part. The conspirators thought that he signaled that he would support a new German government once Hitler was removed, and his name had emerged from Gestapo interrogations of the conspirators. On July 23 Rommel was recovering at home from wounds suffered in an Allied strafing when he received word that he had been implicated in the conspiracy. He was an enormously popular commander, a genuine military hero, and the regime was willing to offer him a choice: he could commit suicide and be given a state funeral with all the military honors, and his wife and children would not be separated and sent to concentration camps (as were Stauffenberg's). If he refused the offer of suicide, he would be tried before the People's Court. He chose suicide.

Hitler drew two paradoxical conclusions from the events of July 20. On the one hand, he was convinced that his survival was an act of providence, a sign from the fates that he was meant to complete the great work of his life. It contributed massively to his already overdeveloped messianic self-perception, reaffirming his conviction that his chosen path was preordained. It also reinforced Hitler's deep-seated suspicion—turning it into an almost primeval conviction—that he was surrounded by treachery and betrayal on all sides, but especially in the army and its High Command. Second, and not so reassuring, he had believed at the outset that the Putsch was the work of a tiny clique of officers, many of whom were aristocratic and hence remote from the people. That was the official interpretation of the conspiracy spun by Goebbels after July 20, but the results of the Gestapo's far-reaching investigation and the mass arrests revealed something quite different. Most Germans were shocked by the attempted assassination and rallied to their embattled Führer, and support for the conspirators within the Wehrmacht was minimal at best. Still, the extent of the conspiracy and the evidence of widespread disaffection with the regime was troubling, especially at a juncture in the war when the Reich's military fortunes were in sharp decline. The conspirators were themselves aware that most Germans would hate them as traitors and that the plot would in all probability fail, but it was important to demonstrate to the world that there were Germans willing to take a stand against this evil regime. As Henning von Tresckow said to Stauffenberg, "The assassination must be attempted at any cost. Even should that fail, the attempt to seize power . . . must be undertaken. We must prove to the world and to future generations that the men of the German resistance movement dared to take the decisive step and to hazard their lives upon it. Compared with this object, nothing else matters."

Throughout the summer the Allied air forces escalated their assault on the German homeland. Although the Anglo-American bombing campaign had had an undeniable effect on German morale in 1943, its impact on German war production was less obvious. In fact, German munitions production actually increased in 1942–43, especially after Hitler's appointment of Albert Speer to head the Ministry of Armaments and Munitions in February 1942. In an effort to rationalize German production, Speer, using his access to Hitler as leverage, was able to supplant Göring's Four Year Plan and the Wehrmacht's War Economy and Armaments Office, headed by General Georg Thomas. He launched a drive to standardize production, tighten control over the uses of raw materials, factory, and labor, and to reduce the number of different types of weapons. Rationalization of production did not begin with Speer, but working with the powerful Erhard Milch, in charge of Luftwaffe production, as well as industrialists and local officials, he was able to bring the disparate elements of war production under something that approached central control. By 1943 this strategy was paying huge dividends, and by early 1944 Germany was producing twice as many rifles as in 1941, over three times as many hand grenades, over seven times as many howitzers, and more than three times as many aircraft. Speer was a star, his achievements touted as the "Speer miracle." At a time when the Nazis had few military triumphs to parade before the public, the striking upward curve of munitions production served as a propaganda tool to demonstrate to the German people that the war could still be won. In the process, Speer, already a Hitler favorite, became a public darling.

But Speer's reputation—and German war production—peaked in the first half of 1944 and began a drastic slide thereafter. Following the invasion of France, the Allies were at last able to execute a sustained air assault against German industry, especially oil and transportation, staging raids of five, six, seven hundred planes against synthetic fuel complexes, railyards, and other related targets. Over half the bomb tonnage dropped by the Allies on Germany fell between D-Day and the end of the war, and German industrial output plunged precipitously in every important category—aircraft production by 62 percent; armor by 54 percent; motor vehicles by 72 percent; ammunition by 62 percent; and weapons by 42 percent. From its peak in 1944 to March 1945, total munitions production fell by 55 percent.

The main thrust of the Allied air campaign between May and September 1944 was directed against Germany's synthetic oil installations, which produced 90 percent of the Reich's aviation fuel and 30 percent of its motor gasoline. As a result of the bombing, synthetic oil production plummeted from an average of 359,000 tons in the four months preceding the onset of the raids to 24,000 tons in September. The output of aviation fuel from these plants tumbled from 175,000 tons in April to 5,000 tons in the same period, while oil and aviation fuel stocks fell by two thirds. By the close of the year, the German war machine was literally running on empty.

After September 1944, the focus of the air offensive shifted to Germany's transportation and communication system. Raids on rail, road, and water transport were, in many respects, more effective than the assault on oil, reducing traffic by 50 percent during the last year of the war. Since 1943, much of German production had been dispersed to different sites to prevent a single blow from destroying a key industrial choke point. By the close of 1944, however, even if crucial parts or weapons were produced, they could not reach assembly areas or soldiers at the front. With the transportation system in tatters, the national economy dissolved into a handful of relatively isolated regional economic zones. The Ruhr was largely severed from the remainder of Germany, and total coal shipments, on which so much of German industry depended, were reduced from 75,000 carloads in June 1944 to 39,000 in January 1945, to 28,000 in March. "Our entire military trouble can be traced back to the enemy's air superiority," Goebbels noted forlornly in his diary in March 1945. "In practice a coordinated conduct [of the war] is no longer possible in the Reich. We no longer have control over transportation and communication links. Not only our cities, but also our industries are for the most part destroyed. The result is a deep break in Germany's war morale."

Resentment against the Nazi authorities, especially Göring and the Luftwaffe, simmered. With a cynicism born of bitter experience, many Germans recalled that there was a time early in the war when the bombing actually seemed to have bonded the people with the regime. Party and state agencies rushed to provide all sorts of services, collecting relief, distributing food and blankets, finding shelter for families whose homes were destroyed in the raids. Even the skeptics, and there were many, had to admit that life beneath the bombs created a sense of communal closeness, of shared hardship, as people found themselves increasingly thrown back on one another, on family and neighbors. But as the bombing escalated to almost apocalyptic proportions that sense of solidarity with the regime was steadily eroded by mass suffering and the increasingly obvious failure of the regime to protect its people.

By the end of 1944 German air defenses were simply overwhelmed. The flak continued to shoot down bombers in large numbers—and sometimes the Luftwaffe, starved for fuel, mustered the new jet fighters, the Me 262 *Dusenjäger*—to attack the formations. After almost every raid the charred fuselages and rudders and wings of enemy bombers were scattered among the boughs of trees or jutted from devastated buildings, bits of bodies strewn among the debris. Children played in the wreckage; scavengers stripped away boots or heavy jackets from the dead; they took parachutes for the silk. But always the bombers came back, more and more of them.

Of the Nazi leaders, only Goebbels toured the devastated city neighborhoods. He talked to the thousands left homeless by the bombs. The Führer was nowhere to be seen. People still heard his voice on rare occasions, rasping through the static of the *Volksempfänger*, but he avoided the bombed-out cities. Even the great war criminal Churchill had gone out among the people of London during the Blitz, people noted. They had seen it in the newsreels. But Hitler had vanished. He appeared rarely in public and he spoke only rarely on the radio. When on November 9 he did not give his annual speech on the anniversary of the Beer Hall Putsch, the disappointed public worried that he was ill, or dead, or held captive by the SS. Goebbels begged him to speak to the people, to show himself; it would be a tremendous boost to morale. But he would not, and his absence was deeply felt. He was safe, many assumed, deep in a bunker in Berlin or in the Alps or in his secret headquarters in East Prussia, directing the war. "The Greatest General of All Times," people whispered in scorn.

For a time in the summer and fall of 1944, with the war sliding unmistakably toward catastrophe on all fronts, spirits were briefly raised by the prospect of new "wonder weapons" that would turn the tide of the war. The regime sought to boost sagging morale by promising retaliation with new, secret weapons. The V-1 rockets, the first of the "vengeance weapons," began landing in England in June 1944, and their use was closely followed by the German public. But within weeks it became obvious that the new wonder weapons had no deterrent effect on the Anglo-American air forces and could not impede the Allied advance in the West. The much heralded introduction of the V-2 rocket in the fall was again met with great anticipation, but by December Nazi regional officials had to report that "it has had as yet no real effect on morale. The people have also grown skeptical about the introduction of more weapons." The general feeling was that it was simply too late.

As the bombing intensified and the regime proved itself helpless to protect the populace, uneasiness, fatigue, and resentment against the Nazis mounted. The RAF's nighttime raids were more unnerving than the American daylight attacks, but the sight of large formations of enemy bombers sweeping across the midday sky, apparently unmolested by the Luftwaffe, had a particularly demoralizing effect. An SD report of July 14, 1944, sounded what would become a characteristic refrain: "The fact that the Terror Fliers could make their way in broad daylight to their targets in important war industries without being hindered by German fighters . . . has had quite a negative impact on morale and strengthened the feeling that we are delivered over to the whims of the enemy."

By the close of 1944 reports from regional districts were punctuated with worries about the debilitating effects of the bombing in cities and strafing in the countryside. "Signs of war weariness and apathy concerning the course of the war can be detected," the authorities commented in December 1944, "especially in the rural population." There was widespread fear that "the small towns and villages will soon be sought out by terror fliers." By spring of 1945 that fear had become a grim reality. Commenting on the mood of the people in early 1945, a similar report concluded that "an upswing in general morale will only come about if success can be attained in breaking the enemy's air superiority, thus . . . protecting the homeland from the actions of the enemy air forces." The reasons given for the military defeats were "everywhere attributed to Russian tank superiority as well as enemy air superiority. Especially the air superiority of the enemy leads again and again to the sharpest condemnation of the German Luftwaffe, in which the person of the supreme commander of the Luftwaffe himself has increasingly come in for criticism."

"The people are beginning to suffer from what is called Bunker fever and inability to work," the Wuppertal Gestapo reported in January 1945. "The faith in our leading men, including the Führer, is rapidly disappearing. They are thoroughly fed up with Goebbels' articles and speeches and say that he too often has lied to the German people and talked too big. The attitude towards National Socialism is characterized by the following saying: 'If we have not yet collapsed, it is not *because* of National Socialism but *in spite of* National Socialism.'" An elderly Hamburg woman who worked with her husband as a hotel manager remembered that "the most remarkable thing one noticed when one sat in the air raid shelter was how the people cursed the Nazis more and more as time went on, without inhibitions or reservations. . . . Never was the cursing about England or America. Always it was about the Nazis. And it got worse and worse." Watching his city consumed in flames, a Lübeck man and his neighbors "were all of the opinion that we had Hitler to thank for all this misery."

Earlier in the war, the regime organized evacuations of children from the cities to small towns and rural retreats. Bewildered children from Munich and Nuremberg or as far away as Hamburg appeared in the streets of bucolic villages, sometimes accompanied by a teacher and an official from the Reich Air Defense League. No longer. In the spring of 1945, low-flying Allied fighters were everywhere. Day and night Thunderbolts and Mustangs and twin-engine Lightnings would roar in just above the treetops, strafing the roads and rail lines. They fired at farmers plowing their fields, at tractors and horse-drawn wagons on nearly deserted country lanes. No one was safe.

German morale did not crack under this onslaught—given the oppressive nature of the National Socialist state, serious unrest was unlikely, an uprising hardly possible—but the bombing did have a corrosive, demoralizing effect on civilian attitudes. Repeated heavy bombardment did not engender feelings of rebellion but a mood of sullen apathy and a devouring absorption with the basic task of survival. Deeply ingrained work habits, Nazi propaganda, and fear of the regime all played a role to keep weary Germans at their jobs. "During the last months of the war," a woman from Wetzlar explained, "my only thought was to keep alive, to keep safe in the cellar, and to get a little food cooked." Survival was the order of the day—a sentiment reflected in the common Berlin farewell of 1944–45: "*Bleib übrig!*" (Survive!)

By fall 1944 Germany's strategic situation was desperate. Allied troops had penetrated the border territory of the Reich in both the East and West and were poised for a drive into the heart of the Third Reich. Hitler decided that one last dramatic stroke in the West might yet save the situation. His plan called for a massive counterattack in the Ardennes area, then sending armored spearheads dashing across the Meuse to Antwerp, depriving the Allies of their most important port and driving a wedge between the British forces in the north and the Americans farther south. To accomplish this he would deploy thirty new and rebuilt divisions, including two reoutfitted panzer armies—a larger force than 1940. Guderian, now chief of the General Staff, objected to the entire undertaking, which, he argued, would waste Germany's last armored reserves for a dubious objective in the West when all available forces were desperately needed in the East as the Soviets prepared a major winter offensive. Both Rundstedt and General Alfred Model, Rommel's replacement, were also wary of deploying these important armored formations in the West and preferred a more limited operation. They were overruled by Hitler.

On December 16, under overcast skies, the Germans launched Operation Autumn Fog. Two hundred thousand German troops and six hundred tanks were thrown into the offensive against approximately eighty thousand unsuspecting American troops backed by four hundred tanks. The surprise was complete. German troops sliced through the overmatched Americans along a seventy-mile front and headed for the Meuse River, creating a bulge in Allied lines sixty-five miles deep and forty miles wide. Fighting was intense and conditions terrible—a heavy, wet snow fell as the coldest winter in half a century settled over Western Europe. Among the forces marshaled for the attack were SS units that had been transferred from the Eastern Front, and on December 17 the First SS Panzer Division brought a taste of the Russian campaign to the West. In what had been a common procedure in Russia, the SS massacred eighty-six American prisoners in a field at Malmedy. Until then the Wehrmacht had for the most part fought what one historian has called "a war with rules" against Anglo-American forces, largely adhering to the Geneva Conventions. But in the East, the Germans had engaged in a vicious "war without rules." At Malmedy that distinction was erased.

Much of the early success of the German offensive came as a result of bad weather that neutralized Allied airpower, but on Christmas Eve the skies cleared, and Allied aircraft decimated the German spearheads. The German thrust was also slowed by stiffening American resistance and a serious shortage of fuel. Military planners had counted on seizing American oil depots, but that proved impossible. The panzers literally ran out of gas. The offensive was a total failure. The Germans had failed to reach the Meuse, and Antwerp, the main objective of the offensive, was still more than a hundred miles away. By mid-January, the Allies had eliminated the "bulge" in their lines. Casualties on both sides were heavy, roughly 80,000 Germans and 70,000 Americans, but Hitler had exhausted the last of the Wehrmacht's reserves on a wildly ambitious project that from the start virtually all the High Command thought had little chance of success. In the process, it desperately weakened the German defensive position in the East on the eve of a massive Russian offensive in Poland. It was the last desperate gasp of the Third Reich.

In the aftermath of the catastrophic Ardennes offensive, Hitler realized that the war could not be won militarily. "I know the war is lost," he confided to his military aide Nicolaus von Below. But, he added, "We'll not capitulate. Never. We can go down. But we'll take a world with us." His only hope was to achieve a political settlement, which he thought might be possible by inflicting such devastating losses on the Western Allies that they would seek a separate peace or even agree to join Germany in its "heroic struggle to save Western Civilization from the ravages of Bolshevism." But even that fanciful hope was extinguished by the failure of the Ardennes offensive.

The drumbeat of bad news continued into February and March. On February 13, Allied aircraft dropped 2,658 tons of bombs on Dresden, 1,181 of which were incendiaries, turning that beautiful Renaissance city into an inferno and killing 25,000 civilians. Among those in the city that night was the Jewish philologist Viktor Klemperer. As he and his wife made their way through the burning city trying to reach the Elbe, he saw that "fires were still burning in many of the buildings on the road above." The dead, "small, and no more than a bundle of clothes . . . were scattered across our path. The skull of one had been torn away, the top of the head was a dark red bowl. Once an arm lay there with a pale, quite fine hand, like a model made of wax." Crowds streamed unceasingly between "the corpses and smashed vehicles, up and down the Elbe, a silent, agitated procession." At one point his wife wanted to light a cigarette but had no matches. "Something was glowing on the ground, she wanted to use it—it was a burning corpse." The city was not a major industrial center, but the Allies claimed that it was an important transit center for German troops moving east and so they attacked as a sign of the West's willingness to help the advance of Stalin's forces.

On March 7, 1945, American troops found the only remaining intact bridge over the Rhine at Remagen, fifteen miles south of Cologne, and poured across. Three weeks later all Allied armies were across the Rhine— the last natural barrier to the interior of the Reich. In the first days of April the Ruhr was encircled by British and American forces, trapping 430,000 German troops. The Ruhr pocket held out until April 12–13 before surrendering. Allied commanders were eager to launch a drive for Berlin, to beat the Russians into the capital of the Third Reich. They were fifty miles from Berlin, but General Dwight Eisenhower, supreme commander of allied forces, refused to give the order to advance on the city. In February at Yalta, the Big Three—Churchill, Roosevelt, and Stalin—had come to an agreement about zones of occupation for defeated Germany, and Berlin was deep inside the Soviet zone. Eisenhower was not about to sacrifice thousands of British and American lives to take the Nazi capital only to turn it over to the Russians. He also understood that while the Americans were only fifty miles from Berlin, they were overextended and at a troop strength of only fifty thousand. The Soviets, with a far greater force, were forty miles from Berlin and would have launched their offensive earlier had the Western Allies pressed on. As events later in the month would demonstrate, the price the Soviets paid for taking the city would be extremely high.

From January onward, German roads were clogged with long straggling columns of Allied POWs and concentration camp inmates herded on desperate marches deeper into the dwindling territory of the Reich. A flood tide of panicked civilians fleeing the rampaging Red Army surged westward, inundating Germany's already ravaged cities and exacerbating the mounting chaos. They brought with them hair-raising tales of rape, wanton destruction, and uncontrolled pillaging by the marauding Red Army. The barbarian hordes were approaching, pushing before them a wave of suicides by local Nazi leaders and ordinary party members. In East Prussia, Silesia, and Pomerania, ancient German cities fell to the Soviets. Instead of allowing German forces there to retreat to more realistic defensive lines, Hitler called for Königsberg, Breslau, and other cities to become fortresses to hold back the Russians. His generals thought this foolish but, as usual, they complied. The Red Army simply bypassed them and continued toward Berlin.

At the same time, the Allied bombing of Germany reached its deadly crescendo. Massive raids by the Anglo-American air forces devastated Dresden, Pforzheim, Würzburg, Magdeburg, Nuremberg, and other cities, large and small, laying waste to much of the country and leaving hundreds of thousands of German civilians dead or homeless. Most of the Germans killed by Allied bombing in the war died in 1945. In fact, January and February were the deadliest months of the Second World War; in addition to the civilian casualties, 1.4 million German soldiers fell in the last four months of the war, roughly 14,000 every day. Soldiers of the once-mighty Wehrmacht also deserted in alarming numbers, discarding their uniforms, hoping to be swallowed up in the torrent of refugees. Thousands were caught and summarily shot or hanged. By mid-1944 more than 26,000 death sentences had been imposed on Wehrmacht personnel for desertion or undermining of the war effort, although the exact number of those executed is impossible to determine with confidence. But between January and May 1945 the number of soldiers sentenced to death in the regular military court system stood at approximately 4,000, while the figures for those executed by the "flying courts-martial" may have been closer to 6,000 or 7,000. As the troops quickly realized, these "flying courts" were little more than roaming death squads.

Nor were such draconian measures reserved for the military. Civilian morale was in a free fall. One report from regional authorities in early February spoke for many when it stated that in December morale had improved due to the Ardennes offensive and the New Year's radio address by the

Führer. But then the Soviet winter offensive in January sent Russian troops deep into Germany, producing in the public "deep disappointment and . . . a great horror. Because of these developments the public has been gripped by strong disappointment . . . as well as fear and worry. Many consider the war already lost." The situation was so dire that the regime felt compelled to create special courts that operated on roughly the same principles as the military drumhead tribunals but were intended for civilians. Any German— man, woman, or child—who in any way failed to support the war effort, disrupted military operations, or showed "defeatist tendencies" could be tried and executed on the spot as a traitor. In these final, increasingly chaotic months more than ten thousand civilians were executed by such tribunals for "defeatism," treason, or "undermining military operations."

Faced with festering resentment from the exhausted population and gripped by a mounting sense of desperation, the Nazis issued fanatical appeals—and threats—to fight "to the last bullet." The only hope for the Reich, Hitler believed, was to hold out until the "unnatural" alliance against him broke apart and a separate peace with either the Western powers or with the Soviets could be negotiated. Consequently, as the ground war moved into Germany, every farm and hamlet, every village, town, and city was to be turned into a fortress; soldiers and civilians were exhorted to fight fanatically to the last man, woman, and child, inflicting maximum casual- ties on the enemy and slowing the Allied advance. In an appeal typical of this apocalyptic policy, the Nazi *Gauleiter* of Upper Franconia warned his beleaguered population that "if coal, gas, and electricity are in short supply now, what is all that compared to our enemies' sadistic Jewish plans for our destruction. And even if our food rations were cut still further, we would look back at these reduced living conditions as a paradise if the Bolshevik and his plutocratic helpers become masters of the Reich. . . . All our men will be taken to Siberia. Our women will be violated, our children dragged away." There could be only one answer: "Fight, Fight, and Fight still more." Defeatism would not be tolerated. "Cowards, trouble makers and traitors," he warned, would be ruthlessly "exterminated."

To augment the army now fighting on German soil, the Nazis mobilized a home guard, the *Volkssturm*, pressing all males between the ages of sixteen and sixty into military service. Poorly equipped and hardly trained at all, some of these ragtag units did fight with dogged determination, especially in the East, but most were quickly crushed; many simply evaporated in the heat of battle, melting away before the enemy. It is estimated that 50 percent of German military losses in 1945 were from *Volkssturm* personnel.

As the vise gradually closed on the Third Reich in the first four months of 1945, the cataclysmic violence of Hitler's war engulfed the German heartland with unimaginable force, and life in the Third Reich assumed an apocalyptic, almost surreal quality. The war-weary population found itself trapped between the onrushing Allied armies, a remorseless assault from the air, and a fanatical regime that in its death throes turned on its own people. The vicious Nazi reign of terror that had spread across Europe since 1939 came home to the Reich, and Germans discovered that they had as much to fear from their own criminal regime as from their onrushing enemies. "Now Hitler has declared war on us," one woman dolefully observed.

On April 7, Himmler sounded the alarm, issuing an order that reflected the desperate state of affairs: "At the present moment in the war everything depends above all else on the stubborn, unflinching will to hold on. Hanging out white sheets, opening already closed tank barriers, failing to report to the *Volkssturm* and other displays [of defeatism] are to be met with the harshest measures. If a white flag appears on any dwelling, all men of that house are to be shot. There can be not a moment of hesitation in carrying out this action." But in these final weeks of madness, a volatile compound of fatalism, fear, and desperation ignited a spark of open rebellion in a number of towns in western and southern Germany. Localized clashes between Nazi officials and German civilians occurred in numerous villages and towns, as ordinary Germans tried to save their communities from certain destruction in what was clearly a futile effort to stave off the invaders. In many locales, it was women, accompanied by their children, who confronted the Nazi leadership, marching into village squares to demand that their town or village be spared. These uprisings were not ideological in nature. They were not protests against the Nazi system or Hitler's leadership. They were inspired by a desire to survive, to save their towns or villages from needless destruction.

Although citizen revolts had taken place in a number of villages and small towns, by far the largest of these women's revolts took place in the cathedral city of Regensburg on April 23, 1945. Responding angrily to the *Gauleiter*'s call for fanatical resistance, some one thousand women accompanied by their children, many in baby carriages, and a sprinkling of men gathered in the market square, demanding that the city be handed over to the Americans without resistance. The Nazis broke up the demonstration and arrested about thirty of the protesters, many more or less at random. By evening all had been released except for a local timber merchant and Johann Maier, a Catholic priest who spoke at the demonstration. The agitated *Gauleiter* phoned from his headquarters south of the city and ordered that "the leaders of these rabble rousers be hanged immediately." When the local party leader objected that, legally speaking [!], a special tribunal must be held, the *Gauleiter* bellowed, "Fine. Hang them first, then convene the tribunal!" The priest was hanged in the dead of night, and his body left dangling on the gallows in the market square throughout the following day. Around his neck the Nazis had hung a sign reading: "Here dies a saboteur." Two days later the Nazi leadership slipped quietly out of town, and on April 27 the Americans entered the city. Not a shot was fired.

In the spring of 1945 towns and cities over the Reich were falling one after another, overrun by Allied forces or surrendered by the local military authorities. Just a day before the women's demonstration in Regensburg American troops staged a victory parade through the ruins of Nuremberg, site of the huge Nazi rallies of prewar days. The city was a desolate sight. More than 90 percent of its buildings lay in ruins, a grisly testament to the devastating Allied air raids and the savage house-to-house fighting as the city fell. To mark the defeat of this city so closely associated with Hitler, the American 3rd Infantry Division marched into the main arena of the party congress grounds, moving in formation beneath the speaker's tribunal where Hitler had mesmerized mammoth crowds before the war. Following the parade, American engineers exploded the huge stone wreath and swastika that looked down over the grounds. It was a moment of high symbolism.

In January, Soviet forces had encountered the virtually deserted camp at Auschwitz. In the sprawling complex where more than a million human beings had been murdered, they discovered 7,500 prisoners miraculously still clinging to life and some 600 corpses. Ten days earlier Himmler had ordered the evacuation of all the camps in the East, stressing that "not a single prisoner from the concentration camps falls alive into the hands of the enemy." He also ordered the destruction of the gas chambers and crematoria, in fact, all traces of the vast crimes committed there. They were not successful in this, but on January 17 roughly 60,000 inmates of the camp were evacuated, sent on forced marches in the bitter cold and snow to the west. Two thirds of them never reached their destination, first at the camp at Gross-Rosen, then the giant camp at Bergen-Belsen in Germany.

As Anglo-American forces moved deeper into Germany, they encountered the Nazi concentration camps located on German soil—Ohrdruf (April 9), Buchenwald (April 11), Bergen-Belsen (April 15), and Flossenbürg (April 23). The Soviets had come upon Majdanek in the previous July, with its gas chambers and crematoria still in place, though that information was not widely shared. The horrors they found in these hellholes revealed the raw ideological core of the Third Reich—mass graves, bodies piled in heaps, the living little more than skeletons, crematoria, some still clogged with bodies, storage bins of gold extracted from teeth, bags of women's hair, spectacles, suitcases, dentures, clothing, including in one camp thousands of pairs of baby shoes. In between Allied troops stumbled upon scores of smaller satellite camps where the horrors were as gruesome as in the larger main camps; only the scale of suffering was smaller. The hideous scenes that greeted the soldiers sent shockwaves through the Allied High Command, the political establishment in the United States and Britain, and a dazed international public numbed by five years of total war. Unlike Auschwitz, which was no longer in operation when the Russians reached it in January, the camps inside Nazi Germany had not been evacuated. In fact, in the spring of 1945 their populations were swollen by arrivals from the extermination camps in the East. By mid-April, Dachau, built to hold 5,000 inmates, was swamped by 30,000 men and women, all existing in conditions of unimaginable filth, disease, and starvation. More than 10,000 prisoners had already died in Dachau and its subsidiary camps since January; hundreds were dying each day.

The camp's Jewish prisoners were for the most part recent arrivals, survivors of the death camps in the East. Most had been evacuated to Buchenwald just days before its liberation, and then marched on foot or crammed into boxcars and open coal cars to begin a long nightmarish journey south. Throughout central and western Germany, in the ever-shrinking territory controlled by the Reich, the SS forced tens of thousands of prisoners on torturous "death marches" from concentration camps, large and small. Barely clinging to life, the exhausted new arrivals found themselves delivered into a filthy, hellish compound literally overflowing with the living and the dead. Among the thousands of inmates who milled listlessly about, hundreds of bodies littered the grounds; corpses were stacked like cordwood beside the long rows of squalid barracks and were piled high against the walls of the crematorium, which had long since ceased to operate. There were simply too many dead to burn. Since the beginning of April transports from Buchenwald, Flossenbürg, and other camps to the north and east had swamped the SS authorities, who no longer bothered to record the thousands of new prisoners that were dumped inside the gates.

On a railway siding just beside the main gate the Americans came upon some fifty boxcars. The transport had arrived on April 27 from Buchenwald via Flossenbürg. Its cargo, two thousand men and women, piled in a ghastly tangle of skeletal limbs and shrunken torsos, had died en route or were left to starve at the very gates of Dachau. The American colonel in command recalled that "the first thing I saw was that terrible train. I walked past car after car. It was all I could do to believe it. Suddenly, a soldier about ten or fifteen yards behind me, yelled, 'Hey, Colonel! Here's a live one!' Immediately, I ran back to the car. There, almost buried under a mass of dead bodies, was a hand that was waving so feebly you could hardly notice it. But it was moving!" One survivor among the two thousand. When he was finally untangled from the bodies around him, the man, hardly more than a skeleton, looked frantically from one soldier to another, repeating in sheer disbelief, *"Frei? Frei?"*

As the Red Army breached the frontiers of the Reich and charged westward, a wave of terror swept over the German population. A stampede of panicked refugees poured into the roads, some two million in all, fleeing the Russians. With them they carried hair-raising tales—many of them true—of rape, random violence, summary executions, and barbaric behavior. By February Soviet spearheads were within sixty miles of Berlin, preparing for a titanic assault on the German capital. Three giant army groups—fronts, the Russians called them—were assembled along the Oder—1.5 million troops, 3,300 tanks, 10,000 aircraft, and 28,000 heavy guns and the dreaded Katyusha rocket launchers—"Stalin Organs," they were called. Arrayed against them were 600,000 German troops, composed for the most part of old men and boys from the *Volkssturm* and the Hitler Youth. In April 1945 Berlin was a city of women, old men, and children. Military units were drained of personnel, so that what appeared on the briefing maps as divisions or regiments were mere shells, some only phantoms.

Hitler did not trust his generals, especially after the attempted Putsch, and they, even the most loyal, were appalled at his lack of judgment. Virtually all agreed that Autumn Fog had been an "incomprehensible" disaster, followed by his order for German troops to fight on the west bank of the Rhine. In January, as the Red Army approached Berlin, he ordered the Sixth Panzer Army to Hungary, where he argued he would surprise the Russians and inflict on them a game-changing defeat. Madness, the generals believed, but they complied. On January 21 he appointed Himmler, who despite his abiding affection for uniforms, had no military experience, as the commander of the newly formed Army Group Vistula.

Since Stalingrad, Hitler had had no comprehensive military strategy. Neither did the professionals of the General Staff. All that Hitler had to offer was an apocalyptic "fight to the last man." His generals recognized the awful consequences of such a death wish, but nonetheless acquiesced in Hitler's suicidal decisions. Hitler's judgment was rarely challenged, and when it was, his reaction was unbridled fury. When at a military conference in early February, Guderian had confronted the Führer, questioning the wisdom of appointing Himmler to lead Army Group Vistula, he was treated to one of the colossal outbursts that all close to the Führer had witnessed before. To the horror of Keitel and others in Hitler's entourage, Guderian refused to back down, and Hitler completely lost control. How dare the general speak to him in such a manner, how dare he contradict his strategic judgment! "His fists raised, his cheeks flushed with rage, his whole body trembling, [Hitler] stood there in front of me," Guderian remembered, "beside himself with fury and having lost all self-control. After each outburst of rage Hitler would stride up and down the carpet edge, then suddenly stop immediately before me and hurl his next accusation in my face. He was almost screaming, his eyes seemed about to pop out of his head, and the veins stood out on his temples." Himmler, as Guderian predicted, was quickly overwhelmed by the responsibility of command and resigned after only a few weeks, unable to master the deteriorating military situation and the attendant stress. Guderian was sacked in March.

One feeble ray of hope did manage to pierce the gloom of the *Führerbunker*. On April 12, Franklin Roosevelt died. When Goebbels received the news, he telephoned the Führer. Only days before he had read to Hitler Thomas Carlyle's depiction of Frederick the Great's apparently hopeless position in the Seven Years' War. A mighty alliance was arrayed against him; defeat was certain. But suddenly the czarina Catherine of Russia, a key figure in the anti-Prussian alliance, died, the coalition against Frederick frayed, and, against all odds, he emerged victorious. Hitler was so moved that he sent for his horoscopes (there were two), which were kept in Himmler's research departments. Both predicted great triumphs in 1941, followed by a series of setbacks, and near catastrophe in the first half 1945. But then would come a turnaround in the second half of April and a respite until peace would be attained in August. Hard times were in store for the Reich, but Germany would rise again; it would again find greatness. When Goebbels now spoke to Hitler, he gushed, "My Führer, I congratulate you. Roosevelt is dead. It is written in the stars that the second half of April will be the turning point for us." The Grand Alliance did not collapse, as Hitler predicted it would, but this is what passed for good news in April 1945.

On April 16, the Russians crossed the Oder at Küstrin, initiating the opening phase of the battle for Berlin. At 3 a.m. a massive barrage of a thousand heavy guns broke the silence; the bone-jarring concussions from the bursting shells could be felt in the eastern suburbs of Berlin forty-five miles away. German forces put up a tenacious defense on the Seelow Heights east of the city, inflicting terrible losses on the advancing Soviets, but after a four-day battle, the German defenses were overrun and the Red Army advanced on Berlin in a sweeping pincer movement. Meanwhile, on April 20, deep beneath the surface of the bomb-shattered Reich Chancellery, Adolf Hitler was marking his fifty-sixth birthday in the bunker to which he had retreated. All the major figures of the Third Reich—Goebbels, Göring, Himmler, Speer, Bormann, Admiral Karl Dönitz, Keitel, and Jodl—made their way through the ruins of the city to

Hitler's subterranean headquarters to pay their respects. In previous years, the Führer's birthday had been an occasion for national celebration—parades, concerts, public tributes. Not today. There was no fanfare, no talk of victory.

After greeting a group of Hitler Youth in the cratered Chancellery garden (the boys had distinguished themselves in combat against the Russians; the youngest was twelve), he descended again into the dank concrete chambers of the bunker for a review of the military situation. The Russians were closing fast on the capital of the Reich. Soon the city would be completely encircled. His cronies and commanders urged him to escape to the south, to continue leading the war from Alpine Berchtesgaden. Hitler refused. The others could go, he insisted, but he would remain at his post in Berlin. To his chief of operations, General Alfred Jodl, he confided, "I will fight as long as the faithful fight next to me and then I will shoot myself." That afternoon convoys of government bureaucrats, high-ranking soldiers, and party officials—"the golden pheasants," ordinary Berliners called them scornfully—began a frantic exodus from the doomed city. Time was running out.

That night an exhausted Hitler retired early, but Eva Braun, Hitler's long time mistress, who had joined him in the bunker earlier in the month and was intent on staying until the end, had other ideas. She wanted to have a good time, perhaps her last, a break in the almost suffocating tension and claustrophobia of life in the bunker. With the sound of Russian artillery thudding dully around them, she moved through the narrow corridors of the bunker, gaily inviting all within earshot to a party in her room above in the Chancellery. As Hitler's longtime secretary Traudl Junge recalled, "Eva Braun wanted to deaden the fear that had grown in her heart. She wanted to celebrate, when there was nothing more to celebrate—dancing, drinking, forgetting." Wehrmacht officers and orderlies, secretaries, Dr. Theodor Morell, Hitler's portly physician, even humorless Martin Bormann happily climbed the stairs for a bit of revelry. A number of SS men arrived with young women in tow. Flowers adorned the large circular table Speer had designed for her, champagne flowed, cigarette smoke, unheard of in the *Führerbunker*, clouded the room; giddy laughter bubbled throughout the crowd. An ancient phonograph materialized, but only one record could be found: "Blood Red Roses Speak to You of Love." It played over and over again. Dancing and intimacies were everywhere, interrupted only briefly by a loud explosion nearby. Eva wanted to dance, and it didn't matter with whom. The determination to release the oppressive tension that jangled their nerves was an almost physical presence in the room. Artillery fire continued to thump all around them. "Blood Red Roses" could not drown it out. Watching the frantic scene, joining in at times, Traudl Junge felt a surge of nausea and fled to her room in the bunker below. This sort of frivolity seemed out of place under the circumstances.

On April 21, amid fierce fighting, Marshal Georgy Zhukov's First White Russian Front reached the northern suburbs of the Reich capital. The fighting was intense, street by street, house to house. Buildings crumbled. Masonry and glass covered the streets. Bodies lay in the rubble. Casualties were high. Four days later, Russian forces completed the encirclement of the city. On that same day, eighty miles to the south, Russian and American troops met at Torgau on the Elbe. The Third Reich was now cut in half. Hitler listened to the reports at his daily military briefing, but seemed not to grasp the seriousness of the situation. While his generals presented the dire predicament they confronted, the military situation, they implied but would not express directly, was hopeless. Hitler resisted the obvious conclusion. Instead he clung to the fantasy that Walther Wenck's Twelfth Army to the southwest could wheel about, join with Theodor Busse's Ninth Army, and relieve the city while Felix Steiner's Waffen-SS units to the north would launch a counterattack against Zhukov's spearhead. Together they would crush the Russians and save Berlin. None of the military men present at the briefings dared state the obvious. Expecting salvation from these much depleted forces was utter fantasy.

At the situation briefing the next day, General Hans Krebs, Guderian's successor as army chief of staff, had reluctantly to confess that Steiner had not yet begun to move. He was unable to marshal the necessary forces. At first Hitler sat motionless, reeling from the news. In a subdued voice, he ordered everyone out, except his close circle, Bormann, Krebs, Keitel, and Wilhelm Burgdorf, Hitler's ranking military adjutant. When the door was closed, he exploded in a quivering rage. He spewed venom on the army and its generals, liars and traitors all. They had no understanding of his grand design, his historic mission, he shrieked, his voice crackling with fury. They were responsible for this disastrous turn of events. He shook violently, his pallid face white as a corpse. Then, exhausted, he dropped abruptly into his chair and uttered words that none had ever expected to hear from him: "The war is lost!" The Third Reich had ended in failure and all that was left for him was to die. "Gentlemen," he said, "this is the end. I shall remain here in Berlin and shoot myself when the time comes. Each of you must make his own decision on when to leave."

All pleaded with him to escape to the Obersalzberg, to lead the fight from there, but he again refused. "Everything is falling to pieces anyway and I can do no more." Göring would now act as his personal representative. There was little fighting left to be done, and if it came to negotiating with the Allies, Göring could do a better job of it than he could. He would either fight and win the Battle of Berlin or die in Berlin. He could not risk falling into Russian hands, and would shoot himself at the last minute. It was his "final, irrevocable decision." When someone pointed to the portrait of Frederick the Great and mentioned the "miracle" that had saved him, Hitler could only shake his head. "The Army has betrayed me, my generals are good for nothing. My orders are not carried out. It is all finished. National Socialism is dead and will never rise again!" The German nation had failed him, and now "Germany is lost. It actually was not quite ready or quite strong enough for the mission I set for the nation."

The next day, April 23, a cable from Göring arrived. The Reich Marshal had taken up residence on the Obersalzberg, where most of the party's and state's ministries were now located. He was officially second in command of the National Socialist state, Hitler's designated successor, and he interpreted Hitler's outburst on the previous day as meaning that the Führer had, in effect, abdicated. The cable asked if that was correct and concluded by saying that if he did not hear back by 10 p.m. (eight hours) he would assume that Hitler had lost freedom of action and was no longer in a position to lead. He would therefore assume leadership of the Reich. When Hitler read through the cable he erupted in a volcanic rage, stoked by Bormann's insistence that the message was clear evidence of Göring's treachery. Hitler immediately ordered the SS to place the Reich Marshal under house arrest, expelled him from the party, and stripped him of all state offices. Bormann, always scheming, pressed for execution, but Hitler could not do it. Göring had been with him since the early days of the party, had marched with him in the Beer Hall Putsch, and played a critical role in creating the Nazi police state.

With bad news cascading all around him, Hitler was increasingly out of touch with reality. He had retreated into the bunker beneath the old Reich Chancellery on January 16 and emerged only twice in the remaining months of the war—105 days lived fifty feet beneath the surface of the Chancellery garden. A penumbra of the surreal surrounded him and all he did. He was living on a diet of amphetamines and sedatives, and ever since the bomb attack on July 20, 1944, his health had deteriorated and his paranoia mounted. Those who had not seen him for a period of time were shocked at his appearance. His eyes were swollen and red, his skin pasty, his shoulders stooped, his uniform, always so immaculate, now bore stains, and his left arm visibly trembled—an early sign of Parkinson's. He had, Albert Speer remarked, "reached the last stage in his flight from reality, a reality he had refused to acknowledge since his youth. At the time I had a name for this unreal world of the bunker: I called it the Isle of the Departed."

Hitler was convinced that he was surrounded by traitors and liars, but Speer, Hitler's favorite, was not among them. A bond of mutual admiration bound them together, but on April 23 the Führer received another unwelcome surprise. In March he had issued an order stating that if the Allies should enter the Reich, Germany's infrastructure—bridges, factories, the communications and transportation systems, as well as all material assets, everything that might be of use to the enemy—was to be destroyed. Speer had protested that such actions would eliminate "all further possibility for the German people to survive," to which Hitler responded: "If the war is lost, the people will also be lost [and] it is not necessary to worry about their needs for elemental survival. On the contrary, it is best for us to destroy even those things. For the nation has proved to be weak, and the future belongs entirely to the strong people of the east. Whatever remains after this battle is in any case only the inadequate, because the good ones will be dead." He was determined to die in Berlin. So complete was Hitler's identification with the German people that if he had no future, neither did they. Since receiving the "Nero order," as it came to be called, Speer had done everything possible to sabotage Hitler's plans. He had worked with industrialists, military leaders, and local officials to ensure that Hitler's scorched-earth policy would not be carried out. He had even contemplated assassinating Hitler by introducing poison gas into the bunker's ventilation system. Now he had come to Berlin for a last leave-taking and to admit that he had disobeyed his Führer's order. It was a tense situation, but Hitler received the news with an air of resignation. The man who had ruled Germany for twelve years, who had created a vast European empire, who was one of the most powerful men in the world, was now "empty, burned out, lifeless."

Speer's admission of disobedience was disappointing and Göring's "betrayal" was a shock, but they were as nothing compared to the news that reached him on April 27. From a foreign press report he discovered that Himmler, his "loyal Heinrich," was attempting to negotiate peace with the Western Allies. He had been carrying on secret talks with Count Folke Bernadotte, head of the Swedish Red Cross in Germany, in hopes of arranging a peace deal with the West while continuing the fight against the Soviets in the East. He was convinced that the Allies would need him and the SS to maintain order in Europe. Besides, he knew more about the Communist underground all over the continent than any Allied intelligence service. His assistance would be invaluable. He even wondered at one point whether when he met Eisenhower, he should offer the general his hand or give him the Nazi salute. Hitler was not the only one in the top echelons of the Third Reich whose grip on reality was tenuous.

Hitler was stunned. He immediately dismissed Himmler from his position as chief of the SS, voided his party membership, and ordered his arrest. Himmler managed to evade arrest, but for Hitler his "betrayal" was a terrible blow, the final straw. Alone among the Führer's inner circle whose loyalty remained unshakable was Goebbels. He had earlier moved into the *Führerbunker*, and days later, Hitler invited Magda and their six children to take up residence in the bunker as well. They had come, Goebbels told Speer, "in order . . . to end their lives at this historic site." Hitler had always been solicitous of Frau Goebbels and was happy to have her and the children join the dwindling group in the bunker. In these final days he gave her his gold party pin as a token of his appreciation for her loyalty and commitment.

April 29 was a day of dramatic developments. The Russians were now only a half mile away and would be at the bunker within a day. Hitler decided that the time had come for him to put his affairs in order: he would marry his longtime mistress, Eva Braun, and would compose his last will and testament. A festive table, with fine "AH" monogrammed linen, silver service, and champagne glasses, had been placed in the corridor where the wedding ceremony would be held. But before the wedding ceremony got under way, Hitler retreated to the small conference room, where he dictated his last will and testament. It contained no confessions or explanations or revelations. For the most part, he reprised the recriminations and accusations of the previous days. But he did return to the theme that had obsessed him throughout his political life: the Jews and their nefarious world conspiracy. In one last scalding blast of hate, he wrote:

> It is untrue that I or anyone else in Germany wanted war in 1939. It was wanted and provoked solely by international statesmen either of Jewish origin or working for Jewish interests. I have made too many offers for the limitation and control of armaments, which posterity will not be cowardly always to disregard, for responsibility for the outbreak of this war to be placed on me. Nor have I ever wished that, after the appalling First World War, there would be a second against either England or America. Centuries will go by, but from the ruins of our towns and monuments the hatred of those ultimately responsible will grow anew against the people whom we have to thank for all this: international Jewry and its henchmen.

The testament concluded with low Hitlerian melodrama, stating that "My wife and I choose to die in order to escape the shame of overthrow or capitulation. It is our wish that our bodies be burned immediately, here where I have performed the greater part of my daily work during the twelve years I served my people." A bit later Hitler surprised his inner circle and married Eva Braun in a brief civil ceremony. The nervous official who performed the ceremony was plucked from a nearby *Volkssturm* unit and had, by law, to ask both parties if they were of pure Aryan heritage. The situation was awkward—the bride wearing black as if for a funeral; halfhearted toasts; the rumbling of artillery fire; the signing of the legal documents, to which the new bride could at last write "Eva Hitler."

Hitler had already decided that this was his day to die, but the news of Mussolini's execution by partisans was perhaps the final straw. It is not clear whether Hitler was informed of the details of the Duce's demise—his pummeled body and that of his mistress strung up by the feet in front of a gas station in Milan—but they could have only confirmed the decision he had already made. He and his wife would commit suicide in the bunker and their bodies would be burned in the Chancellery garden. He still held a final military briefing, where he was told that there would definitely be no rescue. The Russians were at the Reichstag, in the Tiergarten, at the Potsdamer Platz. They would be at the Chancellery no later than May 1.

At a little past 2 a.m., Hitler bade farewell to the two dozen or so guards, servants, and medical personnel still in the bunker; he shook hands with each of them, and released them from their oaths of loyalty. He hoped that they could escape to American or British lines. Around noon he ordered his SS adjutant Otto Günsche to collect as much petrol as possible. Shortly after 3 p.m. he disappeared into his study along with Eva Braun. Goebbels, Bormann, and Günsche gathered in the eerily quiet corridor and waited. No noise escaped the study. Finally, after ten minutes Günsche and Bormann pushed open the door. Hitler and his bride were slumped on the sofa. A strong odor of cyanide rose from Eva's body. To her right on the sofa was the body of Adolf Hitler. His head drooped forward. Blood spilled from a bullet hole in his right temple; his pistol lay at his feet.

The loyal Günsche carried the Führer's body, wrapped in a dark army blanket, into the Chancellery garden, placed it into a shallow shell hole, brimming with gasoline. Then Hitler's chauffeur and Günsche struggled up the four flights of stairs with the body of Eva Braun, now Eva Hitler. She was placed alongside Hitler and their bodies doused by more gasoline. Then, during a lull in the artillery barrage, the chauffeur tossed a lighted rag into the depression, igniting a towering fireball—one of hundreds around the blasted city. From the entrance to the bunker stairwell, Bormann and Goebbels witnessed the scene. Günsche returned every three hours or so to pour gasoline onto the corpses.

One last macabre event remained for the denizens of the *Führerbunker*. Early on that same day, Goebbels had attempted to negotiate with the Russians, who were having none of it. They had conquered the city at a great loss of life. The Third Reich was destroyed, its leader, as Goebbels informed them, was dead. What was there to negotiate? The Russians insisted on unconditional surrender. Upon hearing this, Goebbels moved decisively. This was the moment for him to join his Führer in a "hero's death." Frau Goebbels woke their six children from their beds, told them not to be afraid, that a doctor was going to give them an injection, a kind that was now given to all children and soldiers. It was morphine, which made the children drowsy. Then Frau Goebbels, moving methodically from one child to the next, placed a vile of cyanide in their mouths and crushed it. "My children should die rather than live in shame and scorn," she had told Traudl Junge. "In a Germany as it will be after the war, there will be no place for our children." She could not imagine a world without Hitler, without National Socialism. Immediately thereafter Joseph and Magda Goebbels climbed the stairs to the Chancellery garden. Stories of exactly how they died vary, but they either took cyanide together or were shot by Goebbels's aide. In either case, they were gone. The sorcerer's apprentice who from the early days of the NSDAP had tirelessly, fanatically promoted the National Socialist cause had come to an ignominious end. Their bodies were hurriedly burned, though not beyond recognition, and left unburied. The Russians found them the next day.

On May 1, a red flag flew over the battered Reichstag, and Russian troops at last reached the devastated Reich Chancellery. They discovered, then entered, the bunker. There they found the bodies of adjutant Burgdorf and General Krebs in the deserted corridor. They, too, had committed suicide. Nothing remained but the shabby wreckage of the Führer's last headquarters, papers strewn about, furniture overturned, bottles, scraps of food. And ghosts. Although they were later to deny it, the Russians soon discovered Hitler's corpse. What they did with it remains something of a mystery, though a skull with a bullet hole in the right temple, discovered by Russian troops in the Chancellery garden, resides in a shoebox in a Moscow archive. The Battle of Berlin was over. A tidal wave of rape swept the ruined city. It is estimated that between 95,000 and 130,000 women and girls were raped, some 10,000 of whom died, mostly by suicide. The Russians paid a very high price for their victory: more than 300,000 casualties; the heaviest losses suffered by the Red Army in any battle of the war. Upward of 150,000 Germans perished in the ruined city and its environs, while Hitler waited in vain for the miracle that would save his profoundly evil regime.

The war in Europe did not end on May 1. Hitler had chosen Grand Admiral Karl Dönitz to be his successor, and from his headquarters in Flensburg in Schleswig-Holstein, the admiral held out for another week in the hope of allowing as many of his countrymen as possible to flee to the West ahead of the Russians. In that time, he flushed the leading Nazis out of his government, although he retained Speer. He was especially eager to rid himself and the country of Himmler, who had moved to Flensburg with a large retinue of chauffeurs, secretaries, and SS guards. Still suffering from the abiding delusion that he would be indispensable to the new post-Hitler government, he was stunned to discover that Dönitz wanted no part of him. Astonished, he contemplated reaching out to General Bernard Montgomery, whose British forces were nearby and closing, in an attempt to negotiate a peace agreement—and to hold on to power. He was dissuaded from that fantastical move by his embarrassed aides. When it became painfully obvious that he was not wanted, that he had been stripped of his power and position, he shaved his mustache, donned the uniform of a simple soldier, and tried to pass as a displaced person. He did not, however, dispose of the rimless spectacles that more than anything else identified him as the *Reichsmarschall SS*. Still incredulous, he had no intention of taking his own life, no martyr he. But on May 21, he was captured by the British and was passed on for interrogation near Lüneburg. Before he could be questioned properly, he bit into a cyanide capsule he had hidden behind his teeth, and died convulsing on the dusty floor of a British interrogation camp.

In the south, Hermann Göring was freed from house arrest by a passing Luftwaffe unit, and on May 5 he was taken into custody by the Americans. His arrest probably saved his life since Bormann had ordered his execution as a traitor. At first treated as something of a celebrity, he gave an interview to the international press. Eisenhower quickly called a halt to that, and Göring was sent to a prisoner of war camp in Luxembourg, where he was held until he was transferred to Nuremberg to stand trial as a war criminal. He was tried by the Allied Military Tribunal and condemned to death in 1946 along with Rosenberg, Ribbentrop, Seyss-Inquart, Julius Streicher, Ernst Kaltenbrunner, Hans Frank, and Wilhelm Frick. Robert Ley was also sentenced to death but took his own life before his execution could take place. Walther Funk and Rudolf Hess were given life sentences. Dönitz was condemned to ten years in prison, Speer to a term of twenty years. On the morning Göring was to be hanged, he cheated the hangman by biting into a cyanide capsule he had managed to conceal. Martin Bormann had disappeared in an effort to escape the bunker but was killed in the ruins of the city. His body was not discovered until 2002. Trials of other Nazi criminals would stretch out across decades, tried first by the victorious Allies and then later by German courts.

On May 8, General Jodl signed the unconditional surrender at Reims; a day later Keitel signed a similar capitulation with the Russians, and Hitler's war came at last to an end. Much of Europe was in ruins, thousands upon thousands of bewildered, uprooted persons roamed the devastated continent, many finding their way into crowded displaced persons camps. The roll call of the dead began—in Germany, 1,800,000 military dead, 500,000 civilians, and 1,240 missing; in the Soviet Union, 11,000,000 military dead, 2,500,000 POWs killed in German captivity, and 7,000,000 civilians—10 percent of the population. In the slaughterhouse that was Poland, 4,520,000 dead, over 4,000,000 of whom were civilians, 20 percent of the prewar Polish population. Six million Jews perished in what has come to be called the Holocaust. British, French, and American losses were lower, France 810,000, Britain 300,000, and the United States 259,000. Sixty million more were wounded or maimed, either mentally or physically. It was the largest, most destructive war in human history.

There are many lessons to be drawn from the Nazi experience, lessons about nationalism and racism, about ideological fanaticism and the fragility of democracy, about the dark recesses of human nature that are implicit in the preceding pages, but I would like to close with this thought. On May 9, 1945, the Third Reich ceased to exist. When the last Anglo-American bomb had exploded on Central Europe, and the last Russian shell had detonated, and the German people began emerging from their hiding places to survey the smoking heaps of rubble that had once been Berlin, Dresden, or Hamburg, there must have been a moment, however fleeting, when the grisly reality of all that had happened fell in upon them and they asked themselves the question, How had it ever come to this? It was a question that must also have come to the ghostlike human shells that had suffered the unspeakable agonies of Auschwitz or Buchenwald or Treblinka. It must have come to them in countless ways, in the endless days and nights in boxcars or barracks or prison cells, standing naked on the cusp of mass graves, or in the gas chambers. For the Germans that haunting question, if they dared confront it, was accompanied by an enormous burden of guilt, shame, and horror at what was done in the name of the German people. For them, no less than for the victims of National Socialism whose only crime was to have been a Jew or a Pole or a Russian, there is another legacy, a legacy that must be ours as well. It is a political, but even more a moral imperative: that this must never happen again. Be vigilant about your rights; when the rights of any group, no matter how small or marginal, are threatened, everyone's liberty is put at risk. Let there never come a time when we must cast about and ask how it ever came to this.

ACKNOWLEDGMENTS

The writing of this book has consumed more than five years. I owe much to friends, family, and colleagues for their intellectual counsel and unflagging support when, at times, it seemed the book would never be finished. I could name many, in Britain, Germany, and the U.S., but some deserve special mention.

Bruce Kuklick and Jonathan Steinberg, good friends and excellent critics, were always there with sound advice, goodwill, and encouragement. Over the years the many long discussions with Carl-Ludwig Holtfrerich in Berlin have been an inspiration, and along the way, Hans Mommsen and Gerald Feldman remained solid sources of supportive criticism. I can't quite believe that they are gone.

My agent, John Wright, believed in this project from beginning. He is all an agent should be and more. His insights into the manuscript were of great importance, and his unflagging sense of humor has lightened many a sober day spent with Hitler and the Nazis. John also led me to Bob Bender, my editor at Simon & Schuster, who has been a paragon of patience and who always offered encouragement and sound advice.

But my deepest gratitude I owe to my wife, Kristen Stromberg Childers. She read the pages of the manuscript as the printer spewed them out and offered a careful chapter-by-chapter reading that proved indispensable. I don't know what I would do without her. Finally, this book is also for my children, Nick, Ava, James, and Tim; they are my inspiration.

NOTES

Chapter 1: The Serpent's Egg

2   *"almost pathologically sensitive about anything concerning the body"*: Franz Jetzinger, *Hitler's Youth*, London, 1958; August Kubizek, *The Young Hitler I Knew*, new expanded edition and translation (Barnsley, UK, 2011), p. 163.

3   *"a bolt from the blue"*: Adolf Hitler, *Mein Kampf* (American edition, Boston: Houghton Mifflin, 1971), p. 20.

3   *no chance that he could study painting or architecture*: Konrad Heiden, *Der Fuehrer: Hitler's Rise to Power* (Boston: Houghton Mifflin, 1944), pp. 52–54.

3   *with grief as eighteen-year-old Adolf*: Eduard Bloch, "My Patient Hitler," *Collier's Weekly*, March 15–22, 1941; and his interview with the OSS, in *Hitler Source Book*. See also Brigitte Hamann, *Hitlers Edeljude. Das Leben des Armenarztes Eduard Bloch* (Munich, 2008).

3   *He would tolerate no dissent*: Kubizek, *The Young Hitler I Knew*, p. 78.

4   *did not include mingling or interacting with them*: Ibid., pp. 163–64.

4   *not . . . on the brink of starvation or in desperate straits*: Jetzinger, *Hitler's Youth*, pp. 117, 131–34.

4   *employed to great effect in Nazi propaganda*: Brigitte Hamann, *Hitlers Wien. Lehrjahre eines Diktators* (Munich, 1997), pp. 96–97.

5   *Hitler seemed calm and at peace*: Kubizek, *The Young Hitler I Knew*, p. 94.

5   *"by whom he was persecuted"*: Ibid., p. 157.

5   *"ought to be blown up"*: Ibid., p. 160.

6   *would not see him again for thirty years*: After Hitler disappeared from their Vienna apartment, Kubizek did not meet him again until 1938 when Germany absorbed Austria and Hitler returned to his hometown in glory. Ibid., pp. 246–59.

6   *He had hit rock bottom*: Hamann, *Hitlers Wien*, pp. 208–9, 226–27; Jetzinger, *Hitler's Youth*, pp. 131–32; Bradley F. Smith, *Adolf Hitler: His Family, Childhood and Youth* (Stanford, CA, 1967), pp. 123–24.

6   *Carrying luggage and shoveling snow*: He understood the plight of the working class, he claimed imaginatively in a 1934 speech, because "I myself was a laboring man for years in the building trade and had to earn my own bread." Hitler's address delivered at the First Congress of German Workers on May 10, 1933, in Norman H. Baynes, ed., *The Speeches of Adolf Hitler, April 1922–August*

1939, vol. I (New York, 1969), p. 862. See also Jetzinger, *Hitler's Youth*, 131–32; Reinhold Hanisch, "I Was Hitler's Buddy," *New Republic*, April 5, 12, 19, 1939, pp. 193–99, 270–72, 297–300.

7 *found on the library shelves:* Hamann, *Hitlers Wien*, pp. 285–88.

7 *more than a modicum of comfort:* Jetzinger, *Hitler's Youth*, pp. 132–42.

8 *to be consoled by Hanisch:* Hanisch, "I Was Hitler's Buddy"; Heiden, *Der Fuehrer*, p. 69.

8 *a fin de siècle cultural flowering:* See Carl Schorske, *Fin-de-Siècle Vienna* (New York, 1979).

9 *"to help . . . eliminate Jewry":* Quoted in Hamann, *Hitlers Wien*. For her treatment of Schönerer and Lueger, see p. 337 ff.

9 *the country's political lexicon:* Ibid., p. 334.

10 *"must not become greater Jerusalem":* Lueger quoted in Volker Ullrich, *Hitler's Ascent, 1889–1939* (New York, 2016), p. 44.

11 *"Down with the Terrorism of Jewry":* Ibid., p. 490.

11 *"the entire Marxist worldview":* Kubizek, *The Young Hitler I Knew* (New York: 2011); Hitler, *Mein Kampf*, pp. 37–51.

12 *planned a trip to Munich together:* Hanisch, "I Was Hitler's Buddy," p. 271.

12 *"but which never left me":* Hitler, *Mein Kampf*, p. 125.

13 *"for primarily political reasons":* Ernst Günther Schenck, *Patient Hitler. Eine medizinische biographie* (Düsseldorf, 1989), p. 163.

14 *"by far the most contented of my life":* Hitler, *Mein Kampf*, p. 126.

14 *physically unfit for military service:* Schenck, *Patient Hitler*, p. 297.

14–15 *"the good fortune of being permitted to live at this time":* Hitler, *Mein Kampf*, p. 161.

15–16 *singlehandedly capturing seven French soldiers:* Hitler related the story to American correspondent H. R. Knickerbocker. See Knickerbocker's *Is Tomorrow Hitler's?* (New York, 1941), pp. 31–32. For the many embellishments and outright fabrications of Hitler's war record in Nazi propaganda, see Thomas Weber, *Hitler's First War*, pp. 272–77.

16 *"weakness and narrow-mindedness":* Hitler, *Mein Kampf*, pp. 192–93.

18 *the vicious accusations from the right continued unabated:* For details, see Werner T. Angress, "The German Army's 'Jüdenzählung' of 1916-Genesis-Consequences-Significance," *Leo Baeck Yearbook* 23 (1978), pp. 117–38.

18 *revolution would engulf the country:* Hans Mommsen, *The Rise and Fall of Weimar Democracy* (Chapel Hill, 1996), pp. 15–19.

18 *"and shirkers were losing the war":* Ernst Schmidt, Hitler's closest comrade among the messengers, quoted in John Toland, *Adolf Hitler* (New York, 1976), p. 70.

18 *"goes on strike against it":* Hitler, *Mein Kampf*, p. 195.

18 *"than the biggest cannon of the enemy":* Hans Mend, quoted in Alan Bullock, *Hitler* (New York, 1953), p. 53.

19 *"internationalism will be broken up":* Letter to Josh Popp, his Munich landlord, cited in Toland, *Adolf Hitler*, p. 62.

19 *"damned the war to hell":* Heiden, *Der Fuehrer*, p. 84.

19 *a morbid fear of syphilis:* He would return time and again in speeches, private conversations, and in the pages of *Mein Kampf* to the scourge of prostitution and syphilis, which he attributed to the Jews. *Mein Kampf*, pp. 246–56.

19 *"not the time for it":* Ibid., p. 160. His sergeant, Max Amann, who would later become Hitler's business manager and editor, confirmed that Hitler rarely discussed politics during the war.

19   *a pathological obsession by war's end:* See the recollections of Hans Mend from
       Hitler's regiment, in Rudolf Olden, *Hitler the Pawn* (London, 1936), pp. 70–71.
20   *"without spitefulness":* Ignaz Westenkirchner, quoted in Toland, *Adolf Hitler*, p. 66.
20   *"hatred of Jews dated back to that time":* Fritz Wiedemann, *Der Mann, der
       Feldherr werden wollte* (Velbert/Kettig, 1964), pp. 33–34.
20   *"his mental instability":* Heiden, *Der Fuehrer*, p. 84.
20   *lacked "the capacity for leadership":* Wiedemann, quoted in Toland, *Adolf
       Hitler*, p. 67.
21   *"psychopath suffering from hysteria":* Thomas Weber, pp. 220–21.
23   *"the shame of indignation":* Hitler, *Mein Kampf*, p. 250.
23   *"in the world of war he felt at home":* Heiden, *Der Fuehrer*, p. 78.
23   *"for the time being regular pay":* Hitler, *Mein Kampf*, p. 206.

Chapter 2: Hitler and the Chaos of Postwar Germany

27   *four times the size of the regular army:* Mommsen, *The Rise and Fall of
       Weimar Democracy*, pp. 38–42.
27   *Bolshevik terror and counterrevolutionary suppression:* Evans, *The Coming of
       the Third Reich* (New York, 2004), p. 160.
28   *a task he performed with his usual zeal:* Hitler, *Mein Kampf*, pp. 207–8.
28   *The courses . . . included such offerings:* Ian Kershaw, *Hitler, 1889–1936:
       Hubris*, vol. I (New York, 1998), pp. 121–23.
28   *"immense importance for the future of the German people":* Hitler, *Mein
       Kampf*, p. 213.
29   *"a natural orator in your group?":* The instructor was Karl Alexander von
       Müller, the archconservative historian who later joined the NSDAP. See Müller,
       Mars und Venus. Erinnerungen, 1914–1919 (Stuttgart, 1954), p. 339, quoted
       in David Clay Large, *Where Ghosts Walked* (New York, 1997), p. 128.
29   *"I could 'speak' ":* Hitler, *Mein Kampf*, p. 215.
29   *"and makes them think his way":* Joachim Remak, *The Nazi Years* (Englewood
       Cliffs, NJ, 1969), p. 25.
29   *tone down his anti-Semitic rhetoric:* Kershaw, *Hitler*, vol. I, p. 12.
30   *"removal of the Jews in general":* Hitler's letter is reproduced in Eberhard
       Jäckel, ed., *Hitler. Sämtliche Aufzeichnungen, 1905–1924* (Stuttgart, 1980),
       pp. 88–90.
31   *Hitler left underwhelmed:* Georg Franz-Willig, *Die Hitlerbewegung. Der
       Ursprung 1919–1922*, second edition (Hamburg, 1962), pp. 66–67. Drexler's
       account of that meeting and his impressions of Hitler are also found in Jeremy
       Noakes and Geoffry Pridham, eds., *Nazism 1919–1945*, vol. I: *The Rise to
       Power* (Exeter, UK, 1983), p. 11.
32   *at which Hitler spoke again:* Franz-Willig, *Die Hitlerbewegung*, p. 71.
34   *a new government had to be formed:* Mommsen, *The Rise and Fall of Weimar
       Democracy*, pp. 72–74.
34   *The Versailles Treaty and its impact on the fledgling Weimar Republic:* Ibid., pp. 87–91.
35   *It was, Hitler charged:* Ibid. Such attacks on the hated peace treaty were staples
       of Hitler's rhetoric throughout his career.
35   *He had stolen the show:* Franz-Willig, *Die Hitlerbewegung*, pp. 73–74.
36   *"the voice of the people were speaking":* Heiden, *Der Fuehrer*, pp. 105–10.
37   *"only to religious conversion":* Kurt Ludecke, *I Knew Hitler* (New York, 1937),
       p. 268.

38   *the "Twenty-five Points":* The Twenty-five Points and the DAP's original program can be found in Anson Rabinbach and Sander Gilman, eds., *The Third Reich Source Book* (Berkeley, 2013), pp. 5–6, 12–14.

39   *unrelenting anti-Semitism:* Franz-Willig, *Die Hitlerbewegung,* p. 83.

40   *"There can only be the hard 'either—or' ":* Hitler, *Mein Kampf,* p. 203.

40   *cut from the same cloth as Hitler:* Franz-Willig, *Die Hitlerbewegung,* pp. 67–68.

41   Protocols of the Elders of Zion: A highly successful forgery, published in pamphlet form in Russia in 1903, claiming the existence of a Jewish conspiracy to ensure world domination. It was widely circulated in Europe before the war and enthusiastically seized upon by German far-right, anti-Semitic circles. By 1921 it was fully exposed as a fraud, though this discovery had little effect on its lingering popularity across Europe. See Benjamin Segel and Richard S. Levy, *A Lie and a Libel: The History of the* Protocols of the Elders of Zion (Lincoln, NE, 1995); and Esther Webman, *The Global Impact of "The Protocols of the Elders of Zion"* (London, 2011).

43   *but because it was revolutionary:* Göring, Hanfstaengl recalled, was "not the intellectual type." In those early postwar years, he was "a complete condottiere, the pure soldier of fortune." Ernst Hanfstaengl, *Hitler: The Memoir of a Nazi Insider Who Turned Against the Führer* (New York, 1957), pp. 71–72.

43   *"the orderly life of your respectable burgher":* Ernst Röhm, *Die Geschichte eines Hochverräters,* quoted in Toland, *Adolf Hitler,* p. 98.

45   *German nationalist and racist:* Chamberlain was the author of *The Foundations of the Nineteenth Century,* a pseudo-intellectual work first published in Germany in 1899 that provided a racist, nationalist interpretation of Germany's past. It was greatly admired by anti-Semites everywhere. Among its many enthusiasts was Adolf Hitler.

46   *seen in a dinner jacket and white tie:* Hanfstaengl, *Hitler,* pp. 42–43.

46   *notably absent:* Henry Ashby Turner, Jr., *German Big Business and the Rise of Hitler* (Oxford, NY, 1985), pp. 47–60.

46   *from anti-Marxist groups abroad:* Kershaw, *Hitler,* vol. I, pp. 188–91.

47   *were collected in celebration of Hitler's birthday:* Borsig soon soured on Hitler after reading the Nazi program and refused to offer further financial support. Thyssen's contributions were made not directly to the NSDAP but to Ludendorff, who dispensed the funds to different counterrevolutionary groups, including the Nazis. Turner, *German Big Business and the Rise of Hitler,* p. 60.

48   *executing many and murdering others:* James Diehl, *Paramilitary Politics in the Weimar Republic* (Bloomington, IN, 1977), pp. 29–30.

49   *were committed by leftists:* Toland, *Adolf Hitler,* p. 110.

49   *"when murder could be had for small change":* Heiden, *Der Fuehrer,* p. 113.

50   *the schedule of installments:* Mommsen, *The Rise and Fall of Weimar Democracy,* pp. 112–13.

51   *"madness, nightmare, desperation and chaos":* Fritz Ringer, ed., *The German Inflation of 1923* (London, 1969), p. 144. See also Gerald D. Feldman, *The Great Disorder: Politics, Economics, and Society in the German Inflation, 1914–1924* (Oxford, NY, 1997); and Carl-Ludwig Holtfrerich, *Die Deutsche Inflation 1914–1923* (Berlin, 1980).

51   *"the death of money":* Heiden, *Der Fuehrer,* p. 126.

51   *flock to hear him speak:* Kershaw, *Hitler,* vol. I, pp. 196–98; Large, *Where Ghosts Walked,* pp. 168–72.

52   *coup swept throughout Munich*: Diehl, *Paramilitary Politics in the Weimar Republic*, p. 143; Kershaw, *Hitler*, vol. I, p. 191.

52   *the party had to act*: Harold J. Gordon, Jr., *Hitler and the Beer Hall Putsch*, (Princeton, 1962), pp. 241–42.

53   *no time for unilateral moves*: Ibid., pp. 246–56.

53   *Kahr's hand would have to be forced*: Ibid., pp. 258–59.

54   *"a revolution by sheer bluff"*: Alan Bullock, *Hitler: A Study in Tyranny* (New York, 1953), p. 85.

55   *"with all his medals clinking"*: Hanfstaengl, *Hitler*, p. 97.

55   *training it directly on the audience*: David Clay Large, *Where Ghosts Walked: Munich's Road to the Third Reich* (New York, 1997), p. 176

55   *"This hall is surrounded"*: Adolf Hitler quoted in ibid., p. 177.

55   *"Charlie Chaplin and a headwaiter"*: Quoted in ibid., p. 177.

55   *no laughing matter*: Otto Gritschneder, *Bewährungsfrist für den Terroristen Adolf H. Der Hitler Putsch und die bayerische Justiz* (Munich, 1990), p. 14, quoted in Large, *Where Ghosts Walked*, p. 177.

56   *"cannot now be undone"*: Hitler quoted in Gordon, *Hitler and the Beer Hall Putsch*, p. 286.

56   *"every province in Germany"*: Hitler, quoted in Large, *Where Ghosts Walked*, p. 178.

57   *boisterous cries of "Yes, yes!"*: Müller, *Im Wandel der Zeit*, pp. 162–63, quoted in Gordon, *Hitler and the Beer Hall Putsch*, pp. 287–88.

59   *"ditch of some obscure country lane"*: Hanfstaengl, *Hitler*, p. 104.

60   *almost all were armed*: Large, *Where Ghosts Walked*, pp. 185–86.

65   *"for she acquits us"*: Hitler's closing statement in *Der Hitler Prozess 1924. Wortlaut der Hauptverhandlung vor dem Volksgericht München I*, Teil 4: 19–25. Verhandlungstag, Lothard Grunchmann and Reinhard Weber, eds., p. 159; English translation in Heiden, *Der Fuehrer*, p. 206.

65   *"impossible to keep Hitler from talking"*: Toland, *Adolf Hitler*, p. 189.

65   *"an excellent joke for All Fools Day"*: *New York Times*, April 1, 1924.

66   *"the Law for the Protection of the Republic"*: Toland, *Adolf Hitler*, pp. 188–93.

Chapter 3: On the Fringe, 1925–28

67   "all the stuff started in there": Hanfstaengl, *Hitler*, p. 114.

68   *"made even the smallest disturbance"*: H. Kallenbach, *Mit Adolf Hitler auf Festung Landsberg* (Munich, 1933), quoted in Werner Maser, *Hitler's Mein Kampf* (London, 1970), 22–23.

68   *"sat around him like schoolboys"*: O. Lurker, *Hitler hinter Festungsmauern* (Berlin, 1933), quoted in Maser, p. 23.

69   *a shorter, pithier title*: Mein Kampf (My Struggle): Maser, *Hitler's Mein Kampf*, p. 26.

69   *Rosenberg was in no danger*: Wolfgang Horn, *Der Marsch zur Machtergreifung*; Ian Kershaw, *Hitler, vol. I*,

70   *to the stabilization crisis of 1924*: For details, see Thomas Childers, "Inflation, Stabilization, and Political Realignment in Germany, 1924–1928," in Gerald D. Feldman et al., eds., *Die Deutsche inflation* (Berlin, 1982); and Feldman, *The Great Disorder*, pp. 754–802.

70   *loomed over the negotiations*: Feldman, *The Great Disorder*, p. 821ff.

71   *cooperated and accepted the report*: Mommsen, *The Rise and Fall of Weimar Democracy*, pp. 172–73.

71 *by the vindictive Allied governments:* See J. W. Reichert, ed., *Helferrichs Reichstagsreden 1922–1924*, pp. 323–24; for the Communist reaction, *Die Rote Fahne*, March 22, 1924.

71 *all the enemies of the Republic:* Childers, "Inflation, Stabilization, and Political Realignment in Germany, 1920–1928," pp. 409–43.

72 *in the original classical Greek:* Peter D. Stachura, *Gregor Strasser and the Rise of Nazism* (London: George Allen & Unwin, 1983), pp. 30–31.

72 *burgeoning regional stature:* Ibid.

73 *"for or against the Jews":* "Aus dem Schulbuch der Marxisten," *Völkisch* coalition leaflet, 1924, Bundesarchiv (BA) ZSg. I, 45/13, and "Zu den Stadtverordnetenwahl," *Völkisch* leaflet, 1924, BA, ZSg. I, 45/14.

74 *onset of the Great Depression in 1929:* Stachura, *Gregor Strasser and the Rise of Nazism*, pp. 30–31.

75 *manage events from the confines of prison:* Kershaw, *Hitler*, vol. I, pp. 228–29.

75 *the rudderless party to disintegrate:* Heiden, *Der Fuerher*, p. 251.

76 *"the country of his birth":* New York Times, December 20, 1924.

76 *stormed out of the meeting:* Horn, p. 165ff.

77 *"allied with or supportive of them":* Völkischer Beobachter, February 26, 1925.

78 *"world pestilence and scourge, the Jew":* Adolf Hitler, *Reden, Schriften, Anordnungen*, vol. I, pp. 14ff, 28.

80 *collapse of German democracy:* Wolfgang Horn, *Der Marsch zur Machtergreifung* (Düsseldorf, 1980), pp. 216–18; see also Peter Fritzsche, *Rehearsals for Fascism* (New York and Oxford, 1990).

81 *owing allegiance to him personally:* Diehl, *Paramilitary Politics in the Weimar Republic*, pp. 158–60; Peter Longerich, *Die braunen Bataillone* (Munich, 1989), pp. 39–40.

81 *an instrument for political agitation:* Hitler. RSA, vol. 2, p. 9.

82 *never offered a response of any kind to his old comrade:* Longerich, *Die braunen Bataillone*, pp. 48–52.

82 *"from your personal friendship":* See Ernst Röhm, *Die Memoiren des Stabschef Röhm* (Saarbrücken, 1934), p. 160.

82 *"those worms around him":* Kurt Ludecke, *I Knew Hitler* (New York, 1937), p. 287.

82 *the vast majority in the north:* Stachura, *Gregor Strasser and the Rise of Nazism*, p. 41.

83 *"move an audience by his very personality":* Heiden, *Der Fuehrer*, p. 285.

83 *most visible Nazi leader in the country:* Kershaw, *Hitler*, vol. I, p. 270.

83 *rather than a follower:* Stachura, *Gregor Strasser and the Rise of Nazism*, p. 38.

84 *"to bring about the national revolution":* Strasser's Reichstag speech, November 25, 1925, quoted in ibid., p. 42.

86 *"thus national suicide":* February 14, 1926, Hitler. RSA, vol. I, pp. 294–95.

86 *"to see you in this company":* Joseph Goebbels, *Tagebücher 1924–25*, I/II, February 14, 1926, p. 55.

87 *been so wrong about Hitler:* Horn, *Der Marsch zur Machtergreifung*, p. 241.

87 *firmly under Hitler's control:* Noakes and Pridham, eds., *Nazism*, vol. I, pp. 55–56.

88 *"the greater man, the political genius":* Goebbels, *Tagebücher*, I/II, April 13, 1926, p. 73.

89 *executing the party's campaign directives:* Stachura, *Gregor Strasser and the Rise of Nazism,* pp. 68–73.

89 *"and after that Germany":* Ludecke, *I Knew Hitler,* pp. 234–35.

90 *"repeat them over and over":* Hitler, *Mein Kampf,* pp. 179–84.

90 *so too should the National Socialists:* Ibid., p. 230.

91 *the Propaganda Leadership in Munich:* NS Rundschreiben, March 20, 1926, HA/70/1529.

91 *assault on the surrounding countryside:* Joseph Goebbels, "Neue Methoden der Propaganda," *Nationalsozialistische Briefe,* August 15, 1926.

92 *propaganda and campaign strategy:* Dietrich Orlow, *The History of the Nazi Party* (Pittsburgh, 1973), vol. 1, pp. 112–26.

93 *forms of agitational activity:* "Propaganda," Munich 1927, BA/NS12/40.

94 *a rough form of local entertainment:* E. Stark, *Moderne Politische Propaganda, Propagandaschriften der NSDAP,* Heft 1, BA, NSD 12/1. For the impact of such Nazi activities at the local level, see William Sheridan Allen, *The Nazi Seizure of Power* (Chicago, 1965).

94 *not so out of bounds after all:* See Rudy Koshar, *Social Life, Local Politics, and Nazism: Marburg, 1880–1935* (Chapel Hill, 1986).

94 *grandiosity in Nuremberg:* See Wolfgang Benz, Hermann Graml, and Hermann Weiss, eds., *Enzyklopädie des National Sozialismus,* expanded edition (Munich, 2007), p. 445.

95 *nothing to discourage it:* Hanfstaengl, *Hitler,* pp. 131–32.

96 *"the symbol of a great mission":* Hitler, *Mein Kampf,* p. 3.

97 *"the heart of a people":* Ibid., pp. 106–7.

98 *required to subscribe:* Memorandum of May 7, 1928, to *"alle Gau und selbstständige Ortsgruppen der NSDAP,"* HA/24A/1758; Oran Hale, *The Captive Press in the Third Reich,* pp. 40–42.

98 *The first national election since 1924:* See Gerhard Paul, *Aufstand der Bilder. Die NS-Propaganda vor 1933,* Bonn, 1990, pp. 61–69.

98 *"the revolution is fine by us":* J. Goebbels, "Why Do We Want to Join the Reichstag?," *Der Angriff,* April 30, 1928.

99 *but right-of-center DVP:* See Mommsen, *The Rise and Fall of Weimar Democracy,* pp. 217–67.

100 *ideological framework of National Socialism:* Childers, "Interest and Ideology. Anti-System Politics in the Era of Stabilization, 1924–1928," in Gerald D. Feldman, ed., *Die Nachwirkungen der Inflation auf die deutsche Geschichte, 1921–1933* (Munich, 1985), pp. 1–20.

101 *searching for political alternatives:* Childers, "Inflation, Stabilization, and Political Realignment in Germany, 1920–1928," pp. 409–43.

101 *"the course of political events":* BA, R 43, Vol. 528.

Chapter 4: Into the Mainstream

104 *"disappear and are forgotten":* *Völkischer Beobachter,* May 31, 1928.

104 *need for a shift in emphasis:* Stachura, *Gregor Strasser and the Rise of Nazism,* pp. 64–68.

105 *rural landowning population:* Thomas Childers, *The Nazi Voter* (Chapel Hill, 1983), pp. 127–28.

105 *promising foundation on which to build:* Ibid.

105 *fallow periods between elections:* Ibid.

106 *against the proposed settlement:* Mommsen, *The Rise and Fall of Weimar Democracy*, pp. 278–82.

107 *occupied center stage throughout:* "Wahlaufruf der NSDAP," *Reichstags-Handbuch, V. Wahlperiode*, Berlin, 1930; Gottfried Feder, "Betrachtungen zum Youngplan," *Nationalsozialistische Monatshefte*, (NSHF), Heft 6, September 1930, pp. 249–56; "Das Dritte Versailles, leaflet of the Reichausschuss für das Deutsche Volksbegehren," BA, ZSg. 1, 83/2; "Sklaverei Bedeutet der Pariser Tributplan," BA, ZSg. I, 83/4.

107 *"so-called better classes are seen":* Police Report to the Hanoverian Interior Minister, quoted in Childers, *The Nazi Voter* (Chapel Hill, 1983), p. 130.

108 majority government of the Weimar era: Mommsen, *The Rise and Fall of Weimar Democracy*, p. 282.

110 *for the approaching battle:* Childers, *The Nazi Voter*, pp. 135–38.

110 *the party's campaign directives:* Stachura, *Gregor Strasser and the Rise of Nazism* (London, 1983); and Paul, *Aufstand der Bilder* (Bonn, 1990), pp. 64–68.

111 *"a man who burns like a flame":* Heiden, *Der Fuehrer*, p. 289.

111 *had reached the boiling point:* Stachura, *Gregor Strasser and the Rise of Nazism*, p. 61.

112 *"but lets things happen":* Goebbels, *Tagebücher*, March 16, 1930.

112 *"Forever putting things off!":* Ibid., June 29, 1930.

112 *had resolved itself:* Stachura, *Gregor Strasser and the Rise of Nazism*, pp. 165–71.

112 *"country with propaganda material":* Nazi Propaganda circular of August 5, 1930, NSDAP Hauptarchiv (HA), 701/1529.

113 *coordinating the party's propaganda activities:* Goebbels, *Tagebücher*, March 18, 1932.

113 *"parties of enslaving capitalism":* Paul, *Aufstand der Bilder*, pp. 95–99.

113 *closely monitored and coordinated:* RPL circular of July 4, 1932, *National-sozialistische*s Hauptarchiv (NSDAP HA)/15/289; RPL circular of April 2,1932, NSDAP HA/15286.

114 *serve the party well in the following campaigns:* Childers, *The Nazi Voter*, p. 138.

115 "to expedite the death of this system": Stachura, *Gregor Strasser and the Rise of Nazism*, p. 76.

115 *"these miserable Twenty-Five Points":* Heiden, *Der Fuehrer*, p. 410.

115 *"have never seen before":* Paul, *Aufstand der Bilder*, pp. 91, 283.

116 *he didn't trust Stennes:* Goebbels, *Tagebücher*, August 24, 1930.

116 *"Stennes is a traitor":* Goebbels, *Tagebücher*, August 30 and September 1, 1930.

117 *their fighting spirit essential:* Ibid., September 1, 1930.

117 *ready to erupt again at any moment:* Ralf Georg Reuth, *Goebbels* (San Diego, 1993), pp. 118–19.

117 *"judgment day for the Young parties":* Childers, *The Nazi Voter*, p. 317.

118 *"joy and fighting spirit":* Goebbels, *Tagebücher*, September 15, 1930, p. 239.

119 *"the pestilence of Jewish department stores":* Hans Buchner, "Die sozialkapitalistischen Konsumvereine," *Nationalsozialistische Bibliothek* (1929), pp. 42–59; also Childers, *The Nazi Voter*, pp. 151–52; and "Gewerbetreibende, Handwerker," *Der Angriff*, May 7, 1928.

120 *the Nazis claimed, had been fulfilled:* "An den deutschen Bauern," *Der Angriff*, May 7, 1928; "Bauern!," NS leaflet, Bayerisches Hauptstaatsarchiv (BHStA), Abt. V, F 9.

120 *less class bound, more dangerous:* The consensus in the recent literature is

reflected in Childers, *The Nazi Voter*; Richard Hamilton, *Who Voted for Hitler?* (Princeton, 1982); and Jürgen Falter, *Hitlers Wähler* (Munich, 1991).

120 *yielded the same desolate view:* Childers, *The Nazi Voter*, pp. 180–81.

121 *"hunger, misery, and slavery":* "Der Youngverrat der Marxisten," *Der Angriff*, July 7, 31, 1930.

121 *"tradition of class conflict":* See, for example, "Ein Wort an die KPD-Proleten!" "Bürger und Proletarier," and "Wo steht die Arbeiter Jugend!," all in *Der Angriff*, August 24, 1930; July 21, 1930; and July 3, 1930.

122 *"Jews in the German Fatherland":* Report of the Polizeiverwaltung Bocholt, September 1, 1930, to the Regierungspräsident; also Landrat Lüdinghause an Regierungspräsidenten, August 30, 1930, Staatsarchiv Münster, Nationalsozialismus, VII-67, Bd. 1.

123 *Christianity and the Catholic Church:* Klaus Schölder, *Die Kirchen und das Dritte Reich*, vol. 1 (Frankfurt, 1977), pp. 167–69.

123 *This would prove to be a tall order:* Childers, *The Nazi Voter*, pp. 188–91.

123 *Brüning's emergency rule:* Mommsen, *The Rise and Fall of Weimar Democracy*, pp. 357–63.

124 *parliamentary government in Germany:* Evans, *The Coming of the Third Reich*, pp. 275–76; Bracher, *Auflösung*, p. 373.

125 *the story and the official interpretation:* Report on Nazi activities in Westphalia, Polizeipräsident Bochum an Regierungspräsidenten, September 11, 1930, Westphalisches Staatsarchiv, Münster, XII-67, Bd. 1. See also Longerich, *Die braunen Bataillone*, 117–18.

126 *into the Valhalla of Nazi heroes:* Jay W. Baird, *To Die for Germany* (Bloomington, IN, 1990), pp. 73–90.

126 *pitch-perfect propaganda for the party:* Ibid., pp. 83–84.

127 *There would be no Nazi Putsch:* Horn, *Der Marsch zur Machtergreifung*, pp. 330–34.

127 *"heads will roll":* Heiden, *Der Fuehrer*, pp. 405–6.

127 *"against the sentiments of the SA":* Stennes, quoted in Peter Langerich, *Die Braunen Bataillone*, p. 110.

128 *party bosses in Munich and their local functionaries:* Longerich, *Die braunen Bataillone*, pp. 102–3, 109–12.

128 *"party has had to go through":* Goebbels, *Tagebücher*, February 1 and March 31, 1931.

128 *"Supreme Leader of your SA, Adolf Hitler":* Hitler. RSA, p. 258.

128 *episode continued to simmer:* Kershaw, *Hitler*, vol. I, pp. 349–50.

129 *"but a band of rough fighters":* Toland, *Adolf Hitler*, p. 250; Longerich, *Die braunen Bataillonen*, pp. 109–10, 147–48.

129 *by year's end, 260,000:* See Röhm, *Memoiren des Stabschefs Röhm*; and Longerich, *Die braunen Bataillone*.

130 *administering it to the patient:* See William L. Patch, Jr., *Heinrich Brüning and the Dissolution of the Weimar Republic* (Cambridge, UK: Cambridge University Press, 2006).

130 *too little, too late:* Mommsen, *The Rise and Fall of Weimar Democracy*, pp. 396–97.

131 *they were apt to throw rocks:* Michael Burleigh, *The Third Reich* (New York, 2000), pp. 137–38.

132 *a membership of almost 1.5 million:* Martin Broszat, *Der Staat Hitlers. Grundlegung und Entwicklung seiner inneren Verfasung* (Munich: Deutscher Taschenbuch Verlag, 1971), pp. 49–52. See also Michael Kater, *The Nazi Party* (Oxford, 1983).

132 *"intensify our propaganda work"*: Rundschreiben Gau Rheinland, May 9, 1931, Landesarchiv Koblenz, 403/16734.

133 *Goebbels gloated:* Goebbels, *Tagebücher*, December 11, 13, and 14, 1930.

134 *nostalgic yearning, hardly existed:* See Erich Weitz, *Weimar Germany: Promise and Tragedy* (Princeton, 2009).

134 *"in the Jewish backwash":* Hitler's views of art, and especially modern art, which he branded as reflections of Jewish-Bolshevist influence, are reflected most vividly in two similar speeches given in March 1933 and at the Nuremberg party rally in September 1934. See Norman H. Baynes, *The Speeches of Adolf Hitler: April 1922–August 1938* (Oxford, 1946, reissued in New York, 1968), pp. 568; 569–92.

135 *opportunity for national exposure:* Kershaw, *Hitler*, vol. I, pp. 310–11.

135 *in traditional conservative circles:* Ibid., pp. 356–57.

136 *in fact, all private property:* Boxheim Documents, Ibid.

136 *"the blood plans of Hessen":* Vorwärts, November 26, 1931.

136 *"to take an illegal step":* Mommsen, *The Rise and Fall of Weimar Democracy*, pp. 424–25.

137 *this remained a mystery:* Turner, *German Big Business and the Rise of Hitler*, pp. 213–14.

138 *leadership of the state:* Mommsen, *The Rise and Fall of Weimar Democracy*, p. 342.

139 *seemed one of calculated ambiguity:* Ibid., p. 180ff.

139 *Nazi economic thinking:* Full text of the Düsseldorf speech in Domarus, ed., *Hitler Speeches*, vol. 1, pp. 88–114; reactions of the industrialists present in Turner, *German Big Business and the Rise of Hitler*, 210–19; and Bullock, *Hitler*, pp. 161–63.

139 *especially the DNVP and DVP:* Turner, *German Big Business and the Rise of Hitler*, p. 21ff.

140 *loans or direct contributions:* Ibid. Local reports on funding in Staatsarchiv, Münster, August 28 and 30, 1930, Landrat Ludwingshausen to Regional President; Police report on NS meeting in Coesfled (1931) to Regional President; Police report on NS Wahlversammlung in Beckum, September 9, 1930; Landrat report on Nazi activities in Ludwighausen, September 10, 1930; "Arbeiter sieht eure Führer," Bayerisches Hauptstaatsarchiv (BHstA), A, F 11-NS 1930.

Chapter 5: Making Germany Great Again

143 *"We must give it to him":* Goebbels, *Tagebücher*, January 30, 1932.

143 *"Hitler is hesitating too long":* Goebbels, *Tagebücher*, February 20 and 22, 1932.

144 *"End it now!":* Sonderschreiben der RPL an alle Gaue und Gaupropagandaleitungen, February 20, 1932.

144 *"Poor Hindenburg":* Goebbels, *Tagebücher*, February 3 and 12, 1932.

145 *would evaluate them:* Paul, *Aufstand der Bilder*, pp. 70–79.

147 *No detail was to be ignored:* See the RPL communiqué for the fall Reichstag campaign, HA/14/263, and the RPL circulars of March 1, 1932, HA/15/287; July 4, 1932, NSDAP HA/12/288; and June 16, 1932, HA/15/289.

147 *He also carried a revolver:* Hanfstaengl, *Hitler*, p. 176.

147 *well-choreographed appearances:* See, for example, descriptions of Hitler's *Deutschlandflug* in Paul, *Aufstand der Bilder*, pp. 204–10, and Hanfstaengl, *Hitler*, p. 178.

148 *It was time for new leadership:* "Wer Hindenburg wählt, wählt Brüning," NS leaflet, HA/15/287.

148 *"Evening should find us joyful":* Goebbels, *Tagebücher*, March 13, 1932.

148 *"In that he is great"*: Goebbels, *Tagebücher*, March 14, 1932.

149 *"wagered beyond his means"*: Ernst Hanfstaengl, *Zwischen Weissem und Braunem Haus* (Munich, 1970), pp. 270–71.

149 *"I will lead it"*: *Völkischer Beobachter*, March 14, 1932.

150 *to precisely these groups*: RPL circular, March 3–23, 1932, HA/16/290.

150 *"for the emergency decrees"*: See the "Anordnung für die 2. Wahlgang und die kommende Preussenwahl)," Reg. Münster, Abt. N11, Nr. 67, Bd. 3, Staatsarchiv Münster.

150 *series of leaflets*: BA/NSD 13/7.

151 *"to show me wrong"*: "Mein Programm," April 2, 1932; full text in *Hitler. RSA,* vol. 1, p. 2.

151 *a half million people*: Otto Dietrich, *Mit Hitler an die Macht. Persönliche Erlebnisse mit meinem Führer* (Munich, 1934), pp. 65–70.

152 *"a springboard for the Prussian elections"*: Goebbels, *Tagebücher*, April 11, 1932, p. 259.

153 *"the war of 1914–1918"*: Delmer, who was the Berlin correspondent of the London *Daily Express*, spoke fluent German and in 1932 managed to gain Hitler's trust. Why Hitler allowed him such close access remained a mystery to Delmer. Sefton Delmer, *Trail Sinister*, vol. I (London, 1961), p. 153.

154 *varied sorts made the rounds*: Almost all of what is known about Hitler's relationship with Geli is based on speculation and innuendo, especially the testimony Otto Strasser, a bitter enemy of Hitler's, gave to the OSS in 1943 and in his book, *Hitler und ich* (Constance, 1948). See also Ronald Hayman, *Hitler and Geli* (New York, 1998).

154 *well into the Third Reich*: Kershaw, *Hitler*, vol. I, pp. 352–55. See also Heike B. Görtemaker, *Eva Braun: Life with Hitler* (New York, 2011).

156 *"and you belong to me"*: Hitler. *RSA*, pp. 54–56.

156 *"against centralization and godlessness"*: RPL circular to Prussian Gauleitungen, April 2, 1932, in HA/15/286; and circular of the Wahlpropagandaleitung Bayern, April 1932, HA/30/576.

157 *a Nazi majority was in sight*: Childers, *The Nazi Voter*, pp. 208–9.

157 *"agrarian Bolshevism"*: Mommsen, *The Rise and Fall of Weimar Democracy*, pp. 431–33.

158 *put to productive use*: Ibid., pp. 428–29.

159 *to be all too true*: André François-Poncet, *The Fateful Years: Memoirs of a French Ambassador in Berlin, 1931–1938*, translation, Howard Fertig (New York, 1972), p. 23.

160 *"We're all very happy"*: Kershaw, *Hitler*, vol. I, p. 367; Goebbels, *Tagebücher*, May 30, 1932.

161 *"the iron roofs of latrines"*: Christopher Isherwood, *The Berlin Stories* (New York, 1935), 2008 edition, p. 86.

161 *"Bloody Sunday" came as a shock*: Mommsen, *The Rise and Fall of Weimar Democracy*, p. 442.

162 *"from power once and for all"*: Denkschrift der RPL zur Reichstagswahl 1932, June 18, 1932, in HA/15/289.

162 *humiliating international oppression?*: Hitler. *RSA*, vol. 8, p. 8.

164 *developed at headquarters*: Bernard Köhler, "Arbeitsbeschaffung in Politik und Propaganda," *Unser Wille und Weg, Heft* 10 (1932), p. 303.

165 *political plight on target*: Michael Geyer, "Reichswehr, NSDAP and the Seizure of Power," in Peter D. Stachura, ed., *The Nazi Machtergreifung* (London, 1983), p. 111.

165 *storms of applause:* Hitler speech, Eberswalde, July 26, 1932, *Hitler. RSA*, vol. 8, pp. 274–75.

166 *country's popular picture press:* See "Die Rassenfrage ist der Schüssel zur Weltgeschichte" from the *Illustriert Beobachter*, December 10, 1932.

167 *"of this Jew Republic":* "Das Heckerlied." See also Longerich, *Die braunen Bataillone*, pp. 121–22; and Eberhard Frommann, *Die Lieder der NS-Zeit, Untersuchungen zuer nationalsozialistischen Liederpropaganda von den Anfängen bis zum Zweiten Weltkrieg* (Cologne, 1999).

167 *appeared with regularity:* BA, NSD, 13/7.

167 *"Jewish religion up to contempt":* Goebbels, *Tagebücher*, January 7, 1932, p. 101; and Christian T. Barth, *Goebbels und die Juden* (Paderborn, 2003), pp. 56–77.

167 *and there is much truth to that:* Allen, *The Nazi Seizure of Power*, p. 71.

168 *"but quickly burns out":* Childers, *The Nazi Voter*, pp. 267.

168 *"and contradictory currents":* "Der völkischer Block," NS circular, February 8, 1923, BA, ZSg I, 45/13.

170 *have been posed ten years later:* Thomas Childers, "The Middle Classes and National Socialism," in David Blackbourn and Richard Evans, eds., *The German Bourgeoisie: Essays on the Social History of the German Middle Class from the Late Eighteenth to the Early Twentieth Century* (London, 1991), pp. 318–37.

171 *elements of the working class:* Falter, *Hitlers Wähler*, pp. 198–230; Childers, *The Nazi Voter*, pp. 243–49.

171 *a work in progress:* Childers, *The Nazi Voter*, pp. 258–61. The *Gauleiter*'s report of March 15, 1932, is found in BA/NS22/105.

171 *between thirty and forty:* Only the Communists could match the NSDAP's youthful character. See Martin Broszat, *Der Staat Hitlers. Grundlegung und Entwicklung seiner inneren Verfassung*, second edition, 1971, pp. 49–50.

171 *the League of German Girls:* In 1932 the BdM claimed nine thousand members. Claudia Koonz, *Mothers in the Fatherland: Women, the Family and Nazi Politics* (New York: St. Martin's Press, 1987), p. 112. See also Michael Kater, *Hitler Youth,* (Cambridge, MA: Harvard University Press, 2004), pp. 70–112.

172 *trying to stay afloat:* Childers, *The Nazi Voter*, pp. 224–28.

173 *emancipation from emancipation:* Julia Sneeringer, *Winning Women's Votes* (Chapel Hill, 2002).

173 *"the spoken or written word":* Hildegard Passow, "Die propagandistische Erfassung und Bearbeitung der Frau," *Unsere Wille und Weg*, Heft 5, May 1932; and the guidelines for the organization and work of women's groups in East Prussia, "Richtlinien für die Organisation und Arbeit der Frauengruppen," May 1930, Geheime Staatsarchiv Preussischer Kulturbesitz (GStAB), Berlin, XXHA, Rep. 240, B 31.

173 *searching for alternatives:* Childers, *The Nazi Voter*, p. 259ff; Helen Boak, " 'Our Last Hope': Women's Votes for Hitler—A Reappraisal," *German Studies Review* 12 (1989), pp. 289–310.

174 *"Now action!":* Goebbels, *Tagebücher*, August 1, 1932.

Chapter 6: The Nazis Hit a Wall

176 *"be a terrible setback":* Goebbels, *Tagebücher*, August 8, 1932.

176 *"are carried from office":* Goebbels, *Tagebücher*, July 6, 1932.

177 *"the purpose of the exercise":* Goebbels, *Tagebücher*, August 8, 1932.

178 *"one iron in the fire"*: Ibid.

178 *"a grotesque absurdity"*: Goebbels, *Tagebücher*, August 13, 1932.

179 *"his oath and his conscience"*: Full text in Domarus, ed., *Hitler Speeches*, vol. 3, p. 152.

180 *"has come to naught"*: Goebbels, *Tagebücher*, August 13, 1932.

180 " 'Next time I won't vote' ": Tätigskeitsbericht der RPL, August 1932, BA/55/38; BA, Sammlung Schumacher/382.

181 *violence to unparalleled heights*: Richard Bessel, *Political Violence and the Rise of Nazism* (New Haven, 1984).

181 *"was possible is our duty"*: Ibid.

182 "has no rights at all": Hitler. *RSA*, Berlin speech, August 29, 1932.

182 *stumbled off that line*: Bessel, *Political Violence and the Rise of Nazism*, pp. 75–96.

183 *"The elections have no value"*: Stimmungsbericht der RPL, BA/NS22/347.

183 *"demand an act of deliverance"*: National Archives (NA), Series T-81, Reel 1, frames 11565, Untergruppe Ostholstein, September 24, 1932; and 105001, Untergruppe Baden, September 22, 1932. For a vivid description of the desperate financial situation of many Storm Troopers, see Jeremy Noakes, *The Nazi Party in Lower Saxony, 1921–1933* (Oxford, 1971), pp. 182–85.

184 *"debased in this way"*: NA-T81, 106209, Gruppe Mitte, Dessau, September 22, 1932; and NA-T81, 105199, Untergruppe München-Oberbayern, September 22, 1932. See also the report of Untergruppe Magdeburg-Anhalt, September 22, 1932, NA-T081, 105212.

185 *"the wavering middle class"*: RPL Communiqué, October 27, 1932, HA/14/263.

186 *hardly do to alienate them*: "Bemerkungen zur Propaganda für den Reichstagswahlkampf, undated, NA-T-81, 11427–432.

186 *"and that is Hitler and the NSDAP"*: RPL Streng vertrauliche Information, No. 11, October 20, 1932, BA 26/263.

187 *"they'd have been lost forever"*: Goebbels, *Tagebücher*, November 2, 1932.

187 *"and that one must therefore vote NSDAP"*: RPL Communiqué, October 20, 1932, HA/14/263.

187 *Crowds were smaller*: Domarus, ed., *Hitler Speeches*, vol. 3, pp. 169–74.

188 *"allow them to take it away from us again"*: Hitler. *RSA*, speech in Königsberg, October 17, 1932.

189 *"the old momentum"*: See Childers, *The Nazi Voter*, p. 210; For Goebbels's concern about the party's flagging energy, see RPL communiqué of October 20, HA/14/263.

189 *"throw into the fray"*: Goebbels, *Tagebücher*, November 1, 1932, Aufzeichnunen, Teil 1, p. 267.

189 *"word of another defeat"*: Goebbels, *Tagebücher*, November 6, 1932, Aufzeichnungen, Teil 1, p. 172.

189 *"We have suffered a blow"*: Goebbels, *Tagebücher*, November 6, 1932.

190 *"the events of that day"*: Stimmungsbericht, November 1932.

190 *"found an enthusiastic audience"*: Stimmungsbericht der RPL, November 1932, BA/NS22/I.

191 *reversal of roles since the spring and summer*: Ibid.

192 *"bourgeois masses had to follow"*: Ibid.

192 *"our movement will deliver"*: Kreisbefehl of November 9, 1932, Heilsberg, Ostpreussen, in Geheime Staatsarchiv, Berlin (GStA)/JA XX/Re/240/C50a-c.

193 *"working class must cease"*: Stimmungsbericht der RPL, November 1932, BA/NSA22/1.

193   *than to the National Socialists:* Childers, *The Nazi Voter,* pp. 184–85.

193   *"we find trouble, conflicts, and dissension":* Goebbels, *Tagebücher,* November 10, 1932.

193   *to the Storm Troopers:* Stimmungsbericht der RPL, November 1932, BA, NS 222.

194   *"rather than out of ideological conviction":* Tätigkeitsbericht der RPL, November 1932, BA/NS22.

194   *"urgently demand a revolutionary act":* Report of the Bavarian Staatsministerium, November 9, 1932, HA/24A/1759.

195   *"by no means wavered":* Ibid.

195   *over time was tenuous at best:* Goebbels, *Tagebücher,* April 25, 1932.

196   *"all the consequences this implies":* Mommsen, *The Rise and Fall of Weimar Democracy,* p. 486.

196   *"a house painter in Bismarck's chair":* Toland, *Adolf Hitler,* p. 276.

199   *The situation, he lamented, was a disaster:* Hans Frank, *Im Angesicht des Galgens: Deutung Hitlers und seiner Zeit auf Grund eigener Erlebnisse* (Munich, 1953), p. 108.

199   *"not to bring it about":* John Toland, *Adolf Hitler,* p. 280; also Peter Stachura, *Gregor Strasser,* pp. 288–90.

200   *"leaving Germany for a considerable period":* Stachura, *Gregor Strasser and the Rise of Nazism,* pp. 113–14.

200   *"deserves it, too":* Goebbels, *Tagebücher,* Teil I/Aufzeichnungen, 1924–1941, September 2, 1932, pp. 298–99.

201   *"with a pistol within three minutes":* Ibid., p. 297.

201   *"all our work will have been done for nothing":* Ibid., December 8, 1932, p. 295.

201   *" 'Give something to the wicked Nazis!' ":* Heiden, *Der Fuehrer,* p. 500.

202   *"Now we must act!":* Stimmungsbericht der RPL, November 1932.

202   *"hopes have completely failed":* Goebbels, *Tagebücher,* Teil I/Aufzeichnungen, 2, December 23, 1932, p. 314. Adding to Goebbels's depression was a serious illness of his wife, Magda. His political and personal worries are tightly interwoven in his diary entries from this period.

Chapter 7: The Impossible Happens

203   *"has been repulsed":* "Ein Jahr deutscher Politik," *Frankfurter Zeitung,* January 1, 1933.

205   *country's industrial and financial elites:* Mommsen, *The Rise and Fall of Weimar Democracy,* pp. 499–504.

207   *marriage of convenience:* Goebbels, *Tagebücher,* January 6, 1933, p. 99; background to the meeting in Mommsen, *The Rise and Fall of Weimar Democracy,* pp. 511–15.

207   *"Bravo! We can use him":* Goebbels, *Tagebücher,* January 6, 1933, p. 99; and Franz von Papen, *Memoirs* (London, 1952), pp. 225–29.

208   *"committed another blunder":* Turner, *Hitler's Thirty Days to Power,* p. 50.

209   *"it can still be victorious":* Goebbels, *Tagebücher,* March 1, 1933, Teil I/Aufzeichnungen, p. 326.

209   *"most seem convinced":* Goebbels, *Tagebücher,* January 10, 1933, p. 103.

209   *"Down with Marxism":* Paul, *Aufstand der Bilder,* pp. 109–10.

210   *all the countries in Europe:* "Adolf Hitlers Neujahrsbotschaft," December 31, 1932, in *Hitler. RSA,* vol. 3, p. 297.

210   *"the life of a people is constructed":* Ibid.

210 *"The masses . . . were delirious"*: Goebbels, *Tagebücher*, January 8, 1933, p. 101.

211 *"did his speech stir interest"*: *Lippische Landeszeitung*, quoted in *Hitler. RSA*, vol. 3, January 12, 1933, p. 352.

211 *beyond suspicion*: Anordnung December 14, 1932, *Hitler. RSA*, vol. 3, pp. 261–65.

211 *"but fanatical apostles"*: Denkschrift über die inneren Gründe für die Verfügungen zur Herstellung einer erhöhten Schlagkraft der Bewegung, December 15, 1932, pp. 273–78.

212 *"But he will pay for this"*: Goebbels, *Tagebücher, Aufzeichnungen*, January 31 and 14, 1933, p. 325.

212 *"Everything now hangs on Lippe"*: Goebbels, *Tagebücher*, January 11, 13, 14, 15, and 16, 1933.

213 *the trouble was far from over*: Longerich, *Die Braune Bataillone*, pp. 163–64; and Heiden, *Der Fuehrer*, p. 523.

213 *"it has paid off after all"*: Goebbels, *Tagebücher*, January 16, 1933, p. 107.

213 *"impaled on the tip of his sword"*: Heiden, *Der Fuehrer*, pp. 523–25; Jutta Ciolek-Kümper, *Wahlkampf in Lippe*, Munich, 1976; *Berliner Tageblatt* as quoted in Turner, *Hitler's Thirty Days to Power*, p. 65.

214 *"have slaughtered him"*: Goebbels, *Tagebücher*, January 17, 1933, p. 108.

214 *"and achieve results"*: Stachura, *Gregor Strasser and the Rise of Nazism*, p. 115.

215 *the meeting ended inconclusively*: Kershaw, *Hitler: A Biography* (New York, 2010), pp. 250–51.

217 *"be eating out of my hand"*: Turner, *Hitler's Thirty Days to Power*, p. 86.

217 *asunder at a critical juncture*: Longerich, *Die braunen Bataillone*, pp. 163–64; and Conan Fischer, *Stormtroopers* (London, 1983), p. 210.

218 *have to find ways to economize*: Goebbels, *Tagebücher*, January 6, 1933, p. 99.

218 *securing a loan for the party in the United States*: Turner, *Hitler's Thirty Days to Power*, p. 71.

218 *Papen would be the best alternative*: Ibid., pp. 116–17.

218 *he had no intention of naming Hitler chancellor*: Ibid., p. 130.

219 *"to the strength of his party"*: *Hitler's Table Talk*, p. 496.

219 *seen him in such a state*: Joachim von Ribbentrop, *The Ribbentrop Memoirs* (London, 1954), pp. 24–26.

220 *produce Hitler at eleven*: Ibid., pp. 25–26.

220 *arranged for the following morning*: Ibid., pp. 24–26.

221 *minister of the interior in Prussia*: Papen, *Memoirs*, p. 239; and *The Ribbentrop Memoirs*, p. 25.

221 *"so far into a corner he'll squeal"*: Turner, *Hitler's Thirty Days to Power*, p. 147.

221 *"in your underpants to avoid arrest"*: Duesterberg, *Der Stahlhelm und Hitler* (Wolfenbüttel/Hanover, 1949), pp. 38–39.

221 *"the tug of war [for power] begins"*: Goebbels, *Tagebücher*, January 29, 1933, p. 118.

222 *"Is Papen honest? Who knows"*: Goebbels, *Tagebücher*, Aufzeichnungen, Teil 1, January 30, 1933, p. 355.

222 *a showdown with army troops*: Goebbels, *Tagebücher*, *Sämtliche Fragmente. Teil I, Aufzeichnungen*, January 30, 1933, pp. 356–57.

223 *"then the great moment will be here"*: Ibid.

223 *to suppress an imminent coup d'état*: Mommsen, *The Rise and Fall of Weimar Democracy*, p. 526.

223–24 "establish a military dictatorship": Toland, *Hitler*, pp. 288–90.

224 "may retire at any moment": Toland, *Adolf Hitler*, p. 289.

224 "forward with God!": Ibid., pp. 290–91; Kershaw, *Hitler*, vol. I, pp. 421–23; Otto Meissner, *Staatssekretär unter Ebert, Hindenburg, und Hitler* (Hamburg, 1950), pp. 269–70.

225 "like a dream, a fairy tale": Goebbels, *Tagebücher*, January 31, 1933, p. 120.

226 "the greatest demagogue in world history": Larry Eugene Jones, " 'The Greatest Stupidity of My Life.' Alfred Hugenberg and the Formation of the Hitler Cabinet, January 1933," *Journal of Contemporary History*, 27 (1992), pp. 63–87.

226 "burst into a vast clamor": François-Poncet, *The Fateful Years*, p. 48.

226 "Germany has awakened": Goebbels, *Tagebücher, Aufzeichnungen*, January 30, 1933, p. 358.

227 "for what you have done": Ernst Deuerlein, ed., *Der Aufstieg der NSDAP in Augenzeugenberichten* (Düsseldorf, 1968), p. 418.

Chapter 8: Seizing Power

229 "the road to freedom for the German people": *Der Angriff*, January 31, 1933.

229 so little had changed: "Four Die in Reich in Party Clashes," *New York Times*, February 2, 1933.

230 "Government led by National Socialist": *New York Times*, January 1, 1933.

230 ". . . Hitler may attempt to undertake": "Centrists Demand Hitler Make Clear His Cabinet, Policy," *New York Times*, February 1, 1933.

230 "the support of the German people": Quoted in "Sees Hitler Facing Fall," *New York Times*, February 1, 1933.

230 and big agriculture Alfred Hugenberg: Evans, *The Coming of the Third Reich*, p. 314.

230 "will now come to Hitler's followers": Quoted in *New York Times*, January 31, 1933.

233 "not fighting for ourselves but for Germany!": Full text of Hitler's address in Domarus, ed., *Hitler Speeches*, vol. I, pp. 232–35.

233 that was no choice at all: Kershaw, *Hitler*, vol. I, pp. 441–44.

234 " 'legal' harassment of opposing parties": Karl Dietrich Bracher, *Die national-sozialistische Machtergreifung*, pp. 91–94.

235 official in the Interior Ministry: Hans Buchheim, *Anatomie des SS Staates*, vol. I, Munich, 1967, pp. 34–36.

235 with Nazis and hard-line conservatives: Broszat, *Der Staat Hitlers*, pp. 89–91.

236 "for following the new course": Göring's instructions quoted in Baynes, ed., *The Speeches of Adolf Hitler*, vol. I, pp. 219–20.

236 "before the final election": Turner, *Big Business*, p. 330.

237 "for the next hundred years": Turner, *Big Business*, p. 331.

237 naming him Reich minister of economics: Turner, *German Big Business and the Rise of Hitler*, pp. 329–31.

237 did not seem at all far-fetched: Goebbels, *Tagebücher, Aufzeichnungen, 2, III*, entry of February 22, 1933.

238 Now they were the law: Broszat, *Der Staat Hitlers*, p. 95.

238 "no other idea shall be expressed through it": Helmut Heiber, ed., *Goebbels Reden*, 1971, pp. 87, 89, 106; quoted in Reuth, *Goebbels*, p. 177.

238 "our huge demonstrations": Goebbels, *Tagebücher, Aufzeichnungen, 2, I*, entry of February 3, 1933, p. 365.

238 *"'stuff shut your lying Jewish mouths'"*: Goebbels speech, NS Newsreel, February 10, 1933.

240 *"And Germany will triumph"*: Domarus, ed., *Hitler Speeches*, vol. I, pp. 244–50.

240 *"the real balance of power"*: Viktor Klemperer, *I Will Bear Witness: A Diary of the Nazi Years, 1933–1941* (New York: Random House, 1998), p. 4.

240 *imminent Communist uprising*: Bracher, *Die nationalsozialistische Machtergreifung*, pp. 123–24.

241 *"with an iron fist!"*: Delmer, *Trail Sinister*, pp. 187–88.

242 *"This is a madhouse"*: Rudolf Diels, *Lucifer ante Portas* (Stuttgart, 1950), pp. 192–93.

242 *and fellow travelers were arrested*: Ibid.

243 *"beyond the legal limits otherwise proscribed"*: Akten der Reichskanzlei. Regierung Hitler, 1933–1938, Teil I, 1933/34 (Boppard, 1983), pp. 132–33.

244 *"we must crush Communism out of existence"*: Delmer, *Trail Sinister*, p. 194.

244 *It remains a plausible case*: Benjamin Carter Hett, a historian and attorney, has presented the most recent and strongest case for the Nazis having set the fire, in his *Burning the Reichstag* (New York, 2014). Writing almost as a prosecutor in a criminal case, Hett argues that the Nazis were, in fact, the arsonists.

245 *"Göring has set everything in motion"*: Goebbels, *Tagebücher*, I, 2, February 27, 1933, p. 383.

245 *their own feverish fantasies*: See Fritz Tobias, *The Reichstag Fire* (New York, 1964); and Hans Mommsen, "Van der Lubbe und sein Weg in den Reichstag— der Ablauf der Ereignisse," in Uwe Beck et al., eds., *Reichstagsbrand. Aufklärung einer historischen Legend* (Munich/Zurich, 1986), pp. 33–57.

245 *show trial of the first order*: Bracher, *Machtergreifung*, pp. 123–24.

246 *beheaded in January 1934*: Werner Maser, *Hermann Göring. Hitlers janusköpftiger Paladin. Die politische Biographie* (Berlin, 2000), p. 168. Here Maser draws on *Die neue Weltbühne*, Nr. 28, July 13 1933, p. 863.

246 *no matter how insignificant, to the regime*: Broszat, *Der Staat Hitlers*, p. 103.

246 *murdered in a forest near Berlin*: Diels, *Lucifer ante Portas*, p. 304.

246 *"one day they were just there"*: Ibid., p. 257.

247 *"everyone trembles, keeps out of sight"*: Klemperer, *I Will Bear Witness*, vol. II, diary entries of March 10 and 17, 1933, pp. 6–7.

247 *to cast their ballots publicly*: Heiden, *Der Fuehrer*, pp. 562–63.

247 *"Everything else sinks to insignificance"*: Goebbels, *Tagebücher*, 2/III, March 6, 1933, p. 140.

248 *"the united will of the National Socialists"*: Heiden, *Der Fuehrer*, p. 564.

248 *throwing a single master switch*: Evans, *The Coming of the Third Reich*, p. 381.

248 *a growing source of concern*: Broszat, *Der Staat Hitlers*, pp. 144–50; Kershaw, *Hitler*, vol. I, pp. 469–70.

250 *"acting consciously against the regime"*: Hitler's remarks, March 10, 1933, Domarus, ed., *Hitler Speeches*, vol. I, p. 263.

250 *had read him correctly*: Diels, *Lucifer ante Portas*, p. 269.

251 *"the more powerful of the two personages"*: François-Poncet, *The Fateful Years*, p. 62.

252 *"old glory and young strength"*: Domarus, ed., *Hitler Speeches*, vol. I, p. 272.

253 *overcrowding in the prisons:* Karola Fings, "The Public Face of the Camps," in Jane Caplan and Nicholaus Wachsmann, eds., *Concentration Camps in Nazi Germany* (New York, 2010), pp. 110–11.

253 *The first of these installations:* On the early camps, see Robert Gellately, *Backing Hitler* (Oxford, 2001), pp. 51–53; and Fings, "The Public Face of the Camps," in Caplan and Wachsmann, eds., *Concentration Camps in Nazi Germany*, pp. 114–15.

254 *relations with the Vatican:* Domarus, ed., *Hitler Speeches*, vol. I, p. 283.

254 *"in and of itself, limited":* Ibid., p. 285.

255 *on an almost daily basis:* Longerich, *Die braunen Bataillone*, p. 170.

255 *was intended to go on indefinitely:* "Boycott Manifesto Includes 11 Orders," *New York Times*, May 29, 1933.

256 *"declaration of economic warfare" against Germany:* See Goebbels's diary notes on the boycott from March 26 to April 2, 1933, Goebbels, *Tagebücher*, I, 2, pp. 398–401.

256–57 *"enemies of the people and cunning slanderers":* *Völkischer Beobachter*, quoted in Saul Friedländer, *Nazi Germany and the Jews*, vol. I: *The Years of Persecution, 1933–1939* (New York, 1997), p. 22.

257 *was classified a Jew:* Friedländer, *Nazi Germany and the Jews*, vol. I, pp. 27–28.

258 *beleaguered Jewish community:* Ibid., pp. 29–30.

258 *"opposition of the November system":* Baynes, ed., *The Speeches of Adolf Hitler*, p. 209.

259 *"completely in our hands":* Notes from March 24, 1933, Goebbels, *Tagebücher, Aufzeichnungen*, 2, I, p. 397.

260 *on into the night:* Hitler's remarks in Domarus, ed., *Hitler Speeches*, vol. I, pp. 311–16.

260 *"won't be able to hold out for long":* Goebbels, *Tagebücher, Aufzeichnungen I*, 2, entry of April 17, p. 408.

261 *the number had doubled:* Kershaw, *Hitler*, vol. I, pp. 462–63.

263 *in short, was to be a Nazi church:* See Doris L. Bergen, *Twisted Cross: The German Christian Movement in the Third Reich* (Chapel Hill, 1996); Victoria Barnett, *For the Soul of the People: Protestant Protest Against Hitler* (Oxford, 1992). See also J. S. Conway, *The Nazi Persecution of the Churches, 1933–1945* (London, 1968). For a useful summary, see Richard Steigmann Gall, "Religion and the Churches," in Jane Caplan, ed., *Nazi Germany* (Oxford, 2008), pp. 146–67.

264 *It was July 14, Bastille Day:* See Klaus Scholder, *Die Kirchen und das Dritte Reich*, vol. I (Frankfurt a.M., 1977), pp. 482–525.

Chapter 9: Consolidation of Power

265 *"if it must be!":* Longerich, *Die braunen Bataillone*, pp. 178–81.

266 *joined since the March 5 election:* Broszat, *Der Staat Hitlers*, pp. 252–53.

267 *"blood week of Köpernick":* Richard Evans, *The Coming of the Third Reich*, p. 360.

268 *"had never witnessed such horror":* Diels, *Lucifer ante Portas*, pp. 254–55.

268 *"understands nothing about business":* Hans-Adolf Jacobsen and Werner Jochmann, eds., *Ausgewählte Dokumente zur Geschichtge des Nationalsozialismus, 1933–1945* (Bielefeld, 1961), p. 2.

268 *"lies in the foreign press"*: Longerich, *Die braunen Bataillone*, pp. 182–83.

269 *in Prussia sharply reduced*: Broszat, *Der Staat Hitlers*, pp. 260.

269 *"as the Führer wishes"*: Jeremy Noakes and Geoffry Pridham, eds., *Nazism 1919–1945*, vol. 2, *State, Economy and Society, 1933–1939* (Exeter, 1984), p. 529.

269 *to be snooping around for atrocity stories*: Karl Dietrich Bracher, *Die nationalsozialistische Machtergreifung* (Frankfurt, 1962), pp. 190–202.

270 *confusion streaming behind him*: Ibid.

271 *came in February and March 1933*. See Beatrice and Helmut Heiber, eds., *Die Rückseite des Hakenkreuzes. Absonderliches aus den Akten des "Dritten Reiches"* (Munich, 1993), pp. 123, 125–26.

272 *and the public was impressed*: Adam Tooze, *The Wages of Destruction*, pp. 42–47.

273 *"with equal thoroughness"*: Baynes, *The Speeches of Adolf Hitler*, vol. II, pp. 1049–53.

273 *"while maintaining its honor"*: Domarus, ed., *Hitler Speeches*, vol. I, p. 365.

273 *"the hiss of a traveling bullet"*: Ibid., p. 392.

274 *"so why be a martyr?"*: Klemperer, *I Will Bear Witness*, vol. I, diary entries of November 2 and November 11, pp. 40–41.

274 *"Nazifying society was progressing"*: New Beginning was an organization of the Socialist left that had sought to bring about a common front between the KPD and SPD in the last years of the Weimar Republic. It maintained a network of cells that submitted monthly reports on life in the Third Reich from 1933 to 1936. Those reports are collected in Bernd Stöver, ed., *Berichte über die Lage in Deutschland. Die Meldungen der Gruppe Neu Beginnen aus dem Dritten Reich, 1933–1936* (Bonn, 1996), p. 2.

274 *elements of the working class*: New Beginning's Report for February 1934, in ibid., p. 51.

275 *his successor follow his footsteps*: Sopade, *Deutschland-Berichte der Sozialdemokratischen Partei Deutschlands, 1934–1940, Erster Jahrgang 1934* (Frankfurt a. M., 1989), pp. 54–55. Between 1934 and 1940 the Socialist underground organization smuggled reports on life inside Nazi Germany to the SPD's exiled leadership in Prague and later Paris. The reports from all around Germany blended insightful, hardheaded realism with a generous admixture of wishful thinking. These valuable reports are collected in four volumes under the title *Deutschland-Berichte der Sozialdemokratischen Partei Deutschlands, 1934–1940*.

275 *refrain in local political discourse*: Ian Kershaw, *The "Hitler Myth": Image and Reality in the Third Reich* (New York, 1987), pp. 83–86.

276 *"until our final goal is reached"*: Meissner, *Staatssekretär unter Ebert, Hindenburg, und Hitler* (Hamburg, 1950), p. 363.

277 *"They'll never have a new idea"*: Klaus P. Fischer, *Nazi Germany: A New History* (New York, 1995), pp. 285–86; Broszat, *Der Staat Hitlers*, pp. 251–52.

279 *broke into stormy applause*: Papen's remarks are found in Joachim Päzold, *Franz von Papen, ein deutsches Verhängnis* (Munich, 1995), pp. 208–18.

279 *open to a change of government*: Delmer, *Trail Sinister*, p. 233.

279 *"the slightest attempt at sabotage"*: Domarus, ed., *Hitler Speeches*, vol. I, pp. 463–64; Kershaw, *Hitler*, vol. I, p. 510.

280 *sternly reinforced that position:* See Sefton Delmer, *Trail Sinister*, pp. 233–34; Kershaw, *Hitler*, vol. I, pp. 510–11.

280 *to carry out the operation:* Longerich, *Die braunen Bataillone*, pp. 194–95.

281 *"revolutionary agitation from below":* Domarus, ed., *Hitler Speeches*, vol. 1 January 25, 1934, p. 466.

281 *"has put his own head in a noose":* Domarus, ed., *Hitler Speeches*, vol. I, p. 466.

282 *on that long murderous night:* Ibid., p. 469ff.

283 *no idea that anything unusual was taking place:* Toland, *Adolf Hitler*, p. 345.

283 *It was not safe in the capital today:* Ibid., p. 341; Kershaw, *Hitler*, vol. I, pp. 515.

284 *he could only mutter: "crazy":* Toland, *Adolf Hitler*, p. 340.

285 *"circles of pretentious characters":* This account was the first to be issued by the Nazis on the events of June 30. Domarus, ed., *Hitler Speeches*, vol. I, p. 473.

285 *"My Führer, my Führer":* Toland, *Adolf Hitler*, p. 345.

286 *made retroactively legal:* Domarus, ed., *Hitler Speeches*, vol. I, p. 481.

287 *"having to overcome a difficult crisis":* Ibid., p. 500.

287 *"makes itself guilty":* Ibid., p. 501.

287 *"it is itself supreme justice":* Claudia Koonz, *The Nazi Conscience* (New York, 1988), p. 98. For a full exposition of Schmitt's defense of Hitler's actions, see Schmitt's "Der Führer schützt das Recht": zur Reichstagsrede Adolf Hitlers von 13. Juli 1934, translated in Rabinbach and Gilman, eds., *The Third Reich Source Book*, pp. 63–67.

288 *"extremely unfavorable response":* See, for example, the police report for July 1934 on the negative reaction of the population in Catholic Münster, Joachim Kuropka, *Meldungen aus Münster 1924–1944* (Münster, 1992), p. 151.

288 *A similar telegram went to Göring:* Domarus, ed., *Hitler Speeches*, vol. I, p. 480. Hindenburg was no doubt enormously relieved to see the SA throttled, but the laudatory text of the telegram, some believe, was composed by an aide.

288 *"the traitors and mutineers":* Blomberg quoted in Kershaw, *Hitler*, vol. 2, p. 512.

289 *lost 40 percent of its troops:* Kershaw, *Hitler*, vol. I, p. 517.

289 *"a brave soldier for this oath":* Domarus, ed., *Hitler Speeches*, vol. I, p. 509.

Chapter 10: The People's Community

292 *"become the source of artistic intuition":* Domarus, ed., *Hitler Speeches*, vol. I, pp. 13–14, 279.

292 *"a revival and resurrection of German art":* Baynes, ed., *The Speeches of Adolf Hitler*, vol. I, p. 569.

293 *four thousand works had been banned in that year alone:* Richard Evans, *The Third Reich in Power*, pp. 158–59.

293 *Mozart's Italian librettist was of Jewish origin:* Friedländer, *Nazi Germany and the Jews*, vol. I, pp. 133–34.

294 *Dancers: German Modern Dance and the Third Reich* (New York, 2003).

294 Inspired by the Nazis: For treatments of Weimar's challenge to traditional values, see Eric D. Weitz, *Weimar Germany: Promises and Tragedy* (Princeton, 2007); Peter Gay, *Weimar Culture: The Outsider as Insider* (New York, 1968); Walter Laqueur, *Weimar: A Cultural History* (New York, 1974); John Willett, *Art and Politics in the Weimar Period: The New Sobriety, 1917–1933* (New York, 1978); and Lilian Karina and Marion Kant, *Tanz unter dem Hakenkreuz. Eine Dokumentation* (Berlin, 1999), pp. 122–44, Fritz Böhme quote, p. 135.

294   *mounted in sixteen different cities:* Frederic Spotts, *Hitler and the Power of Aesthetics* (London, 2002), p. 153ff.

294   *seized seventeen thousand pieces of forbidden art:* Jonathan Petropoulos, *Art as Politics in the Third Reich* (Chapel Hill, 1994), pp. 55–56.

295   *architects, Paul Ludwig Troost and Albert Speer:* Eric Michand, *The Cult of Art in Nazi Germany* (Palo Alto, 2004), pp. 110–11.

295   *"hard-earned money and displayed as art":* Fritz Kaiser, *Führer durch die Ausstellung Enartete Kunst,* in Joseph Wulf, ed., *Die Bildenden Künste im Dritten Reich,* pp. 358–60.

295   *a freak show:* Jonathan Petropoulos, *Art as Politics in the Third Reich,* pp. 51–58; Frederic Spotts, *Hitler and the Power of Aesthetics,* pp. 152–54.

296   *"their last opportunity to see modern art":* New York Times, August 6, 1937.

296   *"the ever-open jaws of the perpetrators of these atrocities":* Karl Heinz Schmeer, *Die Regie des öffentlichen Lebens im Dritten Reich* (Munich, 1956), p. 109.

296   *performed a service for the Reich:* Goebbels, *Tagebücher, Aufzeichnungen,* vol. 4, November 5, 1937, p. 392.

296   *bound for extinction is impossible to know:* Frankfurter Zeitung, February 27, 1938, in Wulf, *Die bildenden Künste im Dritten Reich,* p. 364.

297   *burned in the courtyard of a Berlin fire station:* Petropoulos, *Art as Politics in the Third Reich,* pp. 51–58.

297   *"big-city night clubs and international bordellos":* Der SA-Mann, September 18, 1937, quoted in George L. Mosse, *Nazi Culture* (New York, 1966), pp. 50–52.

297   *"conquer the soul of the nation":* "Erobert die Seele der Nation," in "Goebbels Spricht." *Reden aus Kampf und Sieg* (Oldenburg, 1933), pp. 74–75.

298   *Nazism's core values:* Anselm Faust, "Professoren für die NSDAP. Zum politischen Verhalten der Hochschullehrer 1932/33," in Manfred Heinemann, *Erziehung und Schulung im Dritten Reich, Teil 2. Hochschulen, Erwachsenbildung* (Stuttgart, 1980), pp. 31–49.

298   *including eleven Nobel laureates:* Evans, *The Coming of the Third Reich,* pp. 422–26.

298   *"it just doesn't exist anymore":* Richard Grunberger, *The 12-Year Reich: A Social History of the Third Reich, 1933–1945* (New York, 1971), p. 309.

299   *encountered problems finding positions:* Laqueur, *Weimar,* p. 257.

299   *assault on "the Weimar system":* Geoffrey J. Giles, "The Rise of the National Socialist Students Association and the Failure of Political Education in the Third Reich," in Peter D. Stachura, *The Shaping of the Nazi State* (London, 1978), pp. 160–85. See also Anselm Faust, *Der Nationalsozialistische Deutsche Studentenbund: Studenten und Nationalsozialismus in der Weimarer Republik,* 2 vols. (Düsseldorf, 1973).

300   *"their thinking in the German spirit":* Anselm Faust, "Die Hochschulen und der 'undeutsche Geist': Die Bücherverbrennungen am 10. Mai 1933 und ihre Vorgeschichte," in Hermann Haarmann, Walter Huder, and Klaus Siebenhaar, eds., *"Das war ein Vorspiel nur . . ." Bücherverbrennung Deutschland 1933: Voraussetzungen und Folgen,* Berlin and Vienna, 1983, pp. 31–50.

301   *disappeared into the bonfire:* Philip Metcalfe, *1933* (New York, 1988), pp. 121–23.

301 *it had come to this: Neuköllner Tageblatt*, May 12, 1933, quoted in Albert Wucher, *Die Fahne Hoch. Das Ende der Republik und Hitlers Machtüber-nahme. Ein Dokumentarbericht* (Munich, 1963), pp. 210–12; see also Philip Metcalfe's vivid account in his *1933*, pp. 121–24.

301 *the low quality of their educational preparedness:* Grunberger, *The 12-Year Reich*, p. 402.

301 *"the schools but the nation as a whole":* Wucher, *Die Fahne Hoch*, p. 209.

302 *to political reliability tests:* Grunberger, *The 12-Year Reich*, p. 399.

302 *more than five million by the close of 1934:* Kater, *Hitler Youth*, p. 19.

302 *"I will create the New Order":* Quoted in David G. Williams, *The Hitler Youth*, self-published, 2014.

302 *"to die for Germany":* The Jungvolk swearing-in pledge of ten-year-old boys. April 20, 1936, *The Hitler Youth*. Prelude to War. The History Place.com. On Nazi indoctrination of youth, see Burleigh and Wippermann, *The Racial State*, pp. 199–241, and Claudia Koonz, *The Nazi Conscience*, pp. 131–62.

303 *"never be free for the rest of their lives":* Hitler speaking to the Reichstag in December 1938, quoted in H. W. Koch, *The Hitler Youth: Origins and Devel-opment, 1922–1945* (New York: Cooper Square Press, 1975), p. 127.

303 *activities cut into study time:* Grunberger, *The 12-Year Reich*, pp. 402–6.

304 *teacher and student, priest and parishioner:* W. Klosse, *Generation im Gleich-tritt* (Oldenburg, 1964); and Koch, *The Hitler Youth*, pp. 127–30.

304 *"the loss of parental rights and personal freedom":* Sopade, *Deutschland-Bericht*, December 1938, pp. 1400–1401.

304 *"began to envy the childless":* Burleigh, *The Third Reich*, p. 237.

304 *League of German Girls (BdM):* See Michael Kater, *The Nazi Party: A Social Profile of Members and Leaders* (Oxford, 1989), and his *Hitler Youth* (Cam-bridge, MA, 2006).

304 *young women became pregnant:* New Beginning's monthly report for June/July 1934, in Stöver, ed., *Berichte über die Lage in Deutschland*, p. 209.

305 *"Baldur, squeeze me":* Kater, *Hitler Youth*, pp. 73–85; Grunberger, *The 12-Year Reich*, p. 356ff.

305 *"that the man's world can be formed and can grow":* Hitler speech, September 8, 1934, in Domarus, ed., *Hitler Speeches*, vol. I, p. 532.

305 *an official national holiday:* See Karen Hausen, "Mother's Day in the Weimar Re-public," in Renate Bridenthal, Atina Grossmann, and Marion Kaplan, eds., *When Biology Became Destiny: Women in Weimar and Nazi Germany* (New York, 1984), pp. 131–33; also Irmgard Weyrather, *Muttertag und Mutterkreuz. Der Kult um die "deutsche Mutter" im Nationalsozialismus* (Frankfurt am.M., 1993).

306 *removed from higher administrative posts in education:* Ute Frevert, *Women in German History: From Bourgeois Emancipation to Sexual Liberation* (New York, 1989), p. 219.

306 *policy toward women and the family:* Ibid., pp. 217–18; and Koonz, *Mothers in the Fatherland*, pp. 177–83. See also Jill Stephenson, *Women in Nazi Germany* (London, 2001), and her earlier *The Nazi Organization of Women* (London, 1981). The most succinct treatment of Nazi women's organizations can be found in Stephenson, "The Nazi Organization of Women 1933–1939," in Peter Stachura, ed., *The Shaping of the Nazi State* (London, 1978), pp. 186–209.

306 *"the woman stands up for the family":* Mosse, *Nazi Culture*, pp. 39–40.

306   *"is a comrade, a fellow combatant"*: Hanns Anderlahn, *Gegner erkannt!
Kampferlebnisse der SA* (Munich, 1937), pp. 60–63, quoted in ibid., p. 31.

307   *"more useful than lipstick in promoting health"*: Report in the *Frankfurter
Zeitung*, June 1, 1937, quoted in ibid., p. 43.

307   *were working outside the home than in 1933:* Frevert, *Women in German
History*, pp. 218–19.

307   *not welcome in Nazi factory gatherings:* Report of the *Frankfurter Zeitung*,
August 11, 1933, cited in Mosse, *Nazi Culture*, p. 45.

308   *until the collapse of the Third Reich:* Koonz, *Mothers in the Fatherland*, p. 197.

308   *"every year at the party rally in Nürnberg"*: " 'Did You Hear the One About
Hitler?,' " *Spiegel Online*, August 30, 2006. See also F. K. M. Hillenbrand,
Underground Humor in Nazi Germany, 1933–1945 (London: Routledge,
1995); and Rudolph Herzog and Jefferson Chase, *Dead Funny: Telling Jokes in
Hitler's Germany* (Brooklyn, NY: Melville House, reprint, 2012).

309   *families could not afford:* Tooze, *The Wages of Destruction*, pp. 148–49.

309   *by 1939 it was one in two:* Ibid.

310   *including swimming pools:* Shelley Baranowski, *Strength Through Joy* (Cambridge, UK: Cambridge University Press, 2007), pp. 55–56. See also Albert
Speer, *Inside the Third Reich* (New York, 1970), pp. 94–95.

310   *beyond the borders of the Third Reich:* Speer, *Inside the Third Reich*, pp. 94–95.

310   *availed themselves of KdF trips:* Baranowski, *Strength Through Joy*, pp. 48–50; and
Wolfgang König, *Volkswagen, Volksempfänger, Volksgemeinschaft*, pp. 192–219.

311   *"the German worker whom we show to the world"*: Schoenbaum, *Hitler's
Social Revolution*, p. 105.

311   *"with a depressing [economic] situation"*: Noakes and Pridham, eds., *Nazism*,
vol. II, pp. 352–53.

311   *during the Third Reich was made in 1960:* Tooze, *The Wages of Destruction*, pp.
148–50; also König, *Volkswagen, Volksempfänger, Volksgemeinschaft*, pp. 151–91.

312   *"there will be no more 'good days' in Germany"*: Hans-Jochen Gamm, *Der
Flusterwitz im Dritten Reich. Mündliche Dokumente zur Lage der Deutschen
während des Nationalsozialismus* (Munich, 1990), p. 57.

312   *"ball with the swastika in a toy shop"*: Klemperer, *I Will Bear Witness*, diary
entries for March 22 and March 30, 1933, pp. 9–10.

312   *a new people's community supported by all:* Peter Fritzsche, *Life and Death in
the Third Reich* (Cambridge, MA, 2008), pp. 20–23.

312   *"need only inquire at the local party office"*: Grunberger, *The 12-Year Reich*, p. 111.

313   *transcending the now irrelevant boundaries of class:* On the political significance of National Socialist Holidays, see Spotts, *Hitler and the Power of
Aesthetics*, pp. 100–7.

315   *a sea of Storm Troopers and Hitler Youth:* Ibid., pp. 65–66.

317   *every year down to the outbreak of the war:* Franz Janke, *Die braune Gesellschaft. Ein Volk wird Formatiert* (Stuttgart, 1997), pp. 370–77; and Spotts,
Hitler and the Power of Aesthetics, pp. 104–6.

318   *class and region had disappeared:* Franz Janke, *Die braune Gesellschaft*, p. 143ff.

318   *the figure had plunged to 500,000:* Tooze, *The Wages of Destruction*, pp. 47–48.
See also Harold James, *The German Slump: Politics and Economics, 1924–1936*
(Oxford, 1986); and Richard J. Overy, *The Nazi Economic Recovery, 1932–
1938* (London, 1982).

319 *and relied heavily on such denunciations:* Robert Gellately, *The Gestapo and German Society: Enforcing Racial Policy, 1933–1945* (Oxford, 1990). See also his article "The Gestapo and German Society: Political Denunciations in the Gestapo Case Files," *Journal of Modern History*, 60 (1988), pp. 654–94.

321 *foundation of the Nazi system of terror:* For the early development of the concentration camp system, see Nikolaus Wachsmann, *The History of the Nazi Concentration Camps* (New York, 2015).

321 *"which twisted and blighted all human relations":* Erik Larson, *In the Garden of the Beast* (New York, 2011), p. 223.

321 *"watch for the telephone and speak in whispers":* Ibid., p. 236.

322 *was the slogan of one group:* Kater, *Hitler Youth*, p. 137.

322 *"We're the fighting Navajos":* Petlev Peukert, *Die Edelweisspiraten: Protestbewegungen jugendlicher Arbeiter im Dritten Reich. Eine Dokumentation* (Cologne, 1985), p. 71; and Evans, *The Third Reich in Power*, pp. 244–45.

322 *"disintegration of the youth":* Detlev Peukert, *Volksgenossen und Gesellschaftsfremde*, pp. 173–218, quote from p. 183; and Kater, *Hitler Youth*, pp. 113–66.

324 *caution when dealing with the Church:* See the Gestapo reports and assorted correspondence from the predominantly Catholic area around Münster in Westphalia for 1934–37, in Joachim Kuropka, ed., *Meldungen aus Münster 1924–1944* (Münster, 1992), pp. 427–501; also Jeremy Noakes, "The Oldenburg Crucifix Struggle of November 1936," in Stachura, ed., *The Shaping of the Nazi State*, pp. 210–33.

324 *a revival of the Nordic "blood soul":* Rosenberg's *The Myth of the Twentieth Century*, published in 1930, was a ferocious assault on Christianity, especially the Catholic Church. The book was little read, even within National Socialist circles, and Rosenberg was widely ridiculed by many in the party's elite, but it represented a clarion call to arms against both Protestantism and Catholicism and was roundly condemned by both. Rosenberg was also perhaps the most vociferous purveyor of *The Protocols of the Elders of Zion*. Joachim C. Fest, *The Face of the Third Reich: Portraits of the Nazi Leadership* (Boston: Da Capo, 1999), pp. 163–74. Rosenberg's *Myth* provoked Cardinal Clemens von Galen to write a closely argued pamphlet against the book that was widely disseminated in Germany. It was only a small step from there to his open denunciation of the regime's euthanasia program. Grunberger, *The 12-Year Reich*, p. 451.

324 *it was widely circulated nonetheless:* Sopade, *Deutschland-Bericht*, July 1935, report from Rheinland-Westfalen, pp. 571–72.

325 *"The time for the cross is now over":* Sopade, *Deutschland-Bericht*, June 1935, report from Southern Bavaria, pp. 674–75.

325 *all across Germany on Palm Sunday, March 21, 1937:* Guenter Lewy, *The Catholic Church and Nazi Germany* (New York, 1964). See Michael Burleigh and Wolfgang Wippermann, *The Racial State, 1933–1945* (Cambridge, UK, 1991), pp. 152–53.

325 *"the premature hymns of the enemies of Christ":* "Mit brennender Sorge," Rome, 1938.

326 *"but the law of the German people":* Evans, *The Third Reich in Power*, pp. 244–45.

326 *its oppressive intervention in everyday life:* Ian Kershaw, *Popular Opinion and Political Dissent in the Third Reich, 1933–1945* (Oxford, 1983), p. 223.

327 *ran into trouble almost immediately:* See Richard Steigmann-Gall, "Religion and the Churches, in Caplan, ed., *Nazi Germany*, pp. 146–67.

328 *liberated by the Americans in spring 1945:* Ibid.; and Scholder, *Die Kirchen und das Dritte Reich*, pp. 701–42.

329 *"I can promise them":* Hitler's *Table Talk*, from July 11–12, 1941, and February 8, 1942, pp. 6–7, 30.

330 *Nazis closed the Catacombe:* Peter Jelavich, *Berlin Cabaret* (Cambridge, MA, 1993), pp. 236–37.

331 *"You are compromised beyond repair":* Milton Mayer, *They Thought They Were Free: The Germans, 1933–45* (Chicago, 1955), pp. 167–72.

331 *"The revolution that we have made":* Helmut Heiber, ed., *The Early Goebbels Diaries* (London, 1962).

Chapter 11: A Racial Revolution

333 *under different—"Aryan"—management:* Heiden, *Der Fuehrer*, p. 587.

333 *the lower reaches of German society:* David Schoenbaum, *Hitler's Social Revolution* (New York, 1966), p. 55.

334 *"died out from blood poisoning":* Hitler, *Mein Kampf*, pp. 286–90.

335 *"the total victory of the former":* Ibid., p. 296.

335 *"hence worthy of existence":* Ibid., p. 327.

335 *the first task of National Socialism:* Ibid., pp. 325–26.

336 *found among the party's militants and the SA:* Fritzsche, *Life and Death in the Third Reich*, pp. 90, 105–6.

337 *regional variations existed:* Hermann Graml, *Antisemitism in the Third Reich* (London, 1992), pp. 97–98.

337 *"confronted with a concrete solution":* Friedländer, *Nazi Germany and the Jews*, vol. I, p. 28.

338 *"we're from Prenzlau":* Fritzsche, *Life and Death in the Third Reich*, p. 78.

338 *or a legal guardian:* Robert E. Proctor, *Racial Hygiene: Medicine Under the Nazis* (Cambridge, MA, 1988), pp. 46–49.

338 *"the use of force is permissible":* Burleigh and Wippermann, *The Racial State*, p. 137.

339 *the new order of things:* Koonz, *The Nazi Conscience*, p. 104.

339 *fall into one of these categories:* Fritzsche, *Life and Death in the Third Reich*, pp. 87–88.

339 *such appeals were successful:* Proctor, *Racial Hygiene*, pp. 72–73, 102–4.

339 *"never have been born at all":* Hitler's *Table Talk, 1941–1944*, entry of August 29, 1942, p. 675. For a partial list of test questions, see Burleigh and Wipperman, *The Racial State*, pp. 138–39. Convinced that the brilliance of the Führer should be recorded for posterity, Bormann had begun transcribing Hitler's dinner and luncheon conversations. A Bormann aide unobtrusively took notes, which were then typed out, and read by Bormann to eliminate any possible faux pas or embarrassing comments.

340 *first six months of pregnancy:* Giesela Bock, *Zwangssterilisation im Nationalsozialismus. Studien zur Rassenpolitik und Frauenpolitik* (Opladen, 1986), pp. 230–46; and Burleigh and Wippermann, *The Racial State*, p. 140.

340 *lead to compulsory sterilization:* Fritzsche, *Life and Death in the Third Reich*, pp. 80–81.

340 *"Hope for as many children as possible":* Claudia Koonz, "Eugenics, Gender, and Ethics in Nazi Germany: The Debate about Involuntary Sterilization,

1933–1936," in Childers and Caplan, eds., *Reevaluating the Third Reich*, pp. 70–71.

340 *"preservation of high-grade germ plasma"*: Hermann Paull, "Deutsche Rassen-hygiene: Ein Gemeinverständliches Gespräch über Vererbungslehre, Eugenik, Familie, Sippe, Rasse und Volkstum," in C. A. Starke, *Erbegesundheitspflege und Wappenkunde*, Part II (Berlin 1934), pp. 17–21; and Mosse, ed., *Nazi Culture*, pp. 35–38.

341 *race, eugenics, and preventive medicine*: Michael Kater, *Doctors Under Hitler* (Chapel Hill: University of North Carolina Press, 1989), pp. 54–59.

341 *organically grown vegetables and whole wheat bread*: See Robert E. Proctor, *The Nazi War Against Cancer* (Princeton: Princeton University Press, 2000).

341 *new lifestyle for the* Volksgemeinschaft: *Hitler's Table Talk*, pp. 114–15, 230–31, 360–61.

342 *awaiting admission were processed*: Proctor, *Racial Hygiene*, p. 65.

342 *offering courses in the subject*: Ibid., pp. 79–81.

342 *Aryan, Germanic, and Nordic peoples*: See, for example, Dr. H. Meinshausen, *Erziehung zum Dritten Reich. Reden und Aufsätze* (Berlin, 1934).

343 *"engaged in by the Jews of your acquaintance?"*: From Jakob Graf, *Famil-ienkunde und Rassenbiologie für Schüler*, second edition (Munich 1935), pp. 107–14, 115, quoted in Mosse, *Nazi Culture*, pp. 80–81.

343 *to create "a new moral order"*: Koonz, *The Nazi Conscience*, p. 110.

344 *"The healthy preserve the Volk"*: For examples, see Koonz, *The Nazi Con-science*, pp. 118–20.

344 *staffed by 3,600 workers*: Proctor, *Racial Hygiene*, pp. 87–89.

344 *to deal with racial affairs*: Koonz, *The Nazi Conscience*, p. 115.

345 *a nationwide program of euthanasia*: Burleigh and Wippermann, *The Racial State*, p. 142; Proctor, *Racial Hygiene*, pp. 181–82.

345 *No visitations were permitted*: Burleigh, *The Third Reich*, p. 284.

346 *Genetically Determined Illness*: Burleigh and Wippermann, *Life and Death in the Third Reich*, pp. 142–50. See also Michael Burleigh, *Death and Deliver-ance: Euthanasia in Germany 1900–1945* (New York: Cambridge University Press, 1994).

346 *victims in Germany and beyond*: See Henry Friedlander, *The Origins of Nazi Genocide: From Euthanasia to the Final Solution* (Chapel Hill, 1995).

347 *30,000 had received decorations for bravery*: Burleigh, *The Third Reich*, p. 284.

347 *by the close of 1938, there were none*: Friedländer, *Nazi Germany and the Jews*, vol. I, pp. 283–84.

347 *"whose idea is Bolshevism"*: Ibid., p. 182.

348 *many who were not committed Nazis*: Graml, *Antisemitism in the Third Reich*, pp. 108–9.

348 *thrown into the street*: Report of the Stapostelle Regierungsbezirk Köln, March 4, 1935, in Otto Dov Kulka and Eberhard Jäckel, eds., *Die Juden in den gehei-men NS-Stimmungsberichten, 1933–1945* (Düsseldorf, 2004), p. 122.

349 *would no longer be admitted to theaters*: Sopade, *Deutschland-Berichte*, re-ports from September 1935, pp. 1021, 1027, 1031.

349 *"this persecution of the Jews"*: Sopade, *Deutschland-Berichte*, September 1935, pp. 1028–29.

349 *well-ordered, and happy Germany*: Friedländer, *Nazi Germany and the Jews*, vol. I, pp. 180–81.

350 *Hitler's long-cherished ideas:* Graml, *Antisemitism in the Third Reich*, pp. 109–11.

350 *his or her impending blunder:* Noakes and Pridham, eds., *Nazism*, vol. II, p. 533.

351 *the honor of reading out the text:* Ibid., pp. 531–37.

351 *Aryan women of child-bearing age:* Cornelie Essner, *Die "Nürnberger Gesetze" oder Die Verwaltung des Rassenwahns, 1933–1945* (Paderborn, 2002).

353 *Führer about the details:* Noakes and Pridham, eds., *Nazism*, vol. II, p. 538.

353 *quarter Jews at 25,000 to 130,000:* Friedländer, *Nazi Germany and the Jews*, vol. I, pp. 150–51.

354 *Wannsee Conference in January 1942:* Graml, *Antisemitism in the Third Reich*, pp. 121–23; and Friedländer, *Nazi Germany and the Jews*, vol. I, p. 152. For the many contradictions and perplexities arising from the Nuremberg Laws, see Friedländer, ibid., pp. 148–49. For Wannsee, see chapter 16 of this book.

354 *"at least one of the partners":* For the unanticipated complexities of Nazi racial policy, see Robert Procter, *Racial Hygiene*, pp. 64–125; and Michael Burleigh, *The Racial State*, pp. 44–199.

354 *without first being sentenced in court:* Graml, *Antisemitism in the Third Reich*, p. 125.

355 *"Aryan customers entering Jewish businesses":* Report of the Stapostelle Breslau, May 5, 1935, in Kulka and Jäckel, *Die Juden in den geheimen NS-Stimmungsberichten*, p. 129.

355 *warnings against frivolous denunciations:* Grunberger, *The 12-Year Reich*, pp. 108–15; Robert Gellately, *The Gestapo and German Society*.

356 *to slip back into the German mainstream:* Friedländer, *Nazi Germany and the Jews*, vol. I, p. 116; Graml, *Antisemitism in the Third Reich*, pp. 112–13.

356 *"to speak like that in public":* Quoted in Marion Kaplan, *From Dignity to Despair* (New York, 1998), p. 21.

357 *their position deteriorated:* Graml, *Antisemitism in the Third Reich*, pp. 123–24.

358 *to have a passable knowledge of Hebrew:* Friedländer, *Nazi Germany and the Jews*, vol. I, pp. 197–99.

358 *"but with poison gas":* Michael Wildt, *Die Judenpolitik des SD 1935 bis 1938* (Munich, 1995), pp. 66–67; also in Susanne Heim, "Deutschland muss ihnen ein Land ohne Zukunft. Die Zwangsemigration der Juden, 1933–1938," in *Beiträge zur Nationalsozialistischen Gesundheits und Sozialpolitik*, vol. 11, *Arbeitsemigration und Flucht* (Berlin, 1993).

359 *"None of it should remain":* Barth, *Goebbels und die Juden*, pp. 110–17.

359 *"left the population perpetually on edge":* Sopade, *Deutschland-Berichte*, Report for September 1938, pp. 913–32.

360 *to add Israel or Sara to their names:* Friedländer, *Nazi Germany and the Jews*, vol. I, pp. 98–99.

360 *It worked:* Karl Dietrich Bracher, Schulz, and Wolfgang Sauer, *Die nationalsozialistische Machtergreifung*, part I, Bracher, *Stufen der Machtergreifung* (Frankfurt a.M., 1974 ed.), pp. 80–81.

360 *nonetheless to Heydrich and the SD:* Burleigh, *The Third Reich*, pp. 321–32.

361 *"Nobody wants them":* Friedländer, *Nazi Germany and the Jews*, vol. I, p. 94.

361 *"for incompetent party members":* Peter Longerich, *Holocaust: The Nazi Persecution and Murder of the Jews* (Oxford, 2010), p. 109.

362 *"our tragedy and that of the 12,000":* Friedländer, *Nazi Germany and the Jews*, vol. I, p. 268.

362 *"chased like an animal":* Toland, *Adolf Hitler*, p. 502.

362 *"sizzled with white-hot fury"*: Peter Longerich, *Joseph Goebbels. Eine Biographie* (Munich, 2010), p. 394ff; Barth, *Goebbels und die Juden*, p. 132.

363 *action of an enraged nation*: Peter Longerich, *Der ungeschriebene Befehl. Hitler und Weg zur "Endlösung"* (Munich, 2001), p. 61ff; Longerich, *Holocaust*, pp. 109–13.

363 *"difficult diplomatic situation"*: Uwe Dietrich Adam, "Wie Spontan war der Pogrom?," in Walter H. Pehle, ed., *Der Judenpogrom 1938: Von der "Reichskristallnacht" zum Völkermord* (Frankfurt, 1988), pp. 74–80; also Goebbels's diary entry from November 10, 1938, in Goebbels, *Tagebücher*, I. Aufzeichnungnen, 1923–1944, vol. VI, p. 80.

364 *watching but not intervening*: Friedländer, *Nazi Germany and the Jews*, vol I., pp. 277–78.

365 *a train that would take them to Dachau:* Simon Ackermann file, Leo Baeck Institute, New York.

365 *"and had to pay"*: Sally Schlesinger File, Leo Baeck Institute, New York.

366 *in Hitler's good graces:* Reuth, *Goebbels*, pp. 224–25, 239–40; and Longerich, *Joseph Goebbels*, pp. 389–96.

366 *"sixty percent of the population thought like this"*: Report of the mayor, Borgentreich, November 17, 1938, ibid., p. 322.

367 *in the regime's overall Jewish policy:* Longerich, *Holocaust*, pp. 114–17.

367 *"it will have to be tackled"*: Noakes and Pridham, eds., *Nazism*, vol. II, pp. 565–66.

368 *"I would not wish to be a Jew in Germany tonight"*: Friedländer, *Nazi Germany and the Jews*, vol. I, p. 283.

368 *"on the Jewish question to be undertaken"*: Noakes and Pridham, eds., *Nazism*, vol. II, p. 565.

368 *the effects of the Great Depression:* Konrad Kwiet, "Gehen oder Bleiben. Die deutschen Juden am Wendepunkt," in Pehle, ed., *Der Judenpogrom 1938*, pp. 132–45.

368 *"practical purposes been realized"*: Heinz Boberach, ed., *Meldungen aus dem Reich. Die geheimen Lageberichte des Sicherheitsdienstes der SS*, vol. II, Berlin, 1984, pp. 20–21.

368 *"a country without a future"*: Burleigh, *The Third Reich*, p. 316.

Chapter 12: Courting Disaster

370 *"their side to do the same"*: Baynes, ed., *The Speeches of Adolf Hitler*, vol. II, pp. 1049–53.

371 *withdrawal from the League of Nations:* Domarus, ed., *Hitler Speeches*, vol. I, p. 36.

371 *forfeit its strategic advantage:* Hitler's "Proclamation to the German People," October 14, 1933, in Baynes, ed., *The Speeches of Adolf Hitler*, vol. II, p. 1091.

371 *"be so mad as to want a war"*: Domarus, ed., *Hitler Speeches*, vol. II, p. 392.

372 *Hitler gladly endorsed:* Wilhelm Deist, "Die Aufrüstung der Wehrmacht," in Wilhelm Deist et al., *Das Deutsche Reich un der Zweite Weltkrieg*, vol. I (Stuttgart, 1979), pp. 400–409; and Noakes and Pridham, eds., *Nazism*, vol. III, p. 676.

373   *Hitler meanwhile continued:* Domarus, ed., *Hitler Speeches*, vol. II, pp. 613–34.

373   *an immense program of rearmament:* Ian Kershaw, *Hitler, 1936–1945: Nemesis*, vol. II (New York, 2000), p. xxxviii.

373   Lebensraum *in the East:* Domarus, ed., *Hitler Speeches*, vol. I.

374   *"the preservation of peace":* Domarus, ed., *Hitler Speeches*, vol. II, p. 656.

374   *"with such enthusiasm":* Sopade, *Deutschland-Berichte*, 1935, p. 279.

374   *"strengthened its army by 30 percent":* Ibid., pp. 115–17.

377   *The Stresa Front was dead:* Hans-Henning Abendroth, "Deutschlands Rolle im Spanischen Bürgerkrieg," in Manfred Funke, ed., *Hitler, Deutschland und die Mächte* (Düsseldorf, 1978), pp. 471–88; and Hans-Adolf Jacobsen, *Nationalsozialistische Aussenpolitik, 1933–1938* (Frankfurt a.M.), pp. 421–28.

377   *"its creed" was "world revolution":* Baynes, ed., *The Speeches of Adolf Hitler*, vol. II, pp. 1287–88.

378   *and then a withdrawal:* See Kershaw, *Hitler*, vol. I, pp. 587–89. Also Max Braubach, *Der Einmarsch deutscher Truppen in die entmilitarisierte Zone am Rhein im März 1936* (Cologne/Opladen, 1956).

378   *resounded through the crowded chamber:* Baynes, ed., *The Speeches of Adolf Hitler*, vol. II, p. 1297.

379   *"no territorial claims to put forward in Europe":* Ibid., pp. 1298–1300.

380   *"with the assurance of a sleepwalker":* Völkischer Beobachter, March 14, 1936.

380   *could really be true:* For the largely favorable response of American visitors, see Shirer, *Berlin Diary*, pp. 65–66.

381   *"the rulers of Jewish Bolshevism":* Friedländer, *Nazi Germany and the Jews*, vol. I, pp. 180, 184.

381   *Germany's growing global influence:* Jacobsen, *Nationalsozialistische Aussenpolitik*, pp. 424–34.

382   *"even for vital imports":* Shirer, *Berlin Diary*, p. 35.

382   *"offices of the party and state":* Joachim Kuropka, ed., *Meldungen aus Münster, 1924–1944* (Münster, Germany, 1992), pp. 16–162.

383   *other armored vehicles:* Evans, *The Third Reich in Power*, pp. 354–57.

383   *services purchased by the Reich:* Tooze, *The Wages of Destruction*, pp. 206–7.

384   *"a cancerous shadow on our politics":* Goebbels, *Tagebücher, Aufzeichnungen*, vol. 4, November 4, 1937, p. 390.

384   *for the good of the nation:* Tooze, *The Wages of Destruction*, pp. 219–30.

385   *complications for economic planning:* Ibid., pp. 209–11.

385   *"of the preparations being made":* Ibid., pp. 210–13.

385   *were encouraged to do the same:* Goebbels, *Tagebücher, Aufzeichnungen*, vol. 4, pp. 319–23; and Sopade, *Deutschland-Berichte*, 1937, p. 9.

386   *"nourishment for the war psychosis":* Sopade, *Deutschland-Berichte*, vol., 4, See report of February 1937, pp. 9–20.

386   *"I am completely happy":* Goebbels, *Tagebücher, Aufzeichnungen*, vol.3, entry of September 29, 1937.

387   *" 'when and how' ":* Hossbach's firsthand account, referred to historically as the Hossbach Memorandum, is reproduced in Friedrich Hossbach, *Zwischen Wehrmacht und Hitler, 1934–1938* (Göttingen, 1965), pp. 181–89.

389   *"the Führer to reverse a decision":* The Ribbentrop Memoirs, p. 79.

389–90   *was the pistol:* Kershaw, *Hitler*, vol. II, p. 53.

390   *submitted his resignation:* Ibid., pp. 51–53.

391 *Hitler turned to replace Neurath:* Evans, *The Third Reich in Power,* pp. 644–45.

391 *his new foreign minister brilliant:* François-Poncet, *The Fateful Years,* p. 212.

392 *"considers itself a German state":* Kurt Schuschnigg, *Austrian Requiem* (London: G. P. Putnam's Sons, 1947), p. 7.

392 *and skilled workforce into the Four Year Plan:* Tooze, *The Wages of Destruction,* pp. 245–46.

392 *to broach the topic with Schuschnigg:* Papen, *Memoirs,* pp. 406–9.

393 *"Then you'll see something":* Schuschnigg, *Austrian Requiem,* pp. 11–19.

394 *"the Agreement goes into effect":* Ibid., pp. 24–25.

394 *"there was little room for any hope":* Ibid., p. 27.

394 *"to serve the interests of both countries":* Kershaw, *Hitler,* vol. II, p. 72.

395 *"its fate, and its world view":* Domarus, ed., *Hitler Speeches,* vol. II, pp. 1031–32.

396 *" 'What do we get out of it?' ":* Sopade, *Deutschland-Berichte,* March 15, 1938.

396 *"ruthlessness by force of arms":* Domarus, ed., *Hitler Speeches,* vol. II, pp. 1039–49.

397 *the modus operandi of Nazi diplomacy:* Schuschnigg, *Austrian Requiem,* pp. 43, 45–46.

397 *He had spoken for ten minutes:* Ibid., pp. 51–52.

398 *"I believe I have now fulfilled it":* David Faber, *Munich, 1938: Appeasement and World War II* (New York: Simon & Schuster, 2008), pp. 140–42.

399 *"my homeland into the German Reich":* Ibid., pp. 146–47.

399 *colossal building projects in Berlin and Nuremberg:* Jens-Christian Wagner, "Work and Extermination in the Concentration Camps," in Caplan and Wachsmann, eds., *Concentration Camps in Nazi Germany,* pp. 130–31.

400 *The violence of the rampaging Nazi:* Graml, *Antisemitism in the Third Reich,* pp. 135–44.

400 *fluttered from steeple after steeple:* Kershaw, *Hitler,* vol. II, p. 81.

401 *"no war because of Austria":* Sopade, *Deutschland-Bericht,* 1938, pp. 263–64.

403 *"and wear down their power of resistance":* Toland, *Adolf Hitler,* pp. 464–66.

404 *at this point an isolated minority:* Kershaw, *Hitler,* vol. II, pp. 101–4.

405 *the Reich stood on the brink of war:* Domarus, ed., *Hitler Speeches,* vol. II, p. 1124.

405 *deeply ambivalent about Hitler's course of action:* Sopade, *Deutschland-Bericht* 1938, p. 930.

405 *and the offensive was unrelenting:* Shirer, *Berlin Diary,* pp. 126, 134–35.

406 *"German Volksgenossen (people's commander) in Czechoslovakia:* Domarus, ed., *Hitler Speeches,* vol. II, pp. 1158–59.

407 *"matters into my own hands":* Paul Schmidt, *Hitler's Interpreter* (New York, 1950), p. 92.

407 *"when he had given his word":* Ibid., p. 94.

407 *"we found ourselves alone":* Toland, *Adolf Hitler,* p. 478.

408 *"he would intervene at once":* Schmidt, *Hitler's Interpreter,* p. 96.

409 *and the Czechs as "war mongers":* Ibid., pp. 102–3.

409 *"will go get it for ourselves":* Domarus, ed., *Hitler Speeches,* vol. II, pp. 1187–92.

410 *down in his chair thoroughly spent:* Leo Amery, *My Political Life,* vol. III, *The Unforgiving Years, 1929–1940,* p. 276; and Shirer, *Berlin Diary,* p. 142.

410 *"by next Monday we will all be at war":* Faber, *Munich, 1938,* pp. 370–71.

411 *"are dead set against war":* Shirer, *Berlin Diary,* September 27, 1938; and Faber, *Munich, 1938,* p. 380.

411 *"in a war on her account"*: Faber, *Munich, 1938*, p. 378.

412 *clouded by his "blind hatred against England"*: Goebbels, *Tagebücher*, September 29, 1938, 6, Teil I, p. 119.

413 *a "hugger-bugger affair"*: Faber, *Munich, 1938*, p. 405.

414 *"and we were allowed to go"*: Ibid., pp. 412–13.

415 *"means peace in our time"*: Schmidt, *Hitler's Interpreter*, p. 112.

415 *"and Daladier, outside their hotels"*: Ibid., pp. 113–14.

417 *"things cannot go on like this"*: Domarus, ed., *Hitler Speeches*, vol. 2, Hitler comments November 19, 1938, pp. 1245–46.

Chapter 13: Early Success

420 *". . . recognize your common enemy!"*: Baynes, ed., *Speeches of Adolf Hitler*, vol. II, pp. 740–41.

420 *"the annihilation of the Jewish race in Europe"*: Domarus, ed., *Hitler Speeches*, vol. III, p. 1449.

420 *"The day of reckoning has come"*: Toland, *Adolf Hitler*, p. 510.

423 *"I shall go down in history as the greatest German"*: Ibid., pp. 516–17; and Bullock, *Hitler*, pp. 430–31.

424 *"war is inevitable"*: Sopade, *Deutschland-Berichte*, 1939, p. 284.

425 *"all support in their power"*: Bullock, *Hitler*, p. 444.

425 *to isolate Poland diplomatically*: Jeremy Noakes and Geoffrey Pridham, eds., *Nazism, 1919–1945*, vol. III, *Foreign Policy, War and Racial Extermination* (Exeter, 1988), pp. 735–36.

426 *"two fully equipped divisions in the field?"*: Domarus, ed., *Hitler Speeches*, vol. III, p. 1555.

426 *was widely viewed as already allied with Great Britain*: Friedländer, *Nazi Germany and the Jews*, p. 128; Goebbels quoted in Jeffrey Herf, *The Jewish Enemy: Nazi Propaganda During World War II and the Holocaust* (Cambridge, MA, 2006), p. 54.

426 *composed by the "charlatan from Washington"*: Goebbels, *Tagebücher*, 6, I, April 17 and 18, 1939, p. 319. The text of Roosevelt's letter is found in Domarus, *Hitler Speeches*, vol. III, pp. 1548–50.

427 *and he renounced that as well*: Domarus, ed., *Hitler Speeches*, vol. III, pp. 1574–75.

428 *It was a bravura performance*: See Shirer's firsthand account of the scene in the Reichstag, Shirer, *Berlin Diary*, pp. 165–67.

428 *"what a dwarf is a man like Roosevelt"*: Goebbels, *Tagebücher*, 6, I, April 19, 1939, p. 332.

428 *Its purpose was to intimidate the West*: Text in Domarus, ed., *Hitler Speeches*, vol. III, pp. 1612–15.

429 *"not to be for 80,000,000 people"*: Hitler's remarks, in Noakes and Pridham, eds., *Nazism*, vol. 3, pp. 736–38.

431 *" 'I've got them! I've got them' "*: Speer, *Inside the Third Reich*, p. 223.

432 *"Pursuit until complete annihilation"*: Norman Rich, *Hitler's War Aims* (New York, 1978), vol. I, p. 129.

433 *translated into a military alliance*: Christopher Thorne, *The Approach of War, 1938–39* (New York, 1967).

433 *the Corridor must be resolved without delay*: Schmidt, *Hitler's Interpreter*, pp. 141–45.

434 *to work for moderation in Warsaw*: Ibid., p. 144.

434 *made a sustained military effort impossible:* Ibid., pp. 145–46.

435 *"a calamity without parallel in history":* Ibid., pp. 145–46, 148.

435 *"for the sake of one city":* Sopade, *Deutschland-Bericht 1939*, pp. 190–92.

435 *The Poles must accept this condition:* Toland, *Adolf Hitler*, pp. 562–63; and Nevile Henderson, *The Failure of a Mission* (London, 1944).

436 *They were prepared to fight:* Toland, *Adolf Hitler*, pp. 563, 566–67.

436 *"I had done everything to maintain peace":* Schmidt, *Hitler's Interpreter*, pp. 154–55.

436 *reinforcing the Führer's gambling instincts:* Kershaw, *Hitler*, vol. II, pp. 90–91.

437 *a completely abnormal person:* Bullock, *A Study in Tyranny*, p. 487.

437 *" 'Idiots, have I ever told a lie in my life?' ":* Domarus, ed., *Hitler Speeches*, vol. III, pp. 1700–1707.

438 *self-defense against a rapacious Poland:* Toland, *Adolf Hitler*, pp. 566–67.

438 *"with a population so dead set against it":* Shirer, *Berlin Diary*, p. 191.

439 *"never be another November 1918 in German history":* The full text of Hitler's speech is found in Domarus, ed., *Hitler Speeches*, vol. III, pp. 1750–56.

440 *"exist between Great Britain and Germany":* Schmidt, *Hitler's Interpreter*, pp. 156–57.

440 *He was correct:* Ibid., pp. 156–58.

440 *"I saw them at Munich":* David Faber, *Munich, 1938: Appeasement and World War II* (New York, 2010).

441 *in both the East and West:* See François-Poncet, *The Fateful Years*, pp. 175–76.

441 *It was a rout:* Richard J. Evans, *The Third Reich at War* (New York, 2009), pp. 4–5.

441 *executed and deposited in mass graves:* Mazower, *Hitler's Empire: How the Nazis Ruled Europe* (New York, 2008), pp. 100–101; and Timothy Snyder, *Bloodlands: Europe Between Hitler and Stalin* (New York, 2008), pp. 287, 298.

441 *and 130,000 wounded:* Evans, *The Third Reich at War*, p. 7.

442 *"win the* Lebensraum *we need":* Max Hastings, *Inferno: The World at War, 1939–1945* (New York, 2012), p. 18.

442 *"Final Solution" to the "Jewish problem" in Europe:* Longerich, *Holocaust*, pp. 134–47.

442–43 *with a German governor:* After the invasion of the Soviet Union, the frontiers of the General Government were extended to include Radom and Galicia.

443 *roughly half were murdered by the militias:* Evans, *The Third Reich at War*, pp. 14–15.

443 *murdered nearly 200 people:* Snyder, *Bloodlands*, pp. 126–27.

444 *to compose the country's intelligentsia:* Mazower, *Hitler's Empire*, 78–79.

444 *settlers imported from the Baltic:* Ibid., pp. 92–93.

445 *murdered 560 Jews in the vicinity:* Snyder, *Bloodlands*, p. 67.

445 *beyond the providence of local army commanders:* Ibid., p. 70.

445–46 *"a one year prison sentence":* The Halder War Diary, 1939–1942, eds. Charles Burdick and Hans-Adolf Jacobsen (Presidio, CA, 1988), September 10, 1939, pp. 52–53.

446 *"how such things can go unpunished":* General Alexander Ulex, infantry general, quoted in Graml, *Antisemitism in the Third Reich*, p. 158; Blaskowitz, quoted p. 159.

446 *civilians while trudging eastward:* Mazower, *Hitler's Empire*, pp. 68–69.

446 *the ideologically trained SS:* Saul Friedländer, *Nazi Germany and the Jews*, vol. II, *The Years of Extermination, 1939–1945* (New York, 2008), pp. 26–27; Martin Broszat, *Nationalsozialistische Polenpolitik, 1939–1945* (Stuttgart, 1961), pp. 19–20.

447 *photographs and sent them home:* Friedländer, *Nazi Germany and the Jews,* vol. II, pp. 27–28.

447 "judenrein" *(free of Jews):* Graml, *Antisemitism in the Third Reich,* pp. 152–54.

Chapter 14: Hitler Turns West

452 *would be a catastrophe:* Ernest R. May, *Strange Victory: Hitler's Conquest of France* (New York, 2000), p. 22.

452 *"ground forces cannot be expected":* Franz Halder, *Kriegstagebuch,* vol. I, p. 118.

453 *"He would have them shot":* Ibid., p. 78.

453 *an immediate attack in the West:* May, *Strange Victory,* p. 222.

453 *nothing came of their plans:* Peter Hoffmann, *Widerstand, Staatsstreich, Attentat,* pp. 74–130; and May, *Strange Victory,* pp. 217–28.

454 *static warfare of the Great War:* May, *Strange Victory,* pp. 216–17.

455 *reinforcements and defeated:* See Erich von Manstein, *Lost Victories* (Presidio, 1958, 1985 edition), pp. 94–126.

456 *"wishes me to attain my goals":* Domarus, ed., *Hitler Speeches,* vol. III, p. 1876.

456 *"when we have won":* Hitler address, November 23, 1939, in ibid., p. 1887.

457 *commenced immediately:* Tooze, *The Wages of Destruction,* pp. 381–85.

458 *ports of Calais, Bolougne, and Dunkirk: The Halder War Diary,* May 17–18, 1940, pp. 147–51.

459 *The Germans readily accepted:* Evans, *The Third Reich at War,* pp. 127–31.

460 *"in the twenty-two years hence":* Shirer, *Berlin Diary,* pp. 422–23.

460 *He would never see Paris again:* Speer, *Inside the Third Reich,* pp. 236–37.

460 *"France's gravediggers":* Herf, *The Jewish Enemy,* p. 68.

461 *still mired in the mud of the Great War:* May, *Strange Victory,* pp. 256.

461 *"the greatest and most glorious victory of all time":* Domarus, ed., *Hitler Speeches,* vol. III, p. 2042.

462 *"except when he gave his word":* John Wheeler-Bennett, *The Nemesis of Power: The German Army and Politics 1918–1945* (London, 1954), p. 461.

462 *"He wants to keep on fighting alone":* Goebbels, *Tagebücher,* June 19, 1940, pp. 180–81.

463 *"and stockjobbers" wanted this war:* Domarus, ed., *Hitler Speeches,* vol. III, p. 2062.

463 *"state of war against Germany":* Domarus, ed., *Hitler Speeches,* vol. II, July 16, 1937.

463 *"and the democracies and plutocracies":* Herf, *The Jewish Enemy,* p. 60.

463 *"what the German people want":* Goebbels quoted in Ibid., pp. 66, 70.

464 *out in front of Hitler and the Nazi leadership:* See John Lukacs, *The Duel: The Eighty-Day Struggle Between Hitler and Churchill* (New York, 1991), pp. 173–76.

464 *"unwilling to 'choose the way to peace' ": The Halder War Diary,* July 13, p. 227.

464 *for an invasion of Britain:* Evans, *The Third Reich at War,* pp. 139–45.

465 *subdue the Royal Air Force in five weeks:* Kershaw, *Hitler,* vol. II, pp. 309–10.

465 *underestimated their importance:* Williamson Murray, *Luftwaffe* (Baltimore: National Nautical & Aviation Publishing Co. of America), p. 52. For more on the course of the Battle of Britain and the ensuing Blitz, see Richard Overy, *The Air War, 1939–1945* (Stein & Day, 1980), pp. 30–37.

Chapter 15: The Crusade Against Judeo-Bolshevism

470 *White Russia, and the Baltic States: The Halder War Diary*, July 31, 1940, p. 244ff.

471 *no better in the spring:* Ibid., December 5, 1940, p. 297.

471 *"Russian tanks are poorly armored":* Ibid. Also *Das Deutsche Reich und der Zweite Weltkrieg*, vol. 4, *Der Angriff auf die Sowjetunion*, pp. 191–202.

471 *"will come crashing down":* Alan Clark, *Barbarossa: The Russian-German Conflict, 1941–1945* (New York, 1965), p. 43.

472 *the Führer had other ideas:* Walter Warlimont, *Inside Hitler's Headquarters, 1939–45* (Novato, CA), p. 138.

472 *"of no great importance":* The Halder War Diary, December 5, 1940, pp. 293–94.

472 *understood the thrust of his remarks:* Brauchitsch instructed army commanders that "the troops must be clear that the struggle will be carried out from race to race (*von Rasse zu Rasse*) and proceed with necessary severity." Ibid., March 30, 1941, p. 346.

473 *to operate from the same script:* Helmut Krausnick, "Kommisarbefehl und 'Gerichtsbarkeiterlass Barbarossa' in neuer Sicht," in *Vierteljahreshefte zur Zeitgeschichte*, 2 (1977), p. 628ff.

473 *told a very different story:* In the autumn of 1939 Soviet forces under General Georgy Zhukov soundly defeated the Japanese in a major tank battle that ended Japanese ambitions in the north.

474 *every fifth man in the Army:* Heinz Guderian, *Panzer Leader* (New York, 1996), p. 151.

474 *"The world," Hitler said, "will hold its breath":* Anthony Beevor, *Stalingrad: The Fateful Siege, 1942–1943* (New York, 1998), p. 12.

475 *what it needed as it moved along:* Evans, *The Third Reich at War*, pp. 324–25.

475 *"many of them Jews, would starve":* Götz Aly and Susanne Heim, *Architects of Annihilation: Auschwitz and the Logic of Destruction* (Princeton, 2002), pp. 234–42; Longerich, *Holocaust*, p. 181.

476 *"also Muscovite nationalism, of their centers":* The Halder War Diary, July 8, 1941, p. 458.

476 *had attacked Western Europe in the summer of 1940:* Gerhard Weinberg, *A World at Arms: A Global History World War II* (Cambridge, UK, 1994), pp. 193–94.

477 *"I am going to see the Marx Brothers":* Toland, *Adolf Hitler*, pp. 659–66.

478 *the solitary inmate in Germany's Spandau Prison, in 1987:* Kershaw, *Hitler*, vol. II, pp. 338–69.

478 *heard throughout the Berghof:* Speer, *Inside the Third Reich*, p. 239.

478 *"Hitler," Goebbels recorded in his diary, "is completely shaken":* Goebbels, *Tagebücher, Aufzeichnungen, Teil 1*, May 14, 1941, p. 640.

478 *"be the second man after the Führer":* Goebbels, *Tagebücher, Aufzeichnungen, Teil I*, May 1, 1941, pp. 640–41.

479 *"to be disposed of by arms":* English translation in Lucy S. Dawidowicz, *The War Against the Jews, 1933–1945* (seventh edition, New York, 1981), p. 165. See also Friedländer, *Nazi Germany and the Jews*, vol. II, pp. 134–35.

479 *"every active or passive resistance":* Dawidowicz, *The War Against the Jews*, p. 166.

480 *"just atonement on Jewish subhumanity"*: Quoted in Dawidowicz, *The War Against the Jews*, pp. 164, 166, 167.

481 *the Einsatzgruppen on the ground*: Longerich, *Holocaust*, pp. 221–23; Hermann Graml, "Hitler und die Befehle an die Einsatzgruppen im Sommer 1941," in Eberhard Jäckel und Jürgen Rohwer, *Der Mord an die Juden im Zweiten Weltkrieg. Entschlussbildung und Verwirklichung* (Stuttgart, 1985), p. 88ff. Also Graml, *Antisemitism in the Third Reich*, p. 169.

481 *in intensity as the war progressed*: Jürgen Förster, "The German Army and the Ideological War Against the Soviet Union," in Gerhard Hirschfeld, ed., *The Policies of Genocide: Jews and Soviet Prisoners of War in Nazi Germany* (London, 1986), pp. 15–29; Longerich, *Holocaust*, pp. 196–205.

482 *"for many more weeks to come"*: *The Halder War Diary*, July 3, 1941, pp. 446–47.

483 *claimed 95,000 victims by December 1*: Graml, *Antisemitism in the Third Reich*, pp. 170–71.

484 *were shot in a single day*: Noakes and Pridham, eds., *Nazism*, vol. III, pp. 1098–99.

485 *already descending into the pit*: Ibid., pp. 1100–101.

485 *murder of 700,000 Jews*: Raul Hilberg, *The Destruction of the European Jews* (New York, 1985), pp. 108–9.

485 *"in another killing operation"*: OKWA Wehrwirtschaftsund Rüstungsamt Stab 1a Tridrnrtivhy über Besuch im Abschnitt der Heeresgruppe Mitte, July 21, 1941, in Kulka and Jäckel, *Die Juden in den geheimen NS-Stimmungsberichten, 1933–1945*, p. 451.

486 *with which he had been involved*: Hilberg, *The Destruction of the European Jews*, pp. 131–33.

486 *across German-occupied Eastern Europe*: Noakes and Pridham, eds., *Nazism*, vol. III, p. 1138.

486 *not informed about the casualties*: Gestapo report, June 26, 1941, in H. Boberach, *Meldungen aus dem Reich*, vol. 7, p. 2044.

487 *"and thirdly exploit it"*: Kershaw, *Hitler*, vol. II, p. 405.

487 *a German "garden of Eden"*: Hitler monologue, July 27, 1941, in *Hitler's Table Talk*, pp. 15–16.

488 *German empire into the future*: Mazower, *Hitler's Empire*, pp. 204–11.

489 *but to Himmler's SS*: Kershaw, *Hitler*, vol. II, pp. 406–7.

489 *spoke openly about it with foreign statesmen*: Friedländer, *Nazi Germany and the Jews*, vol. II, pp. 272–82.

489 *Jewish plutocrats and Bolsheviks who controlled both*: Herf, *The Jewish Enemy*, pp. 97–99.

490 *whose jurisdiction would be affected*: Friedländer, *Nazi Germany and the Jews*, vol. II, pp. 237–38; Mazower, *Hitler's Empire*, pp. 80–81; and Robert Gerwarth, *Hitler's Hangman: The Life of Heydrich* (New Haven, 2011), pp. 197–98.

491 *"German space by the end of the year"*: Gerwarth, *Hitler's Hangman*, pp. 204–5.

492 *all of whom were doomed to a short hopeless future*: Moorehouse, *Berlin at War*, pp. 162–65.

492 *marched into nearby woods and shot*: Friedländer, *Nazi Germany and the Jews*, vol. II, pp. 266–67.

493 *"clusters of sparse trees stretching to the horizon"*: Gottlob Herbert

Bidermann, *In Deadly Combat: A German Soldier's Memoir of the Eastern Front* (Lawrence, KS, 2000), pp. 13–18.

494 *"horse drawn equipment reminiscent of World War I"*: Ibid., p. 15.

494 *their primary operational objectives:* Omer Bartov, *Hitler's Army: Soldiers, Nazis and War in the Third Reich* (New York, 1991), p. 36. See also Catherine Merridale, *Ivan's War: Life and Death in the Red Army, 1939–1945* (New York, 2006).

494 *dangers lurked everywhere around them:* Kenneth Slepyan, *Stalin's Guerrillas: Soviet Partisans in World War II* (Lawrence, KS, 2006), especially pp. 15–59.

495 *"wounded men caught in the flames":* Clark, *Barbarossa*, pp. 138–39.

495 *"anyone who doesn't give us a straight look":* Friedländer, *Nazi Germany and the Jews*, vol. II, p. 200.

495 *"the greatest field commander of all times":* Beevor, *Stalingrad*, pp. 28–29.

496 *"put a damper on all higher headquarters":* The Halder War Diary, July 20, 1941, p. 482.

496 *"the Russians simply put up another dozen":* Ibid., August 11, 1941, p. 506.

496 *overall manpower of 3,200,000:* Bartov, *Hitler's Army*, pp. 37, 38, 43–44.

496 *"will not be available to us again":* The Halder War Diary, November 23, 1941, p. 562.

496 *"demolished in fourteen days":* Friedländer, *Nazi Germany and the Jews*, vol. II, p. 267.

497 *"a scourge which will eventually be intolerable":* Warlimont, *Inside Hitler's Headquarters*, p. 183.

497 *a distant third in Hitler's thinking:* Guderian, *Panzer Leader*, pp. 189–90.

497 *"the absurdity of Hitler's orders":* Warlimont, *Inside Hitler's Headquarters*, p. 185.

497 *"zigzag course caused by his successive orders":* The Halder War Diary, August 22, 1941, p. 515.

498 *"You can't deny that":* Warlimont, *Inside Hitler's Headquarters*, p. 189.

498 *operational by the late fall:* Overy, *The Air War*, pp. 49–51.

498 *"have suffered heavy losses":* The Halder War Diary, August 10, p. 505.

498 *"distant end is not yet in view":* Gestapo report of August 31, 1941, in Boberach, ed., *Meldungen aus dem Reich*, vol. 11, p. 4146.

499 *more than were lost to combat wounds:* Beevor, *Stalingrad*, p. 40.

499 *bombing of western German cities:* Gestapo report of January 5, 1942, in Boberach, ed., *Meldungen aus dem Reich*, vol. 9, p. 3120.

499 *highest rate coming among junior combat officers:* The Halder War Diary, pp. 38–39.

500 *"discussion was out of the question":* H. R. Trevor-Roper, *The Last Days of Hitler*, fourth edition, New York, 1962, p. 72.

500 *more serious than officially communicated:* Gestapo report of January 5, 1942, in Boberach, ed., *Meldungen aus dem Reich*, vol. 9, pp. 3120–21.

500 *delusional imagination was doomed to failure:* Manstein, *Lost Victories*, pp. 276–77.

501 *and the Soviet Union—were saved: Das Deutsche Reich und der Zweite Weltkrieg*, vol. 4, pp. 600–605; Beevor, *Stalingrad*, pp. 42–43.

501 *"has never been conquered in 3,000 years":* Kershaw, *Hitler*, vol. II, p. 442.

Chapter 16: Holocaust and Total War

505 *"as free of Jews as the Reich is"*: Noakes and Pridham, eds., *Nazism*, vol. III, pp. 1126–27.

506 *had been settled in only ninety minutes*: Longerich, *Holocaust*, pp. 305–10.

506 *got under way almost immediately*: Ibid., p. 313ff.

507 *a Star of David had been installed on the roof*: Noakes and Pridham, eds., *Nazism*, vol. III, pp. 1146–47.

508 *"only the occasional head or arms stick out"*: Kurt Gerstein quoted in Noakes and Pridham, eds., *Nazism*, vol. III, pp. 1151–53.

508 *the largest murder campaign of the Holocaust*: Saul Friedländer, *Nazi Germany and the Jews 1939–1945: The Years of Extermination* (New York, 2007), pp. 479–80. By December 1942, 1,274,166 Jews had perished in the camps of Operation Reinhard.

509 *"as much between individuals as between peoples"*: *Hitler's Table Talk*, January 27, 1942, evening, p. 260.

509 *"only by eliminating the Jews"*: Ibid., February 22, 1942, evening, p. 332.

509 *"unswerving champion and spokesman of a radical solution"*: Louis P. Lochner, ed., *The Goebbels Diaries, 1942–1943* (New York, 1948), March 27, 1942, pp. 147–48.

510 *"the most elementary principles of National Socialism"*: Reports of SD *Aussenstelle* Minden, December 6 and 12, 1941, in Kulka and Jäckel, eds., *Die Juden in den geheimen NS-Stimmungsberichte 1933–1945*, pp. 476–77; and Report of the Stapostelle Bremen, November 11, 1941, in ibid., p. 471.

511 *only two and one third million*: Longerich, *Joseph Goebbels*, pp. 541–42.

511 *The Jews, Goebbels claimed, were behind the attack*: Evans, *The Third Reich at War*, pp. 275–80.

512 *strategy of area bombing*: Max Hastings, *Bomber Command* (London, 1980), pp. 1–34.

512 *devastation and industrial man-hours lost*: Tami Davis Biddle, *Rhetoric and Reality in Air Warfare*, pp. 200–201.

513 *"to destroy one industrial city after another"*: Gestapo report of July 27, 1942, in Boberach, *Meldungen aus dem Reich*, vol. 11, p. 4006.

514 *"attrition whose distant end is not yet in view"*: Gestapo report of August 31, 1942, in Boberach, ed., *Meldungen aus dem Reich*, vol. 11, p. 4146.

515 *even the sober Halder agreed*: Clark, *Barbarossa*, p. 209.

515 *forces moving south across the Don*: After the war General Kleist claimed that "the Fourth Panzer Army . . . could have taken Stalingrad without a fight at the end of July but was diverted to help me in crossing the Don. I did not need its aid, and it simply got in the way and congested the roads that I was using." Clark, *Barbarossa*, p. 209.

516 *" 'All of us feel that the end, victory, is near' "*: Ibid., p. 21.

516 *"That's what the Russians need, to stop them resisting"*: Ibid., p. 218.

517 *"the desire for an end to the war soon"*: Gestapo report, September 3, 1942, in Boberach, ed., *Meldungen aus dem Reich*, vol. 11, p. 4164.

517 *"only a few very small places left not captured"*: Noakes and Pridham, eds., *Nazism*, vol. III, p. 842.

518 *for Hitler's ambitions in the East*: Beevor, *Stalingrad*, p. 398.

520 *"rise up, and storm burst forth!"*: W. A. Boelcke, ed., *Wollt Ihr Den Totalen Krieg? Die geheimen Goebbels-Konferenzen, 1939–1943* (Munich, 1969).

520 *"of the Columbus House they would have done it"*: Toland, *Adolf Hitler*, p. 735.

520   *the regime was ebbing away:* Kershaw, *The "Hitler Myth,"* pp. 192–98.

521   *the people's faith in the regime was badly shaken:* Ibid., pp. 180–89.

521   *the Führer and his people began to loosen:* Ibid., pp. 169–99.

522   *the shrunken, blackened corpse of her child:* Richard Overy, *The Bombers and the Bombed: Allied Air War over Europe, 1940–1945* (New York, 2014), pp. 259–62; and especially Hans Nossack, *The End: Hamburg, 1943* (Chicago, 2004).

522   *never "straighten all that out again":* Speer, *Inside the Third Reich,* p. 370; see Overy, *The Bombers and the Bombed,* pp. 144–48.

523   *"the Jews will destroy the German people":* Rudolf Höss, quoted in Pridham and Noakes, eds., *Nazism,* vol. III, pp. 1175–76.

524   *a smoothly functioning European-wide industrial operation:* Graml, *Antisemitism in the Third Reich,* pp. 181–83.

526   *"has never been written and can never be written":* Noakes and Pridham, eds., *Nazism,* vol. III, p. 1199.

527   *Untermenschen (subhumans) all:* See Longerich, *The Holocaust;* Friedländer, *Nazi Germany and the Jews,* vol. II; Hilberg, *The Destruction of the European Jews;* and Yehuda Bauer, *A History of the Holocaust* (New York, 1982).

527   *"in undisputed possession of the initiative":* Guderian, *Panzer Leader,* p. 312.

Chapter 17: Apocalypse

529   *weighed heavily on the home front:* Gestapo report, March 16, 1944, in Boberach, ed., *Meldungen aus dem Reich,* vol. 16, p. 6412.

529   *"to strengthen the defenses in the West":* Reprinted in Warlimont, *Inside Hitler's Headquarters,* p. 400.

531   *only Hitler could release them:* Ibid., pp. 408–9.

531   *somewhere between the Scheldt and the Seine:* Ibid., pp. 434–37; Weinberg, *A World at Arms,* pp. 681, 684–85.

531   *was staggering, on the cusp of defeat:* Weinberg, *A World at Arms,* pp. 700–702; and Cornelius Ryan, *A Bridge Too Far* (New York, 1974).

532   *not in the end political in nature:* See Arno Klönne, "Jugendprotest und Jugendopposition. Von der HJ-Erziehung zum Cliquenwesen der Kriegszeit," in Broszat, Fröhlich, and Grossmann, *Bayern in der NS-Zeit,* pp. 589–620; and Detlev Peukert, *Inside Nazi Germany: Conformity, Opposition, and Racism in Everyday Life* (New Haven, 1989).

532   *paranoia flourished:* Ian Kershaw, *The End: The Defiance and Destruction of Hitler's Germany, 1944–1945* (New York: Penguin, 2011), pp. 207–46.

533   *one step ahead of the Gestapo:* See Shareen Brysac, *Resisting Hitler: Mildred Fish-Harnack and the Red Orchestra* (Oxford, 2000); Anne Nelson, *Red Orchestra: The Story of the Berlin Underground and the Circle of Friends who Resisted Hitler* (New York, 2009); and Peter Hoffmann, *The History of the German Resistance, 1933–1945* (Toronto, 1996).

533   *were arrested and sent to Dachau:* Regierungsbericht, Munich, June 7, 1944, in BHSTA, MA 106 695.

534   *"the National Socialist Party and its dictatorship":* Toby Axelrod, *Hans and Sophie Scholl: German Resisters of the White Rose* (New York, 2001); and Ulrich Chaussey and Franz Josef Miller, eds., *The White Rose: The Resistance by Students Against Hitler, 1942/43* (Munich, 1991).

535 *"Manifesto of the Munich Students"*: See Ulrich Chaussy and Gerd R. Ueber-schär, eds., *"Es lebe die Freiheit!," Die Geschichte der Weissen Rose und ihrer Mitglieder in Dokumente und Berichten* (Munich: Fischer Verlag, 2013).

535 *could convince the Führer to step aside:* For an analysis of the various plans for a post-Hitler government, see Hans Mommsen, "The Social Views and Constitutional Plans of the Resistance," in Hermann Graml et al., *The German Resistance to Hitler* (London, 1967), pp. 55–147.

536 *Hitler and his regime must go:* Peter Hoffmann, *The History of the German Resistance, 1933–1945* (MIT Press, 1977), and Peter Hoffmann, *The German Resistance to Hitler* (Cambridge, MA: Harvard University Press, 1988).

537 *participants in the plot to kill the Führer:* Thomas Childers, "The Kreisau Circle and the Twentieth of July," in David Large, ed., *Killing Hitler* (Cambridge, UK), pp. 104–17.

538 *would support it at the appropriate time:* Hoffmann, *The History of the German Resistance*; see also his *Stauffenberg* (Toronto, 2008).

538 *Again he carried a bomb:* For the most detailed account of the plot and Stauffenberg's role in it, see Peter Hoffmann, *Widerstand, Staatsstreich, Attentat* (Munich, 1970).

540 *about Freisler's outrageous conduct:* Evans, *The Third Reich at War*, p. 643; Kershaw, *Hitler*, vol. II, pp. 691–93.

540 *"we would have won long ago"*: Ibid., p. 687.

541 *He chose suicide:* Ibid., p. 733.

542 *"nothing else matters"*: Evans, *The Third Reich at War*, p. 638.

542 *touted as the "Speer miracle"*: Richard Bessell, *Nazism and War* (London, 2004), pp. 127–29. See also Richard Overy, *War and Economy in the Third Reich* (New York, 1994), pp. 268–71.

542 *Hitler favorite, became a public darling:* Tooze, *The Wages of Destruction*, pp. 552–89.

543 *total munitions production fell by 55 percent:* United States Strategic Bombing Survey, *The Effects of Strategic Bombing on the German War Economy*, vol. VI, p. 143; Anthony Beevor, *The Fall of Berlin 1945* (New York, 2002), p. 162.

543 *was literally running on empty:* United States Strategic Bombing Survey, *The Effects of Strategic Bombing on the German War Economy*, vol. VI, p. 12.

543 *assembly areas or soldiers at the front:* See Alfred C. Mierzejewski, *The Collapse of the German War Economy, 1944–1945: Allied Air Power and the German National Railway* (Chapel Hill: University of North Carolina Press, 1988), pp. 124–76.

543 *in January 1945, to 28,000 in March:* United States Strategic Bombing Survey, *The Effects of Strategic Bombing on the German War Economy*, vol. X, p. 127.

543 *"break in Germany's war morale"*: Goebbels, *Tagebücher*, March 22, 1945, vol. 15, Part II, p. 569.

544 *people whispered in scorn:* Kershaw, *The Hitler Myth: Image and Reality in the Third Reich* (Oxford, 1987), pp. 169–99.

545 *impede the Allied advance in the West:* United States Strategic Bombing Survey, *The Effects of Strategic Bombing on German Morale*, vol. II, pp. 44–45.

545 *it was simply too late:* Report of the Regierungspräsident, December 11, 1944, BHSTA, MA 106 696.

545 *"delivered over to the whims of the enemy"*: Gestapo report, July 14, 1944, in Boberach, ed., *Meldungen aus dem Reich*, vol. 17, pp. 6650–51.

545 *that fear had become a grim reality:* Report of the Regierungspräsident München-Oberbayern, December 7, 1944, and Regensburg, March 10, 1945, both in BHSTA, MA 106 695 and MA 106 696.

546 *"has increasingly come in for criticism":* District report for Regensburg, March 10, 1945, BHSTA MA 106 696. See a similar report for München-Oberbayern, November 8, 1944, BHSTA MA, 106 695.

546 *" 'but* in spite of *National Socialism' ":* United States Strategic Bombing Survey, *The Effects of Strategic Bombing on German Morale,* vol. I, p. 51.

546 *"Hitler to thank for all this misery":* Schedule B Interviews, Numbers 61294 and 61154, National Archives, RG 23.

546 *to keep weary Germans at their jobs:* United States Strategic Bombing Survey, *The Effects of Strategic Bombing on German Morale,* vol. I, pp. 14–15.

547 *"to get a little food cooked":* Schedule B, Interview Number 61890k, NARA, USSB, RG 23.

547 *"Bleib übrig!" (Survive!):* Beevor, *The Fall of Berlin 1945,* p. 2.

547 *They were overruled by Hitler:* Weinberg, *A World at Arms,* pp. 765–71.

548 *At Malmedy that distinction was erased:* Gerald F. Linderman, *The World Within War: America's Combat Experience in World War II* (New York, 1997), pp. 135–36.

548 *the last desperate gasp of the Third Reich:* Evans, *The Third Reich at War,* pp. 657–58; see also Anthony Beevor, *The Ardennes 1944: The Battle of the Bulge* (New York, 2015).

548 *by the failure of the Ardennes offensive:* Nicolaus von Below, *Als Hitlers Adjutant, 1937–1945* (Frankfurt, 1980), p. 398.

549 *"it was a burning corpse":* Klemperer, *I Will Bear Witness,* vol. II, pp. 409–10.

550 *"were little more than roaming death squads":* Stephen G. Fritz, *Endkampf: Soldiers, Civilians and the Death of the Third Reich* (Lexington, KY, 2004), pp. 190–91.

551 *"Many consider the war already lost":* Report of the Regierungspräsident Regensburg, February 9, 1945, BHSTA, BA-MA.

551 *"undermining military operations":* Fritz, *Endkampf,* pp. 117, 191.

551 *would be ruthlessly "exterminated":* "Für Freiheit und Ehre," Fritz Wächter, *Gauleiter,* in *Regensburger Kurier. Amtliche Tageszeitung des Gaues Bayreuth der NSDAP,* February 6, 1945.

552 *were from* Volkssturm *personnel:* Fritz, *Endkampf,* p. 191.

552 *"hesitation in carrying out this action":* Childers, " 'Facilis descensus averni est.' The Bombing of Germany and Issue of German Suffering," *Central European History,* vol. 38, no. 1, 2005, pp. 75–105.

552 *villages from needless destruction:* For the uprisings in Ochsenfurt and Bad Windsheim and the role of women in those events, see Fritz, *Endkampf,* pp. 120, 142.

553 *Not a shot was fired:* This account is taken largely from Ruckdeschel's postwar trial in Adelheid L. Rüter-Ehlermann, C. F. Rütter, et al., eds., *Justiz und NS-Verbrechen: Sammlung deutscher Strafurteile wegen nationalsozialistischer Tötungsverbrechen, 1945–1966* (Amsterdam and Munich, 1968–1998), pp. 236–51. Also see Hildebrand Troll, "Aktionen zur Kriegsbeendigung im Frühjahr 1945," in Martin Broszat, Elke Fröhlich, and Anton Grossmann, eds., *Bayern in der NS Zeit. Herrschaft und Gesellschaft im Konflikt,* vol. IV (Munich, 1981), pp. 645–84; and Kershaw, *The End,* pp. 324–26.

553 *It was a moment of high symbolism:* Fritz, *Endkampf,* pp. 174–75.

554 *then the giant camp at Bergen-Belsen in Germany:* Longerich, *Holocaust,* pp. 410–16.

554 *"death marches" from concentration camps, large and small:* Kershaw, *The End,* pp. 331–36.

555 *repeating in sheer disbelief, "Frei? Frei?":* Colonel Donald Downard, quoted in Sam Dann, ed., *Dachau, 29 April 1945: The Rainbow Liberation Memoirs* (Lubbock, TX, 1998), p. 74.

557 *Guderian was sacked in March:* Guderian, *Panzer Leader,* pp. 412–14.

557 *"April will be the turning point for us":* The Grand Alliance did not collapse, as Hitler predicted it would, but this is what passed for good news in the *Führerbunker* in April 1945. Toland, *Adolf Hitler,* pp. 860–61.

558 *Time was running out:* Beevor, *The Fall of Berlin, 1945.*

559 *frivolity seemed out of place under the circumstances:* Traudl Junge, *Bis zur letzten Stunde. Hitlers Sekretärin erzählt ihr Leben* (Munich, 2002), p. 177.

560 *"the mission I set for the nation":* Toland, *Adolf Hitler,* p. 870.

561 *"I called it the Isle of the Departed":* Speer, *Inside the Third Reich,* p. 598.

561 *if he had no future, neither did they:* Ibid., p. 800ff.

562 *"empty, burned out, lifeless":* Ibid., pp. 605–6.

562 *whose grip on reality was tenuous:* Toland, *Adolf Hitler.*

562 *"to end their lives at this historic site":* Speer, *Inside the Third Reich,* p. 607.

564 *his pistol lay at his feet:* There are many accounts of these last few hours of Hitler's life. I have drawn on Junge, *Bis zur letzten Stunde,* pp. 165–206; Kershaw, *Hitler,* vol. II, pp. 827–28; Toland, *Adolf Hitler,* pp. 881–91; and still very useful, Trevor-Roper's *The Last Days of Hitler,* pp. 255–89.

565 *a world without Hitler, without National Socialism:* Junge, *Bis zur letzten Stunde,* p. 193.

565 *10,000 of whom died, mostly by suicide:* Anonymous, *A Woman in Berlin: Eight Weeks in the Conquered City* (New York, 2005); and Beevor, *The Fall of Berlin 1945,* p. 326ff.

BIBLIOGRAPHY

Books and Journal Articles

Abel, Theodore. *Why Hitler Came into Power*. Cambridge, MA, 1938, 1986.

Adam, Uwe. *Judenpolitik im Dritten Reich*. Düsseldorf, Germany, 1972.

Allen, William Sheridan. *The Nazi Seizure of Power*. Chicago, 1965.

Aly, Götz, and Susanne Heim. *Architects of Annihilation: Auschwitz and the Logic of Destruction*. Translated by Allan Blunden. Princeton, NJ, 2002.

Amery, L. S. *My Political Life: The Unforgiving Years, 1929–1940*, vol. III. London, 1955.

Angress, Werner T. "The German Army's 'Judenzählung' of 1916: Genesis – Consequences – Significance." *Leo Baeck Yearbook* 23 (1978), pp. 117–38.

Anonymous. *A Woman in Berlin: Eight Weeks in the Conquered City, A Diary*. New York, 2005.

Axelrod, Toby. *Hans and Sophie Scholl: German Resisters of the White Rose*. New York, 2001.

Baird, Jay W. *To Die for Germany: Heroes in the Nazi Pantheon*. Bloomington, IN, 1992.

Bankier, David. *The Germans and the Final Solution: Public Opinion Under the Nazis*. Oxford, UK, 1992.

Baranowski, Shelley. *The Confessing Church, Conservative Elite, and the Nazi State*. Lewiston/Queenston, NY, 1986.

Barnett, Victoria. *For the Soul of the People: Protestant Protest Against Hitler*. New York, 1992.

Barth, Christian. *Goebbels und die Juden*. Paderborn, Germany, 2003.

Bartov, Omer. *Germany's War and the Holocaust: Disputed Histories*. Ithaca, NY, 2003.

———. *Hitler's Army: Soldiers, Nazis, and War in the Third Reich*. New York, 1991.

Bauer, Yehuda. *A History of the Holocaust*. New York, 1982.

Baynes, Norman H., ed. *Speeches of Adolf Hitler*. New York, 2006.

Beevor, Anthony. *Ardennes 1944: The Battle of the Bulge*. New York, 2015.

———. *The Fall of Berlin 1945*. New York, 2003.

———. *Stalingrad: The Fateful Siege, 1942–1943*. New York, 1999.

von Below, Nicolaus. *Als Hitlers Adjutant, 1937–1945*. Frankfurt, Germany, 1980.

Benz, Wolfgang, Hermann Graml, and Hermann Weiss, eds. *Enzyklopädie des Nationalsozialismus*. Munich, Germany, 2007.

Bergen, Doris L. *Twisted Cross: The German Christian Movement in the Third Reich*. Chapel Hill, NC, 1996.

Bessel, Richard. *Nazism and War*. London, 2004.

———. *Political Violence and the Rise of Nazism: The Storm Troopers in Eastern Germany, 1925–1934*. New Haven, CT, 1984.

———. "Violence as Propaganda: The Role of the Storm Troopers in the Rise of National Socialism." In Thomas Childers, ed., *The Formation of the Nazi Constituency*. London, 1986, pp. 131–46.

Biddle, Tami Davis. *Rhetoric and Reality in Air Warfare*. Princeton, NJ, 2002.

Bidermann, Gottlob Herbert. *In Deadly Combat: A German Soldier's Memoir of the Eastern Front*. Translated and edited by Derek S. Zumbro. Lawrence, KS, 2000, pp. 13–18.

Bloch, Eduard. "My Patient Hitler." *Collier's Weekly*, March 15–22, 1941.

Boberach, Heinz, ed. *Meldungen aus dem Reich: Die geheimen Lageberichte des Sicherheitsdienstes der SS, 1938–1945*, 17 vols. Herrsching, Germany, 1984.

Bock, Gisela. *Zwangssterilisation im Nationalsozialismus*. Opladen, Germany, 1986.

Boelcke, Willi A., ed. *Wollt Ihr den totalen Krieg?: Die geheimen Goebbels-Konferenzen 1939–1943*. Munich, Germany, 1969.

Boog, Horst, Jürgen Föster, Joachim Hoffmann, Ernst Klink, Rolf-Dieter Müller, and Gerd R. Ueberschär, eds. *Das Deutsche Reich und der Zweite Weltkrieg: Der Angriff auf die Sowjetunion*, vol. 4. Stuttgart, Germany, 1983.

Bracher, Karl Dietrich. *Die Auflösung der Weimarer Republik: Eine Studie zum Problem des Machtverfalls in der Demokratie*. Düsseldorf, Germany, 1978.

———. *Die nationalsozialistische Machtergreifung: Stufen der Machtergreifung*. Cologne and Opladen, Germany, 1962.

Braubach, Max. *Der Einmarsch deutscher Truppen in die entmilitarisierte Zone am Rhein im März 1936*. Cologne, Germany, 1956.

Bridenthal, Renate, Atina Grossmann, and Marion Kaplan, eds. *When Biology Became Destiny: Women in Weimar and Nazi Germany*. New York, 1984.

Broszat, Martin, Elke Fröhlich, and Anton Grossmann, eds. *Bayern in der NS Zeit: Herrschaft und Gesellschaft im Konflik*, vol. IV. Munich, Germany, 1981.

———. *Der Staat Hitlers: Grundlegung und Entwicklung seiner inneren Verfassung*. Munich, Germany, 1969.

———. *Nationalsozialistische Polenpolitik, 1939–1945*. Stuttgart, Germany, 1961.

———, ed. *Studien zur Geschichte der Konzentrationslager*. Stuttgart, Germany, 1970.

Brysac, Shareen Blair. *Resisting Hitler: Mildred Harnack and the Red Orchestra*. New York, 2000.

Buchheim, Hans, Martin Broszat, Hans-Adolf Jacobsen, and Helmut Krausnick. *Anatomie des SS-Staates*, 2 vols. Munich, Germany, 1967.

Bullock, Alan. *Hitler: A Study in Tyranny*. New York, 1953.

Burdick, Charles, and Hans-Adolf Jacobsen, eds. *The Halder War Diary, 1939–1942*. Novato, CA, 1988.

Burleigh, Michael. *Death and Deliverance: Euthanasia in Germany 1900–1945*. New York, 1994.

———. *The Third Reich: A New History*. New York, 2000.

Burleigh, Michael, and Wolfgang Wippermann. *The Racial State, 1933–1945.* Cambridge, UK, 1991.

Caplan, Jane. *Government Without Administration.* New York, 1988.

Caplan, Jane, ed. *Nazi Germany.* Oxford, UK, 2008.

Caplan, Jane, and Nikolaus Wachsmann, eds. *Concentration Camps in Nazi Germany: The New Histories.* New York, 2010.

Chaussy, Ulrich, and Franz Josef Miller, eds. *The White Rose: The Resistance by Students Against Hitler, 1942–1943.* Munich, Germany, 1991.

Childers, Thomas. "Inflation, Stablization, and Political Realignment in Germany, 1924–1928." In Gerald D. Feldman, Carl-Ludwig Holtfrerich, Gerhard A. Ritter, and Peter Christian Witt, eds., *Die Deutsche Inflation: Eine Zwischenbilanz.* Berlin, 1982, pp. 409–31.

———. "Interest and Ideology: Anti-System Politics in the Era of Stabilization, 1924–1928." In Gerald D. Feldman, ed., *Die Nachwirkung der Inflation auf die deutsche Geschichte, 1924–1933.* Munich, 1985, pp. 1–20.

———. "The Limits of National Socialist Mobilization: The Elections of 6 November 1932 and Fragmentation of the Nazi Constituency." In Thomas Childers, ed., *The Formation of the Nazi Constituency, 1919–1933.* London, 1986.

———. "The Middle Classes and National Socialism." In David Blackbourn and Richard Evans, eds., *The German Bourgeoisie: Essays on the Social History of the German Middle Class from the Late Eighteenth to the Early Twentieth Century.* London, 1991, pp. 318–37.

———. *The Nazi Voter: The Social Foundations of Fascism, 1919–1933.* Chapel Hill, NC, 1983.

Childers, Thomas, ed. *The Formation of the Nazi Constituency.* London, 1986.

Childers, Thomas, and Jane Caplan, eds. *Reevaluating the Third Reich.* New York, 1993.

Childers, Thomas, and Eugene Weiss. "Voters and Violence: Political Violence and the Limits of National Socialist Mass Mobilization." *German Studies Review* XIII, no. 3 (1990): pp. 481–98.

Ciolek-Kümper, Jutta. *Wahlkampf in Lippe: die Wahlkampfpropaganda der NSDAP zur Landtagswahl am 15. Januar 1933.* Munich, Germany, 1976.

Clark, Alan. *Barbarossa: The Russian-German Conflict, 1941–1945.* New York, 1965.

Conway, J. S. *The Nazi Persecution of the Churches 1933–1945.* London, 1968.

Dahlerus, Birger. *Der letzte Versuch, London-Berlin, Sommer 1939.* Munich, Germany, 1948.

Dawidowicz, Lucy S. *The War Against the Jews, 1933–1945.* 7th ed. New York, 1981.

Deist, Wilhelm, ed. *The German Military in the Age of Total War.* Worcester, UK, 1985.

Deist, Wilhelm, Manfred Messerschmidt, Hans-Erich Volkmann, and Wolffram Wette, eds. *Das Deutsche Reich und der Zweite Weltkrieg: Ursachen und Voraussetzungen der deutschen Kriegspolitik,* vol. 1. Stuttgart, Germany, 1979.

Delmer, Sefton. *Trail Sinister,* vol. I. London, 1961.

Deuerlein, Ernst. *Der Aufstieg der NSDAP 1919–1933 in Augenzeugenberichten.* Düsseldorf, Germany, 1968.

Das Deutsche Reich und der Zweite Weltkrieg: Ursachen und Voraussetzungen der deutschen Kriegspolitik, vol. 1. Stuttgart, Germany, 1979.

Deutschland-Berichte der Sozialdemokratischen Partei Deutschlands, 1934–1940. 7 vols. Frankfurt, Germany, 1980.

Diehl, James. *Parliamentary Politics in the Weimar Republic.* Bloomington, IN, 1977.

Diels, Rudolf. *Lucifer ante Portas.* Stuttgart, Germany, 1950.

Dietrich, Otto. *Mit Hitler in die Macht. Persönliche Erlebnisse mit meinem Führer.* Munich, Germany, 1934.

Domarus, Max, ed. *Hitler: Reden und Proklamationen, 1932–1945.* Wiesbaden, Germany, 1973. English: *Speeches and Proclamations, 1932–1945: The Chronicle of a Dictatorship,* 4 vols. Wauconda, IL, 1990.

Dov Kulka, Otto, and Eberhard Jäckel, eds. *Die Juden in den geheimen NS Stimmungsberichten, 1933–1945.* Düsseldorf, Germany, 2004.

Echternkamp, Jörg, ed. *Das Deutsche Reich und der Zweite Weltkrieg: Die Deutsche Kriegsgesellschaft, 1939–1945, Politisierung, Vernichtung, Überleben,* vol. 9/1. Munich, Germany, 2004.

The Effects of Strategic Bombing on the German War Economy, 2 vols. United States Strategic Bombing Survey, Overall Economic Effects Division. Washington, DC, 1945.

Essner, Cornelia. *Die "Nürnberger Gesetze" oder die Verwaltung des Rassenwahns, 1933–1945.* Paderborn, Germany, 2002.

Evans, Richard J. *The Coming of the Third Reich.* New York, 2004.

———. *The Third Reich at War.* New York, 2009.

———. *The Third Reich in Power.* New York, 2008.

Evans, Richard J., and David Blackborn, eds. *The German Middle Class.*

Faber, David. *Munich, 1938: Appeasement and World War II.* New York, 2008.

Falter, Jürgen W. *Hitlers Wähler.* Munich, Germany, 1991.

Faust, Anselm. *Der Nationalsozialistische Deutsche Studentenbund: Studenten und Nationalsozialismus in der Weimarer Republik,* 2 vols. Düsseldorf, Germany, 1973.

Feldman, Gerald D. *The Great Disorder: Politics, Economics, and Society in the German Inflation, 1914–1924.* New York, 1993.

Fest, Joachim E. *The Face of the Third Reich: Portraits of the Nazi Leadership.* New York, 1999.

———. *Hitler: Eine Biographie.* Frankfurt, Germany, 2000.

Fings, Karola. "The Public Face of the Camps." In Jane Caplan and Nikolaus Wachsmann, eds., *Concentration Camps in Nazi Germany.* New York, 2010, pp. 108–26.

Fischer, Conan. *Stormtroopers: A Social, Economic and Ideological Analysis, 1929–1935.* London, 1983.

Fischer, Klaus P. *Nazi Germany: A New History.* New York, 1995.

Fleming, Gerald. *Hitler and the Final Solution.* Oxford, UK, 1986.

Förster, Jürgen. *Der Angriff auf die Soviet Union.* Stuttgart, Germany, 1983.

———. "Operation Barbarossa as a War of Conquest and Annihilation." In Horst Boog et al., eds., *Germany and the Second World War: The Attack on the Soviet Union,* vol. 4. Oxford, UK, 1998.

François-Poncet, André. *The Fateful Years: Memoirs of a French Ambassador in Berlin 1931–1938.* New York, 1972.

Frank, Hans. *Im Angesicht des Galgens. Deutung Hitlers und seiner Zeit auf Grund eigener Erlebnisse und Erkenntnisse.* Munich, Germany, 1953.

Franz-Willig, Georg. *Die Hitlerbewegung Der Ursprung, 1919–1922*. 2nd ed. Hamburg, Germany, 1962.

———. *Kreisenjahr der Hitlerbewegung 1923*. Preussisch Oldendorf, Germany, 1975.

———. *The Origins of Nazi Genocide: From Euthanasia to the Final Solution*. Chapel Hill, NC, 1995.

Frevert, Ute. *Women in German History: From Bourgeois Emancipation to Sexual Liberation*. New York, 1989.

Friedländer, Saul. *Nazi Germany and the Jews: The Years of Persecution, 1933–1939*, vol. I. New York, 1997.

———. *Nazi Germany and the Jews: The Years of Extermination, 1939–1945*, vol. II. New York, 2008.

Fritz, Stephen G. *Endkampf: Soldiers, Civilians, and the Death of the Third Reich*. Lexington, KY, 2004.

Fritzsche, Peter. *Life and Death in the Third Reich*. Cambridge, MA, 2008.

———. *Rehearsals for Fascism: Populism and Political Mobilization in Weimar Germany*. New York and Oxford, 1990.

Fröhlich, Elke, ed. *Die Tagebücher von Joseph Goebbels. Aufzeichnungen 1923–1941, Teil I., Band 2/II, Juni 1931–September 1932*. Munich, Germany, 2004.

———. *Die Tagebücher von Joseph Goebbels. Sämtliche Fragmente, Teil I, Aufzeichnungen 1924–1941, Band 2*. Munich, Germany, 1987.

Frommann, Eberhard. *Die Lieder der NS-Zeit. Untersuchungen zur nationalsozialistischen Liedpropaganda von den Anfängen bis zum Zweiten Weltkrieg*. Cologne, Germany, 1999.

Funke, Manfred, ed. *Hitler, Deutschland und die Mächte. Materialien zur Ausspolitik des Dritten Reiches*. Düsseldorf, Germany, 1978.

Gamm, Hans-Jochen. *Der Flüsterwitz im Dritten Reich: Mündliche Dokumente zur Lage der Deutschen während des Nationalsozialismus*. Munich, Germany, 1990.

Gay, Peter. *Weimar Culture: The Outsider as Insider*. New York, 1968.

Gellately, Robert. *Backing Hitler: Consent and Coercion in Nazi Germany*. Oxford, UK, 2001.

———. *The Gestapo and German Society: Enforcing Racial Policy, 1933–1945*. Oxford, UK, 1990.

———. "The Gestapo and German Society: Political Denunciation in the Gestapo Case Files." *The Journal of Modern History* 60, no. 4 (1988): 654–94.

Gerwath, Robert. *Hitler's Hangman: The Life of Heydrich*. New Haven, CT, 2011.

Geyer, Michael. *Aufrüstung oder Sicherheit. Die Reichswehr in der Krise der Machtpolitik, 1924–1936*. Wiesbaden, Germany, 1980.

Glanz, David. *Colossus Reborn: The Red Army, 1941–1943*. Lawrence, KS, 2005.

Goebbels, Joseph. "Neue Methoden der Propaganda." *Nationalsozialistische Briefe*, August 15, 1926.

———. "Das patriotische Bürgertum." *Nationalsozialistische Monatshefte*, Heft 5 (1930).

———. *Tagebücher 1924–1945. Die letzten Aufzeichnungen*. Hamburg, Germany, 1977.

———. *Vom Kaiserhof zum Reichskanzlei*. Berlin, 1934.

Gordon, Harold J., Jr. *Hitler and the Beer Hall Putsch*. Princeton, NJ, 1962.

Görtemaker, Heike B. *Eva Braun: Life with Hitler.* Translated by Damion Searls. New York, 2011.

Graml, Hermann. *Antisemitism in the Third Reich.* Translated by Tim Kirk. London, 1992.

Graml, Hermann, et al. *The German Resistance to Hitler.* London, 1967.

Gritschneder, Otto. *Bewährungsfrist für den Terroristen Adolf H. Der Hitler-Putsch und die bayerische Justiz.* Munich, Germany, 1990.

Grunberger, Richard. *The 12-Year Reich: A Social History of the Third Reich, 1933–1945.* New York, 1987.

Guderian, Heinz. *Panzer Leader.* New York, 1996.

Haarmann, Hermann, Walter Huder, and Klaus Siebenhaar, eds. *Bücherverbrennung Deutschland 1933: Voraussetzungen und Folgen.* Berlin and Vienna, 1983.

Hale, Oron J. *The Captive Press in the Third Reich.* Princeton, NJ, 1964.

Hamann, Brigitte. *Hitlers Edeljude. Das Leben des Armenarztes Eduard Bloch.* Munich, Germany, 2008.

———. *Hitlers Wien. Lehrjahre eines Diktators.* Munich, Germany, 1997.

Hamilton, Richard F. *Who Voted for Hitler?* Princeton, NJ, 1982.

Hanfstaengl, Ernst. *Hitler: The Memoir of a Nazi Insider Who Turned Against the Führer.* New York, 1957.

———. *Zwischen Weissem Haus und Braunem Haus,* 2nd ed. Munich, Germany, 1970.

Hänisch, Reinhold. "I Was Hitler's Buddy." Series. *The New Republic,* April 5–12, 1939, pp. 193–99, 239, 270–72, 297–300.

Hastings, Max. *Armageddon: The Battle for Germany, 1944–1945.* New York, 2005.

———. *Bomber Command.* London, 1986.

———. *Industry and Ideology: IG Farben in the Nazi Era.* Cambridge, UK, 1987.

———. *Inferno: The World at War, 1939–1945.* New York, 2012.

Hayes, Peter. "Auschwitz, Capital of the Holocaust." *Holocaust and Genocide Studies* 17, no. 2 (2003).

Hayman, Ronald. *Hitler & Geli.* London, 1998.

Heiden, Konrad. *Der Fuehrer: Hitler's Rise to Power.* Boston, 1944.

Heinemann, Manfred. *Erziehung und Schulung im Dritten Reich, Teil 2, Hochschulen, Erwachsenbildung.* Stuttgart, Germany, 1980.

Henderson, Sir Nevile. *Failure of a Mission: Berlin, 1937–1939.* London, 1940.

Herf, Jeffrey. *The Jewish Enemy: Nazi Propaganda During World War II and the Holocaust.* Cambridge, MA, 2006.

Herzog, Rudolf. *Dead Funny: Humor in Hitler's Germany.* Translated by Jefferson Chase. Melville House reprint, New York, 2011.

Hett, Benjamin Carter. *Burning the Reichstag: An Investigation into the Third Reich's Enduring Mystery.* New York, 2014.

Hilberg, Raul. *The Destruction of the European Jews.* New York, 1985.

Hildebrand, Klaus. *The Foreign Policy of the Third Reich.* London, 1973.

Hillenbrand, F. K. M. *Underground Humor in Nazi Germany 1933–1945.* Abingdon, UK, 1995.

Hillgruber, Andreas. *Hitlers Strategie, Politik und Kriegsführung, 1940–1941.* Bonn, Germany, 1993 edition.

Hirschfeld, Gerhard. *The Policies of Genocide: Jews and Soviet Prisoners of War in Nazi Germany.* London, 1986.

Hitler, Adolf. *Der Hitler Prozess 1934. Wortlaut der Hauptverhandlungen vor dem Volksgericht München I, Teil 4*. Munich, Germany, 1997.

———. *Hitler. Reden, Schriften, Anordnungen*. Februar 1925 bis Januar 1933, vol. V. Von der Reichspräsidentenwahl bis zur Machtergreifung April 1932–Januar 1933. Teil 2: Oktober 1932–Januar 1933.

———. *Hitlers Politisches Testament: Die Bormann Diktate vom Februar und April 1945*. Hamburg, 1981.

———. *Mein Kampf*. Munich, Germany, 1927, 1929; New York, 1971 edition.

Hoess, Rudolf. *Commandant at Auschwitz*. London, 1959.

Hofer, Walther. *Die Entfesselung des Zweiten Weltkrieges*. Frankfurt, Germany, 1964.

Hoffmann, Peter. *The History of the German Resistance, 1933–1945*. Cambridge, MA, 1977.

———. *Stauffenberg: A Family History, 1905–1944*. Toronto, Canada, 2008.

———. *Widerstand, Staatsstreich, Attentat*. Munich, Germany, 1970.

Höhne, Hans. *The Order of the Death's Head: The Story of Hitler's SS*. London, 1969.

Holtfrerich, Carl-Ludwig. *Die Deutsche Inflation, 1914–1923*. Berlin, 1980.

Horn, Wolfgang. *Der Marsch zur Machtergreifung. Die NSDAP bis 1933*. Düsseldorf, Germany, 1980.

Hossbach, Friedrich. *Zwischen Wehrmacht und Hitler, 1934–1938*. Wolfenbüttel/Hanover, Germany, 1949.

Isherwood, Christopher. *The Berlin Stories*. New York, 2008 edition (1935).

Jäckel, Eberhard, ed. *Hitler: Sämtliche Aufzeichnungen, 1905–1924*. Stuttgart, Germany, 1980.

Jacobsen, Hans-Adolf. *Fall Gelb: Der Kampf um den deutschen Operationsplan zur Wesoffensive 1940*. Wiesbaden, Germany, 1957.

———. *Nationalsozialistische Aussenpolitik, 1933–1938*. Frankfurt, Germany, 1968.

Jacobsen, Hans-Adolf, and Werner Jochmann, eds. *Ausgewählte Dokumente zur Geschichte des Nationalsozialismus 1933–1945*. Bielefeld, Germany, 1961.

James, Harold. *The German Slump: Politics and Economics, 1924–1936*. Oxford, 1986.

Janka, Franz. *Die braune Gesellschaft: Ein Volk wird Formatiert*. Stuttgart, Germany, 1997.

Jelavich, Peter. *Berlin Cabaret*. Cambridge, MA, 1993.

Jetzinger, Franz. *Hitler Jugend*. Vienna, 1956.

Johnson, Eric A. *Nazi Terror: The Gestapo, Jews, and Ordinary Germans*. New York, 1999.

Jones, Larry Eugene. *German Liberalism and the Dissolution of the Weimar Party System*. Chapel Hill, NC, 1988.

Junge, Traudl. *Bis zur letzten Stunde: Hitlers Sekretärin erzählt ihr Leben*. Munich, Germany, 2002.

Justiz und NA-Verbrechen, Sammlung deutscher Strafurteil wegen nationalsozialistischer Tötungsverbrechen, 1945–1966, 20 vols. Amsterdam, 1979.

Kaplan, Marion. *Between Dignity and Despair: Jewish Life in Nazi Germany*. New York, 1998.

———. *Hitler Youth*. Cambridge, MA, 1999.

———. *The Nazi Party: A Social Profile of Members and Leaders, 1919–1945*. Cambridge, MA, 1983.

Karina, Lilian, and Marion Kant. *Tanz Unterm Hakenkreuz: Eine Dokumentation.* Berlin, 1999.

Kater, Michael H. *Doctors Under Hitler.* Chapel Hill, NC, 1989.

Kershaw, Ian. *The End: The Defiance and Destruction of Hitler's Germany, 1944–1945.* New York, 2011.

———. *Hitler: A Biography.* New York, 1998.

———. *Hitler, 1889–1936: Hubris,* vol. I. New York, 1998.

———. *The Hitler Myth: Image and Reality in the Third Reich.* Oxford, UK, 1987.

———. *Hitler, 1939–1945: Nemesis,* vol. II. New York, 2000.

———. *Popular Opinion and Political Dissent in the Third Reich: Bavaria, 1933–1945.* Oxford, UK, 1983.

Klee, Ernst, ed. *Dokumente zur "Euthanasie."* Frankfurt, Germany, 1985.

Klee, Ernst. *"Euthanasie" im NS-Staat: Die "Vernichtung lebensunwerten Lebens."* Frankfurt, Germany, 1983.

von Klemperer, Klemens. *German Resistance Against Hitler: The Search for Allies Abroad, 1938–1945.* Oxford, UK, 1992.

Klemperer, Viktor. *I Will Bear Witness: A Diary of the Nazi Years, 1933–1941,* 2 vols. Translated by Martin Chalmers. New York, 1998.

Klose, W. *Generation im Gleichschritt.* Oldenburg, Germany, 1964.

Knickerbocker, H. R. *Is Tomorrow Hitler's?* New York, 1941.

Koch, H. W. *The Hitler Youth: Origins and Development, 1922–1945.* New York, 1975.

König, Wolfgang. *Volkswagen, Volksempfänger, Volksgemeinschaft.* Munich, Germany, 2004.

Koonz, Claudia. *Mothers in the Fatherland, Women, the Family, and Nazi Politics.* New York, 1987.

———. *The Nazi Conscience.* Cambridge, MA, 2003.

Koshar, Rudy D. *Social Life, Local Politics, and Nazism: Marburg, 1880–1935.* Chapel Hill, NC, 1986.

Kubizek, August. *The Young Hitler I Knew.* Introduction by Ian Kershaw, 3rd ed. Translated by Lionel Leventhal. New York, 2006.

Kuropka, Joachim. *Meldungen aus Münster, 1924–1944.* Münster, Germany, 1992.

Laqueur, Walter. *Weimar: A Cultural History.* New York, 1974.

Large, David Clay, ed. *Contending with Hitler: Varieties of German Resistance in the Third Reich.* Cambridge, UK, 1991.

———. *Where Ghosts Walked: Munich's Road to the Third Reich.* New York, 1997.

Larson, Erik. *In the Garden of Beasts: Love, Terror, and an American Family in Hitler's Berlin.* New York, 2011.

Lewy, Guenter. *The Catholic Church and Nazi Germany.* New York, 1964.

Linderman, Gerald F. *The World Within War: America's Combat Experience in World War II.* New York, 1997.

Lochner, Louis P., ed. and trans. *The Goebbels Diaries, 1942–1943.* New York, 1948.

Longerich, Peter. *Der ungeschriebene Befehl: Hitler und der Weg zur "Endlösung."* Munich, Germany, 2001.

———. *Die braunen Bataillone: Geschichte der SA.* Munich, Germany, 1989.

———. *Goebbels: Biographie.* Munich, Germany, 2010.

———. *Heinrich Himmler.* New York, 2012.

————. *Holocaust: The Nazi Persecution and Murder of the Jews.* New York, 2010.

————. *The Unwritten Order: Hitler's Role in the Final Solution.* Charleston, SC, 2001.

Lubrich, Oliver. *Reisen ins Reich, 1933–1945.* Frankfurt, Germany, 2004.

Ludecke, Kurt. *I Knew Hitler.* New York, 1937.

Lukacs, John. *The Duel: The Eighty-Day Struggle Between Hitler and Churchill.* New York, 1991.

Lurker, Otto. *Hitler hinter Festungsmauern.* Berlin, 1933.

Mandell, Richard D. *The Nazi Olympics.* London, 1972.

von Manstein, Erich. *Lost Victories.* American edition, Novato, CA, 1985.

Maser, Werner. *Hermann Göring: Hitlers janusköpfiger Paladin. Die politische Biographie.* Berlin, 2000.

————. *Hitler's Mein Kampf: An Analysis.* London, 1970.

Mason, Tim W. *Arbeiterklasse und Volksgemeinschaft.* Opladen, Germany, 1975.

May, Ernest R. *Strange Victory: Hitler's Conquest of France.* New York, 2000.

Mayer, Arno. *Why Did the Heavens Not Darken?: The "Final Solution" in History.* New York, 1988.

Mayer, Milton. *They Thought They Were Free: The Germans, 1933–45.* Chicago, 1955.

Mazower, Mark. *Hitler's Empire: How the Nazis Ruled Europe.* New York, 2008.

Meinshausen, Hans. *Erziehung zum Dritten Reich. Reden und Aufsätze.* Berlin, 1934.

Meissner, Otto. *Staatssekretär unter Ebert, Hindenburg, und Hitler: Der Schicksals-weg des deutschen Volkes, 1918–1945.* Hamburg, Germany, 1950.

Merkl, Peter. *Political Violence Under the Swastika: 581 Early Nazis.* Princeton, NJ, 1975.

Merridale, Catherine. *Ivan's War: Life and Death in the Red Army, 1939–1945.* New York, 2006.

Metcalfe, Philip. *1933.* New York, 1988.

Michaud, Eric. *The Cult of Art in Nazi Germany.* Translated by Janet Lloyd. Palo Alto, CA, 2004.

Middlebrook, Martin. *The Battle of Hamburg: Allied Bomber Forces Against a German City in 1943.* New York, 1981.

Mierzejewski, Alfred C. *The Collapse of the German War Economy, 1944–1945: Allied Air Power and the German National Railway.* Chapel Hill, NC, 1988.

Moltmann, Günter. "Goebbels Speech on Total War, February 18, 1943." In Hajo Holborn, ed., *Republic to Reich: The Making of the Nazi Revolution.* New York, 1973, pp. 298–342.

————. *The Rise and Fall of Weimar Democracy.* Chapel Hill, NC, 1996.

Mommsen, Hans. "Die Realisierung des Utopischen: Die 'Endlösung der Judenfrage im Dritten Reich.'" *Geschichte und Gesellschaft* 9 (1983), pp. 381–420.

————. "Van der Lubbe und sein Weg in den Reichstag—der Ablauf der Ereignisse." In Uwe Beckes et al., eds., *Reichstagsbrand. Aufklärung einer historischen Legende.* Munich, Germany, 1986.

Mosse, George L. *Nazi Culture: Intellectual, Cultural and Social Life in the Third Reich.* New York, 1966.

Murray, Williamson. *Luftwaffe,* 2nd ed. Baltimore, 1989.

Noakes, Jeremy. *The Nazi Party in Lower Saxony, 1921–1933.* Oxford, UK, 1971.

Noakes, Jeremy, and Geoffrey Pridham, eds. *Nazism, 1919–1945: The Rise to Power, 1919–1933,* vol. I. Exeter, UK, 1983.

———. *Nazism, 1919–1945: State, Economy and Society, 1933–1939*, vol. II. Exeter, UK, 1984.

———. *Nazism, 1919–1945: Foreign Policy, War and Racial Extermination*, vol. III. Exeter, UK, 1988.

Nossack, Hans Erich. *The End: Hamburg 1943*. Translated by Joel Agee. Chicago, 2004.

Orlow, Dietrich. *The History of the Nazi Party*. Pittsburgh, PA, 1973.

Overy, Richard. *The Air War, 1939–1945*. New York, 1980.

———. *The Bombers and the Bombed: Allied Air War over Europe, 1940–1945*. New York, 2014.

———. *The Nazi Economic Recovery, 1993–1938*. London, 1982.

———. *War and Economy in the Third Reich*. New York, 1994.

von Papen, Franz. *Memoirs*. Translated by Brian Connell. London, 1952.

Patch, William L., Jr. *Heinrich Brüning and the Dissolution of the Weimar Republic*. Cambridge, UK, 1998.

Paul, Gerhard. *Aufstand der Bilder. Die NS-Propaganda vor 1933*. Bonn, Germany, 1990.

Petropoulos, Jonathan. *Art as Politics in the Third Reich*. Chapel Hill, NC, 1996.

Petzold, Joachim. *Franz von Papen: Ein Deutsches Verhängnis*. Munich, Germany, 1995.

Peukert, Detlev. *Die Edelweisspiraten: Protestbewegungen jugendlicher Arbeiter im Dritten Reich eine Dokumentation*. Cologne, Germany, 1983.

———. "The Genesis of the 'Final Solution' from the Spirit of Science." In Thomas Childers and Jane Caplan, eds., *Reevaluating the Third Reich*. New York, 1993.

———. *Inside Nazi Germany: Conformity, Opposition, and Racism in Everyday Life*. Translated by Richard Deveson. New Haven, CT, 1987.

Proctor, Robert N. *The Nazi War on Cancer*. Princeton, NJ, 1999.

———. *Racial Hygiene: Medicine Under the Nazis*. Cambridge, MA, 1988.

Rabinbach, Anson, and Sander L. Gilman, eds. *The Third Reich Sourcebook*. Berkeley, CA, 2013.

Reichert, J. W., ed. *Helferrichs Reichstagsreden, 1922–1924*. Berlin, 1925.

Remak, Joachim, ed. *The Nazi Years*. New York, 1969.

Rempel, Gerhard. *Hitler's Children: The Hitler Youth and the SS*. Chapel Hill, NC, 1989.

Reuth, Ralf Georg. *Goebbels*. San Diego, 1990.

von Ribbentrop, Joachim. *The Ribbentrop Memoirs*. London, 1954.

Rich, Norman. *Hitler's War Aims: Ideology, the Nazi State, and the Course of Expansion*, vol. 1. New York, 1973.

Richarz, Monika, ed. *Judisches Leben in Deutschland, Bd. 3. Selbstzeugnisse zur Sozialgeschichte, 1918–1945*. Stuttgart, Germany, 1982.

Ringer, Fritz, ed. *The German Inflation of 1923*. London, 1969.

Röhm, Ernst. *Die Geschichte eines Hochverräters*. Munich, Germany, 1978.

———. *Die Memoiren des Stabschef Röhm*. Saarbrücken, Germany, 1934.

Rothfels, Hans. *The German Opposition to Hitler: An Assessment*. London, 1970.

Ryan, Cornelius. *A Bridge Too Far: The Classic History of the Greatest Battle of World War II*. New York, 1974.

———. *The Last Battle*. New York, 1966.

———. *The Longest Day*. New York, 1960.

Schacht, Hjalmar. *Abrechnung mit Hitler*. Berlin, 1949.

Schenck, Ernst Günther. *Patient Hitler: Eine Medizinisch Biographie.* Düsseldorf, Germany, 1989.

von Schlabrendorff, Fabian. *Offiziere gegen Hitler.* Berlin, 1946; 2nd ed., 1984.

Schleunes, Karl A. *The Twisted Road to Auschwitz: Nazi Policy Toward German Jews, 1933–1939.* Urbana, IL, 1970.

Schmeer, Karlheinz. *Die Regie des öffentlichen Lebens im Dritten Reich.* Munich, Germany, 1956.

Schmidt, Paul. *Hitler's Interpreter.* New York, 1951.

Schmitthenner, Walter, and Hans Buchheim, eds. *Der Deutsche Widerstand. Vier historisch-kritische Studien von Hermann Graml, Hans Mommsen, Hans-Joachim Reichhardt und Ernst Wolf.* Cologne, Germany, 1966.

Schoenbaum, David. *Hitler's Social Revolution: Class and Status in Nazi Germany, 1933–1939.* New York, 1966.

Scholder, Klaus. *Die Kirchen und das Dritte Reich. Vorgeschichte und Zeit der Illusionen,* vol. 1. Frankfurt, Germany, 1977.

Schorske, Carl E. *Fin-de-Siècle Vienna.* New York, 1979.

Schuschnigg, Kurt. *Austrian Requiem.* London, 1947.

Segel, Binjamin W. *A Lie and a Libel: The History of the Protocols of the Elders of Zion.* Translated and edited by Richard S. Levy. Lincoln, NE, 1995.

Shirer, William L. *Berlin Diary, 1934–1941.* New York, 1941.

———. *The Rise and Fall of the Third Reich.* New York, 1966.

———. *This Is Berlin: Reporting from Nazi Germany, 1938–40.* London, 1999.

Smelser, Ronald. *Robert Ley: Hitler's Labor Front Leader.* New York, 1988.

Smith, Bradley F. *Adolf Hitler: His Family, Childhood, and Youth.* Palo Alto, CA, 1967.

Sneeringer, Julia. *Winning Women's Votes: Propaganda and Politics in Weimar Germany.* Chapel Hill, NC, 2002.

Snyder, Timothy. *Bloodlands: Europe Between Hitler and Stalin.* New York, 2008.

Speer, Albert. *Inside the Third Reich.* New York, 1970.

Spotts, Frederic. *Hitler and the Power of Aesthetics.* London, 2002.

Stachura, Peter D. *Gregor Strasser and the Rise of Nazism.* London, 1983.

———. *The Shaping of the Nazi State.* Abingdon, UK, 1978.

Stachura, Peter D., ed. *The Nazi Machtergreifung.* London, 1983.

Stephenson, Jill. "The Nazi Organization of Women." In Peter Stachura, ed., *The Shaping of the Nazi State,* vol. 8. Abingdon, UK, 1978.

———. *Women in Nazi Germany.* New York, 2001.

Stöver, Bernd. *Berichte über die Lage in Deutschland: Die Lagemeldungen der Gruppe Neu Beginnen aus dem Dritten Reich, 1933–1936.* Bonn, Germany, 1996.

Strasser, Otto. *Hitler und ich.* Constance, Germany, 1948.

Taylor, A. J. P. *The Origins of the Second World War.* New York, 1966.

Thorne, Christopher. *The Approach of War, 1938–1939.* New York, 1967.

Tobias, Fritz. *The Reichstag Fire.* New York, 1964.

Toland, John. *Adolf Hitler.* New York, 1976.

Tooze, Adam. *The Wages of Destruction: The Making and Breaking of the Nazi Economy.* London, 2006.

Trevor-Roper, Hugh, ed. *Hitler's Table Talk 1941–1944,* 3rd ed. New York, 2000.

———. *The Last Days of Hitler,* 4th ed. New York, 1962.

Turner, Henry Ashby, Jr. *German Big Business and the Rise of Hitler.* New York, 1985.
——. *Hitler's Thirty Days to Power: January 1933.* Reading, MA, 1996.
Tyrell, Albrecht. *Führer befiehl . . . Selbstzeugnisse aus der "Kampfzeit" der NSDAP.* Düsseldorf, Germany, 1969.
——. *Vom "Trommler" zum "Führer."* Munich, Germany, 1975.
Ullrich, Volker. *Hitler: The Ascent.* New York, 2016.
Wachsmann, Nikolaus. *KL: A History of the Nazi Concentration Camps.* New York, 2015.
Wagener, Otto. *Hitler aus nächster Nähe: Aufzeichnungen eines Vertrauten, 1929–1932,* 2nd ed. Edited by Henry A. Turner. Kiel, Germany, 1987.
Warlimont, Walter. *Inside Hitler's Headquarters, 1939–45.* Novato, CA, 1998; first edition in London, 1962.
Weber, Thomas. *Hitler's First War: Adolf Hitler, the Men of the List Regiment, and the First World War.* Oxford, UK, 2010.
Webman, Esther, ed. *The Global Impact of the Protocols of the Elders of Zion.* Abingdon, UK, 2011.
Wehler, Hans-Ulrich. *Deutsche Gesellschaftsgeschichte, 1871–1914,* vol. 3. Munich, Germany, 1995.
Weinberg, Gerhard L. *The Foreign Policy of Hitler's Germany: Diplomatic Revolution in Europe, 1933–1936.* Chicago, 1970.
——. *A World at Arms: A Global History of World War II.* Cambridge, UK, 1994.
Weitz, Eric D. *Weimar Germany: Promise and Tragedy.* Princeton, NJ, 2007.
Weyrather, Irmgard. *Muttertag und Mutterkreuz: Der Kult um die "deutsche Mutter" im Nationalsozialismus.* Frankfurt, Germany, 1993.
Wiedemann, Fritz. *Der Mann, der Feldherr warden wollte.* Velbert/Kettig, Germany, 1964.
Wildt, Michael. *Die Judenpolitik des SD 1935 bis 1938.* Munich, Germany, 1995.
Willett, John. *Art & Politics in the Weimar Period: The New Sobriety, 1917–1933.* New York, 1978.
Wucher, Albert. *Die Fahne hoch: Das Ende der Republik und Hitlers Machtübernahme.* Munich, Germany, 1963.
Wulf, Joseph. *Die bildenden Künste im Dritten Reich.* Berlin, 1999.

Archival Sources

Bundesarchiv (Koblenz/Berlin)

Zeitgeschictliche Sammlung (ZSg), Leaflets and Pamphlets of the NSDAP 3334, 1, 45, 13 NSDAP

National Archives, Washington, DC

T580: Captured German Documents/Rolls

Geheime Staatsarchiv Preussischer Kulturbesitz GStA (Berlin)

Bayerisches Hauptstaatsarchiv BHStA (Munich)

Abt. V, F9

Leo Baeck Institute (New York)

Personal Histories

National Holocaust Museum (Washington, DC)
Personal Histories

Landesarchiv Berlin
Acc. 1941
Acc. 1962
Acc. 1964
Acc. 2088

Landesarchiv Koblenz
403/16734

Hoover Institution
Theodor Abel Collection
Weimar Republic Collection

NSDAP Hauptarchiv (Microfilm)
Reels 14–15 Rundschreiben der RPL
Reels 29–30 Rundschreiben der RPL
Reel 58 Propaganda

Staatsarchiv Münster
Nationalsozialismus, VII-67 Bd. 1
Abt. N11, Nr. 67, Bd. 3

Westphalisches Staatsarchiv, Münster
XII-67, Bd. 1

INDEX